NTC's
AMERICAN
IDIOMS
Dictionary

NTC's AMERICAN IDIOMS Dictionary

RICHARD A. SPEARS

Associate Editor
LINDA SCHINKE-LLANO

NATIONAL TEXTBOOK COMPANY
4255 West Touhy Avenue
Lincolnwood, Illinois 60646-1975 U.S.A.

1988 Printing

Copyright © 1987 by National Textbook Company
4255 West Touhy Avenue
Lincolnwood (Chicago), Illinois 60646-1975 U.S.A.
All rights reserved. No part of this book may
be reproduced, stored in a retrieval system, or
transmitted in any form or by any means, electronic,
mechanical, photocopying, recording or otherwise,
without the prior permission of National Textbook Company.
Manufactured in the United States of America.
Library of Congress Catalog Number: 86-63996

890 WK 9 8 7 6 5 4 3

CONTENTS

ACKNOWLEDGMENTS

We are grateful to Sylvia Aruffo for her efforts in systematically gathering idiomatic phrases from the students in her English classes. In addition, we wish to thank the students who brought in long lists of expressions they did not understand, and who tested a pilot version of this dictionary.

TO THE USER

Every language has phrases or sentences that cannot be understood literally. Even if you know the meanings of all the words in a phrase and understand the grammar completely, the meaning of the phrase may still be confusing. Many clichés, proverbs, slang phrases, phrasal verbs, and common sayings offer this kind of problem. A phrase or sentence of this type is usually said to be *idiomatic*. This Dictionary is a collection of the idiomatic phrases and sentences that occur frequently in American English.

How to Use This Dictionary

1. First, try looking up the phrase in the Dictionary. Each expression is alphabetized by the first word of the phrase. For example, **in so many words** will be found in the section dealing with the letter "i." Entry phrases are never inverted or reordered like **so many words, in; words, in so many;** or **many words, in so**. Remember that in the entry phrase, the words "someone" or "one" are used to stand for persons and "something" stands for things.

2. If you do not find the phrase or if you cannot decide exactly what the phrase is, look up any major word in the phrase in the **Phrase-Finder Index** which begins on page 361. There you will find all of the phrases that contain the key word you have looked up. Pick out the phrase you want and look it up. The Index has its own instructions for use.

3. A main entry may have one or more alternate forms. The main entry and its alternates are printed in **boldface type**, and the alternate forms are preceded by "AND." (Two or more alternate forms are separated by a semicolon.) For example:

save someone's skin* AND **save someone's neck*** to save someone from injury, embarrassment, or punishment. (Informal.) □ *I saved my skin by getting the job done on time.* □ *Thanks for saving my neck! I would have fallen down the stairs if you hadn't held my arm.*

4. Many of the entry phrases have more than one major sense or meaning. These meanings are numbered with boldface numerals. For example:

settle down 1. to calm down. □ *Now, children, it's time to settle down and start class.* □ *If you don't settle down, I'll send you all home.* **2.** to settle into a stable way of life; to get married and settle into a stable way of life. □ *Tom, don't you think it's about time you settled down and stopped all of this running around?* □ *Bill and Ann decided to settle down and raise some children.*

5. Numbered senses may have additional forms which are shown in boldface type, in which case the AND and the additional form(s) follow the numeral. For example:

make a point of something 1. AND **make a point** to state an item of importance. □ *You made a point which we all should remember.* □ *He spoke for an hour without making a point.* **2.** AND **make a point of doing something** to make an effort to do something. □ *Please make a point of mailing this letter. It's very important.* □ *The hostess made a point of thanking me for bringing flowers.* **3.** AND **make an issue of someone or something** to turn someone or something into an important matter. □ *Please don't make a point of John's comment. It wasn't that important.* □ *I hope you make an issue of Tom's success and* *the reasons for it.* □ *Tom has a lot of problems. Please don't make an issue of him.*

6. Some entries have additional related forms within the entry. These are introduced by "ALSO:" and are in boldface type. For example:

make sense out of someone or something to understand or interpret someone or something. (Also with *some,* as in the examples.) □ *I can hardly make sense out of John.* □ *I'm trying to make some sense out of what John is saying.* ALSO: **make sense** to be understandable. □ *John doesn't make sense.* □ *What John says makes sense.*

7. Some entry phrases are followed by an asterisk (*) which suggests caution in their use. The comments in parentheses after the definition will tell what special kind of phrase the entry is. Clichés, slang expressions, folksy expressions, and some other phrases are marked with this caution. You may not want to use these expressions in formal writing. For example:

cut class* to skip going to class. (Informal.) □ *If Mary keeps cutting classes, she'll fail the course.* □ *I can't cut that class. I've missed too many already.*

8. Where there are numbered senses in an entry and only some of the senses need caution, the asterisk is placed after the number of the sense that requires caution. The explanation for the caution follows the definition. For example:

in the groove 1. in a notch or a long slit. (*In* can be replaced with *into.* See *in a bind* and the examples below.) □ *The record won't play unless the needle is in the groove.* □ *Put this part into this groove, and then screw down the other part.* **2.*** AND **groovy** good and satisfying; exactly what is needed; attractive. (Slang.) □ *This music is really in the groove.* □ *What a groovy hat!*

9. The boldface entry is usually followed by a definition. Alternate forms of the definition are separated by a semicolon (;). These additional definitions are usually given to show slight differences in meaning or interpretation. Sometimes an alternate definition is given when the vocabulary of the first definition is difficult. For example:

> **dead on one's or its feet** exhausted; worn out; no longer useful. □ *Ann is so tired. She's really dead on her feet.* □ *He can't teach well anymore. He's dead on his feet.* □ *This inefficient company is dead on its feet.*

10. Some entries are followed by instructions to look up some other phrase. For example:

> **in someone's behalf** See *in behalf of someone.*

11. A definition may be followed by comments in parentheses. These comments tell about some of the variations of a phrase, give other useful information, and indicate cross-referencing. For example:

> **in advance of someone or something** AND **in advance** before someone or something. (Refers to both time and space.) □ *They reached the station in advance of the 7:00 train.* □ *It's good to be there in advance.* □ *I boarded the train in advance of Mr. Jones.*

12. When comments apply to all numbered senses of an entry, the comments are found before the numbered senses. For example:

> **in the money*** (Informal. See also *on the money.*) **1.** wealthy. □ *John is really in the money. He's worth millions.* □ *If I am ever in the money, I'll be generous.* **2.** in the winning position in a race or contest. (As if one had won the prize money.) □ *I knew when Jane came around the final turn that she was in the money.* □ *The horses coming in first, second, and third are said to be in the money.*

13. Comments that apply to only one numbered sense are found within the numbered sense, after the definition. For example:

> **in the money*** (Informal. See also *on the money*.) **1.** wealthy. □ *John is really in the money. He's worth millions.* □ *If I am ever in the money, I'll be generous.* **2.** in the winning position in a race or contest. (As if one had won the prize money.) □ *I knew when Jane came around the final turn that she was in the money.* □ *The horses coming in first, second, and third are said to be in the money.*

14. Some definitions contain additional comments in parentheses which help make the definition more clear. These comments provide part of the context in which the entry phrase is usually used. For example:

> **serve someone right** (for an act or event) to punish someone fairly (for doing something). □ *John copied off my test paper. It would serve him right if he fails the test.* □ *It'd serve John right if he got arrested.*

15. Many entries are cross-referenced to additional idiomatic phrases that are related in form or meaning. For example:

> **in the black** not in debt; in a financially profitable condition. (Compare to *in the red. In* can be replaced with *into*. See *in a bind* and the examples below.) □ *I wish my accounts were in the black.* □ *Sally moved the company into the black.*

16. Sometimes the numbered senses refer to only people or things, but not both. In such cases the numeral is followed by "[with *something*]" or "[with *someone*]". For example:

> **nail someone or something down** AND **nail down someone or something 1.*** [with *someone*] to get a firm and final decision from some-

one (on something). (Informal.) □ *I want you to find Bob and get an answer from him. Nail him down one way or the other.* □ *Please nail down John on the question of signing the contract.* **2.*** [with *something*] to get a firm and final decision (from someone) on something. (Informal.) □ *Find Bob and nail down an answer.* □ *Let's get in touch with John and nail down this contract.* **3.** [with *something*] to nail (with a hammer) something which is loose. □ *Nail down this loose floor board.* □ *Please nail this thing down.*

17. Each main entry has at least two examples. Examples are in *italic* type, and each example begins with a □ symbol. The examples show how the idiomatic phrases are used and the types of contexts in which they are found.

18. Entry phrases and their variants appear in **boldface type.** Examples and emphasized words appear in *italic type.* An entry phrase appears in *italic sans serif type* whenever the phrase is referred to in a definition or cross reference.

TERMS AND SYMBOLS

☐ (a box) marks the beginning of an example.

ALSO: introduces additional forms within an entry that are related to the main entry, but have different meanings.

AND indicates that an entry has variant forms that are the same or almost the same in meaning. One or more variant forms are preceded by AND.

cliché indicates an expression that is used too frequently and too casually. You may not want to use clichés in writing.

folksy refers to expressions that are rural, old-fashioned, or quaint. You may not want to use folksy expressions in writing.

formal indicates an expression that is literary in origin or usually reserved for writing.

informal refers to a very casual expression that is most likely to be spoken and not written.

proverb refers to a fixed saying that is often quoted.

see means to look up the entry indicated.

see also means to go to the entry indicated for additional information or to find similar expressions.

slang refers to expressions that are recognized as casual or playful. You may not want to use slang expressions in writing.

ABOUT THIS DICTIONARY

Some idiomatic phrases—especially proverbs and clichés—do not usually vary in form. People will say "A bird in the hand is worth two in the bush," but never "A bird in the hand is worth two in the tree" or "Two birds in the hand are worth four in the bush." Most phrases show some kind of variation, however, and many are highly variable. Phrasal verbs may occur in two different orders. For instance, **ask someone out** or **ask out someone**. Some idiomatic phrases can take a variety of modifiers. For instance, "The audience gave the performer a hand" and "The audience gave the performer a <u>very nice</u> hand." And, of course, verbs in idiomatic phrases can occur in a variety of tenses and aspects. The Dictionary unites the variant forms of an idiomatic phrase at one entry and calls attention to the major types of variation the user is likely to encounter.

In English it is important to know whether an idiomatic phrase includes an object as part of the phrase and it is just as important to know whether the object is a person or a thing. You can say "send someone packing" (with a human object), but not "send something packing" (with a non-human object). Many idioms are like **bail someone or something out**, where the basic *form* of the idiom is the same whether the object is a person or a thing, but the meaning is different for persons and things. **Bail someone out** means to "pay money to get someone out of jail" and **bail something out** means to "remove water from something, such as a boat or canoe." These are really two different idioms that look similar. The Dictionary uses *form* (rather than meaning) for indexing the idioms so that you can more easily locate them to find out what they mean.

Typically an idiomatic phrase will be listed in a dictionary or a word list in its simplest or shortest form, such as **try out**. If you have spoken English all your life, you probably know that this simple entry, **try out**, really stands for **try someone out, try out someone, try something out, try out something, try out for something,** and just **try out**. The phrase **try out** is the common element in all these forms, but knowing only the common element is not adequate for most people. This Dictionary lists the fullest form as the entry phrase, with the variant and shortened forms listed afterward. When one is seeking only the short form, one looks up the phrase that *includes* the short form.

It is often difficult to decide what the basic form of an idiom is. Textbooks, idiom dictionaries, and lists of useful phrases show little agreement on the basic forms of idiomatic phrases. If it has not been decided what the basic form of an idiom is, how will anyone know what to look up in a dictionary? This Dictionary uses a Phrase-Finder Index to allow the user to determine how an idiomatic phrase is listed in the Dictionary simply by looking up any major word in the Phrase-Finder Index. If you know that the idiom you want has the word **cloud** in it, just look up **cloud** in the Phrase-Finder Index and you will find **cloud up; Every cloud has a silver lining; have one's head in the clouds; on cloud nine; under a cloud of suspicion.** The user does not have to guess at the form of the idiom.

There is an important distinction made between *one* and *someone* in the entry phrases. *Someone* is used to refer to someone other than the subject of the sentence, as with **acknowledge someone to be right.** For example, "I acknowledged her to be right" or "She acknowledged me to be right." One does not acknowledge oneself to be right. *One* is used where the *one* is the same person as the subject of the sentence (or the conversation), as with **act one's age** and **know one's ABCs.** For example, "You should learn to act your age." or "He doesn't know his ABCs." One is not said to act someone else's age or know someone else's ABCs. Where there are two *ones* in a phrase they both must refer to the same person, as with **set one back on one's heels.** For example, "The scolding set him back on his heels." or "That bill really set John back on his heels." You cannot set one person back on another person's heels.

Each entry is accompanied by two or more examples. The examples illustrate the types of variation one might encounter and the typical ways in which the phrase is used, including passives and reflexives. The Dictionary indicates special types of phrases—slang, folksy, informal—and suggests caution with their use. It is difficult to instruct people on the proper or appropriate use of slang and folksy material because in some situations, especially in writing, they are often most effectively used when they are not quite appropriate. Perceptions of appropriateness are culturally bound and are tied to personality traits such as sense of humor, risk-taking, position or rank, and many other factors. No book can advise people—in any culture—how to act in all situations. For this reason, slang, folksy, and informal expressions, as well as clichés, are marked with an * which indicates caution. If in doubt or in a situation where the wrong word may cause difficulty, do not use expressions marked with an *.

In general, there is no attempt to instruct the user in English grammar or explain the grammatical structure of the expressions in the Dictionary. Usually, when an idiomatic expression is of the type that can be included in a sentence, it follows regular grammatical rules. Exceptions to this are noted in the Dictionary, as with **Them's fighting words!** If the dictionary user is moderately competent in the construction of English sentences, the grammatical use of the phrases in the Dictionary should cause no special difficulty. If the dictionary user lacks competence with the construction of English sentences, the Dictionary should be used to help in the *comprehension* of phrases until more competence in the use of the language is achieved.

Very few symbols and special terms are used in the Dictionary. Variation is indicated simply by listing the whole variant form. For instance, just after **get something off** you will find AND **get off something.** This provides immediate visual verification that this phrasal verb allows third-person singular objects to occur both before and after the preposition. This makes the information in the Dictionary available to those who may not yet have mastered the grammatical explanations of English structure well enough to understand the syntactic explanations of idiomatic expressions. The Dictionary assumes no grammatical skills other than the ability to identify a few parts of speech such as nouns, adjectives, and verbs, and to recognize the similarity between the phrases listed in the Dictionary and those found in everyday language use.

The phrases in the Dictionary come from many sources. Many have been collected from current newspapers and magazines. Others have come from existing dictionaries and reference books. Dictionary users have helped collect idioms for this Dictionary, also. Students in English as a foreign language classes at Northwestern University kept lists of expressions they could not understand and submitted them to their instructor. These phrases became the basis of classroom instruction and also became a part of this book.

The Dictionary should prove useful for people who are learning how to understand idiomatic English, the hearing impaired, and for all speakers of English who want to know more about the language.

A

A bird in the hand is worth two in the bush. a proverb meaning that something you already have is better than something you might get. □ *Bill has offered to buy my car for $3,000. Someone else might pay more, but a bird in the hand is worth two in the bush.* □ *I might be able to find a better offer, but a bird in the hand is worth two in the bush.*

a chip off the old block* a person (usually a male) who behaves in the same way as his father or resembles his father. (Usually informal.) □ *John looks like his father—a real chip off the old block.* □ *Bill Jones Jr. is a chip off the old block. He's a banker just like his father.*

a cut above someone or something a measure or degree better than someone or something else. (Especially with *average*, as in the examples.) □ *Your shirt is beautiful, but mine is a cut above yours.* □ *John isn't the best mechanic in town, but he's a cut above average.*

a drop in the bucket See the following entry.

a drop in the ocean AND **a drop in the bucket** just a little bit; not enough of something to make a difference. □ *But one dollar isn't enough! That's just a drop in the ocean.* □ *At this point your help is nothing more than a drop in the ocean. I need far more help than twenty people could give.* □ *I won't accept your offer. It's just a drop in the bucket.*

A fool and his money are soon parted. a proverb meaning that a person who acts unwisely with money soon loses it. (Often said about a person who has just lost a sum of money because of poor judgement.) □ *When Bill lost a $400 bet on a horse race, Mary said, "A fool and his money are soon parted."* □ *When John bought a cheap used car that fell apart the next day, he said, "Oh well, a fool and his money are soon parted."*

A friend in need is a friend indeed. a proverb meaning that a true friend is a person who will help you when you really need someone. (Compare to *fair-weather friend*.) □ *When Bill helped me with geometry, I really learned the meaning of "A friend in need is a friend indeed."* □ *"A friend in need is a friend indeed" sounds silly until you need someone very badly.*

a little bird told me learned from a mysterious or secret source. (Often given as an evasive answer to someone who asks how you learned something. Rude in some circumstances.) □ *"All right," said Mary, "where did you get that information?" John replied, "A little bird told me."* □ *A little bird told me where I might find you.*

A little knowledge is a dangerous thing. a proverb meaning that incomplete knowledge can embarrass or harm someone or something. □ *The doctor said, "Just because you've had a course in first aid, you shouldn't have treated your own illness. A little knowledge is a dangerous thing."* □ *John thought he knew how to take care of the garden, but he killed all the flowers. A little knowledge is a dangerous thing.*

A penny saved is a penny earned. a proverb meaning that money saved through thrift is the same as money earned by employment. (Sometimes used to explain stinginess.) □ *"I didn't want to pay that much for the book,"* said Mary. "*After all, a penny saved is a penny earned.*" □ *Bob put his money in a new bank which pays more interest than his old bank, saying, "A penny saved is a penny earned.*"

A rolling stone gathers no moss. a proverb which describes a person who keeps changing jobs or residences and, therefore, accumulates no possessions or responsibilities. □ "*John just can't seem to stay in one place,*" *said Sally. "Oh well, a rolling stone gathers no moss.*" □ *Bill has no furniture to bother with because he keeps on the move. He keeps saying that a rolling stone gathers no moss.*

a stone's throw away* a short distance; a relatively short distance. (Informal. May refer to distances in feet or miles.) □ *John saw Mary across the street, just a stone's throw away.* □ *Philadelphia is just a stone's throw away from New York City.*

A watched pot never boils. a proverb meaning that concentration on a problem will not help solve it. (Refers to the seemingly long time it takes water to boil when you are waiting for it. Said about a problem which a person is watching very closely.) □ *John was looking out the window, waiting eagerly for the mail to be delivered. Ann said, "Be patient. A watched pot never boils.*" □ *Billy weighed himself four times a day while he was trying to lose weight. His mother said, "Relax. A watched pot never boils.*"

abandon oneself to someone or something to give up and accept a situation; to yield to a person. □ *Ann gave up and abandoned herself to the flu.* □ *Bill saw the gun and abandoned himself to the robber.*

abide by something to follow the rules of something; to obey someone's orders. □ *John felt that he had to abide by his father's wishes.* □ *All drivers are expected to abide by the rules of the road.*

able to breathe again AND **able to breathe easily again; able to breathe freely again** able to relax and recover from a busy or stressful time; able to catch one's breath. (*Able to* can be replaced with *can.*) □ *Now that the lion*

has been caught, we'll be able to breathe freely again. □ *Now that the annual sale is over, the sales staff will be able to breathe again.* □ *Final exams are over, so I can breathe easily again.*

able to do something blindfolded AND **able to do something standing on one's head** able to do something easily and quickly, possibly without even looking. (Informal. Rarely used literally. *Able to* can be replaced with *can.*) □ *Bill boasted that he could pass his driver's test blindfolded.* □ *Mary is very good with computers. She can program blindfolded.* □ *Dr. Jones is a great surgeon. He can take out an appendix standing on his head.*

able to do something standing on one's head See the previous entry.

able to make something* able to attend an event. (Informal. Also used literally. *Able to* can be replaced with *can.*) □ *I don't think I'll be able to make your party, but thanks for asking me.* □ *We are having another one next month. We hope you can make it then.*

able to take a joke to be able to accept ridicule good-naturedly; to be the object or butt of a joke willingly. (*Able to* can be replaced with *can.*) □ *Let's play a trick on Bill and see if he's able to take a joke.* □ *Better not tease Ann. She can't take a joke.*

able to take something able to endure something; able to endure abuse. (Often in the negative. *Able to* can be replaced with *can.* See also the previous entry.) □ *Stop yelling like that. I'm not able to take it anymore.* □ *Go ahead, hit me again. I can take it.* ALSO: **able to take just so much** able to endure only a limited amount of discomfort. (*Able to* can be replaced with *can.*) □ *Please stop hurting my feelings. I'm able to take just so much.* □ *I can take just so much.*

abound with something AND **abound in something** to be plentiful with something. □ *The forest abounds with small animals.* □ *The medical system abounds with problems.*

about to do something ready to do something; on the verge of doing something. □ *Our old dog is about to die.* □ *The apple tree is about to bloom.*

above and beyond the call of duty AND **beyond the call of duty** in addition to what is required; more than is required in one's job. □ *We didn't expect the police officer to drive us home. That was above and beyond the call of duty.* □ *The English teacher helped students after school every day, even though it was beyond the call of duty.*

above board AND **honest and above board; open and above board** in the open; visible to the public; honest. (Especially with *keep*, as in the examples.) □ *Don't keep it a secret. Let's make sure that everything is above board.* □ *You can do whatever you wish, as long as you keep it honest and above board.* □ *The inspector had to make sure that everything was open and above board.*

above suspicion to be honest enough that no one would suspect you; to be in a position where you could not be suspected. □ *The general is a fine old man, completely above suspicion.* □ *Mary was at work at the time of the accident, so she's above suspicion.*

absent without leave AND **AWOL** absent from a military unit without permission; absent from anything without permission. (**AWOL** is an abbreviation. This is a serious offense in the military.) □ *The soldier was taken away by the military police because he was absent without leave.* □ *John was AWOL from school and got into a lot of trouble with his parents.* ALSO: **go AWOL** to become absent without leave. □ *Private Smith went AWOL last Wednesday. Now he's in a military prison.*

according to all accounts AND **by all accounts** from all the reports; everyone is saying. □ *According to all accounts, the police were on the scene immediately.* □ *According to all accounts, the meeting broke up over a very minor matter.* □ *By all accounts, it was a very poor performance.*

according to Hoyle according to the rules; in keeping with the way it is normally done. (Refers to the rules for playing the card game *bridge*. Mr. Hoyle wrote a book about bridge. This expression is usually used for something other than bridge.) □ *That's wrong. Accord-ing to Hoyle, this is the way to do it.* □ *The carpenter said, "This is the way to drive a nail, according to Hoyle."*

according to one's own lights according to the way one believes; according to the way one's conscience or inclinations lead one. (Rarely used informally.) □ *People must act on this matter according to their own lights.* □ *John may have been wrong, but he did what he did according to his own lights.*

according to someone or something as said or indicated by someone or something. □ *According to the weather forecast, this should be a beautiful day.* □ *According to my father, this is a very good car to buy.* □ *It's too cold to go for a walk, according to the thermometer.*

account for someone or something to explain what happened to someone or something; to explain the state of someone or something. □ *How do you account for the $100 you started out with?* □ *How do you account for that mud on your dress?* □ *Something must account for that elderly woman who keeps following us around.*

accustomed to someone or something to be used to or comfortable with someone or something; to accept someone or something as common and usual. □ *We are accustomed to wearing shoes.* □ *They aren't accustomed to paying a visit without bringing a gift.* □ *I'll never become accustomed to you.*

ace in the hole* something or someone held (secretly) in reserve; anything which can help in an emergency. (Slang. Refers to the ace of spades in card playing.) □ *The hostages served as the terrorists' ace in the hole for getting what they wanted.* □ *The twenty-dollar bill in my shoe is my ace in the hole.*

acknowledge receipt of something AND **acknowledge receipt** to inform the sender that what was sent was received. (Commonly used in business correspondence.) □ *In a letter to a shoe company, Mary wrote, "I'm happy to acknowledge receipt of four dozen pairs of shoes."* □ *John acknowledged receipt of the bill.* □ *The package hasn't arrived, so I'm unable to acknowledge receipt.*

acknowledge someone to be right

to admit or state that someone is correct about something. □ *Mary acknowledged Bill to be right about the name of the store.* □ *Bill said that the car was useless, and the mechanic acknowledged him to be right.*

acquainted with someone or something to know someone or something by name, not necessarily well; to know of the existence of someone or something. □ *I'm acquainted with John, but I've only met him once.* □ *I'm acquainted with the street you describe, but I don't know how to get there.*

acquire a taste for something to develop a liking for food, drink, or something else; to learn to like something. □ *One acquires a taste for fine wines.* □ *Many people are not able to acquire a taste for foreign food.* □ *Mary acquired a taste for art when she was very young.*

across from someone or something facing or opposite someone or something. □ *At the table, Mary sat across from John.* □ *The shoe store is across from the bank.*

across the board equally for everyone or everything. □ *The school board raised the pay of all the teachers across the board.* □ *Congress cut the budget by reducing the money for each department ten percent across the board.*

act as someone to perform in the capacity of someone, temporarily or permanently. □ *I'll act as your supervisor until Mrs. Brown returns from vacation.* □ *This is Mr. Smith. He'll act as manager from now on.*

act high and mighty to act proud and powerful. (Informal.) □ *Why does the doctor always have to act so high and mighty?* □ *If Sally wouldn't act so high and mighty, she'd have more friends.*

act of faith an act or deed demonstrating religious faith; an act or deed showing trust in someone or something. □ *He lit candles in church as an act of faith.* □ *For him to trust you with his safety was a real act of faith.*

act of God an occurrence (usually an accident) for which no human is responsible; an act of nature such as a storm, earthquake, or windstorm. □ *My insurance company wouldn't pay for the dam-*

age because it was an act of God. □ *The thief tried to convince the judge that the diamonds were in his pocket due to an act of God.*

act of war an international act of violence for which war is considered a suitable response; (figuratively) any hostile act between two people. □ *To bomb a ship is an act of war.* □ *Can spying be considered an act of war?* □ *"You just broke my stereo," yelled John. "That's an act of war!"*

act on something to deal with a problem; to perform a task which needs doing. □ *We hope congress will act on this bill soon.* □ *We can do nothing until the manager acts on our request.*

act one's age to behave more maturely; to act as grown up as one really is. (This is frequently said to a child.) □ *Come on, John, act your age. Stop throwing rocks.* □ *Mary! Stop picking on your little brother. Act your age!*

act something out AND **act out something** to perform an imaginary event as if one were in a play. □ *Bill always acted his anger out by shouting and pounding his fists.* □ *The psychiatrist asked Bill to act out the way he felt about getting fired.*

act up to misbehave; to run or act badly. □ *John, why do you always have to act up when your father and I take you out to eat?* □ *My arthritis is acting up. It really hurts.* □ *My car is acting up. I could hardly get it started this morning.*

Actions speak louder than words. a proverb meaning that it is better to do something about a problem than just talk about it. □ *Mary kept promising to get a job. John finally looked her in the eye and said, "Actions speak louder than words!"* □ *After listening to the senator promising to cut federal spending, Ann wrote a simple note saying, "Actions speak louder than words."*

add fuel to the fire* AND **add fuel to the flame*** to make a problem worse; to say or do something which makes a bad situation worse; to make an angry person get even more angry. (A cliché.) □ *To spank a crying child just adds fuel to the fire.* □ *Bill was shouting angrily, and Bob tried to get him to stop by laugh-*

ing at him. Of course, that was just adding fuel to the flame.

add insult to injury* to make a bad situation worse; to hurt the feelings of a person who has already been hurt. (A cliché.) □ *First, the basement flooded, and then, to add insult to injury, a pipe burst in the kitchen.* □ *My car barely started this morning, and to add insult to injury, I got a flat tire in the driveway.*

add something up AND **add up something; total something up; total up something** to make a mathematical total; to combine facts in order to figure something out. (See also *add up to something*.) □ *I've got to finish adding the figures up.* □ *Hurry and add up the numbers.* □ *When you total up all the facts, you see things entirely differently.*

add up to something AND **add up 1.** to total up to a particular amount. (See also *add something up*.) □ *The bill added up to $200.* □ *These groceries will add up to almost sixty dollars.* □ *These numbers just won't add up.* **2.** to mean something; to signify or represent something; to result in something. □ *All this adds up to trouble!* □ *I don't understand. What does all this add up to?* □ *If you think about it carefully, these facts add up perfectly.*

address someone as something 1. to talk to or write to a person using a particular title. □ *They addressed Abraham Lincoln as "Mr. President."* □ *A physician is usually addressed as "Doctor."* **2.** to treat a person you are talking with in a particular manner. □ *You should address him as your equal.* □ *Do not address me as your superior.*

advanced in years See *up in years*.

afraid of one's own shadow easily frightened; always frightened, timid, or suspicious. (Never used literally.) □ *After Tom was robbed, he was even afraid of his own shadow.* □ *Jane has always been a shy child. She has been afraid of her own shadow since she was three.*

after a fashion in a manner which is just barely adequate; poorly. □ *He thanked me—after a fashion—for my help.* □ *Oh yes, I can swim, after a fashion.*

after all anyway; in spite of what had been decided. (Often refers to a change in plans or a reversal of plans.) □ *Mary had planned to go to the bank first, but she came here after all.* □ *It looks like Tom will go to law school after all.*

after all is said and done* when everything is settled or concluded; finally. (A cliché.) □ *After all was said and done, it was a lovely party.* □ *After all is said and done, it will turn out just as I said.*

after hours after the regular closing time; after any normal or regular time, such as one's bedtime. □ *John was arrested in a bar after hours.* □ *The soldier was caught sneaking into the barracks after hours.* □ *John got a job sweeping floors in the bank after hours.*

after the fact after something has happened; after something, especially a crime, has taken place. (Primarily a legal phrase.) □ *John is always making excuses after the fact.* □ *Remember to lock your car whenever you leave it. If it's stolen, there is nothing you can do after the fact.*

after the fashion of someone or something in the manner or style of someone or something. See also *after a fashion*. □ *She walks down the street after the fashion of a grand lady.* □ *The church was built after the fashion of an English cathedral.*

against someone's will without a person's consent or agreement. □ *You cannot force me to come with you against my will!* □ *Against their will, the men were made to stand up against the wall and be searched.*

against the clock in a race with time; in a great hurry to get something done before a particular time. (See also *race against time*.) □ *Bill set a new track record running against the clock. He lost the actual race, however.* □ *In a race against the clock, they rushed the special medicine to the hospital.*

agree on someone or something to agree on the choice of a particular person or thing. □ *They needed to find a new candidate. They finally agreed on John.* □ *They agreed on yellow as the new color for the kitchen.*

agree to something to agree to do

something; to agree to let something happen. □ *Mary agreed to serve as president.* □ *Bill won't agree to mow the lawn.*

agree with someone or something **1.** to reach accord with someone; to come to an understanding with someone. □ *I'm glad you agree with me about the problem.* □ *John and Mary both agree with us on this issue.* **2.** to complement, harmonize with, or act positively on someone or something. □ *That skirt is lovely, Mary. Red certainly agrees with you.* □ *Cold weather agrees with me very nicely.* ALSO: **not agree with someone** to make someone ill; to give someone minor stomach distress. □ *Fried foods don't agree with Tom.* □ *I always have onions in my garden, but I never eat them. They just don't agree with me.*

ahead of someone or something **1.** in front of or before a person; with an advantage over a person. (See *get ahead of someone or something.*) □ *In the footrace, I came in ahead of Tom.* □ *You're certainly ahead of me when it comes to math.* **2.** before or in advance of something; having something under control or on schedule. □ *I feel good because I'm ahead of my work schedule.* □ *Our car arrived ahead of yours.*

ahead of the game* being early; having an advantage over a situation; having done more than necessary. (Informal or slang. Also used literally.) □ *Whenever we go to a movie, we show up ahead of the game and have to wait.* □ *Bill has to study math very hard to keep ahead of the game.* □ *Bob does extra work so he's always ahead of the game.*

ahead of time beforehand; before the announced time. □ *If you show up ahead of time, you will have to wait.* □ *Be there ahead of time if you want to get a good seat.*

aid and abet someone* to help someone; to incite someone to do something which is wrong. (A cliché.) □ *He was scolded for aiding and abetting those boys who were fighting.* □ *It's illegal to aid and abet a thief.*

aim at someone or something AND **aim for someone or something; aim something at someone or something** **1.** to point (something, such as a weapon) at a person or thing. □ *Aim at the target, not below it.* □ *Aim the telescope right at the moon.* □ *Aim for the center of the target.* **2.** [with *something*] to hold something as one's model or goal. □ *I try to aim at success in everything I do.* □ *Aim for the good things in life.* □ *I'll aim for the best paying job I can get.*

aim to do something* to mean to do something; to intend to do something in the future. (Folksy.) □ *I aim to paint the house as soon as I can find a brush.* □ *He aims to take a few days off and go fishing.*

air one's grievances to complain; to make a public complaint. □ *I know how you feel, John, but it isn't necessary to air your grievances over and over.* □ *I know you're busy, sir, but I must air my grievances. This matter is very serious.*

air someone's dirty linen in public to discuss private or embarrassing matters in public, especially when quarreling. (This *linen* refers to sheets and tablecloths or other soiled cloth.) □ *John's mother had asked him repeatedly not to air the family's dirty linen in public.* □ *Mr. and Mrs. Johnson are arguing again. Why must they always air their dirty linen in public?*

air something out AND **air out something** to freshen up something by placing it in the open air; to freshen a room by letting air move through it. □ *It's so stale in here. Mary, please open a window and air this place out.* □ *Please take this pillow outside and air it out.* □ *I'll have to air out the car. Someone has been smoking in it.*

alive and kicking* AND **alive and well*** well and healthy. (Informal.) □ JANE: *How is Bill?* MARY: *Oh, he's alive and kicking.* □ *The last time I saw Tom, he was alive and well.*

alive with someone or something covered with, filled with, or active with people or things. □ *Look! Ants everywhere. The floor is alive with ants!* □ *When we got to the ballroom, the place was alive with dancing.* □ *The campground was alive with campers from all over the country.*

all and sundry* everyone; one and all. (Folksy.) □ *Cold drinks were served to all and sundry.* □ *All and sundry came to the village fair.*

all at once 1. suddenly. □ *All at once the chair broke, and Bob fell to the floor.* □ *All at once she tripped on a stone.* **2.** all at the same time. □ *The entire group spoke all at once.* □ *They were trying to cook dinner, clean house, and paint the closet all at once.*

all balled up* troubled; confused; in a mess. (Slang.) □ *Look at you! You're really all balled up!* □ *John is all balled up because his car was stolen.* □ *Of course this typewriter won't work. It's all balled up.*

all better now* improved; cured. (Folksy or juvenile.) □ *My leg was sore, but it's all better now.* □ *I fell off my tricycle and bumped my knee. Mommy kissed it, and it's all better now.*

all day long throughout the day; during the entire day. □ *We waited for you at the station all day long.* □ *I can't keep smiling all day long.*

all dressed up dressed in one's best clothes; dressed formally. (See also *dress up; get dolled up.*) □ *We're all dressed up to go out to dinner.* □ *I really hate to get all dressed up just to go somewhere to eat.*

all for something very much in favor of something. (*For* is usually emphasized.) □ *Bill is all for stopping off to get ice cream.* □ *Mary suggested that they sell their house. They weren't all for it, but they did it anyway.*

all for the best See *for the best.*

all gone used up; finished; over with. □ *Oh, the strawberry jelly is all gone.* □ *We used to have wonderful parties, but those days are all gone.*

all hours of the day and night AND **all hours** very late in the night or very early in the morning. □ *Why do you always stay out until all hours of the day and night?* □ *I like to stay out till all hours.*

all in tired; exhausted; *all tuckered out.* □ *I just walked all the way from town. I'm all in.* □ *"What a day!" said Sally. "I'm all in."*

all in a day's work part of what is expected; typical or normal. □ *I don't particularly like to cook, but it's all in a day's work.* □ *Putting up with rude customers isn't pleasant, but it's all in a day's work.* □ *Cleaning up after other people is all in a day's work for a chambermaid.*

all in all considering everything which has happened; in summary and in spite of any unpleasantness. □ *All in all, it was a very good party.* □ *All in all, I'm glad that I visited New York City.*

all in good time at some future time; *in good time;* soon. (This phrase is used to encourage people to be patient and wait quietly.) □ *When will the baby be born? All in good time.* □ MARY: *I'm starved! When will Bill get here with the pizza?* TOM: *All in good time, Mary, all in good time.*

all in one breath AND **in one breath** spoken very rapidly, usually while one is very excited. □ *Ann said all in one breath, "Hurry, quick! The parade is coming!"* □ *Jane was in a play, and she was so excited that she said her whole speech in one breath.* □ *Tom can say the alphabet all in one breath.*

all in one piece safely; without damage. (Informal.) □ *Her son came home from school all in one piece, even though he had been in a fight.* □ *The package was handled carelessly, but the vase inside arrived all in one piece.*

all in the family AND **in the family** restricted to one's own family, as with private or embarrassing information. (Especially with *keep.*) □ *Don't tell anyone else. Please keep it all in the family.* □ *He only told his brother because he wanted it to remain in the family.*

all kinds of someone or something* a great number of people or things; a great amount of something, especially money. (Informal. Also used literally to mean all types.) □ *There were all kinds of people there, probably thousands.* □ *The Smith family has all kinds of money.*

all manner of someone or something all types of people or things. □ *We saw all manner of people there. They came from every country in the world.* □ *They were selling all manner of things in the country store.*

all night long throughout the whole night. □ *I couldn't sleep all night long.* □ *John was sick all night long.*

all of a sudden suddenly. □ *All of a sudden lightning struck the tree we were sitting under.* □ *I felt a sharp pain in my side all of a sudden.*

all-out effort a very good and thorough effort. □ *We need an all-out effort to get this job done on time.* □ *The government began an all-out effort to reduce the federal budget.* ALSO: **make an all-out effort** to make a thorough and energetic effort. □ *Sally made an all-out effort to get to class on time.* □ *In my job, I have to make an all-out effort every day.*

all-out war total war, as opposed to small, warlike acts or threats of war. □ *We are now concerned about all-out war in the Middle East.* □ *Threats of all-out war caused many tourists to leave the country immediately.*

all over 1. finished; dead. (Compare to *all over with*.) □ *Dinner is all over. I'm sorry you didn't get any.* □ *It's all over. He's dead now.* **2.** everywhere. (See also *all over the earth.*) □ *Oh, I just itch all over.* □ *She's spreading the rumor all over.*

all over but the shouting decided and concluded; finished except for a celebration. (An elaboration of *all over* which means finished.) □ *The last goal was made just as the final whistle sounded. Tom said, "Well, it's all over but the shouting."* □ *Tom worked hard in college and graduated last month. When he got his diploma, he said, "It's all over but the shouting."*

all over the earth AND **all over the world** everywhere. □ *Grass grows all over the earth.* □ *It's the same way all over the world.*

all over the place* everywhere; in all parts of a particular location. (Informal. An elaboration of *all over.*) □ *Tom, stop leaving your dirty clothes all over the place.* □ *We keep finding this kind of problem all over the place.*

all over town 1. everywhere in town. □ *Our dog got loose and ran all over town.* □ *Jane looked all over town for a dress to wear to the party.* **2.** known

to everyone in town. □ *Now keep this a secret. I don't want it all over town.* □ *In a short time the secret was known all over town.*

all over with finished. (See also *all over.*) □ *His problems are all over with now.* □ *After dinner is all over with, we can play cards.*

all right* well, good, or okay, but not excellent. (Informal. This phrase has all the uses that *okay* has.) □ *I was a little sick, but now I'm all right.* □ *His work is all right, but nothing to brag about.* □ *All right, it's time to go.*

All right for you!* That's it for you!; That's the last chance for you! (Juvenile and informal. Usually said by a child who is angry at a playmate.) □ *All right for you, John. See if I ever play with you again.* □ *All right for you! I'm telling your mother what you did.*

all right with someone agreeable to someone. □ *If you want to ruin your life and marry Tom, it's all right with me.* □ *I'll see if it's all right with my father.*

All roads lead to Rome. a proverb meaning that there are many different routes to the same goal. □ *Mary was criticizing the way that Jane was planting the flowers. John said, "Never mind, Mary, all roads lead to Rome."* □ *Some people learn by doing. Others have to be taught. In the long run, all roads lead to Rome.*

all set ready to begin; okay. (See also *set to do something.*) □ TOM: *Is everything all right?* JANE: *Yes, we are all set.* □ *We are ready to leave now. Are you all set?*

all systems are go* AND **all systems go*** everything is ready. (Informal. Originally said when preparing to launch a rocket.) □ *The rocket is ready to blast off—all systems are go.* □ TOM: *Are you guys ready to start playing?* BILL: *Sure, Tom, all systems go.*

all talk and no action AND **all talk** talking about doing something, but never actually doing it. (See also *Actions speak louder than words.*) □ *The car needs washing, but Bill is all talk and no action on this matter.* □ *Bill keeps saying he'll get a job soon, but he's all* *talk and no action.* □ *Bill won't do it. He's just all talk.*

All that glitters is not gold. a proverb meaning that many attractive and alluring things have no value. □ *The used car looked fine but didn't run well at all. "Ah yes," thought Bill, "all that glitters is not gold." □ When Mary was disappointed about losing Tom, Jane reminded her, "All that glitters is not gold."*

all the live-long day* throughout the whole day. (Folksy.) □ *They kept at their work all the live-long day.* □ *Bob just sat by the creek fishing, all the live-long day.*

all the rage* in current fashion. (Slang and informal.) □ *A new dance called the "floppy disc" is all the rage.* □ *Wearing a rope instead of a belt is all the rage these days.*

all the same AND **just the same** **1.** nevertheless; anyhow. (Also used literally.) □ *They were told not to bring presents, but they brought them all the same.* □ *His parents said no, but John went out just the same.* **2.** See the following entry.

all the same to someone AND **all the same; just the same to someone; just the same** of no consequence to someone; immaterial to someone. □ *It's all the same to me whether we win or lose.* □ *If it's just the same to you, I'd rather walk than ride.* □ *If it's all the same, I'd rather you didn't smoke.*

all the time **1.** throughout a specific period of time. □ *Bill was stealing money for the last two years, and Tom knew it all the time.* □ *Throughout December and January, Jane had two jobs all the time.* **2.** at all times; continuously. □ *Your blood keeps flowing all the time.* □ *That electric motor runs all the time.* **3.** repeatedly; habitually. □ *She keeps a handkerchief in her hand all the time.* □ *She hums softly all the time.*

all the way from the beginning to the end; the entire distance, from start to finish. (See also *go all the way with someone*.) □ *The ladder reaches all the way to the top of the house.* □ *I walked all the way home.*

all thumbs very awkward and clumsy, especially with one's hands. □ *Poor Bob can't play the piano at all. He's all thumbs.* □ *Mary is all thumbs when it comes to gardening.*

all to the good for the best; for one's benefit. □ *He missed the train, but it was all to the good because the train had a wreck.* □ *It was all to the good that he died without suffering.*

all told totaled up; including all parts. □ *All told, he earned about $700 last week.* □ *All told, he has many fine characteristics.*

all tuckered out* AND **tuckered out*** tired out; worn out. (Folksy.) □ *Poor John worked so hard that he's all tuckered out.* □ *Look at that little baby sleeping. She's really tuckered out.*

all walks of life all social, economic, and ethnic groups. □ *We saw people there from all walks of life.* □ *The people who came to the art exhibit represented all walks of life.*

all wet* mistaken; wrong-headed; on the wrong track. (Slang. Also used literally.) □ *It's not that way, John. You're all wet.* □ *If you think that prices will come down, you're all wet.*

all wool and a yard wide* genuinely warm-hearted and friendly. (Informal and folksy. Refers to woolen cloth which is 100% wool and exactly the standard width of one yard.) □ *Old Bob is a true gentleman—all wool and a yard wide.* □ *The banker, hardly all wool and a yard wide, wouldn't give us a loan.*

All work and no play makes Jack a dull boy. a proverb meaning that one should have recreation as well as work. (*Jack* does not refer to anyone in particular, and the phrase can be used for persons of either sex.) □ *Stop reading that book and go out and play! All work and no play makes Jack a dull boy.* □ *The doctor told Mr. Jones to stop working on weekends and start playing golf, because all work and no play makes Jack a dull boy.*

all worked up over something AND **all worked up about something; all worked up** excited and agitated about something. □ *Tom is all worked up over the threats of a new war.* □ *Don't get all worked up about something which you* *can't do anything about.* □ *Bill is all worked up again. It's bad for his health.*

all year round   throughout all the seasons of the year; during the entire year. □ *The public swimming pool is enclosed so that it can be used all year round.* □ *In the South they can grow flowers all year round.*

All's well that ends well.*   a proverb meaning that an event which has a good ending is good even if some things went wrong along the way. (This is the name of a play by Shakespeare. It is now used as a cliché.) □ *I'm glad you finally got here even though your car had a flat tire on the way. Oh well. All's well that ends well.* □ *The groom was late for the wedding, but everything worked out all right. All's well that ends well.*

allow for someone or something   **1.** to plan on having enough of something (such as food, space, etc.) for someone. □ *Mary is bringing Bill on the picnic, so be sure to allow for him when buying the food.* □ *Allow for an extra person when setting the table tonight.* **2.** to plan on the possibility of something. □ *Allow for a few rainy days on your vacation.* □ *Be sure to allow for future growth when you plant the rose bushes.*

along in years   See *get along in years; up in years.*

alongside of someone or something AND **alongside someone or something**   **1.** beside or moving beside a person or a thing. □ *Our driveway is alongside our house.* □ *John is running alongside of Tom.* □ *The car is traveling alongside the fence.* **2.** as compared to a person or a thing. (Informal. The things being compared need not be beside one another.) □ *Our car looks quite small alongside of theirs.* □ *My power of concentration is quite limited alongside of yours.*

amount to something   (for someone or something) to be or to become valuable or successful. □ *Most parents hope that their children will amount to something.* □ *I put $200 in the bank, and I hope it will amount to something in twenty years.* □ *I'm glad to see that Bill Jones finally amounts to something.*

An eye for an eye, a tooth for a tooth.
a Biblical theme indicating that punishment should equal the offense. (Now used as a proverb.) □ *Little John pulled Jane's hair, so the teacher pulled John's hair as punishment, saying, "An eye for an eye, a tooth for a tooth."* □ *He kicked me in the leg, so I kicked him in the leg. After all, an eye for an eye, a tooth for a tooth.*

An ounce of prevention is worth a pound of cure.   a proverb meaning that it is easier and better to prevent something bad than to deal with the results. □ *When you ride in a car, buckle your seat belt. An ounce of prevention is worth a pound of cure.* □ *Every child should be vaccinated against polio. An ounce of prevention is worth a pound of cure.*

and the like*   and other similar things. (Informal.) □ *Whenever we go on a picnic, we take potato chips, hot dogs, soda pop, and the like.* □ *I'm very tired of being yelled at, pushed around, and the like.*

and then some*   and even more; more than has been mentioned. (Folksy.) □ *John is going to have to run like a deer and then some to win this race.* □ *The cook put the amount of salt called for into the soup and then some.*

another country heard from*   a catch phrase said when someone makes a comment or interrupts. (Folksy.) □ *Jane and Bill were discussing business when Bob interrupted to offer an opinion. "Another country heard from," said Jane.* □ *In the middle of the discussion, the baby started crying. "Another country heard from," said Tom.*

answer for someone or something to assume responsibility for someone or something; to vouch for someone; to tell of the goodness of someone's character. □ *John had to answer for the theft of the bicycle since it was found at his house.* □ *Mr. Jones, who had known the girl all her life, answered for her. He knew she was innocent.* □ *Someday we'll all have to answer for our wrongdoings.*

answer someone's purpose AND **serve someone's purpose**   to fit or suit someone's purpose. □ *This piece of wood will answer my purpose quite nicely.* □ *The new car serves our purpose perfectly.*

answer to someone to explain to someone; to justify one's actions to someone. (Usually with *have to*.) □ *If John cannot behave properly, he'll have to answer to me.* □ *The car thief will have to answer to the judge.*

any number of someone or something a large number; a sufficiently large number. (Used when the exact number is not important.) □ *Any number of people can vouch for my honesty.* □ *I can give you any number of reasons why I should join the army.* □ *I ate there any number of times and never became ill.*

appear as something to act a certain part in a play, opera, etc. □ *Madame Smith-Franklin appeared as Carmen at the City Opera last season.* □ *The actor refused to appear as a villain in the play.*

apple of someone's eye someone's favorite person or thing; a boyfriend or a girlfriend. □ *Tom is the apple of Mary's eye. She thinks he's great.* □ *John's new stereo is the apple of his eye.*

arise from something to get up from something; to improve one's situation. □ *Jane arose from bed refreshed by a good night's sleep.* □ *Bob arose from poverty to become a successful banker.*

arm in arm linked or hooked together by the arms. □ *The two lovers walked arm in arm down the street.* □ *Arm in arm, the line of dancers kicked high, and the audience roared its approval.*

armed to the teeth* heavily armed with deadly weapons. (A cliché.) □ *The bank robber was armed to the teeth when he was caught.* □ *There are too many guns around. The entire country is armed to the teeth.*

around the clock AND **round the clock** continuously for twenty-four hours at a time. □ *The priceless jewels were guarded around the clock.* □ *Grandfather was so sick that he had to have nurses round the clock.* ALSO: **around-the-clock** constant; day and night. □ *Grandfather required around-the-clock care.*

arrange something with someone 1. AND **arrange to do something with someone** to plan an event to include another person or persons. □ *Jane arranged a meeting with Ann.* □ *Bill arranged to go to the station with Tom and Mary.* **2.** to get someone's consent for something. □ *Mary arranged the entire affair with her employer.* □ *The new mother arranged the christening with the pastor.*

as a duck takes to water* easily and naturally. (Informal.) □ *She took to singing, just as a duck takes to water.* □ *The baby adapted to bottle feeding as a duck takes to water.*

as a general rule AND **as a rule** usually; almost always. □ *He can be found in his office as a general rule.* □ *As a general rule, Jane plays golf on Wednesdays.* □ *As a rule, things tend to get less busy after supper time.*

as a last resort as the last choice; if everything else fails. □ *Call the doctor at home only as a last resort.* □ *As a last resort, she will perform surgery.*

as a matter of course normally; as a normal procedure. □ *The nurse always takes your temperature as a matter of course.* □ *You are expected to make your own bed as a matter of course.*

as a matter of fact in addition to what has been said; in reference to what has been said. (See also *matter-of-fact*.) □ *As a matter of fact, John came into the room while you were talking about him.* □ *I'm not a poor worker. As a matter of fact, I'm very efficient.*

as a result of something because of something which has happened. □ *As a result of the accident, Tom couldn't walk for six months.* □ *We couldn't afford to borrow money for a house as a result of the rise in interest rates.*

as a rule See *as a general rule*.

as a token of something AND **as a token** symbolic of something, especially of gratitude; as a memento of something. □ *He gave me a rose as a token of the time we spent together.* □ *Here, take this $100 as a token of my appreciation.* □ *I can't thank you enough. Please accept this money as a token.*

as an aside as a comment; as a comment which is not supposed to be heard by everyone. □ *At the wedding, Tom said as an aside, "The bride doesn't look well."* □ *At the ballet, Billy said as an aside to his mother, "I hope the dancers fall off the stage!"*

as bad as all that as bad as reported; as bad as it seems. (Usually expressed in the negative.) □ *Come on! Nothing could be as bad as all that.* □ *Stop crying. It can't be as bad as all that.*

as big as all outdoors* very big, usually referring to a space of some kind. (Folksy.) □ *You should see Bob's living room. It's as big as all outdoors.* □ *The new movie theater is as big as all outdoors.*

as big as life* AND **as big as life and twice as ugly*** an exaggerated way of saying that a person or a thing appeared in a particular place. (Folksy. The second phrase is slang.) □ *The little child just stood there as big as life and laughed very hard.* □ *I opened the door, and there was Tom as big as life.* □ *I came home and found this cat in my chair, as big as life and twice as ugly.*

as blind as a bat with imperfect sight; blind. (The first *as* can be omitted.) □ *My grandmother is as blind as a bat.* □ *I'm getting blind as a bat. I can hardly read this page.*

as busy as a beaver AND **as busy as a bee** very busy. (The first *as* can be omitted.) □ *I don't have time to talk to you. I'm as busy as a beaver.* □ *You don't look busy as a beaver to me.* □ *Whenever there is a holiday, we are all as busy as bees.*

as busy as a bee See the previous entry.

as busy as Grand Central Station very busy; crowded with customers or other people. (The first *as* can be omitted. This refers to Grand Central Station in New York City.) □ *This house is as busy as Grand Central Station.* □ *When the tourist season starts, this store is busy as Grand Central Station.*

as clear as mud* not understandable. (Informal. The first *as* can be omitted.) □ *Your explanation is as clear as mud.* □ *This doesn't make sense. It's clear as mud.*

as comfortable as an old shoe very comfortable; very comforting and familiar. (The first *as* can be omitted.) □ *This old house is fine. It's as comfortable as an old shoe.* □ *That's a great tradition—comfortable as an old shoe.*

as cool as a cucumber* calm and not agitated; with one's wits about one. (Informal. The first *as* can be omitted.) □ *The captain remained as cool as a cucumber as the passengers boarded the lifeboats.* □ *During the fire the homeowner was cool as a cucumber.*

as crazy as a loon* very silly; completely insane. (Folksy. The first *as* can be omitted.) □ *If you think you can get away with that, you're as crazy as a loon.* □ *Poor old John is crazy as a loon.*

as dead as a dodo* dead; no longer in existence. (Informal. The first *as* can be omitted.) □ *Yes, Adolph Hitler is really dead—as dead as a dodo.* □ *That silly old idea is dead as a dodo.*

as dead as a doornail* dead. (Informal. The first *as* can be omitted.) □ *This fish is as dead as a doornail.* □ *John kept twisting the chicken's neck even though it was dead as a doornail.*

as different as night and day completely different. (The first *as* can be omitted.) □ *Although Bobby and Billy are twins, they are as different as night and day.* □ *Birds and bats appear to be similar, but they are different as night and day.*

as easy as apple pie See *as easy as pie*.

as easy as duck soup* very easy; requiring no effort. (Informal. When a duck is cooked, it releases a lot of fat and juices, making a "soup" without effort. The first *as* can be omitted.) □ *Finding your way to the shopping center is easy as duck soup.* □ *Getting Bob to eat fried chicken is as easy as duck soup.*

as easy as falling off a log* very easy. (Folksy. The first *as* can be omitted.) □ *Passing that exam was as easy as falling off a log.* □ *Getting out of jail was easy as falling off a log.*

as easy as pie* AND **as easy as apple pie*** very easy. (Informal. The first *as* can be omitted.) □ *Mountain climbing is as easy as pie.* □ *Making a simple dress out of cotton cloth is easy as pie.*

as far as anyone knows* AND **so far as anyone knows*** to the limits of anyone's knowledge. (Informal. The *any-*

one can be replaced with a more specific noun or pronoun. The first *as* can be omitted.) □ *As far as anyone knows, this is the last of the great herds of buffalo.* □ *Far as I know, this is the best one.* □ *These are the only keys to the house so far as anyone knows.*

as far as I'm concerned* AND **so far as I'm concerned*** for all I care; if I'm to make the decision. (Informal. The first *as* can be omitted.) □ *You can take your old dog and leave as far as I'm concerned.* □ *Far as I'm concerned, you can get out and never come back.* □ *So far as I'm concerned, you're okay.*

as far as it goes as much as something does, covers, or accomplishes. (Usually said of something which is inadequate.) □ *Your plan is fine as far as it goes. It doesn't seem to take care of everything, though.* □ *As far as it goes, this law is a good one. It should require stiffer penalties, however.*

as far as possible AND **so far as possible** as much as possible; to whatever degree is possible. □ *We must try, as far as possible, to get people to stop smoking in buses.* □ *As far as possible, the police will issue tickets to all speeding drivers.* □ *I'll follow your instructions so far as possible.*

as fit as a fiddle* healthy and physically fit. (Informal. The first *as* can be omitted.) □ *Mary is as fit as a fiddle.* □ *Tom used to be fit as a fiddle. Look at him now!*

as flat as a pancake* very flat. (Informal. The first *as* can be omitted.) □ *The punctured tire was as flat as a pancake.* □ *Bobby squashed the ant flat as a pancake.*

as for someone or something 1. AND **as to someone or something** regarding someone or something. □ *As for the mayor, he can pay for his own dinner.* □ *As for you, Bobby, there will be no dessert tonight.* □ *As for this chair, there is nothing to do but throw it away.* □ *As to your idea about building a new house, forget it.* **2.** [with *someone*] quoting someone; speaking for someone. □ *As for me, I prefer vegetables to meat.* □ *As for Tom, he refuses to attend the concert.*

as free as a bird carefree; completely free. (The first *as* can be omitted.) □ *Jane is always happy and free as a bird.* □ *The convict escaped from jail and was as free as a bird for two days.* □ *In the summer I feel free as a bird.*

as full as a tick* AND **as tight as a tick*** very full of food or drink. (Informal. Refers to a tick which has filled itself full of blood. The first *as* can be omitted.) □ *Little Billy ate and ate until he was as full as a tick.* □ *Our cat drank the cream until he became full as a tick.*

as funny as a crutch* not funny at all. (Informal. Compare to *as clear as mud*. The first *as* can be omitted.) □ *Your trick is about as funny as a crutch. Nobody thought it was funny.* □ *The well-dressed lady slipped and fell in the gutter, which was funny as a crutch.*

as good as done the same as being done; almost done. (Many different past participles can replace *done* in this phrase: *cooked, dead, finished, painted, typed,* etc.) □ *This job is as good as done. It'll just take another second.* □ *Yes sir, if you hire me to paint your house, it's as good as painted.* □ *When I hand my secretary a letter to be typed, I know that it's as good as typed right then and there.*

as good as gold* genuine; authentic. (A cliché. The first *as* can be omitted.) □ *Mary's promise is as good as gold.* □ *Yes, this diamond is genuine—good as gold.*

as happy as a clam happy and content. (The first *as* can be omitted. Note the variations in the examples.) □ *Tom sat there smiling, as happy as a clam.* □ *There they all sat eating corn on the cob and looking happy as clams.*

as happy as a lark visibly happy and cheerful. (The first *as* can be omitted. Note the variations in the examples.) □ *Sally walked along whistling, as happy as a lark.* □ *The children danced and sang, happy as larks.*

as hard as nails very hard; cold and cruel. (Refers to the nails which are used with a hammer. The first *as* can be omitted.) □ *The old loaf of bread was dried out and became as hard as nails.* □ *Ann was unpleasant and hard as nails.*

as high as a kite AND **as high as the sky** (The first *as* can be omitted.) **1.** very high. □ *The tree grew as high as a kite.* □ *Our pet bird got outside and flew up high as the sky.* **2.** drunk or drugged. □ *Bill drank beer until he got as high as a kite.* □ *The thieves were high as the sky on drugs.*

as high as the sky See the previous entry.

as hot as hell* very hot. (Informal. Use *hell* with caution. The first *as* can be omitted.) □ *It's as hot as hell outside. It must be near 100 degrees.* □ *I hate to get into a car that has been parked in the sun. It's hot as hell.*

as hungry as a bear* very hungry. (Informal. The first *as* can be omitted.) □ *I'm as hungry as a bear. I could eat anything!* □ *Whenever I jog, I get hungry as a bear.*

as innocent as a lamb* guiltless; naive. (A cliché. The first *as* can be omitted.) □ *"Hey! You can't throw me in jail," cried the robber. "I'm innocent as a lamb."* □ *Look at the baby, as innocent as a lamb.*

as it were as one might say. (Sometimes used to qualify an assertion which may not sound reasonable.) □ *He carefully constructed, as it were, a huge sandwich.* □ *The Franklins live in a small, as it were, exquisite house.*

as light as a feather* of little weight. (Informal. The first *as* can be omitted.) □ *Sally dieted until she was as light as a feather.* □ *Of course I can lift the box. It's light as a feather.*

as likely as not probably; with an even chance either way. (The first *as* can be omitted.) □ *He will as likely as not arrive without warning.* □ *Likely as not, the game will be cancelled.*

as long as 1. AND **so long as** since; because. □ *As long as you're going to the bakery, please buy some fresh bread.* □ *So long as you're here, please stay for dinner.* **2.** AND **so long as** if; only if. □ *You may have dessert so long as you eat all your vegetables.* □ *You can go out this evening as long as you promise to be home by midnight.* **3.** for a specified length of time. □ *You may stay out as long as you like.* □ *I didn't go to school as long as Bill did.*

as luck would have it by good or bad luck; as it turned out; by chance. □ *As luck would have it, we had a flat tire.* □ *As luck would have it, the check came in the mail today.*

as mad as a hatter 1. crazy. (From the character called the Mad Hatter in Lewis Carroll's *Alice in Wonderland*. The first *as* can be omitted.) □ *Poor old John is as mad as a hatter.* □ *All these screaming children are driving me mad as a hatter.* **2.*** angry. (This is a misunderstanding of *mad* in the first sense. Folksy. The first *as* can be omitted.) □ *You make me so angry! I'm as mad as a hatter.* □ *John can't control his temper. He's always mad as a hatter.*

as mad as a hornet* angry. (Informal. The first *as* can be omitted.) □ *You make me so angry. I'm as mad as a hornet.* □ *Jane can get mad as a hornet when somebody criticizes her.*

as mad as a March hare crazy. (From the name of a character in Lewis Carroll's *Alice in Wonderland*. The first *as* can be omitted.) □ *Sally is getting as mad as a March hare.* □ *My Uncle Bill is mad as a March hare.*

as mad as a wet hen* angry. (Folksy. The first *as* can be omitted.) □ *Bob was screaming and shouting—as mad as a wet hen.* □ *What you said made Mary mad as a wet hen.*

as mad as hell* very angry. (Informal. Use *hell* with caution. The first *as* can be omitted.) □ *He made his wife as mad as hell.* □ *Those terrorists make me mad as hell.*

as naked as a jaybird* naked. (Folksy. A jaybird is a parrot, in this case, one which has plucked out its feathers. The first *as* can be omitted.) □ *"Billy," called Mrs. Franklin, "get back in the house and get some clothes on. You're as naked as a jaybird."* □ *Tom had to get naked as a jaybird for the doctor to examine him.*

as one as if a group were one person. (Especially with *act, move,* or *speak.*) □ *All the dancers moved as one.* □ *The chorus spoke as one.*

as plain as day* (Informal. The first *as* can be omitted.) **1.** very plain and simple. □ *Although his face was as plain as* *day, his smile made him look interesting and friendly.* □ *Our house is plain as day, but it's comfortable.* **2.** clear and understandable. □ *The lecture was as plain as day. No one had to ask questions.* □ *His statement was plain as day.*

as plain as the nose on one's face* obvious; clearly evident. (Informal. The first *as* can be omitted.) □ *What do you mean you don't understand? It's as plain as the nose on your face.* □ *Your guilt is plain as the nose on your face.*

as poor as a church mouse* very poor. (A cliché. The first *as* can be omitted.) □ *My Aunt is as poor as a church mouse.* □ *The Browns are poor as church mice.*

as pretty as a picture* very pretty. (A cliché. The first *as* can be omitted.) □ *Sweet little Mary is as pretty as a picture.* □ *Their new house is pretty as a picture.*

as proud as a peacock* very proud; haughty. (A cliché. The first *as* can be omitted.) □ *John is so arrogant. He's as proud as a peacock.* □ *The new father was proud as a peacock.*

as quick as a wink* very quickly. (A cliché. The first *as* can be omitted.) □ *As quick as a wink, the thief took the lady's purse.* □ *I'll finish this work quick as a wink.*

as quick as greased lightning* very quickly; very fast. (Folksy. The first *as* can be omitted.) □ *Jane can really run. She's as quick as greased lightning.* □ *Quick as greased lightning, the thief stole my wallet.*

as quiet as a mouse* very quiet; shy and silent. (Informal. Often used with children. The first *as* can be omitted.) □ *Don't yell; whisper. Be as quiet as a mouse.* □ *Mary hardly ever says anything. She's quiet as a mouse.*

as regular as clockwork* dependably regular. (Informal. The first *as* can be omitted. See also *go like clockwork*.) □ *She comes into this store everyday, as regular as clockwork.* □ *Our tulips come up every year, regular as clockwork.*

as right as rain* correct; genuine. (Folksy. The first *as* can be omitted.) □ *Your answer is as right as rain.* □ *John is very dependable. He's right as rain.*

as scarce as hen's teeth* AND **scarcer than hen's teeth*** very scarce or nonexistent. (A cliché. Chickens don't have teeth. The first *as* can be omitted.) □ *I've never seen one of those. They're as scarce as hen's teeth.* □ *I was told that the part needed for my car is scarcer than hen's teeth, and it would take a long time to find one.*

as sick as a dog* very sick; sick and vomiting. (Informal. The first *as* can be omitted.) □ *We've never been so ill. The whole family was sick as dogs.* □ *Sally was as sick as a dog and couldn't go to the party.*

as slick as a whistle* quickly and cleanly; quickly and skillfully. (Folksy. The first *as* can be omitted.) □ *Tom took a broom and a mop and cleaned the place up as slick as a whistle.* □ *Slick as a whistle, Sally pulled off the bandage.*

as slippery as an eel* devious; undependable. (Informal. Also used literally. The first *as* can be omitted.) □ *Tom can't be trusted. He's as slippery as an eel.* □ *It's hard to catch Joe in his office because he's slippery as an eel.*

as smart as a fox* smart and clever. (Informal. The first *as* can be omitted.) □ *My nephew is as smart as a fox.* □ *You have to be smart as a fox to outwit me.*

as snug as a bug in a rug* cozy and snug. (Informal. The kind of thing said when putting a child to bed. The first *as* can be omitted.) □ *Let's pull up the covers. There you are, Bobby, as snug as a bug in a rug.* □ *What a lovely little house! I know I'll be snug as a bug in a rug.*

as sober as a judge* (A cliché. The first *as* can be omitted.) **1.** very formal, somber, or stuffy. □ *You certainly look gloomy, Bill. You're sober as a judge.* □ *Tom's as sober as a judge. I think he's angry.* **2.** not drunk; alert and completely sober. □ *John's drunk? No, he's as sober as a judge.* □ *You should be sober as a judge when you drive a car.*

as soft as a baby's bottom* very soft and smooth to the touch. (Informal. The first *as* can be omitted.) □ *This cloth is as soft as a baby's bottom.* □ *No, Bob* *doesn't shave yet. His cheeks are soft as a baby's bottom.*

as soon as possible at the earliest time. □ *I'm leaving now. I'll be there as soon as possible.* □ *Please pay me as soon as possible.*

as strong as an ox* very strong. (Informal. The first *as* can be omitted.) □ *Tom lifts weights and is as strong as an ox.* □ *Now that Ann has recovered from her illness, she's strong as an ox.*

as stubborn as a mule* very stubborn. (Informal. The first *as* can be omitted.) □ *My husband is as stubborn as a mule.* □ *Our cat is stubborn as a mule.*

as the crow flies* straight across the land, as opposed to distances measured on a road, river, etc. (Folksy.) □ *It's twenty miles to town on the highway, but only ten miles as the crow flies.* □ *Our house is only a few miles from the lake as the crow flies.*

as thick as pea soup* very thick. (Informal. Usually used in reference to fog. The first *as* can be omitted.) □ *This fog is as thick as pea soup.* □ *Wow, this coffee is strong! It's thick as pea soup.*

as thick as thieves* very close-knit; friendly; allied. (A cliché. The first *as* can be omitted.) □ *Mary, Tom, and Sally are as thick as thieves. They go everywhere together.* □ *Those two families are thick as thieves.*

as tight as a tick See *as full as a tick.*

as tight as Dick's hatband* very tight. (A cliché. The first *as* can be omitted.) □ *I've got to lose some weight. My belt is as tight as Dick's hatband.* □ *This window is stuck tight as Dick's hatband.*

as to someone or something See *as for someone or something.*

as weak as a kitten* weak; weak and sickly. (Informal. The first *as* can be omitted.) □ *John is as weak as a kitten because he doesn't eat well.* □ *Oh! Suddenly I feel weak as a kitten.*

as white as the driven snow* very white. (A cliché. The first *as* can be omitted.) □ *I like my bed sheets to be as white as the driven snow.* □ *We have a new kitten whose fur is white as the driven snow.*

as wise as an owl* very wise. (A cliché. The first *as* can be omitted.) □ *Grandfather is as wise as an owl.* □ *My goal is to be wise as an owl.*

ashamed of someone or something having shame about someone or something. □ *I'm ashamed of my ragged clothing.* □ *There is no need to be ashamed of your brother.*

aside from someone or something not including someone or something. □ *Aside from a small bank account, I have no money at all.* □ *Aside from Mary, I have no friends.*

ask about someone or something to inquire about someone or something; to ask about the state of someone or something. □ *John asked about Mary's brother. Mary replied that he was fine.* □ *Mary asked about the house we were building. We told her that it was coming along nicely.*

ask for someone or something 1. to request someone or something; to request that someone make an appearance. □ *You must go out on stage, Mary. They are asking for you.* □ *They are all standing there asking for more ice cream.* **2.** to do something which will cause trouble. (See also *ask for trouble.*) □ *Don't talk to me that way! You're really asking for it.* □ *Anyone who acts like that is just asking for a good talking to.*

ask for the moon to ask for too much; to make great demands. □ *When you're trying to get a job, it's unwise to ask for the moon.* □ *Please lend me the money. I'm not asking for the moon!*

ask for trouble to do or say something which will cause trouble. □ *Stop talking to me that way, John. You're just asking for trouble.* □ *Anybody who threatens a police officer is just asking for trouble.*

ask someone for something to request that a person give you something. □ *I asked you for some help. Hurry up and help me!* □ *Please go and ask the butcher for a soup bone.*

ask someone out AND **ask out someone** to ask a person for a date. □ *Mary hopes that John will ask her out.* □ *John doesn't want to ask out his best friend's girl.*

asleep at the switch not attending to one's job; failing to do one's duty at the proper time. □ *The guard was asleep at the switch when the robber broke in.* □ *If I hadn't been asleep at the switch, I'd have seen the stolen car.*

astonished at someone or something very much surprised by someone or something. □ *Bill was astonished at Mary and the way she acted.* □ *Mary was astonished at the size of John's new car.*

at a loss for words AND **at a loss** unable to speak; speechless; befuddled. □ *I was so surprised that I was at a loss for words.* □ *Tom was terribly confused—really at a loss.*

at a premium at a high price; priced high because of something special. □ *Sally bought the shoes at a premium because they were of very high quality.* □ *This model of car is selling at a premium because so many people want to buy it.*

at a set time at a particular time; at an assigned time. □ *Each person has to show up at a set time.* □ *Do I have to be there at a set time, or can I come whenever I want?*

at a sitting at one time; during one period. (Usually refers to an activity which takes place while a person is seated.) □ *The restaurant could feed only sixty people at a sitting.* □ *I can read about 300 pages at a sitting.*

at a snail's pace very slowly. □ *When you watch a clock, time seems to move at a snail's pace.* □ *You always eat at a snail's pace. I'm tired of waiting for you.*

at all without distinguishing; without qualification. (See the examples for word order variations.) □ *It really wasn't very cold at all.* □ *It really wasn't at all cold.* □ *Tom will eat anything at all.* □ *Jane isn't at all hungry.* □ *Grandma was always ready to go anywhere at all.*

at all costs AND **at any cost** regardless of the difficulty or cost; no matter what. □ *I intend to have that car at all costs.* □ *I'll get there by six o'clock at all costs.* □ *Mary was going to get that job at any cost.*

at all times constantly; continuously. □ *You must keep your passport handy at all times when you are traveling in a foreign country.* □ *When you're in a crowd, you must watch your child at all times.*

at an early date soon; some day soon. □ *The note said, "Please call me at an early date."* □ *You're expected to return the form to the office at an early date.*

at any cost See *at all costs.*

at any rate* anyway. (Informal. Frequently used as an introduction to a conclusion or a final statement. Also used literally.) □ *At any rate, we had a nice time at your party. We are grateful that you asked us.* □ *It's not much at any rate, but it's the best we can do.*

at best AND **at most; at the best; at the most** in the best view; in the most positive judgement; as the best one can say. □ *I believe her to be totally negligent. Her actions were careless at best.* □ *At best we found their visit pleasantly short.* □ *The dinner was not at all pleasant. At the best the food was not burned.* □ *At the most she was careless, but not criminal.* □ *We found their visit pleasingly short at most.*

at close range very near; in close proximity. (Usually used in regard to shooting.) □ *The hunter fired at the deer at close range.* □ *The powder burns tell us that the gun was fired at close range.*

at cross purposes with opposing purposes; with goals which interfere with each other. □ *We are arguing at cross purposes. We aren't even discussing the same thing.* □ *Bill and Tom are working at cross purposes. They'll never get the job done right.*

at death's door near death. (Euphemistic.) □ *I was so ill that I was at death's door.* □ *The family dog was at death's door for three days, and then it finally died.*

at ease relaxed and comfortable. □ *I don't feel at ease driving when there is lots of traffic.* □ *Mary is most at ease when she's near the sea.*

at every turn everywhere; everywhere one looks. □ *There is a new problem at every turn.* □ *Life holds new adventures at every turn.*

at first initially; at the beginning. □ *He was shy at first. Then he became more friendly.* □ *At first we chose the red one. Later we switched to the blue one.*

at first blush See the following entry.

at first glance AND **at first blush** when first examined; at an early stage. □ *At first glance, the problem appeared quite simple. Later we learned just how complex it really was.* □ *He appeared quite healthy at first glance.* □ *At first blush, she appeared to be quite old.*

at full speed AND **at full tilt** as fast as possible. □ *The motor was running at full speed.* □ *John finished his running at full speed.* □ *Things are now operating at full tilt.*

at full tilt See the previous entry.

at half mast halfway up or down. (Primarily referring to flags. Can be used for things other than flags as a joke.) □ *The flag was flying at half mast because the general had died.* □ *Americans fly flags at half mast on Memorial Day.* □ *The little boy ran out of the house with his pants at half mast.*

at hand close by. (Used with both time and distance.) □ *I don't happen to have your application at hand at the moment.* □ *With the holiday season at hand, everyone is very excited.*

at home at or in one's dwelling. □ *Is Mary at home, or is she still at work?* □ *What time will she be at home?*

at home with someone or something comfortable with someone or something; comfortable doing something. □ *Tom is very much at home with my parents.* □ *Sally seems to be very much at home with her car.* □ *Mary seems to be at home with selling stock.*

at it again* doing something again. (Informal.) □ *I asked Tom to stop playing his trumpet, but he's at it again.* □ *They are at it again. Why are they always fighting?*

at large **1.** free; uncaptured. (Usually said of criminals running loose.) □ *At noon the day after the robbery, the thieves were still at large.* □ *There is a murderer at large in the city.* **2.** in general; according to a general sample. □ *Truck drivers at large don't like the new law.* □ *Students at large felt that the rule was too strict.* **3.** representing the whole group rather than its subsections. (Always refers to a special kind of elective office.) □ *He ran for representative at large.* □ *She represented shareholders at large on the governing board.*

at last AND **at long last** after a long wait; finally. □ *At last the hostages were released.* □ *Sally earned her diploma at long last.*

at least **1.** no less than; no fewer than. □ *There were at least four people there that I knew.* □ *I want to spend at least three weeks in Mexico.* **2.** anyway; in spite of difficulties. □ *At least we had a good evening, even though the afternoon was rainy.* □ *At least we came away with some of our money left.*

at leisure **1.** resting; not working. □ *What do you usually do when you are at leisure?* □ *During the summer when you are at leisure, you ought to play golf.* **2.** AND **at one's leisure** at one's convenience. □ *Choose one or the other at your leisure.* □ *Please drop by at your leisure.*

at length **1.** after some time; finally. □ *At length, the roses bloomed, and the tomatoes ripened.* □ *And at length, the wizard spoke.* **2.** AND **at some length** for quite a long time. □ *He spoke on and on at some length.* □ *He described the history of his village at length.*

at liberty free; unrestrained. □ *The criminal was set at liberty by the judge.* □ *You're at liberty to go anywhere you wish.* □ *I'm not at liberty to discuss the matter.*

at loggerheads in opposition; at an impasse; in a quarrel. □ *Mr. and Mrs. Franklin have been at loggerheads for years.* □ *The two political parties were at loggerheads during the entire legislative session.*

at long last See *at last*.

at loose ends restless and unsettled; unemployed. □ *Just before school starts, all the children are at loose ends.* □ *When Tom is home on the weekends, he's always at loose ends.* □ *Jane has been at loose ends ever since she lost her job.*

at most See *at best*.

at odds with someone AND **at odds** in opposition to someone; *at loggerheads* with someone. □ *Mary is always at odds with her father about how late she can stay out.* □ *John and his father are always at odds, too.*

at once immediately; at this very moment. □ *John, come here at once!* □ *Bring me my coffee at once!* □ *Shall I do it at once or wait until morning?*

at one fell swoop* AND **in one fell swoop*** in a single incident; as a single event. (This phrase preserves the old word *fell*, meaning terrible. Now a cliché, sometimes with humorous overtones.) □ *The party guests ate up all the snacks at one fell swoop.* □ *When the stock market crashed, many large fortunes were wiped out in one fell swoop.*

at one's best in the best of health; displaying the most civilized behavior. (Often in the negative.) □ *I'm not at my best when I'm angry.* □ *He's at his best after a good nap.*

at one's wits' end at the limits of one's mental resources. □ *I'm at my wits' end with this problem. I cannot figure it out.* □ *Tom could do no more. He was at his wits' end.*

at present now; at this point in time. □ *We are not able to do any more at present.* □ *We may be able to lend you money next week, but not at present.*

at random without sequence or order. □ *Sally picked four names at random from the telephone book.* □ *The gunman walked into the crowded restaurant and fired at random.* □ *Jane will read almost anything. She selects four novels at random at the library each week and reads them all.*

at sea about something AND **at sea** confused; lost and bewildered. □ *Mary is all at sea about getting married.* □ *When it comes to higher math, John is totally at sea.*

at sixes and sevens disorderly; lost and bewildered; *at loose ends.* □ *Mrs. Smith is at sixes and sevens since the death of her husband.* □ *Bill is always at sixes and sevens when he's home by himself.*

at someone's beck and call ready to obey someone. □ *What makes you think I wait around here at your beck and call? I live here, too, you know!* □ *It was a fine hotel. There were dozens of maids and waiters at our beck and call.*

at someone's doorstep AND **on someone's doorstep** in someone's care; as someone's responsibility. □ *Why do you always have to lay your problems at my doorstep?* □ *I shall put this issue on someone else's doorstep.* □ *I don't want it on my doorstep.*

at someone's earliest convenience as soon as it is easy or convenient for someone. (This is also a polite way of saying *immediately.*) □ *Please stop by my office at your earliest convenience.* □ *Bill, please have the oil changed at your earliest convenience.*

at someone's request due to someone's request; on being asked by someone. □ *At his mother's request, Tom stopped playing the saxophone.* □ *At the request of the police officer, Bill pulled his car over to the side of the road.*

at sometime sharp exactly at a named time. □ *You must be here at noon sharp.* □ *The plane is expected to arrive at 7:45 sharp.*

at stake to be won or lost; at risk; hanging in the balance. □ *That's a very risky investment. How much money is at stake?* □ *I have everything at stake on this wager.*

at that rate in that manner; at that speed. (See also *at this rate.*) □ *If things keep progressing at that rate, we'll be rich by next year.* □ *At that rate we'll never get the money which is owed us.*

at the appointed time at the announced or assigned time. □ *The cab pulled up in the driveway at the appointed time.* □ *We all met at the hotel at the appointed time.*

at the best See *at best.*

at the bottom of the ladder at the lowest level of pay and status. □ *Most people start work at the bottom of the ladder.* □ *When Ann got fired, she had to start all over again at the bottom of the ladder.*

at the break of dawn See the following entry.

at the crack of dawn AND **at the break of dawn** at the earliest light of the day. □ *Jane was always up at the crack of dawn.* □ *The birds start singing at the break of dawn.*

at the drop of a hat immediately and without urging. □ *John was always ready to go fishing at the drop of a hat.*

☐ *If you need help, just call on me. I can come at the drop of a hat.*

at the eleventh hour at the last possible moment. (See also *eleventh-hour decision*.) ☐ *She always turned her term papers in at the eleventh hour.* ☐ *We don't worry about death until the eleventh hour.*

at the end of nowhere at a remote place; at some distance from civilization. ☐ *They live way out in the country at the end of nowhere.* ☐ *The police will never find us here at the end of nowhere.*

at the end of one's rope AND **at the end of one's tether** at the limits of one's endurance. ☐ *I'm at the end of my rope! I just can't go on this way!* ☐ *These kids are driving me out of my mind. I'm at the end of my tether.*

at the end of one's tether See the previous entry.

at the expense of someone or something to the detriment of someone or something; to the harm of someone or something. ☐ *He had a good laugh at the expense of his brother.* ☐ *He took a job in a better place at the expense of a larger income.*

at the last minute at the last possible chance. (Compare to *at the eleventh hour*.) ☐ *Please don't make reservations at the last minute.* ☐ *Why do you ask all your questions at the last minute?*

at the latest no later than. ☐ *Please pay this bill in ten days at the latest.* ☐ *I'll be home by midnight at the latest.*

at the mercy of someone AND **at someone's mercy** under the control of someone; without defense against someone. ☐ *We were left at the mercy of the arresting officer.* ☐ *Mrs. Franklin wanted Mr. Franklin at her mercy.*

at the most See *at best.*

at the outset at the beginning. (See also *from the outset*.) ☐ *It seemed like a very simple problem at the outset.* ☐ *At the outset, they were very happy. Then they had money problems.*

at the outside at the very most. ☐ *The car repairs will cost $300 at the outside.* ☐ *I'll be there in three weeks at the outside.*

at the point of doing something See *on the point of doing something.*

at the present time AND **at this point in time; at this point** now; *at present.* (Used often as a wordy replacement for now.) ☐ *We don't know the location of the stolen car at the present time.* ☐ *The tomatoes are doing nicely at the present time.* ☐ *At this point in time, we feel very sad about his death.* ☐ *Yes, it's sad, but there is nothing we can do at this point.*

at the same time 1. simultaneously; together. ☐ *All the campers returned home at the same time.* ☐ *I cannot drive the car and discuss money at the same time.* 2. nevertheless; however. ☐ *Bill was able to make the car payment. At the same time, he was very angry about the bill.* ☐ *We agree to your demands. At the same time, we object strongly to your methods.*

at the top of one's lungs See the following entry.

at the top of one's voice AND **at the top of one's lungs** with a very loud voice. ☐ *Bill called to Mary at the top of his voice.* ☐ *How can I work when you're all talking at the top of your lungs?*

at this point in time See *at the present time.*

at this rate at this speed. (Compare to *at any rate* and *at that rate*.) ☐ *Hurry up! We'll never get there at this rate.* ☐ *At this rate, all the food will be gone before we get there.*

at this stage of the game* AND **at this stage** at the current point in some event; currently. (The first phrase is informal.) ☐ *We'll have to wait and see. There isn't much we can do at this stage of the game.* ☐ *At this stage, we are better off not calling the doctor.*

at times sometimes; occasionally. ☐ *I feel quite sad at times.* ☐ *At times, I wish I had never come here.*

at will whenever one wants; freely. (Compare to *at liberty*.) ☐ *You're free to come and go at will.* ☐ *The soldiers were told to fire their guns at will.* ☐ *You can eat anything you want at will.*

at work 1. working (at something); busy (with something). ☐ *Tom is at work on his project. He'll be finished in a minute.* ☐ *Don't disturb me when I'm busy at work.* 2. at one's place of work. ☐

I'm sorry to call you at work, but this is important. □ *She's at work now. She'll be home at supper time.*

at worst AND **at the worst** in the worst view; in the most negative judgement; as the worst one can say about something. □ *At worst, Tom can be seen as greedy.* □ *Ann will receive a ticket for careless driving, at the worst.*

attend to someone or something to take care of someone or something; give attention to someone or something. □ *The baby is crying. Please attend to her.* □ *First, you must attend to your homework.*

attract someone's attention to cause someone to take notice; to get someone's attention. □ *I called and waved to attract Ann's attention.* □ *A small yellow flower attracted my attention.*

avail oneself of something to take advantage of an opportunity; to use something. □ *I hope you'll be able to avail yourself of the opportunity to make some extra money.* □ *Mary refused to avail herself of the chance to get promoted.*

avoid someone or something like the plague* to avoid someone or something totally. (Informal.) □ *What's wrong with Bob? Everyone avoids him like the plague.* □ *I don't like opera. I avoid it like the plague.*

aware of someone or something conscious of someone or something; knowing of the existence or presence of someone or something. □ *I didn't mean to bump into you. I was not aware of you.* □ *They were all aware of her efforts to win the election.*

away from one's desk not available for a telephone conversation; not available to be seen. (Sometimes said by the person who answers a telephone in an office. It means that the person whom the caller wants is not immediately available due to personal or business reasons.) □ *I'm sorry, but Ann is away from her desk just now. Can you come back later?* □ *Tom is away from his desk, but if you leave your number, he will call you right back.*

B

babe-in-the-woods a naive or innocent person; an inexperienced person. □ *Bill is a babe-in-the-woods when it comes to dealing with plumbers.* □ *As a painter, Mary is fine, but she's a babe-in-the-woods as a musician.*

back and forth backwards and forwards; first one way and then another way. (Compare to *to and fro.*) □ *The young man was pacing back and forth in the hospital waiting room.* □ *The pendulum on the clock swung back and forth.*

back down from someone or something AND **back off from someone or something; back down; back off** to yield to a person or a thing; to fail to carry through on a threat. □ *Jane backed down from her position on the budget.* □ *It's probably better to back down from someone than to have an argument.* □ *John agreed that it was probably better to back down than to risk getting shot.* □ *Bill doesn't like to back off from a fight.* □ *Sometimes it's better to back off than to get hurt.*

back East to or from the eastern United States, often the northeastern or New England states. (See also *down South, out West,* and *up North.* This is used even by people who have never been in the East.) □ *Sally felt that she had to get back East for a few days.* □ *Tom went to school back East, but his brother attended college in the Midwest.*

back in circulation **1.** (of a thing) available to the public again. (Said especially of things which are said to circulate such as money, library books, and magazines.) □ *I've heard that gold coins are back in circulation in Europe.* □ *I would like to read* War and Peace. *Is it back in circulation, or is it still checked out?* **2.** (of a person) socially active again; dating again after a divorce or breakup with one's lover. (Informal.) □ *Now that Bill is a free man, he's back in circulation.* □ *Tom was in the hospital for a month, but now he's back in circulation.*

back off from someone or something See *back down from someone or something.*

back order something (for a merchant) to order something which is not in stock and then make delivery to the customer when the goods become available. (The merchant may hold your money until the order is filled.) □ *The store didn't have the replacement part for my vacuum cleaner, so the manager back ordered it for me.* □ *The shop had to back order some of the items on my list.*

back out of something AND **back out** **1.** to move out of something backwards. (See also *back something out.*) □ *Mary started the car and backed out of the garage.* □ *Bob slowly backed out of the room keeping his eye on the angry dog at all times.* **2.** to withdraw from something you have agreed to do; to break an agreement. □ *The buyer tried to back out of the sale, but the seller wouldn't permit it.* □ *Please don't back out of our date.* □ *Mary backed out at the last minute.*

back someone or something up AND **back up someone or something** **1.** to cause someone or something to move backwards or back. □ *Mary backed the car up.* □ *Mary backed up*

22

the car. □ *Bob backed Mary up careful-ly. She couldn't see where she was going.* **2.** to support someone or something; to concur with someone. □ *Please back me up in this argument.* □ *I would like you to back up John in this discussion.*

back something out AND **back out something** to cause something to move out backwards. □ *Mary backed the car out of the garage.* □ *Bob backed the bicycle out of the parking stand.* □ *Hurry up! Back that car out! I want that parking space.*

back-to-back **1.** adjacent and touch-ing backs. □ *They started the duel by standing back-to-back.* □ *Two people who stand back-to-back can manage to see in all directions.* **2.** following imme-diately. (Said of things or events.) □ *The doctor had appointments set up back-to-back all day long.* □ *I have three lecture courses back-to-back every day of the week.*

back to the drawing board* time to start over again; it is time to plan some-thing over again. (A cliché. Take note of the variation shown in the exam-ples.) □ *It didn't work. Back to the draw-ing board.* □ *I flunked English this semester. Well, back to the old drawing board.*

back to the salt mines* time to return to work, school, or something else which might be unpleasant. (A cliché. The phrase implies that the speaker is a slave who works in the salt mines.) □ *It's eight o'clock. Time to go to work! Back to the salt mines.* □ *School starts again in the fall, and then it's back to the salt mines again.*

bad-mouth someone or something* to say bad things about someone or something; to libel someone. (Slang.) □ *Mr. Smith was always bad-mouthing Mrs. Smith. They didn't get along.* □ *John bad-mouths his car constantly because it doesn't run.*

bag and baggage* AND **part and par-cel*** with one's luggage; with all one's possessions. (Informal. See also *part and parcel of something*.) □ *Sally showed up at our door bag and baggage one Sunday morning.* □ *All right, if you won't pay the rent, out with you, bag and baggage!* □ *Get all your stuff—part and parcel—out of here!*

bag of tricks a collection of special tech-niques or methods. □ *What have you got in your bag of tricks that could help me with this problem?* □ *Here comes Mother with her bag of tricks. I'm sure she can help us.*

bail out of something AND **bail out** **1.** to jump out of an airplane (with a parachute). □ *John still remembers the first time he bailed out of a plane.* □ *When we get to 8,000 feet, we'll all bail out and drift down together. We'll open our parachutes at 2,000 feet.* **2.*** to aban-don a situation; to get out of some-thing. (Informal.) □ *John got tired of school, so he just bailed out.* □ *Please stay, Bill. You've been with us too long to bail out now.*

bail someone or something out AND **bail out someone or something** **1.** [with *someone*] to deposit a sum of money which allows someone to get out of jail while waiting for a trial; to get a person out of trouble. □ *John was in jail. I had to go down to the police station to bail him out.* □ *You kids are always getting in trouble. Do you really expect me to bail out the whole gang of you every time you have a problem?* **2.** [with *something*] to remove water from the bottom of a boat by dipping or scoop-ing. □ *Tom has to bail the boat out before we get in.* □ *You should always bail out a boat before using it.*

balance the accounts **1.** AND **balance the books** to determine through accounting that accounts are in bal-ance, that all money is accounted for. □ *Jane was up all night balancing the accounts.* □ *The cashier was not allowed to leave the bank until the manager bal-anced the books.* **2.** to get even with someone. □ *Tom hit Bob. Bob bal-anced the accounts by breaking Tom's toy car.* □ *Once we have balanced the accounts, we can shake hands and be friends again.*

ball and chain* a person's special bur-den; a job. (Usually considered slang. Prisoners are sometimes fettered with a chain attached to a leg on one end and a heavy metal ball on the other.) □

23

Tom wanted to quit his job. He said he was tired of that old ball and chain. □ *Mr. Franklin always referred to his wife as his ball and chain.*

ball of fire* a very active and energetic person who always succeeds. (Usually considered slang.) □ *Sally is a real ball of fire—she works late every night.* □ *Ann is no ball of fire, but she does get the job done.*

ball someone or something up AND **ball up someone or something** 1. [with *something*] to wad something up into a ball. □ *John balled up the gum and stuck it under his chair.* □ *The baker balled the dough up and put it in a pan.* 2.* [with *someone*] to confuse someone. (Slang.) □ *The explosion balled up the whole crowd.* ALSO: **balled up*** confused. (Slang.) □ *They were totally balled up.*

bandy something about AND **bandy about something** to utter or speak gossip freely; to spread rumors or tell secrets. (Informal.) □ *Don't tell Tom. He bandies everything about.* □ *They bandied about the story until everyone in the town had heard it.*

bang one's head against a brick wall See *beat one's head against the wall.*

bank on something to count on something; to rely on something. □ *The weather service said it wouldn't rain, but I wouldn't bank on it.* □ *My word is to be trusted. You can bank on it.*

bargain for something AND **bargain on something** to plan for something; to expect something. (Informal.) □ *We knew it would be difficult, but we didn't bargain for this kind of trouble.* □ *I bargained on an easier time of it than this.*

barge in on someone or something AND **barge in** to break in on someone or something; to interrupt someone or something. □ *Oh! I'm sorry. I didn't mean to barge in on you.* □ *They barged in on the church service and caused a commotion.* □ *You can't just barge in like that!*

bark up the wrong tree* to make the wrong choice; to ask the wrong person; to follow the wrong course. (A cliché.) □ *If you think I'm the guilty person,*

you're barking up the wrong tree. □ *The baseball players blamed their bad record on the pitcher, but they were barking up the wrong tree.*

base one's opinion on something to make a judgement or form an opinion from something. □ *You must not base your opinion on one bad experience.* □ *I base my opinion on many years of studying the problem.*

bawl someone out AND **bawl out someone** to scold someone in a loud voice. □ *The teacher bawled the student out for arriving late.* □ *Teachers don't usually bawl out students.*

be a cold fish* to be a person who is distant and unfeeling. (Informal or slang.) □ *Bob is so dull—a real cold fish.* □ *She hardly ever speaks to anyone. She's a cold fish.*

be a copy-cat to be a person who copies or mimics what someone else does. (Usually juvenile.) □ *Sally wore a pink dress just like Mary's. Mary called Sally a copy-cat.* □ *Bill is such a copy-cat. He bought a coat just like mine.*

be a dead duck* to be finished; to have failed or lost a contest; dead. (Slang.) □ *He missed the exam. He's a dead duck.* □ *Yes, John's a dead duck. He drove his car into a tree.*

be a drag on someone* AND **be a drag*** to be a burden to someone; to bore someone. (Slang.) □ *Mr. Franklin is a drag on Mrs. Franklin.* □ *Yes, I'd expect him to be a drag.*

be a fan of someone to be a follower of someone; to idolize someone. □ *My mother is still a fan of the Beatles.* □ *I'm a great fan of the mayor of the town.*

be a goner* to be dead or finished; to be as good as dead or nearly dead. (Slang.) □ *The boy brought the sick fish back to the pet store to get his money back. "This one is a goner," he said.* □ *John thought he was a goner when his parachute didn't open.*

be a must* to be something that you must do. (Informal.) □ *When you're in San Francisco, see the Golden Gate Bridge. It's a must.* □ *It's a must that you brush your teeth after every meal.*

be a thorn in someone's side to be a constant bother or annoyance to someone. □ *This problem is a thorn in my side. I wish I had a solution to it.* □ *John was a thorn in my side for years before I finally got rid of him.*

be about something 1. to get busy doing something, especially doing one's business. □ *It's 8:00 and it's time I was about my homework.* □ *Goodbye, Jane. I must be about my business.* **2.** to be almost at a particular time. □ *It's about three o'clock.* □ *Isn't it about time to go to work?*

be about to do something to be ready to do something; to be on the verge of doing something. □ *Our old dog is about to die.* □ *The apple tree is about to bloom.*

be against someone to be opposed to someone; to be prejudiced against someone. (Also used literally. See also *hold something against someone* and *turn against someone or something*.) □ *Sally is against John since he ran into her car.* □ *I'm sorry! Please don't be against me anymore.*

be all ears to be listening eagerly and carefully. (See also the following entry.) □ *Well, hurry up and tell me. I'm all ears.* □ *Be careful what you say. The children are all ears.*

be all eyes AND **be all eyes and ears** to be alert for something to happen; to await eagerly for something to happen or for someone or something to appear. (See also the previous entry.) □ *There they were, sitting at the table, all eyes. The birthday cake was soon to be served.* □ *Nothing can escape my notice. I'm all eyes and ears.*

be an unknown quantity to be a person or thing about which no one is certain. □ *John is an unknown quantity. We don't know how he's going to act.* □ *The new clerk is an unknown quantity. Things may not turn out all right.*

be at someone's service to be ready to help someone in any way. (This is rarely meant literally. It probably indicates an offer of minimal help, except when said by a servant.) □ *The count greeted me warmly and said, "Welcome to my home. Just let me know what you need. I'm at your service."* □ *The desk clerk said, "Good morning, madam. I'm at your service."*

be bushed* to be tired or exhausted. (Informal.) □ *I can't go on, Mary. I'm just bushed.* □ *Oh, John, you look bushed! Whatever have you been doing?*

be careful about someone or something AND **be careful** to be cautious with someone or something; to try to avoid difficulties with someone or something. (Compare this entry to the following one.) □ *Please be careful about Mr. Franklin. He can be such a problem.* □ *Please be careful with the vase. It's old and valuable.* □ *Be careful about speaking too loudly.* □ *That's too big of a load. Be careful!*

be careful not to do something AND **be careful with someone or something; be careful** to use care in avoiding difficulties. (Similar to the previous entry, but is more specific about what is to be avoided.) □ *Please be careful not to discuss politics with Mr. Brown.* □ *Please be careful not to break the vase.* □ SALLY: *Your load is too big. Try not to drop it!* TOM: *I'm being careful.*

be certain of someone or something AND **be certain about someone or something; be certain** to be sure of a fact about someone or something. □ *I need to be certain of when the train arrives.* □ *Mary may or may not come. I need to be certain about Mary.* □ *Yes, try to be certain.*

be death on something* to be very harmful to something. (Informal or slang.) □ *The salt they put on the roads in the winter is death on cars.* □ *That teacher is death on slow learners.*

be done with someone or something AND **be done with** to be finished with someone or something. (Informal.) □ *Mary is done with Bill. She has found another boyfriend.* □ *I can't wait until I'm done with school forever.* □ *I agree. I'll be glad when it's done with.*

be even-steven* to be even (with someone or something). (Informal or slang.) □ *Bill hit Tom; then Tom hit Bill. Now they are even-steven.* □ *Mary paid Ann the $100 she owed her. Ann said, "Good, we are even-steven."*

be for someone or something to support or be in favor of someone or something. □ *Ann is for going out for dinner.* □ *Mary is running for congress, and the whole family is for her.*

be friends with someone to be a friend of someone. □ *Sally is friends with Bill.* □ *Mary and Bill are friends with one another.*

be from Missouri* to require proof; to have to be shown (something). (A cliché. From the motto of the state of Missouri, the "Show-Me State.") □ *You'll have to prove it to me. I'm from Missouri.* □ *She's from Missouri and has to be shown.*

be half-hearted about someone or something AND **be half-hearted** to be unenthusiastic about someone or something. □ *Ann was half-hearted about the choice of Sally for president.* □ *She didn't look half-hearted to me. She looked angry.*

be into something* AND **into something*** to be interested in something; to be involved in something. (Slang. See also *get into something.*) □ *Did you hear? Tom is into sky-diving!* □ *Too many people are into drugs.*

be of age to be old enough to marry or to sign legal agreements. (See also *come of age.*) □ *Now that Mary is of age, she can buy her own car.* □ *When I'm of age, I'm going to get married and move to the city.*

be of service to someone AND **be of service** to help someone; to serve someone. (A phrase often used by salesclerks. See also *be at someone's service.*) □ *Good morning, madam. May I be of service to you?* □ *Welcome to the Warwick Hotel. May I be of service?*

be off **1.** to be spoiled; to be running incorrectly, as with a mechanical device. □ *Oh! I'm afraid that this meat is off. Don't eat it.* □ *I don't have the exact time. My watch is off.* **2.** to leave; to depart. □ *Well, I must be off. Goodbye.* □ *The train leaves in an hour, so I must be off.*

be old hat to be old fashioned; to be outmoded. (Informal.) □ *That's a silly idea. It's old hat.* □ *Nobody does that anymore. That's just old hat.*

be oneself again to be healthy again;

to be calm again; to be restored. □ *After such a long illness, it's good to be myself again.* □ *I'm sorry that I lost my temper. I think I'm myself again now.*

be poles apart to be very different; to be far from coming to an agreement. □ *Mr. and Mrs. Jones don't get along well. They are poles apart.* □ *They'll never sign the contract because they are poles apart.*

be sick to vomit. (Euphemistic. Also with *get,* as in the examples. Also used literally.) □ *Mommy, Billy just got sick on the floor.* □ *Oh, excuse me! I think I'm going to be sick.* □ *Bob was sick all over the carpet.*

be talked out to have gotten tired of talking. (Folksy. See also *talk oneself out.*) □ *I can't go on. I'm all talked out.* □ *She was talked out in the first hour of discussion.*

be the spit and image of someone* AND **be the spitting image of someone*** to look very much like someone; to resemble someone very closely. (Folksy. The second version is a frequent error.) □ *John is the spit and image of his father.* □ *I'm not the spit and image of anyone.* □ *At first, I thought you were saying spitting image.*

be the teacher's pet to be the teacher's favorite student. □ *Sally is the teacher's pet. She always gets special treatment.* □ *The other students don't like the teacher's pet.*

be too AND **be so** to be something (despite anything to the contrary). (An emphatic form of *is, am, are, was, were.* See also *do too, have too.*) □ MOTHER: *Billy, you aren't old enough to be up this late.* BILLY: *I am too!* □ *I was so! I was there exactly when I said I would be!*

be with someone to be on someone's side; to be allied with someone. (Also used literally.) □ *Keep on trying, John. We are all with you.* □ *I'm with you in your efforts to win re-election.*

bear a grudge against someone AND **have a grudge against someone; hold a grudge against someone; bear a grudge** to have an old resentment for someone; to have continual anger for someone. □ *She bears a grudge against* *the judge who sentenced her.* □ *I have a grudge against my landlord for over-charging me.* □ *How long can a person hold a grudge? Let's be friends.*

bear down on someone or something AND **bear down** to put (literal or figurative) pressure on someone or something. □ *My boss really bears down on me when he's in a bad mood.* □ *Billy, please don't bear down on your pencil so hard. You'll break it.* □ *You're making three carbon copies, so bear down as you write.*

bear fruit to yield results; to give (literal or figurative) fruit. □ *Our apple tree didn't bear fruit this year.* □ *I hope your new plan bears fruit.* □ *We've had many good ideas, but none of them has borne fruit.*

bear one's cross AND **carry one's cross** to carry or bear one's burden; to endure one's difficulties. (This is a Biblical theme. It is always used figuratively except in the Biblical context.) □ *It's a very bad disease, but I'll bear my cross.* □ *I can't help you with it. You'll just have to carry your cross.*

bear someone or something in mind See *keep someone or something in mind.*

bear someone or something up AND **bear up someone or something** to support someone or something (literally or figuratively). (See also *bear up.*) □ *I hope the chair can bear John up.* □ *I hope John can bear up Tom. He can't carry heavy loads.* □ *The bridge was not able to bear up the traffic, so it collapsed.*

bear something out AND **bear out something** to demonstrate or prove that something is right. □ *I hope that the facts will bear your story out.* □ *I'm sure that the facts will bear out my story.* ALSO: **borne out** shown to be true. □ *My story will be borne out by the facts.*

bear the brunt of something AND **bear the brunt** to withstand the worst part or the strongest part of something, such as an attack. □ *I had to bear the brunt of her screaming and yelling.* □ *Why don't you talk with her the next time? I'm tired of bearing the brunt.*

bear up to endure; to hold up in a bad situation; to retain strength and continue supporting yourself or something else. □ *This is such a trying time. I don't see how she can bear up.* □ *The chair is very old. I don't believe that it will bear up much longer.* □ *How long will that bridge bear up under all that heavy traffic?*

bear watching to need watching; to deserve observation or monitoring. □ *This problem will bear watching.* □ *This is a very serious disease, and it will bear watching for further developments.*

bear with someone or something to be patient with someone or something; to endure someone or something. □ *Please bear with me while I fill out this form.* □ *Please bear with my old car. It'll get us there sooner or later.*

beard the lion in his den* to face an adversary on the adversary's home ground. (A cliché.) □ *I went to the tax collector's office to beard the lion in his den.* □ *He said he hadn't wanted to come to my home, but it was better to beard the lion in his den.*

beat a dead horse* to continue fighting a battle which has been won; to continue to argue a point which is settled. (A cliché meaning that a dead horse will not run no matter how hard it is beaten.) □ *Stop arguing! You have won your point. You are just beating a dead horse.* □ *Oh, be quiet. Stop beating a dead horse.*

beat a path to someone's door* (for people) to come to someone in great numbers. (A cliché meaning that so many people will wish to come and see you that they will wear down a pathway to your door.) □ *I have a product so good that everyone is beating a path to my door.* □ *If you really become famous, people will beat a path to your door.*

beat a retreat AND **beat a hasty retreat** to retreat or withdraw very quickly. □ *We went out into the cold weather, but beat a retreat to the warmth of our fire.* □ *The dog beat a hasty retreat to its own yard.*

beat about the bush See the following entry.

beat around the bush AND **beat about the bush** to avoid answering a question; to stall; to waste time. □ *Stop beating around the bush and answer my question.* □ *Let's stop beating about the bush and discuss this matter.*

beat one's gums* to waste one's time talking; to talk and get no results. (Slang.) □ *Pay attention to me. I'm not just standing here beating my gums.* □ *Stop beating your gums. I'm not listening to you.*

beat one's head against the wall AND **bang one's head against a brick wall** to waste one's time trying to accomplish something which is completely hopeless. □ *You're wasting your time trying to fix up this house. You're just beating your head against the wall.* □ *You're banging your head against a brick wall trying to get that dog to behave properly.*

beat someone down to size AND **beat someone down; knock someone down to size** to make a person more humble, possibly by beating. (See also *cut someone down to size.*) □ *If you keep acting so arrogant, someone is going to beat you down to size.* □ *It's time someone knocked you down to size.* □ *I'll try to be more thoughtful. I don't want anyone to beat me down.*

beat someone to the draw See the following entry.

beat someone to the punch AND **beat someone to the draw** to do something before someone else does it. □ *I wanted to have the first new car, but Sally beat me to the punch.* □ *I planned to write a book about computers, but someone else beat me to the draw.*

beat someone up AND **beat up someone** to harm or subdue a person by beating and striking. □ *The robber beat me up and took my money.* □ *I really want to beat up that robber.*

beat someone's brains out* 1. to beat someone severely. (Usually considered slang. This threatens violence and should not be used casually.) □ *If I catch him, I'll beat his brains out.* □ *Take it easy. Just punch him a bit. You don't want to beat his brains out.* 2. to work very hard (to do something). (This

sense is figurative and involves no violence. Informal or slang.) □ *I beat my brains out to solve the problem.* □ *That's the last time I'll beat my brains out trying to cook a nice dinner for you.*

beat something into someone's head* to force someone to learn something, possibly through violence. (This can be a threat of violence and should not be used casually.) □ *I studied for hours. I have never beat so much stuff into my head in such a short time.* □ *You're going to learn this math if I have to beat it into your head.*

beat the band* very much; very fast. (Folksy. This has no literal meaning.) □ *The carpenter sawed and hammered to beat the band.* □ *They baked cookies and pies to beat the band.*

beat the gun* to manage to do something before the ending signal. (Originally from sports, referring to making a goal in the last seconds of a game. See also *jump the gun.*) □ *The ball beat the gun and dropped through the hoop just in time.* □ *Tom tried to beat the gun, but he was one second too slow.*

beat the living daylights out of someone* AND **beat the stuffing out of someone*; beat the tar out of someone*** to beat or spank someone, probably a child. (Folksy. These are all threats to do violence and should not be used casually.) □ *If you do that again, I'll beat the living daylights out of you.* □ *The last time Bobby put the cat in the refrigerator, his mother beat the living daylights out of him.* □ *If you continue to act that way, I'll beat the tar out of you.* □ *He wouldn't stop, so I beat the stuffing out of him.*

beat the pants off someone* 1. to beat someone severely. (Informal. Refers to physical violence, not the removal of someone's pants.) □ *The thugs beat the pants off their victim.* □ *If you do that again, I'll beat the pants off you.* 2. to win out over someone. (Informal. This has nothing to do with violence or removing pants.) □ *In the footrace, Sally beat the pants off Jane.* □ *Tom beats the pants off Bob when it comes to writing poetry.*

beat the rap* to escape conviction and

punishment (for a crime). (Slang, especially criminal slang.) □ *He was charged with drunk driving, but he beat the rap.* □ *The police hauled Tom in and charged him with a crime. His lawyer helped him beat the rap.*

beat the stuffing out of someone See *beat the living daylights out of someone.*

beat the tar out of someone See *beat the living daylights out of someone.*

Beauty is only skin deep. a proverb meaning that looks are only superficial. □ BOB: *Isn't Jane lovely?* TOM: *Yes, but beauty is only skin deep.* □ *I know that she looks like a million dollars, but beauty is only skin deep.*

becoming to someone complimentary to someone; enhancing one's good looks. (Usually refers to clothing, hair, and other personal ornaments.) □ *That hair style is very becoming to you.* □ *Your new fur coat is becoming to you.*

beef something up* AND **beef up something*** to make something stronger; to supplement something. (Informal or slang.) □ *The government decided to beef the army up by buying hundreds of new tanks.* □ *Okay, let's beef up the opening song. Please, everyone, sing louder!*

been had* been mistreated; been cheated or dealt with badly. (Informal or slang.) □ *They were cheated out of a thousand dollars. They've really been had.* □ *Look what they did to my car. Boy, have I been had.*

been through the mill* been badly treated; exhausted. (Informal.) □ *This has been a rough day. I've really been through the mill.* □ *This old car is banged up, and it hardly runs. It's been through the mill.*

before long soon. □ *Billy will be grown up before long.* □ *Before long, we'll be without any money if we keep spending so much.*

before you can say Jack Robinson* almost immediately. (A cliché. Often found in children's stories.) □ *And before you could say Jack Robinson, the bird flew away.* □ *I'll catch a plane and be there before you can say Jack Robinson.*

before you know it almost immediately. □ *I'll be there before you know it.* □ *If you keep spending money like that, you'll be broke before you know it.*

beg something off AND **beg off something; beg off** to ask to be released from something; to refuse an invitation. □ *I'm sorry. I'll have to beg off your invitation.* □ *I have an important meeting, so I'll have to beg off.* □ *I wanted to go to the party, but I had to beg it off.*

beg the question to evade the issue; to carry on a false argument where one assumes as proved the very point which is being argued. □ *Stop arguing in circles. You're begging the question.* □ *It's hopeless to argue with Sally. She always begs the question.*

Beggars can't be choosers. a proverb meaning that one should not criticize something one gets for free. □ *I don't like the old hat that you gave me, but beggars can't be choosers.* □ *It doesn't matter whether people like the free food or not. Beggars can't be choosers.*

begin to see daylight to begin to see the end of a long task. (See also *see the light at the end of the tunnel.*) □ *I've been working on my thesis for two years, and at last I'm beginning to see daylight.* □ *I've been so busy. Only in the last week have I begun to see daylight.*

begin to see the light to begin to understand (something). □ *My algebra class is hard for me, but I'm beginning to see the light.* □ *I was totally confused, but I began to see the light after your explanation.*

behind someone's back in secret; without someone's knowledge. □ *Please don't talk about me behind my back.* □ *She sold the car behind his back.*

behind the eight ball* in a difficult or awkward position. (Informal.) □ *Bob broke his wife's crystal vase and is really behind the eight ball.* □ *I ran over the neighbor's lawn with my car, so I'm really behind the eight ball.*

behind the scenes privately; out of public view. □ *The people who worked behind the scenes are the real heroes of this project.* □ *I worked behind the scenes in the play.* □ *We don't usually thank the people who are behind the scenes.*

believe in someone or something to believe that someone or something exists; to have confidence in someone or something. □ *Tommy still believes in Santa Claus.* □ *I don't believe in making too much money.* □ *I believe in my friends and their judgement.*

believe it or not* to choose to believe something or not. (A cliché.) □ *Believe it or not, I just got home from work.* □ *I'm over fifty years old, believe it or not.*

belong to someone to be someone's property. □ *That book belongs to me. It isn't yours.* □ *This one belongs to you.*

belt something out AND **belt out something** to sing or play a song loudly and with spirit. □ *She really knows how to belt out a song.* □ *When she's playing the piano, she really belts the music out.*

bend over backwards to do something See *fall over backwards to do something.*

bend someone's ear to talk to someone, perhaps annoyingly. □ *Tom is over there bending Jane's ear about something.* □ *I'm sorry. I didn't mean to bend your ear for an hour.*

bent on doing something - determined to do something. □ *Jane was bent on having her own apartment.* □ *Her mother was bent on keeping her at home.*

beside oneself excited; disturbed; emotionally uncontrolled. □ *He was beside himself with grief.* □ *She laughed and laughed until she was beside herself.*

beside the point AND **beside the question** irrelevant; of no importance. □ *That's very interesting, but beside the point.* □ *That's beside the point. You're evading the issue.* □ *Your observation is beside the question.*

beside the question See the previous entry.

best bib and tucker* one's best clothing. (Folksy.) □ *I always put on my best bib and tucker on Sundays.* □ *Put on your best bib and tucker, and let's go to the city.*

bet one's bottom dollar* AND **bet one's life*** to be quite certain (about something). (Both are informal and folksy. A *bottom dollar* is the last dollar.) □ *I'll*

be there. You bet your bottom dollar.* □ *I bet my bottom dollar you can't swim across the pool.* □ *You bet your life I can't swim that far.* □ *I bet my life on it.*

bet one's life See the previous entry.

better late than never* better to do something late than not at all. (A cliché.) □ *I wish you had come here sooner, but better late than never.* □ *She bought a house when she was quite old. Better late than never.*

better off See the following two entries.

better off doing something AND **better off if something were done; better off in a better position if something were done.** □ *She'd be better off selling her house.* □ *They are better off flying to Detroit.* □ *They would be better off if they flew to Detroit.* □ *I'm better off now.*

better off somewhere AND **better off if one were somewhere else; better off in a better position somewhere else.** □ *They would be better off in Florida.* □ *We'd all be better off if we were in Florida.* □ *I know I'd be better off.*

better to do something preferable to do something. □ *It's better to go there now than to wait.* □ *It's never better to wait too long.*

between a rock and a hard place* AND **between the devil and the deep blue sea*** in a very difficult position; facing a hard decision. (Slang or informal.) □ *I couldn't make up my mind. I was caught between a rock and a hard place.* □ *He had a dilemma on his hands. He was clearly between the devil and the deep blue sea.*

between life and death in a position where living or dying is an even possibility. (Especially with *caught* or *hovering.*) □ *And there I was on the operating table, hovering between life and death.* □ *The mountain climber hung by his rope, caught between life and death.*

between the devil and the deep blue sea See *between a rock and a hard place.*

betwixt and between* (A cliché.) **1.** between (people or things). □ *I liked the soup and the dessert and all that* *came betwixt and between.* □ *I sat betwixt and between all the actors who weren't on stage.* **2.** undecided. □ *I wish she would choose. She has been betwixt and between for three weeks.* □ *Tom is so betwixt and between about getting married. I don't think he's ready.*

beyond a reasonable doubt almost without any doubt. (A legal phrase.) □ *The jury decided beyond a reasonable doubt that she had committed the crime.* □ *She was also found guilty beyond a reasonable doubt.*

beyond measure more than can be measured; in a very large amount. □ *They brought in hams, turkeys, and roasts, and then they brought vegetables and salads beyond measure.* □ *They thanked all of us beyond measure.*

beyond one's depth **1.** in water which is too deep. (See also *in over one's head.*) □ *Sally swam out until she was beyond her depth.* □ *Jane swam out to get her even though it was beyond her depth, too.* **2.** beyond one's understanding or capabilities. □ *I'm beyond my depth in algebra class.* □ *Poor John was involved in a problem that was really beyond his depth.*

beyond one's means more than one can afford. □ *I'm sorry, but this house is beyond our means. Please show us a cheaper one.* □ *Mr. and Mrs. Brown are living beyond their means.*

beyond the pale unacceptable; outlawed. □ *Your behavior is simply beyond the pale.* □ *Because of Tom's rudeness, he's considered beyond the pale and is never asked to parties anymore.*

beyond the shadow of a doubt completely without doubt. (Said of a fact, not a person. See also *beyond a reasonable doubt.*) □ *We accepted her story as true beyond the shadow of a doubt.* □ *Please assure us that you are certain of the facts beyond the shadow of a doubt.*

beyond words more than one can say. (Especially with *grateful* and *thankful.*) □ *Sally was thankful beyond words.* □ *I don't know how to thank you. I'm grateful beyond words.*

bid adieu to someone or something* AND **bid someone or something adieu*** to say goodbye to someone or something. (A cliché. This *adieu* is French for *goodbye* and should not be confused with *ado.*) □ *Now it's time to bid adieu to all of you gathered here.* □ *He silently bid adieu to his favorite hat as the wind carried it down the street.*

bide one's time to wait patiently. □ *I've been biding my time for years, just waiting for a chance like this.* □ *He's not the type to just sit there and bide his time. He wants some action.*

big frog in a small pond* to be an important person in the midst of less important people. (A cliché.) □ *I'd rather be a big frog in a small pond than the opposite.* □ *The trouble with Tom is that he's a big frog in a small pond. He needs more competition.*

birds and the bees human reproduction. (A euphemistic way of referring to human sex and reproduction.) □ *My father tried to teach me about the birds and the bees.* □ *He's twenty years old and doesn't understand about the birds and the bees.*

Birds of a feather flock together. a proverb meaning that people of the same type seem to gather together. □ *Bob and Tom are just alike. They like each other's company because birds of a feather flock together.* □ *When Mary joined a club for redheaded people, she said, "Birds of a feather flock together."*

bite off more than one can chew* to take (on) more than one can deal with; to be overconfident. (A cliché. This is used literally for food and figuratively for other things, especially difficult projects.) □ *Billy, stop biting off more than you can chew. You're going to choke on your food someday.* □ *Ann is exhausted again. She's always biting off more than she can chew.*

bite one's nails to be nervous or anxious; to bite one's nails from nervousness or anxiety. (Used both literally and figuratively.) □ *I spent all afternoon biting my nails, worrying about you.* □ *We've all been biting our nails from worry.*

bite one's tongue to struggle not to say something which you really want to say. (Used literally only to refer to an accidental biting of one's tongue.) □ *I had to bite my tongue to keep from telling her what I really thought.* □ *I sat through that whole conversation biting my tongue.*

bite something off AND **bite off something** to remove something by biting; to take a bite. □ *Tom bit off a piece of the turkey leg.* □ *The dog tried to bite the man's ear off.*

bite the bullet* to put up with or endure (something). (Informal or slang.) □ *I didn't want to go to the doctor, but I bit the bullet and went.* □ *John, you just have to bite the bullet and do what you're told.*

bite the dust* to fall to defeat; to die. (A cliché. Typically heard in movies about the U.S. Western frontier.) □ *A bullet hit the sheriff in the chest, and he bit the dust.* □ *Poor old Bill bit the dust while mowing the lawn. They buried him yesterday.*

bite the hand that feeds one* to do harm to someone who does good things for you. (A cliché. Not used literally.) □ *I'm your mother! How can you bite the hand that feeds you?* □ *She can hardly expect much when she bites the hand that feeds her.*

black out to faint or pass out. □ *Sally blacked out just before the crash.* □ *I was so frightened that I blacked out for a minute.*

black sheep of the family the worst member of the family. □ *Mary is the black sheep of the family. She's always in trouble with the police.* □ *He keeps making a nuisance of himself. What do you expect from the black sheep of the family?*

blame someone for something to declare that someone is the cause of something wrong. □ *Please don't blame me for the accident.* □ *You can't blame Sally for the mistake. She didn't work here when it happened.* ALSO: **to blame for something** (for someone) to be the cause of something wrong. □ *Tom is to blame for the accident.* □ *Sally isn't to blame for the mistake.*

blame something on someone to declare that something wrong was caused by someone. □ *Please don't*

blame the accident on me. □ *You can't blame the mistake on Sally.*

blast off (for a rocket) to shoot into the sky. □ *What time does the rocket blast off?* □ *It won't blast off today. It has been canceled.* ALSO: **blast-off** an act of blasting off. □ *When is the blast-off?* □ *There will be no blast-off today.*

blaze a trail to make and mark a trail. (Either literally or figuratively.) □ *The scout blazed a trail through the forest.* □ *Professor Williams blazed a trail in the study of physics.*

bleep something out AND **bleep out something** to replace a word or phrase in a radio or television broadcast with some sort of a musical noise. (This is sometimes done to prevent a bad word or other information from being broadcast.) □ *He tried to say the word on television, but they bleeped it out.* □ *They tried to bleep out the whole sentence.*

blind leading the blind having to do with a situation where people who don't know how to do something try to explain it to other people. □ *Tom doesn't know anything about cars, but he's trying to teach Sally how to change the oil. It's a case of the blind leading the blind.* □ *When I tried to show Mary how to use a computer, it was the blind leading the blind.*

blow a fuse See the following entry.

blow a gasket* AND **blow a fuse*; blow one's cool*; blow one's cork*; blow one's top*; blow one's stack*** to become very angry; to lose one's temper. (Slang.) □ *I was so mad I almost blew a gasket.* □ *I've never heard such a thing. I'm going to blow a fuse.* □ *It was just too much for her. She blew her cool.* □ *I blew my cork when he hit me.* □ *I was so mad I could have blown my top.* □ *It makes me so mad I could blow my stack.*

blow-by-blow account AND **blow-by-blow description** a detailed description (of an event) given as the event takes place. (This referred originally to boxing.) □ *I want to listen to a blow-by-blow account of the prize fight.* □ *The lawyer got the witness to give a blow-by-blow description of the argument.*

blow hot and cold to be changeable or uncertain (about something). □ *He keeps blowing hot and cold on the question of moving to the country.* □ *He blows hot and cold about this. I wish he'd make up his mind.*

blow off steam See *let off steam.*

blow one's cookies See *blow one's lunch.*

blow one's cool See *blow a gasket.*

blow one's cork See *blow a gasket.*

blow one's lines See *fluff one's lines.*

blow one's lunch* AND **blow one's cookies*** to vomit. (Slang.) □ *The accident was so horrible I almost blew my lunch.* □ *Don't run so hard, or you'll blow your cookies.*

blow one's own horn See *toot one's own horn.*

blow one's stack See *blow a gasket.*

blow one's top See *blow a gasket.*

blow over to go away without causing harm. □ *If we are lucky, the storm will blow over.* □ *Given time, all this controversy will blow over.*

blow someone or something away AND **blow away someone or something** **1.** (for the wind) to carry someone or something away. □ *The wind blew my hat away.* □ *The wind was so strong that it almost blew me away.* **2.*** to kill or destroy someone or something. (Slang.) □ *He drew his gun and blew the thief away.* □ *His bad attitude blew away the whole deal.* □ *The bad news really blew me away.*

blow someone or something off* AND **blow off someone or something*** **1.** [with *something*] to neglect or bumble something. (Slang.) □ *He blew off his homework.* □ *He would do better in school if he didn't blow his math class off.* **2.** [with *someone*] to deceive or cheat someone. (Slang.) □ *She really blew me off on the question of grades. She was really failing all the time.* □ *She blew off the teacher by cheating on the test.*

blow someone's brains out* AND **blow out someone's brains*** to kill someone with a gun. (Slang and quite shocking.) □ *The robber grabbed the gun and blew her brains out.* □ *He went into the back yard and blew out his brains with a shotgun.*

blow someone's cover to reveal someone's true identity or purpose. □ *The spy was very careful not to blow her cover.* □ *I tried to disguise myself, but my dog recognized me and blew my cover.*

blow someone's mind* (Slang.) **1.** to destroy the function of one's brain. □ *It was a terrible experience. It nearly blew my mind.* □ *She blew her mind on drugs.* **2.** to overwhelm someone; to excite someone. □ *It was so beautiful, it nearly blew my mind.* □ *The music was so wild. It blew my mind.*

blow something down AND **blow down something** (for the wind) to knock something over. □ *The wind blew the sign down.* □ *The storm blew down the tree.*

blow something out of all proportion See *out of all proportion.*

blow something up AND **blow up something** **1.** to destroy something with an explosion. □ *They used dynamite to blow the old house up.* □ *We'll blow up the barn tomorrow.* **2.** to inflate something. □ *I'll blow up this balloon and then pop it.* □ *Please don't blow up the balloon.* ALSO: **blow up** to explode. □ *The bomb won't blow up by itself.* □ *The house blew up because of a gas leak.*

blow the lid off something AND **blow the lid off** to reveal something, especially wrongdoing; to make wrongdoing public. □ *The police blew the lid off the smuggling ring.* □ *The government is glad that they blew the lid off.*

blow the whistle on someone AND **blow the whistle** to report someone's wrongdoing to someone (such as the police) who can stop the wrongdoing. □ *The citizen's group blew the whistle on the street gangs by calling the police.* □ *The gangs were getting very bad. It was definitely time to blow the whistle.*

blow up **1.** See *blow something up.* **2.** to get angry; to lose one's temper and yell (at someone). □ *I'm sorry. I didn't mean to blow up.* □ *You'd blow up, too, if you'd had a day like mine.* **3.** to fall apart or get ruined. □ *The whole project blew up. It will have to be canceled.* □ *All my planning was blown up this afternoon.*

blow up in someone's face **1.** to blow

up or explode suddenly. □ *The bomb blew up in the robber's face.* □ *The firecracker blew up in his face and injured him.* **2.** (for something) to get ruined while someone is working on it. □ *All my plans blew up in my face.* □ *It is terrible for your life to get ruined and blow up in your face.*

blue around the gills See *pale around the gills.*

blurt something out AND **blurt out something** to say something suddenly and rapidly, even when one is expected to keep quiet. □ *She blurted the story out right in the middle of the movie.* □ *The witness blurted out the name of the killer even though the judge told him to keep quiet.*

boast of someone or something to brag about someone or something. □ *She always boasted of her luck at gambling.* □ *She boasts a lot about her children.*

bog down to slow down; to become stuck. □ *The project bogged down because of so much red tape.* □ *We bog down every year at this time because many of our workers go on vacation.*

boggle someone's mind to confuse someone; to overwhelm someone; to *blow someone's mind.* □ *The size of the house boggles my mind.* □ *She said that his arrogance boggled her mind.*

boil down to something to reduce to something; to come down to something; to be essentially something. □ *It all boils down to whether you wish to buy a car.* □ *It boils down to a question of good health.*

bone of contention the subject or point of an argument; an unsettled point of disagreement. □ *We've fought for so long that we've forgotten what the bone of contention is.* □ *The question of a fence between the houses has become quite a bone of contention.*

bone up on something AND **bone up** to study something thoroughly; to review the facts about something. □ *I have to bone up on the state driving laws because I have to take my driving test tomorrow.* □ *I take mine next month, so I'll have to bone up, too.*

boot someone or something out See *kick someone or something out.*

bore someone stiff AND **bore someone to death** to bore someone very much. (*Stiff* is an old slang word meaning dead.) □ *The play bored me stiff.* □ *The lecture bored everyone to death.* ALSO: **bored stiff** very bored. □ *We were all bored stiff.* □ *During the first half of the opera, Bill was bored stiff. He slept during the second half.* ALSO: **bored to death** very bored. □ *The children were bored to death.* □ *I've never been so bored to death in my life.*

bore someone to death See *bore someone stiff.*

born out of wedlock born to an unmarried mother. □ *The child was born out of wedlock.* □ *In the city many children are born out of wedlock.*

born with a silver spoon in one's mouth* born with many advantages; born to a wealthy family. (A cliché.) □ *Sally was born with a silver spoon in her mouth.* □ *I'm glad I was not born with a silver spoon in my mouth.*

borrow trouble to worry needlessly; to make trouble for oneself. □ *Worrying too much about death is just borrowing trouble.* □ *Do not get involved with politics. That's borrowing trouble.*

boss someone around AND **boss around someone** to give orders to someone; to keep telling someone what to do. □ *Stop bossing me around. I'm not your employee.* □ *Captain Smith bosses around the whole crew. That's his job.*

botch something up AND **botch up something** to ruin something; to mess something up. □ *I botched the whole project up.* □ *I hope you don't botch up anything else.*

bother oneself about someone or something AND **bother oneself** to trouble oneself about someone or something. □ *Please don't bother yourself about my brother. I'll take care of him.* □ *If he's all right, I won't bother myself.*

bother with someone or something to concern oneself with someone or something. □ *Please don't bother with my brother. I'll take care of him.* □ *Don't bother with the dishes. I'll do them later.*

bottle something up AND **bottle up something 1.** to constrict something as if it were put in a bottle. □ *The* police bottled up the traffic while they searched the cars for the thieves. □ The patrol boats bottled the other boats up at the locks on the river. **2.** to hold one's feelings within; to keep from saying something which one feels strongly about. □ Let's talk about it, John. You shouldn't bottle it up. □ Don't bottle up your problems. It's better to talk them out.

bottom out to reach the lowest point. □ The price of wheat bottomed out last week. Now it's rising again. □ My interest in school bottomed out in my junior year, so I quit and got a job.

bound and determined* determined. (A cliché.) □ We were bound and determined to get there on time. □ I'm bound and determined that this won't happen again.

bound for somewhere on the way to somewhere; planning to go somewhere. □ I'm bound for Mexico. In fact, I'm leaving this afternoon. □ I'm bound for the bank. Do you want to go, too?

bound hand and foot with hands and feet tied up. □ The robbers left us bound hand and foot. □ We remained bound hand and foot until the maid found us and untied us.

bound to do something AND **bound to** to be certain to do something. □ They are bound to come home soon. They always come home early. □ Oh, yes. They are bound to.

bow and scrape to be very humble and subservient. □ Please don't bow and scrape. We are all equal here. □ The salesclerk came in, bowing and scraping, and asked if he could help us.

bow out to quit and depart; to resign; to retire. □ I've done all that I can do. Now is the time to bow out. □ Most workers bow out at the normal retirement age.

bowl someone over **1.** to knock someone over. □ The blow struck him in the chest and bowled him over. □ The wind blew the door into her and bowled her over. **2.** to surprise or overwhelm someone. □ The news bowled me over. □ The details of the proposed project bowled everyone over.

brag about someone or something

to boast about or praise someone or something. □ Mr. Smith often brags about his children. □ He also brags about his new job.

branch off to move off in a new direction. □ The river branched off to the South. □ The road branches off here and goes on to the next town. □ Tom branched off into the study of law.

branch out to reach out or spread out. □ As the tree grew, it branched out widely. □ She branched out into a new line of work.

bread and butter (a person's) livelihood or income. □ Selling cars is a lot of hard work, but it's my bread and butter. □ It was hard to give up my bread and butter, but I felt it was time to retire.

Break a leg!* good luck. (Theatrical slang. This is said to actors before a performance instead of Good luck. Also used literally.) □ Before the play, John said to Mary, "Break a leg!" □ Saying "Break a leg!" before a performance is an old theatrical tradition.

break away from someone or something AND **break away** to get away or pull away from someone or something. □ It was hard for John to break away from his mother. □ John finally broke away. His mother cried and cried. □ The dog broke away from its owner. □ The iceberg broke away from the glacier.

break camp to close down a campsite; to pack up and move on. □ Early this morning we broke camp and moved on northward. □ Okay, everyone. It's time to break camp. Take those tents down and fold them neatly.

break down **1.** to fall apart; to stop operating. (See also break someone or something down.) □ The air conditioning broke down, and we got very warm. □ The car broke down in the parking lot. **2.** to lose control of one's emotions; to have a nervous collapse. □ He couldn't keep going. He finally broke down and wept. □ I was afraid I'd break down.

break even for income to equal expenses. (This implies that money was not earned or lost.) □ Unfortunately my business just managed to break even *last year.* □ *I made a bad investment, but I broke even.*

break ground for something AND **break ground** to start digging the foundation for a building. (See also *break new ground*.) □ *The president of the company came to break ground for the new building.* □ *This was the third building this year for which this company has broken ground.* □ *When will they break ground?*

break in on someone or something AND **break in** to interrupt someone or something; to come in suddenly and interrupt someone or something. □ *I'm sorry. I didn't mean to break in on your conference.* □ *Tom frequently broke in on his sister and her boyfriend.* □ *I think he broke in on purpose.*

break into something AND **break in** to enter into a place (illegally) by the use of force. □ *The robber broke into the house.* □ *If the door had been left unlocked, he wouldn't have had to break in.*

break loose from someone or something AND **break loose** to get away from a person or a thing which is holding one. (See also *break away from someone or something*.) □ *The criminal broke loose from the police officer.* □ *It's hard to break loose from home.* □ *I was twenty years old before I could break loose.*

break new ground to begin to do something which no one else has done; to pioneer (in an enterprise). (See also *break ground for something*.) □ *Dr. Anderson was breaking new ground in cancer research.* □ *They were breaking new ground in consumer electronics.*

break off with someone AND **break off** to end a friendship with someone, especially a boyfriend or a girlfriend. □ *Tom has finally broken off with Mary.* □ *I knew it couldn't last. He was bound to break off.*

break one's back to do something See the following entry.

break one's neck to do something AND **break one's back to do something; break one's back; break one's neck** to work very hard to do something. (Never used in its literal sense.) □ *I*

broke my neck to get here on time. □ *That's the last time I'll break my neck to help you.* □ *There is no point in breaking your back. Take your time.*

break out 1. See *break out of something*. **2.** (for one's face) to erupt in pimples. □ *Bob's face has started breaking out badly.* □ *My face breaks out when I eat a lot of chocolate.*

break out in a cold sweat to perspire from fever, fear, or anxiety. □ *I was so frightened I broke out in a cold sweat.* □ *The patient broke out in a cold sweat.*

break out in something AND **break out** to erupt with something such as a rash, a cold sweat, or pimples. (See also *break out in a cold sweat*.) □ *After being in the woods, I broke out in a rash. I think it's poison ivy.* □ *I hate to break out like that.* □ *When I eat chocolate, I break out in pimples.*

break out into tears AND **break into tears; break out in tears** to start crying suddenly. □ *I was so sad that I broke out into tears.* □ *I always break into tears at a funeral.* □ *It's hard not to break out in tears under those circumstances.*

break out of something AND **break out** to force one's way out of a place. □ *The criminal broke out of jail.* □ *The lion broke out of its cage and terrorized the village.* □ *I've always been afraid that the lion would break out.*

break someone or something down AND **break down someone or something** **1.** [with *someone*] to force someone to give up and tell secrets or agree to do something. □ *After threats of torture, they broke the spy down.* □ *They broke down the agent by threatening violence.* **2.** [with *something*] to tear something down; to destroy something. □ *They used an ax to break the door down.* □ *We broke down the wall with big hammers.*

break someone or something in AND **break in someone or something; break in** **1.** [with *someone*] to train someone to do a job; to supervise a new person learning a new job. □ *I have to break in a new worker.* □ *It takes time to break a new worker in.* □ *Are they hard to break in?* **2.** [with *something*] to make something fit by wearing or using it. □ *I'll be glad when I've finished breaking in these shoes.* □ *Yes, it takes time to break them in.* □ *They are easy to break in, though.* □ *The car will run better after I break it in.*

break someone or something up AND **break up someone or something** **1.** [with *someone*] to cause a person to laugh, perhaps at an inappropriate time. (Informal.) □ *John told a joke which really broke Mary up.* □ *The comedian's job was to break up the audience by telling jokes.* **2.** [with *something*] to destroy something. □ *The police broke up the gambling ring.* □ *The storm broke the docks up on the lake.*

break someone's fall to cushion a falling person; to lessen the impact of a falling person. □ *When the little boy fell out of the window, the bushes broke his fall.* □ *The old lady slipped on the ice, but a snowbank broke her fall.*

break someone's heart to cause someone emotional pain. □ *It just broke my heart when Tom ran away from home.* □ *Sally broke John's heart when she refused to marry him.*

break something away AND **break something loose; break something off; break off something** to break and dislodge a piece of something. □ *Break the glass away from the frame, and then put in the new pane of glass.* □ *I broke a tooth loose.* □ *Have some of this candy. Break a piece off.* □ *Okay, I'll break off a piece.*

break something loose See *break something away.*

break something off See *break something away.*

break something to pieces* to shatter something. (Informal.) □ *I broke my crystal vase to pieces.* □ *I dropped a glass and broke it to pieces.*

break the back of something to end the domination of something; to reduce the power of something. □ *The government has worked for years to break the back of organized crime.* □ *This new medicine should break the back of the epidemic.*

break the ice to initiate social interchanges and conversation; to get some-

thing started. (The *ice* sometimes refers to social coldness. Also used literally.) □ *Tom is so outgoing. He's always the first one to break the ice at parties.* □ *It's hard to break the ice at formal events.* □ *Sally broke the ice by bidding $20,000 for the painting.*

break the news to someone AND **break the news** to tell someone some important news, usually bad news. □ *The doctor had to break the news to Jane about her husband's cancer.* □ *I hope that the doctor broke the news gently.*

break through something AND **break through** to break something and pass through; to overcome something. (Used both literally and figuratively.) □ *Tom was able to break through racial barriers.* □ *They are hard to break through in some places.* □ *The scientists broke through the mystery surrounding the disease and found the cause.* ALSO: **breakthrough** the discovery of a solution to a problem. □ *The scientists working on cancer made a major break-through.*

break up with someone AND **break up** to end a love affair or a romance. □ *Tom finally broke up with Mary.* □ *I thought they would break up. He has been so moody lately.*

breath of fresh air **1.** air which is not stale or smelly. (This is the literal sense.) □ *I feel faint. I think I need a breath of fresh air.* □ *You look ill, John. What you need is a breath of fresh air.* **2.** air which is not (figuratively) contaminated with unpleasant people or situations. (This is a sarcastic version of sense 1.) □ *You people are disgusting. I have to get out of here and get a breath of fresh air.* □ *I believe I'll go get a breath of fresh air. The intellectual atmosphere in here is stifling.* **3.** a new, fresh, and imaginative approach (to something). (Usually with *like*.) □ *Sally, with all her wonderful ideas, is a breath of fresh air.* □ *New furniture in this room is like a breath of fresh air.*

breathe down someone's neck **1.** to keep close watch on someone; to watch someone's activities. (Refers to standing very close behind a person.) □ *I can't work with you breathing down my neck all the time. Go away.* □ *I will get* *through my life without your help. Stop breathing down my neck.* **2.** to try to hurry someone along; to make someone get something done on time. (The subject does not have to be a person. See the second example.) □ *I have to finish my taxes today. The tax collector is breathing down my neck.* □ *I have a deadline breathing down my neck.*

breathe one's last* to die; to breathe one's last breath. (A cliché.) □ *Mrs. Smith breathed her last this morning.* □ *I'll keep running every day until I breathe my last.*

bright and early very early. □ *Yes, I'll be there bright and early.* □ *I want to see you here on time tomorrow, bright and early, or you're fired!*

bring home the bacon* to earn a salary. (Folksy.) □ *I've got to get to work if I'm going to bring home the bacon.* □ *Go out and get a job so you can bring home the bacon.*

bring someone around **1.** to bring someone for a visit; to bring someone for someone (else) to meet. □ *Please bring your wife around sometime. I'd love to meet her.* □ *You've just got to bring the doctor around for dinner.* **2.** to bring someone to consciousness. □ *The doctor brought Tom around with smelling salts.* □ *The boxer was knocked out, but the doctor brought him around.*

bring someone or something back AND **bring back someone or something** to return someone or something (to here or the present). □ *Please bring Ann back when you come.* □ *Okay, I'll bring her back.* □ *I wish I could bring back the good old days.* □ *Sorry, you can't bring them back.*

bring someone or something out AND **bring out someone or something** **1.** to expose someone or something to the public or to the outdoors. □ *It's a lovely day. I think I'll bring Grandmother out.* □ *Please bring out the car, and I'll wash it.* **2.** [with *someone*] to formally introduce one's daughter to society at a special party. □ *Mr. and Mrs. Johnson are bringing their daughter out this autumn.* □ *They brought out her sister last season.* **3.** [with *something*] to publish a book; to intro-

duce a new product. □ *The University Press is bringing out a book on Shakespeare this month.* □ *My company has just brought a new computer out.*

bring someone or something up AND **bring up someone or something** **1.** to mention a person or a thing. □ *Please don't bring up that matter again.* □ *Please don't bring up John Jones' name again.* □ *I'm sorry. I won't bring him up again.* **2.** to raise a child or an animal. □ *Her uncle brought her up.* □ *It's difficult to bring up a pet monkey.*

bring someone or something up to date to make someone or something more modern. (See also *bring someone up to date on someone or something.*) □ *Let's buy some new furniture and bring this room up to date.* □ *John tried to bring himself up to date by changing his hair style. He still looked like the same old John.*

bring someone to to bring someone to consciousness; to wake someone up. (See also *bring someone around; come to.*) □ *The nurse brought the patient to.* □ *She's hurt! Come on, help me bring her to.*

bring someone to account AND **call someone to account** to demand an accounting or an explanation from someone. □ *Tom was brought to account because of his horrible behavior.* □ *They called him to account.*

bring someone up to date on someone or something AND **bring someone up to date** to tell someone the news about something. □ *Please bring me up to date on the Middle East situation.* □ *Please bring me up to date on John. I want to hear all the news.* □ *And bring me up to date, too.*

bring something about AND **bring about something** to make something happen. (Compare to *bring something off.*) □ *Is she clever enough to bring it about?* □ *Oh yes, she can bring about anything she wants.*

bring something crashing down around one AND **bring something crashing down** to destroy something that one has built; to destroy something that one has a special interest in. □ *She brought her whole life crashing down around her.*

□ *Bob's low grade in English brought everything crashing down.*

bring something into question to question something; to express suspicion about something. □ *It was necessary to bring your part in this matter into question.* □ *The city council brought the building project into question.*

bring something off AND **bring off something** to make something happen; to produce a great event. □ *She managed to bring the party off with no difficulty.* □ *She brought off a similar party last season.*

bring something to a close See *bring something to an end.*

bring something to a halt **1.** to make something stop moving. □ *Sally brought the car to a halt.* □ *Ann will bring the horse to a halt in front of the barn.* **2.** See the following entry.

bring something to an end AND **bring something to a close; bring something to a halt** to make an event come to an end. □ *They brought the party to an end.* □ *We brought the evening to a close at midnight.* □ *I must bring this activity to a halt.*

bring something to light to make something known; to discover something. □ *The scientists brought their findings to light.* □ *We must bring this new evidence to light.*

bring the house down AND **bring down the house** to excite a theatrical audience to laughter or applause or both. □ *This is a great joke. The last time I told it, it brought the house down.* □ *It didn't bring down the house; it emptied it.*

bring up the rear to move along behind everyone else; to be at the end of the line. (Originally referred to marching soldiers.) □ *Here comes John, bringing up the rear.* □ *Hurry up, Tom! Why are you always bringing up the rear?*

brush up on something AND **brush up** to learn something; to review something. (See also *bone up on something.*) □ *I think I should brush up on my Spanish before I go to Mexico.* □ *I've heard you speak Spanish. You need to do more than brush up.*

buck for something to aim, try, or strike for a goal. (Originally referred to

trying to get a higher military rank.) □ *Bill acts that way because he's bucking for corporal.* □ *Tom is bucking for a larger office.*

buck up* cheer up. (Slang.) □ *Buck up, old friend! Things can't be all that bad.* □ *I know I have to buck up. Life must go on.*

buckle down to something AND **buckle down** to settle down to something; to begin to work seriously at something. □ *If you don't buckle down to your job, you'll be fired.* □ *You had better buckle down and get busy.*

bug out* to leave; to pack up and get out. (Slang.) □ *It's time to bug out. Let's get out of here.* □ *I just got a call from headquarters. They say to bug out immediately.*

bug someone* to irritate someone; to bother someone. (Slang.) □ *Go away! Stop bugging me!* □ *Leave me alone. Go bug someone else.*

build a fire under someone* to do something to make someone start doing something. (Informal.) □ *The teacher built a fire under the students, and they really started working.* □ *Somebody built a fire under Bill, so he finally went out and got a job.*

build castles in Spain See the following entry.

build castles in the air AND **build castles in Spain** to daydream; to make plans which can never come true. (Neither phrase is used literally.) □ *Ann spends most of her time building castles in Spain.* □ *I really like to sit on the porch in the evening, just building castles in the air.*

build someone or something up AND **build up someone or something; build up** **1.** to make someone or something bigger or stronger. □ *Tom is eating lots of fresh fruits and vegetables to build himself up for basketball.* □ *Tom needs to build up.* □ *The farmer built up his stone fences where they had weakened.* **2.** to advertise, praise, or promote someone or something. □ *Theatrical agents work very hard to build up their clients.* □ *An advertising agency can build up a product so much that everyone will want it.*

39

build something to order to build something especially for someone. (See also *make something to order*.) □ *Our new car was built to order just for us.* □ *My company builds computers to order. No two are alike.*

build up to something to lead up to something; to work up to something. □ *You could tell by the way she was talking that she was building up to something.* □ *The sky was building up to a storm.*

bull in a china shop* a very clumsy person around breakable things; a thoughtless or tactless person. (A cliché. *China* is fine crockery.) □ *Look at Bill, as awkward as a bull in a china shop.* □ *Get that big dog out of my garden. It's like a bull in a china shop.* □ *Bob is so rude, a regular bull in a china shop.*

bump into someone or something AND **run into someone or something** **1.** [with *someone*] to chance on someone; to meet someone by chance. □ *Guess who I bumped into downtown today?* □ *I ran into Bob Jones yesterday.* **2.** to move or steer into someone or something; to crash into someone or something. □ *I ran into a bus yesterday. I dented it badly.* □ *My car bumped into the side of the house. I think that the accident is going to cost a lot of money.*

bump someone off* AND **bump off someone***; **knock someone off***; **knock off someone*** to kill someone. (Slang, especially criminal slang.) □ *They tried to bump her off, but she was too clever and got away.* □ *The crooks bumped off the witness to the crime.* □ *They tried to knock them all off.*

bundle someone up AND **bundle up someone** to dress someone in warm winter clothing; to put warm bedcovers on someone. □ *Mother bundled up Tom before he went to school.* □ *Father put Mary into bed and bundled her up well.* ALSO: **bundle up** to wrap oneself up. □ *I bundled up well before I went outside.* □ *I always bundle up in extra covers during the winter months.*

burn one's bridges behind one AND **burn one's bridges** **1.** to make decisions which cannot be changed in the future. □ *If you drop out of school now, you'll be burning your bridges behind you.* □ *You're too young to burn your bridges that way.* **2.** to be unpleasant in a situation which you are leaving, insuring that you'll never be welcome to return. □ *If you get mad and quit your job, you'll be burning your bridges behind you.* □ *No sense burning your bridges. Be polite and leave quietly.* **3.** to cut off the way back to where you came from, making it impossible to retreat. □ *The army, which had burned its bridges behind it, couldn't go back.* □ *By blowing up the road, the spies had burned their bridges behind them.*

burn oneself out AND **burn out** to do something so long and so intensely that one gets sick and tired of doing it. (See also *burn something out*.) □ *I burned myself out as an opera singer. I just cannot do it anymore.* □ *Tom burned himself out playing golf. He can't stand it anymore.* □ *Tom burned out too young.*

burn someone at the stake **1.** to set fire to a person tied to a post (as a form of execution). □ *They used to burn witches at the stake.* □ *Look, officer, I only ran a stop sign. What are you going to do, burn me at the stake?* **2.** to chastise or denounce someone severely, but without violence. □ *Stop yelling. I made a simple mistake, and you're burning me at the stake for it.* □ *Sally only spilled her milk. There is no need to shout. Don't burn her at the stake for it.*

burn someone in effigy to burn a dummy or other figure which represents a hated person. (See also *hang someone in effigy*.) □ *For the third day in a row, they burned the king in effigy.* □ *Until they have burned you in effigy, you can't really be considered a famous leader.*

burn someone or something to a crisp to burn someone or something totally or very badly. □ *The flames burned him to a crisp.* □ *The cook burned the meat to a crisp.*

burn someone or something up AND **burn up someone or something** **1.** to incinerate someone or something; to destroy someone or something with flames. □ *Don't burn up the steak.* □

I won't burn it up. □ *They burned up the witch.* **2.*** [with *someone*] to make someone very angry. (Informal.) □ *People like that just burn me up!* □ *It burns me up to hear you talk that way.* □ *Talk like that really burns John up, too.* ALSO: **burned up** very angry. □ *I've never been so burned up in my life.* □ *I'm really burned up at Bob.*

burn something down AND **burn down something** to destroy something with fire. □ *Someone burned down the supermarket.* □ *They don't know who burned it down.*

burn something out AND **burn out something** to wear out or render useless something electrical or certain other mechanical things like bearings. (See also *burn oneself out.*) □ *I just burned out my hair dryer.* □ *Why did you burn it out?* □ *I just burned the fan's bearings out, too.* ALSO: **burn out** (for electrical or mechanical devices) to break down and become useless. □ *I hope the light bulb in the ceiling doesn't burn out. I can't reach it.*

burn the candle at both ends to work very hard and stay up very late at night. □ *No wonder Mary is ill. She has been burning the candle at both ends for a long time.* □ *You can't keep on burning the candle at both ends.*

burn the midnight oil* to stay up working, especially studying, late at night. (A cliché. Refers to working by the light of an oil lamp.) □ *I have to go home and burn the midnight oil tonight.* □ *If you burn the midnight oil night after night, you'll probably become ill.*

burn with a low blue flame to be very angry. (Refers to the imaginary heat caused by extreme anger.) □ *By the time she showed up three hours late, I was burning with a low blue flame.* □ *Whenever Ann gets mad, she just presses her lips together and burns with a low blue flame.*

burned up See *burn someone or something up.*

burst at the seams **1.** [with *someone*] to explode (figuratively) with pride or laughter. □ *Tom nearly burst at the seams with pride.* □ *We laughed so hard we just about burst at the seams.* **2.** to explode from fullness. □ *The room was so crowded that it almost burst at the seams.* □ *I ate so much I almost burst at the seams.*

burst in on someone or something AND **burst in** to rush in suddenly and interrupt someone or something. (See also *break in on someone or something.*) □ *I didn't mean to burst in on your discussion.* □ *It's rude to burst in like that.* □ *Tom burst in on his sister while she was doing her hair. After apologizing, he told her the bad news.*

burst into flames to catch fire suddenly; to ignite all at once. □ *Suddenly, the car burst into flames.* □ *It was so hot in the forest fire that a few trees literally burst into flames.*

burst into tears AND **burst out crying** to suddenly begin to cry. (See also *break out into tears.*) □ *After the last notes of her song, the audience burst into tears, such was its beauty and tenderness.* □ *The brother and sister burst into tears on hearing of the death of their dog.* □ *Some people find themselves bursting out crying for no reason at all.*

burst out crying See the previous entry.

burst out laughing to suddenly begin to laugh. □ *The entire audience burst out laughing at exactly the wrong time, and so did the actors.* □ *Every time I think of you sitting there with a lap full of noodle soup, I burst out laughing.*

burst with joy to be full to the bursting point with happiness. (See also *burst at the seams.*) □ *When I got my grades, I could have burst with joy.* □ *Joe was not exactly bursting with joy when he got the news.*

burst with pride to be full to the bursting point with pride. (See also *burst at the seams.*) □ *My parents were bursting with pride when I graduated from college.* □ *I almost burst with pride when I was chosen to go up in the space shuttle.*

bury one's head in the sand AND **hide one's head in the sand** to ignore or hide from obvious signs of danger. (Refers to an ostrich which we picture with its head stuck into the sand or the ground.) □ *Stop burying your head in the sand. Look at the statistics on smok-*

ing and cancer. □ *And stop hiding your head in the sand. All of us will die somehow whether we smoke or not.*

bury the hatchet to stop fighting or arguing; to end old resentments. □ *All right you two. Calm down and bury the hatchet.* □ *I wish Mr. and Mrs. Franklin would bury the hatchet. They argue all the time.*

bust a gut* to work very hard; to strain oneself to do something. (Slang. The word *gut* is considered impolite in some circumstances. *Bust* is an informal form of *burst.*) □ *I don't intend to bust a gut to get there on time.* □ *I busted a gut to get there the last time, and I was the first one there.*

but for someone or something if it were not for someone or something. □ *But for the railing, I'd have fallen down the stairs.* □ *But for the children, Mrs. Smith would have left her husband years ago.*

butt in on someone or something AND **butt in** to interrupt someone or something. (See also *break in on someone or something; burst in on someone or something.*) □ *Pardon me for butting in on your conversation, but this is important.* □ *John butted in on Tom and Jane to tell them that the mail had come.* □ *That's a strange reason to butt in. What was in the mail?*

butter someone up AND **butter up someone** to flatter someone. □ *If I butter up the landlady, she allows me to be a few days late with my rent.* □ *I believe she prefers me to butter her up to getting the rent on time.*

button one's lip to get quiet and stay quiet. (Often used with children.) □ *All right now, let's button our lips and listen to the story.* □ *Button your lip, Tom! I'll tell you when you can talk.*

buy a pig in a poke* to purchase or accept something without having seen or examined it. (A cliché. *Poke* means bag. Compare to *buy something sight unseen.*) □ *Buying a car without test-driving it is like buying a pig in a poke.* □ *He bought a pig in a poke when he ordered a diamond ring by mail.*

buy someone off AND **buy off someone** to bribe someone; to win someone over by gifts or favors. □ *They bought off the whole city council with campaign contributions.* □ *It's not hard to buy politicians off.*

buy someone or something out AND **buy out someone or something** 1. [with *someone*] to buy all of something that someone has. □ *He didn't have much ice cream, and he wouldn't let us buy him out, so we had to go elsewhere to get as much as we wanted.* □ *We bought each merchant out of ice cream.* 2. [with *something*] to buy all of something that someone has. □ *We bought out all the ice cream that he had.* □ *We bought it all out.* 3. [with *something*] to buy all of something which a store has. □ *We bought the store out of ice cream.* □ *When you buy out a whole store, that's a lot of ice cream.*

buy something* to believe someone; to accept something to be a fact. (Informal. Also used literally.) □ *It may be true, but I don't buy it.* □ *I just don't buy the idea that you can swim that far.*

buy something for a song to buy something cheaply. □ *No one else wanted it, so I bought it for a song.* □ *I could buy this house for a song, because it's so ugly.*

buy something on credit to purchase something now and pay for it later (plus interest). (See also *sell something on credit.*) □ *Almost everyone who buys a house buys it on credit.* □ *I didn't have any cash with me, so I used my credit card and bought a new coat on credit.*

buy something sight unseen to buy something without seeing it first. (Compare to *buy a pig in a poke.*) □ *I bought this land sight unseen. I didn't know it was so rocky.* □ *It isn't usually safe to buy something sight unseen.*

buy something to go AND **get something to go; have something to go; order something to go** to purchase food to take out; to make a purchase of cooked food to be taken elsewhere to be eaten. □ *Let's stop here and buy six hamburgers to go.* □ *I didn't thaw anything for dinner. Let's stop off on the way home and get something to go.* □ *No, I don't want to sit at a table. I'll just have a cup of coffee to go.*

buy something up AND **buy up something** to buy a lot of or most of something. □ *We bought up a lot of land in Florida many years ago.* □ *Now we wish we had bought more up.*

by a great deal by a lot; by a large amount. □ *I increased my investment by a great deal.* □ *The patient hasn't improved by a great deal.*

by a hair's breadth AND **by a whisker*** just barely; by a very small distance. (The *whisker* phrase is folksy.) □ *I just missed getting on the plane by a hair's breadth.* □ *The arrow missed the deer by a whisker.*

by a mile by a great distance. (An exaggeration in this case. Also used literally.) □ *You missed the target by a mile.* □ *Your estimate of the budget deficit was off by a mile.*

by a whisker See *by a hair's breadth.*

by all accounts See *according to all accounts.*

by all appearances apparently; according to what one sees. □ *She is, by all appearances, ready to resume work.* □ *By all appearances, we ought to be approaching the airport.*

by all means certainly; yes; absolutely. (Compare to *by any means.*) □ *I will attempt to get there by all means.* □ BOB: *Can you come to dinner tomorrow?* JANE: *By all means. I'd love to.*

by all means of something using every possible manner of something to do something. □ *People will be arriving by all means of transportation.* □ *The surgeon performed the operation by all means of instruments.*

by and by after a period of time has passed. (Most often seen in children's stories.) □ *By and by the bears returned home, and can you guess what they found?* □ *And by and by the little boy became a tall and handsome prince.*

by and large generally; usually. (Originally a nautical expression.) □ *I find that, by and large, people tend to do what they are told to do.* □ *By and large, rose bushes need lots of care.*

by any means by any way possible. □ *I need to get there soon by any means.* □ *I must win this contest by any means, fair or unfair.* □ *It cannot be done by any means.*

by chance by accident; without cause; randomly. □ *The contestants were chosen by chance.* □ *We met only by chance, and now we are the closest of friends.*

by choice due to conscious choice; on purpose. □ *I do this kind of thing by choice. No one makes me do it.* □ *I didn't go to this college by choice. It was the closest one to home.*

by coincidence by an accidental and strange similarity; by an unplanned pair of similar events or occurrences. □ *We just happened to be in the same place at the same time by coincidence.* □ *By coincidence, the circus was in town when I was there. I'm glad because I love circuses.*

by dint of something because of something; due to the efforts of something. (*Dint* is an old word meaning force, and it is never used except in this phrase.) □ *They got the building finished on time by dint of hard work and good organization.* □ *By dint of much studying, John got through college.*

by fits and starts* irregularly; unevenly; with much stopping and starting. (Informal.) □ *Somehow, they got the job done by fits and starts.* □ *By fits and starts, the old car finally got us to town.*

by guess and by golly* by luck; with the help of God. (Folksy. *Golly* is a disguise of *God.*) □ *They managed to get the shed built by guess and by golly.* □ *I lost my ruler and had to install the new floor tile by guess and by golly.*

by hook or by crook* by any means, legal or illegal. (Folksy.) □ *I'll get the job done by hook or by crook.* □ *I must have that house. I intend to get it by hook or by crook.*

by leaps and bounds rapidly; by large movements forward. (Not often used literally, but it could be.) □ *Our garden is growing by leaps and bounds.* □ *The profits of my company are increasing by leaps and bounds.*

by means of something using something; with the use of something. □ *I opened the bottle by means of a bottle opener.* □ *I was able to afford a car by means of a loan.*

by mistake in error; accidentally. □ *I'm sorry. I came into the wrong room by* mistake. □ *I chose the wrong road by mistake. Now we are lost.*

by no means absolutely no; certainly not. □ *I'm by no means angry with you.* □ BOB: *Did you put this box here?* TOM: *By no means. I didn't do it, I'm sure.*

by return mail by a subsequent mailing (back to the sender). (A phrase indicating that an answer is expected soon, by mail.) □ *Since this bill is overdue, would you kindly send us your check by return mail?* □ *I answered your request by return mail over a year ago. Please check your records.*

by shank's mare* by foot. (*Shank* refers to the shank of the leg. Folksy.) □ *My car isn't working, so I'll have to travel by shank's mare.* □ *I'm sore because I've been getting around by shank's mare.*

by the book See *by the numbers.*

by the day one day at a time. □ *I don't know when I'll have to leave town, so I rent this room by the day.* □ *Sally is in such distress. She manages to live only by the day.*

by the dozen twelve at a time; in a group of twelve. (Almost the same as the following entry.) □ *I purchase socks by the dozen.* □ *Eggs are usually sold by the dozen.* □ *Around here we have problems by the dozen.*

by the dozens many; by some large, indefinite number. (Similar to but less than *hundreds.* Almost the same as the previous entry.) □ *Just then people began showing up by the dozens.* □ *I baked cakes and pies by the dozens.*

by the handful in measurements equal to a handful; lots. □ *Billy is eating candy by the handful.* □ *People began leaving by the handful at midnight.*

by the hour at each hour; after each hour. □ *It kept growing darker by the hour.* □ *I have to take this medicine by the hour.* □ *The illness is getting worse by the hour.*

by the month one month at a time. □ *Not many apartments are rented by the month.* □ *I needed a car for a short while, so I rented one by the month.*

by the nape of the neck by the back of the neck. (Mostly found in real or mock threats.) □ *He grabbed me by the nape*

of the neck and told me not to turn around if I valued my life. I stood very still. □ *If you do that again, I'll pick you up by the nape of the neck and throw you out the door.*

by the numbers* AND **by the book*** according to the rules. (Informal.) □ *He always plays the game by the numbers. He never cheats.* □ *I want all my people to go by the numbers. This place is totally honest.* □ *We always go by the book in matters like this.*

by the same token* in the same way; reciprocally. (A cliché.) □ *Tom must be good when he comes here, and, by the same token, I expect you to behave properly when you go to his house.* □ *The mayor votes for his friend's causes. By the same token, the friend votes for the mayor's causes.*

by the seat of one's pants* by sheer luck and very little skill. (Informal. Especially with *fly.*) □ *I got through school by the seat of my pants.* □ *The jungle pilot spent most of his days flying by the seat of his pants.*

by the skin of one's teeth* just barely; by an amount equal to the thickness of the (imaginary) skin on one's teeth. (Informal or slang.) □ *I got through that class by the skin of my teeth.* □ *I got to the airport late and missed the plane by the skin of my teeth.*

by the sweat of one's brow by one's efforts; by one's hard work. □ *Tom raised these vegetables by the sweat of his brow.* □ *Sally polished the car by the sweat of her brow.*

by the way incidentally; in addition; while I think of it. □ *By the way, I'm not going to the bank today.* □ *Oh, by the way, your shoes need polishing.*

by the week one week at a time. □ *I plan my schedules by the week.* □ *Where can I rent a room by the week?*

by the year one year at a time. □ *Most apartments are available by the year.* □ *We budget by the year.*

by virtue of something because of something; due to something. □ *She's permitted to vote by virtue of her age.* □ *They are members of the club by virtue of their great wealth.*

by way of something 1. passing through

something; via something. □ *He came home by way of Toledo.* □ *She went to the bank by way of the drugstore.* **2.** in illustration; as an example. □ *By way of illustration, the professor drew a picture on the board.* □ *He read them a passage from Shakespeare by way of example.*

by word of mouth by speaking rather than writing. □ *I learned about it by word of mouth.* □ *I need it in writing. I don't trust things I hear about by word of mouth.*

C

call a halt to something AND **call a halt** to bring something to an end; to request or demand that something be stopped. (Never used to refer to stopping a moving object.) □ *The town council called a halt to the building project.* □ *The umpire called a halt to the game while the injured player was removed.*

call a meeting to ask that people assemble for a meeting; to request that a meeting be held. □ *The mayor called a meeting to discuss the problem.* □ *I'll be calling a meeting of the town council to discuss the new building project.*

call a spade a spade* to call something by its right name; to speak frankly about something, even if it is unpleasant. (A cliché.) □ *Well, I believe it's time to call a spade a spade. We are just avoiding the issue.* □ *Let's call a spade a spade. The man is a liar.*

call for someone or something to arrive to collect or pick up a person or a thing. (Used especially when you are to pick someone up and are acting as an escort.) □ *I will call for you about eight this evening.* □ *The messenger will call for your reply in the morning.*

call it a day to quit work and go home; to say that a day's work has been completed. □ *I'm tired. Let's call it a day.* □ *The boss was mad because Tom called it a day at noon and went home.*

call it quits* to quit; to resign from something; to announce that one is quitting. (Informal.) □ *Okay! I've had enough! I'm calling it quits.* □ *Time to go home, John. Let's call it quits.*

call on someone See *call upon someone.*

call someone back AND **call back someone 1.** to ask a person to return. □ *The audience called the orchestra conductor back to the stage.* □ *The general called back the whole platoon.* **2.** to return someone's telephone call; to repeat a telephone call. □ *I'll call the doctor back in the morning.* □ *Do I have to return her call? I don't want to call her back.* □ *Why should I call back her secretary? I want to talk to her.*

call someone down to reprimand a person; to *bawl someone out.* □ *The teacher had to call Sally down in front of everybody.* □ *"I wish you wouldn't call me down in public," cried Sally.*

call someone names to call a person unpleasant or insulting names. (Usually viewed as a juvenile act.) □ *Mommy! John is calling me names again!* □ *We'll never get anywhere by calling one another names.*

call someone on the carpet to reprimand a person. (The phrase presents images of a person called into the boss's carpeted office for a reprimand.) □ *One more error like that and the boss will call you on the carpet.* □ *I'm sorry it went wrong. I really hope he doesn't call me on the carpet again.*

call someone or something in AND **call in someone or something** to call on the special talents, abilities, or power of someone or something. □ *They had to call a new doctor in.* □ *Yes, they had to call in a specialist.* □ *They had to call in a huge tractor to move the boulder.*

call someone or something into question AND **call into question someone or something** to cause someone or something to be evaluated; to examine or reexamine the qualifications or value of someone or something. (Do not confuse this phrase with *call someone or something in for questioning.*) □ *Because of her poor record, we were forced to call Dr. Jones into question.* □ *We called Dr. Jones's qualifications into question.* □ *They called the whole project into question.* □ *I cannot call into question the entire medical profession.*

call someone or something off AND **call off someone or something 1.** to call a halt to an attack by someone or something. □ *Please call your dog off. It's trying to bite me!* □ *Okay, you can call off the police. I surrender.* □ *It's time to call off the manhunt. The criminal has given himself up.* **2.** to cancel an event. □ *Because of rain, they called off the baseball game.* □ *It's too late to call the party off. The first guests have already arrived.*

call someone or something up AND **call up someone or something 1.** to call a person, business, or office on the telephone. □ *Mary called the company up and ordered a new supply of medicine.* □ *John picked up the telephone and called his girlfriend up.* □ *Tom called up Mary.* **2.** to summon information from a computer. □ *John used a computer to call up the information.* □ *With a few strokes on the computer keyboard, Sally called up the figures she was looking for.*

call someone to account See *bring someone to account.*

call someone's attention to something to make someone aware of something; to cause someone to take notice of something. □ *May I call your attention to the paragraph at the bottom of the page?* □ *He called my attention to the car parked by the drugstore.*

call someone's bluff to demand that someone prove a claim; to demonstrate that a person is or is not being deceptive. □ *All right, I'll call your bluff. Show me you can do it!* □ *Tom said, "I've got a gun here in my pocket, and I'll shoot if you come any closer!" "Go ahead," said Bill, calling his bluff.*

call the dogs off* AND **call off the dogs*** to stop threatening, chasing, or hounding (a person); (literally), to order dogs

away from the chase. (Informal. Note the variations in the examples) □ *All right, I surrender. You can call your dogs off.* □ *Tell the sheriff to call off the dogs. We caught the robber.* □ *Please call off your dogs!*

call the meeting to order to officially start a meeting; to announce that the meeting has started. □ *The president called the meeting to order shortly after noon.* □ *We cannot do anything until someone calls the meeting to order.*

call the shots* AND **call the tune*** to make the decisions; to decide what is to be done. (Informal.) □ *Sally always wants to call the shots, and Mary doesn't like to be bossed around. They don't get along well.* □ *Sally always wants to call the tune.* □ *Look here, friend, I'm calling the shots. You just be quiet.*

call the tune See the previous entry.

call upon someone AND **call on someone 1.** to visit someone. □ *I called upon Mary last week. We had a fine visit.* □ *It's too late to call on the Browns. They have left for Florida.* **2.** to make a special appeal to God or another deity. □ *They called upon God to help in the freeing of the hostages.* □ *The old wizard chanted, "I call upon you, evil spirits. Come now and do my bidding!"*

Can it!* Be quiet!; Shut up! (Rude slang.) □ *Stop your noise, Bob. Can it!* □ *That's enough, you brat. Can it!*

can't See the expressions listed at *not able,* as well as those listed below.

can't carry a tune unable to sing a simple melody; lacking musical ability. (Almost always negative. Also with *cannot.*) □ *I wish that Tom wouldn't try to sing. He can't carry a tune.* □ *Listen to poor old John. He really cannot carry a tune.*

can't do anything with someone or something not able to manage or control someone or something. (Also with *cannot.*) □ *Bill is such a problem. I can't do anything with him.* □ *My hair is such a mess. I just can't do anything with it.*

can't help but do something unable to choose any but one course of action. (Also with *cannot.*) □ *Her parents live nearby, so she can't help but go there on* *holidays.* □ *Bob is a tennis fan and can't help but travel to Wimbledon each year.*

can't hold a candle to someone not equal to someone; unable to measure up to someone. (Also with *cannot.*) □ *Mary can't hold a candle to Ann when it comes to auto racing.* □ *As for singing, John can't hold a candle to Jane.*

can't make heads or tails of someone or something* AND **can't make heads or tails out of someone or something*** unable to understand someone or something. (A cliché. Also with *cannot.*) □ *John is so strange. I can't make heads or tails of him.* □ *Do this report again. I can't make heads or tails out of it.*

can't see beyond the end of one's nose unaware of the things which might happen in the future; not farsighted; self-centered. (Also with *cannot.*) □ *John is a very poor planner. He can't see beyond the end of his nose.* □ *Ann can't see beyond the end of her nose. She is very self-centered.*

can't see one's hand in front of one's face* unable to see very far, usually due to darkness or fog. (A cliché. Also with *cannot.*) □ *It was so dark that I couldn't see my hand in front of my face.* □ *Bob said that the fog was so thick he couldn't see his hand in front of his face.*

can't stand someone or something See the following entry.

can't stand the sight of someone or something AND **can't stand someone or something; can't stomach someone or something** unable to tolerate someone or something; disliking someone or something extremely. (Also with *cannot.*) □ *I can't stand the sight of cooked carrots.* □ *Mr. Jones can't stand the sight of blood.* □ *None of us can stand this place.* □ *Nobody can stand Tom when he smokes a cigar.* □ *I can't stomach your foul language.* □ *I just can't stomach Mr. Smith.*

can't stomach someone or something See the previous entry.

cancel something out AND **cancel out something** to destroy the effect of something; to balance something. □ *This last payment cancels out my debt.*

□ *Yes, your last payment cancels it out.* □ *Bob's two good grades canceled out his two failing grades.* □ *Give me some medicine to cancel the pain out.*

care about someone or something AND **care for someone or something** to have feelings for someone or something; to love or respect someone or something. □ *It's hard to believe, but Bill cares about Jane.* □ *Bob really cares about the welfare of the town.* □ *Yes, Bob cares for our welfare.*

care for someone or something **1.** to take care of someone or something. □ *Tom cares for his dog and keeps it healthy.* □ *The mother is busy caring for her child.* **2.** See *care about someone or something.*

care nothing about someone or something AND **care nothing for someone or something** to have no feelings at all about someone or something. □ *Jane cares nothing about Tom.* □ *Bill cares nothing for the welfare of the community.* □ *The father cared nothing for his own children.*

carried away excited or moved to (extreme) action (by someone or something). □ *The crowd got carried away and did a lot of damage to the park.* □ *I know that planning a party is fun, but don't get carried away.*

carry a torch for someone AND **carry a torch; carry the torch** to be in love with someone who is not in love with you; to brood over a hopeless love affair. □ *John is carrying a torch for Jane.* □ *Is John still carrying a torch?* □ *Yes, he'll carry the torch for months.*

carry coals to Newcastle* to do something unnecessary; to do something which is redundant or duplicative. (An old cliché from England. Newcastle was a town from which coal was shipped to other parts of England.) □ *Taking food to a farmer is like carrying coals to Newcastle.* □ *Mr. Smith is so rich he doesn't need any more money. To give him money is like carrying coals to Newcastle.*

carry on about someone or something AND **carry on** to make a great fuss over someone or something; to cry and become out of control about someone or something. (Note the variation in the examples.) □ *Billy, stop carrying on about your tummy ache like that.* □ *Billy, you must stop carrying on so.* □ *The child carried on endlessly about his mother.*

carry on with someone or something AND **carry on** 1. [with *something*] to continue with something. □ *Can I please carry on with my work now?* □ *Yes, please carry on.* 2. [with *someone*] to behave improperly with someone; to be affectionate in public. □ *Look at Jane carrying on with Tom. They ought to be ashamed.* □ *Jane, stop carrying on like that!*

carry one's cross See *bear one's cross.*

carry one's own weight AND **carry one's weight; pull one's weight** to do one's share; to earn one's keep. □ *Tom, you must be more helpful around the house. We all have to carry our own weight.* □ *Bill, I'm afraid that you can't work here anymore. You just haven't been carrying your weight.* □ *If you would just pull your weight, we would finish this by noon.*

carry someone or something away AND **carry away someone or something** to move a person or a thing to another place. (See also *get carried away.*) □ *The wind carried the leaves away.* □ *The river carried away the boat.* □ *The taxi carried Sally away.*

carry someone or something off AND **carry off someone or something** 1. to gather up and remove someone or something; to *carry someone or something away.* □ *Sally picked up the papers and carried them off.* □ *The wind carried off the leaves.* □ *The kidnapper carried the child off.* 2. [with *something*] to make a planned event work out successfully. (See also *bring something off.*) □ *The magician carried off the trick with great skill.* □ *It was a huge party, but the hostess carried it off beautifully.*

carry someone or something out AND **carry out someone or something** 1. to move someone or something out of a place. □ *The lady fainted, and they had to carry her out.* □ *They carried out a man who had a heart attack.* □ *The maid carried out the dirty dishes.* 2. [with

something] to perform a task; to perform an assignment. □ *The students didn't carry out their assignments.* □ *"This is a very important job," said Jane. "Do you think you can carry it out?"*

carry something over AND **carry over something** to let something like a bill extend into another period of time; to extend to another location. □ *We'll carry the amount of money due over into the next month.* □ *Yes, please carry over the balance.* □ *We'll have to carry this paragraph over to the next page.* ALSO: **carry over** to extend into another time period or location. □ *I don't like for bills to carry over into the next month.* □ *Please do not let the paragraph carry over.*

carry the ball 1. (in sports) to be the player holding the ball, especially in football when a goal is made. □ *It was the fullback carrying the ball.* □ *Yes, Tom always carries the ball.* 2. to be in charge; to make sure that a job gets done. (See also *drop the ball.*) □ *We need someone who knows how to get the job done. Hey, Sally! Why don't you carry the ball for us?* □ *John can't carry the ball. He isn't organized enough.*

carry the torch 1. to uphold a set of goals; to lead or participate in a (figurative) crusade. □ *The battle was over, but John continued to carry the torch.* □ *If Jane hadn't carried the torch, no one would have followed, and the whole thing would have failed.* 2. See *carry a torch for someone.*

carry the weight of the world on one's shoulders to appear to be burdened by all the problems in the whole world. □ *Look at Tom. He appears to be carrying the weight of the world on his shoulders.* □ *Cheer up, Tom! You don't need to carry the weight of the world on your shoulders.*

carry through on something See *follow through on something.*

carry weight with someone AND **carry weight** (for someone) to have influence with someone; (for something) to have significance for someone. (Often in the negative.) □ *Everything Mary says carries weight with me.* □ *Don't pay any attention to John.*

What he says carries no weight around here. □ *Your proposal is quite good, but since you're not a member of the club, it carries no weight.*

case in point an example of what one is talking about. □ *Now, as a case in point, let's look at 19th century England.* □ *Fireworks can be dangerous. For a case in point, look what happened to Bob Smith last week.*

cash-and-carry having to do with a sale of goods or a way of selling that requires payment at the time of sale and requires that you take the goods with you. (See also *cash on the barrelhead.*) □ *I'm sorry. We don't deliver. It's strictly cash-and-carry.* □ *You cannot get credit at drugstores. They are all cash-and-carry.*

cash in on something AND **cash in** to earn a lot of money at something; to make a profit at something. (See also *cash something in.*) □ *This is a good year for farming, and you can cash in on it if you're smart.* □ *It's too late to cash in on that particular clothing fad.*

cash in one's chips* to die. (Slang. From an expression in the card game poker.) □ *Bob cashed in his chips yesterday.* □ *I'm too young to cash in my chips.*

cash on the barrelhead* money paid for something when it is purchased; money paid at the time of sale. (Folksy. See also *cash-and-carry.*) □ *I don't extend credit. It's cash on the barrelhead only.* □ *I paid $12,000 for this car—cash on the barrelhead.*

cash something in AND **cash in something** to exchange something with cash value for the amount of money it is worth. □ *I need to cash in an insurance policy.* □ *It's time to cash in your U. S. savings bonds.* □ *I should have cashed them in years ago.*

cast around for someone or something AND **cast about for someone or something** to seek someone or something; to seek a thought or an idea. (Refers to a type of a person rather than a specific person.) □ *John is casting around for a new cook. The old one quit.* □ *Bob is casting about for a new car.* □ *Mary cast about for a way to win the contest.*

cast doubt on someone or something AND **cast doubt; cast doubts** to cause someone or something to be doubted. □ *The police cast doubt on my story.* □ *How can they cast doubt? They haven't looked into it yet.* □ *The city council cast doubt on John and his plan.* □ *They are always casting doubts.*

cast one's lot in with someone AND **cast in one's lot with someone** to join in with someone and accept whatever happens. (Also with *in.*) □ *I decided to cast in my lot with the home team this year.* □ *Mary cast her lot with the group going to Spain. They had a wonderful time.*

cast pearls before swine AND **cast one's pearls before swine** a proverb meaning to waste something good on someone who doesn't care about it. (It is considered insulting to refer to people as swine.) □ *To sing for them is to cast pearls before swine.* □ *To serve them French cuisine is like casting one's pearls before swine.*

cast someone or something out AND **cast out someone or something** to send someone or something away; to throw someone or something out. (Formal and literary.) □ *The guards cast the whole group out.* □ *They shouldn't cast out people like that.* □ *I had a loaf of bread, but it got dry so I cast it out.*

cast the first stone to make the first criticism; to be the first to attack. (From a Biblical quotation.) □ *Well, I don't want to be the one to cast the first stone, but she sang horribly.* □ *John always casts the first stone. Does he think he's perfect?*

Cat got your tongue? Why do you not speak?; Speak up and answer my question! (Folksy.) □ *Answer me! What's the matter, cat got your tongue?* □ *Why don't you speak up? Cat got your tongue?*

catch-as-catch-can the best one can do with whatever is available. □ *We went hitchhiking for a week and lived catch-as-catch-can.* □ *There were ten children in our family, and every meal was catch-as-catch-can.*

catch cold AND **take cold** to contract a cold (the disease). □ *Please close the window, or we'll all catch cold.* □ *I take cold every year at this time.*

catch fire AND **catch on fire** to ignite

and burn with flames. □ *Keep your coat away from the flames, or it will catch fire.* □ *Lightning struck the prairie, and the grass caught on fire.*

catch forty winks* AND **catch some Zs*** to take a nap; to get some sleep. (Informal or slang.) □ *I'll just catch forty winks before getting ready for the party.* □ *Tom always tries to catch some Zs before going out for a late evening.*

catch hell See *get the devil.*

catch hold of someone or something AND **catch a hold of someone or something; catch hold** to grasp someone or something. □ *She caught hold of Billy just as he slipped and fell.* □ *She almost failed to catch hold.* □ *Here, catch a hold of this rope.*

catch it* to get into trouble and receive punishment. (Informal. See also *get the devil.* Also used literally.) □ *I know I'm going to catch it when I get home.* □ *Bob hit Billy in the face. He really caught it from the teacher.*

catch on fire See *catch fire.*

catch on to someone or something AND **catch on** to figure someone or something out; to solve a puzzle; to see through an act of deception. □ *Mary caught on to Bob and his tricks.* □ *Ann caught on to the woman's dishonest plan.* □ *The woman thought that Ann wouldn't catch on.*

catch one with one's pants down* to catch someone doing something, especially something that ought to be done in secret or in private. (Informal. Use with caution. This probably refers indirectly to having one's pants down in the bathroom.) □ *John couldn't convince them he was innocent. They caught him with his pants down.* □ *Did you hear that John took the camera? The store owner caught him with his pants down.*

catch one's breath to resume one's normal breathing after exertion; to return to normal after being busy or very active. □ *I don't have time to catch my breath.* □ *I ran so fast that it took ten minutes to catch my breath.*

catch one's death of cold AND **catch one's death; take one's death of cold** to contract a cold; to catch a serious cold. (See *catch cold.*) □ *If I go out in this weather, I'll catch my death of cold.* □ *Dress up warm or you'll take your death of cold.* □ *Put on your raincoat, or you'll catch your death.*

catch sight of someone or something to see someone or something briefly; to get a glimpse of someone or something. □ *I caught sight of the rocket just before it flew out of sight.* □ *Ann caught sight of the robber as he ran out of the bank.*

catch some Zs See *catch forty winks.*

catch someone in the act of doing something AND **catch someone in the act** to catch a person doing something illegal or private. (See also *in the act of doing something.*) □ *They know who set the fire. They caught someone in the act.* □ *I caught Tom in the act of stealing a car.* ALSO: **caught in the act** seen doing something illegal or private. □ *Tom was caught in the act.* □ *She's guilty. She was caught in the act.*

catch someone off balance to catch a person who is not prepared; to surprise someone. (Also used literally.) □ *Sorry I acted so flustered. You caught me off balance.* □ *The robbers caught Ann off balance and stole her purse.*

catch someone off guard AND **catch one off one's guard** to catch a person at a time of carelessness. (Compare to *catch someone off balance.*) □ *Tom caught Ann off guard and frightened her.* □ *She caught me off my guard, and I told her the location of the jewels.*

catch someone red-handed to catch a person in the act of doing something wrong. (Compare to *catch someone in the act of doing something.*) □ *Tom was stealing the car when the police drove by and caught him red-handed.* □ *Mary tried to cash a forged check at the bank, and the teller caught her red-handed.* ALSO: **caught red-handed** caught in the act of doing something wrong. □ *Tom was caught red-handed.* □ *Many car thieves are caught red-handed.*

catch someone's eye AND **get someone's eye** to establish eye contact with someone; to attract someone's attention. (Also with *have*, as in the examples.) □ *The shiny red car caught Mary's eye.* □ *Tom got Mary's eye and waved* *to her.* □ *When Tom had her eye, he smiled at her.*

catch the devil See *get the devil.*

catch up to someone or something AND **catch up with someone or something; catch up** to move faster in order to reach someone or something who is moving in the same direction. □ *The red car caught up with the blue one.* □ *Bill caught up with Ann, and they walked to the bank together.* □ *He had to run to catch up to her.*

catch up with someone or something See the previous entry.

caught in the act See *catch someone in the act of doing something.*

caught in the cross-fire **1.** caught between two fighting people or groups. □ *In Western movies, innocent people are always getting caught in the cross-fire.* □ *In the war, Corporal Smith was killed when he got caught in the cross-fire.* **2.** See the following entry.

caught in the middle AND **caught in the cross-fire** caught between two arguing people or groups, making it difficult to remain neutral. □ *The cook and the dishwasher were having an argument, and Tom got caught in the middle. All he wanted was his dinner.* □ *Mr. and Mrs. Smith tried to draw me into their argument. I don't like being caught in the middle.* □ *Bill and Ann were arguing, and poor Bobby, their son, was caught in the cross-fire.*

caught short to be without something you need, especially money. □ *I needed eggs for my cake, but I was caught short.* □ *Bob had to borrow money from John to pay for the meal. Bob is caught short quite often.*

cause a commotion See the following entry.

cause a stir AND **cause a commotion** to cause people to become agitated; to cause trouble in a group of people; to shock or alarm people. (Notice the example with *quite.*) □ *When Bob appeared without his evening jacket, it caused a stir in the dining room.* □ *The dog ran through the church and caused quite a commotion.*

cause eyebrows to raise AND **cause some eyebrows to raise** to shock people; to surprise and dismay people. (See also *raise some eyebrows.*) □ *John caused eyebrows to raise when he married a poor girl from Toledo.* □ *If you want to cause some eyebrows to raise, just start singing as you walk down the street.*

cause tongues to wag AND **cause some tongues to wag** to cause people to gossip; to give people something to gossip about. □ *The way John was looking at Mary will surely cause some tongues to wag.* □ *The way Mary was dressed will also cause tongues to wag.*

cave in **1.** to collapse; (for the roof of a cave, tunnel, or house) to collapse. □ *The tunnel caved in killing three people.* □ *The ground caved in dropping the house into a vast cavern.* **2.** See the following entry.

cave in to someone or something AND **cave in** for someone to collapse and give in to someone else or to something. □ *Mr. Franklin always caves in to Mrs. Franklin.* □ *It's easier to cave in than to go on fighting.* □ *Tom caved in to the pressure of work.*

chalk something up to something AND **chalk up something to something** to recognize something as the cause of something else. □ *We chalked her bad behavior up to her recent illness.* □ *She chalked up her behavior to her headache.* □ *I chalked up my defeat to my impatience.*

champ at the bit to be ready and anxious to do something. (Originally said about horses.) □ *The kids were champing at the bit to get into the swimming pool.* □ *The dogs were champing at the bit to begin the hunt.*

chance on someone or something AND **chance upon someone or something** to find someone or something by chance. □ *I just happened to chance upon this excellent restaurant down by the river. The food is superb.* □ *We were exploring a small Kentucky town when we chanced on an old man who turned out to be my great uncle.*

chance something to risk doing something; to try doing something. □ *I don't usually ride horses, but this time I will chance it.* □ *Bob didn't have reserva-*

tions, but he went to the airport anyway, chancing a cancellation.

change horses in midstream to make major changes in an activity which has already begun; to choose someone or something else after it is too late. □ *I'm already baking a cherry pie. I can't bake an apple pie. It's too late to change horses in midstream.* □ *The house is half-built. It's too late to hire a different architect. You can't change horses in midstream.*

change someone's mind to cause a person to think differently (about someone or something). □ *Tom thought Mary was unkind, but an evening out with her changed his mind.* □ *I can change my mind if I want to. I don't have to stick with an idea.*

change someone's tune to change the manner of a person, usually from bad to good, or from rude to pleasant. □ *The teller was most unpleasant until she learned that I'm a bank director. Then she changed her tune.* □ *"I will help change your tune by fining you $150," said the judge to the rude defendant.* ALSO: **sing a different tune** to change one's manner, usually from bad to good. □ *When she learned that I was a bank director, she began to sing a different tune.*

charge off to leave rapidly and with a sense of purpose, or in anger. □ *"Oh Bob," cried Mary, "why do you always get mad and charge off when I talk to you?"* □ *The knight said goodbye to the king and charged off into the forest.*

charge someone or something up AND **charge up someone or something 1.** [with *someone*] to get someone excited and enthusiastic. □ *The speaker charged up the crowd to go out and raise money.* □ *Mrs. Smith tried to charge her husband up about getting a job.* **2.** [with *something*] to restore a charge to an electrical storage battery. (Also without *up*.) □ *They charged up the battery overnight.* □ *My car charges the battery up whenever the engine runs.* ALSO: **charged up 1.** (of someone) excited; enthusiastic □ *The crowd was really charged up.* □ *Tom is so tired that he cannot get charged up about anything.*

2. (of something) full of electrical power. (Also without *up*.) □ *The battery is completely charged up.* □ *If the battery isn't charged up, the car won't start.*

charge something to someone or something to buy something and place the cost on the account of someone or something (such as a business). □ *He charged his new suit to his mother.* □ *Mary charged her vacation to the company she worked for.*

charge something up to someone or something to blame something on someone or something. □ *Mary charged her problems up to her lack of patience.* □ *Her mother charged it up to herself.*

Charity begins at home. a proverb meaning that one should be kind to one's own family, friends, or fellow citizens before trying to help others. □ *"Mother, may I please have some pie?" asked Mary. "Remember, charity begins at home."* □ *At church, the minister reminded us that charity begins at home, but we must remember others also.*

chase after someone or something AND **chase around after someone or something; chase around; run after someone or something; run around after someone or something; run around 1.** to pursue someone or something. □ *The dog ran after the car.* □ *I've been chasing around after your birthday present all day. I finally found the right thing.* □ *Bill, when are you going to stop running around and settle down?* **2.** [with *someone*] to flirt with someone; to follow someone around to ask for a date. □ *Tom is still chasing after Jane. Can't he see that she doesn't care for him?* □ *He shouldn't run around like that!*

chase around after someone or something See the previous entry.

chase someone or something around AND **chase around someone or something** to chase (and try to catch) someone or something. □ *The dogs chased one another around until they both got tired.* □ *The mothers chased around their children in the park.*

cheat on someone to commit adultery; to be unfaithful to one's lover. □ *"Have you been cheating on me?" cried*

Mrs. Franklin. □ "No, I haven't been cheating on you," said Mr. Franklin.

check in See *check into something; look in on someone or something.*

check in on someone or something See *look in on someone or something.*

check into something 1. AND **check in** to register or sign into a place, such as a hotel. □ *I'll call you just after I check into the hotel.* □ *I can't get to a telephone until I check in.* 2. See *look into something.*

check on someone or something to examine or investigate someone or something. □ *I'll have to check on your facts.* □ *I'll check on the baby and make sure she's asleep.*

check out of something AND **check out** to sign out of a place and leave. □ *What time do you have to check out?* □ *I have to check out of the hotel by 2:00 p.m.*

check someone in AND **check in someone** to make a record of someone's arrival; in a hotel, to assign a person to a room. □ *The room clerk was waiting to check me in.* □ *He had just checked in another gentleman named Smith.*

check someone or something off AND **check off someone or something** to record some fact about someone or something on a list. (The *someone* refers to someone's name on a list, not a person.) □ *I have the hot dogs right here. You can check them off.* □ *Look at your list of the people who can't come to the party. Have you checked off the Smiths?*

check someone or something out AND **check out someone or something** 1. [with *someone*] to look closely at or investigate someone, especially a man or woman with whom you might wish to make a date. (Slang.) □ *Look at Tom checking Mary out. Do you think he will ask her out?* □ *Tom is always checking out the girls.* 2. [with *someone*] to make a record of someone's departure. □ *The desk clerk checked out the guests when they left the hotel.* □ *I'm leaving the building now. Please check me out.* 3. [with *something*] to record the lending of something. □ *I checked out a library book.* □ *The librarian found the book I wanted and checked it out so I could read it at home.* 4. [with *something*] to

determine the truth of something. □ *I didn't believe her story, so I checked it out. It was true after all.* □ *This reference may be wrong. Go to the library and check out the date.*

check up on someone or something AND **check up** to investigate someone or something. □ *The police are checking up on my story.* □ *When they want to check up on someone, they don't waste any time.* □ *An investigator spends the whole day just checking up.* ALSO: **have some checking up to do** to have the task of checking up (on someone or something). □ *Please excuse the officer. He has some checking up to do.*

check with someone to ask someone (about something); to get permission from someone (to do something). □ *Yes, I think I can drive us to the party. I'll have to check with my parents, however.* □ *Please check with Mr. Brown, the city manager, about that problem.*

cheer someone on to give words or shouts of encouragement to someone who is trying to do something. □ *John was leading in the race, and the whole crowd was cheering him on.* □ *Sally was doing so well in her performance that I wanted to cheer her on.*

cheer someone up AND **cheer up someone** to make a sad person happy. □ *When Bill was sick, Ann tried to cheer him up by reading to him.* □ *Interest rates went up, and that cheered up all the bankers.* ALSO: **cheer up** to become more happy. □ *Things are bad for you now, but you'll cheer up when they get better.* □ *Cheer up, Tom! Things can't be that bad.*

cheer up See the previous entry.

chew someone or something up AND **chew up someone or something** to grind, chew, or crush someone or something. (Usually in reference to chewing up food.) □ *Bob, chew your food up.* □ *The food processor chewed up the carrots into tiny strips.* □ *The dog chewed up my new shoes.* □ *The machine chewed Bill up very badly.*

chew someone out* AND **chew out someone*; eat out someone*; eat someone out*** to scold someone; to bawl someone out thoroughly. (Informal. Used much in the military.) □ *The sergeant chewed the corporal out; then the corporal chewed the private out.* □ *The boss is always chewing out somebody.* □ *The coach ate out the entire football team because of their poor playing.*

chew something off AND **chew off something** to pull or tear something off (of something else) by biting or chewing. □ *My coat is ruined! The puppy chewed the buttons off.* □ *My puppy would chew the knob off the door if she could reach it.* □ *Bob picked up the turkey leg and chewed off a big piece.*

chew the fat* AND **chew the rag*** to have a chat with someone; to talk very informally with one's close friends. (Slang.) □ *Hi, old buddy! Come in and let's chew the fat.* □ *They usually just sat around and chewed the rag. They never did get much done.*

chew the rag See the previous entry.

chicken out of something* AND **chicken out*** to withdraw from something due to fear or cowardice. (Slang.) □ *Jane was going to go parachuting with us, but she chickened out at the last minute.* □ *I'd never chicken out of parachute jumping, because I'd never agree to do it in the first place!*

chime in with something AND **chime in** to add one's voice to something; to add something to the discussion, usually by interrupting. □ *Billy chimed in by reminding us to come to dinner.* □ *Everyone chimed in on the final chorus of the song.*

chip in on something AND **chip in something on something; chip something in on something; chip in** to contribute a small amount of money to a fund which will be used to buy something. □ *Would you care to chip in on a gift for the teacher?* □ *Yes, I'd be happy to chip in.* □ *Could you chip in a dollar on the gift please?*

chip something in on something See the previous entry.

choke someone up* AND **choke up someone*** to make a person become over-emotional and speechless; to make a person begin to cry. (Informal.) □ *The sight of all those smiling people*

choked Bob up, and he couldn't go on speaking. □ *The funeral procession choked up Jane.* ALSO: **choked up*** speechless due to one's emotions. (Informal.) □ *Bob was choked up by the smiling people.* □ *Jane got all choked up at the funeral.*

choke something off AND **choke off something** to stifle something; to force something to an end. □ *The car ran over the hose and choked the water off.* □ *The president choked off the debate.*

choose up sides to form into two opposing teams by having a leader or captain take turns choosing players. □ *Let's choose up sides and play baseball.* □ *When I choose up sides, all the best players don't end up on the same team.*

chop someone or something up AND **cut up someone or something** to cut someone or something into pieces. □ *The murderer chopped the body up and hid the pieces in the forest.* □ *The food processor cut up the carrots quickly and neatly.*

clam up* to shut up; to refuse to talk; to close one's mouth (as tightly as a clam closes its shell). (Slang.) □ *You talk too much, John. Clam up!* □ *When they tried to question her, she clammed up.*

clamp down on someone or something AND **clamp down** to become strict with someone; to become strict about something. □ *Because Bob's grades were getting worse, his parents clamped down on him.* □ *The police have clamped down on speeders in this town.* □ *Things have already gone too far. It's too late to clamp down.*

clean out of something See *fresh out of something.*

clean someone or something out AND **clean out someone or something 1.** to remove everything from inside someone or something; to clean out the inside of someone or something. □ *We cleaned out our garage last weekend.* □ *The laxative cleaned out Bill in a few hours.* **2.*** [with *someone*] to take everything—especially the money—that a person has. (Informal.) □ *I'm sorry I don't have any change. My children cleaned me out this morning.* □ *The* *robber cleaned the man out without hurting him.*

clean someone or something up AND **clean up someone or something; clean up** to make someone or something clean. □ *This house is a mess. Let's clean it up.* □ *The mother cleaned up the baby after dinner.* □ *It's nearly supper time. I have to go clean up.* □ *After you finish cooking, you must clean up.*

clean up 1. to make a great profit. (Informal.) □ *John won at the races and really cleaned up.* □ *Ann cleaned up by taking a job selling encyclopedias.* **2.** See *clean someone or something up.*

clean up one's act* AND **clean one's act up*** to reform one's conduct; to improve one's performance. (Slang. Originally referred to polishing one's stage performance.) □ *If you don't clean up your act, you'll be sent home.* □ *Since Sally cleaned up her act, she has become very productive.*

clear out to get out (of someplace); to leave. □ *All right you people, clear out of here, now.* □ *I knew right then that it was time to clear out.*

clear something off AND **clear off something** to clean something off; to remove something from the top of something. □ *It's time to clear off the table.* □ *There is too much music stacked on the piano. Please clear it off.*

clear something out AND **clear out something** to make something or someplace empty. □ *We have to make room for the car in this garage. Clear everything out!* □ *They had to clear out the entire closet in order to find the broom.*

clear something up AND **clear up something 1.** to make the sky bright and clear. □ *The wind will blow away the clouds and clear things up very quickly.* □ *A fresh breeze always clears up the air.* **2.** to explain something; to solve a mystery. □ *I think that we can clear this matter up without calling in the police.* □ *First we have to clear up the problem of the missing jewels.* **3.** to cure a disease or a medical condition. (Especially facial pimples.) □ *The doctor will give you something to clear up your cold.* □ *There is no medicine which will clear pimples up.* ALSO: **clear up**

1. (for the sky) to become clear. □ *Look! It's beginning to clear up already.* □ *It usually clears up by noon.* **2.** (for a problem) to become solved. □ *This matter won't clear up by itself.* **3.** (for a disease) to cure itself or run its course. □ *I told you your pimples would clear up without special medicine.* □ *My rash cleared up in a week.*

clear the air to get rid of doubts or hard feelings. (Sometimes this is said about an argument or other unpleasantness. The literal meaning is also used.) □ *All right, let's discuss this frankly. It'll be better if we clear the air.* □ *Mr. and Mrs. Brown always seem to have to clear the air with a big argument before they can be sociable.*

clear the table to remove the dishes and other eating utensils from the table after a meal. □ *Will you please help clear the table?* □ *After you clear the table, we'll play cards.*

clear up See *clear something up.*

climb on the bandwagon to join others in supporting someone or something. □ *Come join us! Climb on the bandwagon and support Senator Smith!* □ *Look at all those people climb on the bandwagon! They don't know what they are getting into!*

climb the wall* AND **climb the walls*** to do something desperate when one is extremely anxious, bored, or excited. (Informal or slang.) □ *I'm so upset I could climb the wall.* □ *The meeting was so long and the speaker so boring that most of the audience wanted to climb the wall.*

clip someone's wings* to restrain someone; to reduce or put an end to a teenager's privileges. (Informal.) □ *You had better learn to get home on time, or I will clip your wings.* □ *My mother clipped my wings. I can't go out tonight.*

clip something out AND **clip out something** to cut something out of a sheet of paper, usually with scissors. □ *Jane clipped out the news article about her uncle.* □ *Bob always clips coupons out to use at the supermarket.*

clog someone or something up AND **clog up someone or something 1.** [with *something*] to fill up something such as a drain pipe, water pipe, or blood vessel. □ *The blood clogged up your arteries.* □ *The roots clogged the sewer up totally.* **2.*** [with *someone*] to constipate someone. (Informal.) □ *I can't eat foods which clog me up.* □ *That horrible stuff clogged up the whole army.*

close at hand within reach; handy. □ *I'm sorry, but your letter isn't close at hand. Please remind me what you said in it.* □ *When you're cooking, you should keep all the ingredients close at hand.*

close in on someone or something AND **close in** to overwhelm or surround someone or something. □ *My problems are closing in on me.* □ *The wolves closed in on the elk.* □ *They howled as they closed in.*

close one's eyes to something to ignore something; to pretend that something is not really happening. □ *You can't close your eyes to hunger in the world.* □ *I just closed my eyes to the problem and pretended that it wasn't there.*

close ranks 1. to move closer together in a military formation. □ *The soldiers closed ranks and marched on the enemy.* □ *All right! Stop that talking and close ranks.* **2.** to join (with someone). □ *We can fight this menace only if we close ranks.* □ *Let's all close ranks behind Ann and get her elected.*

close someone out of something to prevent someone from joining in a class, an excursion, etc., because there is no more room. □ *They closed me out of the class I wanted.* □ *They closed twelve people out of the trip to China.*

close something down AND **close down something; shut down something; shut something down** to make something stop operating; to put something out of business. □ *The city council closed down the amusement park.* □ *The police closed the factory down.* □ *The manager shut down the factory for the holidays.*

close something out AND **close out something 1.** [with *something*] (for a merchant) to sell off all of one kind of goods. □ *We'll have to close out all the spring dresses in May.* □ *I'm sorry. We closed that item out last month.* **2.** to

cease offering a course, an excursion, etc., because there is no more room. □ *They closed that course out last week.* □ *The travel agency closed out the trip to China because it was full.*

close the books on someone or something AND **close the books** to put an end to a matter which concerns someone or something. (The *books* here refers to financial accounting records.) □ *It's time to close the books on the Franklin case.* □ *Yes, let's close the books on Mr. Franklin.* □ *You closed the books too soon. Here is some new information.*

close the door on someone or something See *shut the door on someone or something.*

close to home 1. close to one's personal situation, such as in one's family or neighborhood. □ *When those things happen close to home, we are always surprised.* □ *We never expect tragedy to strike close to home.* **2.** See *hit one where one lives.*

close to someone fond of someone; very good friends with someone. □ *Tom is very close to Mary. They may get married.* □ *Mr. Smith isn't exactly close to Mrs. Smith.*

close up shop* to quit working, for the day or forever. (Informal.) □ *It's five o'clock. Time to close up shop.* □ *I can't make any money in this town. The time has come to close up shop and move to another town.*

cloud up 1. (for the sky) to get cloudy, as if it were going to rain. □ *All of a sudden it clouded up and began to rain.* □ *It usually clouds up at sunset.* **2.** (for someone) to grow very sad, as if to cry. (See also *turn on the waterworks.*) □ *The baby clouded up and let out a howl.* □ *Whenever Mary got homesick, she'd cloud up. She really wanted to go home.*

clue someone in on something* AND **clue someone in*** to inform someone of something. (Informal.) □ *Please clue me in on what's going on.* □ *Yes, clue her in.*

coast-to-coast from the Atlantic to the Pacific Ocean (in the U.S.A.); all the land between the Atlantic and Pacific Oceans. □ *My voice was once heard on a coast-to-coast radio broadcast.* □ *Our* *car made the coast-to-coast trip in eighty hours.*

cock-and-bull story a silly, made up story; a story which is a lie. □ *Don't give me that cock-and-bull story.* □ *I asked for an explanation, and all I got was your ridiculous cock-and-bull story!*

cold, hard cash* cash, not checks or promises. (Informal.) □ *I want to be paid in cold, hard cash, and I want to be paid now!* □ *Pay me now! Cash on the barrelhead—cold, hard cash.*

come a cropper to have a misfortune; to fail. (Literally, to fall off one's horse.) □ *Bob invested all his money in the stock market just before it fell. Boy, did he come a cropper.* □ *Jane was out all night before she took her tests. She really came a cropper.*

come about 1. to happen. □ *How did this come about?* □ *This came about due to the severe weather.* **2.** (for a sailboat) to turn. □ *Look how easily this boat comes about.* □ *Now, practice making the boat come about.*

come across someone or something AND **run across someone or something** to find someone or something by accident. □ *In Kentucky, I came across this beautiful little stream just full of fish.* □ *Guess who I ran across on Main Street this afternoon?*

Come again?* 1. Say it again. I did not hear you. (Folksy.) □ TOM: *Hello, Grandfather.* GRANDFATHER: *Come again? You'll have to talk louder.* □ *The farmer looked at me and said, "Come again?"* **2.** to come back; to return some other time. □ *I'm so glad you enjoyed our party. Please come again sometime.* □ *The store clerk gave me my change and my purchase and said, "Thank you. Come again."*

come along with one AND **come along** to accompany one to someplace. □ *Come along with me, young man. We are going to the principal's office.* □ *All right. I'll come along.*

Come and get it!* Dinner is ready. Come and eat it! (Folksy.) □ *A shout was heard from the kitchen, "Come and get it!"* □ *No one says "Come and get it!" at a formal dinner.*

come apart at the seams to suddenly lose one's emotional self-control. (Informal. From the literal sense referring to a garment falling apart. See also *burst at the seams*.) □ *Bill was so upset that he almost came apart at the seams.* □ *I couldn't take anymore. I just came apart at the seams.*

come around AND **come round 1.** to finally agree or consent (to something). □ *I thought he'd never agree, but in the end he came around.* □ *She came round only after we argued for an hour.* **2.** to return to consciousness; to wake up. □ *He came around after we threw cold water in his face.* □ *The boxer was knocked out, but came round in a few seconds.* **3.** to come for a visit; to stop by (somewhere). □ *Why don't you come around about eight? I'll be home then.* □ *Come round some weekend when you aren't busy.*

come at someone or something to threaten or attack someone or something. □ *The dog snarled and came at me, but I didn't get bitten.* □ *The bull turned and came at the matador's cape.*

come away empty-handed to return without anything. (See also *go away empty-handed*.) □ *All right, go gambling. Don't come away empty-handed, though.* □ *Go to the bank and ask for the loan again. This time don't come away empty-handed.*

come back to return. (Compare to *go back*.) □ *We must go now. Please come back with me.* □ *Come back! Do not go any farther.*

come between someone and someone else to interfere with the relationship between two people. □ *Mary Jones is coming between Mr. and Mrs. Franklin.* □ *I'll stay at home. I don't want to come between Tom and his brother.*

come by something 1. to travel by a specific carrier, such as a plane, boat, or car. □ *We came by train. It's more relaxing.* □ *Next time, we'll come by plane. It's faster.* **2.** to find or get something. □ *How did you come by that haircut?* □ *Where did you come by that new shirt?*

come by something honestly 1. to get something honestly. □ *Don't worry. I came by this watch honestly.* □ *I have* *a feeling she didn't come by it honestly.* **2.** to inherit something—a character trait—from one's parents. □ *I know I'm mean. I came by it honestly, though.* □ *She came by her kindness honestly.*

come clean with someone* AND **come clean*** to be completely honest with someone; to confess (everything) to someone. (Slang.) □ *The lawyer said, "I can help you only if you come clean with me."* □ *All right, I'll come clean. Here is the whole story.*

come down 1. (for something) to descend (to someone) through inheritance. □ *All my silverware came down to me from my great grandmother.* □ *The antique furniture came down through my mother's family.* **2.** to return to normal. (Slang. Often used to refer to drug use.) □ *He's very excited about his new job. He'll come down when he finds out how difficult it is.* □ *He's talking nonsense now. He'll make sense when he comes down.*

come down hard on someone or something AND **come down on someone or something hard** to attack vigorously; to scold someone severely. □ *Tom's parents really came down hard on him for coming home late.* □ *Yes, they came down on him hard.*

come down in the world to lose one's social position or financial standing. □ *Mr. Jones has really come down in the world since he lost his job.* □ *If I were unemployed, I'm sure I'd come down in the world, too.*

come down to earth to become realistic; to become alert to what is going on around one. (Informal.) □ *You have very good ideas, John, but you must come down to earth. We can't possibly afford any of your suggestions.* □ *Pay attention to what is going on. Come down to earth and join the discussion.*

come down to something* to be reduced to something; to amount to no more than something. (Informal. Similar to *boil down to something*.) □ *It comes down to whether you want to go to the movies or stay at home and watch television.* □ *It came down to either getting a job or going back to college.*

come down with something to become

ill with some disease. □ *I'm afraid I'm coming down with a cold.* □ *I'll probably come down with pneumonia.*

come from far and wide to come from many different places. □ *Everyone was there. They came from far and wide.* □ *We have foods that come from far and wide.*

come hell or high water* no matter what happens. (Informal. Use *hell* with caution.) □ *I'll be there tomorrow, come hell or high water.* □ *Come hell or high water, I intend to have my own home.*

come home 1. (for one) to return to one's home. □ *What time do you think you'll come home?* □ *I'll come home after the ball game.* **2.** See the following entry.

come home to roost AND **come home** to return to cause trouble (for someone). □ *As I feared, all my problems came home to roost.* □ *Yes, problems all come home eventually.*

come in to enter (into a place where the speaker is). □ *Ann said as she opened the door, "Come in. Make yourself at home."* □ *"Thank you," said Bob, "I'd love to come in."*

come in a body AND **arrive in a body** to arrive as a group. □ *All the guests came in a body.* □ *Things become very busy when everyone arrives in a body.*

come in for something AND **fall in for something** to receive something; to acquire something. □ *Billy came in for a good bawling out when he arrived home.* □ *Mary came in for a tremendous amount of money when her aunt died.* □ *Sally fell in for a lot of trouble when she bought a used car.*

come in handy* to be useful or convenient. (Informal.) □ *A small television set in the bedroom would come in handy.* □ *A good hammer always comes in handy.* □ *A nice cool drink would come in handy about now.*

come in out of the rain to become alert and sensible; to *come down to earth.* (Also used literally. See also *not know enough to come in out of the rain.*) □ *Pay attention, Sally! Come in out of the rain!* □ *Bill will fail if he doesn't come in out of the rain and study.*

come into one's or its own **1.** (for one)

to achieve one's proper recognition. □ *Sally finally came into her own.* □ *After years of trying, she finally came into her own.* **2.** (for something) to achieve its proper recognition. □ *The idea of an electric car finally came into its own.* □ *Film as an art medium finally came into its own.*

come into something to inherit something. (Also used literally. See also *come in for something* which is very close in meaning.) □ *Jane came into a small fortune when her aunt died.* □ *Mary came into a house and a new car when her rich uncle died.*

come of age to reach an age when one is old enough to own property, get married, and sign legal contracts. □ *When Jane comes of age, she will buy her own car.* □ *Sally, who came of age last month, entered into an agreement to purchase a house.*

come off **1.** to become detached (from something). □ *Whoops! My coat button came off.* □ *His wig came off. How embarrassing!* **2.*** to happen; to take place. (Informal.) □ *What time does this party come off?* □ *How did your speech come off?* □ *It came off very well.*

Come off it!* Tell the truth!; Be serious! (Slang.) □ *Come off it, Bill! I don't believe you!* □ *Come on, Jane. Come off it! That can't be true.*

come off second best to win second place or worse; to lose out to someone else. □ *John came off second best in the race.* □ *Why do I always come off second best in an argument with you?*

come on **1.** to hurry up; to follow (someone). □ *Come on! I'm in a hurry.* □ *If you don't come on, we'll miss the train.* **2.** See the following entry.

come on somehow* AND **come on*** to appear somehow to other people. (Informal. Especially with *strong* which means intense.) □ *Jane comes on like a very unpleasant person.* □ *She really comes on strong.* □ *John doesn't care how he comes on.*

come out **1.** to leave the inside and move to the outside; to exit. □ *My friend went into the store, and I'm waiting for her to come out.* □ *How long will it be until she comes out?* **2.** to

become; to turn out. □ *We'll just have to wait and see how things come out.* □ *I'm baking a cake. I hope it comes out okay.* **3.** to be presented to the public; to be released to the public. □ *My new book came out last month.* □ *Mary Ann Smith came out last fall at a lovely party.*

come out ahead to end up with a profit; to improve one's situation. (Compare to *break even.*) □ *I hope you come out ahead with your investments.* □ *It took a lot of money to buy the house, but I think I'll come out ahead.*

come out for someone or something to announce one's support for someone or something. □ *I'm coming out for Senator Brown's reelection.* □ *All the employees came out for a longer work week.*

come out in the wash* to work out all right. (Informal. This means that problems or difficulties will go away as dirt goes away in the process of washing.) □ *Don't worry about that problem. It'll all come out in the wash.* □ *This trouble will go away. It'll come out in the wash.*

come out of nowhere to appear suddenly. □ *Suddenly, a truck came out of nowhere.* □ *Without warning, the storm came out of nowhere.*

come out of one's shell to become more friendly; to be more sociable. □ *Ann, you should come out of your shell and spend more time with your friends.* □ *Come out of your shell, Tom. Go out and make some friends.*

come out of the closet **1.** to reveal one's secret interests. □ *Tom Brown came out of the closet and admitted that he likes to knit.* □ *It's time that all of you lovers of chamber music came out of the closet and attended our concerts.* **2.** to reveal that one is a homosexual. □ *Tom surprised his parents when he came out of the closet.* □ *It was difficult for him to come out of the closet.*

come out with something to say something; to announce something. □ *Sometimes Jane comes out with the most interesting comments.* □ *Jane came out with a long string of curse words.*

come over **1.** to join this party or side; to change sides or affiliation. □ *Tom* *was formerly an enemy spy, but last year he came over.* □ *I thought that Bill was a Republican. When did he come over?* **2.** to come for a visit. □ *See if Ann wants to come over.* □ *I can't come over. I'm busy.*

come round See *come around.*

come someone's way to come to someone. □ *I wish a large sum of money would come my way.* □ *I hope that no bad luck comes my way.*

come through **1.** to penetrate (from the other side to this side). □ *There is a tree branch scraping on the roof. I hope that it doesn't come through.* □ *There is a tack in the sole of my shoe. It had better not come through.* **2.** to do what one is expected to do, especially under difficult conditions. □ *You can depend on Jane. She'll always come through.* □ *We thought that there would be no food, but Tom came through at the last minute with everything we needed.*

come to to become conscious; to wake up. □ *We threw a little cold water in his face, and he came to immediately.* □ *Come to, John! You act as if you were in a daze.*

come to a bad end to have a disaster, perhaps one which is deserved or expected; to die an unfortunate death. □ *My old car came to a bad end. Its engine burned up.* □ *The evil merchant came to a bad end.*

come to a dead end to come to an absolute stopping point. □ *The building project came to a dead end.* □ *The street came to a dead end.* □ *We were driving along and came to a dead end.*

come to a head to come to a crucial point; to come to a point when a problem must be solved. □ *Remember my problem with my neighbors? Well, last night the whole thing came to a head.* □ *The battle between the two factions of the city council came to a head yesterday.*

come to a standstill to stop, temporarily or permanently. □ *The building project came to a standstill because the workers went on strike.* □ *The party came to a standstill until the lights were turned on again.*

come to an end to stop; to finish. □

The party came to an end at midnight. □ *Her life came to an end late yesterday.*

come to an untimely end to come to an early death. □ *Poor Mr. Jones came to an untimely end in a car accident.* □ *Cancer caused Mrs. Smith to come to an untimely end.*

come to blows over something AND **come to blows** to fight about something, usually by striking blows, or verbally. □ *They got excited about the accident, but they never actually came to blows over it.* □ *Yes, they aren't the kind of people who come to blows.*

come to grief to fail; to have trouble or grief. □ *The artist wept when her canvas came to grief.* □ *The wedding party came to grief when the bride passed out.*

come to grips with something to face something; to comprehend something. □ *He found it difficult to come to grips with his grandmother's death.* □ *Many students have a hard time coming to grips with algebra.*

come to life to become alive or lively. (Usually used in a figurative sense.) □ *The party came to life about midnight.* □ *As the anesthetic wore off, the patient came to life.*

come to light to become known. □ *Some interesting facts about your past have just come to light.* □ *If too many bad things come to light, you may lose your job.*

come to mind (for a thought or idea) to enter one's mind. (Compare to *cross someone's mind.*) □ *Do I know a good barber? No one comes to mind right now.* □ *Another idea comes to mind. Why not cut your own hair?*

come to naught See the following entry.

come to nothing AND **come to naught** to amount to nothing; to be worthless. □ *So all my hard work comes to nothing.* □ *Yes, the whole project comes to naught.*

come to one's senses to wake up; to become conscious; to start thinking clearly. □ *John, come to your senses. You're being quite stupid.* □ *In the morning I don't come to my senses until I have had two cups of coffee.*

come to pass to happen. (Formal.) □

When did all of this come to pass? □ When will this event come to pass?

come to rest to stop moving. □ When the car comes to rest, you can get in. □ The leaf fell and came to rest at my feet.

come to terms with someone or something AND **come to terms** **1.** to come to an agreement with someone. □ I finally came to terms with my lawyer about his fee. □ Bob, you have to come to terms with your father. **2.** to learn to accept someone or something. □ She had to come to terms with the loss of her sight. □ She couldn't come to terms with her unemployed husband.

come to the fore to become prominent; to become important. □ The question of salary has now come to the fore. □ Since his great showing in court, my lawyer has really come to the fore in city politics.

come to the point AND **get to the point** to get to the important part (of something). □ He has been talking a long time. I wish he would come to the point. □ Quit wasting time! Get to the point! □ We are talking about money, Bob! Come on, get to the point.

come to think of it I just remembered. □ Come to think of it, I know someone who can help. □ I have a screwdriver in the trunk of my car, come to think of it.

come true to become real; for a dream or a wish to actually happen. □ When I got married, all my dreams came true. □ Coming to the big city was like having my wish come true.

come unglued* to lose emotional control; to have a mental breakdown; to break out into tears or laughter. (Slang.) □ When Sally heard the joke, she almost came unglued. □ When the bank took away my car, I came unglued and cried and cried.

come up to happen unexpectedly. (Also used literally.) □ I'm sorry, I cannot come to your party. Something has come up. □ The storm came up so quickly that I almost got blown away.

come up from behind to approach someone or something from the rear; to move from a poor position to a better one. □ As the horses came to the finish line, my horse came up from behind and won. □ In my math class, I worked and worked and finally came up from behind.

come up in the world to improve one's status or situation in life. □ Since Mary got her new job, she has really come up in the world. □ A good education helped my brother come up in the world.

come up with someone or something to find or supply someone or something. □ I came up with a date at the last minute. □ My mom is always able to come up with a snack for me in the afternoon. □ I don't have the tool you need, but I'll see if I can come up with something.

come upon someone or something AND **come on someone or something** to find someone or something by accident. □ I came upon an interesting fact in my reading last week. □ It is unusual for a teacher to come on a student who is so bright and yet so lazy.

come what may* no matter what might happen. (A cliché.) □ I'll be home for the holidays, come what may. □ Come what may, the mail will get delivered.

come with See the following entry.

come with someone or something to accompany someone or something. □ Where is John? Did he come with Bill? □ Who did John come with? □ The chocolate sundae comes with whipped cream. □ What else does the sundae come with? ALSO: **come with*** to come with someone. (May be regarded as incomplete or informal in parts of the U.S.) □ Mind if I come with? □ John is coming with.

come within an ace of doing something See the following entry.

come within an inch of doing something AND **come within an ace of doing something** to almost do something; to come very close to doing something. (The reference to distance is usually metaphorical.) □ I came within an inch of going into the army. □ I came within an inch of falling off the roof. □ She came within an ace of buying the house.

commit something to memory to memorize something. □ We all committed the Gettysburg Address to memory. □ I committed your telephone number to memory.

compare someone to someone AND **compare someone with someone** to compare two or more people. □ *Please don't compare me to my brother.* □ *Don't compare me with anyone.*

compare someone with someone See the previous entry.

compare something to something AND **compare something with something** to compare two or more things. □ *If you compare this coat to that one, you'll see that this one is better.* □ *He compared the old car with the new one and decided to keep what he had.*

compare something with something See the previous entry.

compel someone to do something to force someone to do something. □ *The law compels you to go to school.* □ *Mary's father compelled her to take a course in driving.*

confide in someone to tell secrets or personal matters to someone. □ *Sally always confided in her sister Ann.* □ *She didn't feel that she could confide in her mother.*

conk out* to pass out; to go to sleep. (Slang.) □ *Bob bumped his head on a tree branch and conked out.* □ *I usually conk out just after the late news at 11:00 p.m.*

conspicuous by one's absence to have one's absence noticed (at an event). □ *We missed you last night. You were conspicuous by your absence.* □ *How could the bride's father miss the wedding party? He was certainly conspicuous by his absence.*

contend with someone or something to endure someone or something; to argue with someone. □ *I cannot contend with John for another instant.* □ *I prefer not to contend with this old television set anymore. I want a new one.*

control the purse strings to be in charge of the money in a business or a household. □ *I control the purse strings at our house.* □ *Mr. Williams is the treasurer. He controls the purse strings.*

convince someone of something to make someone believe something. □ *She convinced me of her sincerity.* □ *I convinced her of the need to study.*

cook someone's goose to damage or ruin someone. □ *I cooked my own goose by not showing up on time.* □ *Sally cooked Bob's goose for treating her the way he did.*

cook something up AND **cook up something** to plot something; to improvise something. (Also used literally.) □ *Mary cooked an interesting party up at the last minute.* □ *Let me see if I can cook up a way to get you some money.*

cook the accounts to cheat in bookkeeping; to make the accounts appear to balance when they do not. □ *Jane was sent to jail for cooking the accounts of her mother's store.* □ *It's hard to tell whether she really cooked the accounts or just didn't know how to add.*

Cool it!* Calm down!; Take it easy! (Slang.) □ *Don't get mad, Bob. Cool it!* □ *Cool it you guys! No fighting around here.*

cool off AND **cool down** 1. to lose or reduce heat. □ *I wish my soup would cool off. I'm hungry.* □ *It'll cool down this evening, after dusk.* 2. to let one's anger die away. □ *I'm sorry I got angry. I'll cool off in a minute.* □ *Cool off, Tom. There is no sense getting so excited.* 3. to let one's passion or love die away. □ TED: *Is Bob still in love with Jane?* BILL: *No, he's cooled off a lot.* □ TED: *I thought that they were both cooling down.*

cool one's heels* to wait (for someone). (Informal.) □ *I spent all afternoon cooling my heels in the waiting room while the doctor talked on the telephone.* □ *All right. If you can't behave properly, just sit down here and cool your heels until I call you.*

cool someone or something down AND **cool down someone or something**; **cool off someone or something**; **cool someone or something off** 1. to reduce the heat of someone or something. (See *cool off*.) □ *A cold drink is what I need to cool me down.* □ *She took a shower to cool herself off.* □ *She cooled down her tea by putting an ice cube in it.* 2. [with *someone*] to reduce someone's anger. □ *I just stared at him while he was yelling. I knew that would cool him down.* □ *The coach talked to them for a long time. That cooled them* *off.* **3.** [with *someone*] to reduce someone's passion or love. □ *When she slapped him, that really cooled him down.* □ *Bill cooled Mary off by dating Sally for a while.*

cool someone or something off See the previous entry.

cop a plea* to plead guilty to a crime in hopes of receiving a lighter punishment. (Slang, especially criminal slang.) □ *The robber copped a plea and got only two years in jail.* □ *When you cop a plea, it saves the court system a lot of money.*

cop out* to get out of a difficult situation; to sneak out of a difficult situation. (Slang.) □ *At the last minute she copped out on us.* □ *Things were going badly for Senator Phillips, so he copped out by resigning.*

cost a pretty penny* to cost a lot of money. (A cliché.) □ *I'll bet that diamond cost a pretty penny.* □ *You can be sure that house cost a pretty penny. It has seven bathrooms.*

cost an arm and a leg See *pay an arm and a leg for something.*

cough something up* AND **cough up something*** to produce something (which someone has requested). (Slang.) □ *All right, Bill. Cough up the stolen diamonds or else.* □ *Okay, okay. I'll cough them up.* □ *Bill had to cough up forty dollars to pay for the broken window.*

could do with someone or something to want or need someone or something; to benefit from someone or something. (Compare to *go for someone or something.*) □ *I could do with a nice cool drink right now.* □ *I could do with some help on this project.* □ *This house could do with some cleaning up.* □ *They said they could do with John to help them finish faster.* □ *My car could do with a bigger engine.*

couldn't care less* AND **could care less*** unable to care at all. (Informal.) □ *John couldn't care less whether he goes to the party or not.* □ *So she won first place. I couldn't care less.* □ *I could care less if I live or die.*

count noses to count people. □ *I'll tell you how many people are here after I* count noses. □ *Everyone is here. Let's count noses so we can order hamburgers.*

count off See *count someone or something off.*

count on someone or something to rely on someone or something. □ *Can I count on you to be there at noon?* □ *I want to buy a car I can count on in winter weather.*

count one's chickens before they hatch* to plan how to utilize good results of something before those results have occurred. (A cliché. Frequently used in the negative.) □ *You're way ahead of yourself. Don't count your chickens before they hatch.* □ *You may be disappointed if you count your chickens before they hatch.*

count someone in for something AND **count in someone for something; count someone in on something; count in someone on something; count in someone; count someone in** to include someone in something. (Compare to *count someone out for something.*) □ *If you're looking for a group to go mountain climbing, count me in on it.* □ *I would like to count in your entire family, but there isn't enough room.* □ *Please count me in.*

count someone or something off AND **count off someone or something** to count or enumerate someone or something. □ *He went down the line counting the houses off, one by one.* □ *They counted off the people who were waiting to get into the movie.* ALSO: **count off** for a line of people (often soldiers) to count themselves off, thus dividing themselves into groups. (This can be done with any number: *by twos, by threes,* etc.) □ SERGEANT: *Count off by twos!* FIRST SOLDIER: *One!* SECOND SOLDIER: *Two!* THIRD SOLDIER: *One!* □ *When I ask you to count off by twos, I want it done fast!*

count someone out for something AND **count someone out** to exclude someone from something. (Compare to *count someone in for something.*) □ *Please count me out for the party next Saturday. I have other plans.* □ *You should count the whole family out. We are going to the beach for the weekend.*

count something up AND **count up something** to total something; to count something. (Also without *up*.) □ *Please count your packages up and make sure you have them all.* □ *Count up your change before you leave the cashier.*

cover a lot of ground 1. to travel over a great distance; to investigate a wide expanse of land. □ *The prospectors covered a lot of ground looking for gold.* □ *My car can cover a lot of ground in one day.* 2. to deal with much information and many facts. □ *The history lecture covered a lot of ground today.* □ *Mr. and Mrs. Franklin always cover a lot of ground when they argue.*

cover for someone 1. to make excuses for someone; to conceal someone's errors. □ *If I miss class, please cover for me.* □ *If you're late, I'll cover for you.* 2. to handle someone else's work. □ *Dr. Johnson's partner agreed to cover for him during his vacation.* □ *I'm on duty this afternoon. Will you please cover for me? I have a doctor's appointment.*

cover someone or something up AND **cover up someone or something** 1. to shield or protect someone or something for safety or warmth. (Also without *up*.) □ *There will be frost tonight so I had better cover up the roses.* □ *Don't forget to cover up the baby before coming to bed.* 2. [with *something*] to conceal something. □ *They covered up the truth about the crime.* □ *We'll cover up this little matter and make up a story for the press.*

cover someone's tracks up AND **cover up someone's tracks; cover someone's tracks** to conceal one's trail; to conceal one's past activities. □ *She was able to cover her tracks up so that they couldn't find her.* □ *It's easy to cover your tracks if you aren't well known.*

cover the territory See the following entry.

cover the waterfront* AND **cover the territory*** to deal with many things, much space, or much information from many points of view. (Informal.) □ *That lecture really covered the waterfront. I could hardly follow it.* □ *Why can't she stick to the point? She has to cover the territory every time she talks.*

cozy up to someone* AND **cozy up*** to be extra friendly with someone, perhaps in hope of special favors in return. (Informal or slang.) □ *Look at that lawyer cozying up to the judge!* □ *Lawyers who cozy up like that usually get in big trouble.*

crack a book* to open a book to study. (Slang. Almost always in the negative.) □ *I passed that test with an A, and I didn't even crack a book.* □ *If you think you can get through college without cracking a book, you're wrong.*

crack a joke* to tell a joke. (Informal.) □ *She's never serious. She's always cracking jokes.* □ *As long as she's cracking jokes, she's okay.*

crack a smile* to smile a little, perhaps reluctantly. (Informal.) □ *She cracked a smile so I knew she was kidding.* □ *The soldier cracked a smile at the wrong time and had to march for an hour as punishment.*

crack down on someone or something AND **crack down** to be hard on someone or something; to enforce a rule or law more strenuously. □ *They are cracking down on speeding around here.* □ *It's about time they cracked down.*

crack someone or something up AND **crack up someone or something** 1. [with *something*] to shatter something in small pieces. □ *I cracked the candy up and gave it to the children.* □ *We cracked up the stones and used them to build the wall.* 2. [with *something*] to crash something; to destroy something (in an accident). □ *The pilot cracked up the plane.* □ *The driver cracked the car up in an accident.* 3. [with *someone*] to make someone laugh. □ *She told a joke which really cracked us up.* □ *I cracked up my history class with a silly remark.* ALSO: **crack up** 1. (for a plane, boat, car, etc.) to crash. □ *The plane cracked up in the storm.* □ *The boat cracked up on the rocks.* 2. (for someone) to break out in laughter. □ *The audience really cracked up during the second act.* □ *The class cracked up when I told my joke, but the teacher didn't like it.*

crack something wide open 1. to crack or split something. □ *The earthquake* cracked the field wide open. □ They used dynamite to crack the boulder wide open. **2.** to expose and reveal some great wrongdoing. □ The police cracked the drug ring wide open. □ The newspaper story cracked the trouble at city hall wide open.

crack up* 1. to go crazy. (Slang.) □ The mayor cracked up after only a year in office. □ I was afraid the mayor would crack up because of too much work. **2.** See crack someone or something up.

cramp someone's style to limit someone in some way. □ I hope this doesn't cramp your style, but could you please not hum while you work? □ To ask him to keep regular hours would really be cramping his style.

crank something out* AND **crank out something*** to produce something; to make something in a casual and mechanical way. (Slang.) □ John can crank a lot of work out in a single day. □ That factory keeps cranking out cars even though no one buys them.

crazy about someone or something* AND **mad about someone or something*; nuts about someone or something*** very fond of someone or something. (Slang.) □ Ann is crazy about John. □ He's crazy about her, too. □ I'm mad about their new song. □ Our whole family is nuts about homemade ice cream.

cream of the crop* the best of all. (A cliché.) □ This particular car is the cream of the crop. □ The kids are very bright. They are the cream of the crop.

create a stink about something* AND **create a stink*; make a stink about something*; make a stink*; raise a stink about something*; raise a stink*** to make a major issue out of something; to make much over something; to make a lot of complaints and criticisms about something. (Slang. Compare to make a big deal about something.) □ Tom created a stink about Bob's remarks. □ Why did he make a stink about that? □ Tom is always trying to raise a stink.

create an uproar AND **make an uproar** to cause an outburst or sensation. (Especially with such.) □ The dog got into

church and made an uproar. □ Her poodle created an uproar in the restaurant. □ Why did you make such an uproar?

creep up on someone or something to move up quietly and slowly on someone or something. □ Age creeps up on all of us. □ The cat crept up on the bird.

Crime doesn't pay. a proverb meaning that crime will not benefit a person. □ At the end of the radio program, a voice said, "Remember, crime doesn't pay." □ No matter how tempting it may appear, crime doesn't pay.

crop out to appear at the surface. □ His real feelings began to crop out during the interview. □ There is a lot of sandstone cropping out along the river.

crop up to appear without warning. □ Bad luck will often crop up when you aren't ready for it. □ We are waiting for something good to crop up.

cross a bridge before one comes to it to worry excessively about something before it happens. (Note the variations in the examples.) □ There is no sense in crossing that bridge before you come to it. □ She's always crossing bridges before coming to them. She needs to learn to relax.

cross a bridge when one comes to it to deal with a problem only when one is faced with the problem. (Note the variations in the examples.) □ Please wait and cross that bridge when you come to it. □ He shouldn't worry about it now. He can cross that bridge when he comes to it.

cross-examine someone to ask someone questions in great detail; to question a suspect or a witness at great length. □ The police cross-examined the suspect for three hours. □ The lawyer plans to cross-examine the witness tomorrow morning.

cross one's fingers See keep one's fingers crossed for someone.

cross one's heart and hope to die AND **cross one's heart** to pledge or vow that the truth is being told. □ It's true, cross my heart and hope to die. □ It's really true—cross my heart.

cross someone See cross someone up.

cross someone or something off AND **cross off someone or something**

to take the name of someone or something off a list; to disregard or eliminate someone or something. (Compare to the following entry.) □ *We had to cross the Franklins off our guest list.* □ *They crossed off ice cream from the grocery list. It's just too cold for ice cream.*

cross someone or something out AND **cross out someone or something** to draw a line through the name of someone or something on a list. (Almost the same as the previous entry, but more specific about physically drawing a line.) □ *We crossed out the Franklins and wrote in the Smiths instead.* □ *They crossed the ice cream out and put cake on the list instead.*

cross someone up to give someone trouble; to defy or betray someone. (Also without *up*.) □ *You really crossed me up when you told Tom what I said.* □ *Please don't cross me up again.*

cross someone's mind See *pass through someone's mind*.

cross swords with someone AND **cross swords** to enter into an argument with someone. □ *I don't want to cross swords with Tom.* □ *The last time we crossed swords, we had a terrible time.*

crushed by something - demoralized; with hurt feelings. (Also used literally.) □ *The whole family was completely crushed by the news.* □ *I was just crushed by your attitude. I thought we were friends.*

crux of the matter the central issue of the matter. (*Crux* is an old word meaning *cross*.) □ *All right, this is the crux of the matter.* □ *It's about time that we looked at the crux of the matter.*

cry before one is hurt to cry or complain before one is injured. □ *Bill always cries before he's hurt.* □ *There is no point in crying before one is hurt.*

cry bloody murder to scream as if something very serious has happened. □ *Now that Bill is really hurt, he's crying bloody murder.* □ *There is no point in crying bloody murder about the bill if you aren't going to pay it.*

cry one's eyes out to cry very hard. □ *When we heard the news, we cried our eyes out with joy.* □ *She cried her eyes out after his death.*

cry over spilled milk.* to be unhappy about having done something which cannot be undone. (A cliché. *Spilled* can also be spelled *spilt*.) □ *I'm sorry that you broke your bicycle, Tom. But there is nothing that can be done now. Don't cry over spilled milk.* □ *Ann is always crying over spilt milk.*

cry wolf to cry or complain about something when nothing is really wrong. □ *Pay no attention. She's just crying wolf again.* □ *Don't cry wolf too often. No one will come.*

cue someone in AND **cue in someone** **1.** to give someone a cue; to indicate to someone that the time has come. □ *All right, cue in the announcer.* □ *Now, cue the orchestra director in.* **2.*** to tell someone what is going on. (Informal. Almost the same as *clue someone in on something*.) □ *I want to know what's going on. Cue me in.* □ *Cue in the general about the troop movement.*

Curiosity killed the cat. a proverb meaning that it is dangerous to be curious. (A cliché.) □ *Don't ask so many questions, Billy. Curiosity killed the cat.* □ *Curiosity killed the cat. Mind your own business.*

curl someone's hair to really frighten or alarm someone; to shock someone with sight, sound, or taste. (Also used literally.) □ *Don't ever sneak up on me like that again. You really curled my hair.* □ *The horror film curled my hair.*

curl up to curl, twist, or bend. □ *The cat went over and curled up in front of the fire.* □ *The fallen leaves curl up in the fall.*

curl up and die* to retreat and die. (A cliché.) □ *When I heard you say that, I could have curled up and died.* □ *No, it wasn't an illness. She just curled up and died.*

curry favor with someone AND **curry favor** to try to win favor from someone. □ *The lawyer tried to curry favor with the judge.* □ *It's silly to curry favor. Just act yourself.*

cut a fine figure to look good; to look elegant. (Formal. Usually said of a male.) □ *Tom really cuts a fine figure on the dance floor.* □ *Bill cuts a fine figure since he bought some new clothes.*

cut a wide swath AND **cut a big swath** to seem important; to attract a lot of attention. □ *In social matters, Mrs. Smith cuts a wide swath.* □ *Bob cuts a big swath whenever he appears in his military uniform.*

cut across something 1. to slice across something physically, as with a knife. □ *Cut across the grain with a good sawing motion.* □ *Cut across each loaf of dough; then pour on some melted butter.* 2. AND **cut across** to move across an area on foot or by other transportation. □ *You can get there faster if you cut across the vacant lot.* □ *I don't like to cut across when someone is playing baseball there.* 3. to reach beyond something; to embrace a wide variety; to slice across a figurative boundary or barrier. □ *His teaching cut across all human cultures and races.* □ *This rule cuts across all social barriers.*

cut and dried fixed; determined beforehand; usual and uninteresting. □ *I find your writing quite boring. It's too cut and dried.* □ *The lecture was, as usual, cut and dried. It was the same thing we've heard for years.* ALSO: **cut-and-dried** routine; dull. □ *I don't care for cut-and-dried writing.* □ *We are all bored by cut-and-dried lectures.*

cut back 1. to turn back; to reverse direction. □ *Suddenly, the bull cut back in our direction and began chasing us.* □ *The road cuts back about a mile ahead, and it goes west again.* 2. See the following entry.

cut back on something AND **cut back** to reduce something; to use less of something. □ *The government has to cut back on its spending.* □ *It's very difficult for the government to cut back.*

cut class* to skip going to class. (Informal.) □ *If Mary keeps cutting classes, she'll fail the course.* □ *I can't cut that class. I've missed too many already.*

cut corners to reduce efforts or expenditures; to do things poorly or incompletely. (From the phrase *cut the corner* meaning to avoid going to an intersection to make a turn.) □ *You cannot cut corners when you are dealing with public safety.* □ *Don't cut corners, Sally. Let's do the job right.*

cut down on something AND **cut down** to reduce or limit use or consumption. □ *The doctor told Jane to cut down on sweets.* □ *It's very hard to cut down.*

cut in on someone or something AND **cut in** 1. to interrupt someone or something. (See also *cut into something.*) □ *The telephone operator cut in on our call.* □ *I wish the operator hadn't cut in on us.* □ *May I cut in on your conversation?* □ *You have just cut in.* 2. [with *someone*] to signal, by tapping on the shoulder, one member of a dancing couple to indicate that you wish to dance with the other member of the pair. □ *Tom cut in on Bob and Jane.* □ *Jane was sorry that Tom cut in.*

cut into something AND **cut in** 1. to slice or dig into something. □ *The sharp knife cut into the apple.* □ *The spade cut into the rich soil.* □ *The spade couldn't cut in. The ground was too hard.* 2. to interrupt; to break into something. □ *John cut into the line and made a lot of people mad.* □ *John is always cutting in.* □ *The operator cut in on our call.*

Cut it out! See *cut someone or something out.*

cut loose from someone or something AND **cut loose** to break away from someone or something; to break ties with someone or something; to act in a free manner. □ *Jane is finding it hard to cut loose from her family.* □ *Cutting loose is part of growing up.* □ *When those farm boys get to town, they really cut loose from convention.* □ *They sure are wild when they cut loose.*

cut loose with something See *let go with something.*

cut off* to stop by itself or oneself. (Informal. See also *cut someone or something off.*) □ *The machine got hot and cut off.* □ *Bob cut off in mid-sentence.*

cut off one's nose to spite one's face a proverb meaning that one harms oneself in trying to punish another person. (The phrase is variable in form. Note the examples.) □ *Billy loves the zoo, but he refused to go with his mother because he was mad at her. He cut off his nose to spite his face.* □ *Find a better way to be angry. It is silly to cut your nose off to spite your face.*

cut one's eyeteeth on something* to have done something since one was very young; to have much experience at something. (Folksy.) □ *Do I know about cars? I cut my eyeteeth on cars.* □ *I cut my eyeteeth on Bach. I can whistle everything he wrote.*

cut out for something well-suited for something; with a talent for something. (Compare to the following entry.) □ *Tom was not cut out for banking.* □ *Sally was cut out for the medical profession.*

cut out to be something well-suited for a particular role or a particular occupation. (Compare to the previous entry.) □ *Tom was not cut out to be a banker.* □ *Sally was cut out to be a doctor.*

cut someone down to size AND **cut someone down; take someone down to size** to make a person humble; to *put one in one's place.* (See also *beat someone down to size.*) □ *John's remarks really cut me down to size.* □ *Jane is too conceited. I think her new boss will take her down to size.* □ *The boss's angry stare will really cut her down.*

cut someone or something in* AND **cut in someone or something*** 1. [with *someone*] to give someone a share of something. (Informal or slang.) □ *Shall we cut Bill in on this deal?* □ *I don't think we should cut anybody in.* □ *Pretty soon we'll have to cut in the whole town.* 2. [with *something*] to turn something on; to make something join other similar things. □ *At midnight they cut the large generator in.* □ *The director cut in the music too soon, and the audience didn't hear the rest of the radio play.*

cut someone or something loose to detach someone or something; to free someone or something. □ *The father cut his kids loose in the park.* □ *The vandals cut the boat loose, and it drifted away.*

cut someone or something off AND **cut off someone or something** to cut or sever a connection to someone or something. □ *The telephone operator cut us off because we had talked too long.* □ *We cut off the flowers which had wilted.*

cut someone or something out AND **cut out someone or something** to eliminate someone or something; to remove someone or something. □ *We had to cut Bob out. There was no more room.* □ *Uncle Bob left Sally nothing in his will. He cut her out years ago.* □ *The doctor cut out the growth.* ALSO: **Cut it out!** Stop it! □ *Stop that noise! Cut it out!*

cut someone or something short AND **cut someone or something off short** to end something before it is finished; to end one's speaking before one is finished. □ *We cut the picnic short because of the storm.* □ *I'm sorry to cut you off short, but I must go now.*

cut someone or something to pieces* to cut someone or something much or severely. (Informal.) □ *Ann just cut herself to pieces on the broken glass.* □ *My tie went into the grinder which cut it to pieces.*

cut someone or something to the bone 1. to slice deep to a bone. □ *The knife cut John to the bone. He had to be sewed up.* □ *Cut each slice of ham to the bone. Then each slice will be as big as possible.* 2. [with *something*] to cut down severely (on something). □ *We cut our expenses to the bone and are still losing money.* □ *Congress had to cut the budget to the bone in order to balance it.*

cut someone or something up AND **cut up someone or something** 1. to cut severely or thoroughly; to *cut someone or something to pieces.* □ *The flying glass cut John up severely.* □ *The cook cut up the meat for a stew.* 2.* to criticize someone or something severely. (Slang.) □ *Jane is such a gossip. She was really cutting up Mrs. Jones.* □ *The professor really cut up my essay.*

cut someone to the quick to hurt someone's feelings very badly. (Can be used literally when *quick* refers to the tender flesh at the base of finger- and toenails.) □ *Your criticism cut me to the quick.* □ *Tom's sharp words to Mary cut her to the quick.*

cut someone's losses to reduce someone's losses of money, goods, or other things of value. □ *I sold the stock as it went down, thus cutting my losses.* □ *He cut his losses by putting better locks* on the doors. There were fewer robberies. □ The mayor's reputation suffered because of the scandal. He finally resigned to cut his losses.

cut someone's throat* (for someone) to experience certain failure; to do damage to someone. (Informal. Also used literally.) □ If I were to run for office, I'd just be cutting my throat. □ Judges who take bribes are cutting their own throats.

cut teeth (for a baby or young person) to grow teeth. □ Billy is cranky because he's cutting teeth. □ Ann cut her first tooth this week.

cut the ground out from under someone AND **cut out the ground from under someone** to destroy the foundation of someone's plans or someone's argument. □ The politician cut the ground out from under his opponent. □ Congress cut out the ground from under the President.

cut up* to act wildly; to show off and be troublesome; to act like a clown. (Slang. See also cut someone or something up.) □ Tom, Billy! Stop cutting up, or I'll send you to the principal's office. □ If you spent more time studying than cutting up, you'd get better grades.

cuts no ice* has no effect; makes no sense; has no influence. (Slang.) □ That idea cuts no ice. It won't help at all. □ It cuts no ice that your mother is the mayor.

D

dance to another tune to shift quickly to different behavior; to change one's behavior or attitude. (See also *change someone's tune.*) □ *After being yelled at, Ann danced to another tune.* □ *A stern talking to will make her dance to another tune.*

dare someone to do something AND **dare someone** to challenge someone to do something. □ *Sally dared Jane to race her to the corner.* □ *You wouldn't do that, would you? I dare you.*

darken someone's door* AND **go and never darken my door again*** to go away and not come back. (A cliché.) □ *The heroine of the drama told the villain never to darken her door again.* □ *She touched the back of her hand to her forehead and said, "Go and never darken my door again!"*

dash cold water on something See *pour cold water on something.*

dash off to leave in a hurry; to depart quickly. □ *Bye bye. I must dash off.* □ *Must you dash off so soon?*

dash something off AND **dash off something** to send something off, usually quickly. □ *I'll dash a quick note off to Aunt Mary.* □ *Ann just dashed off a message to her parents.*

date back to sometime AND **date back** to extend back to a particular time; to have been alive at a particular time in the past. □ *My late grandmother dated back to the Civil War.* □ *This record dates back to the sixties.* □ *How far do you date back?*

dawn on someone to occur to someone; to *cross someone's mind.* □ *It just dawned on me that I forgot my books.* □ *When will it dawn on him that his audience is bored?*

day after day every day; daily; all the time. □ *He wears the same clothes day after day.* □ *She visits her husband in the hospital day after day.*

day and night AND **night and day** all the time; around the clock. □ *The nurse was with her day and night.* □ *The house is guarded night and day.*

day in and day out AND **day in, day out** on every day; for each day. □ *She smokes day in and day out.* □ *They eat nothing but vegetables, day in, day out.*

day-to-day daily; everyday; common. □ *They update their accounts on a day-to-day basis.* □ *Just wear your regular day-to-day clothing.*

dead ahead straight ahead; directly ahead. □ *Look out! There is a cow in the road dead ahead.* □ *The farmer said that the town we wanted was dead ahead.*

dead and buried gone forever. (Refers literally to persons and figuratively to ideas and other things.) □ *Now that Uncle Bill is dead and buried, we can read his will.* □ *That kind of thinking is dead and buried.*

dead in someone's or something's tracks exactly where someone or something is at the moment; at this instant. (This does not usually have anything to do with death. The phrase is often used with *stop.*) □ *Her unkind words stopped me dead in my tracks.* □ *When I heard the rattlesnake, I stopped dead in my tracks.* □ *The project came to a halt dead in its tracks.*

dead loss a total loss. □ *My investment was a dead loss.* □ *This car is a dead loss. It was a waste of money.*

dead on one's or its feet exhausted; worn out; no longer useful.

71

□ *He can't teach well anymore. He's dead on his feet.* □ *This inefficient company is dead on its feet.*

dead set against someone or something totally opposed to someone or something. □ *I'm dead set against the new tax proposal.* □ *Everyone is dead set against the mayor.*

dead to the world tired; exhausted; sleeping soundly. (Compare to *dead on one's feet.*) □ *I've had such a hard day. I'm really dead to the world.* □ *Look at her sleep. She's dead to the world.*

deal in something to buy and sell something. □ *My uncle is a stock broker. He deals in stocks and bonds.* □ *My aunt deals in antiques.*

deal someone in* AND **deal in someone*** to include someone in something, especially a card game. (Informal.) □ *Sit down, Bill. We'll deal you in.* □ *John, deal in Bill. He's going to play.*

deal something out* AND **deal out something*** to pass out or hand out something. (Informal.) □ *Here, Bob, deal out these cards.* □ *I'm going to deal the candy out now.*

deal with someone or something to manage someone or something; to handle someone or something. □ *I'm afraid that you'll have to deal with this problem, Tom.* □ *Could you please deal with Mrs. Franklin? She's on the telephone.*

death on someone or something 1. very effective in acting against someone or something. □ *This road is terribly bumpy. It's death on tires.* □ *The sergeant is death on lazy soldiers.* **2.** [with *something*] accurate or deadly at doing something requiring skill or great effort. □ *John is death on curve balls. He's our best pitcher.* □ *The boxing champ is really death on those fast punches.*

decide in favor of someone or something to determine that someone or something is the winner. □ *The judge decided in favor of the defendant.* □ *I decided in favor of the red one.*

deep-six someone or something* to get rid of someone or something; to dispose of someone or something. (Slang. Means to bury someone or some-

thing six feet deep, the standard depth for a grave.) □ *Take this horrible food out and deep-six it.* □ *That guy is a pain. Deep-six him so the cops will never find him.*

depend on someone or something to rely on someone or something; to not be able to get along without someone or something. □ *Children depend on their parents.* □ *Many people depend on their cars to get them to work.*

desert a sinking ship* AND **leave a sinking ship*** to leave a place, a person, or a situation when things become difficult or unpleasant. (A cliché. Rats are said to be the first to leave a ship which is sinking.) □ *I hate to be the one to desert a sinking ship, but I can't stand it around here any more.* □ *There goes Tom. Wouldn't you know he'd leave a sinking ship rather than stay around and try to help?*

devil-may-care attitude AND **devil-may-care manner** a very casual attitude; a worry free or carefree attitude. □ *You must get rid of your devil-may-care attitude if you want to succeed.* □ *She acts so thoughtless with her devil-may-care manner.*

diamond in the rough a valuable or potentially excellent person or thing hidden by an unpolished or rough exterior. □ *Ann looks like a stupid woman, but she's a fine person—a real diamond in the rough.* □ *That piece of property is a diamond in the rough. Someday it will be valuable.*

die a natural death 1. (for someone) to die by disease or old age rather than violence or foul play. □ *I hope to live to 100 and die a natural death.* □ *The police say she didn't die a natural death, and they are investigating.* **2.** (for something) to fade away or die down. □ *I expect that all this excitement about computers will die a natural death.* □ *Most fads die a natural death.*

die away See *die out.*

die down See *die out.*

die in one's boots* AND **die with one's boots on*** to go down fighting; to die in some fashion other than in bed; to die fighting. (A cliché popularized by Western movies. The villains of these movies said they preferred death by gunshot or hanging to dying in bed. See also *go down fighting*.) □ *I won't let him get me. I'll die in my boots.* □ *He may give me a hard time, but I won't be overcome. I'll fight him and die with my boots on.*

die laughing 1. to meet one's death laughing—in good spirits, revenge, or irony. □ *Sally is such an optimist that she'll probably die laughing.* □ *Bob poisoned his rich aunt who then died laughing because she had taken Bob out of her will.* 2. to laugh very long and hard. (Informal.) □ *The joke was so funny that I almost died laughing.* □ *The play was meant to be funny, but the audience didn't exactly die laughing.*

die of a broken heart 1. to die of emotional distress. □ *I was not surprised to hear of her death. They say she died of a broken heart.* □ *In the movie, the heroine appeared to die of a broken heart, but the audience knew she was poisoned.* 2. to suffer from emotional distress, especially from a failed romance. □ *Tom and Mary broke off their romance and both died of broken hearts.* □ *Please don't leave me. I know I'll die of a broken heart.*

die of boredom to suffer from boredom; to be very bored. □ *No one has ever really died of boredom.* □ *We sat there and listened politely, even though we almost died of boredom.*

die off See *die out.*

die on the vine See *wither on the vine.*

die out AND **die away; die off** 1. AND **die down** to come slowly to an end; to subside. □ *All this talk about war will eventually die out.* □ *The flames of the fire slowly died away.* □ *This trouble will die down soon.* 2. (for a group of living things) to die one by one until all are dead. □ *The dinosaurs died out millions of years ago.* □ *Why did they die away?* □ *Some scientists think that a change in climate caused them to die off.*

die with one's boots on See *die in one's boots.*

dig in 1. (for soldiers) to prepare for a long battle by digging trenches and getting into them. □ *The soldiers dug in* and prepared to fight. □ *The entire platoon was still digging in when the first shots were fired.* 2. to get ready for a very long job or session. (Informal.) □ *There is a long agenda today. Better dig in for a long meeting.* □ *The delegates arrived on Monday and began to dig in for a long convention.* 3. to eat a meal; to begin eating a meal. (Informal. Out of place in formal situations. See also *Come and get it!*) □ *Dinner's ready, Tom. Sit down and dig in.* □ *The cowboy helped himself to some beans and dug in.* 4. to apply oneself to a task; to tackle (something) vigorously. □ *Sally looked at the big job ahead of her. Then she rolled up her sleeves and dug in.* □ *"Tom," hollered Mrs. Smith, "you get to that pile of homework and dig in this very minute."*

dig some dirt up on someone AND **dig up some dirt on someone** to find out something bad about someone. (Informal.) □ *If you don't stop trying to dig some dirt up on me, I'll get a lawyer and sue you.* □ *The citizens' group dug up some dirt on the mayor and used it against her at election time.*

dig someone or something* to understand something; to relate to a person or a thing. (Slang.) □ *I really dig Tom. He's a special guy.* □ *I really dig rock music.*

dig someone or something out AND **dig out someone or something** 1. to get someone or something out by digging; to free someone or something by digging. □ *The prisoner dug himself out of the cell.* □ *The rescuers dug out the avalanche victim from the snow.* □ *The prospectors dug all the gold out. Then the mine was useless.* 2. [with *something*] to work hard to locate something and bring it forth. □ *They dug the contract out of the file cabinet.* □ *I dug this old suit out of a box in the attic.*

dig someone or something up AND **dig up someone or something** to go to great effort to find someone or something. (There is an implication that the thing or person dug up is not the most desirable, but it is all that could be found.) □ *Mary dug a date up for the dance next Friday.* □ *I dug up a recipe* *for roast pork with pineapple.* □ *I dug up a carpenter who doesn't charge very much.*

dime a dozen* abundant; cheap and common. (A cliché.) □ *People who can write good books are not a dime a dozen.* □ *Romantic movies are a dime a dozen.*

dine out See *eat a meal out.*

dip into something AND **dip in** to take or borrow from a supply of something, especially a supply of money. (Also used literally.) □ *I had to dip into my savings account to pay for the car.* □ *I hate to dip in like that.* □ *She put out her hand and dipped into the chocolate box.*

dirty one's hands See *get one's hands dirty.*

disagree with someone to hold an opinion different from someone else's opinion; to argue with someone. □ *I'm sorry, but I disagree with you about that.* □ *Tom was disagreeing with Ann very loudly.*

dish something out AND **dish out something** to give something out, especially food or punishment. □ *The cook dished out the stew as if he were feeding hogs.* □ *The teacher dished punishment out whenever things got too noisy.*

dish something up AND **dish up something** to serve something, especially food or opinions (to someone). □ *The cook dished up large portions of the stew.* □ *The teacher dished her opinions up for the whole class.*

dispose of someone or something **1.** to get rid of someone or something. (Note that this sense may easily by confused with the other two senses.) □ *Please dispose of these papers.* □ *There is a salesman at the door. Please dispose of him as quickly as possible.* **2.** [with *something*] to settle or terminate something. □ *It's necessary to dispose of this matter as soon as possible.* □ *It's time to dispose of this matter of interest rates once and for all.* **3.** [with *someone*] to kill someone. □ *It may become necessary to dispose of Mr. Jones, especially if he continues snooping.* □ *The crooks disposed of the witness to the crime.*

divide something fifty-fifty* AND **split something fifty-fifty*** to divide something into two equal parts. (Informal. The *fifty* means 50%.) □ *Tommy and Billy divided the candy fifty-fifty.* □ *The robbers split the money fifty-fifty.*

divide something in two to divide a (single) thing into two parts. (Do not confuse *in two* with *into*.) □ *He divided the cake in two.* □ *The farmer divided his farm in two and gave half to his children.*

divide something into something **1.** divide one number into another number. □ *We'll now practice dividing seven into all these other numbers.* □ *I can't divide 300 into 540 from memory.* **2.** to separate something into a number of parts. □ *They divided their property into seven sections.* □ *Let us divide the pie into six pieces.*

do a double take* to react with surprise; to have to look twice to make sure that one really saw correctly. (Informal.) □ *When the boy led a goat into the park, everyone did a double take.* □ *When the nurse saw that the man had six toes, she did a double take.*

do a flip-flop on something* AND **do a flip-flop*; do an about face*** to make a total reversal of opinion. (Informal or slang.) □ *Without warning, the government did a flip-flop on taxation.* □ *It had done an about face on the question of deductions last year.*

do a job on someone or something* **1.** to damage someone or something; to mess up someone or something. (Informal or slang.) □ *The robbers really did a job on the bank guard. They beat him when they robbed the bank.* □ *The puppy did a job on my shoes. They are all chewed to pieces.* **2.** [with *something*] to defecate on something. (Informal and euphemistic. Note the variation in the second example.) □ *The puppy did a job on the living room carpet.* □ *It's supposed to do its job on the newspapers in the basement.*

do a land office business* to do a large amount of business in a short period of time. (A cliché.) □ *The ice cream shop always does a land office business on a hot day.* □ *The tax collector's office did a land office business on the day that taxes were due.*

do a number on someone or some-

thing* to damage or harm someone or something. (Slang.) □ *The teacher did a number on the whole class. That test was terrible.* □ *Tom did a number on Mary when he went out with Ann.*

do a snow job on someone* to deceive or confuse someone. (Informal or slang.) □ *Tom did a snow job on the teacher when he said that he was sick yesterday.* □ *I hate it when someone does a snow job on me. I find it harder and harder to trust people.*

do an about-face See *do a flip-flop on something.*

do away with someone or something 1. [with *someone*] to kill someone; to *dispose of someone or something.* □ *The crooks did away with the witness.* □ *I was there, too. I hope they don't try to do away with me.* **2.** [with *something*] to get rid of something; to dispose of something. □ *This chemical will do away with the stain in your sink.* □ *The time has come to do away with that old building.*

do credit to someone AND **do someone credit** to add to the reputation of someone. (See also *do someone proud.*) □ *Your new job really does credit to you.* □ *Yes, it really does you credit.*

do justice to something 1. to do something well; to represent or portray something accurately. □ *Sally did justice to the contract negotiations.* □ *This photograph doesn't do justice to the beauty of the mountains.* **2.** to eat or drink a great deal. □ *Bill always does justice to the turkey on Thanksgiving.* □ *The party didn't do justice to the roast pig. There were nearly ten pounds left over.*

do one's best to do (something) as well as one can. □ *Just do your best. That's all we can ask of you.* □ *Tom isn't doing his best. We may have to replace him.*

do one's bit See *do one's part.*

do one's duty to do one's job; to do what is expected of one. □ *Please don't thank me. I'm just doing my duty.* □ *Soldiers who fight in wars are doing their duty.*

do one's own thing* AND **do one's thing*** to do what one likes or what one pleases. (Informal or slang.) □ *Tom doesn't like being told what to do. He prefers to do*

his own thing. □ *When you do your thing, you have no one but yourself to blame if things don't work out.*

do one's part AND **do one's bit** to do one's share of the work; to do whatever one can do to help. □ *All people everywhere must do their part to help get things under control.* □ *I always try to do my bit. How can I help this time?*

do one's thing See *do one's own thing.*

do so See *do too.*

do somehow by someone* to treat someone in a particular manner. (Informal. Do not confuse this with a passive construction. The *someone* is not the actor but the object.) □ *Tom did all right by Ann when he brought her red roses.* □ *I did badly by Tom. I fired him.*

do someone damage* to harm someone. (Informal.) □ *I hope she doesn't plan to do me damage.* □ *They did us damage by telling the whole story to the newspapers.*

do someone good* to benefit someone. (Informal.) □ *A nice hot bath really does me good.* □ *A few years in the army would do you good.*

do someone one better See *go someone one better.*

do someone or something in AND **do in someone or something 1.** [with *someone*] to make someone tired. □ *That tennis game really did me in.* □ *Yes, hard activity will do you in.* **2.** [with *someone*] to cheat someone; to *take someone in.* □ *The crooks did the widow in.* □ *They did in the widow by talking her into giving them all the money in her bank account.* **3.** [with *someone*] to kill someone. □ *The crooks did in the bank guard.* □ *They'll probably do in the witnesses soon.* **4.** [with *something*] to destroy something. □ *The huge waves totally did in the seaside community.* □ *The fire did in the wooden building.*

do someone or something over AND **do over someone or something; make someone or something over; make over someone or something** (See also *make a fuss over someone or something.*) **1.** [with *someone*] to buy a new wardrobe for someone; to redo someone's hair. □ *Sally's mother did Sally over for the play tryouts.* □ *It's very expensive to completely do a person over.* □ *She went to the beauty salon where they made her over.* **2.** [with *something*] to rebuild, redesign, or redecorate something. □ *We did over our living room for the holidays.* □ *We had to do the plans over because the first plans were unacceptable.* □ *We made over the family room because it was looking shabby.*

do someone or something up AND **do up someone or something** to put someone or something in order; to straighten up someone or something; to dress up someone or something. □ *The mother did her little girl up in new clothes.* □ *The maids did up my room while I was at breakfast.* □ *The clerk did up the present in beautiful silver paper.*

do someone out of something* to cheat someone out of something. (Informal or slang.) □ *They did the widow out of her life savings.* □ *I won't let anyone do me out of anything. I'm a very cautious and suspicious person.*

do someone proud* to make someone proud. (Folksy. See *do credit to someone.*) □ *Well, Bill really did himself proud in the horse race.* □ *That fine looking, prize-winning hog ought to do you proud. Did you raise it all by yourself?*

do someone's heart good* to make someone feel good emotionally. (Informal. Also used literally.) □ *It does my heart good to hear you talk that way.* □ *When she sent me a get-well card, it really did my heart good.*

do something by hand to do something with one's hands rather than with a machine. □ *The computer was broken so I had to do the calculations by hand.* □ *All this tiny stitching was done by hand. Machines cannot do this kind of work.*

do something fair and square* to do something fairly. (Folksy.) □ *He always plays the game fair and square.* □ *I try to treat all people fair and square.*

do something hands down to do something easily and without opposition. □

□ *The mayor won the election hands down.* □ *She was the choice of the people hands down.*

do something in person to appear somewhere and do something oneself rather than sending someone or doing something over the telephone or by mail. □ *I know the money should be in his account. I saw him put it there in person.* □ *The famous actor came to the hospital and greeted each patient in person.*

do something in public to do something where anyone looking could see it. (Compare to *in private.*) □ *You should dress neatly when you appear in public.* □ *I wish that you wouldn't talk to me so rudely in public.* □ *Bob, you must behave properly in public.*

do something in secret to do something privately or secretly. □ *Why do you always do things like that in secret?* □ *There is no need to count your money in secret.*

do something in vain to do something for no purpose; to do something which fails. □ *They rushed her to the hospital, but they did it in vain.* □ *We tried in vain to get her there on time.* ALSO: **be in vain** (for one's efforts or hopes) to be purposeless or futile. □ *They tried and tried, but their efforts were in vain.*

do something on purpose to do something with purpose or intent; to do something intentionally and not accidentally. □ *You hit me on purpose!* □ *I wouldn't hit anybody on purpose.*

do something on the fly* to do something while one is moving; to do something (to something which is in motion). (Slang. This has nothing to do with actual flight.) □ *We can't stop the machine to oil it now. You'll have to do it on the fly.* □ *We will have to find the break in the film on the fly—while we are showing it.*

do something on the run* to do something while one is moving hurriedly; to do something while one is going rapidly from one place to another. (Informal.) □ *I was very busy today and had to eat on the run.* □ *I didn't have time to meet with Bill, but I was able to talk to him on the run.*

do something on the sly* to do something slyly or sneakily. (Informal.) □ *He was seeing Mrs. Smith on the sly.* □ *She was supposed to be losing weight, but she was snacking on the sly.*

do something over again AND **do something over** to redo something; to repeat the doing of something. □ *This isn't right. You'll have to do it over again.* □ *The teacher made me do my paper over.*

do something the hard way to do something in an awkward fashion; to do something the wrong way. □ *No, you can't pound in nails like that. You're doing it the hard way.* □ *I'm sorry. I learn things the hard way.*

do something up brown* to do something just right. (Folksy. As if one were cooking and trying to make something to have just the right amount of brownish color.) □ *Of course I can do it right. I'll really do it up brown.* □ *Come on, Bob. Let's do it right this time. I know you can do it up brown.*

do something with a vengeance* to do something with vigor; to do something energetically as if one were angry with it. (Folksy.) □ *Bob is building that fence with a vengeance.* □ *Mary is really weeding her garden with a vengeance.*

do the dishes to wash the dishes; to wash and dry the dishes. □ *Bill, you cannot go out and play until you've done the dishes.* □ *Why am I always the one who has to do the dishes?*

do the honors to act as host or hostess and serve one's guests by pouring drinks, slicing meat, making (drinking) toasts, etc. □ *All the guests were seated, and a huge juicy turkey sat on the table. Jane Thomas turned to her husband and said, "Bob, will you do the honors?" Mr. Jones smiled and began slicing thick slices of meat from the turkey.* □ *The mayor stood up and addressed the people who were still eating their salads. "I'm delighted to do the honors this evening and propose a toast to your friend and mine, Bill Jones. Bill, good luck and best wishes in your new job in Washington." And everyone sipped a bit of wine.*

do the trick* to do exactly what needs to be done. (Folksy.) □ *Push it just a little more to the left. There, that does the trick.* □ *If you give me two dollars, I'll have enough to do the trick.*

do too AND **do so** to do something (despite anything to the contrary). (An emphatic way of saying *do.* See *be too, have too.*) □ BOB: *You don't have your money with you.* BILL: *I do too!* □ *He does so! I saw him put it in his pocket.* □ *She did too. I saw her do it.*

do without someone or something AND **do without** to manage to get through life without someone or something which you want or need. □ *I guess I'll just have to do without a car.* □ *I don't know how I can do without.* □ *The boss can't do without a secretary.*

dollar for dollar* considering the amount of money involved; considering the cost. (Informal. Often seen in advertising.) □ *Dollar for dollar, you cannot buy a better car.* □ *Dollar for dollar, this laundry detergent washes cleaner and brighter than any other product on the market.*

Don't hold your breath.* Do not stop breathing (while waiting for something to happen). (Informal.) □ *You think he'll get a job? Ha! Don't hold your breath.* □ *I'll finish building the fence as soon as I have time, but don't hold your breath.*

Don't let someone or something get you down. Do not allow yourself to be overcome by someone or something. □ *Don't let their constant teasing get you down.* □ *Don't let Tom get you down. He's not always unpleasant.*

Don't look a gift horse in the mouth. a proverb meaning that one should not expect perfect gifts. (Usually stated in the negative. Note the variation in the examples. The age of a horse and, therefore, its usefulness can be determined by looking at its teeth. It would be greedy to inspect the teeth of a horse given as a gift to make sure the horse is of the best quality.) □ *Don't complain. You shouldn't look a gift horse in the mouth.* □ *John complained that the television set he got for his birthday was black and white rather than color. He was told, "Don't look a gift horse in the mouth."*

done to a T* AND **done to a turn*** cooked just right. (Folksy. See also *fit someone to a T; suit someone to a T.*) □ *Yummy! This meat is done to a T.* □ *I like it done to a turn, not too done and not too raw.*

door to door (from) one person's house to the next person's house. (Used as an adverb.) □ *Ann is selling books from door to door.* □ *We went from door to door trying to get people to sign the petition.* ALSO: **door-to-door** moving from door to door. □ *John is a door-to-door salesman.* □ *We spent two weeks making a door-to-door survey.*

dose of one's own medicine the same kind of treatment which one gives to other people. (Often with *get* or *have*.) □ *Sally never is very friendly. Someone is going to give her a dose of her own medicine someday.* □ *He didn't like getting a dose of his own medicine.*

double back on someone or something AND **double back** (for a person or animal) to reverse motion, moving toward someone or something (rather than away from someone or something). (Refers primarily to a person or animal which is being pursued by someone or something.) □ *The deer doubled back on the hunter.* □ *The robber doubled back on the police, and they lost track of him.* □ *He doubled back in his tracks.*

double-cross someone* to betray someone by doing the opposite of what was promised; to betray a person by not doing what was promised. (Slang. Originally criminal slang.) □ *If you double-cross me again, I'll kill you.* □ *Tom is mad at Jane because she double-crossed him on the sale of his car.*

double in brass* to serve two purposes; to be useful for two different things. (A cliché. Refers to a musician who can play a trumpet or trombone, etc., in addition to some other instrument.) □ *The English teacher also doubles in brass as the football coach.* □ *The drummer doubles in brass as a violinist.*

double up with someone AND **double up** to share something with someone. □ *We don't have enough books. Tom,* will you double up with Jane? □ *When we get more books, we won't have to double up anymore.* □ *We'll share hotel rooms to save money. Tom and Bill will double up in room twenty.*

down at the heels shabby; poorly dressed. □ *The hobo was really down at the heels.* □ *Tom's house needs paint. It looks down at the heels.* ALSO: **down-at-the-heels** run-down. □ *Look at that down-at-the-heels hobo.*

down in the dumps* sad or depressed. (Informal.) □ *I've been down in the dumps for the past few days.* □ *Try to cheer Jane up. She's down in the dumps for some reason.*

down in the mouth sad-faced; depressed and unsmiling. □ *Since her dog died, Barbara has been down in the mouth.* □ *Bob has been down in the mouth since the car wreck.*

down on one's luck without any money; unlucky. (Euphemistic for *broke*.) □ *Can you loan me twenty dollars? I've been down on my luck lately.* □ *The gambler had to get a job because he had been down on his luck and didn't earn enough money to live on.*

down on someone or something against someone or something; negative about someone or something. □ *I've been down on red meat lately. It's better to eat chicken or fish.* □ *The teacher was down on Tom because he acts badly in class.*

down South to or at the Southeastern United States. (See also *back East; out West; up North.*) □ *I used to live down South.* □ *We are going down South for the winter.*

down the drain* lost forever; wasted. (Informal. Also used literally.) □ *I just hate to see all that money go down the drain.* □ *Well, there goes the whole project, right down the drain.*

down the hatch* swallow (something). (Informal or slang. Sometimes said when someone takes a drink of alcohol.) □ *Come on, Billy. Eat your dinner. Down the hatch!* □ *John raised his glass of beer and said, "Down the hatch."*

down the street a short distance away on this same street. □ *Sally lives just down the street.* □ *There is a drugstore down the street. It's very convenient.*

down to earth direct, frank, and honest. □ *You can depend on Ann. She's very down to earth.* □ *It's good that she's down to earth.* ALSO: **down-to-earth** direct, frank, and honest. □ *Ann is a very down-to-earth person.*

down to the wire at the very last minute; up to the very last instant. (Refers to a wire which marks the end of a horse race.) □ *I have to turn this in tomorrow, and I'll be working down to the wire.* □ *When we get down to the wire, we'll know better what to do.*

down with a disease ill; sick at home. (Can be said about many diseases.) □ *Tom isn't here. He's down with a cold.* □ *Sally is down with the flu.* □ *The whole office has come down with something.*

downhill all the way* easy all the way. (Informal. Also used literally.) □ *Don't worry about your algebra course. It's downhill all the way.* □ *The mayor said that the job of mayor is easy—in fact, downhill all the way.*

downhill from here on* easy from this point on. (Informal.) □ *The worst part is over. It's downhill from here on.* □ *The painful part of this procedure is over. It's downhill from here on.*

doze off to sleep AND **doze off; drift off to sleep; drift off** to go slowly and gently to sleep. □ *When the room gets warm, I usually doze off to sleep.* □ *I hate to doze off like that.* □ *The baby drifted off to sleep.* □ *It's easy to drift off when you're a baby.*

drag on See *drag something on.*

drag out See *drag something on.*

drag someone or something in AND **drag in someone or something** to forcibly include someone or something. □ *A crime has been committed, and the police were told to drag in the usual suspects.* □ *I hope they don't drag me in this time.*

drag someone or something off AND **drag off someone or something** to carry someone or something away by force. □ *The lion dragged the antelope off in order to eat it in peace.* □ *The mother dragged off the little boy to the dentist's office.*

drag something on AND **drag something out** to make something last longer than it should. □ *The actors seem to drag this play on endlessly.* □ *The lawyers are dragging this trial on much too long.* □ *Why do people have to drag things out like this?* □ *They are dragging it out.* ALSO: **drag on; drag out** to last too long; to last long and be boring. □ *Winter always seems to drag on too long.* □ *Why do operas drag on for hours?* □ *I don't know what makes them drag out like that.*

drag something out See the previous entry.

draw a bead on someone or something* to aim at someone or something; to pick out someone or something for special treatment. (Informal.) □ *Ann wants a new car, and she has drawn a bead on a red convertible.* □ *Jane wants to get married, and she has drawn a bead on Tom.*

draw a blank* (Informal.) **1.** to get no response; to find nothing. □ *I asked him about Tom's financial problems, and I just drew a blank.* □ *We looked in the files for an hour, but we drew a blank.* **2.** to fail to remember (something). □ *I tried to remember her telephone number, but I could only draw a blank.* □ *It was a very hard test with just one question to answer, and I drew a blank.*

draw a line between something and something else to separate two things; to distinguish or differentiate between two things. (The *a* can be replaced with *the*. See also *draw the line at something.*) □ *It's necessary to draw a line between bumping into people and striking them.* □ *It's very hard to draw the line between slamming a door and just closing it loudly.*

draw blood 1. to hit or bite (a person or an animal) and make a wound that bleeds. □ *The dog chased me and bit me hard, but it didn't draw blood.* □ *The boxer landed just one punch and drew blood immediately.* **2.** to anger or insult a person. □ *Sally screamed out a terrible insult at Tom. Judging by the look on his face, she really drew blood.* □ *Tom started yelling and cursing, trying to insult Sally. He wouldn't be satisfied until he had drawn blood, too.*

draw fire away from someone or something AND **draw fire; draw someone's fire away from someone or something; draw someone's fire** to make oneself a target in order to protect someone or something. (Refers literally to gunfire or figuratively to any kind of attack.) □ *The mother bird drew fire away from her chicks.* □ *The hen drew the hunter's fire away from her nest.* □ *Birds draw fire by flapping their wings to get attention.* □ *The President drew fire away from Congress by proposing a compromise.* □ *The airplanes drew the soldier's fire away from the ships in the harbor.*

draw interest 1. to appear interesting and get (someone's) attention. (Note the variation in the examples.) □ *This kind of event isn't likely to draw a lot of interest.* □ *What kind of thing will draw interest?* 2. (for money) to earn interest while on deposit. □ *Put your money in the bank so it will draw interest.* □ *The cash value of some insurance policies also draws interest.*

draw near to come close (in space or time). (Formal or literary.) □ *Christmastime is drawing near.* □ *Draw near to me, and I will recount my days as Queen of this great and beautiful land.*

draw oneself up to stand up straighter and taller to show that one is insulted or angry. □ *Bill didn't say a word. He simply drew himself up and walked straight out of the room. John knew he was very angry.* □ *You could tell that Mary overheard us talking about her because she drew herself up for a moment.*

draw someone or something out AND **draw out someone or something** 1. [with *someone*] to lure someone out (of somewhere); to bring someone out (of somewhere). □ *The smell of bacon and coffee drew Mary out of her bedroom.* □ *The sound of sirens drew out everyone into the street.* 2. [with *someone*] to coax someone to speak or answer; to bring someone into a conversation or other social interaction. □ *Jane is usually very shy with older men, but Tom really drew her out last evening.* □ *John drew out Mr. Smith on*

the question of tax increases. 3. [with *something*] to make something longer, (literally or figuratively.) □ *Jane drew the conversation out for more than twenty minutes.* □ *Bill drew the taffy candy out into a long string.*

draw something to a close to make something end. □ *It is now time to draw this evening to a close.* □ *What a lovely vacation. It's a shame that we must draw it to a close.* ALSO: **draw to a close** to end; to come to an end. □ *This evening is drawing to a close.* □ *It's a shame that our vacation is drawing to a close.*

draw something up AND **draw up something** 1. to put something into writing; to prepare a written document; to put plans on paper. (Used especially with legal documents prepared by a lawyer.) □ *I went to see my lawyer this morning about drawing up a will.* □ *You should draw a will up as soon as you can.* □ *The architect is drawing up plans for the new city hall.* 2. to drive something up (to somewhere). □ *The driver drew the car up to the door.* □ *In the dim gas lights I could see the horses draw the empty carriage up to the mouth of a darkened alley.* 3. to pull something up; to raise something. □ *The old man used a long rope and a bucket to draw up the water out of the well.* □ *Each morning the maid drew the blinds up.* ALSO: **draw up** to drive up (to or toward something). □ *The car drew up to the door.* □ *The carriage drew up to the mouth of the alley.*

draw the line at something AND **draw the line** to set a limit at something; to decide when a limit has been reached. □ *You can make as much noise as you want, but I draw the line at fighting.* □ *It's hard to keep young people under control, but you have to draw the line somewhere.*

draw to a close See *draw something to a close.*

draw up See *draw something up.*

dream about someone or something AND **dream of someone or something** to have a dream concerning someone or something. □ *I dreamed about living in a palace with lots of servants.* □ *Do you dream of people or places?*

dream come true a wish or a dream which has become real. □ *Going to Hawaii is like having a dream come true.* □ *Having you for a friend is a dream come true.*

dream of someone or something See *dream about someone or something.*

dream something up AND **dream up something** to think of something; to invent something; to make up something. □ *That's a great idea. Did you dream it up yourself?* □ *I like to dream up ways to make money.*

dress someone down to bawl someone out; to give someone a good scolding. (Primarily military.) □ *The sergeant dressed the soldier down severely.* □ *I know they'll dress me down when I get home.* ALSO: **dressing-down** a scolding. □ *The sergeant gave the soldier a good dressing-down.* □ *I will get a dressing-down when I get home.*

dress someone or something up AND **dress up someone or something** 1. [with *someone*] to provide fancy or better clothing for someone. □ *Sally's mother dressed her up for the party.* □ *Sally's mother likes to dress up her daughter.* 2. [with *something*] to make something look or seem better. □ *I think we can dress this car up with a new paint job and sell it.* □ *Mary is good at dressing up old ideas to make them sound new.* ALSO: **dress up** (for someone) to dress in fancy or better clothing. □ *Sally knew it was time to dress up for the party.* □ *I like to dress up and go out.* ALSO: **dressed up** wearing fancy or better clothing. □ *Sally looks so nice when she's dressed up.* □ *I feel good when I'm dressed up in new clothes.*

dress up See *dress someone or something up.*

dressed to kill* dressed in fancy or stylish clothes. (Slang.) □ *Wow, look at Sally! She's really dressed to kill.* □ *A person doesn't go to church dressed to kill.*

drift off to sleep See *doze off to sleep.*

drink something up AND **drink up something** to drink all of something. □ *Who drank all the orange juice up?* □ *Come on, Billy. Drink up your milk.*

ALSO: **drink up** to drink quickly; to take a drink. (Often said of alcoholic drinks.) □ *The bartender said, "Drink up. I have to close the bar."* □ *When the hostess had served punch to all the guests, she said, "Drink up!"*

drink to excess to drink too much alcohol; to drink alcohol continually. □ *Mr. Franklin drinks to excess.* □ *Some people drink to excess only at parties.*

drive a hard bargain* to work hard to negotiate prices or agreements in one's own favor. (Informal.) □ *I saved $200 by driving a hard bargain when I bought my new car.* □ *All right, sir, you drive a hard bargain. I'll sell you this car for $12,450.* □ *You drive a hard bargain, Jane, but I'll sign the contract.*

drive someone crazy* AND **drive someone mad*** (Informal.) 1. to make someone insane. □ *He's so strange that he actually drove his wife crazy.* □ *Doctor, there are little green people following me around trying to drive me mad.* 2. to annoy or irritate someone. □ *This itch is driving me crazy.* □ *All these telephone calls are driving me mad.*

drive someone mad See the previous entry.

drive someone or something back AND **drive back someone or something** 1. to bring someone or something back by driving. □ *Bob is taking me to work. Someone else is driving me back.* □ *After he takes us to the station, he'll drive the car back.* 2. to force someone or something to retreat or move back. □ *The enemy attacked in great numbers, but we drove them back.* □ *We used long sticks to drive back the dogs when they came at us.*

drive someone or something home AND **drive home someone or something** 1. [with *someone*] to take someone home in a car or other vehicle. □ *Will you please drive Bill home?* □ *I must drive home two other people first.* 2. [with *something*] to make something clearly understood. □ *Why do I always have to shout at you to drive something home?* □ *Sometimes you have to be forceful to drive home a point.*

drive someone to the wall See *force someone to the wall.*

drive someone up the wall* (Slang.) **1.** to make someone insane. □ *Mr. Franklin drove his wife up the wall.* □ *All my problems will drive me up the wall someday.* **2.** to annoy or irritate someone. □ *Stop whistling that tune. You're driving me up the wall.* □ *All his talk about moving to California nearly drove me up the wall.*

drive something into the ground See *run something into the ground.*

drive up to something AND **drive up** (for a car or other vehicle) to move to something and stop. □ *The car drove up to the house and honked.* □ *Is anyone expecting a car to drive up?*

driving force behind someone or something AND **driving force** a person or a thing that motivates or directs someone or something. □ *Money is the driving force behind most businesses.* □ *Ambition is the driving force behind Tom.* □ *Love can also be a driving force.*

drop a bombshell* AND **drop a bomb***; **explode a bombshell***; **drop a brick*** to announce shocking or startling news. (Informal or slang.) □ *They really dropped a bombshell when they announced that the mayor had cancer.* □ *Friday is a good day to drop a bomb like that. It gives the business world the weekend to recover.* □ *They must speak very carefully when they explode a bombshell like that.* □ *They really dropped a brick when they told the cause of her illness.*

drop a brick* See the previous entry.

drop around sometime AND **drop around; drop by** to come and visit (someone) at some future time. (Similar to *drop in on someone.*) □ *Nice to see you, Mary. You and Bob must drop around sometime.* □ *Please do drop around when you're out driving.* □ *We'd love to have you drop by.*

drop back to go back or remain back; to fall behind. □ *As the crowd moved forward, the weaker ones dropped back.* □ *Sometimes it's a good idea to move forward. At other times one should drop back.*

drop by See *drop around sometime.*

drop by the wayside See *fall by the wayside.*

drop dead 1. to die suddenly. □ *I understand that Tom Anderson dropped dead at his desk yesterday.* □ *No one knows why Uncle Bob suddenly dropped dead.* **2.*** Go away and stop bothering me. (Rude slang.) □ *If you think I'm going to put up with your rudeness all afternoon, you can just drop dead!* □ *Drop dead! I'm not your slave!*

drop in on someone AND **drop in; drop in to say hello** to pay someone a casual visit, perhaps a surprise visit. □ *I hate to drop in on people when they aren't expecting me.* □ *You're welcome to drop in at any time.* □ *We won't stay a minute. We just dropped in to say hello.*

drop in one's tracks to stop or collapse from exhaustion; to die suddenly. □ *If I keep working this way, I'll drop in my tracks.* □ *Uncle Bob was working in the garden and dropped in his tracks. We are all sorry that he's dead.*

drop in to say hello See *drop in on someone.*

drop off to sleep AND **drop off** to go to sleep without difficulty; to fall asleep. (See also *drift off to sleep; doze off to sleep.*) □ *I sat in the warm room for five minutes, and then I dropped off to sleep.* □ *After I've eaten dinner, I can drop off with no trouble at all.*

drop out of something AND **drop out** to stop being a member of something; to stop attending or participating in something. □ *I'm working part time so that I won't have to drop out of college.* □ *I don't want to drop out at this time.*

drop someone to stop being friends with someone, especially with one's boyfriend or girlfriend. □ *Bob finally dropped Jane. I don't know what he saw in her.* □ *I'm surprised that she didn't drop him first.*

drop someone a line AND **drop someone a few lines** to write a letter or a note to someone. (The *line* refers to lines of writing.) □ *I dropped Aunt Jane a line last Thanksgiving.* □ *She usually drops me a few lines around the first of the year.*

drop someone or something off AND **drop off someone or something** to deliver someone or something to a place which is part way to one's final destination. □ *If you're going to the bank, please drop off my paycheck on the way.* □ *Please drop Mary off at her office.*

drop the ball to make a blunder; to fail in some way. (Also literally, in sports: to drop a ball in error.) □ *Everything was going fine in the election until my campaign manager dropped the ball.* □ *You can't trust John to do the job right. He's always dropping the ball.*

drop the other shoe to do the deed that completes something; to do the expected remaining part of something. (Refers to the removal of shoes at bedtime. One shoe is dropped, and then the process is completed when the second shoe drops.) □ *Mr. Franklin has left his wife. Soon he'll drop the other shoe and divorce her.* □ *Tommy has just failed three classes in school. We expect him to drop the other shoe and quit altogether any day now.*

drown one's sorrows See the following entry.

drown one's troubles* AND **drown one's sorrows*** to try to forget one's problems by drinking a lot of alcohol. (Informal.) □ *Bill is in the bar drowning his troubles.* □ *Jane is at home drowning her sorrows.*

drown someone or something out AND **drown out someone or something** to make so much noise that someone or something cannot be heard. □ *I can't hear what you said. The radio drowned you out.* □ *We couldn't hear all the concert because the airplanes drowned out the quiet parts.*

drug on the market something available on the market in great abundance; a glut on the market. □ *Right now, small computers are a drug on the market.* □ *Ten years ago, small transistor radios were a drug on the market.*

drum some business up AND **drum up some business** to stimulate people to buy what you are selling. (See also *drum something up.*) □ *I need to do something to drum some business up.* □ *A little bit of advertising would drum up some business.*

drum something into someone AND **drum something into someone's head** to make someone learn something through persistent repetition. □ *Yes, I know that. They drummed it into me as a child.* □ *Now I'm drumming it into my own children.* □ *I will drum it into their heads day and night.*

drum something up AND **drum up something** to invent something; to come up with something; to make up something. □ *Have no fear. I'll drum a date up for Tom.* □ *Don't worry. I'll drum up some excuse.*

dry behind the ears* very young and immature. (Informal. Usually expressed as a negative.) □ *Tom is going into business by himself? Why, he's hardly dry behind the ears.* □ *That kid isn't dry behind the ears. He'll go broke in a month.*

dry someone or something off AND **dry off someone or something** to make someone or something dry. □ *A dog shakes to dry itself off.* □ *I use a towel to dry off my face.*

dry someone or something out AND **dry out someone or something 1.** to permit someone or something to dry. □ *We dried the towels out by hanging them in the sun.* □ *We dried out the children by standing them in front of the fire.* **2.** [with *someone*] to help a drunk person get sober. □ *We had to call the doctor to help dry Mr. Franklin out.* □ *It takes time to dry out someone who has been drinking for a week.*

dry something up AND **dry up something** to make a liquid evaporate; to let or cause a liquid to dry. □ *The sun came out and dried up the puddles left by the rain.* □ *The sun will never dry the oceans up.* ALSO: **dry up 1.** to become dry; to evaporate. □ *The puddles will dry up.* □ *The ink will dry up in the bottle if you don't tighten the lid.* □ *My source of funds dried up, and I have no more money.* **2.*** to shut up and go away; to *drop dead.* (Rude slang.) □ *Quit bothering me! Dry up!* □ *Dry up! I'm tired of listening to you.*

dry up See the previous entry.

due to someone or something because of someone or something. □ *Due to forces beyond our control, the concert is cancelled.* □ *We are here* *tonight due to Tom and his talent for organization.*

dust someone or something off AND **dust off someone or something** to remove the dust from someone or something; to freshen or renew someone or something by removing dust. □ *Bob got up from the ground and dusted himself off.* □ *She found the book on the bottom shelf. She took it from its place and dusted it off.* □ *It's time to dust off some of your old ideas about the best way to build cities.*

duty bound to do something AND **duty bound** forced by a sense of duty and honor to do something. □ *Good evening, madam. I'm duty bound to inform you that we have arrested your husband.* □ *No one made me say that. I was duty bound.*

dwell on something AND **dwell upon something** to linger overly long on a thought, sight, or sound; to concentrate on something. □ *I wish you wouldn't dwell upon death so much.* □ *Don't spend so much of your time dwelling on your mistakes.*

dyed-in-the-wool permanent; indelible; stubborn. (Usually said of a person.) □ *My uncle was a dyed-in-the-wool farmer. He wouldn't change for anything.* □ *Sally is a dyed-in-the-wool socialist.*

dying to do something very anxious to do something. □ *I'm just dying to go sailing in your new boat.* □ *After a long hot day like this one, I'm just dying for a cool drink of water.*

E

early on early; at an early stage. □ *We recognized the problem early on, but we waited too long to do something about it.* □ *This doesn't surprise me. I knew about it early on.*

Early to bed, early to rise, makes a man healthy, wealthy, and wise. AND **early to bed, early to rise** a proverb which claims that going to bed and getting up early is good for you. (Sometimes said to explain why a person is going to bed early. The last part of the saying is sometimes left out.) □ *Tom left the party at 10:00 p.m. saying, "Early to bed, early to rise, makes a man healthy, wealthy, and wise."* □ *I always get up at 6:00 a.m. After all, early to bed, early to rise.*

earn one's keep to help out with chores in return for food and a place to live; to earn one's pay by doing what is expected. □ *I earn my keep at college by shoveling snow in the winter.* □ *Tom hardly earns his keep around here. He should be fired.*

ease off on someone or something AND **ease off; ease up on someone or something; ease up** to reduce the urgency with which one deals with someone or something; to put less pressure on someone or something. □ *Ease off on John. He has been yelled at enough today.* □ *Yes, please ease off. I can't stand any more.* □ *Tell them to ease up on the horses. They are getting tired.* □ *Tell them to ease up now! They are making the horses work too hard.*

ease someone out AND **ease out someone** to remove a person from a job or an office gently and quietly. □ *They eased out the mayor without a scandal.* □ *It is very difficult to ease a senator out of office.*

ease up on someone or something See *ease off on someone or something.*

easier said than done* said of a task which is easier to talk about than to do. (A cliché.) □ *Yes, we must find a cure for cancer, but it's easier said than done.* □ *Finding a good job is easier said than done.*

easy come, easy go* said to explain the loss of something which required only a small amount of effort to get in the first place. (A cliché.) □ *Ann found twenty dollars in the morning and spent it foolishly at noon. "Easy come, easy go," she said.* □ *John spends his money as fast as he can earn it. With John it's easy come, easy go.*

Easy does it. Act with care. (Informal.) □ *Be careful with that glass vase. Easy does it!* □ *Now, now, Tom. Don't get angry. Easy does it.*

easy to come by easily found; easily purchased; readily available. □ *Please be careful with that phonograph record. It was not easy to come by.* □ *A good dictionary is very easy to come by.*

eat a meal out AND **eat out; dine out** to eat a meal at a restaurant. □ *I like to eat a meal out every now and then.* □ *Yes, it's good to eat out and try different kinds of food.* □ *It costs a lot of money to dine out often.*

eat away at someone or something **1.** to remove parts, bit by bit. □ *John's disease was eating away at him.* □ *The acid in the rain slowly ate away at the stone wall.* **2.** [with *someone*] to bother or worry someone. □ *Her failure to pass the exam was eating away at her.* □ *Fear of appearing in court was eating away at Tom.*

eat high on the hog* to eat good or expensive food. (Folksy. Compare to *live high on the hog*. Note the *so* in the second example.) □ *The Smith family has been eating pretty high on the hog since they had a good corn harvest.* □ *John would have more money to spend on clothing if he didn't eat so high on the hog.*

eat humble pie* (Informal.) **1.** to act very humble when one is shown to be wrong. □ *I think I'm right, but if I'm wrong, I'll eat humble pie.* □ *You think you're so smart. I hope you have to eat humble pie.* **2.** to accept insults and humiliation. □ *John, stand up for your rights. You don't have to eat humble pie all the time.* □ *Beth seems quite happy to eat humble pie. She should stand up for her rights.*

eat like a bird to eat only small amounts of food; to peck at one's food. □ *Jane is very slim because she eats like a bird.* □ *Bill is trying to lose weight by eating like a bird.*

eat like a horse* to eat large amounts of food. (Informal.) □ *No wonder he's so fat. He eats like a horse.* □ *John works like a horse and eats like a horse, so he never gets fat.*

eat one's cake and have it too See *have one's cake and eat it too.*

eat one's hat* a phrase telling the kind of thing that one would do if a very unlikely event really happens. (Informal. Always used with *if*. Never used literally.) □ *If we get there on time, I'll eat my hat.* □ *I'll eat my hat if you get a raise.* □ *He said he'd eat his hat if she got elected.*

eat one's heart out **1.** to be very sad (about someone or something). □ *Bill spent a lot of time eating his heart out after his divorce.* □ *Sally ate her heart out when she had to sell her house.* **2.*** to be envious (of someone or something). (Informal.) □ *Do you like my new watch? Well, eat your heart out. It was the last one in the store.* □ *Don't eat your heart out about my new car. Go get one of your own.*

eat one's words to have to take back one's statements; to confess that one's predictions were wrong. □ *You shouldn't say that to me. I'll make you eat your words.* □ *John was wrong about the election and had to eat his words.*

eat out See *eat a meal out.*

eat out of someone's hands to do what someone else wants; to obey someone eagerly. (Often with *have.*) □ *Just wait! I'll have everyone eating out of my hands. They'll do whatever I ask.* □ *The President has Congress eating out of his hands.* □ *A lot of people are eating out of his hands.*

eat someone out See *chew someone out.*

eat someone out of house and home* to eat a lot of food (in someone's home); to eat all the food in the house. (A cliché.) □ *Billy has a huge appetite. He almost eats us out of house and home.* □ *When the kids come home from college, they always eat us out of house and home.*

eat something away AND **eat away something** to remove parts of something bit by bit. (Almost the same as *eat away at someone or something.*) □ *The rain ate the stone carving away.* □ *The river ate away parts of the river bank.*

eat something up AND **eat up something** **1.** to eat all of something. (Also without *up.*) □ *Who ate up the ice cream?* □ *Every time I buy ice cream, someone eats it up before I get any.* **2.*** to enjoy, absorb, or appreciate. (Informal.) □ *The audience loved the comedian. They ate up his act and demanded more.* □ *The children ate up grandfather's stories. They listened to him for hours.*

edge someone out AND **edge out someone** to remove a person from a job, office, or position, usually by beating the person in competition. □ *The Vice President edged the President out during the last election.* □ *Tom edged out Bob as the new cook at the restaurant.*

egg someone on to encourage, urge, or dare someone to continue doing something, usually something unwise. □ *John wouldn't have done the dangerous experiment if his brother hadn't egged him on.* □ *The two boys kept throwing stones because the other children were egging them on.*

either feast or famine* either too much (of something) or not enough (of something). (A cliché. Also without *either*.) □ *This month is very dry, and last month it rained almost every day. Our weather is either feast or famine.* □ *Sometimes we are busy, and sometimes we have nothing to do. It's feast or famine.*

eleventh-hour decision a decision made at the last possible minute. (See also *at the eleventh hour*.) □ *Eleventh-hour decisions are seldom satisfactory.* □ *The president's eleventh-hour decision was made in a great hurry, but it turned out to be correct.*

end in itself for its own sake; toward its own ends; toward no purpose but its own. □ *For Bob, art is an end in itself. He doesn't hope to make any money from it.* □ *Learning is an end in itself. Knowledge does not have to have a practical application.*

end of the line See the following entry.

end of the road AND **end of the line** the end; the end of the whole process; death. (*Line* originally referred to railroad tracks.) □ *Our house is at the end of the road.* □ *We rode the train to the end of the line.* □ *When we reach the end of the road on this project, we'll get paid.* □ *You've come to the end of the line. I'll not lend you another penny.* □ *When I reach the end of the road, I wish to be buried in a quiet place, near some trees.*

end something up* AND **end up something*** to bring something to an end. (Informal. Also without *up*.) □ *I want you to end your game up and come in for dinner.* □ *We can't end up the game until someone scores.*

end up AND **end up somehow** to end something at a particular place, in a particular state, or by having to do something. (Compare to *end up by doing something*.) □ *I ended up having to pay for everyone's dinner.* □ *After paying for dinner, I ended up broke.* □ *We all ended up at my house.* □ *After playing in the rain, we all ended up with colds.*

end up by doing something AND **wind up by doing something** to conclude something by doing something. (Also without *by*.) □ *We ended up by going back to my house.* □ *After playing in the rain, we all wound up catching colds.*

end up somehow See *end up*.

end up somewhere AND **wind up somewhere** to finish at a certain place. □ *If you don't get straightened out, you'll end up in jail.* □ *I fell and hurt myself. I wound up in the hospital.*

engage in small talk to talk only about minor matters rather than important matters or personal matters. □ *All the people at the party were engaging in small talk.* □ *They chatted about the weather and otherwise engaged in small talk.*

enlarge on something AND **expand on something** to make a more detailed explanation of something; to explain one's previous comments. □ *Mary was asked to enlarge on her remarks.* □ *I'd now like to enlarge on my earlier statement about the growth of the economy.* □ *I would be happy to expand on my remarks.*

Enough is enough. That is enough, and there should be no more. □ *Stop asking for money! Enough is enough!* □ *I've heard all the complaining from you that I can take. Stop! Enough is enough!*

enough to go around AND **enough to go round** a supply adequate to serve everyone. (Informal.) □ *Don't take too much. There's not enough to go around.* □ *I cooked some extra potatoes, so there should be enough to go around.*

enter one's mind to come to one's mind; (for an idea or memory) to come into one's consciousness. □ *Leave you behind? The thought never even entered my mind.* □ *A very interesting idea just entered my mind. What if I ran for Congress?*

equal to someone or something **1.** (literally) the same as someone or something. □ *This car is equal to that car in value.* □ *Tom is equal to John as a runner.* **2.** able to handle or deal with someone or something. □ *I'm afraid that I'm not equal to Mrs. Smith's problem right now. Please ask her to come back later.* □ *That's a very difficult task, but I'm sure Bill is equal to it.*

escape someone's notice to go unnoticed; to not have been noticed. (Usually a way to point out that someone has failed to see or respond to something.) □ *I suppose my earlier request escaped your notice, so I'm writing again.* □ *I'm sorry. Your letter escaped my notice.*

Every cloud has a silver lining. a proverb meaning that there is something good in every bad thing. □ *Jane was upset when she saw that all her flowers had died from the frost. But when she saw that the weeds had died, too, she said, "Every cloud has a silver lining."* □ *Sally had a sore throat and had to stay home from school. When she learned she missed a math test, she said, "Every cloud has a silver lining."*

Every dog has its day. AND **Every dog has his day.** a proverb meaning that everyone will get a chance. □ *Don't worry, you'll get chosen for the team. Every dog has its day.* □ *You may become famous some day. Every dog has his day.*

every last one* every one; every single one. (Informal.) □ *You must eat all your peas! Every last one!* □ *Each of you—every last one—has to take some medicine.*

every living soul* every person. (Informal.) □ *I expect every living soul to be there and be there on time.* □ *This is the kind of problem that affects every living soul.*

Every minute counts. AND **Every moment counts.** Time is very important.; It is urgent. □ *Doctor, please try to get here quickly. Every minute counts.* □ *When you take a test, you must work rapidly because every minute counts.* □ *When you're trying to meet a deadline, every moment counts.*

every now and again See the following entry.

every now and then AND **every now and again; every once in a while** occasionally; once in a while. □ *We eat lamb every now and then.* □ *I read a novel every now and again.* □ *We don't go to the movies except maybe every now and then.* □ *I drink coffee every once in a while.*

every once in a while See the previous entry.

every time one turns around* frequently; at every turn; with annoying frequency. (Informal.) □ *Somebody asks me for money every time I turn around.* □ *Something goes wrong with Bill's car every time he turns around.*

every which way* in all directions. (Folksy.) □ *The children were all running every which way.* □ *The wind scattered the leaves every which way.*

everything but the kitchen sink* almost everything one can think of. (A cliché.) □ *When Sally went off to college, she took everything but the kitchen sink.* □ *John orders everything but the kitchen sink when he goes out to dinner, especially if someone else is paying for it.*

everything from A to Z See the following entry.

everything from soup to nuts* AND **everything from A to Z*** almost everything one can think of. (A cliché.) □ *For dinner we had everything from soup to nuts.* □ *In college I studied everything from soup to nuts.* □ *She mentioned everything from A to Z.*

except for someone or something all but someone or something. □ *It's all finished except for giving out the awards.* □ *Everyone is here except for Bill.*

excuse someone **1.** to forgive someone. (Usually with *me*. Said when interrupting or when some other minor offense has been committed. There are many mannerly uses of this expression.) □ *John came in late and said, "Excuse me, please."* □ *John said "excuse me" when he interrupted our conversation.* □ *When John made a strange noise at the table, he said quietly, "Excuse me."* □ *John suddenly left the room saying, "Excuse me. I'll be right back."* **2.** to permit someone to leave; to permit someone to remain away from an event. □ *The coach excused John from practice yesterday.* □ *The teacher excused John, and he ran quickly from the room.*

expand on something See *enlarge on something.*

expecting a child AND **expecting** pregnant. (A euphemism.) □ *Tommy's* *mother is expecting a child.* □ *Oh, I didn't know she was expecting.*

explain oneself **1.** to explain what one has said or done. (Formal and polite.) □ *Please take a moment to explain yourself. I'm sure we are interested in your ideas.* □ *Yes, if you give me a moment to explain myself, I think you'll agree with my idea.* **2.** to give an explanation or excuse for something wrong which one may have done. (Usually said in anger.) □ *Young man! Come in here and explain yourself this instant.* □ *Why did you do that, Tom Smith? You had better explain yourself, and it had better be good.*

explain something away AND **explain away something** to give a good explanation for something; to explain something so that it seems less important; to make excuses for something. □ *John couldn't explain away his low grades.* □ *This is a very serious matter, and you cannot just explain it away.*

explode a bombshell See *drop a bombshell.*

extend credit to someone AND **extend credit** to allow someone to purchase something on credit. □ *I'm sorry, Mr. Smith, but because of your poor record of payment, we are no longer able to extend credit to you.* □ *Look at this letter, Jane. The store won't extend credit any more.*

extend one's sympathy to someone AND **extend one's sympathy** to express sympathy to someone. (A very polite and formal way to tell someone that you are sorry about a misfortune.) □ *Please permit me to extend my sympathy to you and your children. I'm very sorry to hear of the death of your husband.* □ *Let's extend our sympathy to Bill Jones who is in the hospital with a broken leg. We should send him some flowers.*

extenuating circumstances special circumstances which account for an irregular or improper way of doing something. □ *Mary was permitted to arrive late because of extenuating circumstances.* □ *Due to extenuating circumstances, the teacher will not meet class today.*

F

face someone down AND **face down someone** to overcome someone by being bold; to disconcert someone by displaying great confidence. □ *The teacher faced the angry student down without saying anything.* □ *The mayor couldn't face down the entire city council.*

face someone or something to meet or confront someone or something in spite of fear or embarrassment. □ *I can hardly face going to the dentist.* □ *Face it, John. You must go to the dentist.* □ *The students couldn't face the teacher after their bad behavior.*

face the music to receive punishment; to accept the unpleasant results of one's actions. □ *Mary broke a dining room window and had to face the music when her father got home.* □ *After failing a math test, Tom had to go home and face the music.*

face to face in person; in the same location. (Said only of people. An adverb.) □ *Let's talk about this face to face. I don't like talking over the telephone.* □ *Many people prefer to talk face to face.* ALSO: **face-to-face** facing one another; in the same location. □ *I prefer to have a face-to-face meeting.* □ *They work better on a face-to-face basis.*

face up to someone or something AND **face up 1.** to confess to something; to confess (something) to someone. (See also *face someone or something*.) □ *Tom had to face up to breaking Mr. Brown's window.* □ *He had to face up to Mr. Brown.* □ *His father told him, "Tom, you've just got to face up." ***2.** to confront something bravely. □ *Tom had to face up to going to the dentist.* □ *Bill doesn't want to face up to his problems.*

facts of life 1. the facts of sex and reproduction, especially human reproduction. (See also *birds and the bees*.) □ *My parents told me the facts of life when I was nine years old.* □ *Bill learned the facts of life from his classmates.* **2.*** the truth about the unpleasant ways that the world works. (A cliché.) □ *Mary really learned the facts of life when she got her first job.* □ *Tom couldn't accept the facts of life in business, so he quit.*

fail to do something to not do something that you were supposed to do. □ *John failed to carry out the garbage for three days in a row.* □ *If you fail to show up for a test, you'll be in trouble.*

fair to middling* only fair or okay; a little better than acceptable. (Folksy.) □ *I don't feel sick, just fair to middling.* □ *The play wasn't really good. It was just fair to middling.*

fair-weather friend someone who is your friend only when things are going well for you. (This person will desert you when things go badly for you. Compare to *A friend in need is a friend indeed*.) □ *Bill wouldn't help me with my homework. He's just a fair-weather friend.* □ *A fair-weather friend isn't much help in an emergency.*

fake someone out* AND **fake out someone*** to deceive or bluff someone; to outmaneuver someone. (Slang.) □ *Wow, you really faked me out when you hid my book under my chair!* □ *You'll never be able to fake out someone twice with the same trick.*

fall all over oneself AND **fall over oneself** to behave awkwardly and eagerly in an attempt to please someone. (See also *fall over backwards to do*

something.) □ *Tom fell all over himself trying to make Jane feel at home.* □ *I fall over myself when I'm doing something that makes me nervous.*
fall all over someone to give a lot of attention, affection, or praise to someone. (Informal. See also the following entry.) □ *My aunt falls all over me whenever she comes to visit.* □ *I hate for someone to fall all over me. It embarrasses me.*
fall apart AND **fall to pieces** to break into pieces; to disband; to become disorganized. (Compare to *go to pieces.*) □ *This old car is about ready to fall apart.* □ *One of the clubs which I belong to fell apart.* □ *It began to fall apart last spring when most of the members quit.* □ *All my plans fell to pieces.*
fall apart at the seams to break into pieces; to *fall apart;* for material which is sewn together to separate at the seams. (Both literal and figurative uses.) □ *My new jacket fell apart at the seams.* □ *This old car is about ready to fall apart at the seams.*
fall asleep to go to sleep. □ *The baby cried and cried and finally fell asleep.* □ *Tom fell asleep in class yesterday.*
fall back from something AND **fall back** to move back from something; to back away from something. □ *Suddenly the opposing team fell back from the end of the field.* □ *On orders from the fire chief, the crowd fell back.*
fall back on someone or something to turn to someone or something for help. (Also used literally.) □ *Bill fell back on his brother for help.* □ *John ran out of ink and had to fall back on his pencil.*
fall behind See the following entry.
fall behind in something AND **fall behind on something; fall behind; get behind in something; get behind on something; get behind** to fail to do a task on time; to fail to do enough of something; to move more slowly than others, letting them move ahead of you. □ *I fell behind on my car payments, so the bank took my car back.* □ *Ann fell behind in her work and had to explain to the manager.* □ *Try not to get behind.* □ *When we were hiking, I fell behind*

and got lost. ALSO: **be behind in something** to have failed to do enough. (The *in* can be replaced with *on.*) □ *I'm behind in my car payments.* □ *She's behind on her work.*
fall behind on something See the previous entry.
fall by the wayside AND **drop by the wayside** to give up and quit before the end (of something). (As if one became exhausted and couldn't finish a foot race. Also used literally.) □ *John fell by the wayside and didn't finish college.* □ *Many people start out to train for a career in medicine, but some of them drop by the wayside.*
fall down on the job to fail to do something properly; to fail to do one's job adequately. (Also used literally.) □ *The team kept losing because the coach was falling down on the job.* □ *Tom was fired because he fell down on the job.*
fall flat on one's face* AND **fall flat on its face*; fall flat*** to be completely unsuccessful. (Informal.) □ *I fell flat on my face when I tried to give my speech.* □ *The play fell flat on its face.* □ *My jokes fall flat most of the time.*
fall for someone or something 1. [with *someone*] to fall in love with someone. □ *Tom fell for Ann after only two dates. He wants to marry her.* □ *Some men always fall for women with blond hair.* 2. [with *something*] to be deceived by something. □ *I can't believe you fell for that old trick.* □ *Jane didn't fall for Ann's story.*
fall in 1. to line up in a row, standing shoulder to shoulder. (Usually refers to people in scouting or the military. Compare to *fall in line* and *fall out.*) □ *The boy scouts were told to fall in behind the scout master.* □ *The soldiers fell in quickly.* 2. to cave in; to collapse. □ *Because of the heavy snow, the roof fell in.* □ *Don't jump up and down on the floor. It might fall in.*
fall in for something See *come in for something.*
fall in line AND **fall into line** 1. to line up with each person (except the first person) standing behind someone. (The same as *line up.* Compare to *fall in.*) □ *The teacher told the students to fall in*

line for lunch. □ *Hungry students fall into line very quickly.* **2.** to conform; to **fall in place.** □ *All the parts of the problem finally fell into line.* □ *Bill's behavior began to fall in line.*

fall in love with someone AND **fall in love** to develop the emotion of love for someone. □ *Tom fell in love with Mary, but she only wanted to be friends.* □ *John is too young to really fall in love.*

fall in place AND **fall into place** to fit together; to become organized. □ *After we heard the whole story, things began to fall in place.* □ *When you get older, the different parts of your life begin to fall into place.*

fall in with someone or something 1. [with *someone*] to meet someone by accident; to join with someone. □ *John has fallen in with a strange group of people.* □ *We fell in with some people from our home town when we went on vacation.* **2.** to agree with someone or something. □ *Bill was not able to fall in with our ideas about painting the house red.* □ *Bob fell in with Mary's plans to move to Texas.*

fall into a trap AND **fall into the trap; fall into someone's trap** to become trapped. (Also used literally.) □ *We fell into a trap by asking for an explanation.* □ *I fell into his trap when I agreed to drive him home.* □ *We fell into the trap of thinking he was honest.*

fall off 1. to decline or diminish. □ *Business falls off during the summer months.* □ *My interest in school fell off when I became twenty.* **2.** See the following entry.

fall off something AND **fall off of something; fall off** to fall down from something. □ *The baby fell off the bed.* □ *My coat fell off of the hanger.* □ *It wouldn't have fallen off if you had been more careful.*

fall on someone or something See *fall upon someone or something.*

fall out 1. to happen; to result; to *work out.* □ *As things fell out, we had a wonderful trip.* □ *What fell out of our discussion was a decision to continue.* **2.** to leave one's place in a formation when dismissed. (Usually in scouting or the

military. The opposite of *fall in.*) □ *The scouts fell out and ran to the campfire.* □ *All the soldiers fell out and talked among themselves.* **3.** See the following entry.

fall out with someone over something AND **fall out with someone about something; fall out** to quarrel or disagree about something. □ *Bill fell out with Sally over the question of buying a new car.* □ *Bill fell out with John about who would sleep on the bottom bunk.* □ *They are always arguing. They fall out about once a week.* ALSO: **have a falling-out with someone over something; have a falling-out over something; have a falling-out** to have a disagreement with someone about something. □ *Bill had a falling-out with Sally over buying a new car.* □ *They had a falling-out over a car.*

fall over to tip over and fall; to fall down. □ *The flagpole fell over.* □ *Tom fell over and hurt himself.*

fall over backwards to do something* AND **fall over backwards*; bend over backwards to do something*; bend over backwards*; lean over backwards to do something; lean over backwards*** to do everything possible to please someone. (Informal. See also *fall all over oneself.*) □ *The taxi driver fell over backwards to be helpful.* □ *The teacher bent over backwards to help the students understand.* □ *The principal said that it was not necessary to bend over backwards.* □ *You don't have to lean over backwards to get me to help. Just ask.*

fall over someone or something to trip and fall down because of someone or something in the way. (The person or thing is the cause of the fall.) □ *The quarterback fell over the center and went out of bounds.* □ *Tommy's mother was always falling over his toys.* □ *Bill fell over Tom, and they were both hurt.*

fall short of something AND **fall short 1.** to lack something; to lack enough of something. □ *We fell short of money at the end of the month.* □ *When baking a cake, the cook fell short of eggs and had to go to the store for more.* **2.** to fail to achieve a goal. □ *We fell short of our* goal of collecting a thousand dollars. □ *Ann ran a fast race, but fell short of the record.*

fall through* to not happen; to come to nothing. (Informal.) □ *Our plans fell through, and we won't be going to Texas after all.* □ *The party fell through at the last minute.*

fall to to begin (to do something). (Compare to *turn to*.) □ *The hungry children took their knives and forks and fell to.* □ *The carpenter unpacked his saw and hammer and fell to.* □ *The boys wanted to fight, so the coach put boxing gloves on them and told them to fall to.* □ *John fell to and cleaned up his room after he got yelled at.*

fall to pieces See *fall apart.*

fall upon someone or something AND **fall on someone or something 1.** to attack someone or something. □ *The cat fell upon the mouse and killed it.* □ *The children fell on the birthday cake and ate it all.* **2.** [with *someone*] (for a task) to become the duty of someone. □ *The task of telling mother about the broken vase fell upon Jane.* □ *The job of cleaning up the spill fell upon Tom.*

Familiarity breeds contempt. a proverb meaning that knowing a person closely for a long time leads to bad feelings. □ *Bill and his brothers are always fighting. Like they say: "Familiarity breeds contempt."* □ *Mary and John were good friends for many years. Finally they got into a big argument and became enemies. That just shows that familiarity breeds contempt.*

far and away the best* unquestionably the best. (A cliché.) □ *This soap is far and away the best.* □ *Sally is good, but Ann is far and away the best.*

far be it from me to do something* it is not really my place to do something. (A cliché. Always with *but*, as in the examples.) □ *Far be it from me to tell you what to do, but I think you should buy the book.* □ *Far be it from me to attempt to advise you, but you're making a big mistake.*

far cry from something* a thing which is very different from something else. (Informal.) □ *What you did was a far cry from what you said you were going to do.* □ *The song they played was a far cry from what I call music.*

Far from it. That is not it at all.; That is not nearly correct. □ *Do I think you need a new car? Far from it. The old one is fine.* □ *BILL: Does this hat look strange? TOM: Far from it. It looks good.*

far into the night late into the night; late. □ *She sat up and read far into the night.* □ *The party went on far into the night.*

far out 1. far from the center of things; far from town. □ *The Smiths live sort of far out.* □ *The restaurant is nice, but too far out.* **2.*** strange. (Slang.) □ *Ann acts pretty far out sometimes.* □ *The whole group of people seemed pretty far out.*

farm someone or something out AND **farm out someone or something 1.** [with *someone*] to send someone (somewhere) for care or development. □ *When my mother died, they farmed me out to my aunt and uncle.* □ *The team manager farmed out the baseball player to the minor leagues until he improved.* **2.** [with *something*] to send something (elsewhere) to be dealt with. □ *I farmed out various parts of work to different people.* □ *Bill farmed his chores out to his brothers and sisters and went to a movie.*

feast one's eyes on someone or something AND **feast one's eyes** to look at someone or something with pleasure, envy, or admiration. □ *Just feast your eyes on that beautiful juicy steak!* □ *Yes, feast your eyes. You won't see one like that again for a long time.*

feather in one's cap an honor; a reward for something. □ *Getting a new client was really a feather in my cap.* □ *John earned a feather in his cap by getting an A in physics.*

feather one's nest AND **feather one's own nest 1.** to decorate and furnish one's home in style and comfort. (Birds line their nests with feathers to make them warm and comfortable.) □ *Mr. and Mrs. Simpson have feathered their nest quite comfortably.* □ *It costs a great deal of money to feather one's nest these days.* **2.** to use power and prestige to selfishly provide for oneself. (Said especially of politicians who use their offices to make money for themselves.) □ *The mayor seemed to be helping people, but was really feathering her own nest.* □ *The building contractor used a lot of public money to feather his nest.*

fed up with someone or something* AND **fed up to someplace with someone or something*; fed up*** bored with or disgusted with someone or something. (Informal. The *someplace* can be *here, the teeth, the gills,* or other places.) □ *I'm fed up with Tom and his silly tricks.* □ *I'm fed up to here with high taxes.* □ *They are fed up to the teeth with screaming children.* □ *I'm really fed up!*

feed one's face* to eat. (Slang.) □ *Come on everyone. It's time to feed your faces.* □ *Bill, if you keep feeding your face all the time, you'll get fat.*

feed someone a line See *give someone a line.*

feed the kitty to contribute money. (The *kitty* is a container into which money is put. See also *pass the hat.*) □ *Please feed the kitty. Make a contribution to help sick children.* □ *Come on, Bill. Feed the kitty. You can afford a dollar for a good cause.*

feel compelled to do something to feel that it is necessary to do something. □ *I feel compelled to report your bad behavior.* □ *For some reason, John felt compelled to study history.*

feel dragged out* to feel exhausted. (Informal.) □ *What a day! I really feel dragged out.* □ *If he runs too much, he ends up feeling dragged out.*

feel fit to feel well and healthy. □ *If you want to feel fit, you must eat the proper food and get enough rest.* □ *I hope I still feel fit when I get old.*

feel free to do something AND **feel free** to feel like one is permitted to do something or take something. □ *Please feel free to stay for dinner.* □ *If you see something you want in the refrigerator, please feel free.*

feel it beneath one to do something AND **feel it beneath one** to feel that one would be lowering oneself to do something. □ *Tom feels it beneath him to scrub the floor.* □ *Ann feels it beneath*

her to carry her own luggage. □ *I would do it, but I feel it beneath me.*

feel like a million dollars* AND **feel like a million*** to feel well and healthy, both physically and mentally. (A cliché.) □ *A quick swim in the morning makes me feel like a million dollars.* □ *What a beautiful day! It makes you feel like a million.*

feel like a new person to feel refreshed and renewed, especially after getting well or getting dressed up. □ *I bought a new suit, and now I feel like a new person.* □ *Bob felt like a new person when he got out of the hospital.*

feel like something 1. to feel well enough to do something. □ *I believe I'm getting well. I feel like getting out of bed.* □ *I don't feel like going to the party. I have a headache.* **2.** to want to have something or do something. □ *I feel like having a nice cool drink.* □ *I feel like a nice cool drink.* □ *I don't feel like going to the party. It sounds boring.*

feel out of place to feel that one does not belong in a place. □ *I feel out of place at formal dances.* □ *Bob and Ann felt out of place at the picnic, so they went home.*

feel put upon to feel taken advantage of or exploited. □ *Bill refused to help because he felt put upon.* □ *Sally's mother felt put upon, but she took each of the children home after the birthday party.*

feel someone out* to try to find out how someone feels (about something). (Informal. This does not involve touching anyone.) □ *Sally tried to feel out Tom on whether he'd make a contribution.* □ *The students felt out their parents to find out what they thought about the proposed party.*

feel something in one's bones* AND **know something in one's bones*** (Informal.) to sense something; to have an intuition about something. □ *The train will be late. I feel it in my bones.* □ *I failed the test. I know it in my bones.*

feel up to something to feel well enough or prepared enough to do something. (Often in the negative.) □ *I don't feel up to jogging today.* □ *Aunt Mary didn't feel up to making the visit.* □ *Do you feel up to going out today?*

fence someone in* to restrict someone in some way. (Informal. See also *hem someone or something in*.) □ *I don't want to fence you in, but you have to get home earlier at night.* □ *Don't try to fence me in. I need a lot of freedom.* ALSO: **fenced in** restricted or restrained. □ *I don't like to be fenced in.* □ *I need lots of space and lots of freedom. I can't stand being fenced in.*

fenced in See the previous entry.

fend for oneself See *shift for oneself*.

ferret something out of someone or something AND **ferret out something from someone or something** to remove or retrieve something from someone or something, usually with cunning and persistence. □ *I tried very hard, but I couldn't ferret the information out of the clerk.* □ *I had to ferret out the answer from a book in the library.*

few and far between* very few; few and widely scattered. (Informal.) □ *Get some gasoline now. Service stations on this highway are few and far between.* □ *Some people think that good movies are few and far between.*

fiddle around with someone or something AND **fiddle about with someone or something; fiddle around; fiddle about** (See also *mess around with someone or something*.) **1.** [with *someone*] to tease, annoy, or play with someone; to waste someone's time. □ *All right, stop fiddling around with me and tell me how much you will give me for my car.* □ *Now it's time for all of you to quit fiddling around and get to work.* □ *Tom, you have to stop spending your time fiddling about with your friends. It's time to get serious with your studies.* **2.** [with *something*] to play with something; to tinker with something ineptly. □ *My brother is outside fiddling around with his car engine.* □ *He should stop fiddling around and go out and get a job.* □ *Stop fiddling about with that stick. You're going to hurt someone.*

fight against time to hurry to meet a deadline or to do something quickly. □ *The ambulance sped through the city to reach the accident, fighting against time.* □ *All the students fought against time* to complete the test. ALSO: **fight against time** an attempt to meet a deadline or accomplish something quickly. (This is a nominal form of the entry phrase.) □ *The speeding ambulance was in a fight against time.* □ *The surgical operation was completed successfully. The fight against time was won.*

fight someone or something hammer and tongs* AND **fight someone or something tooth and nail; go at it hammer and tongs; go at it tooth and nail*** to fight against someone or something energetically and with great determination. □ *They fought against the robber tooth and nail.* □ *The dogs were fighting each other hammer and tongs.* □ *The mayor fought the new law hammer and tongs.* □ *We'll fight this zoning ordinance tooth and nail.*

fight someone or something off AND **fight off someone or something** to vanquish someone or something; to fight and overcome someone or something. □ *The boy fought the dog off.* □ *The small boy managed to fight the bigger boy off.* □ *The family was unable to fight off the flu.* □ *I was about to catch a cold, but I fought it off.* □ *The mayor fought off the challenger and won the election.*

fight someone or something tooth and nail See *fight someone or something hammer and tongs*.

figure in something (for a person) to play a role in something. (See also *figure someone or something in*.) □ *Tom figures in our plans for a new building.* □ *I don't wish to figure in your future.*

figure on something* to plan on something; to make arrangements for something. (Informal.) □ *We figured on twenty guests at our party.* □ *I didn't figure on so much trouble.*

figure someone or something in AND **figure in someone or something** to add or include someone or something into one's plans. (Compare to *figure in something*.) □ *Please figure Ann in when you plan the party.* □ *Please figure in two extra places when you set the table.*

figure someone or something out AND **figure out someone or something**

1. [with *something*] to solve a problem; to determine the answer to a problem or a question. □ *I figured all the answers out.* □ *I figured out why the machine wouldn't work.* **2.** to understand someone or something; to find an explanation for someone or something. □ *It's hard to figure John out. I don't know what he means.* □ *I can't figure out this recipe.*

figure something up AND **figure up something** to add up or total up a list of prices. □ *Please figure our costs up and send us a statement.* □ *The clerk figured up our bill quickly.*

fill in for someone AND **fill in** to take the place of another person. □ *Bob had to fill in for Tom in the play.* □ *Who filled in when the secretary was sick?*

fill out to grow fuller. (See also *fill something out.*) □ *The tree we planted two years ago is beginning to fill out.* □ *John was very thin, but now he's beginning to fill out.* □ *Mary is beginning to fill out and look like a young lady.*

fill someone in on someone or something AND **fill someone in; fill in someone** to inform someone about someone or something. □ *Please fill me in on what is happening in Washington.* □ *Please fill me in on Ann. How is she doing?* □ *Sit down, and I'll fill you in.* □ *Later, I'll fill in everyone else.*

fill someone or something in AND **fill in someone or something** **1.** [with *something*] to add matter to a hole or cavity. □ *Now we will fill in the hole with dirt.* □ *They filled the bad places in with plaster. Now the wall looks fine.* **2.** [with *something*] to write or type information into blank places on a form or application. (The same as *fill something out.*) □ *Please fill in this application.* □ *You must fill all the blanks in.* □ *Take this home and fill it in.* **3.** [with *someone*] See *fill someone in on someone or something.*

fill someone or something up AND **fill up someone or something** to make a person or thing completely full (of something). □ *Here, have some more food. You haven't eaten enough to fill you up.* □ *Fill your glass up with milk.* □ *Please fill up this hole.* □ *Fill up your pockets with candy and eat it later.*

fill someone's shoes to take the place of some other person and do that person's work satisfactorily. (As if you were wearing the other person's shoes.) □ *I don't know how we'll be able to do without you. No one can fill your shoes.* □ *It'll be difficult to fill Jane's shoes. She did her job very well.*

fill something out AND **fill out something** to write or type information into blank places on a form or application; to complete an application form. (See also *fill someone or something in.*) □ *Take this form home and fill it out please.* □ *Please fill out this application when you have a chance.*

fill the bill* to be exactly the thing that is needed. (A cliché.) □ *Ah, this steak is great. It really fills the bill.* □ *This new pair of shoes fills the bill nicely.*

fill the gap AND **fill in the gap** to fill in an open place; to supply something which was missing; to fill a space of time. □ *Part of our fence blew down, and we had to fill the gap with boards.* □ *We filled in the gap between classes by having a snack.*

find fault with someone or something AND **find fault** to find things wrong with someone or something. □ *We were unable to find fault with the meal.* □ *Sally's father was always finding fault with her.* □ *Some people are always finding fault.*

find it in one's heart to do something AND **find it in one's heart** to have the courage or compassion to do something. □ *She couldn't find it in her heart to refuse to come home to him.* □ *I can't do it! I can't find it in my heart.*

find one's or something's way somewhere **1.** [with *one's*] to discover the route to a place. □ *Mr. Smith found his way to the museum.* □ *Can you find your way home?* **2.** [with *something's*] to end up in a place. (This expression avoids accusing someone of moving the thing to the place.) □ *The money found its way into the mayor's pocket.* □ *The secret plans found their way into the enemy's hands.*

find one's tongue* to be able to talk. (Informal.) □ *Tom was speechless for a moment. Then he found his tongue.*

□ *Ann was unable to find her tongue. She sat there in silence.*

find one's way around AND **find one's way** to be able to move about an area satisfactorily. □ *I can go downtown by myself. I can find my way around.* □ *I know the area well enough to find my way.* □ *He can find his way around when it comes to car engines.*

find oneself to discover what one's talents and preferences are. □ *Bill did better in school after he found himself.* □ *John tried a number of different jobs. He finally found himself when he became a cook.*

find out about someone or something AND **find out** to learn or discover something about someone or something. □ *I need to find out about how to buy life insurance.* □ *I found out about John and his new business.* □ *We found out that Tom ran away from home.* □ *They didn't want us to find out.*

find someone or something out 1. [with *something*] AND **find out something** to discover facts about someone or something; to learn a fact. □ *I found something out that you might be interested in.* □ *We found out that the Smiths are going to sell their house.* **2.** [with *someone*] to discover something bad about someone. □ *John thought he could get away with smoking, but his mother found him out.* □ *Jane was taking a two-hour lunch period until the manager found her out.*

find something out the hard way See *learn something the hard way.*

Finders keepers, losers weepers.* AND **finders keepers*** a phrase said when something is found. (A cliché meaning that the person who finds something gets to keep it. The person who loses it can only weep.) □ *John lost a quarter in the dining room yesterday. Ann found the quarter there today. Ann claimed that since she found it, it was hers. She said, "Finders keepers, losers weepers."* □ *John said, "I'll say finders keepers when I find something of yours!"*

fine kettle of fish* a real mess; an unsatisfactory situation. (A cliché.) □ *The dog has eaten the steak we were going to have for dinner. This is a fine kettle of fish!* □ *This is a fine kettle of fish. It's below freezing outside, and the furnace won't work.*

finish something up AND **finish up something** to complete something. □ *Hurry and finish this up.* □ *Finish up your work and go home.* ALSO: **finish up** to come to the end (of a task). □ *I'll be right there as soon as I finish up.*

finish up See the previous entry.

fire away at someone or something 1. to shoot at someone or something. □ *The hunters fired away at the ducks.* □ *On television, somebody is always firing away at somebody else.* **2.** [with *someone*] to ask many questions of someone; to criticize someone severely. □ *When it came time for questions, the reporters began firing away at the mayor.* □ *Members of the opposite party are always firing away at the President.*

first and foremost* first and most important. (A cliché.) □ *First and foremost, I think you should work harder on your biology.* □ *Have this in mind first and foremost: Keep smiling!*

First come, first served.* The first people to arrive will be served first. (A cliché.) □ *They ran out of tickets before we got there. It was first come, first served, but we didn't know that.* □ *Please line up and take your turn. It's first come, first served.*

first of all the very first thing; before anything else. □ *First of all, put your name on this piece of paper.* □ *First of all, we'll try to find a place to live.*

first off first; the first thing. (Almost the same as *first of all.*) □ *He ordered soup first off.* □ *First off, we'll find a place to live.*

first thing in the morning AND **first thing** before anything else in the morning. □ *Please call me first thing in the morning. I can't help you now.* □ *I'll do that first thing.*

First things first.* The most important things must be taken care of first. (A cliché.) □ *It's more important to get a job than to buy new clothes. First things first!* □ *Do your homework now. Go out and play later. First things first.*

fish for a compliment to try to get someone to pay you a compliment. (Informal.) □ *When she showed me her new dress, I could tell that she was fishing for a compliment.* □ *Tom was certainly fishing for a compliment when he modeled his fancy haircut for his friends.*

fish for something to try to get information (from someone). (Also used literally.) □ *The lawyer was fishing for evidence.* □ *The teacher spent a lot of time fishing for the right answer from the students.*

fish or cut bait* either do the job you are supposed to be doing or quit and let someone else do it. (A cliché.) □ *Mary is doing much better on the job since her manager told her to fish or cut bait.* □ *The boss told Tom, "Quit wasting time! Fish or cut bait!"*

fit for a king* totally suitable. (A cliché.) □ *What a delicious meal. It was fit for a king.* □ *Our room at the hotel was fit for a king.*

fit in with someone or something AND **fit in** to be comfortable with someone or something; to be in accord or harmony with someone or something. □ *I really feel like I fit in with that group of people.* □ *It's good that you fit in.* □ *This chair doesn't fit in with the style of furniture in my house.* □ *I won't buy it if it doesn't fit in.*

fit like a glove* to fit very well; to fit tightly or snugly. (A cliché.) □ *My new shoes fit like a glove.* □ *My new coat is a little tight. It fits like a glove.*

fit someone or something into something AND **fit in someone or something; fit someone or something in** **1.** [with *something*] to manage to put something into an opening. □ *The mechanic fit in the screw without any trouble.* □ *The shelf was crowded, but I fit the book in easily.* **2.** to manage to put someone or something into a schedule. □ *The doctor is busy, but I can fit you into the schedule.* □ *Yes, here's an opening in the schedule. I can fit you in.*

fit someone or something out with something AND **fit someone or something out** to provide or furnish someone or something with something. □ *They fit the camper out with everything they needed.* □ *They fit them out for only $140.* □ *He fit his car out with lots of chrome.*

fit someone to a T See *suit someone to a T.*

fit to be tied* very angry and excited. (Folksy. To be so angry that one has to be restrained with ropes.) □ *If I'm not home on time, my parents will be fit to be tied.* □ *When Ann saw the bill, she was fit to be tied.*

fit to kill* dressed up to look very fancy or sexy. (Folksy.) □ *Mary put on her best clothes and looked fit to kill.* □ *John looked fit to kill in his tuxedo.*

fix someone or something up AND **fix up someone or something** **1.** [with *something*] to repair something; to decorate or refurbish something. □ *The Smiths fixed their yard up.* □ *Bill fixed up his old car, and now it runs very well.* **2.*** [with *someone*] to dress up and otherwise improve the appearance of someone. (Folksy.) □ *The hairdresser fixed up Mary, and she looked lovely.* □ *Sally fixed herself up for the big dance.* **3.** [with *someone*] See *fix someone up with someone or something.*

fix someone up with someone or something* AND **fix someone up*; fix up someone with someone or something*; fix up someone*** **1.** [with *something*] to supply a person with something. (Informal.) □ *We fixed up John with a cold drink.* □ *The usher fixed us up with seats at the front of the theater.* □ *We thanked the usher for fixing us up.* **2.** [with *someone*] AND **line someone up with someone*; line up someone with someone*** to supply a person with a date or a companion. (Informal.) □ *We fixed up Bob with a date.* □ *They lined John up with my cousin, Jane.* □ *John didn't want us to fix him up.*

fix someone's wagon* to punish someone; to get even with someone; to plot against someone. (Informal.) □ *If you ever do that again, I'll fix your wagon!* □ *Tommy! You clean up your room this instant, or I'll fix your wagon!* □ *He reported me to the boss, but I fixed his wagon. I knocked his lunch on the floor.*

fizzle out to die out; to come to a stop shortly after starting; to fail. □ *It started to rain, and the fire fizzled out.* □ *The* *car started in the cold weather, but it fizzled out before we got very far.* □ *My attempt to run for mayor fizzled out.* □ *She started off her job very well, but fizzled out after about a month.*

flag someone or something down AND **flag down someone or something** to signal for someone or something to stop. □ *A police officer flagged her down and gave her the urgent message.* □ *The doctor flagged down a passing car and got a ride to the hospital.* □ *If you want the train to stop here, you have to flag it down.*

flare up to grow intense for a brief period. (Usually said of a flame, someone's anger, or a chronic disease.) □ *Just when we thought we had put the fire out, it flared up again.* □ *Mr. Jones always flares up whenever anyone mentions taxes.* □ *My hay fever usually flares up in August.*

flash in the pan* someone or something which draws a lot of attention for a very brief time. (Informal.) □ *I'm afraid that my success as a painter was just a flash in the pan.* □ *Tom had hoped to be a singer, but his career was only a flash in the pan.*

flat broke* completely broke; with no money at all. (Informal.) □ *I spent my last dollar, and I'm flat broke.* □ *The bank closed its doors to the public. It was flat broke!*

flat out* **1.** clearly and definitely; holding nothing back. (Informal.) □ *I told her flat out that I didn't like her.* □ *They reported flat out that the operation was a failure.* **2.** at top speed. (Slang.) □ *How fast will this car go flat out?* □ *This car will hit about 110 miles per hour flat out.*

flesh and blood **1.** a living human body, especially with reference to its natural limitations; a human being. □ *This cold weather is more than flesh and blood can stand.* □ *Carrying 300 pounds is beyond mere flesh and blood.* **2.** the quality of being alive. □ *The paintings of this artist are lifeless. They lack flesh and blood.* □ *A ghost is not a flesh and blood being.* **3.** one's own relatives; one's own kin. □ *That's no way to treat one's own flesh and blood.* □ *I want to leave*

my money to my own flesh and blood. □ *Grandmother was happier living with her flesh and blood.*

flesh out to become more fleshy. □ *John was very thin after his illness, but he is beginning to flesh out now.* □ *Bill is overeating again. He's fleshing out too much.*

flesh something out AND **flesh out something** to make something more detailed, bigger, or fuller. (As if one were adding flesh to a skeleton.) □ *This is basically a good outline. Now you'll have to flesh it out.* □ *The play was good, except that the author needed to flesh out the third act. It was too short.*

fling oneself at someone See *throw oneself at someone.*

flip one's lid See the following entry.

flip one's wig* AND **flip one's lid*** to suddenly become angry, crazy, or enthusiastic. (Slang.) □ *Whenever anyone mentions taxes, Mr. Jones absolutely flips his wig.* □ *Stop whistling. You're going to make me flip my lid.* □ *When I saw that brand new car and learned it was mine, I just flipped my wig.*

float a loan to get a loan; to arrange for a loan. □ *I couldn't afford to pay cash for the car, so I floated a loan.* □ *They needed money, so they had to float a loan.*

fluff one's lines* AND **blow one's lines***; **muff one's lines*** to speak one's speech badly or forget one's lines when one is in a play. (Informal.) □ *The actress fluffed her lines badly in the last act.* □ *I was in a play once, and I muffed my lines over and over.* □ *It's okay to blow your lines in rehearsal.*

flunk out to fail a course; to fail out of school. □ *Tom didn't study, and he finally flunked out.* □ *Bill is about to flunk out of geometry.*

flunk someone out AND **flunk out someone** to cause someone to leave school by giving a failing grade. □ *The teacher flunked Tom out.* □ *The professor wanted to flunk out the whole class.*

fly-by-night irresponsible; untrustworthy. (Refers to a person who sneaks away secretly in the night.) □ *The carpenter we hired was a fly-by-night worker who did a very bad job.* □

You shouldn't deal with a fly-by-night merchant.

fly in the face of someone or something AND **fly in the teeth of someone or something** to disregard, defy, or show disrespect for someone or something. □ *John loves to fly in the face of tradition.* □ *Ann made it a practice to fly in the face of standard procedures.* □ *John finds great pleasure in flying in the teeth of his father.*

fly in the ointment* a small, unpleasant matter which spoils something; a drawback. (A cliché.) □ *We enjoyed the play, but the fly in the ointment was not being able to find our car afterward.* □ *It sounds like a good idea, but there must be a fly in the ointment somewhere.*

fly in the teeth of someone or something See *fly in the face of someone or something.*

fly off the handle* to lose one's temper. (Informal.) □ *Every time anyone mentions taxes, Mrs. Brown flies off the handle.* □ *If she keeps flying off the handle like that, she'll have a heart attack.*

fly the coop* to escape; to get out or get away. (Informal. Refers to a chicken escaping from a chicken coop.) □ *I couldn't stand the party, so I flew the coop.* □ *The prisoner flew the coop at the first opportunity.*

foam at the mouth* to be very angry. (Informal. Related to a "mad dog"—a dog with rabies—which foams at the mouth.) □ *Bob was raving—foaming at the mouth. I've never seen anyone so angry.* □ *Bill foamed at the mouth in anger.*

fob something off on someone AND **fob off something on someone; fob something off; fob off something** to trick someone into accepting something which is worthless. (Informal.) □ *The car dealer fobbed a junky car off on Tom.* □ *He also fobbed off a bad car on Jane.* □ *Some car dealers are always trying to fob something off.*

fold something up AND **fold up something 1.** to fold something. □ *The children folded the flag up.* □ *Fold up the paper carefully.* **2.** to put an end to some-thing; to close something. □ *The producer decided to fold up the play early. It was losing money.* □ *Mr. Jones was going broke, so he folded his business up.* ALSO: **fold up** to fold; to close up. □ *The ladder folded up and pinched me.* □ *The leaves of this plant fold up at night.* □ *The play folded up after two days.* □ *It's time to fold up and go home.*

follow in someone's footsteps See the following entry.

follow in someone's tracks AND **follow in someone's footsteps** to follow someone's example; to assume someone else's role or occupation. □ *The Vice President was following in the President's footsteps when he called for budget cuts.* □ *She followed in her father's footsteps and went into medicine.*

follow one's heart to act according to one's feelings; to obey one's sympathetic or compassionate inclinations. □ *I couldn't decide what to do, so I just followed my heart.* □ *I trust that you will follow your heart in this matter.*

follow one's nose* 1. to go straight ahead, the direction that one's nose is pointing. (Folksy.) □ *The town that you want is straight ahead on this highway. Just follow your nose.* □ *The chief's office is right around the corner. Turn left and follow your nose.* **2.** to follow an odor to its source. (Informal.) □ *The kitchen is at the back of the building. Just follow your nose.* □ *There was a bad smell in the basement—probably a dead mouse. I followed my nose until I found it.*

follow someone or something up AND **follow up someone or something** (See also *follow up on someone or something.*) **1.** [with *something*] to add more information or detail to something; to follow something through. □ *Bill had to follow my suggestion up.* □ *The police followed up my story.* **2.** [with *someone*] to review someone's work and check it over. □ *When I followed up Mary, I found errors in her work.* □ *The person who follows you up will make sure you're doing the right thing.*

follow suit to follow in the same pattern; to follow someone else's example. (From card games.) □ *Mary went to work for a bank, and Jane followed suit.*

Now they are both head cashiers. □ *The Smiths went out to dinner, but the Browns didn't follow suit. They stayed home.*

follow through on something AND **carry through on something; carry through; follow through; go through on something** to complete a task; to see a task through to its completion. □ *You must follow through on the things that you start.* □ *Don't start the job if you can't follow through.* □ *Ask Sally to carry through on her project.* □ *I hope she goes through on her job.* ALSO: **follow-through** an act of bringing a task to a conclusion. □ *Your problem is that you lack follow-through.* □ *If your follow-through matched your get-up-and-go, you'd be a wonder.*

follow up on someone or something AND **follow up** to find out more about someone or something. (Compare to *follow someone or something up.*) □ *Please follow up on Mr. Brown and his activities.* □ *Bill, Mr. Smith has a complaint. Would you please follow up on it?* □ *We can take care of that when we follow up.*

fond of someone or something to like someone or something. □ *I'm fond of chocolate.* □ *Mary isn't fond of me, but I'm fond of her.*

food for thought something to think about. □ *I don't like your idea very much, but it's food for thought.* □ *Your lecture was very good. It contained much food for thought.*

fool around with someone or something* AND **fool around*** to fiddle, play, or mess with someone or something; to waste time with someone or something. (Informal.) □ *John is out fooling around with his friends again.* □ *That child spends most of his time fooling around.* □ *Please don't fool around with the light switch. You'll break it.* □ *There are lots of interesting things in here, but you must leave them alone. Don't fool around.*

foot the bill to pay the bill; to pay (for something). □ *Let's go out and eat. I'll foot the bill.* □ *If the bank goes broke, don't worry. The government will foot the bill.*

for all I care* I don't care (if something happens). (Informal.) □ *For all I care, the whole city council can go to the devil.* □ *They can all starve for all I care.*

for all I know* according to the information I have; I think; probably. (Informal.) □ *For all I know, the mayor has resigned already.* □ *She may have gone to town for all I know.*

for all it's worth AND **for what it's worth; for whatever it's worth** if it has any value. □ *My idea—for all it's worth—is to offer them only $300.* □ *Here is my thinking, for whatever it's worth.* □ *Ask her to give us her opinion, for what it's worth.*

for all practical purposes as might be reasonably expected; essentially. □ *For all practical purposes, this is simply a matter of right and wrong.* □ *This should be considered final, for all practical purposes.*

for all something in spite of something. □ *For all her complaining, she still seems to be a happy person.* □ *For all my aches and pains, I'm still rather healthy.*

for all the world 1. exactly; precisely. (Especially with *look.*) □ *She sat there looking for all the world like she was going to cry.* □ *It started out seeming for all the world like a beautiful day. Then a storm came up.* 2.* everything. (A cliché. Usually in the negative.) □ *I wouldn't give up my baby for all the world.* □ *They wouldn't sell their property for all the world.*

for better or for worse* under any conditions; no matter what happens. (A cliché.) □ *I married you for better or for worse.* □ *For better or for worse, I'm going to quit my job.*

for chicken feed* AND **for peanuts*** for nearly nothing; for very little money. (Informal. Also used without *for.*) □ *Bob doesn't get paid much. He works for chicken feed.* □ *You can buy an old car for chicken feed.* □ *I won't do that kind of work for peanuts!*

for days on end for many days. □ *We kept on traveling for days on end.* □ *Doctor, I've had this pain for days on end.*

for fear of something out of fear for

101

something; because of fear of something. □ *He doesn't drive for fear of an accident.* □ *They lock their doors for fear of being robbed.*

for good forever; permanently. □ *I finally left home for good.* □ *They tried to repair it many times before they fixed it for good.*

for good measure as extra; adding a little more to make sure there is enough. □ *When I bought a pound of nails, the clerk threw in a few extra nails for good measure.* □ *I always put a little extra salt in the soup for good measure.*

for hours on end for many hours. □ *We sat and waited for the doctor for hours on end.* □ *We listened to the speaker for hours on end.*

for keeps* forever; permanently. (Informal. See also *play for keeps*. Compare to *for good*.) □ *When I get married, it'll be for keeps.* □ *We've moved around a lot. Now I think we'll stay here for keeps.*

for kicks* for fun; just for entertainment; for no good reason. (Slang.) □ *They didn't mean any harm. They just did it for kicks.* □ *We drove over to the next town for kicks.*

for one's own part AND **for one's part** as far as one is concerned; from one's point of view. □ *For my own part, I wish to stay here.* □ *For her part, she prefers chocolate.*

for one's own sake AND **for one's sake** for one's good or benefit; in honor of someone. □ *I have to earn a living for my family's sake.* □ *I did it for my mother's sake.* □ *I didn't do it for my own sake.*

for openers* AND **for starters*** to start with. (Informal.) □ *For openers, they played a song everyone knows.* □ *For starters, I'll serve a delicious soup.*

for peanuts See *for chicken feed*.

for real* authentic; genuine; really. (Informal or slang.) □ *Is this diamond for real?* □ *Are you for real?* □ *Are we there for real?*

for sale available for purchase; buyable. (Compare to *on sale*.) □ *Is this item for sale?* □ *How long has this house been for sale?* □ *My car is for sale. Are you interested?*

For shame! See *shame on someone*.

for short in a short form. (Usually refers to names.) □ *My name is William. They call me Bill for short.* □ *Almost everyone who is named Robert is called Bob for short.*

for something to change hands for something to be sold. (Refers to the changing of owners.) □ *How many times has this house changed hands in the last ten years?* □ *We built this house in 1920, and it has never changed hands.*

for something to sell like hotcakes* for something to be sold very fast. (A cliché.) □ *The delicious candy sold like hotcakes.* □ *The fancy new cars were selling like hotcakes.*

for starters See *for openers*.

for sure* certainly; surely. (Informal or slang.) □ MARY: *Do you like my new jacket?* JANE: *For sure.* □ *For sure, I want to go on the picnic.*

for that matter besides; in addition. □ *If you're hungry, take one of my doughnuts. For that matter, take two.* □ *I don't like this house. The roof leaks. For that matter, the whole place is falling apart.* □ *Tom is quite arrogant. So is his sister, for that matter.*

for the asking if one just asks (for something); simply by asking; on request. □ *Do you want to use my car? It's yours for the asking.* □ *I have an extra winter coat that's yours for the asking.*

for the best AND **all for the best** good in spite of the way it seems; better than you think. (Often said when someone dies after a serious illness.) □ *I'm very sorry to hear of the death of your aunt. Perhaps it's for the best.* □ *I didn't get into the college I wanted, but I couldn't afford it anyway. It's probably all for the best.*

for the better better; an improvement. (See also *take a turn for the better*.) □ *A change of government would be for the better.* □ *A new winter coat would certainly be for the better.*

for the birds* worthless; undesirable. (Slang.) □ *This television program is for the birds.* □ *Winter weather is for the birds.*

for the devil of it* AND **for the heck of it*; for the hell of it*** just for fun;

because it is slightly evil; for no good reason. (Informal. Some people may object to the word *hell*.) □ *We filled their garage with leaves just for the devil of it.* □ *Tom tripped Bill for the heck of it.* □ *John picked a fight with Tom just for hell of it.*

for the heck of it See the previous entry.

for the hell of it See *for the devil of it.*

for the life of one* even if one's life were threatened; even in exchange for one's life. (Informal. Always with a negative, and usually having to do with one's memory.) □ *For the life of me, I don't remember your name.* □ *She couldn't recall the correct numbers for the life of her.* □ *For the life of them, they couldn't remember the way home.*

for the moment AND **for the time being** for the present; for now; temporarily. □ *This will have to do for the moment.* □ *This is all right for the time being. It'll have to be improved next week, however.* □ *This good feeling will last only for the time being.* □ *This solution is satisfactory for the moment.*

for the most part mostly; in general. □ *For the most part, the class is enjoying geometry.* □ *I like working here for the most part.*

for the odds to be against one for things to be against one generally; for one's chances to be slim. □ *You can give it a try, but the odds are against you.* □ *I know the odds are against me, but I wish to run in the race anyway.*

for the record so that (one's own version of) the facts will be known; so there will be a record of a particular fact. (This often is said when there are reporters present.) □ *I'd like to say—for the record—that at no time have I ever accepted a bribe from anyone.* □ *For the record, I've never been able to get anything done around city hall without bribing someone.*

for the sake of someone or something for the good of someone or something; for the honor or recognition of someone or something. (Compare to *for one's own sake*.) □ *I did it for the sake of all those people who helped me get through school.* □ *I'm investing in a house for the sake of my children.* □ *For the sake*

of honesty, Bill shared all the information he had.

for the time being See *for the moment.*

for whatever it's worth See *for all it's worth.*

force someone out of something AND **force someone out** to drive someone out of a place or an office. □ *The city council forced the mayor out of office.* □ *Please leave immediately, or I'll have to force you out.*

force someone to the wall AND **drive someone to the wall** to push someone to an extreme position; to put someone into an awkward position. □ *He wouldn't tell the truth until we forced him to the wall.* □ *They don't pay their bills until you drive them to the wall.*

force someone's hand to force a person to reveal plans, strategies, or secrets. (Refers to a handful of cards in card playing.) □ *We didn't know what she was doing until Tom forced her hand.* □ *We couldn't plan our game until we forced the other team's hand in the last play.*

forever and a day See the following entry.

forever and ever* AND **forever and a day*** forever. (A cliché when used in everyday language.) □ *I will love you forever and ever.* □ *This car won't keep running forever and ever. We'll have to get a new one sometime.* □ *We have enough money to last forever and a day.*

forget oneself to forget one's manners or training. (Said in formal situations in reference to belching, bad table manners, and, in the case of very young children, pants-wetting.) □ *Sorry, mother, I forgot myself.* □ *John, we are going out to dinner tonight. Please don't forget yourself.*

forgive and forget* to forgive someone (for something) and forget that it ever happened. (A cliché.) □ *I'm sorry, John. Let's forgive and forget. What do you say?* □ *It was nothing. We'll just have to forgive and forget.*

fork money out for something AND **fork out money for something; fork money out; fork out money** to pay (perhaps unwillingly) for something. (Informal. Often mention is made about the amount of money. See the examples.) □ *I like that stereo, but I don't want to fork out a lot of money.* □ *Do you think I'm going to fork twenty dollars out for that book?* □ *I hate having to fork out money day after day.* □ *Forking money out to everyone is part of life in a busy economy.*

fork something over* AND **fork over something*** to give something to someone. (Slang. Often refers to money. Usually used in a command.) □ *Okay, Joe. Fork over that twenty dollars you owe me.* □ *Now! Fork it over now!*

form an opinion to think up or decide on an opinion. (Note the variations in the examples.) □ *I don't know enough about the issue to form an opinion.* □ *Don't tell me how to think! I can form my own opinion.* □ *I don't form opinions without careful consideration.*

foul play illegal activity; bad practices. □ *The police investigating the death suspect foul play.* □ *Each student got an A on the test, and the teacher imagined it was the result of foul play.*

foul someone or something up* AND **foul up someone or something*** to cause disorder and confusion for someone or something; to tangle up someone or something; to *mess someone or something up*. (Informal.) □ *You've fouled up my whole day.* □ *Go away! Don't foul me up any more.* □ *Watch out! You're going to foul up my kite strings.* □ *Stay off the field. You're going to foul up the coach.* ALSO: **foul up*** to do (something) badly; to mess something up. (Informal.) □ *At the last minute, he fouled up and failed the course.* □ *Take your time. Plan your moves, and don't foul up.* ALSO: **foul-up** an act of fouling up or messing up. □ *You've created a real foul-up.* □ *Look at this paper. I've never seen such a foul-up.* □ *Your foul-up took me three hours to straighten out.* ALSO: **fouled up** messed up. □ *My fishing line is all fouled up.* □ *The football team got fouled up and lost the game.*

foul up See the previous entry.

free and easy casual. □ *John is so free and easy. How can anyone be so relaxed?* □ *Now, take it easy. Just act free and easy. No one will know you're nervous.*

free-for-all a disorganized fight or contest involving everyone; a brawl. □ *The picnic turned into a free-for-all after midnight.* □ *The race started out in an organized manner, but ended up being a free-for-all.*

fresh out of something* AND **clean out of something***; **clean out***; **fresh out*** just now having sold or used up the last of something. (Folksy.) □ *Sorry, I can't serve you scrambled eggs. We are fresh out of eggs.* □ *We are fresh out of nails. I sold the last box just ten minutes ago.* □ *Lettuce? Sorry. I'm fresh out.* □ *Sorry. We are clean out of dried beans.*

frighten one out of one's wits AND **scare one out of one's wits** to frighten one very badly. (See also *frighten the wits out of someone.*) □ *Oh! That loud noise scared me out of my wits.* □ *I'll give him a good scolding and frighten him out of his wits.*

frighten someone to death AND **scare someone to death** to frighten someone severely. (Also used literally.) □ *The dentist always frightens me to death.* □ *She scared me to death when she screamed.* ALSO: **frightened to death**; **scared to death** severely frightened. (Also used literally.) □ *I don't want to go to the dentist today. I'm frightened to death.* □ *I'm frightened to death of dogs.* □ *She's scared to death she'll fail algebra.*

frighten the wits out of someone AND **frighten the living daylights out of someone**; **scare the living daylights out of someone**; **scare the wits out of someone** to frighten someone very badly. (The *living* can be left out.) □ *We nearly had an accident. It frightened the living daylights out of me.* □ *The incident scared the wits out of me.*

frightened to death See *frighten someone to death.*

fritter something away* AND **fritter away something*** to waste something little by little, especially time or money. (Folksy.) □ *Don't stand around and fritter the whole day away.* □ *Stop frittering away my hard earned money!*

from day to day on a daily basis; one day at a time; occasionally. □ *We face this kind of problem from day to day.* □

I'll have to check into this matter from day to day. □ *When you're very poor, you live from day to day.*

from hand to hand from one person to a series of other persons. □ *The book traveled from hand to hand until it got back to its owner.* □ *By the time the baby had been passed from hand to hand, it was crying.*

from pillar to post* from one place to a series of other places; (figuratively) from person to person, as with gossip. (A cliché.) □ *My father was in the army, and we moved from pillar to post year after year.* □ *After I told one person my secret, it went quickly from pillar to post.*

from rags to riches* from poverty to wealth; from modesty to elegance. (A cliché.) □ *The princess used to be quite poor. She certainly moved from rags to riches.* □ *After I inherited the money, I went from rags to riches.*

from start to finish* from the beginning to the end; throughout. (A cliché.) □ *I disliked the whole business from start to finish.* □ *Mary caused problems from start to finish.*

from stem to stern* from one end to another. (A cliché. Refers to the front and back ends of a ship. Also used literally in reference to ships.) □ *Now, I have to clean the house from stem to stern.* □ *I polished my car carefully from stem to stern.*

from the bottom of one's heart* sincerely. (A cliché. Compare to *with all one's heart and soul.*) □ *When I returned the lost kitten to Mrs. Brown, she thanked me from the bottom of her heart.* □ *Oh, thank you! I'm grateful from the bottom of my heart.*

from the ground up from the beginning; from start to finish. (Used literally in reference to building a house or other building.) □ *We must plan our sales campaign carefully from the ground up.* □ *Sorry, but you'll have to start all over again from the ground up.*

from the heart from a deep and sincere emotional source. □ *I know that your kind words come from the heart.* □ *We don't want your gift unless it comes from the heart.*

from the outset from the beginning. □

We had problems with this machine from the outset. □ *We knew about the unfriendly judge from the outset of our trial.*

from the word go* from the beginning. (Informal.) □ *I knew about the problem from the word go.* □ *She was failing the class from the word go.*

from this day on AND **from this day forward** from today into the future. (Formal.) □ *We'll live in love and peace from this day on.* □ *I'll treasure your gift from this day forward.*

from time to time occasionally. □ *We have pizza from time to time.* □ *From time to time, a visitor comes to our door.*

from top to bottom from the highest point to the lowest point; throughout. (Compare to *from stem to stern.*) □ *I have to clean the house from top to bottom today.* □ *We need to replace our elected officials from top to bottom.*

from way back* from far in the past; from an earlier time. (Informal.) □ *Grandfather comes from way back.* □ *This antique clock is from way back.*

full of beans See *full of hot air.*

full of bull See the following entry.

full of hot air* AND **full of beans*; full of bull*; full of it*; full of prunes*** full of nonsense; talking nonsense. (Slang.) □ *Oh, shut up, Mary. You're full of hot air.* □ *Don't pay any attention to Bill. He's full of beans.* □ *My English professor is full of bull.* □ *You're full of it.* □ *She doesn't know what she's talking about. She's just full of prunes.*

full of Old Nick See *full of the devil.*

full of prunes See *full of hot air.*

full of the devil* AND **full of Old Nick*** always making mischief. (Informal. *Old Nick* is another name for the devil.) □ *Tom is a lot of fun, but he's sure full of the devil.* □ *I've never seen a child get into so much mischief. He's really full of Old Nick.*

fun and games* playing around; doing worthless things. (Informal.) □ *All right, Bill, the fun and games are over. It's time to get down to work.* □ *This isn't a serious course. It's nothing but fun and games.*

fuss over someone or something
See *make a fuss over someone or something.*

G

gain on someone or something to draw nearer to someone or something; to move toward a goal faster than someone or something. □ *In the race, Tom kept gaining on Bob.* □ *The speeding truck was gaining on the automobile.*

game at which two can play* a manner of competing which two competitors can use; a strategy that competing sides can both use. (A cliché.) □ *The mayor shouted at the city council, "Politics is a game at which two can play."* □ *"Flattery is a game at which two can play," said John as he returned Mary's compliment.* ALSO: **two can play at this game; two can play at that game** two players can compete using the same strategy. □ *I'm sorry you're being so hard to deal with. Two can play at that game.*

gang up on someone AND **gang up** to form into a group and attack someone. (Usually a physical attack, but it can also be a verbal attack.) □ *We can't win against the robber unless we gang up on him.* □ *All right you guys, don't gang up on me. Play fair!*

gas up* to fill up one's gasoline tank with gasoline. (Informal.) □ *I have to stop at the next service station and gas up.* □ *The next time you gas up, try some of the gasoline with alcohol in it.*

generous to a fault* too generous; overly generous. (A cliché.) □ *My favorite uncle is generous to a fault.* □ *Sally—always generous to a fault—gave away her sandwiches.*

get a bang out of someone or something See *get a charge out of someone or something.*

get a big send-off to receive or enjoy a happy celebration before departing. (Also with *have*. Note: *Get* can be replaced with *have*. Note variations in the examples. *Get* usually means to become, to acquire, or to cause. *Have* usually means to possess, to be, or to have resulted in.) □ *I had a wonderful send-off before I left.* □ *John got a fine send-off as he left for Europe.* ALSO: **give someone a big send-off** to see someone off on a journey with celebration and encouragement. □ *When I left for college, all my brothers and sisters came to the airport to give me a big send-off.* □ *When the sailors left, everyone went down to the docks and gave them a big send-off.*

get a black eye (Also with *have*. See the note at *get a big send-off.*) **1.** to get a bruise near the eye from being struck. □ *I got a black eye from walking into a door.* □ *I have a black eye where John hit me.* **2.** to have one's character or reputation harmed. □ *Mary got a black eye because of her complaining.* □ *The whole group now has a black eye.* ALSO: **give someone a black eye 1.** to hit someone near the eye so that a dark bruise appears. □ *John became angry and gave me a black eye.* **2.** to harm the character or reputation of someone. □ *The constant complaining gave the whole group a black eye.*

get a break to have good fortune; to receive a bit of luck. (Often with *lucky, nice,* etc. Also with *have*. See the note at *get a big send-off.*) □ *Mary is going to get a break.* □ *I wish I'd get a lucky break.* □ *Why don't I have a lucky break when I need one?* □ *She's got a lucky break and doesn't even know it.* ALSO:

give someone a break to give someone a chance; to give someone another chance or a second chance. □ *I'm sorry. Don't send me home. Give me a break!* □ *They gave me a nice break. They didn't send me home.*

get a bright idea for a clever thought or idea to occur (to someone). (Also with *have*. See the explanation at *get a big send-off*.) □ *Now and then I get a bright idea.* □ *John hardly ever gets a bright idea.* □ *Listen here. I have a bright idea.* ALSO: **give someone a bright idea** to give someone a clever thought or idea. □ *That gives me a bright idea!* □ *Thank you for giving me a bright idea.*

get a charge out of someone or something* AND **get a bang out of someone or something***; **get a kick out of someone or something*** to receive a special pleasure from someone or something. (Informal.) □ *Tom is really funny. I always get a kick out of his jokes.* □ *Bill really got a bang out of the present we gave him.* □ *Mary got a charge out of Bob's visit.* ALSO: **give someone a bang***; **give someone a charge***; **give someone a kick*** to give someone a bit of excitement. (Informal.) □ *John always gives me a bang.*

get a Charley horse to develop a cramp in the arm or leg, usually from strain. (Also with *have*. See the note at *get a big send-off*.) □ *Don't work too hard or you'll get a Charley horse.* □ *Poor Tom is always getting a Charley horse in his leg.* □ *Sally can't play. She has a Charley horse.* ALSO: **give someone a Charley horse** to cause a cramp in someone's arm or leg. □ *All this running is giving me a Charley horse.*

get a check-up to have a physical examination by a physician. (Also with *have*. See the note at *get a big send-off*.) □ *She got a check-up yesterday.* □ *I am going to have a check-up in the morning. I hope I'm okay.* ALSO: **give someone a check-up** (for a physician) to give someone a physical examination. □ *The doctor gave her a check-up.*

get a clean bill of health (for someone) to be pronounced healthy by a physician. (Also with *have*. See the note at

get a big send-off.) □ *Sally got a clean bill of health from the doctor.* □ *Now that Sally has a clean bill of health, she can go back to work.* ALSO: **give someone a clean bill of health** (for a doctor) to pronounce someone well and healthy. □ *The doctor gave Sally a clean bill of health.*

get a crush on someone to become infatuated with someone. (Also with *have*. See the note at *get a big send-off*.) □ *Mary thinks she's getting a crush on Bill.* □ *Sally says she'll never get a crush on anyone again.* □ *John's got a crush on Mary.*

get a dirty look from someone to get frowned at by someone. □ *I stopped whistling when I got a dirty look from Ann.* □ *I got a dirty look from the teacher. I don't know why.* ALSO: **give someone a dirty look** (for a person) to frown or make an angry face at someone. □ *Ann gave me a dirty look.* □ *I gave her a dirty look back.*

get a fair shake from someone to get fair treatment from someone. □ *I hope I get a fair shake when my turn comes.* □ *I got a fair shake. I can't complain.* ALSO: **give someone a fair shake** to give someone fair treatment. □ *He's unpleasant, but we have to give him a fair shake.*

get a fix on something (Also with *have*. See the note at *get a big send-off*.) **1.** to find out the exact location of something. □ *I can't get a fix on your location. Where are you?* □ *We are trying to get a fix on your radio transmission.* **2.** to begin to understand the direction of a discussion. □ *I can't quite get a fix on what you're trying to say.* □ *I can't get a fix on where you're going with this argument.* ALSO: **give someone a fix on something** to tell someone the location of something. □ *Please give me a fix on your location.*

get a free hand with something AND **to get a free hand** to be granted complete control over something. □ *I didn't get a free hand with the last project.* □ *John was in charge then, but he didn't have a free hand either.* ALSO: **give someone a free hand with something**; **give someone a free hand** to give someone complete control over something. □ *They gave me a free hand with the project.* □ *I feel proud that they gave me a free hand. That means that they trust my judgement.*

get a grasp of something to understand something. (Also with *good, solid, sound,* as in the examples. Also with *have.* See the note at *get a big send-off.*) □ *Try to get a grasp of the basic rules.* □ *You don't have a good grasp of the principles yet.* □ *John started out with a solid grasp of the methods used in his work.* ALSO: **give someone a grasp of something** to explain something well. □ *Take your time and give her a good grasp of the basic rules.*

get a hand for something AND **get a hand** (Often with *big, good, nice,* etc.) **1.** to receive applause for something. □ *She got a big hand for singing so well.* □ *That kind of performance always gets a good hand.* **2.** See *give someone a hand with something* in the following entry. ALSO: **give someone a hand for something; give someone a hand** to applaud someone for something. □ *After she sang, they gave her a nice hand.* □ *Come on, give them a hand. They did very well.* ALSO: **have a hand for someone or something** (as a request) to please applaud for someone or something. (Informal. Always with *let's,* as in the examples.) □ *Let's have a big hand for Sally and her lovely voice.*

get a hand with something to receive assistance with something. (Also with *have.* See the note at *get a big send-off.*) □ *Mary would really like to get a hand with that. It's too much for one person.* □ *I'd like to have a hand with this.* ALSO: **give someone a hand with something; give someone a hand** to help someone; to give help to someone, often with the hands. □ *Will somebody please give me a hand with this?*

get a handle on something* to find a way to understand something; to find an aid to understanding something. (Informal. Also with *have.* See the note at *get a big send-off.*) □ *Let me try to get a handle on this.* □ *You can't seem to get a handle on what I'm saying.* □ *Now that I have a handle on the concept, I can begin to understand it.*

get a hard time to experience unnecessary difficulties. (Also with *have.* See the note at *get a big send-off.*) □ *I get a hard time every time I come to this store.* □ *I never have a hard time at the store across the street.* ALSO: **give someone a hard time** to give someone unnecessary difficulty. □ *Please don't give me a hard time.*

get a head start on someone or something AND **get a head start 1.** [with *someone*] to start (something) earlier than someone else. (Also with *have.* See the note at *get a big send-off.*) □ *Bill always gets there first because he gets a head start on everybody else.* □ *I'm doing well in my class because I have a head start.* **2.** [with *something*] to start something earlier (than someone else). □ *I was able to get a head start on my reading during the holidays.* □ *If I hadn't had a head start, I'd be behind in my reading.* ALSO: **give someone a head start on someone or something; give someone a head start 1.** [with *someone*] to allow someone to start (something) earlier than someone else. □ *They gave Bill a head start on everyone else, so he got there early.* **2.** [with *something*] to allow someone to start something earlier (than someone else). □ *We'll give you a head start on the project.*

get a hurry on* AND **get a move on*** to start to hurry. (Informal.) □ *We are going to leave in five minutes, Jane. Get a hurry on!* □ *Mary! Get a move on! We can't wait all day.*

get a kick out of someone or something See *get a charge out of someone or something.*

get a licking* AND **take a licking*** to get a spanking; to get beat in a fight. (Folksy.) □ *Billy, you had better get in here if you don't want a licking.* □ *Bob took a real licking in the stock market.* ALSO: **give someone a licking** to beat someone. □ *Bill gave Tom a licking in a fight.*

Get a life!* Don't act so stupid!; find some purpose for existing. (Slang. Usually rude.) □ *Hey stupid! You want to get run over? Get a life!* □ *You worthless jerk! Get a life!*

Get a load of someone or something.* to look at someone or something. (Informal or slang.) □ *Get a load of that guy. Have you ever seen such arrogance?* □ *Get a load of that car. It's got real wire wheels.*

get a load off one's feet* AND **take a load off one's feet*** to sit down; to enjoy the results of sitting down. (Informal.) □ *Come in, John. Sit down and take a load off your feet.* □ *Yes, I need to get a load off my feet. I'm really tired.*

get a load off one's mind* to say what one is thinking; to *speak one's mind.* (Informal.) □ *He sure talked a long time. I guess he had to get a load off his mind.* □ *You aren't going to like what I'm going to say, but I have to get a load off my mind.*

get a lump in one's throat to have the feeling of something in one's throat— as if one were going to cry. (Also with *have.* See the note at *get a big send-off.*) □ *Whenever they play the national anthem, I get a lump in my throat.* □ *I have a lump in my throat because I'm frightened.*

get a move on See *get a hurry on.*

get a pat on the back See *pat someone on the back.*

get a rain check on something AND **get a rain check; take a rain check on something; take a rain check** (Also with *have.* See the note at *get a big send-off.*) **1.** to accept a piece of paper allowing one to see an event— which has been canceled—at a later time. (Originally said of sporting events which had to be canceled because of rain.) □ *The game was canceled because of the storm, but we all got rain checks on it.* □ *I didn't take a rain check because I'm leaving town for a month.* **2.** to accept (or request) a re-issuance of an invitation at a later date. (Said to someone who has invited you to something which you cannot attend now, but would like to attend at a later time.) □ *We would love to come to your house, but we are busy next Saturday. Could we take a rain check on your kind invitation?* □ *Oh, yes. You have a rain check that's good anytime you can come by*

and visit. **3.** to accept a piece of paper which allows one to purchase an item on sale at a later date. (Stores issue these pieces of paper when they run out of specially priced sale merchandise.) □ *The store was all out of the shampoo they advertised, but I got a rain check.* □ *Yes, you should always take a rain check so you can get it at the sale price later when they have more.* ALSO: **give someone a rain check on something; give someone a rain check** **1.** to give someone a piece of paper allowing admission to an event—which has been canceled—at a later time. □ *The game was canceled because of the rain, but they gave everyone rain checks.* **2.** to tell someone that an invitation to a social event will be re-issued at a later date. □ *We couldn't go to the Williams' party, so they gave us a rain check.* **3.** to issue a piece of paper which allows one to purchase an item on sale at a later date. □ *If you have no more of the sale shampoo, will you give me a rain check on it, please?*

get a raw deal* to receive unfair or bad treatment. (Slang.) □ *Mary got a raw deal on her traffic ticket. She was innocent, but she had to pay a big fine.* □ *I bought a used T.V. which worked for two days and then quit. I sure got a raw deal.* ALSO: **give someone a raw deal** to treat someone unfairly or badly. □ *The judge gave Mary a raw deal.* □ *The students think that the teacher gave them a raw deal.*

get a red face to blush from embarrassment. (Also with *have.* See the note at *get a big send-off.*) □ *When I'm embarrassed, I really get a red face.* □ *He's really got a red face now.* □ *He has a red face because he got caught.* ALSO: **give someone a red face** to embarrass someone. □ *We caught him and really gave him a red face.*

get a reputation as a something AND **get a reputation** to acquire notoriety for being something. (Can be a good or a bad reputation. Also with *have.* See the note at *get a big send-off.*) □ *You'll get a reputation as a cheater.* □ *When did you get a reputation as a singer?* □ *Behave yourself, or you'll get a reputa-*

tion. □ *Unfortunately, Tom's got a reputation.* ALSO: **give someone a reputation as a something; give someone a reputation** to cause someone to be notorious for being something. □ *That evening gave him a reputation as a flirt.* □ *Yes, it gave him a reputation.*

get a reputation for doing something AND **get a reputation** to acquire notoriety for doing something. (Often a bad reputation, as in the examples. Also with *have.* See the note at *get a big send-off.*) □ *You'll get a reputation for cheating.* □ *I don't want to get a reputation.* □ *He's got a bad reputation.* □ *I don't have a reputation for cheating.* ALSO: **give someone a reputation for doing something** to cause someone to be notorious for doing something. □ *Her excellent parties gave Jane a reputation for entertaining well.*

get a rise out of someone* to get a response from someone, usually anger or laughter. (Informal.) □ *Mary really liked my joke. I knew I could get a rise out of her.* □ *I got a rise out of him by telling him to go home.*

get a rough idea about something AND **get a rough idea of something; get a rough idea** to receive a general idea; to receive an estimate. (Also with *have.* See the note at *get a big send-off.*) □ *I need to get a rough idea of how many people will be there.* □ *I don't need to know exactly. Just get a rough idea.* □ *Judy's got a rough idea about who'll be there.* □ *I have a rough idea. That's good enough.* ALSO: **give someone a rough idea about something; give someone a rough idea of something; give someone a rough idea** to give someone a general idea or an estimate about something. □ *I don't need to know exactly. Just give me a rough idea about how big it should be.*

get a run for one's money* (Informal.) **1.** to receive what one deserves, expects, or wants. □ *I get a run for my money at a high school football game.* □ *I get a run for my money in the stock market.* **2.** to receive a challenge. □ *Bob got a run for his money when he tried to convince Mary to go to college.* □ *Bill got a run for his money*

playing cards with John. ALSO: **give one a run for one's money 1.** to give one what one deserves, expects, or wants. □ *High school football gives me a run for my money.* □ *I invest in the stock market, and that really gives me a run for my money.* **2.** give one a challenge. □ *That was some argument. Bill gave John a run for his money.* □ *Tom likes to play cards with Mary because she always gives him a run for his money.*

get a shellacking* AND **take a shellacking*** (Slang.) **1.** to receive a beating. □ *The boxer took a shellacking and lost the fight.* □ *I got a shellacking when I broke the window.* **2.** to be beaten—as in sports. □ *Our team played well, but got a shellacking anyway.* □ *I practiced my tennis game so I wouldn't take a shellacking in the tournament.* ALSO: **give someone a shellacking 1.** to beat someone. □ *My dad gave me a shellacking when I broke his fishing rod.* **2.** to beat someone (in a contest). □ *The other team gave us a shellacking.*

get a slap on the wrist to get a light punishment (for doing something wrong). □ *He created quite a disturbance, but he only got a slap on the wrist.* □ *I thought I'd get a slap on the wrist for speeding, but I got fined $200.* ALSO: **give someone a slap on the wrist; slap someone on the wrist; slap someone's wrist** to give someone a light punishment (for doing something wrong). □ *The judge gave her a slap on the wrist for speeding.* □ *The judge should have done more than slap her wrist.*

get a start 1. to receive help starting one's car. □ *My car is stalled. I need to get a start.* □ *I got my car going. I got a start from John.* **2.** to receive training or a big opportunity in beginning one's career. (The same as *get one's start.* Also with *have.* See the note at *get a big send-off.*) □ *She got a start in show business in Cincinnati.* □ *She had a start when she was only four.* ALSO: **give someone a start 1.** to help start someone's car. □ *John gave me a start when my car was stalled.* **2.** to give someone training or a big opportunity in beginning one's career. □ *My career* *began when my father gave me a start in his act.*

get a swelled head to become conceited. (Also with *have*. See the note at *get a big send-off*.) □ *Now that she's famous, she's getting a swelled head.* □ *She's trying not to get a swelled head.* □ *Who else has got a swelled head?* ALSO: **give someone a swelled head** to make someone conceited. □ *Fame gave John a swelled head.*

get a tongue-lashing* to receive a severe scolding. (Folksy. Also with *have*. See the note at *get a big send-off*.) □ *I really got a tongue-lashing when I got home.* □ *I never had a tongue-lashing like that before.* ALSO: **give someone a tongue-lashing*** (Folksy.) to give someone a severe scolding. □ *I gave Bill a real tongue-lashing when he got home late.*

get a word in edgeways See the following entry.

get a word in edgewise AND **get a word in edgeways** to manage to say something when other people are talking and ignoring you. (Often in the negative.) □ *It was such an exciting conversation that I could hardly get a word in edgewise.* □ *Mary talks so fast that nobody can get a word in edgeways.*

get about AND **get around** to move around; to go from place to place. □ *I can't get about without a car.* □ *Aunt Mary cannot get about when her arthritis is troubling her.* □ *It's very hard for some older people to get around.*

get after someone* to remind, scold, or nag someone (to do something). (Informal.) □ *John hasn't taken out the garbage. I'll have to get after him.* □ *Mary's mother will get after her if she doesn't do the dishes.* ALSO: **keep after someone; keep at someone; keep on someone; stay after someone** to remind or nag someone over and over to do something. □ *I'll keep after you until you do it!* □ *Mother stayed after Bill until he did the dishes.* □ *She kept at him until he dried them and put them away.* □ *She kept on him for forty minutes before he finally finished.*

get ahead of someone or something AND **get ahead** to advance; to move

in front (of someone or something). (See also *ahead of someone or something*.) □ *I have to run hard to get ahead of everyone else.* □ *Most people have to work hard to get ahead.* ALSO: **be ahead of someone or something; be ahead; keep ahead of someone or something; keep ahead; stay ahead of someone or something; stay ahead** to maintain a position in front of someone or something. □ *I kept ahead of everyone by running hard.* □ *So that's how you stay ahead.* □ *We have to work hard to keep ahead of inflation.* □ *It takes a lot of energy to be ahead.*

get along to move along. (See also the following four entries.) □ *All right, everybody. Get along! The excitement is over.* □ *I think I had better get along home now.*

get along in years AND **get along** to grow older. □ *Grandfather is getting along in years.* □ *Yes, he's really getting along.*

get along on a shoestring AND **get along** to be able to afford to live on very little money. □ *For the last two years, we have had to get along on a shoestring.* □ *With so little money, it's hard to get along.*

get along with someone AND **get on with someone; get along; get on** to be friends with someone; to cooperate with someone. (See also *get on with someone or something*.) □ *I just can't seem to get along with you.* □ *We must try harder to get along.* □ *How do you get on with John?* □ *Oh, we get on.*

get along without someone or something AND **get along; get along without** to manage without someone or something; to do without someone or something. □ *I don't think I can get along without my secretary.* □ *My secretary just quit, and I don't think I will be able to get along.* □ *I like steak, but I can't afford it. I guess I'll have to get along without.*

get ants in one's pants* AND **get antsy*** to become nervous and agitated. (Slang. As if ants had crawled into one's pants. Also with *have*. See the note at *get a big send-off*.) □ *I always get ants in my pants before a test.* □ *I wonder if all actors get antsy before they go on stage.*

get around **1.** to be experienced; to know a lot about life. (Informal. Use with caution—especially with females—since this can also refer to sexual experience. See also *have been around.*) □ *That's a hard question. I'll ask Jane. She gets around.* □ *John knows a lot about New York City. He gets around.* **2.** See *get about.*

get around to something to find time to do something; to do something after a long delay. □ *I finally got around to buying a new coat.* □ *It takes Sally years to get around to visiting her aunt.*

get at someone or something **1.** AND **have at someone or something** to attack or strike someone or something. (Compare to *go at someone or something.*) □ *The cat jumped over the wall to get at the mouse.* □ *Ok, you guys. There he is. Have at him!* **2.*** [with *something*] AND **have at something*** to eat food; to gobble up food. (Informal.) □ *I can't wait to get at that cake.* □ *Dinner's ready. Sit down and have at it.* **3.** [with *someone*] to find a way to irritate someone; to manage to wound someone, physically or emotionally. □ *Mr. Smith found a way to get at his wife.* □ *John kept trying to get at his teacher.* **4.** [with *something*] to explain or try to explain something; to hint at something. □ *We spent a long time trying to get at the answer.* □ *I can't understand what you're trying to get at.* **5.** [with *something*] to begin to do something; to *get around to something.* □ *I won't be able to get at it until the weekend.* □ *I'll get at it first thing in the morning.*

get away from it all AND **get away** to get away from one's work or daily routine; to go on a vacation. □ *I just love the summer when I can take time off and get away from it all.* □ *Yes, that's the best time to get away.*

get away from someone or something AND **get away** to move away or escape from someone or something; to remove (oneself) from the influence of someone or something. □ *I need to get away from my job for a few days.* □ *Yes, getting away from it would do you good.* □ *Mary needs to get away from her mother.*

ALSO: **keep away from someone or something; keep away; stay away from someone or something; stay away** to remain distant from someone or something. □ *I stayed away from my job for a week.* □ *Was it all right to stay away?* □ *You should keep away from your uncle until you're over your cold.*

get away with something to do something bad and not get punished or found out. (Informal when the *something* refers figuratively to murder.) □ *Tom did it again and didn't get punished. He's always getting away with murder.* □ *Just because she's so popular, she thinks she can get away with anything.* □ *You'll never get away with it.*

get back **1.** to return (from some place). □ *I can get a ride there, but I can't get back.* □ *What time will you get back?* **2.** See *get back to someone.* **3.** See the following entry.

get back at someone AND **get back; have back at someone*** to repay one for a bad deed; to *get even with someone.* (*Have back at someone* is informal or folksy. Compare to *have at someone or something* at *get at someone or something.*) □ *Tom called me a jerk, but I'll get back at him.* □ *I don't know how I'll get back, but I will.* □ *Just wait. I'll have back at you!*

get back on one's feet to become independent again; to become able to *get around* again. (Note the variations with *own* and *two* in the examples.) □ *He was sick for a while, but now he's getting back on his feet.* □ *My parents helped a lot when I lost my job. I'm glad I'm back on my own feet now.* □ *It feels great to be back on my own two feet again.*

get back to someone AND **get back** to continue talking with someone (at a later time); to find out information and tell it to a person (at a later time). □ *I don't have the answer to that question right now. Let me find out and get back to you.* □ *Okay. Please try to get back early tomorrow.*

get behind in something See *fall behind in something.*

get better to improve. □ *I had a bad*

cold, but it's getting better. □ Business was bad last week, but it's getting better. □ I'm sorry you're ill. I hope you get better.

get busy to start working; to work harder or faster. □ The boss is coming. You'd better get busy. □ I've got to get busy and clean this house up. □ Come on, everybody. Let's get busy and get this job done.

get butterflies in one's stomach* to get a nervous feeling in one's stomach. (Informal. Also with have. See the note at get a big send-off.) □ Whenever I have to go on stage, I get butterflies in my stomach. □ She always has butterflies in her stomach before a test. ALSO: **give one butterflies in one's stomach** to cause someone to have a nervous stomach. □ Tests give me butterflies in my stomach.

get by See the next three entries.

get by on something AND **get by** to manage on the least amount. (Compare to get along on a shoestring.) □ We don't have much money. Can we get by on love? □ I'll get by as long as I have you. □ We don't have very much money, but we'll get by.

get by someone or something AND **get by** to manage to move past someone or something. □ I couldn't get by the fat man holding the large package. □ Excuse me, please. I'd like to get by. □ I'd like to get by the car in front, but there is too much traffic.

get by with something AND **get by** 1. to satisfy the minimum requirements. □ I was failing geometry, but managed to get by with a D. □ I took the bar exam and just barely got by. 2. to do something bad and not get caught or punished; to get away with something. □ Tom cheated on the test and got by with it. □ Maybe you can get by like that once or twice, but you'll get caught.

get carried away to be overcome by emotion or enthusiasm (in one's thinking or actions). (Also used literally.) □ Calm down, Jane. Don't get carried away. □ Here, Bill. Take this money and go to the candy store, but don't get carried away.

get close to someone or something AND **get close** (Also used literally.) 1. [with someone] AND **get next to someone** to be close friends with someone; to get to know someone well. □ I would really like to get close to Jane, but she's so unfriendly. □ We talked for hours and hours, but I never felt that we were getting close. □ It's very hard to get next to someone who won't talk to you. 2. [with something] to almost equal something; to be almost as good as something. (Often in the negative.) □ I practiced and practiced, but my bowling couldn't get close to Mary's. □ Her performance was so good that I couldn't get close.

get cold feet to become timid or frightened. (Also with have. See the note at get a big send-off.) □ I usually get cold feet when I have to speak in public. □ John got cold feet and wouldn't run in the race. □ I can't give my speech now. I have cold feet.

get cracking* to get moving; to get busy. (Folksy.) □ Let's go. Come on, get cracking! □ Move it! We don't have all day. Let's get cracking! □ We'll never get finished if you don't get cracking.

get credit for something AND **get credit** to receive praise or recognition for one's role in something. (Especially with a lot of, much, etc., as in the examples.) □ Mary should get a lot of credit for the team's success. □ Each of the team captains should get credit. ALSO: **give someone credit for something; give someone credit** to praise or recognize someone for doing something. □ The coach gave Mary a lot of credit. □ The director gave John much credit for his fine performance.

get dolled up* AND **get all dolled up*** to dress (oneself) up. (Informal. Usually used for females.) □ I have to get all dolled up for the dance tonight. □ I just love to get dolled up in my best clothes.

get down to brass tacks* to begin to talk about important things; to get down to business. (A cliché.) □ Let's get down to brass tacks. We've wasted too much time chatting. □ Don't you think that it's about time to get down to brass tacks?

get down to business AND **get down to**

work to begin to get serious; to begin to negotiate or conduct business. □ *All right everyone. Let's get down to business. There has been enough playing around.* □ *When the president and vice president arrive, we can get down to business.* □ *They're here. Let's get down to work.*

get down to cases to begin to discuss specific matters; to *get down to business.* □ *When we've finished the general discussion, we'll get down to cases.* □ *Now that everyone is here, we can get down to cases.*

get down to something to begin doing some kind of work in earnest. □ *I have to get down to my typing.* □ *John, you get in here this minute and get down to that homework!*

get down to the facts to begin to talk about things that matter; to get to the truth. □ *The judge told that lawyer that the time had come to get down to the facts.* □ *Let's get down to the facts, Mrs. Brown. Where were you on the night of January 16?*

get down to the nitty-gritty* to *get down to the facts*; to *get down to cases.* (Slang.) □ *Stop fooling around. Get down to the nitty-gritty.* □ *Let's stop wasting time. We have to get down to the nitty-gritty.*

get down to work See *get down to business.*

get even with someone AND **get even** to repay someone's bad deed; to *get back at someone.* □ *Bill hit Bob, and Bob got even with Bill by hitting him back.* □ *Some people always have to get even.*

get fresh with someone AND **get fresh** to become overly bold or impertinent. □ *When I tried to kiss Mary, she slapped me and shouted, "Don't get fresh with me!"* □ *I can't stand people who get fresh.*

get goose bumps AND **get goose pimples** (for one's skin) to feel prickly or become bumpy due to fear or excitement. (Also with *have.* See the note at *get a big send-off.*) □ *When he sings, I get goose bumps.* □ *I never get goose pimples.* □ *That really scared her. Now she's got goose pimples.*

get gray hair AND **get gray hairs** to have one's hair turn gray from stress or frustration. □ *I'm getting gray hair because I have three teenage boys.* □ *Oh, Tom, stop it! I'm going to get gray hairs.* ALSO: **give someone gray hair; give someone gray hairs** □ *My three teenage boys are going to give me gray hairs.* □ *Tom has been giving me gray hair for months now.*

get hold of someone or something AND **get a hold of someone or something** (See also *get one's hands on someone or something; get in touch with someone.* Also with *have.* See the note at *get a big send-off.*) **1.** [with *someone*] to make contact with someone; to call someone on the telephone. □ *I'll try to get hold of you in the morning.* □ *It's very hard to get a hold of John. He's so busy.* **2.** [with *something*] to obtain something. □ *I'm trying to get hold of a glass jar. I need it for school.* □ *Does anyone know where I can get a hold of a spare tire?* □ *I have hold of a very large piece of land.* **3.** See *take hold of someone or something.*

get in on something to become associated with something, such as an organization or an idea; to find out or be told about special plans. (Also with *be,* as in the final example.) □ *There is a party upstairs, and I want to get in on it.* □ *I want to get in on your club's activities.* □ *Mary and Jane know a secret, and I want to get in on it.* □ *I'm happy to be in on your celebration.* □ *There is going to be a surprise party, and I'm in on it.*

get in on the ground floor AND **get in** to become associated with something at its start. □ *If you move fast, you can still get in on the ground floor.* □ *A new business is starting up, and I want to get in early.*

get in someone's hair to bother or irritate someone. □ *Billy is always getting in his mother's hair.* □ *I wish you'd stop getting in my hair.*

get in someone's way to interfere with someone's movement or intentions. □ *Tom is going to back out the car. Please don't get in his way.* □ *I intend to run for Congress. You had better not get in my way.*

get in touch with someone AND **get in touch** to make contact with someone; to telephone or write to someone. □ *I have to get in touch with John and ask him to come over for a visit.* □ *Yes, you must try to get in touch.* ALSO: **keep in touch with someone; keep in touch; stay in touch with someone; stay in touch** to retain friendly contact with someone. □ *I try to keep in touch with my cousins.* □ *All our family tries to stay in touch.*

get into a mess* to get into difficulty or confusion. (Informal. Compare to *get out of a mess.*) □ *Try to keep from getting into a mess.* □ *"Hello, Mom," said John on the telephone. "I'm in a mess down at the police station."*

get into an argument with someone to begin to argue with someone. □ *Let's try to discuss this calmly. I don't want to get into an argument with you.* □ *Tom got into an argument with John.* ALSO: **get into an argument** (for two people) to begin arguing. □ *Tom and John got into an argument.* □ *Let's not get into an argument.* ALSO: **have an argument with someone; have an argument** to argue with someone. □ *Tom and John had an argument.* □ *Let's not have an argument.*

get into full swing* AND **get into high gear*** to move into the peak of activity; to start moving fast or efficiently. (Informal.) □ *In the summer months, things really get into full swing around here.* □ *We go skiing in the mountains each winter. Things get into high gear there in November.*

get into high gear See the previous entry.

get into something to get involved in something; to join something. (See also *be into something.*) □ *I'd like to get into your club.* □ *If I could run faster, I'd get into racing.*

get into the swing of things to join into the routine or the activities. □ *Come on, Bill. Try to get into the swing of things.* □ *John just couldn't seem to get into the swing of things.*

get involved with someone or something AND **get involved** 1. to become concerned or associated with someone or something. □ *Why not try to get involved with a sport?* □ *Be careful and don't get involved with the wrong kind of people.* □ *When it comes to drugs, just don't get involved.* 2. [with someone] to become romantically associated with someone. □ *Sally is getting involved with Bill. They've been seeing a lot of each other.* □ *I hope they don't get too involved.* ALSO: **involved with someone or something** 1. to have established an association with someone or something. □ *Bill is involved with swimming and basketball.* □ *Mary is very much involved with her friends.* 2. [with someone] to be romantically attached to someone; to be in love with someone. □ *Tom and Ann are very much involved.* □ *Tom is also involved with Sally.*

get it See *get something.*

get it all together* AND **get it together*** to become fit or organized; to organize one's thinking; to become relaxed and rational. (Slang. Also with *have*. See the note at *get a big send-off.*) □ *Bill seems to be acting more normal now. I think he's getting it all together.* □ *I hope he gets it together soon. His life is a mess.* □ *When Jane has it all together, she really makes sense.* □ *Sally is a lovely person. She really has it together.*

get it in the neck* to receive something bad, such as punishment or criticism. (Slang. Compare to *get it.*) □ *I don't know why I should get it in the neck. I didn't break the window.* □ *Bill got it in the neck for being late.*

get it together See *get it all together.*

get lost 1. to become lost; to lose one's way. □ *We got lost on the way home.* □ *Follow the path, or you might get lost.* 2.* Go away!; Stop being an annoyance! (Slang. Always a command.) □ *Stop bothering me. Get lost!* □ *Get lost! I don't need your help.* □ *Stop following me. Get lost!*

get mad at someone or something AND **get mad** 1. to become angry at someone or something. □ *Don't get mad at me. I didn't do it.* □ *I'm mad at my car. It won't start.* □ *I get mad every time I think about it.* 2.* [with something] to muster all one's physical and mental resources in order to do something. (Informal or slang.) □ *Come on, Bill. If you're going to lift your end of the piano, you're going to have to get mad at it.* □ *The sergeant kept yelling, "Work, work! Push, push! Come on, you guys, get mad!"*

get mixed up to get confused. □ *I get mixed up easily whenever I take a test.* □ *Sorry, I didn't say the right thing. I got mixed up.*

get moving* to get busy; to get started; to work harder or faster. (Informal.) □ *Come on, everybody. Get moving!* □ *The boss is coming. You had better get moving.*

get next to someone See *get close to someone.*

get nowhere fast* to not make progress; to get nowhere. (Informal or slang.) □ *I can't seem to make any progress. No matter what I do, I'm just getting nowhere fast.* □ *Come on. Speed up this car. We're getting nowhere fast.*

get off (See also *get something off.*) **1.** to climb down from; to disembark. □ *Be careful as you get off the bus.* □ *Get off the roof and come down here this minute!* □ *Stop the train! This is where I get off!* **2.** to depart. □ *Our flight got off on time.* □ *We hope to get off about 4:00 in the morning.* **3.*** to become high or intoxicated, as with drug use. (Slang.) □ *John is acting strange. What did he take to get off this time?* □ *John is always getting off on something.* **4.** to escape or avoid punishment (for doing something wrong). □ *It was a serious crime, but Mary got off with a light sentence.* □ *I was afraid that the robber was going to get off completely.* **5.** to start off (on a friendship). (See also *get off on the wrong foot; get off to a bad start.* Compare to *get on.*) □ *Tom and Bill had never met before. They seemed to get off all right, though.* □ *I'm glad they got off so well.*

get off easy AND **get off lightly** to receive very little punishment (for doing something wrong). (See also *slap someone's wrist.*) □ *It was a serious crime, but Mary got off easy.* □ *Billy's punishment was very light. Considering what he did, he got off lightly.*

Get off it!* Don't talk nonsense!; Don't talk like that! (Usually a command.) □ *Get off it, Tom! You don't know that for a fact.* □ *Oh, get off it! You sound so conceited!*

get off lightly See *get off easy.*

get off on the wrong foot AND **get off to a bad start** to start something (such as a friendship) with negative factors. (See also *get off.*) □ *Bill and Tom got off on the wrong foot. They had a minor car accident just before they were introduced.* □ *Let's work hard to be friends. I hate to get off on the wrong foot.* □ *Bill is getting off to a bad start in geometry. He failed the first test.* ALSO: **be off on the wrong foot; be off to a bad start** to have started something with negative factors. □ *I'm sorry we are off to a bad start. I tried to be friendly.*

Get off someone's back! See the following entry.

Get off someone's case!* AND **Get off someone's back!*; Get off someone's tail!*** Leave someone alone!; Stop picking on someone! (Slang. Usually a command.) □ *I'm tired of your criticism, Bill. Get off my case!* □ *Quit picking on her. Get off her back!* □ *Leave me alone! Get off my tail!*

Get off someone's tail! See the previous entry.

get off to a bad start See *get off on the wrong foot.*

get on **1.** to climb aboard; to board or embark. (See also *get on someone or something.*) □ *The bus stopped, and I got on.* □ *Where did you get on?* **2.** See *get on with someone or something.*

get on someone or something **1.** [with *someone*] to pester someone (about something); to pressure someone. □ *John is supposed to empty the trash every day. He didn't do it, so I will have to get on him.* □ *It's time to get on Bill about his homework. He's falling behind.* **2.** [with *something*] to get aboard something; to climb onto something. □ *They just announced that it's time to get on the airplane.*

get on someone's nerves to irritate someone. □ *Please stop whistling. It's getting on my nerves.* □ *All this arguing is getting on their nerves.*

get on the bandwagon* AND **jump on the bandwagon*** to join the popular side (of an issue); to take a popular position. (A cliché.) □ *You really should get on the bandwagon. Everyone else is.* □ *Jane has always had her own ideas about things. She's not the kind of person to jump on the bandwagon.*

get on the good side of someone to get in someone's favor. □ *You had better behave properly if you want to get on the good side of Mary.* □ *If you want to get on the good side of your teacher, you must do your homework.* ALSO: **keep on the good side of someone** to stay in someone's favor. □ *You have to work hard to keep on the good side of the manager.*

get on with someone or something AND **get along with someone or something; get along; get on** 1. [with *someone*] to be friends with someone; to have a good relationship with someone. (The friendship is *always* assumed to be good unless it is stated to be otherwise.) □ *How do you get on with John?* □ *I get along with John just fine.* □ *We get along.* □ *I don't get on with John.* □ *We don't get along.* 2. [with *something*] to continue with something. (See also *keep on with something*.) □ *I must get on with my work.* □ *Now that the crisis is over, I'll get on with my life.*

get one's act together* to get oneself organized, especially mentally. (Slang. Originally from theatrical use. Also with *have*. See the note at *get a big send-off*.) □ *I'm so confused about life. I have to get my act together.* □ *Bill Smith had a hard time getting his act together after his mother's death.* □ *Mary really has her act together. She handles herself very well.*

get one's best shot* (for something) to receive one's best effort. (Slang. Also with *have*. See the note at *get a big send-off*.) □ *The project should succeed. It got my best shot.* □ *It had my best shot. I couldn't have tried harder.* ALSO: **give something one's best shot** to give a task one's best effort. □ *I gave the project my best shot.* □ *Sure, try it. Give it your best shot!*

get one's comeuppance* to get a reprimand; to get the punishment one deserves. (Folksy.) □ *Tom is always insulting people, but he finally got his comeuppance. Bill hit him.* □ *I hope I don't get my comeuppance like that.*

get one's ducks in a row* to put one's affairs in order; to get things ready. (Informal.) □ *You can't hope to go into a company and sell something until you get your ducks in a row.* □ *As soon as you people get your ducks in a row, we'll leave.*

get one's feet on the ground to get firmly established or reestablished. (Also with *have*. See the note at *get a big send-off*.) □ *He's new at the job, but soon he'll get his feet on the ground.* □ *Her productivity will improve after she gets her feet on the ground again.* □ *Don't worry about Sally. She has her feet on the ground.* ALSO: **keep one's feet on the ground** to remain firmly established. □ *Sally will have no trouble keeping her feet on the ground.*

get one's feet wet* to begin something; to have one's first experience of something. (Informal.) (As if one were wading into water.) □ *Of course he can't do the job right. He's hardly got his feet wet yet.* □ *I'm looking forward to learning to drive. I can't wait to get behind the steering wheel and get my feet wet.*

get one's fill of someone or something to receive enough of someone or something. (Also with *have*. See the note at *get a big send-off*.) □ *You'll soon get your fill of Tom. He can be quite a pest.* □ *I can never get my fill of shrimp. I love it.* □ *Three weeks of visiting grandchildren is enough. I've had my fill of them.*

get one's fingers burned to have a bad experience. (Also used literally.) □ *I tried that once before and got my fingers burned. I won't try it again.* □ *If you go swimming and get your fingers burned, you won't want to swim again.*

get one's foot in the door* to achieve a favorable position (for further action); to take the first step in a process. (A cliché. People selling things from door to door used to block the door with a foot, so it could not be closed on them.

Also with *have*. See the note at *get a big send-off*.) □ *I think I could get the job if I could only get my foot in the door.* □ *It pays to get your foot in the door. Try to get an appointment with the boss.* □ *I have a better chance now that I have my foot in the door.*

get one's hands dirty AND **dirty one's hands; soil one's hands** to become involved with something illegal; to do a shameful thing; to do something which is beneath one. □ *The mayor would never get his hands dirty by giving away political favors.* □ *I will not dirty my hands by breaking the law.* □ *Sally felt that to talk to the hobo was to soil her hands.*

get one's hands off someone or something AND **get one's hands off; take one's hands off someone or something; take one's hands off** to release someone or something; to stop touching someone or something. (Also with *have*. See the note at *get a big send-off*.) □ *Get your hands off my bicycle!* □ *Take your hands off me! Come on! Take them off!* □ *Please ask John to get his hands off the window glass.* ALSO: **keep one's hands off someone or something; keep one's hands off** to refrain from touching or handling something. □ *I'm going to put these cookies here. You keep your hands off them.* □ *Get your hands off my book, and keep them off.*

get one's hands on someone or something* AND **lay one's hands on someone or something*** to *get hold of someone or something*; to get someone or something in one's grasp. (Informal. Sometimes said in anger, as if one may wish to do harm.) □ *Just wait until I get my hands on Tom. I'll really give him something to think about.* □ *When I lay my hands on my book again, I'll never lend it to anyone.*

get one's head above water to get ahead of one's problems; to catch up with one's work or responsibilities. (Also used literally. Also with *have*. See the note at *get a big send-off*.) □ *I can't seem to get my head above water. Work just keeps piling up.* □ *I'll be glad when I have my head above water.* ALSO:

keep one's head above water to stay ahead of one's responsibilities. □ *Now that I have more space to work in, I can easily keep my head above water.*

get one's just desserts* to get what one deserves. (A cliché.) □ *I feel better now that Jane got her just desserts. She really insulted me.* □ *Bill got back exactly the treatment which he gave out. He got his just desserts.*

get one's money's worth to get everything which has been paid for; to get the best quality for the money paid. □ *Weigh that package of meat before you buy it. Be sure you're getting your money's worth.* □ *I didn't get my money's worth with my new camera, so I took it back.*

get one's nose out of someone's business to stop interfering in someone else's business; to mind one's own business. □ *Go away! Get your nose out of my business!* □ *Bob just can't seem to get his nose out of other people's business.* ALSO: **keep one's nose out of someone's business** to refrain from interfering in someone else's business. □ *Let John have his privacy, and keep your nose out of my business, too!*

get one's say AND **have one's say** to be able to state one's position; to be able to say what one thinks. □ *I want to have my say on this matter.* □ *He got his say, and then he was happy.*

get one's second wind (Also with *have*. See the note at *get a big send-off*.) **1.** to have one's breathing become stabilized after exerting oneself for a short time. □ *John was having a hard time running until he got his second wind.* □ *Bill had to quit the race because he never got his second wind.* □ *"At last," thought Ann, "I have my second wind. Now I can really swim fast."* **2.** to become more active or productive (after starting off more slowly). □ *I usually get my second wind early in the afternoon.* □ *Mary is a better worker now that she has her second wind.*

get one's start AND **have one's start** to receive the first major opportunity of one's career. □ *I had my start in painting when I was thirty.* □ *She helped me get my start by recommending me* *to the manager.* ALSO: **give someone a start** to give one one's first opportunity. □ *A teacher gave me my start in woodworking.*

get one's teeth into something* to start on something seriously, especially a difficult task. (Informal.) □ *Come on, Bill. You have to get your teeth into your biology.* □ *I can't wait to get my teeth into this problem.*

get one's walking papers See *give one one's walking papers.*

get one's way with someone or something AND **get one's way** to have someone or something follow one's plans; to control someone or something. (Also with *have.* See the note at *get a big send-off.*) □ *The mayor got his way with the city council.* □ *He seldom gets his way.* □ *How often do you have your way with your own money?* □ *Parents usually have their way with their children.*

get one's wits about one to pull oneself together for action; to set one's mind to work, especially in a time of stress. (Also with *have.* See the note at *get a big send-off.*) □ *Let me get my wits about me so I can figure this out.* □ *I don't have my wits about me at this time of the morning.* ALSO: **keep one's wits about one** to keep one's mind operating in a time of stress. □ *If Jane hadn't kept her wits about her during the fire, things could have been much worse.*

get out 1. See *get out of something.* 2.* to go away or leave a place. (Impolite. A command.) □ *Get out! You're a pest.* □ *That's enough from you. Get out!*

get out from under someone or something 1. to come from beneath someone or something. (Also with verbs other than *get,* as in the examples.) □ *Bill was working on the car. When he got out from under it, he was greasy.* □ *After their fall, one skater had to get out from under the other skater.* □ *The snake got out from under the rock.* 2. [with *someone*] to get free of someone's control. □ *Mary wanted to get out from under her mother.* □ *We started our own business because we needed to get out from under our employer.* 3. [with *something*] to get free of a burdensome

problem. □ *I can't go out tonight until I get out from under this pile of homework.* □ *There is so much work to do! I don't know when I'll ever get out from under it.*

get out of a mess* to get free of a bad situation. (Informal. Also with *this, such a,* etc. See the examples. Compare to *get into a mess.*) □ *How can anyone get out of a mess like this?* □ *Please help me get out of this mess!*

get out of someone's way 1. to remove oneself from someone's pathway. □ *Here I come. Please get out of my way.* □ *He intends to go in. Please get out of his way.* 2. to stop interfering with someone's romance. □ *I intend to marry Jane, so please get out of my way.* □ *I had my eyes on Tom before you did. Get out of my way.*

get out of something 1. AND **get out** to leave; to go (out of a place). □ *We didn't get out of the meeting on time.* □ *I got in, but I couldn't get out.* 2. to not have to do something. □ *I was supposed to go to a wedding, but I got out of it.* □ *Jane was called for jury duty, but she got out if it.*

get out of the wrong side of the bed See *get up on the wrong side of the bed.*

get over someone or something 1. to climb over someone or something. □ *Stay still. I think I can get over you. Then I'll help you up.* □ *Somehow, I managed to get over the pile of rocks.* 2. to recover from someone or something. □ *Now that Bob has left me, I have to learn to get over him.* □ *It was a horrible shock. I don't know when I'll get over it.* □ *It was a serious illness. It took two weeks to get over it.*

get physical with someone AND **get physical** 1. to use physical force against someone. □ *The coach got in trouble for getting physical with some members of the team.* □ *When the suspect wouldn't cooperate, the police were forced to get physical.* 2. to touch someone in love-making. □ *I've heard that Bill tends to get physical with his dates.* □ *I don't care if he gets physical—within reason.*

get ready to do something AND **get**

ready to prepare to do something. □ *Get ready to jump!* □ *It's time to get ready to go to work.* □ *It's time to get ready.*

get religion* to become serious (about something), usually after a powerful experience; to develop a strong religious belief. (Folksy.) □ *When I had an automobile accident, I really got religion. Now I'm a very safe driver.* □ *Soldiers often say they got religion in the midst of a battle.*

get rid of someone or something to get free of someone or something; to dispose of or destroy someone or something. (Also with *be,* as in the examples.) □ *I'm trying to get rid of Mr. Smith. He's bothering me.* □ *I'll be happy when I'm rid of my old car.*

get rolling* to get started. (Informal.) □ *Come on. It's time to leave. Let's get rolling!* □ *Bill, it's 6:30. Time to get up and get rolling!*

get second thoughts about someone or something to have doubts about someone or something. (Also with *have.* See the note at *get a big send-off.*) □ *I'm beginning to get second thoughts about Tom.* □ *Tom is getting second thoughts about it, too.* □ *We now have second thoughts about going to Canada.*

get set to get ready; to get organized. (Also with *be,* as in the examples.) □ *We are going to start. Please get set.* □ *We are set. Let's go.* □ *Hurry up and get set!*

get sick **1.** to become ill (perhaps with vomiting). □ *I got sick and couldn't go to school.* □ *My whole family got sick with the flu.* **2.** to vomit. (A euphemism.) □ *Mommy, the dog just got sick on the carpet.* □ *Bill got sick in the hallway.*

get someone off the hook* AND **get off the hook*** to free someone from an obligation. (Informal.) □ *Thanks for getting me off the hook. I didn't want to attend that meeting.* □ *I couldn't get off the hook by myself.*

get someone or something across See *put someone or something across.*

get someone or something down **1.** to manage to lower someone or some-

thing. □ *After a long struggle, we got the flag down and put it away.* □ *Bill was stuck up in the tree until Sally got him down.* **2.** [with *something*] to manage to swallow something, especially something large or unpleasant. □ *The pill was huge, but I got it down.* □ *It was the worst food I have ever had, but I got it down somehow.* **3.** [with *someone*] to depress a person; to make a person very sad. □ *My dog ran away, and it really got me down.* □ *Oh, that's too bad. Don't let it get you down.* ALSO: **keep someone or something down** **1.** to make someone or something stay down or lowered for a period of time. □ *We had to keep the flag down for a month.* □ *Bobby loves to climb trees. We don't know how we are going to keep him down.* **2.** [with *something*] to keep food in one's stomach (without vomiting it up). □ *I don't know how I managed to keep the pill down.* □ *The food must have been spoiled. I couldn't keep it down.* □ *Sally is ill. She can't keep solid food down.* **3.** [with *someone*] to keep someone depressed for a period of time. □ *It's upsetting, but it shouldn't keep you down for days.* □ *Nothing is too upsetting to keep me down very long.*

get someone or something out of one's mind AND **get someone or something out of one's head** to manage to forget someone or something; to stop thinking about or wanting someone or something. (Almost the same as *put someone or something out of one's mind.*) □ *I can't get him out of my mind.* □ *Mary couldn't get the song out of her mind.* □ *Get that silly idea out of your head!*

get someone or something out of the way to move a person or a thing out of a pathway or away. □ *Get that car out of the way.* □ *Please get your children out of the way.* ALSO: **keep someone or something out of the way** to prevent someone or something from getting in the way. □ *Please keep your children out of the way.*

get someone or something started to cause someone or something to start or begin. (Also with *have.* See the note at *get a big send-off.*) □ *Please help me* *get my car started.* □ *Hurry and get the dishwasher started.* □ *I had my car started by 7:00 this morning.* □ *My teacher got me started on the project.*

get someone or something under control to make someone or something manageable, calm, or peaceful. (Also with *have.* See the note at *get a big send-off.*) □ *Mary, calm down. You must get yourself under control.* □ *I think I have the situation under control.* □ *The teacher quickly got the class under control.*

get someone out of a jam* to free someone from a problem or a bad situation. (Informal. Compare to *in a jam.*) □ *I like John. He got me out of a jam once.* □ *I would be glad to help get you out of a jam.* ALSO: **get out of a jam*** to get free from a problem or a bad situation. □ *Would you lend me five dollars? I need it to get out of a jam.*

get someone over a barrel* AND **get someone under one's thumb*** to put someone *at the mercy of someone* else; to get control over someone. (Informal. Also with *have.* See the note at *get a big send-off.*) □ *He got me over a barrel, and I had to do what he said.* □ *Ann will do exactly what I say. I've got her over a barrel.* □ *All right, John. You've got me under your thumb. What do you want me to do?*

get someone under one's thumb See the previous entry.

get someone's back up See the following entry.

get someone's dander up* AND **get someone's back up*; get someone's goat*; get someone's hackles up*; get someone's Irish up*** to make someone get angry. (Informal. Also with *have.* See the note at *get a big send-off.*) □ *Now, don't get your dander up. Calm down.* □ *I insulted him and really got his hackles up.* □ *Bob had his Irish up all day yesterday. I don't know what was wrong.* □ *She really got her back up when I asked her for money.* □ *Now, now, don't get your hackles up. I didn't mean any harm.*

get someone's ear to get someone to listen (to you). (Also with *have.* See the note at *get a big send-off.* Compare to

bend someone's ear.) □ *He got my ear and talked for an hour.* □ *While I have your ear, I'd like to tell you about something I'm selling.*

get someone's eye See *catch someone's eye.*

get someone's goat See *get someone's dander up.*

get someone's hackles up See *get someone's dander up.*

get someone's Irish up See *get someone's dander up.*

get someone's number (Also with *have.* See the note at *get a big send-off.*) **1.** to find out someone's telephone number. □ *As soon as I get Mary's number, I'll call her.* □ *I have her number. Do you want me to write it down for you?* **2.*** to find out about a person; to learn the key to understanding a person. (Informal.) □ *I'm going to get your number if I can. You're a real puzzle.* □ *I've got Tom's number. He's ambitious.*

get something AND **get it** **1.** to receive or procure something. □ *Tom is supposed to catch his train now. I hope he gets it.* □ *I'm going to get an A in biology.* **2.** to receive punishment. □ *Bill broke the window, and he's really going to get it.* □ *John got it for arriving late at school.* **3.** to receive the meaning of a joke; to understand a joke. □ *John told a joke, but I didn't get it.* □ *Bob laughed very hard, but Mary didn't get it.*

get something across to someone AND **get something across** to convey information to someone; to teach someone. □ *I'm trying to get this across to you. Please pay attention.* □ *I'll keep trying until I get it across.*

get something back to receive something (which was already yours). □ *I lent her my algebra book. I don't know when I'll get it back.* □ *I got my watch back from the jeweler today.*

get something in order See *put something into order.*

get something into someone's thick head See *get something through someone's thick skull.*

get something off AND **get off something** **1.** to remove an article of clothing. □ *Bill, hurry and get off your coat* *and come to dinner.* □ *Mommy! I can't get my boots off.* **2.*** to manage to tell a joke or make a wisecrack. (Slang.) □ *The comedian got off one more joke before the curtain came down.* □ *Bob hadn't finished getting off his wisecrack before the teacher came in. He was sent to the principal's office.* **3.** See *get something off the ground.*

get something off one's chest to tell something that has been bothering you. (Also with *have*. See the note at *get a big send-off.*) □ *I have to get this off my chest. I broke your window with a stone.* □ *I knew I'd feel better when I had that off my chest.*

get something off the ground AND **get something off** to get something started. □ *I can relax after I get this project off the ground.* □ *You'll have a lot of free time when you get the project off.*

get something on someone to learn something potentially damaging to a person. (Also with *have*. See the note at *get a big send-off.*) □ *Tom is always trying to get something on me. I can't imagine why.* □ *If he has something on you, he'll have you over a barrel.* □ *If he gets something on you, you ought to get something on him.*

get something out in the open to make something public; to stop hiding a fact or a secret. □ *We had better get this out in the open before the press gets wind of it.* □ *I'll feel better when it's out in the open. I can't stand all of this secrecy.*

get something out of one's system **1.** to get something like food or medicine out of one's body, usually through natural elimination. □ *He'll be more active once he gets the medicine out of his system.* □ *My baby, Mary, ate applesauce and has been crying for three hours. She'll stop when she gets the applesauce out of her system.* **2.** to be rid of the desire to do something; to do something that you have been wanting to do so that you aren't bothered by wanting to do it anymore. □ *I bought a new car. I've been wanting to for a long time. I'm glad I finally got that out of my system.* □ *I can't get it out of my system! I want to go back to school and earn a degree.*

get something out of something to get some kind of benefit from something. □ *I didn't get anything out of the lecture.* □ *I'm always able to get something helpful out of our conversations.*

get something over with AND **get something over** to complete something, especially something you have dreaded. (Also with *have*. See the note at *get a big send-off.*) □ *Oh, please hurry and get it over with. It hurts.* □ *Please get it over. □ When I have this over with, I can relax.*

get something sewed up (See also *sew something up.* Also with *have*. See the note at *get a big send-off.*) **1.** to have something stitched together (by someone). □ *I want to get this tear sewed up now.* □ *I'll have this hole sewed up tomorrow.* **2.** AND **get something wrapped up** to have something settled or finished. (See also *wrap something up.* Also with *have*.) □ *I'll take the contract to the mayor tomorrow morning. I'll get the whole deal sewed up by noon.* □ *Don't worry about the car loan. I'll have it sewed up in time to make the purchase.* □ *I'll get the loan wrapped up, and you'll have the car this week.*

get something straight to understand something clearly. (Informal. Also with *have*. See the note at *get a big send-off.*) □ *Now get this straight. You're going to fail history.* □ *Let me get this straight. I'm supposed to go there in the morning?* □ *Let me make sure I have this straight.*

get something through someone's thick skull* AND **get something into someone's thick head*** to understand something. (Informal.) □ *He can't seem to get it through his thick skull.* □ *If I could get this into my thick head once, I'd remember it.*

get something to go See *buy something to go.*

get something under one's belt* (Informal. Also with *have*. See the note at *get a big send-off.*) **1.** to eat or drink something. (This means the food goes into one's stomach and is under one's belt.) □ *I'd feel a lot better if I had a cool drink under my belt.* □ *Come in* *out of the cold and get a nice warm meal under your belt.* **2.** to learn something well; to assimilate some information. □ *I have to study tonight. I have to get a lot of algebra under my belt.* □ *Now that I have my lessons under my belt, I can rest easy.*

get something underway to get something started. (Also with *have.* See the note at *get a big send-off.*) □ *The time has come to get this meeting underway.* □ *Now that the president has the meeting underway, I can relax.*

get something wrapped up See *get something sewed up.*

get stars in one's eyes to be obsessed with show business; to be stage struck. (Also with *have.* See the note at *get a big send-off.*) □ *Many young people get stars in their eyes at this age.* □ *Ann has stars in her eyes. She wants to go to Hollywood.*

get the advantage of someone AND **get the advantage over someone; get the edge on someone; get the edge over someone** to achieve a position superior to someone else. (The word *the* can be replaced with *an.* See also the special sense at *have the advantage of someone.* Also with *have.* See the note at *get a big send-off.* See also *take advantage of someone or something.*) □ *Toward the end of the race, I got the advantage over Mary.* □ *She'd had an advantage over me since the start of the race.* □ *I got an edge on Sally, too, and she came in second.* □ *It's speed that counts. You can have the edge over everyone, but if you don't have speed, you lose.*

get the air to be ignored or sent away. □ *Whenever I get around Tom, I end up getting the air.* □ *I hate to get the air. It makes me feel unwanted.* ALSO: **give someone the air** □ *Tom always gives me the air. Is there something wrong with me?*

get the ax See *get the sack.*

get the ball rolling* AND **set the ball rolling; start the ball rolling*** to start something; to get some process going. (Informal. Also with *have.* See the note at *get a big send-off.*) □ *If I could just get the ball rolling, then other people*

would help. □ *Who else would start the ball rolling?* □ *I had the ball rolling, but no one helped me with the project.* □ *Ann set the ball rolling, but didn't follow through.* ALSO: **keep the ball rolling** □ *Tom started the project, and we kept the ball rolling.*

get the benefit of the doubt to receive a judgement in your favor when the evidence is neither for you or against you. (Also with *have.* See the note at *get a big send-off.*) □ *I was right between a B and an A. I got the benefit of the doubt—an A.* □ *I thought I should have had the benefit of the doubt, but the judge made me pay a fine.* ALSO: **give someone the benefit of the doubt** □ *I'm glad the teacher gave me the benefit of the doubt.* □ *Please, judge. Give me the benefit of the doubt.*

get the best of someone See the following entry.

get the better of someone AND **get the best of someone** to win out over someone in a competition or bargain. (Also with *have.* See the note at *get a big send-off.*) □ *Bill got the best of John in the boxing match.* □ *I tried to get the better of John, but he won anyway.* □ *I set out to have the better of Sally, but I didn't have enough skill.*

get the blues to become sad or depressed. (Also with *have.* See the note at *get a big send-off.*) □ *You'll have to excuse Bill. He has the blues tonight.* □ *I get the blues every time I hear that song.*

get the boot* to be sent away (from somewhere); to be dismissed from one's employment; to be kicked out (of a place). (Slang. See also *get the sack.*) □ *I guess I wasn't dressed well enough to go in there. I got the boot.* □ *I'll work harder at my job today. I nearly got the boot yesterday.* ALSO: **give someone the boot*** to dismiss someone; to kick someone out (of a place). (Slang.) □ *You had better behave, or they'll give you the boot.*

get the brushoff* to be ignored or sent away; to be rejected. (Slang.) □ *Don't talk to Tom. You'll just get the brushoff.* □ *I went up to her and asked for a date, but I got the brushoff.* ALSO: **give some-**

one the brushoff* to send someone away; to reject someone. (Slang.) □ *Tom wouldn't talk to her. He just gave her the brushoff.*

get the business* to be harassed; to be given a bad time. (Informal.) □ *Whenever I go to that office, I end up getting the business. They are so rude to me!* □ *They are so inefficient. They can't do their jobs right, so you just get the business.* ALSO: **give someone the business*** to harass someone; to give someone a bad time. (Informal.) □ *The people in that office can't answer your question. They just give you the business.*

get the cold shoulder* to be ignored; to be rejected. (Informal.) □ *If you invite her to a party, you'll just get the cold shoulder.* □ *I thought that Sally and I were friends, but lately I've been getting the cold shoulder.* ALSO: **give someone the cold shoulder** to ignore someone; to reject someone. (Informal.) □ *She gave me the cold shoulder when I asked her to the party.* □ *Sally has been giving me the cold shoulder.*

get the creeps* AND **get the willies*** to become frightened; to become uneasy. (Slang.) (Also with *have*. See the note at *get a big send-off*.) □ *I get the creeps when I see that old house.* □ *I really had the willies when I went down into the basement.* ALSO: **give someone the creeps***; **give someone the willies*** to make someone uneasy; to frighten someone. (Informal.) □ *That old house gives me the creeps.* □ *That strange old man gives him the willies.*

get the day off to have a day free from working. (Also with *have*. See the note at *get a big send-off*. See also *take the day off*.) □ *The next time I get a day off, we'll go to the zoo.* □ *I have the day off. Let's go to the zoo.*

get the devil* AND **catch hell***; **catch the devil***; **get hell*** to receive a severe scolding. (Informal. Use *hell* with caution.) □ *Bill is always getting the devil about something.* □ *I'm late. If I don't get home soon, I'll catch hell!* □ *I caught the devil yesterday for being late.* ALSO: **give someone the devil***; **give someone hell*** to scold someone severely.

(Informal. Use *hell* with caution.) □ *I'm going to give Bill hell when he gets home. He's late again.* □ *Bill, why do I always have to give you the devil?*

get the edge on someone See *get the advantage of someone*.

get the feel of something (for someone) to learn the way something feels (when it is used). (Also with *have*. See the note at *get a big send-off*. See also the special sense at *have the feel of something*.) □ *I haven't yet got the feel of this bat. I hope I don't strike out.* □ *I can drive better now that I have the feel of this car's steering.*

get the floor to receive official permission to address the audience. (Also with *have*. See the note at *get a big send-off*.) □ *When I get the floor, I'll make a short speech.* □ *The last time you had the floor, you talked for an hour.*

get the gate* to be sent away; to be rejected. (Slang.) □ *I thought he liked me, but I got the gate.* □ *I was afraid I'd get the gate, and I was right.* ALSO: **give someone the gate*** to send someone away; to reject someone. (Slang.) □ *Not only was he not friendly, he gave me the gate.*

get the glad hand* to receive an overly friendly welcome; to receive insincere attention. (Informal.) □ *Whenever I go into that store, I get the glad hand.* □ *I hate to go to a party and get the glad hand.* ALSO: **give someone the glad hand*** to give someone an overly friendly welcome; to give someone insincere attention. (Informal.) □ *Here comes Tom. Watch him give us the glad hand and leave.*

get the go-ahead AND **get the green light** to receive a signal to start or continue. □ *We have to wait here until we get the go-ahead.* □ *I hope we get the green light on our project soon.* ALSO: **give someone the go ahead**; **give someone the green light** to give someone the signal to start or continue. □ *It's time to start work. Give everybody the go-ahead.* □ *They gave us the green light to start.*

get the go-by* to be ignored or passed by. (Slang.) □ *It was my turn, but I got the go-by.* □ *Tom stood on the road for* *fifteen minutes trying to get a ride, but all he could get was the go-by.* ALSO: **give someone the go-by*** to pass by or ignore someone. (Slang.) □ *I could see that Tom wanted a ride, but I gave him the go-by.*

get the goods on someone* to find out something potentially damaging or embarrassing about someone. (Slang. Also with *have.* See the note at *get a big send-off.*) □ *John beat me unfairly in tennis, but I'll get even. I'll get the goods on him and his cheating.* □ *The authorities have the goods on Mr. Smith. He has been selling worthless land again.*

get the green light See *get the go-ahead.*

get the hang of something* to learn how to do something; to learn how something works. (Informal. Also with *have.* See the note at *get a big send-off.*) □ *As soon as I get the hang of this computer, I'll be able to work faster.* □ *Now that I have the hang of starting the car in cold weather, I won't have to get up so early.*

get the hard sell* to receive considerable pressure to buy or accept (something). (Informal.) □ *I won't go to that store again. I really got the hard sell.* □ *You'll probably get the hard sell if you go to a used car dealer.* ALSO: **give someone the hard sell*** to put pressure on someone to buy or accept (something). (Informal.) □ *They gave me the hard sell, but I still wouldn't buy the car.*

get the high sign to receive a prearranged signal. (Often refers to a hand signal or some other visual signal.) □ *When I got the high sign, I pulled cautiously out into the roadway.* □ *The train's engineer got the high sign, and began to move the train out of the station.* ALSO: **give someone the high sign** to give someone a prearranged signal. □ *As the robber walked past me, I gave the police officer a high sign. Then the officer arrested the robber.*

get the inside track to get the advantage (over someone) because of special connections, special knowledge, or favoritism. (Also with *have.* See the note at *get a big send-off.*) □ *If I could get the inside track, I could win the con-*

tract. □ *The boss likes me. Since I have the inside track, I'll probably be the new office manager.*

get the jump on someone to do something before someone; to get ahead of someone. (Also with *have.* See the note at *get a big send-off.*) □ *I got the jump on Tom and got a place in line ahead of him.* □ *We'll have to work hard to get the contract, because they have the jump on us.*

get the last laugh* to laugh at or ridicule someone who has laughed at or ridiculed you; to put someone in the same bad position that you were once in; to *turn the tables on someone.* (A cliché. Also with *have.* See the note at *get a big send-off.*) □ *John laughed when I got a D on the final exam. I got the last laugh, though. He failed the course.* □ *Mr. Smith said I was foolish when I bought an old building. I had the last laugh when I sold it a month later for twice what I paid for it.*

get the last word AND **get the final word** to get to make the final point (in an argument); to get to make the final decision (in some matter). (Also with *have.* See the note at *get a big send-off.*) □ *The boss gets the last word in hiring.* □ *Why do you always have to have the final word in an argument?*

get the lead out* AND **shake the lead out*** to hurry; to move faster. (Slang. This means to get the lead weights out of your pants so you can move faster.) □ *Come on, you guys. Get the lead out!* □ *If you're going to sell cars, you're going to have to shake the lead out.*

get the low-down on someone or something* AND **get the low-down*** to receive the full story about someone or something. (Slang.) □ *I need to get the low-down on John. Is he still an accountant?* □ *Sally wants to get the low-down on the new expressway. Please tell her all about it.* ALSO: **give someone the low-down on someone or something*** to tell someone the full story about someone or something. (Slang.) □ *Please give Sally the low-down on the new expressway.*

get the message See *get the word.*
get the nod* to get chosen. (Informal.

Also with *have*. See the note at *get a big send-off*.) □ *The manager is going to pick the new sales manager. I think Ann will get the nod.* □ *I had the nod for captain of the team, but I decided not to do it.*

get the old heave-ho* AND **get the heave-ho*** to get thrown out (of a place); to get dismissed (from one's employment). (Informal. From nautical use where sailors used *heave-ho* to coordinate hard physical labor. One sailor called *heave-ho*, and all the sailors would pull at the same time on the *ho*. Also with *have*. See the note at *get a big send-off*.) □ *I went there to buy a record album, but I got the old heave-ho. That's right. They threw me out!* □ *They fired a number of people today, but I didn't get the heave-ho.* □ *John had the old heave-ho last week. Now he's unemployed.* ALSO: **give someone the old heave-ho***; **give someone the heave-ho*** to throw someone out (of a place); to fire someone. (Informal.) □ *We gave Jane the old heave-ho today.* □ *John was behaving badly at our party, so my father gave him the heave-ho.*

get the once-over to receive a quick visual examination. (With variations, as in the examples.) □ *Every time John walks by I get the once-over. Does he like me?* □ *I went to the doctor yesterday, but I only had a once-over lightly.* □ *I wanted a complete examination, not just a once-over.* ALSO: **give someone the once-over** to examine someone visually quickly. □ *John gives me the once-over every time he walks by me.* □ *Why does he just give me the once-over? Why doesn't he say hello?*

get the picture* to understand the whole situation. (Informal or slang.) □ *Okay, Bob. That's the whole explanation. You get the picture?* □ *Yes, I got the picture.*

get the red carpet treatment to receive very special treatment; to receive royal treatment. (This refers—sometimes literally—to the rolling out of a clean red carpet for someone to walk on.) □ *I love to go to fancy stores where I get the red carpet treatment.* □ *The queen*

expects to get the red carpet treatment wherever she goes. ALSO: **give someone the red carpet treatment** to give someone very special treatment; to give someone royal treatment. □ *We always give the queen the red carpet treatment when she comes to visit.* ALSO: **roll out the red carpet for someone** to provide special treatment for someone. □ *There's no need to roll out the red carpet for me.* □ *We rolled out the red carpet for the king and queen.*

get the runaround to receive a series of excuses, delays, and referrals. □ *You'll get the runaround if you ask to see the manager.* □ *I hate it when I get the runaround.* ALSO: **give someone the runaround** to give someone a series of excuses, delays, and referrals. □ *If you ask to see the manager, they'll give you the runaround.*

get the sack* AND **get the ax*** to get fired; to be dismissed (from one's employment). (Slang.) □ *I got the sack yesterday. Now I have to find a new job.* □ *I tried to work harder, but I got the ax anyway.* ALSO: **give someone the ax**; **give someone the sack** to fire someone; to terminate someone's employment. □ *I gave Tom the sack, and he has to find a new job.* □ *I had to give three people the ax yesterday. We are having to reduce our office staff.*

get the shock of one's life* to receive a serious (emotional) shock. (A cliché. Also with *have*. See the note at *get a big send-off*.) □ *I opened the telegram and got the shock of my life.* □ *I had the shock of my life when I won $5,000.*

get the short end of the stick* AND **end up with the short end of the stick*** to end up with less (than someone else); to end up cheated or deceived. (A cliché. Also with *have*. See the note at *get a big send-off*.) □ *Why do I always get the short end of the stick? I want my fair share!* □ *She's unhappy because she has the short end of the stick again.* □ *I hate to end up with the short end of the stick.*

get the show on the road* to get (something) started. (Slang.) □ *Hurry up, you guys. Let's get the show on the road.* □

If you don't get the show on the road right now, we'll never finish today.

get the slip* (for someone) to elude or escape (someone). (Slang.) □ *We followed her for two blocks, and then got the slip.* □ *The police got the slip, and the criminal got away.* ALSO: **give someone the slip*** to escape from or elude someone. (Slang.) □ *We followed her for two blocks, and then she gave us the slip.*

get the third degree* to be questioned in great detail for a long period. (Slang.) □ *Why is it I get the third degree from you every time I come home late?* □ *Poor Sally spent all night at the police station getting the third degree.* ALSO: **give someone the third degree*** to question someone in great detail for a long period. (Slang.) □ *The police gave Sally the third degree.*

get the upper hand on someone AND **get the upper hand** to get into a position superior to someone; to *get the advantage of someone.* (Also with *have.* See the note at *get a big send-off.*) □ *John is always trying to get the upper hand on someone.* □ *He never ends up having the upper hand, though.*

get the word* AND **get the message*** to receive an explanation; to receive the final and authoritative explanation. (Informal. Also with *have.* See the note at *get a big send-off.*) □ *I'm sorry, I didn't get the word. I didn't know the matter had been settled.* □ *Now that I have the message, I can be more effective in answering questions.*

get the works* to receive a lot of something. (Slang. The *works* can be a lot of food, good treatment, bad treatment, etc.) □ BILL: *Shall we order a snack or a big meal?* JANE: *I'm hungry. Let's get the works.* □ *But, your honor. I shouldn't get the works. I only drove too fast!* ALSO: **give someone the works*** to give someone the full amount or the full treatment. (Slang.) □ *The judge gave her the works for driving too fast.*

get the worst of something to experience the worst aspects of something. (Also with *have.* See the note at *get a big send-off.*) □ *No matter what happens at the office, I seem to get the worst*

of it. □ *He always gets the worst of the bargain.* □ *I got to choose which one I wanted, but I still got the worst of the two.*

get through something 1. to finish something; to work one's way through something. (Compare to *get through with something.*) □ *If I read fast, I can get through this book in an hour.* □ *I don't think I can get through all this work by quitting time.* 2. to survive something; to *go through something.* □ *This is a busy day. I don't know how I'll get through it.* □ *Sally hopes to get through college in three years.*

get through to someone AND **get through** 1. to reach someone; to manage to communicate to someone. □ *I called her on the telephone time after time, but I couldn't get through to her.* □ *I tried every kind of communication, but I couldn't get through.* 2. to pass through (something). □ *The crowd was so thick that I couldn't get through to him.* □ *I tried, but I couldn't get through. The crowd was too heavy.* 3. to make someone understand something; to *get something through someone's thick skull.* □ *Why don't you try to understand me? What do I have to do to get through to you?* □ *Can anybody get through, or are you just stubborn?* □ *Ann is still too sick to understand what I'm saying. Maybe I can get through to her tomorrow.*

get through with something to get finished with something. (Compare to *get through something.*) □ *You can use this pencil when I'm through with it.* □ *Can I have the salt when you're through with it?*

get time for someone or something AND **find time for someone or something** to set aside time for someone or something. (Also with *have.* See the note at *get a big send-off.*) □ *I don't have time for it now. I'll try to do it later.* □ *I'll try to find time for you tomorrow.*

get time off to receive a period of time which is free from employment. (Compare to *get the day off.* See *take time off.* Also with *have.* See the note at *get a big send-off.*) □ *I'll have to get time off for jury duty.* □ *I got time off to go* *downtown and shop.* □ *I don't have time off from work very often.* ALSO: **get time off for good behavior** to have one's prison sentence shortened because of good behavior. □ *Bob will get out of jail tomorrow rather than next week. He got time off for good behavior.*

get time to catch one's breath to find enough time to relax or behave normally. (Also with *have.* See the note at *get a big send-off.*) □ *When things slow down around here, I'll get time to catch my breath.* □ *Sally was so busy she didn't even have time to catch her breath.*

get to first base with someone or something* AND **get to first base; reach first base with someone or something*; reach first base*** to make a major advance with someone or something. (Informal. *First base* refers to baseball.) □ *I wish I could get to first base with this business deal.* □ *John adores Sally, but he can't even reach first base with her. She won't even speak to him.* □ *He smiles and acts friendly, but he can't get to first base.*

get to one's feet to stand up. □ *On a signal from the director, the singers got to their feet.* □ *I was so weak, I could hardly get to my feet.*

get to the bottom of something to get an understanding of the causes of something. □ *We must get to the bottom of this problem immediately.* □ *There is clearly something wrong here, and I want to get to the bottom of it.*

get to the heart of the matter* AND **get at the heart of the matter*** to get to the essentials of a matter. (A cliché.) □ *We have to stop wasting time and get to the heart of the matter.* □ *You've been very helpful. You really seem to be able to get at the heart of the matter.*

get to the point See *come to the point.*

get together to meet with someone; to come together for a social occasion. □ *We are going to get together with the Smiths for bridge next Thursday.* □ *It's good to see you, Bill. We'll have to get together again soon.*

get tough with someone AND **get tough** to become firm with someone; to use physical force against someone. (Compare to *get physical with someone.*) □

The teacher had to get tough with the class because the students were acting badly. □ *I've tried to get you to behave, but it looks like I'll have to get tough.*

get two strikes against one to get a number of things against one; to be in a position where success is unlikely. (From baseball where one is "out" after three strikes. Also with *have.* See the note at *get a big send-off.*) □ *Poor Bob got two strikes against him when he tried to explain where he was last night.* □ *I can't win. I've got two strikes against me before I start.*

get under someone's skin* to bother or irritate someone. (Informal.) □ *John is so annoying. He really gets under my skin.* □ *I know he's bothersome, but don't let him get under your skin.*

get underway to start going; to start. (The word *get* can be replaced with *be.* Compare to *get something underway.*) □ *The ship is leaving soon. It's about to get underway.* □ *Let us get our journey underway.* □ *I'm glad our project is underway.*

get up to wake up and get out of bed. □ *What time do you usually get up?* □ *I get up when I have to.*

get-up-and-go energy; motivation. □ *I must be getting old. I just don't have my old get-up-and-go.* □ *A good breakfast will give you lots of get-up-and-go.*

get up enough nerve to do something AND **get up enough nerve** to get brave enough to do something. □ *I could never get up enough nerve to sing in public.* □ *I'd do it if I could get up enough nerve, but I'm shy.*

get up on the wrong side of the bed AND **get out of the wrong side of the bed** to get up in the morning in a bad mood. □ *What's wrong with you? Did you get up on the wrong side of the bed today?* □ *Excuse me for being grouchy. I got out of the wrong side of the bed.*

get used to someone or something to become accustomed to someone or something. □ *I got used to being short many years ago.* □ *John is nice, but I really can't get used to him. He talks too much.*

get well to become healthy again. □ *Ann had a cold for a week, and then she got well.* □ *Hurry up and get well!*

get wet to become soaked with water. (See also *all wet*.) □ *Get out of the rain or you'll get wet.* □ *Don't get wet, or you'll catch a cold.*

get what for* to get scolded. (Folksy.) □ *If I don't get home on time, I'm really going to get what for.* □ *Billy, if you don't want to get what for, you had better get in this house now.* ALSO: **give someone what for*** to scold someone. (Folksy.) □ *Billy's mother gave him what for because he didn't get home on time.*

get what's coming to one* to get what one deserves. (A cliché.) □ *If you cheat, you'll get in trouble. You'll get what's coming to you.* □ *Billy got what was coming to him.* ALSO: **give one what's coming to one** to give one what one deserves. □ *I'm here to be paid. Give me what's coming to me.*

get wind of something* to hear about something; to receive information about something. (Informal.) □ *I just got wind of your marriage. Congratulations.* □ *Wait until the boss gets wind of this. Somebody is going to get in trouble.*

get wise to someone or something* AND **get wise*** to find out about someone or something; to see through the deception of someone or something. (Informal or slang.) □ *Watch out, John. Your friends are getting wise to your tricks.* □ *John's friends are getting wise. He had better watch out.*

get with something* (Slang. Usually with *it*.) **1.** to become alert. □ *Hey, stupid. Get with it!* □ *Wake up, Bill. Get with what's going on!* **2.** to get up to date on something. □ *You're too old fashioned, Mary. Get with it!* □ *Tom just couldn't get with the newest dance fad.* ALSO: **with it*** (Slang.) **1.** alert and knowledgeable. □ *Jane isn't making any sense. She's not really with it tonight.* □ *When it comes to jazz, John is really with it.* **2.** up-to-date. □ *My parents are so old fashioned. I'm sure they were never with it.* □ *Why do you wear those baggy old clothes? Why aren't you with it?*

get worked up over something AND **get worked up about something; get worked up** to get excited or emotionally distressed about something. □ *Please don't get worked up over this matter.* □ *They get worked up about these things very easily.* □ *I try not to get worked up.*

ghost of a chance* even the slightest chance. (Slang.) □ *She can't do it. She doesn't have a ghost of a chance.* □ *There is just a ghost of a chance that I'll be there on time.*

gild the lily* to add ornament or decoration to something which is pleasing in its original state; to attempt to improve something which is already fine the way it is. (A cliché. Often refers to flattery or exaggeration.) □ *Your house has lovely brickwork. Don't paint it. That would be gilding the lily.* □ *Oh, Sally. You're beautiful the way you are. You don't need makeup. You would be gilding the lily.*

gird one's loins* AND **gird up one's loins*** to get ready; to prepare oneself (for something). (A cliché.) □ *Well, I guess I had better gird up my loins and go to work.* □ *Somebody has to do something about the problem. Why don't you gird your loins and do something?*

give a good account of oneself to do (something) well or thoroughly. □ *John gave a good account of himself when he gave his speech last night.* □ *Mary was not hungry, and she didn't give a good account of herself at dinner.*

give an account of someone or something AND **give someone an account of someone or something** to tell (someone) about someone or something. □ *Mary gave an account of Bill's trip to town.* □ *She gave Ann an account of Bill's trip.* □ *We gave them an account of the new teacher.*

give an ear to someone or something AND **give ear to someone or something; give one's ear to someone or something** to listen to someone or to what someone is saying. (Compare to *get someone's ear*.) □ *I gave an ear to Mary so she could tell me her problems.* □ *She wouldn't give her ear to my story.* □ *He gave ear to the man's request.*

give as good as one gets to give as much as one receives; to pay someone back *in kind*. (Usually in the present tense.) □ *John can take care of himself in a fight. He can give as good as he gets.* □ *Sally usually wins a formal debate. She gives as good as she gets.*

give birth to someone or something
1. AND **give birth** to bear a child. □ *The mother gave birth to her second child last week.* □ *She gave birth last week.* **2.** to give rise to or start something. □ *The composer gave birth to a new kind of music.* □ *They gave birth to a new view of language.*

give chase to someone or something AND **give chase** to chase someone or something. □ *The dogs gave chase to the fox.* □ *A mouse ran by, but the cat was too tired to give chase.* □ *The police gave chase to the robber.*

give credence to something to believe something. □ *He tells lies. Don't give credence to what he says.* □ *Please don't give credence to Mary. She doesn't know what she's talking about.*

give credit where credit is due* to give credit to someone who deserves it; to acknowledge or thank someone who deserves it. (A cliché.) □ *We must give credit where credit is due. Thank you very much, Sally.* □ *Let's give credit where credit is due. Mary is the one who wrote the report, not Jane.*

give free rein to someone AND **give someone free rein** to allow someone to be completely in charge (of something). (See also *get a free hand with something*.) □ *The boss gave the manager free rein with the new project.* □ *The principal gave free rein to Mrs. Brown in her classes.*

give ground to retreat (literally or figuratively). □ *When I argue with Mary, she never gives ground.* □ *I approached the barking dog, but it wouldn't give ground.*

give in to someone or something AND **give in** to yield to someone or something; to give up to someone or something. □ *He argued and argued and finally gave in to my demands.* □ *I thought he'd never give in.*

give it the gun* AND **give her the gun*** to make a motor or engine run faster; to rev up an engine. (Informal or slang. The *her* is often pronounced *'er*.) □

BILL: *How fast will this thing go?* BOB: *I'll give it the gun and see.* □ *Hurry up, driver. Give 'er the gun. I've got to get there immediately.*

give it to someone* AND **give it to someone straight*** to tell something to someone clearly and directly. (Informal.) □ *Come on, give it to me straight. I want to know exactly what happened.* □ *Quit wasting time, and tell me. Give it to me now.*

give of oneself to be generous with one's time and concern. □ *Tom is very good with children because he gives of himself.* □ *If you want to have more friends, you have to learn to give of yourself.*

give one a run for one's money See *get a run for one's money.*

Give one an inch, and one will take a mile.* AND **If you give one an inch, one will take a mile.*** a proverb meaning that a person who is granted a little of something (such as a reprieve or lenience) will want more. (A cliché.) □ *I told John he could turn in his paper one day late, but he turned it in three days late. Give him an inch, and he'll take a mile.* □ *First we let John borrow our car for a day. Now he wants to go on a two-week vacation. If you give him an inch, he'll take a mile.*

give one butterflies in one's stomach See *get butterflies in one's stomach.*

give one one's freedom to set someone free; to divorce someone. □ *Mrs. Brown wanted to give her husband his freedom.* □ *Well, Tom, I hate to break it to you this way, but I have decided to give you your freedom.*

give one one's walking papers* to fire someone; to *give someone the sack.* (Informal.) □ *Tom has proved unsatisfactory. I decided to give him his walking papers.* □ *We might even give Sally her walking papers, too.* ALSO: **get one's walking papers*** to get fired. (Informal.) □ *Well, I'm through. I got my walking papers today.* □ *They are closing down my department. I guess I'll get my walking papers soon.*

give one's right arm for someone or something* AND **give one's right arm*** to be willing to give something of great value for someone or something. (A cliché. Never literal.) □ *I'd give my right arm for a nice cool drink.* □ *I'd give my right arm to be there.* □ *Tom really admired John. Tom would give his right arm for John.*

give oneself airs to act conceited or superior. □ *Sally is always giving herself airs. You'd think she had royal blood.* □ *Come on, John. Don't act so haughty. Stop giving yourself airs.*

give oneself up to someone or something AND **give oneself up** to surrender or yield to someone or something. □ *The suspect gave himself up to the police.* □ *She was innocent, but she gave herself up.* □ *The painter gave himself up to his work.*

give out to wear out; to become exhausted and stop. □ *The old lady's heart finally gave out.* □ *Our television set gave out right in the middle of my favorite program.* □ *Bill gave out in the middle of the race.*

give out with something* to utter or say something. (Informal. Also with *have.* See the example below.) □ *Suddenly, the dog gave out with a horrible growl.* □ *At that point, John gave out with a comment about how boring it all was.* □ *Come on, tell me. Have out with it!*

give rise to something to cause something. □ *The bad performance gave rise to many complaints.* □ *The new law gave rise to violence in the cities.*

give someone a bang See *get a charge out of someone or something.*

give someone a big send-off See *get a big send-off.*

give someone a black eye See *get a black eye.*

give someone a break See *get a break.*

give someone a buzz See *give someone a ring.*

give someone a check-up See *get a check-up.*

give someone a clean bill of health See *get a clean bill of health.*

give someone a dirty look See *get a dirty look from someone.*

give someone a fair shake See *get a fair shake from someone.*

give someone a free hand with some-

thing See *get a free hand with something.*

give someone a grasp of something See *get a grasp of something.*

give someone a hand for something See *get a hand for something.*

give someone a hand with something See *get a hand with something.*

give someone a hard time See *get a hard time.*

give someone a head start on someone or something See *get a head start on someone or something.*

give someone a licking See *get a licking.*

give someone a line AND **feed somebody a line** to lead someone on; to deceive someone with false talk. □ *Don't pay any attention to John. He gives everybody a line.* □ *He's always feeding somebody a line.*

give someone a pain* to annoy or bother someone. (Slang.) □ *Here comes Sally. Oh, she gives me a pain.* □ *She's such a pest. She really gives me a pain.*

give someone a pat on the back See *pat someone on the back.*

give someone a piece of one's mind* to bawl someone out; to *tell someone off.* (A cliché.) □ *I've had enough from John. I'm going to give him a piece of my mind.* □ *Sally, stop it, or I'll give you a piece of my mind.*

give someone a rain check See *get a rain check.*

give someone a raw deal See *get a raw deal.*

give someone a red face See *get a red face.*

give someone a reputation as a something See *get a reputation as something.*

give someone a reputation for doing something See *get a reputation for doing something.*

give someone a ring* AND **give someone a buzz*** to call someone on the telephone. (Informal.) □ *Nice talking to you. Give me a ring some time.* □ *Give me a buzz when you're in town.*

give someone a rough idea about something See *get a rough idea about something.*

give someone a shellacking See *get a shellacking.*

give someone a slap on the wrist See *get a slap on the wrist.*

give someone a start See *get a start; get one's start.*

give someone a swelled head See *get a swelled head.*

give someone a tongue-lashing See *get a tongue-lashing.*

give someone credit for something See *get credit for something.*

give someone gray hair See *get gray hair.*

give someone hell See *get the devil.*

give someone or something a wide berth to keep a reasonable distance from someone or something; to *steer clear of someone or something.* (Originally referred to sailing ships.) □ *The dog we are approaching is very mean. Better give it a wide berth.* □ *Give Mary a wide berth. She's in a very bad mood.*

give someone or something away 1. to reveal a secret about someone or something. □ *I thought no one knew where I was, but my breathing gave me away.* □ *We know that Billy ate the cherry pie. The cherry juice on his shirt gave him away.* □ *I had planned a surprise, but John gave it away.* **2.** AND **give away something** [with *something*] to make a gift of something. (See also *give the bride away.*) □ *Mary gave away the cherry pie.* □ *Mary gave it away.*

give someone or something the once-over See *get the once-over.*

give someone or something up AND **give up someone or something** to release or relinquish someone or something; to give someone or something (to someone else). □ *Tom loved Ann very much, but he had to give her up.* □ *John was forced to give up smoking.*

give someone pause to cause someone to stop and think. □ *When I see a golden sunrise, it gives me pause.* □ *Witnessing an accident is likely to give all of us pause.*

give someone some skin* (for two people) to touch two hands together in a special greeting, like a hand-shake. (Slang. One hand may be slapped down on top of the other, or they may be slapped together palm to palm with the arms held vertically. Usually said as a command.) □ *Hey Bob, give me some skin!* □ *Come over here, you guys. I want you to meet my brother and give him some skin!*

give someone the air See *get the air.*

give someone the ax See *get the sack.*

give someone the benefit of the doubt See *get the benefit of the doubt.*

give someone the boot See *get the boot.*

give someone the brushoff See *get the brushoff.*

give someone the business See *get the business.*

give someone the cold shoulder See *get the cold shoulder.*

give someone the creeps See *get the creeps.*

give someone the eye* to look at someone in a way that communicates romantic interest. (Informal. See also *catch someone's eye.*) □ *Ann gave John the eye. It really surprised him.* □ *Tom kept giving Sally the eye. She finally left.*

give someone the gate See *get the gate.*

give someone the glad hand See *get the glad hand.*

give someone the go-ahead See *get the go-ahead.*

give someone the go-by See *get the go-by.*

give someone the green light See *get the go-ahead.*

give someone the hard sell See *get the hard sell.*

give someone the high sign See *get the high sign.*

give someone the low-down on someone or something See *get the low-down on someone or something.*

give someone the old heave-ho See *get the old heave-ho.*

give someone the red carpet treatment See *get the red carpet treatment.*

give someone the runaround See *get the runaround.*

give someone the sack See *get the sack.*

give someone the shirt off one's back* to be very generous or solicitous to someone. (A cliché.) □ *Tom really likes Bill. He'd give Bill the shirt off his back.* □ *John is so friendly that he'd give anyone the shirt off his back.*

give someone the slip See *get the slip.*

give someone the third degree See *get the third degree.*

give someone the willies See *get the creeps.*

give someone the works See *get the works.*

give someone tit for tat* to give someone something equal to what was given you; to exchange a series of things, one by one with someone. (Informal.) □ *They gave me the same kind of difficulty that I gave them. They gave me tit for tat.* □ *He punched me, so I punched him. Every time he hit me, I hit him. I just gave him tit for tat.*

give someone to understand something to explain something to someone; to imply something to someone. (This may mislead someone, accidentally or intentionally.) □ *Mr. Smith gave Sally to understand that she should be home by midnight.* □ *The mayor gave the citizens to understand that there would be no tax increase. He didn't promise, though.* ALSO: **given to understand** made to believe. □ *They were given to understand that there would be no tax increase, but after the election taxes went up.* □ *She was given to understand that she had to be home by midnight.*

give someone what for See *get what for.*

give something a lick and a promise* to do something poorly—quickly and carelessly. (Informal.) □ *John! You didn't clean your room! You just gave it a lick and a promise.* □ *This time, Tom, comb your hair. It looks like you just gave it a lick and a promise.*

give something off AND **give off something** to release light, a sound, or an odor. □ *This flower give off a lovely smell.* □ *The machine gave a soft hum off.* □ *The crystal gave off a rosy glow.*

give something one's best shot See *get one's best shot.*

give something out AND **give out something** to release something; to distribute something. (See also *have something out with someone.*) □ *The teacher gave the papers out.* □ *The dog gave out a loud growl.*

give the bride away (for a bride's father) to accompany the bride to the groom in a wedding ceremony. □ *Mr. Brown is ill. Who'll give the bride away?* □ *In the traditional wedding ceremony, the bride's father gives the bride away.*

give the devil his due* AND **give the devil her due*** to give your foe proper credit (for something). (A cliché. This usually refers to a person who has acted evil—like the devil.) □ *She's generally impossible, but I have to give the devil her due. She cooks a terrific cherry pie.* □ *John may cheat on his taxes and yell at his wife, but he keeps his car polished. I'll give the devil his due.*

give the game away* to reveal a plan or strategy. (Informal.) □ *Now, all of you have to keep quiet. Please don't give the game away.* □ *If you keep giving out hints, you'll give the game away.*

give up to surrender; to quit. □ *Even though things get hard, don't give up.* □ *The soldiers were surrounded, but they wouldn't give up.*

give up the ghost* to die; to release one's spirit. (A cliché. Considered formal or humorous.) □ *The old man sighed, rolled over, and gave up the ghost.* □ *I'm too young to give up the ghost.*

give vent to something to express anger. (The *something* is usually *anger, ire, irritation,* etc.) □ *John gave vent to his anger by yelling at Sally.* □ *Bill couldn't give vent to his frustration because he had been warned to keep quiet.*

give voice to something to express a feeling or an opinion in words; to speak out about something. □ *The bird gave voice to its joy in the golden sunshine.* □ *All the people gave voice to their anger at Congress.*

give way to someone or something AND **give way** to yield to someone or something; to get out of the way of someone or something. □ *The trees and bushes gave way to the flooding water.* □ *All the cars gave way to the fire engine.* □ *The law requires them to give way.* □ *The children gave way to the teenagers. They didn't want to argue with them.*

given to understand See *give someone to understand something.*

glance at someone or something to look quickly at someone or something. □ *Mary glanced at her watch and then went on with her work.* □ *Tom glanced at Sally and smiled.*

glance something over AND **glance over something** to look at something quickly and casually. □ *When you have time, please glance over this report.* □ *Okay, I'll glance this over this evening.*

gloss something over AND **gloss over something** to cover up or conceal an error; to make something appear right by minimizing or concealing the flaws. □ *When Mr. Brown was selling me the car, he tried to gloss over its defects.* □ *When I asked him not to gloss the flaws over, he got angry.*

go a long way toward doing something AND **go a long way in doing something** to nearly satisfy specific conditions; to be almost right. □ *This machine goes a long way toward meeting our needs.* □ *Your plan went a long way in helping us with our problem.*

go about doing something to do something (in a particular manner); to approach the doing of something. □ *I don't know how to go about painting the house.* □ *That isn't the proper way to go about baking a cake.*

go about one's business to mind one's business; to move elsewhere and mind one's own business. □ *Leave me alone! Just go about your business!* □ *I have no more to say. I would be pleased if you would go about your business.*

go after someone or something to pursue someone or something; to chase someone or something. □ *We were all hungry, so Tom went after pizza.* □ *The entire sales staff is out going after new business.* □ *In the race, Tom is the one to beat. Why not go after him?*

go against the grain to go against the natural direction or inclination. (See also *rub someone's fur the wrong way*.) □ *You can't expect me to help you cheat. That goes against the grain.* □ *Would it go against the grain for you to call in sick for me?*

go ahead with something AND **go ahead** to start something; to continue with something. □ *I hope we can go ahead with this project soon.* □ *If we cannot go ahead, we'll have to make new plans.*

go all out* to use all one's resources; to be very thorough. (Informal. Compare to *make an all-out effort*.) □ *Whenever they have a party, they really go all out.* □ *My cousin is coming for a visit, and she expects us to go all out.*

go all the way to somewhere AND **go all the way** to travel the total distance to a place. □ *I don't want to go all the way to San Francisco.* □ *All right. You don't have to go all the way.*

go all the way with someone* AND **go all the way***; **go to bed with someone***; **go to bed*** to have sexual intercourse. (Euphemistic. Use with caution.) □ *If you go all the way, you stand a chance of getting pregnant.* □ *I've heard that they go to bed all the time.*

go along for the ride to accompany (someone) for the pleasure of riding along. □ *Join us. You can go along for the ride.* □ *I don't really need to go to the grocery store, but I'll go along for the ride.*

go along with someone or something AND **go along** **1.** to move or travel along with someone or something. □ *John is going to California. I think I'll go along with him.* □ *When I go sailing, I love to go along with the wind.* **2.** to agree to something. □ *All right. I'll go along with your plan.* □ *I'm sure that John won't want to go along with it.* **3.** to agree with someone. □ *I go along with Sally. I'm sure she's right.* □ *I can't go along with John. He doesn't know what he's talking about.*

go ape over someone or something* AND **go ape*** to become very excited and enthusiastic about someone or something. (Slang.) □ *I really go ape over chocolate ice cream.* □ *Tom really goes ape over Mary.*

go around in circles* AND **go in circles***; **go round in circles*** to be or act confused. (Informal.) □ *I'm so busy I'm going around in circles.* □ *I can't work anymore. I'm so tired that I'm going in circles.*

go around with someone See *hang around with someone*.

go astray to leave the proper path (literally or figuratively). □ *Stay right on the road. Don't go astray and get lost.* □ *Follow the rules I've given you and don't go astray. That'll keep you out of trouble.*

go at it hammer and tongs See *fight someone or something hammer and tongs.*

go at it tooth and nail See *fight someone or something hammer and tongs.*

go at someone or something to attack someone or something; to move or lunge toward someone or something. □ *The dog went at the visitor and almost bit him.* □ *He went at the door and tried to break it down.*

go away empty-handed to depart with nothing. (Compare to *come away empty-handed.*) □ *I hate for you to go away empty handed, but I cannot afford to contribute any money.* □ *They came hoping for some food, but they had to go away empty-handed.*

go AWOL See *absent without leave.*

go back to return (to that place from which you came). (Compare to *come back.*) □ *I came here for only a short time. Now I must go back.* □ *I miss my home. I can't wait to go back.*

go back on one's word to break a promise which one has made. □ *I hate to go back on my word, but I won't pay you $100 after all.* □ *Going back on your word makes you a liar.*

go bad to become rotten, undesirable, evil, etc. □ *I'm afraid that this milk has gone bad.* □ *Life used to be wonderful. Now it has gone bad.*

go bananas* to go crazy or become silly. (Slang.) □ *Whenever I see Sally, I just go bananas! She's fantastic.* □ *This was a horrible day! I almost went bananas.*

go begging to be unwanted or unused. (As if a thing were begging for an owner or a user.) □ *There is still food left. A whole lobster is going begging. Please eat some more.* □ *There are many excellent books in the library just going begging because people don't know they are there.*

go broke to completely run out of money and other assets. □ *This company is going to go broke if you don't* stop spending money foolishly. □ *I made some bad investments last year, and it looks like I may go broke this year.*

go by the board to get ruined or lost. (This is a nautical expression meaning to fall or be washed overboard.) □ *I hate to see good food go by the board. Please eat up so we won't have to throw it out.* □ *Your plan has gone by the board. The entire project has been canceled.*

go chase oneself* to go away (and stop being a bother). (Slang.) □ *He was bothering me, so I told him to go chase himself.* □ *Get out, you pest! Go chase yourself!*

go cold turkey* to stop (doing something) without tapering off. (Slang. Originally drug slang. Now concerned with breaking any habit.) □ *I had to stop smoking, so I went cold turkey. It's awful!* □ *When heroin addicts go cold turkey, they get terribly sick.*

go down fighting to continue the struggle until one is completely defeated. □ *I won't give up easily. I'll go down fighting.* □ *Sally, who is very determined, went down fighting.*

go down in history* to be remembered as historically important. (A cliché.) □ *Bill is so great. I'm sure that he'll go down in history.* □ *This is the greatest party of the century. I bet it'll go down in history.*

go downhill (for something) to decline and grow worse and worse. (Also used literally.) □ *This industry is going downhill. We lose money every year.* □ *As one gets older, one tends to go downhill.*

go Dutch to share the cost of a meal or some other event. □ JANE: *Let's go out and eat.* MARY: *Okay, but let's go Dutch.* □ *It's getting expensive to have Sally for a friend. She never wants to go Dutch.*

go easy on someone or something AND **go easy** 1. to be kind or gentle with someone or something. □ *Go easy on Tom. He just got out of the hospital.* □ *Go easy on the cat. It doesn't like to be roughed up.* □ *Okay, I'll go easy.* 2. [with *something*] to use something sparingly. □ *Go easy on the mustard. That's all there is.* □ *Please go easy on the onions. I don't like them very well.*

Go fly a kite!* Go away and stop bothering me! (Slang.) □ *You're bothering me. Go fly a kite!* □ *If you think I'm going to waste my time talking to you, go fly a kite.*

go for broke* to risk everything; to try as hard as possible. (Slang.) □ *Okay, this is my last chance. I'm going for broke.* □ *Look at Mary starting to move in the final 100 yards of the race! She is really going for broke.*

go for it* to make a try for something; to decide to do something. (Slang.) □ *I have an offer of a new job. I think I'm going to go for it.* □ *Hey, great. Go for it!*

go for someone or something 1. to move toward someone or something; to reach for someone or something. □ *John was very close to the edge. Bill went for John and caught him just in time.* □ *John went for the door, but turned and came back without opening it.* **2.** to go out and find someone or something. □ *Who went for pizza?* □ *I went for Mary, but she wasn't ready. I'll go back for her later.* **3.** to *go at someone or something;* to attack someone or something. □ *The dog went for the robber and drove him back.* □ *The robber started to go for the guard, but stopped suddenly.* **4.** to desire someone or something. (Usually with *could,* as in the examples. Compare to *fall for someone or something* and *could do with someone or something.*) □ *Look at that cute guy. I could really go for him.* □ *I could go for a nice cool glass of iced tea.*

go from bad to worse* to progress from a bad state to a worse state. (A cliché.) □ *This is a terrible day. Things are going from bad to worse.* □ *My cold is awful. It went from bad to worse in just an hour.*

go great guns* to go fast or energetically. (Folksy.) □ *I'm over my cold and going great guns.* □ *Business is great. We are going great guns selling ice cream.*

go haywire* to go wrong; to malfunction; to break down. (Folksy.) □ *I was talking to Mary when suddenly the telephone went haywire. I haven't heard*

from her since. □ *There we were, driving along, when the engine went haywire. It was two hours before the tow truck came.*

go hog wild* to behave wildly. (Folksy.) □ *Have a good time at the party, but don't go hog wild.* □ *The teacher cannot control a class which is going hog wild.*

go in a body to move in a group. □ *The whole team went in a body to talk to the coach.* □ *Each of us was afraid to go alone, so we went in a body.*

go in for something to take part in something; to enjoy (doing) something. □ *John doesn't go in for sports.* □ *None of them seems to go in for swimming.*

go in one ear and out the other* (for something) to be heard and then forgotten. (A cliché.) □ *Everything I say to you seems to go in one ear and out the other. Why don't you pay attention?* □ *I can't concentrate. Things people say to me just go in one ear and out the other.*

go into a nose dive AND **take a nose dive 1.** (for an airplane) to suddenly dive toward the ground, nose first. □ *It was a bad day for flying, and I was afraid we'd go into a nose dive.* □ *The small plane took a nose dive. The pilot was able to bring it out at the last minute, so the plane didn't crash.* **2.*** to go into a rapid emotional or financial decline, or a decline in health. (Informal.) □ *Our profits took a nose dive last year.* □ *After breaking his hip, Mr. Brown's health went into a nose dive, and he never recovered.*

go into a tailspin 1. (for an airplane) to lose control and spin to the earth, nose first. □ *The plane shook and then suddenly went into a tailspin.* □ *The pilot was not able to bring the plane out of the tailspin, and it crashed into the sea.* **2.*** (for someone) to become disoriented or panicked; (for someone's life) to fall apart. (Informal.) □ *Although John was a great success, his life went into a tailspin. It took him a year to get straightened out.* □ *After her father died, Mary's world fell apart, and she went into a tailspin.*

go into action AND **swing into action**

to start doing something. □ *I usually get to work at 7:45, and I go into action at 8:00.* □ *When the ball is hit in my direction, you should see me swing into action.*

go into effect AND **take effect** (for a law or a rule) to become effective. □ *When does this new law go into effect?* □ *The new tax laws won't go into effect until next year.* □ *This law takes effect almost immediately.*

go into one's song and dance about something* to start giving one's explanations and excuses about something. (A cliché. *One's* can be replaced by *the same old.*) □ *Please don't go into your song and dance about how you always tried to do what was right.* □ *John went into his song and dance about how he won the war all by himself.* □ *He always goes into the same old song and dance every time he makes a mistake.*

go into orbit* to get very excited; to be in ecstasy. (Slang. Also used literally.) □ *When I got a letter from my boyfriend in England, I almost went into orbit.* □ *Tom goes into orbit every time the football team scores.*

go into something to start something new. (Especially a new career, project, product line, etc. Compare to *be into something.*) □ *I may quit selling and go into management.* □ *We are shifting production away from glass bottles, and we are going into vases and other decorative containers.* □ *After she graduated, she went into law.*

go it alone* to do something by oneself. (Informal.) □ *Do you need help, or will you go it alone?* □ *I think I need a little more experience before I go it alone.*

go like clockwork* to progress with regularity and dependability. (Informal.) □ *The building project is progressing nicely. Everything is going like clockwork.* □ *The elaborate pageant was a great success. It went like clockwork from start to finish.*

go off 1. (for someone) to go away (from other people). □ *It was a very busy day. At lunch time, I went off to think.* □ *You need to go off by yourself and do some hard thinking.* 2. (for something) to explode. □ *The fireworks didn't go*

off when they were supposed to. □ *There was a bomb in the building, but it didn't go off.*

go off half-cocked* to proceed without proper preparation; to speak (about something) without adequate knowledge. (Informal or slang.) □ *Don't pay any attention to what John says. He's always going off half-cocked.* □ *Get your facts straight before you make your presentation. There is nothing worse than going off half-cocked.*

go off the deep end* AND **jump off the deep end*** to become deeply involved (with someone or something) before one is ready; to follow one's emotions into a situation. (Informal. Refers to going into a swimming pool at the deep end—rather than the shallow end—and finding oneself *in deep water.* Applies especially to falling in love.) □ *Look at the way Bill is looking at Sally. I think he's about to go off the deep end.* □ *Now, John, I know you really want to go to Australia, but don't go jumping off the deep end. It isn't all perfect there.*

go on 1. See *go on doing something.* 2. Stop saying those things!; Not so!; I don't believe you! (Always a command: *Go on!*) □ *Go on! You don't know what you're talking about!* □ *Oh, go on! You're just trying to flatter me.*

go on a binge* to do too much of something. (Slang. Especially to drink too much.) □ *Jane went on a binge last night and is very sick this morning.* □ *Bill loves to spend money on clothes. He's out on a binge right now—buying everything in sight.*

go on a fishing expedition to attempt to discover information. (Also used literally.) □ *We are going to have to go on a fishing expedition to try to find the facts.* □ *One lawyer went on a fishing expedition in court, and the other lawyer objected.*

go on an errand See *run an errand.*

go on and on* to (seem to) last or go forever. (Folksy.) □ *You talk too much, Bob. You just go on and on.* □ *The road to their house is very boring. It goes on and on with nothing interesting to look at.*

go on doing something AND **go on with**

something; go on to continue doing something. □ *How long can that man go on talking?* □ *Please go on with your reading. I'm finished talking now.* □ *This play is really boring. How long can it go on?* □ *It's safe to cross the street now, so go on and cross.*

go on strike AND **go out on strike** (for a group of people) to quit working at their jobs until certain demands are met. □ *If we don't have a contract by noon tomorrow, we'll go out on strike.* □ *The entire work force went on strike at noon today.*

go on with something See *go on doing something.*

go out for something AND **go out** 1. to leave one's home to do something. (Usually refers to food or entertainment.) □ *Let's go out for dinner.* □ *Mother likes to go out.* □ *Do you want to go out for a movie?* 2. to try out for something. (Usually refers to sports.) □ *Mary went out for the soccer team.* □ *Tom went out for baseball.* □ *He didn't go out last year.*

go out in search of someone or something to go find someone or something. □ *Tom went out in search of a place to get his watch fixed.* □ *Jane and Bob went out in search of their cat.*

go out of fashion See *out of style.*

go out of one's way to do something AND **go out of one's way** 1. to travel an indirect route in order to do something. □ *I'll have to go out of my way to give you a ride home.* □ *I'll give you a ride even though I have to go out of my way.* 2. to make an effort to do something; to accept the bother of doing something. □ *We went out of our way to please the visitor.* □ *We appreciate anything you can do, but don't go out of your way.*

go out of style See *out of style.*

go out with someone AND **go out** 1. to go out with someone for entertainment. □ *The Smiths went out with the Franklins to a movie.* □ *Those guys don't have much time to go out.* 2. to go on a date with someone; to date someone regularly. □ *Is Bob still going out with Sally?* □ *No, they've stopped going out.*

go over like a lead balloon* (for something which is supposed to be funny) to fail to be funny. (Slang. Refers to jokes or performance. See also *go over with a bang.*) □ *Your joke went over like a lead balloon.* □ *If that play was supposed to be a comedy, it went over like a lead balloon.*

go over someone's head (for the intellectual content of something) to be too difficult for someone to understand. □ *All that talk about computers went over my head.* □ *I hope my lecture didn't go over the students' heads.*

go over something 1. AND **go over** to pass above something. □ *The car easily went over the rough road.* □ *Where were you when the plane went over?* 2. to review or explain something. □ *The teacher went over the lesson.* □ *Will you please go over this form? I don't understand it.*

go over something with a fine-tooth comb AND **search something with a fine-tooth comb** to search through something very carefully. (As if one were searching for something very tiny lost in some kind of fiber.) □ *I can't find my calculus book. I went over the whole place with a fine-tooth comb.* □ *I searched this place with a fine-tooth comb and didn't find my ring.*

go over with a bang* (for something) to be funny or entertaining. (Informal. Refers to jokes or performance. Compare to *go over like a lead balloon.*) □ *The play was a success. It really went over with a bang.* □ *That's a great joke. It went over with a bang.*

go overboard 1. to fall off of or out of a boat or ship. □ *My fishing pole just went overboard. I'm afraid it's lost.* □ *That man just went overboard. I think he jumped.* 2. to do too much; to be extravagant. □ *Look, Sally, let's have a nice party, but don't go overboard. It doesn't need to be fancy.* □ *Okay, you can buy a big comfortable car, but don't go overboard.*

go places* to have a good future. (Informal.) □ *Sally shows great promise as a scholar. She's really going to go places.* □ *Tom is as good as we thought. He's certainly going places now.*

go right through someone* (for food) to pass through and out of the body very rapidly. (Informal. Use with caution.) □ *Those little apples go right through me, but I love them.* □ *I can't eat onions. They go right through me.*

go round the bend AND **go around the bend** **1.** to go around a turn or a curve; to make a turn or a curve. □ *You'll see the house you're looking for as you go round the bend.* □ *John waved to his father until the car went round the bend.* **2.*** to go crazy; to lose one's mind. (Informal.) □ *If I don't get some rest, I'll go round the bend.* □ *Poor Bob. He has been having trouble for a long time. He finally went around the bend.*

go scot-free AND **get off scot-free** to go unpunished; to be acquitted of a crime. (This *scot* is an old word meaning tax or tax burden.) □ *The thief went scot-free.* □ *Jane cheated on the test and got caught, but she got off scot-free.*

go sky high* to go very high. (Informal.) □ *Prices go sky high whenever there is inflation.* □ *Oh, it's so hot. The temperature went sky high about noon.*

go so far as to say something to put something into words; to risk saying something. □ *I think that Bob is dishonest, but I wouldn't go so far as to say he's a thief.* □ *Red meat may be harmful, but I can't go so far as to say it causes cancer.*

go someone one better AND **do someone one better** to do something superior to what someone else has done; to top someone. □ *That was a great joke, but I can go you one better.* □ *Your last song was beautifully sung, but Mary can do you one better.*

go stag* to go to an event (which is meant for couples) without a member of the opposite sex. (Informal. Originally referred only to males.) □ *Is Tom going to take you, or are you going stag?* □ *Bob didn't want to go stag, so he took his sister to the party.*

go steady with someone AND **go steady** to date someone on a regular basis. □ *Mary is going steady with John.* □ *Bill went steady for two years before he got married.*

go stir crazy* to become anxious because one is confined. (Slang. *Stir* is an old criminal word for prison.) □ *If I stay around this house much longer, I'm going to go stir crazy.* □ *John left school. He said he was going stir crazy.*

go straight* to begin to obey the law; to become law-abiding. (Slang. Primarily criminal slang. Also used literally.) □ *When John got out of prison, he decided to go straight.* □ *I promised the teacher that I would go straight and that I would never cheat again.*

go the distance* to do the whole amount; to play the entire game; to run the whole race. (Informal. Originally sports use.) □ *That horse runs fast. I hope it can go the distance.* □ *This is going to be a long, hard project. I hope I can go the distance.*

go the limit to do as much as possible. (Compare to *go whole hog*.) □ *What do I want on my hamburger? Go the limit!* □ *Don't hold anything back. Go the limit.*

go through to be approved; to succeed in getting through the approval process. (See also *go through something*.) □ *I sent the board of directors a proposal. I hope it goes through.* □ *We all hope that the new law goes through.*

go through channels to proceed by consulting the proper persons or offices. □ *If you want an answer to your questions, you'll have to go through channels.* □ *If you know the answers, why do I have to go through channels?*

go through something **1.** to pass through something. (See also *go right through someone*.) □ *The speeding car went through the intersection.* □ *The visitor said goodbye and went through the door to the hallway.* **2.** to examine something. □ *Give me a day or two to go through this contract, and then I'll call you with advice.* □ *Don't go through it too fast. Read it carefully, or you might miss something.* **3.** to experience something; to endure something unpleasant; to *get through something*. □ *It was a terrible thing. I don't know how I went through it.* □ *It'll take four years to go through college.*

go through the changes* to experience a rough period in one's life. (Slang.)

□ *Most teenagers spend their time going through the changes.*

go through the motions to make a feeble effort to do something; to do something insincerely. □ *Jane isn't doing her best. She's just going through the motions.* □ *Bill was supposed to be raking the yard, but he was just going through the motions.*

go through the roof* to go very high; to reach a very high degree (of something). (Informal.) □ *It's so hot! The temperature is going through the roof.* □ *Mr. Brown got so angry he almost went through the roof.*

go through with something to decide to do something; to finish something. □ *We decided to go through with the new highway.* □ *I can't do it. I just can't go through with it.*

go to See *go to hell.*

go to any length to do whatever is necessary. □ *I'll go to any length to secure this contract.* □ *I want to get a college degree, but I won't go to any length to get one.*

go to bat for someone* to support or help someone. (Informal. From baseball. See *pinch-hit for someone.*) □ *I tried to go to bat for Bill, but he said he didn't want any help.* □ *I heard them gossiping about Sally, so I went to bat for her.*

go to bed with someone See *go all the way with someone.*

go to bed with the chickens* to go to bed at sundown; to go to bed very early (when the chickens do). (A cliché.) □ *Of course I get enough sleep. I go to bed with the chickens.* □ *Mr. Brown goes to bed with the chickens and gets up with them, too.*

go to Davy Jones's locker to go to the bottom of the sea. (Thought of as a nautical expression.) □ *My camera fell overboard and went to Davy Jones's locker.* □ *My uncle was a sailor. He went to Davy Jones's locker during a terrible storm.*

go to hell* AND **go to***; **go to the devil*** to become ruined; to go away and stop bothering (someone). (Informal. Use caution with *hell.*) □ *This old house is just going to hell. It's falling apart every-*

where. □ *Leave me alone! Go to the devil!* □ *Oh, go to, yourself!*

go to hell in a handbasket* to become totally worthless; to *go to hell.* (Informal. Use caution with *hell.* Not used as a command.) □ *The whole country is going to hell in a handbasket.* □ *Look at my lawn—full of weeds. It's going to hell in a handbasket.*

go to pieces 1. to break into pieces; to *fall apart.* □ *My old winter coat is going to pieces.* □ *I don't want to see a nice vase like that go to pieces.* 2. to break out in tears; to break down mentally. □ *On hearing of the death, we just went to pieces.* □ *I couldn't talk about it any longer. I went to pieces.*

go to pot* AND **go to the dogs*** to go to ruin; to deteriorate. (Informal.) □ *My whole life seems to be going to pot.* □ *My lawn is going to pot. I had better weed it.* □ *The government is going to the dogs.*

go to rack and ruin AND **go to wrack and ruin** to go to ruin. (The words *rack* and *wrack* mean wreckage and are found only in this expression.) □ *That lovely old house on the corner is going to go to rack and ruin.* □ *My lawn is going to wrack and ruin.*

go to seed See *run to seed.*

go to someone's head to make someone conceited; to make someone overly proud. □ *You did a fine job, but don't let it go to your head.* □ *He let his success go to his head, and soon he became a complete failure.*

go to the bathroom 1. to go into a restroom, bathroom, W.C., or toilet. □ BILL: *Where is Bob?* JANE: *He went to the bathroom.* □ *John went to the bathroom to brush his teeth.* 2. to eliminate bodily wastes through defecation and urination. □ *Mommy! The dog went to the bathroom on the carpet!* □ *Billy's in there going to the bathroom. Don't disturb him.*

go to the devil See *go to hell.*

go to the dogs See *go to pot.*

go to the expense of doing something AND **go to the expense** to pay the (large) cost of doing something. □ *I hate to have to go to the expense of painting the house.* □ *It needs to be done, so you'll have to go to the expense.*

go to the limit to do as much as is possible to do. (Compare to *go the limit*.) □ *Okay, we can't afford it, but we'll go to the limit.* □ *How far shall I go? Shall I go to the limit?*

go to the trouble of doing something AND **go to the trouble to do something; go to the trouble** to endure the bother of doing something. □ *I really don't want to go to the trouble to cook.* □ *Should I go to the trouble of cooking something for her to eat?* □ *Don't go to the trouble. She can eat a sandwich.*

go to the trouble to do something See the previous entry.

go to the wall* to be defeated; to fail in business. (Informal.) □ *We really went to the wall on that deal.* □ *The company went to the wall because of that contract. Now it's broke.*

go to town* to work hard or fast. (Informal. Also used literally.) □ *Look at all those ants working. They are really going to town.* □ *Come on, you guys. Let's go to town. We have to finish this job before noon.*

go to waste to be wasted; to be unused (and therefore thrown away). □ *Eat your potatoes! Don't let them go to waste.* □ *We shouldn't let all those nice flowers go to waste. Let's pick some.*

go together 1. (for two things) to look, sound, or taste well together. □ *Do you think that this pink one and this purple one go together?* □ *Milk and grapefruit don't go together.* 2. (for two people) to date each other regularly. □ *Bob and Ann have been going together for months.* □ *Tom and Jane want to go together, but they live too far apart.*

go too far to do more than is acceptable. □ *I didn't mind at first, but now you've gone too far.* □ *If you go too far, I'll slap you.*

go under 1. to pass underneath (someone or something). □ *I couldn't get over it, so I went under.* □ *It was too tall to climb, so we went under.* 2. to fail. □ *The company was weak from the start, and it finally went under.* □ *Tom had a lot of trouble in school, and finally he went under.*

go under the knife* to have a surgical operation. (Informal.) □ *Mary didn't want to go under the knife, but the doctor insisted.* □ *If I go under the knife, I want to be completely asleep.*

go up in flames AND **go up in smoke** to burn up. □ *The whole museum went up in flames.* □ *My paintings—my whole life's work—went up in flames.* □ *What a shame for all that to go up in smoke.*

go up in smoke See the previous entry.

go whole hog* to do everything possible; to be extravagant. (Informal. Compare to *go the limit*.) □ *Let's go whole hog. Order steak and lobster.* □ *Show some restraint. Don't go whole hog all the time.*

go with someone or something 1. AND **go with** [with *someone*] to accompany someone. □ *Daddy is leaving now. Why don't you go with him?* □ *Daddy, can I go with?* 2. [with *something*] to go well with something. □ *Milk doesn't go with grapefruit.* □ *Pink doesn't go with orange.* 3.* [with *something*] to choose something (over something else). (Informal.) □ *I think I'll go with the yellow one.* □ *We decided to go with the oak table rather than the walnut one.*

go without something AND **go without** to manage to get along without something. (Compare to *do without someone or something*.) □ *I went without food for three days.* □ *Some people have to go without a lot longer than that.*

go wrong to fail; (for something bad) to happen. □ *The project failed. I don't know what went wrong.* □ *I'm afraid that everything will go wrong.*

goes to show you* (something) serves to prove (something) to you. (A cliché.) □ *It just goes to show you that too much sugar is bad for you.* □ *Of course you shouldn't have married her. It goes to show you that your parents are always right.*

goes without saying* (something) is so obvious that it need not be said. (A cliché.) □ *It goes without saying that you are to wear formal clothing to dinner each evening.* □ *Of course. That goes without saying.*

gone on died. (Euphemistic.) □ *My husband, Tom—he's gone on, you know—was a great one for golf.* □ *Let* *us remember those who have gone on before.*

good and something very something. (The *something* can be *ready, mad, tired, worn out,* etc.) □ *Now I'm good and mad, and I'm going to fight back.* □ *I'll be there when I'm good and ready.* □ *He'll go to bed when he's good and tired.*

good enough for someone or something adequate for someone or something. □ *This seat is good enough for me. I don't want to move.* □ *I'm happy. It's good enough for me.* □ *That table is good enough for my office.*

good-for-nothing **1.** worthless. □ *Here comes that good-for-nothing boy now.* □ *Where is that good-for-nothing pen of mine?* **2.** a worthless person. □ *Tell that good-for-nothing to go home at once.* □ *Bob can't get a job. He's such a good-for-nothing.*

good riddance* AND **good riddance to bad rubbish*** (it is) good to be rid (of worthless persons or things). (A cliché.) □ *She slammed the door behind me and said, "Good riddance to bad rubbish!"* □ *"Good riddance to you, madam," thought I.*

goof off* to waste time. (Informal or slang.) □ *John is always goofing off.* □ *Quit goofing off and get to work!*

grasp at straws to depend on something which is useless; to make a futile attempt at something. □ *John couldn't answer the teacher's question. He was just grasping at straws.* □ *There I was, grasping at straws, with no one to help me.*

grease someone's palm* to bribe someone. (Slang.) □ *If you want to get something done around here, you have to grease someone's palm.* □ *I'd never grease a policemen's palm. That's illegal.*

Greek to me* unintelligible to me. (A cliché. Usually with some form of *be.*) □ *I can't understand it. It's Greek to me.* □ *It's Greek to me. Maybe Sally knows what it means.*

green around the gills See *pale around the gills.*

green with envy* envious; jealous. (A cliché.) □ *When Sally saw me with Tom, she turned green with envy. She likes*

him a lot. □ *I feel green with envy whenever I see you in your new car.*

grin and bear it* to endure something unpleasant in good humor. (A cliché.) □ *There is nothing you can do but grin and bear it.* □ *I hate having to work for rude people. I guess I have to grin and bear it.*

grind to a halt to slow to a stop; to run down. □ *By the end of the day, the factory had ground to a halt.* □ *The car ground to a halt, and we got out to stretch our legs.*

grit one's teeth to grind one's teeth together in anger or determination. □ *I was so mad, all I could do was stand there and grit my teeth.* □ *All through the race, Sally was gritting her teeth. She was really determined.*

gross someone out* AND **gross out someone*** to revolt someone; to make someone sick. (Slang.) □ *Oh, look at his face. Doesn't it gross you out?* □ *That teacher is such a creep. He grosses out the whole class.*

ground someone* to take away someone's privileges. (Informal. Usually said of a teenager.) □ *My father said that if I didn't get at least C's, he'd ground me.* □ *Guess what! He grounded me!*

grow on someone (for something) to become commonplace to a person. (The *someone* is usually *one, someone, a person,* etc., not a specific person.) □ *That music is strange, but it grows on you.* □ *I didn't think I could ever get used to this town, but after a while it grows on one.*

grow out of something **1.** to grow too big for something. □ *Tommy has grown out of all his pants.* □ *I grew out of my shirts, too.* **2.** to abandon something as one matures. □ *I used to have a lot of allergies, but I grew out of them.* □ *She grew out of the habit of biting her nails.* ALSO: **outgrow something** **1.** to get too big for something. □ *Tom outgrew all his clothes in two months.* □ *The plant outgrew its pot.* **2.** to become too mature for something. □ *I outgrew my allergies.* □ *The boys will outgrow their toys.*

grow up **1.** to become full size. □ *When that plant grows up, it'll need a new pot.*

2. (for a person) to become physically and mentally mature. □ *Oh, grow up, Tom! You act like a child.* □ *When Bill grows up a little more, he'll be a better student.*

guard against someone or something to take care to avoid someone or something. □ *Try to guard against getting a cold.* □ *You should guard against pickpockets.*

guess at something to guess at the answer to something. (The *something* is a question, riddle, etc.) □ *Guess at the answer if you don't know it.* □ *Try to guess at what I have in my hand.*

gum something up* AND **gum up the works***; **gum up something*** to make something inoperable; to ruin someone's plans. (Informal.) □ *Please, Bill, be careful and don't gum up the works.* □ *Tom gummed the whole plan up.*

gum up the works See the previous entry.

gun for someone* to be looking for someone, presumably to harm them. (Informal. Rarely literal. Originally from Western and gangster movies.) □ *The coach is gunning for you. I think he's going to bawl you out.* □ *I've heard that the sheriff is gunning for me, so I'm getting out of town.*

H

hack something* to endure something; to deal with something. (Slang. The *something* is usually *it*.) □ *I don't know if I can hack it.* □ *John works very hard, but he can't seem to hack it.*

hack something up AND **hack up something** to chop or cut something up, usually carelessly. □ *You did a poor job of carving the turkey. You hacked it up.* □ *The workers hacked up the door frame when they took the piano out.*

had as soon do something* AND **would as soon do something*** prefer to do something else; to be content to do something. (The *would* or *had* is usually *'d*. Also with *just*, as in the examples.) □ *They want me to go into town. I'd as soon stay home.* □ *If you're cooking stew tonight, we'd as soon eat somewhere else.* □ *I would just as soon stay home as see a bad movie.* □ *If that's what we're having for dinner, I'd just as soon starve.*

had best do something* ought to do something. (Informal. Almost the same as the following entry.) □ *You had best get that fixed right away.* □ *You had best be at school on time every day.*

had better do something ought to do something (or face the consequences). (Almost the same as the previous entry.) □ *I had better get home for dinner, or I'll get yelled at.* □ *You had better do your homework right now.*

had rather do something AND **had sooner do something** prefer to do something. □ *I'd rather go to town than sit here all evening.* □ *They'd rather not.* □ *I'd sooner not make the trip.*

had sooner do something See the previous entry.

hail fellow well met AND **hail-fellow-well-met** friendly to everyone; falsely friendly to everyone. (Usually said of males. See also *get the glad hand*.) □ *Yes, he's friendly, sort of hail fellow well met.* □ *He's not a very sincere person. Hail fellow well met—you know the type.* □ *What a pain he is. Good old Mr. hail-fellow-well-met. What a phony!*

hail from somewhere (for someone) to come originally from somewhere. □ *I'm from Kansas. Where do you hail from?* □ *I hail from the Southwest.*

hair of the dog that bit one* a drink of liquor taken when one has a hangover; a drink of liquor taken when one is recovering from drinking too much liquor. (Informal.) □ *Oh, I'm miserable. I need some of the hair of the dog that bit me.* □ *That's some hangover you've got there, Bob. Here, drink this. It's some of the hair of the dog that bit you.*

hale and hearty* well and healthy. (A cliché.) □ *Doesn't Ann look hale and hearty?* □ *I don't feel hale and hearty. I'm really tired.*

Half a loaf is better than none. a proverb meaning that having part of something is better than having nothing. □ *When my raise was smaller than I wanted, Sally said, "Half a loaf is better than none."* □ *People who keep saying "Half a loaf is better than none" usually have as much as they need.*

ham something up* AND **ham up something*** to make a performance seem silly by showing off or exaggerating one's part. (Informal. A show-off actor is known as a *ham*.) □ *The play was going fine until Bob got out there and hammed*

145

up his part. □ *Come on, Bob. Don't ham it up!*

hammer away at someone or something AND **hammer away** to keep trying to accomplish something with someone or something. (Also used literally.) □ *John, you've got to keep hammering away at your geometry.* □ *They hammered away at the prisoner until he confessed.* □ *They kept hammering away.*

hammer something out AND **hammer out something** 1. to flatten something by hammering it. □ *The mechanic hammered out the dent in the car's fender.* □ *The mechanic hammered the dent out.* 2. to work hard at writing up an agreement; to work hard at writing something. (As if one were hammering at the keys of a typewriter.) □ *The lawyers sat down to hammer out a contract.* □ *I'm busy hammering my latest novel out.* 3. to play something on the piano. □ *Listen to John hammer out that song on the piano.*

hand in glove with someone AND **hand in glove** very close to someone. □ *John is really hand in glove with Sally.* □ *The teacher and the principal work hand in glove.*

hand in hand 1. holding hands. □ *They walked down the street hand in hand.* □ *Bob and Mary sat there quietly, hand in hand.* 2. together, one with the other. (Said of two things, the presence of either of which implies the other.) □ *Cookies and milk seem to go hand in hand.* □ *Teenagers and back talk go hand in hand.*

hand it to someone* to give credit to someone. (Informal. Often with *have to* or *must*.) □ *I'll hand it to you. You did a fine job.* □ *We must hand it to Sally. She helped us a lot.*

hand-me-down something, such as an article of used clothing, which has been handed down from someone. (See *hand something down to someone.*) □ *Why do I always have to wear my brother's hand-me-downs? I want some new clothes.* □ *This is a nice shirt. It doesn't look like a hand-me-down at all.*

hand over fist (for money and merchandise to be exchanged) very rapidly. □ *What a busy day. We took in money hand over fist.* □ *They were buying things hand over fist.*

hand over hand (moving) one hand after the other (again and again). □ *Sally pulled in the rope hand over hand.* □ *The man climbed the rope hand over hand.*

hand something down to someone AND **hand down something to someone; hand down something; hand something down** 1. to give something to a younger person. (Either at death or during life. See also *hand-me-down.*) □ *John handed his old shirts down to his younger brother.* □ *I hope my uncle will hand down his golf clubs to me when he dies.* 2. to announce or deliver a (legal) verdict or indictment. □ *The grand jury handed down seven indictments last week.* □ *The jury handed down a guilty verdict.*

hand something in AND **hand in something** to turn something in; to submit something by hand. □ *Did you hand your application form in?* □ *I forgot to hand in my test.*

hand something on to someone AND **hand on something to someone; hand on something; hand something on** to pass something on to someone. □ *This watch was given to me by my grandfather. I'll hand it on to my grandson.* □ *Would you please hand the tray of food on to the next person?* □ *Yes, please hand on the tray. I'm hungry.*

hand something out to someone AND **hand out something to someone; hand out something; hand something out** to distribute something; to pass something out to someone. □ *Please hand out these papers to everyone.* □ *Look! They are handing candy out! Get some!*

hand something over AND **hand over something** to give something (to someone); to relinquish something (to someone); to turn something over (to someone). □ *Come on, John! Hand over my wallet.* □ *Please hand this over to the guard.*

handle someone with kid gloves to be very careful with a touchy person. □ *Bill has become so sensitive. You really have to handle him with kid gloves.* □

You don't have to handle me with kid gloves. I can take it.

Hands off! AND **Hands off someone or something!** Do not touch someone or something. □ *Careful! Don't touch that wire. Hands off!* □ *The sign says, "Hands off!" and you had better do what it says.*

Hands up!* □ *Hands off my book!* AND **Stick 'em up!*** Put your hand in the air. (Slang. Said by robbers and police officers.) □ *All right, you, hands up!* □ *Stick 'em up! I got you covered.*

hang a left* to turn to the left. (Slang. See also the following entry.) □ *Hang a left up at that light.* □ *Go three blocks and hang a left.*

hang a right* to turn to the right. (Slang. See the previous entry.) □ *At the next corner, hang a right.* □ *Hang a right at the stop sign.*

hang around with someone AND **go around with someone; hang around** to spend a lot of time with someone; to waste away time with someone. (See also *run around with someone*.) □ *John hangs around with Bill a lot.* □ *They've been going around with the Smiths.* □ *I've asked them all to stop hanging around.*

hang back to stay behind (the others); to hold back (from the others). □ *Walk with the group, Bob. Don't hang back. You'll get left behind.* □ *Three of the marchers hung back and talked to each other.*

hang by a hair* AND **hang by a thread*** to be in an uncertain position; to depend on something very insubstantial; to *hang in the balance.* (Informal. Also with *on*, as in the second example.) □ *Your whole argument is hanging by a thread.* □ *John isn't failing geometry, but he's just hanging on by a hair.*

hang in the balance to be in an undecided state; to be between two equal possibilities. (See also *in the balance*.) □ *The prisoner stood before the judge with his life hanging in the balance.* □ *This whole issue will have to hang in the balance until Jane gets back from her vacation.*

hang in there* to keep trying; to persevere. (Slang.) □ *I know things are tough, John, but hang in there.* □ *I know if I hang in there, things will come out okay.*

hang loose* to relax; to remain calm. (Slang.) □ *I know I can pass this test if I just hang loose.* □ *Hang loose, Bob. Everything is going to be all right.*

Hang on! Be prepared for fast or rough movement. (Compare to *hold tight*.) □ *Hang on! Here we go!* □ *The airplane passengers suddenly seemed weightless. Someone shouted, "Hang on!"*

hang on someone's coattails See *ride on someone's coattails*.

hang on someone's every word to listen carefully to everything someone says. □ *He gave a great lecture. We hung on his every word.* □ *Look at the way John hangs on Mary's every word. He must be in love with her.*

hang on to someone or something AND **hang on; hold on to someone or something; hold on** **1.** to keep someone or something in one's grasp; to *hold on to someone or something;* to hold someone or something tightly. □ *The child held on to her mother and cried and cried.* □ *Please hang on to your purse. It might get stolen.* □ *Hold on tight!* □ *Okay, I'll hang on.* **2.** to remember someone or something for a long time; to be effected very much by someone or something in the past. (Never with the literal sense of grasping or holding.) □ *That's a nice thought, Bob. Hang on to it.* □ *You've been holding on to those bad memories for too long. It's time to let them go.* □ *Yes, I can't keep hanging on.*

Hang on to your hat!* AND **Hold on to your hat!*** Grasp your hat and prepare for a sudden surprise or shock. (Informal.) □ *What a windy day. Hang on to your hat!* □ *Here we go! Hold on to your hat!* □ *Are you ready to hear the final score? Hang on to your hat! We won ten to nothing!*

hang out somewhere AND **hang out** to spend time somewhere; to waste time somewhere. □ *I wish you guys wouldn't hang out around the bowling alley.* □ *Why do you have to hang out near our house?*

hang out with someone AND **hang out** to waste time in the company of someone. □ *I hope Bob isn't hanging out with the wrong people.* □ *He needs to* *spend more time studying and less time hanging out.*

hang someone in effigy to hang a dummy or some other figure of a hated person. (See also *burn someone in effigy*.) □ *They hanged the dictator in effigy.* □ *The angry mob hanged the President in effigy.*

hang something out AND **hang out something** to hang up something out of doors. (The *something* is usually laundry, a sign, or a "shingle" which is a special term for a doctor's or lawyer's sign.) □ *When the sun is shining, I prefer to hang my laundry out on the line rather than using the clothes dryer.* □ *Sally can't wait to get out of law school and hang out her shingle.*

hang something up AND **hang up something** to hang something, as from a hook. (See also *hang up.*) □ *Sally! Go hang up your clothes.* □ *Don't forget to hang the telephone up when you're finished.*

hang together to be or stay (figuratively or literally) united. □ *The little group of children hung together all through school.* □ *If our group hangs together, we can accomplish big things.* □ *Your argument doesn't hang together.*

hang tough* to be firm in one's position; to stick to one's position. (Slang. Compare to *hang in there.*) □ *I know that your parents don't want you to go out tonight, but hang tough. They may change their minds.* □ *Hang tough, Mary. You'll get your way!*

hang up to replace the telephone receiver. (See also *hang something up.*) □ *If you have called a wrong number, you should apologize before you hang up.* □ *When you hear the busy signal, you're supposed to hang up.* ALSO: **hang-up*** a personal problem. (Slang. See also *hung up on someone or something.*) □ *John has a lot of hang-ups he's going to have to get over before he can relax.* □ *I'm tired of hearing about your hang-ups.*

happen on someone or something to find someone or something unexpectedly. □ *I happened on this nice little restaurant on Elm Street yesterday.* □ *Mr. Simpson and I happened on one another in the bank last week.*

hard-and-fast rule* a strict rule. (A cliché.) □ *It's a hard-and-fast rule that you must be home by midnight.* □ *You should have your project completed by the end of the month, but it's not a hard-and-fast rule.*

hard nut to crack* AND **tough nut to crack*** a difficult person or thing to deal with. (Informal.) □ *This problem is getting me down. It's a hard nut to crack.* □ *Tom sure is a hard nut to crack. I can't figure him out.* □ *He sure is a tough nut to crack.*

hard on someone's heels* following someone very close; following very closely to someone's heels. (Informal.) □ *I ran as fast as I could, but the dog was still hard on my heels.* □ *Here comes Sally, and John is hard on her heels.*

hard pressed to do something See the following entry.

hard put to do something AND **hard pressed to do something; hard pressed; hard put** able to do something only with great difficulty. □ *I'm hard put to come up with enough money to pay the rent.* □ *I get hard put like that about once a month.*

hard up for something* AND **hard up*** greatly in need of something. (Informal.) □ *Ann was hard up for the cash to pay the bills.* □ *I was so hard up, I couldn't afford to buy food.*

hardly have time to breathe* to be very busy. (A cliché.) □ *This was such a busy day. I hardly had time to breathe.* □ *They made him work so hard that he hardly had time to breathe.*

hark back to something* AND **harken back to something*** (A cliché. *Harken* is an old form of *hark* which is an old word meaning listen.) **1.** to have originated as something; to have started out as something. □ *The word icebox harks back to refrigerators which were cooled by ice.* □ *Our modern breakfast cereals hark back to the porridge and gruel of our ancestors.* **2.** to remind one of something. □ *Seeing a horse and buggy in the park harks back to the time when horses drew milk wagons.* □ *Sally says it harkens back to the time when everything was delivered by a horse-drawn wagon.*

hash something over* AND **hash over something*** to discuss something in great detail. (Informal.) ☐ *Why don't you come to my office so we can hash over this contract?* ☐ *Okay, we can hash it over this afternoon.*

Haste makes waste. a proverb meaning that time gained in doing something rapidly and carelessly will be lost when one has to do the thing over again correctly. ☐ *Now, take your time. Haste makes waste.* ☐ *Haste makes waste, so be careful as you work.*

hate someone's guts* to hate someone very much. (Informal and rude.) ☐ *Oh, Bob is terrible. I hate his guts!* ☐ *You may hate my guts for saying so, but I think you're getting gray hairs.*

haul someone or something in AND **haul in someone or something 1.** [with *something*] to pull something in. ☐ *I caught a fish so big that it took me twenty minutes to haul it in.* ☐ *I hauled in the anchor and started up the boat's engine.* **2.*** [with *someone*] to arrest someone; (for a police officer) to take someone to the police station. (Slang.) ☐ *The cop hauled the crook in.* ☐ *The traffic officer said, "Do you want me to haul you in?"*

haul someone over the coals See *rake someone over the coals.*

haul up somewhere AND **haul up; pull up somewhere; pull up** to stop somewhere; to come to rest somewhere. ☐ *The car hauled up in front of the house.* ☐ *My hat blew away just as the bus pulled up.* ☐ *The attackers hauled up at the city gates.*

have a bad effect on someone or something AND **have a bad effect** to be bad for someone or something. ☐ *Aspirin has a bad effect on me.* ☐ *Cold weather has a bad effect on roses.*

have a ball* to have a really great time. (Slang. This *ball* is a formal social dancing party.) ☐ *The picnic was fantastic. We had a ball!* ☐ *Hey Mary! Have a ball at the party tonight!*

have a bee in one's bonnet to have an idea or a thought remain in one's mind; to have an obsession. ☐ *I have a bee in my bonnet that you'd be a good manager.* ☐ *I had a bee in my bonnet about swimming. I couldn't stop wanting to go swimming.* ALSO: **put a bee in someone's bonnet** to give someone an idea (about something). ☐ *Somebody put a bee in my bonnet that we should go to a movie.* ☐ *Who put a bee in your bonnet?*

have a big mouth* to be a gossiper; to be a person who tells secrets. (Informal.) ☐ *Mary has a big mouth. She told Bob what I was getting him for his birthday.* ☐ *You shouldn't say things like that about people all the time. Everyone will say you have a big mouth.*

have a blowout to have one of one's car tires burst. ☐ *I had a blowout on the way here. I nearly lost control of the car.* ☐ *If you have a blowout in one tire, you should check the other tires.*

have a bone to pick with someone AND **have a bone to pick** to have a matter to discuss with someone; to have something to argue about with someone. ☐ *Hey, Bill. I've got a bone to pick with you. Where is the money you owe me?* ☐ *I had a bone to pick with her, but she was so sweet that I forgot about it.* ☐ *You always have a bone to pick.*

have a break See *get a break.*

have a bright idea See *get a bright idea.*

have a brush with something to have a brief contact with something; to have an experience with something. (Especially with the law. Sometimes a *close* brush. Compare to *have a scrape with someone or something.*) ☐ *Ann had a close brush with the law. She was nearly arrested for speeding.* ☐ *When I was younger, I had a brush with scarlet fever, but I got over it.*

have a case against someone AND **have a case** to have much evidence which can be used against someone in court. (*Have* can be replaced with *build, gather, assemble,* etc.) ☐ *Do the police have a case against John?* ☐ *No, they don't have a case.* ☐ *They are trying to build a case against him.* ☐ *My lawyer is busy assembling a case against the other driver.*

have a Charley horse See *get a Charley horse.*

have a chip on one's shoulder to be tempting someone to an argument or a fight. ☐ *Who are you mad at? You* *always seem to have a chip on your shoulder.* □ *John's had a chip on his shoulder ever since he got his speeding ticket.*

have a clean conscience about someone or something See the following entry.

have a clear conscience about someone or something AND **have a clean conscience about someone or something; have a clean conscience; have a clear conscience** to be free of guilt about someone or something. □ *I'm sorry that John got the blame. I have a clean conscience about the whole affair.* □ *I have a clear conscience about John and his problems.* □ *I didn't do it. I have a clean conscience.* □ *She can't sleep nights because she doesn't have a clear conscience.*

have a close call See the following entry.

have a close shave AND **have a close call** to have a narrow escape from something dangerous. (See also *have a brush with something.*) □ *What a close shave I had! I nearly fell off the roof when I was working there.* □ *I almost got struck by a speeding car. It was a close shave.*

have a conniption* AND **have a conniption fit*** to get angry or hysterical. (Folksy. See also *have a fit.*) □ *I got so mad I thought I was going to have a conniption.* □ *My father had a conniption fit when I got home this morning.*

have a crush on someone See *get a crush on someone.*

have a falling-out with someone over something See *fall out with someone over something.*

have a familiar ring* (for a story or an explanation) to sound familiar. (A cliché.) □ *Your excuse has a familiar ring. Have you done this before?* □ *This term paper has a familiar ring. I think it has been copied.*

have a fit* to be very angry. (Informal.) □ *The teacher had a fit when the dog ran through the classroom.* □ *John had a fit when he found his car had been damaged.*

have a fix on something See *get a fix on something.*

have a glass jaw* to be susceptible to collapsing when struck on the head. (Informal. Said only of boxers who are frequently knocked down by a blow to the head.) □ *When the prize fighter was knocked out in his third fight, the newspapers said he had a glass jaw.* □ *Once a fighter has a glass jaw, he's finished as a boxer.*

have a go at something AND **have a go** to make a try at something. (See also *take a stab at something.*) □ *I've never fished before, but I'd like to have a go at it.* □ *Great, have a go right now. Take my fishing pole and give it a try.*

have a good command of something to know something well. □ *Bill has a good command of French.* □ *Jane has a good command of economic theory.*

have a good head on one's shoulders to have common sense; to be sensible and intelligent. □ *Mary doesn't do well in school, but she's got a good head on her shoulders.* □ *John has a good head on his shoulders and can be depended on to give good advice.*

have a good thing going* to have something arranged for one's benefit. (Informal.) □ *Sally paints pictures and sells them at art fairs. She has a good thing going, and she makes good money.* □ *John inherited a fortune and doesn't have to work for a living anymore. He's got a good thing going.*

have a grasp of something See *get a grasp of something.*

have a green thumb to have the ability to grow plants well. □ *Just look at Mr. Simpson's garden. He has a green thumb.* □ *My mother has a green thumb when it comes to house plants.*

have a grudge against someone See *bear a grudge against someone.*

have a hand in something See *take a hand in something.*

have a handle on something See *get a handle on something.*

have a head start on someone or something See *get a head start on someone or something.*

have a heart to be compassionate; to be generous and forgiving. □ *Oh, have a heart! Give me some help!* □ *If Ann had a heart, she'd have made us feel more welcome.*

have a heart of gold to be generous, sincere, and friendly. □ *Mary is such a lovely person. She has a heart of gold.* □ *You think Tom stole your watch? Impossible! He has a heart of gold.*

have a heart of stone to be cold and unfriendly. □ *Sally has a heart of stone. She never even smiles.* □ *The villain in the play had a heart of stone. He was an ideal villain.*

have a heart-to-heart talk AND **have a heart-to-heart** to have a sincere and intimate talk. □ *I had a heart-to-heart talk with my father before I went off to college.* □ *I have a problem, John. Let's sit down and have a heart-to-heart.*

have a lot going for one AND **have a lot going** to have many things working to one's benefit. □ *Jane is so lucky. She has a lot going for her.* □ *She has a good job and a nice family. She has a lot going.*

have a lot of promise to be very promising; to have a good future ahead. □ *Sally is quite young, but she has a lot of promise.* □ *This bush is small, but it has a lot of promise.*

have a lot on one's mind to have many things to worry about; to be preoccupied. □ *I'm sorry that I'm so grouchy. I have a lot on my mind.* □ *He forgot to go to his appointment because he had a lot on his mind.*

have a low boiling point* to anger easily. (Informal.) □ *Be nice to John. He's upset and has a low boiling point.* □ *Mr. Jones sure has a low boiling point. I hardly said anything, and he got angry.*

have a lump in one's throat See *get a lump in one's throat.*

have a near miss to nearly crash or collide. □ *The airplanes—flying much too close—had a near miss.* □ *I had a near miss while driving over here.*

have a penchant for doing something to have a taste, desire, or inclination for doing something. □ *John has a penchant for eating fattening foods.* □ *Ann has a penchant for buying clothes.*

have a pick-me-up to eat or drink something stimulating. (The *have* can be replaced with *need, want,* etc. The *me* does not change.) □ *I'd like to have a pick-me-up. I think I'll have a bottle*

of pop. □ *You look tired. You need a pick-me-up.*

have a price on one's head* to be wanted by the authorities who have offered a reward for one's capture. (Informal or folksy. Usually limited to Western and gangster movies.) □ *We captured a thief who had a price on his head, and the sheriff gave us the reward.* □ *The crook was so mean, he turned in his own brother who had a price on his head.*

have a red face See *get a red face.*

have a reputation as a something See *get a reputation as a something.*

have a reputation for doing something See *get a reputation for doing something.*

have a right to do something AND **have the right to do something** to have the freedom to do something; to possess the legal or moral permission or license to do something. □ *You don't have the right to enter my home without my permission.* □ *I have a right to grow anything I want on my farm land.*

have a rough idea about something See *get a rough idea about something.*

have a rough time of it AND **have a rough time** to experience a difficult period. □ *Since his wife died, Mr. Brown has been having a rough time of it.* □ *Be nice to Bob. He's been having a rough time.*

have a say in something See *have a voice in something.*

have a score to settle with someone See *settle a score with someone.*

have a scrape with someone or something AND **have a scrape** to come into contact with someone or something; to have a small battle with someone or something. (Compare to *have a brush with something.*) □ *I had a scrape with the county sheriff.* □ *John and Bill had a scrape, but they are friends again now.*

have a screw loose* to act silly or crazy. (Slang.) □ *John's such a clown. He acts like he has a screw loose.* □ *What's the matter with you? Do you have a screw loose or something?*

have a smoke to smoke a cigarette, cigar, or pipe. (The *have* can be replaced with *need, want,* etc.) □ *Can I have a* *smoke? I'm very nervous.* □ *Do you have a cigarette? I need a smoke.*

have a snowball's chance in hell* to have no chance at all; to have a chance no greater than that of a snowball in hell. (A cliché. A snowball would melt in hell and have no chance of surviving. Use *hell* with caution.) □ *He has a snowball's chance in hell of passing the test.* □ *You don't have a snowball's chance in hell of her agreeing to marry you.*

have a soft spot in one's heart for someone or something to be fond of someone or something. □ *John has a soft spot in his heart for Mary.* □ *I have a soft spot in my heart for chocolate cake.*

have a spaz* to get angry or hysterical; to have a *conniption.* (Slang.) □ *Relax, Bob. Don't have a spaz.* □ *My father had a spaz when I came in late last night.*

have a stab at something See *take a stab at something.*

have a stroke to experience sudden unconsciousness or paralysis due to an interruption in the blood supply to the brain. (Also used as an exaggeration. See the last two examples.) □ *The patient who received an artificial heart had a stroke two days after the operation.* □ *My great uncle Bill—who is very old—had a stroke last May.* □ *Calm down, Bob. You're going to have a stroke.* □ *My father almost had a stroke when I came home at 3:00 this morning.*

have a sweet tooth to desire to eat many sweet foods—especially candy and pastries. □ *I have a sweet tooth, and if I don't watch it, I'll really get fat.* □ *John eats candy all the time. He must have a sweet tooth.*

have a swelled head See *get a swelled head.*

have a thing about someone or something to have strong likes or dislikes about someone or something. □ *I have a thing about celery. I can't stand it.* □ *John can't get enough celery. He has a thing about it.* □ *John has a thing about Mary. He thinks he's in love.*

have a thing going with someone* AND **have a thing going*; have something going with someone*; have something going*** to have a romance or a love affair with someone. (Informal.) □ *John and Mary have a thing going.* □ *Bill has a thing going with Ann.* □ *They have something going.*

have a voice in something AND **have a say in something; have a voice; have a say** to have a part in making a decision. □ *I'd like to have a voice in choosing the carpet.* □ *John wanted to have a say in the issue also.* □ *He says he seldom gets to have a say.*

have a way with someone or something to handle or deal well with someone or something. □ *John has a way with hamburger. It's always delicious.* □ *Mother has a way with Father. She'll get him to paint the house.*

have a weakness for someone or something to be unable to resist someone or something; to be fond of someone or something; to be (figuratively) powerless against someone or something. (Compare to *have a soft spot in one's heart for someone or something.*) □ *I have a weakness for chocolate.* □ *John has a weakness for Mary. I think he's in love.*

have a whale of a time* to have an exciting time; to have a big time. (Slang. *Whale* is a way of saying *big.*) □ *We had a whale of a time at Sally's birthday party.* □ *Enjoy your vacation! I hope you have a whale of a time.*

have a word with someone to speak to someone, usually privately. □ *The manager asked to have a word with me when I was not busy.* □ *John, could I have a word with you? We need to discuss something.*

have an accident 1. to experience something which was not foreseen or intended. □ *Traffic is very bad. I almost had an accident.* □ *Drive carefully. Try to avoid having an accident.* **2.** to lose control of the bowels or the bladder. (Euphemistic. Usually said of a young child.) □ *"Oh, Ann," cried Mother. "It looks like you've had an accident!"* □ *Mother asked Billy to go to the bathroom before they left so that he wouldn't have an accident in the car.*

have an argument to argue (with someone). □ *John and Sally had an argu-*

ment. *Now they aren't speaking.* □ *Every time we sit down to discuss something, we end up having an argument.*

have an ax to grind* to have something to complain about. (Informal.) □ *Tom, I need to talk to you. I have an ax to grind.* □ *Bill and Bob went into the other room to argue. They had an ax to grind.*

have an eye for someone or something to have a taste or an inclination for someone or something. □ *Bob has an eye for beauty.* □ *He has an eye for color.* □ *Ann has an eye for well-dressed men.*

have an eye on someone or something AND **keep an eye on someone or something** to keep watch on someone or something; to keep track of someone or something. (The *an* can be replaced by *one's.*) □ *I have my eye on the apple tree. When the apples ripen, I'll harvest them.* □ *Please keep an eye on the baby.* □ *Will you please keep your eye on my house while I'm on vacation?*

have an eye out for someone or something AND **have an eye out; keep an eye out for someone or something; keep an eye out** to watch for the arrival or appearance of someone or something. (The *an* can be replaced by *one's.*) □ *Please try to have an eye out for the bus.* □ *Keep an eye out for rain.* □ *Have your eye out for a raincoat on sale.* □ *Okay. I'll keep my eye out.*

have an in with someone AND **have an in** to have a way to request a special favor from someone; to have influence with someone; to *have pull with someone.* (The *in* is a noun.) □ *Do you have an in with mayor? I have to ask him a favor.* □ *Sorry, I don't have an in, but I know someone who does.*

have an itchy palm AND **have an itching palm** to be in need of a tip; to tend to ask for tips. (As if placing money in the palm would stop the itching.) □ *All the waiters at that restaurant have itchy palms.* □ *The cab driver was troubled by an itching palm. Since he refused to carry my bags, I gave him nothing.*

have an out* to have an excuse; to have a (literal or figurative) means of escape or avoiding something. (Informal. The

out is a noun.) □ *He's very clever. No matter what happens, he always has an out.* □ *I agreed to go to a party which I don't want to go to now. I'm looking for an out.*

have another guess coming See the following entry.

have another think coming* AND **have another guess coming*** to have to rethink something because one was wrong the first time. (Folksy. *Think* is a noun here.) □ *She's quite wrong. She's got another think coming if she wants to walk in here like that.* □ *You've got another guess coming if you think you can treat me like that!*

have ants in one's pants See *get ants in one's pants.*

have at someone or something See *get at someone or something.*

have back at someone See *get back at someone.*

have bats in one's belfry* to be slightly crazy. (A cliché.) □ *Poor old Tom has bats in his belfry.* □ *Don't act so silly, John. People will think you have bats in your belfry.*

have been around* to be experienced in life. (Informal. Use with caution—especially with females—since this can also refer to sexual experience. See also *get around.*) □ *Ask Sally about how the government works. She's been around.* □ *They all know a lot about life. They've been around.*

have butterflies in one's stomach See *get butterflies in one's stomach.*

have charge of someone or something See *in charge of someone or something.*

have clean hands to be guiltless. (As if the guilty person would have bloody hands.) □ *Don't look at me. I have clean hands.* □ *The police took him in, but let him go again because he had clean hands.*

have cold feet See *get cold feet.*

have come a long way **1.** to have traveled a long distance. □ *You've come a long way. You must be tired and hungry.* □ *I've come a long way. Please let me rest.* **2.** to have accomplished much; to have advanced much. □ *My, how famous you are. You've come a long* *way.* □ *Tom has come a long way in a short time.*

have designs on someone or something to have plans for someone or something. □ *Mrs. Brown has designs on my apple tree. I think she's going to cut off the part that hangs over her fence.* □ *Mary has designs on Bill. I think she'll try to date him.*

have dibs on something* AND **put one's dibs on something*** to reserve something for oneself; to claim something for oneself. (Informal.) □ *I have dibs on the last piece of cake.* □ *John put his dibs on the last piece again. It isn't fair.*

have egg on one's face to be embarrassed because of an error which is obvious to everyone. (Rarely literal.) □ *Bob has egg on his face because he wore jeans to the party and everyone else wore formal clothing.* □ *John was completely wrong about the weather for the picnic. It snowed! Now he has egg on his face.*

have eyes bigger than one's stomach See *one's eyes are bigger than one's stomach.*

have eyes in the back of one's head* to seem to be able to sense what is going on outside of one's vision. (A cliché.) □ *My teacher seems to have eyes in the back of her head.* □ *My teacher doesn't need to have eyes in the back of his head. He watches us very carefully.*

have feet of clay (for a strong person) to have a defect of character. □ *All human beings have feet of clay. No one is perfect.* □ *Sally was popular and successful. She was nearly fifty before she learned that she, too, had feet of clay.*

have foot-in-mouth disease* to embarrass oneself through a silly blunder. (Informal. This is a parody on *foot-and-mouth disease* or *hoof-and-mouth disease* which affects cattle and deer. See also *put one's foot in one's mouth.*) □ *I'm sorry I keep saying stupid things. I guess I have foot-in-mouth disease.* □ *Yes, you really have foot-in-mouth disease tonight.*

have goose bumps See *get goose bumps.*

have got to do something to be obliged to do something. □ *I've got to go to the post office tomorrow.* □ *We've got to go to school.*

have growing pains 1. (for a child) to have pains—which are attributed to growth—in the muscles and joints. □ *The doctor said that all Mary had was growing pains and that nothing was really wrong.* □ *Not everyone has growing pains.* 2. (for an organization) to have difficulties in its growth. □ *The banker apologized for losing my check and said the bank was having growing pains.* □ *Governments have terrible growing pains.*

have had enough to have had as much of something as is needed or will be tolerated. (Compare to the following entry.) □ *Stop yelling at me. I've had enough.* □ *No more potatoes, please. I've had enough.* □ *I'm leaving you, Bill. I've had enough!*

have had it* AND **have had it up to here*** to have reached the end of one's endurance or tolerance. (Informal.) □ *Okay, I've had it. You kids go to bed this instant.* □ *We've all had it with you, John. Get out!* □ *I've had it. I've got to go to bed before I drop dead.* □ *Tom is disgusted. He said that he has had it up to here.*

have had it up to here See the previous entry.

have half a mind to do something See the following entry.

have half a notion to do something* AND **have half a mind to do something*** to have almost decided to do something, especially something unpleasant. (Informal.) □ *I have half a mind to go off and leave you here.* □ *The cook had half a notion to serve cold chicken.*

have hold of someone or something See *get hold of someone or something.*

have it all over someone or something to be much better than someone or something. □ *This cake has it all over that one.* □ *My car has it all over yours.* □ *Sally can really run. She has it all over Bill.*

have it both ways to have both of two incompatible things. (Also used literally. See also *have one's cake and eat it too.*) □ *John wants the security of marriage and the freedom of being single. He wants to have it both ways.* □ *John* *thinks he can have it both ways—the wisdom of age and the vigor of youth.*

have it in for someone to have something against someone; to plan to scold or punish someone. □ *Don't go near Bob. He has it in for you.* □ *Billy! You had better go home. Your mom really has it in for you.*

have mixed feelings about someone or something AND **have mixed feelings** to be uncertain about someone or something. □ *I have mixed feelings about Bob. Sometimes I think he likes me; other times I don't.* □ *I have mixed feelings about my trip to England. I love the people, but the climate upsets me.* □ *Yes, I also have mixed feelings.*

have money to burn to have lots of money; to have more money than one needs. (See also *Money burns a hole in someone's pocket.*) □ *Look at the way Tom buys things. You'd think he had money to burn.* □ *If I had money to burn, I'd just put it in the bank.*

have no business doing something to be wrong to do something; to be extremely unwise to do something. □ *You have no business bursting in on me like that!* □ *You have no business spending money like that!*

have no staying power to lack endurance; to not be able to last. □ *Sally can swim fast for a short distance, but she has no staying power.* □ *That horse can race fairly well, but it has no staying power.*

have no time for someone or something See the following entry.

have no use for someone or something AND **have no time for someone or something** to dislike someone. (The literal senses of both expressions are also used.) □ *I have no use for John. I can't see why Mary likes him.* □ *We have no time for the Smiths. We don't get along.*

have none of something to tolerate or endure no amount of something. □ *I'll have none of your talk about quitting school.* □ *We'll have none of your gossip.* □ *I wish to have none of the sweet potatoes, please.*

have nothing on someone or something 1.* [with *someone*] to lack evidence against someone. (Informal.) □ *The police had nothing on Bob, so they let him loose.* □ *You've got nothing on me! Let me go!* **2.** to have no information about someone or something. □ *The dictionary had nothing on the word I looked up.* □ *The librarian said that the library has nothing on the Jones brothers.*

have nothing to do with someone or something 1. to ignore or avoid someone or something. (Also with *anything*, as in the examples. See also *have something to do with someone or something.*) □ *I will have nothing to do with Ann.* □ *I won't have anything to do with Ann.* □ *Bill would have nothing to do with the clown.* **2.** to not be related to or associated with someone or something. (The negative of *have something to do with someone or something.* Also with *anything*, as in the examples.) □ *"Saddle soap" is a wax. It has nothing to do with soap.* □ *Waterloo? That doesn't have anything to do with water, does it?*

have one's back to the wall* to be in a defensive position. (Informal. See also *push someone to the wall.*) □ *He'll have to give in. He has his back to the wall.* □ *How can I bargain when I've got my back to the wall?*

have one's cake and eat it too AND **eat one's cake and have it too** to enjoy both having something and using it up; to *have it both ways.* (Usually stated in the negative.) □ *Tom wants to have his cake and eat it too. It can't be done.* □ *Don't buy a car if you want to walk and stay healthy. You can't eat your cake and have it too.*

have one's druthers* to get one's choice; to be permitted to have one's preference. (Folksy. The *druthers* is from *rather*.) □ *If I had my druthers, I'd go to France.* □ *Tom said that if he had his druthers, he'd choose to stay home.*

have one's ear to the ground AND **keep one's ear to the ground** to listen carefully hoping to get advance warning of something. (Not used literally.) □ *John had his ear to the ground, hoping to find out about new ideas in computers.* □ *His boss told him to keep his ear to the* ground so that he'd be the first to know of a new idea.

have one's eye on someone or something See *have an eye on someone or something*.

have one's feet on the ground See *get one's feet on the ground*.

have one's fill of someone or something See *get one's fill of someone or something*.

have one's finger in the pie to be involved in something. □ *I like to have my finger in the pie so I can make sure things go my way.* □ *As long as John has his finger in the pie, things will happen slowly.*

have one's foot in the door See *get one's foot in the door*.

have one's hand in the till to be stealing money from a company or an organization. (The *till* is a cash box or drawer.) □ *Mr. Jones had his hand in the till for years before he was caught.* □ *I think that the new clerk has her hand in the till. There is cash missing every morning.*

have one's hands full with someone or something AND **have one's hands full** to be busy or totally occupied with someone or something. □ *I have my hands full with my three children.* □ *You have your hands full with the store.* □ *We both have our hands full.*

have one's hands tied to be prevented from doing something. □ *I can't help you. I was told not to, so I have my hands tied.* □ *John can help. He doesn't have his hands tied.*

have one's head in the clouds to be unaware of what is going on. □ *"Bob, do you have your head in the clouds?"* said the teacher. □ *She walks around all day with her head in the clouds. She must be in love.*

have one's heart go out to someone to have compassion for someone. □ *I can't have my heart go out to everyone.* □ *To have compassion is to have one's heart go out to those who are suffering.* ALSO: **one's heart goes out to someone** one feels compassion for someone. □ *My heart goes out to those starving children I see on television.*

have one's heart in one's mouth to feel strongly emotional about someone or something. □ *"Gosh, Mary,"* said John, *"I have my heart in my mouth whenever I see you."* □ *My heart is in my mouth whenever I hear the national anthem.* ALSO: **one's heart is in one's mouth** (for one) to feel strongly emotional. □ *It was a touching scene. My heart was in my mouth the whole time.*

have one's heart in the right place to have good intentions, even if there are bad results. □ *I don't always do what is right, but my heart is in the right place.* □ *Good old Tom. His heart's in the right place.* □ *It doesn't matter if she lost the game. She has her heart in the right place.* ALSO: **one's heart is in the right place** (for one) to have good intentions, even if the results are bad. □ *She gave it a good try. Her heart was in the right place.*

have one's heart miss a beat AND **have one's heart skip a beat** to be so excited that one's heart flutters or beats unevenly. □ *I hate to have my heart skip a beat. It frightens me.* ALSO: **one's heart misses a beat; one's heart skips a beat** for one's heart to flutter or beat unevenly. □ *Whenever I'm near you, my heart skips a beat.* □ *When the race horse fell, my heart missed a beat.*

have one's heart on one's sleeve See *wear one's heart on one's sleeve*.

have one's heart set against something to be totally against something. (Also with *dead*, as in the example. See also *dead set against someone or something*.) □ *Jane has her heart dead set against going to Australia.* □ *John has his heart set against going to college.* ALSO: **set one's heart against something** to turn against something; to become totally against something. (Cannot be used with *dead* as can the phrase above.) □ *Jane set her heart against going to Australia.* ALSO: **one's heart is set against something** one is totally against something. □ *Jane's heart is set against going there.*

have one's heart set on something to be desiring and expecting something. □ *Jane has her heart set on going to London.* □ *Bob will be disappointed. He had his heart set on going to college* *this year.* □ *His heart is set on it.* ALSO: **set one's heart on something** to become determined about something. □ *Jane set her heart on going to London.* ALSO: **one's heart is set on something** to desire and expect something. □ *Jane's heart is set on going to London.*

have one's heart skip a beat See *have one's heart miss a beat.*

have one's heart stand still* one's heart (figuratively) stops beating because one is feeling strong emotions. (A cliché.) □ *I had my heart stand still once when I was overcome with joy.* □ *Lovers—at least the ones in love songs—usually have their hearts stand still.* ALSO: **one's heart stands still** for one's heart to (figuratively) stop beating because of strong emotions. □ *When I first saw you, my heart stood still.*

have one's luck run out for one's good luck to stop; for one's good fortune to come to an end. □ *I had my luck run out when I was in South America. I nearly starved.* □ *I hate to have my luck run out just when I need it.* ALSO: **one's luck runs out** one's good luck stops. □ *My luck ran out, so I had to come home.*

have one's nose in a book to be reading a book; to read books all the time. □ *Bob has his nose in a book every time I see him.* □ *His nose is always in a book. He never gets any exercise.*

have one's nose in the air to be conceited or aloof. □ *Mary always seems to have her nose in the air.* □ *I wonder if she knows that she has her nose in the air.* ALSO: **one's nose is in the air** one is acting conceited or aloof. (Note the variation with *always.*) □ *Mary's nose is always in the air.* □ *Her mother's nose was always in the air, too.*

have one's say See *get one's say.*

have one's tail between one's legs to be frightened or cowed. (Refers to a frightened dog. Also used literally with dogs.) □ *John seems to lack courage. Whenever there is an argument, he has his tail between his legs.* □ *You can tell that the dog is frightened because it has its tail between its legs.* ALSO: **one's tail is between one's legs** one is act-

ing frightened or cowed. □ *He should have stood up and argued, but—as usual—his tail was between his legs.*

have one's way with someone or something See *get one's way with someone or something.*

have one's wits about one to be alert and responsive to a challenge. □ *You can depend on Sally. She has her wits about her.* □ *Bob never seems to have his wits about him.* ALSO: **one's wits are about one** one is alert and responsive to a challenge. □ *Try to keep your wits about you during the test.* □ *My wits are about me most of the time.*

have one's words stick in one's throat to be so overcome by emotion that one can hardly speak. □ *I sometimes have my words stick in my throat.* □ *John said that he never had his words stick in his throat.* ALSO: **one's words stick in one's throat** to find it difficult to speak because of emotion. □ *My words stick in my throat whenever I try to say something kind or tender.*

have one's work cut out for one to have a large and difficult task prepared for one. □ *They sure have their work cut out for them, and it's going to be hard.* □ *There is a lot for Bob to do. He has his work cut out for him.* ALSO: **one's work is cut out for one** one's task is prepared for one; one has a lot of work to do. □ *This is a big job. My work is cut out for me.*

have oneself something* to select, use, or consume something. (Folksy. Also with non-reflexive pronouns, *me, him, her,* etc., as in the last example.) □ *He had himself a two-hour nap.* □ *I'll have myself one of those red ones.* □ *I think I'll have me a big, cold drink.*

have other fish to fry to have other things to do; to have more important things to do. (*Other* can be replaced by *bigger, better, more important,* etc. The literal sense is not used.) □ *I can't take time for your problem. I have other fish to fry.* □ *I won't waste time on your question. I have bigger fish to fry.*

have pull with someone* to have influence with someone. (Slang. Also with *some, much, lots,* etc.) □ *Let's ask Ann to help us. She has pull with the* mayor. □ *Do you know anyone who has some pull with the bank president? I need a loan.*

have reason to do something AND **have reason** to have a cause or a reason to do something. (Note the variation in the examples.) □ *Tom has reason to act like that.* □ *Yes, he has good reason.* □ *We don't have any reason to do that.*

have rocks in one's head* to be silly or crazy. (Slang.) □ *John is a real nut. He has rocks in his head.* □ *I don't have rocks in my head—I'm just different.*

have second thoughts about someone or something See *get second thoughts about someone or something.*

have seen better days* to be worn or worn out. (Informal.) □ *This coat has seen better days. I need a new one.* □ *Oh, my old legs ache. I've seen better days, but everyone has to grow old.*

have so See *have too.*

have someone dead to rights* to have proven someone unquestionably guilty. (A cliché.) □ *The police burst in on the robbers while they were at work. They had the robbers dead to rights.* □ *All right, Tom! I've got you dead to rights! Get your hands out of the cookie jar.*

have someone in one's pocket* to have control over someone. (Informal.) □ *Don't worry about the mayor. She'll cooperate. I've got her in my pocket.* □ *John will do just what I tell him. I've got him and his brother in my pocket.*

have someone on the string* to have someone waiting for your decision. (Informal.) □ *Sally has John on the string. He has asked her to marry him, but she hasn't replied yet.* □ *Yes, it sounds like she has him on the string.*

have someone or something in one's hands to have control of or responsibility for someone or something. (*Have* can be replaced with *leave* or *put.*) □ *You have the whole project in your hands.* □ *The boss put the whole project in your hands.* □ *I have to leave the baby in your hands while I go to the doctor.*

have someone or something in tow to lead, pull, or tow someone or some-thing around. □ *Mrs. Smith has her son in tow.* □ *That car has a boat in tow.* ALSO: **in tow** □ *Here comes Mrs. Smith with her son Billy in tow.* □ *There goes a car with a boat in tow.*

have someone or something on 1. [with *someone*] to kid or deceive some-one. □ *You can't be serious. You're hav-ing me on!* □ *Bob is such a joker. He's always having someone on.* **2.** [with *something*] to be wearing something. □ *Do you have your coat on?* □ *I don't have anything on, so don't come in.* **3.** [with *something*] See *have something doing.*

have someone or something on one's hands to be burdened with someone or something. (*Have* can be replaced with *leave.* Also used literally.) □ *I run a record store. I sometimes have a large number of unwanted records on my hands.* □ *Please don't leave the chil-dren on my hands.*

have someone or something on one's mind to think often about someone or something; to be obsessed with some-one or something. □ *Bill has chocolate on his mind.* □ *John has Mary on his mind every minute.*

have someone or something started See *get someone or something started.*

have someone or something under con-trol See *get someone or something under control.*

have someone over a barrel See *get someone over a barrel.*

have someone under one's thumb See *get someone over a barrel.*

have someone's ear See *get some-one's ear.*

have someone's hide* to scold or pun-ish someone. (Slang. Refers to skinning an animal. Not used literally. Compare to *skin someone alive.*) □ *If you ever do that again, I'll have your hide.* □ *He said he'd have my hide if I entered his garage again.*

have someone's number See *get someone's number.*

have something against someone or something to possess something (such as prejudice or knowledge) which is harmful to someone or something. (Note the variation in the examples.)

□ *Do you have something against North Americans?* □ *What do you have against me?* □ *I don't have anything against eating beef.*

have something at hand See the following entry.

have something at one's fingertips AND **have something at hand** to have something within (one's) reach. (*Have* can be replaced with *keep*.) □ *I have a dictionary at my fingertips.* □ *I try to have everything I need at hand.* □ *I keep my medicine at my fingertips.*

have something coming 1. to be due to receive something. □ *I have a new car coming. It'll be received by the dealer next week.* □ *I have a contract coming. I look for it every day in the mail.* □ *I paid for a full dinner, so I have a dessert coming.* 2.* to deserve punishment (for something). (Informal.) □ *Bill broke a window, so he has a spanking coming.* □ *That's it, Bill. Now you've got it coming!*

have something doing* AND **have something on*** to have plans for an event. (Informal. Note the variation with *anything* in the examples.) □ *BOB: Are you busy Saturday night? BILL: Yes, I've got something doing.* □ *I don't have anything doing Sunday night.* □ *I have something on almost every Saturday.*

have something going for oneself* AND **have something going*** (for someone) to have a scheme or operation going. (Informal.) □ *John really has something going for himself. He's a travel agent, and he gets to travel everywhere for free.* □ *I wish I could have something like that going.*

have something going with someone* AND **have something going*** (Informal.) 1. to have a business deal with someone. □ *Sally has a new business project going with Ann. They'll announce a new product in the spring.* □ *John and Tom work as stock brokers. I've heard that they have a business deal going.* 2. See *have a thing going with someone.*

have something hanging over one's head* to have something bothering or worrying one; to have a deadline worrying one. (Informal. Also used literal-

ly.) □ *I keep worrying about getting drafted. I hate to have something like that hanging over my head.* □ *I have a history paper which is hanging over my head.*

have something in common with someone or something AND **have something in common** (for groups of people or things) to resemble one another in specific ways. □ *Bill and Bob both have red hair. They have that in common with each other.* □ *Bob and Mary have a lot in common. I can see why they like each other.*

have something in hand to have something in one's hand or close by. (Compare to *have something at hand.*) □ *I have your letter of May tenth in hand.* □ *I have my pen in hand, and I'm ready to write.*

have something in mind to think of something; to have an idea or image (of something) in one's mind. □ *BILL: I would like to purchase some boots. CLERK: Yes, Sir. Did you have something in mind?* □ *I have something in mind, but I don't see it here. Good day.*

have something in stock to have merchandise available and ready for sale. □ *Do you have extra large sizes in stock?* □ *Of course, we have all sizes and colors in stock.*

have something in store for someone AND **have something in store** to have something planned for one's future. □ *Tom has a large inheritance in store for him when his uncle dies.* □ *I wish I had something like that in store.*

have something left to have some part remaining. □ *That cake looks delicious. I hope you have some left.* □ *Is there any left?* □ *Sorry, there isn't any left.* ALSO: **something is left** something remains. □ *Some cake is left. Do you want it?*

have something made 1. to hire someone to make something. □ *Isn't it a lovely coat? I had to have it made because I couldn't find one I liked in a store.* □ *We had the cake made at the bakery. Our oven isn't big enough for a cake that size.* 2.* to have achieved a successful state. (Slang. Usually with *it.*) □ *Mary really has it made. She inher-*

ited one million dollars. □ *I wish I had it made like that.*

have something on file to have a written record of something in storage. □ *I'm sure I have your letter on file. I'll check again.* □ *We have your application on file somewhere.*

have something on someone See *get something on someone.*

have something on the ball* to be smart and clever. (Slang.) □ *Both John and Mary have a lot on the ball. They should go far.* □ *I think I'd do better in school if I had more on the ball. I learn slowly.*

have something on the brain* to be obsessed with something. (Slang.) □ *Bob has chocolate on the brain.* □ *Mary has money on the brain. She wants to earn as much as possible.*

have something out with someone* AND **have something out*** to settle a disagreement or a complaint. (Informal.) □ *John has been mad at Mary for a week. He finally had it out with her today.* □ *I'm glad we are having this out today.*

have something sewed up See *get something sewed up.*

have something stick in one's craw* to have something irritate or displease someone. (Folksy.) □ *I don't like to have someone's words stick in my craw.* □ *He meant to have the problem stick in my craw and upset me.* ALSO: **something sticks in one's craw** something bothers one. □ *Her criticism stuck in my craw.*

have something to do with someone or something to be related to or associated with someone or something. (See *have nothing to do with someone or something.*) □ *Does Waterloo have something to do with water?* □ *No, Waterloo has something to do with Napoleon Bonaparte.*

have something to go See *buy something to go.*

have something to spare* to have more than enough of something. (Informal.) □ *Ask John for some firewood. He has firewood to spare.* □ *Do you have any candy to spare?*

have something up one's sleeve* to have a secret or surprise plan or solution (to a problem). (Slang. Refers to cheating at cards by having a card hidden in one's sleeve.) □ *I've got something up my sleeve, and it should solve all your problems. I'll tell you what it is after I'm elected.* □ *The manager has something up her sleeve. She'll surprise us with it later.*

have something wrapped up See *get something sewed up.*

have stars in one's eyes See *get stars in one's eyes.*

have sticky fingers* to have a tendency to steal. (Slang.) □ *The clerk—who had sticky fingers—got fired.* □ *The little boy had sticky fingers and was always taking his father's small change.*

have the advantage of someone AND **have the advantage over someone** (*The* can be replaced with *an.*) **1.** to know more about a person than the person knows about you; to know the name of a person to whom you have not been formally introduced. (Formal. Sometimes used as a way of asking to be introduced to someone.) □ *I'm sorry, but I'm afraid you have the advantage of me.* □ *You have an advantage over me, sir. I regret that I have never had the pleasure of making your acquaintance.* **2.** See *get the advantage of someone.*

have the blues See *get the blues.*

have the cards stacked against one* to have luck against one. (Informal.) □ *You can't get very far in life if the cards are stacked against you.* □ *I can't seem to get ahead. I always have the cards stacked against me.* ALSO: **the cards are stacked against one*** luck is against one. (Informal.) □ *I have the worst luck. The cards are stacked against me all the time.*

have the courage of one's convictions to have enough courage and determination to carry out one's goals. □ *It's fine to have noble goals in life and to believe in great things. If you don't have the courage of your convictions, you'll never reach your goals.* □ *Jane was successful because she had the courage of her convictions.*

have the day off See *get the day off.*

have the devil to pay* AND **have hell to**

pay* to have a great deal of trouble. (Informal. Use *hell* with caution.) □ *If you cheat on your income taxes, you'll have the devil to pay.* □ *I came home after 3:00 in the morning and had hell to pay.*

have the edge on someone See *get the advantage of someone.*

have the feel of something **1.** (for something) to feel like something (else). □ *This plastic has the feel of fine leather.* □ *The little car has the feel of a much larger one.* **2.** See *get the feel of something.*

have the floor See *get the floor.*

have the gift of gab* to have a great facility with language; to be able to use language very effectively. (Slang.) □ *My brother really has the gift of gab. He can convince anyone of anything.* □ *If I had the gift of gab like you do, I'd achieve more in life.*

have the inside track See *get the inside track.*

have the last laugh See *get the last laugh.*

have the last word See *get the last word.*

have the right-of-way to possess the legal right to occupy a particular space on a public roadway. □ *I had a traffic accident yesterday, but it wasn't my fault. I had the right-of-way.* □ *Don't pull out onto a highway if you don't have the right-of-way.*

have the shoe on the other foot* to experience the opposite situation (from a previous situation). (Informal. Also with *be* instead of *have*. See the examples. Compare to *in someone else's shoes.*) □ *I used to be a student, and now I'm the teacher. Now I have the shoe on the other foot.* □ *You were mean to me when you thought I was cheating. Now that I have caught you cheating, the shoe is on the other foot.*

have the time of one's life to have a very good time; to have the most exciting time in one's life. □ *What a great party! I had the time of my life.* □ *We went to Florida last winter and had the time of our lives.*

have the upper hand on someone See *get the upper hand on someone.*

have the wherewithal to do something* AND **have the wherewithal*** to have the means to do something, especially energy or money. (A cliché.) □ *He has good ideas, but he doesn't have the wherewithal to carry them out.* □ *I could do a lot if I only had the wherewithal.*

have them rolling in the aisles* to make an audience roll in the aisles with laughter. (Slang. Never literal.) □ *I have the best jokes you've ever heard. I'll have them rolling in the aisles.* □ *What a great performance. We had them rolling in the aisles.*

have time for someone or something See *get time for someone or something.*

have time off See *get time off.*

have time to catch one's breath See *get time to catch one's breath.*

have to do something for it to be necessary to do something. □ *I have to go to the doctor today.* □ *We have to pay our taxes this week.*

have to live with something to have to endure something. □ *I have a slight limp in the leg which I broke last year. The doctor says I'll have to live with it.* □ *We don't like the new carpeting in the living room, but we'll have to live with it.*

have too AND **have so** to have done something (despite anything to the contrary). (This is an emphatic way of affirming that something has happened.) □ BILL: *You haven't made your bed.* BOB: *I have too!* □ *I have so turned in my paper! If you don't have it, you lost it!*

have too many irons in the fire* to be doing too many things at once. (A cliché.) □ *Tom had too many irons in the fire and missed some important deadlines.* □ *It's better if you don't have too many irons in the fire.*

have turned the corner to have passed a critical point in a process. □ *The patient has turned the corner. She should begin to show improvement now.* □ *The project has turned the corner. The rest should be easy.*

have two strikes against one See *get two strikes against one.*

have what it takes* to have the courage or stamina (to do something). (A cliché.) □ *Bill has what it takes. He can swim for miles.* □ *Tom won't succeed. He doesn't have what it takes.*

He laughs best who laughs last. See the following entry.

He who laughs last, laughs longest. AND **He laughs best who laughs last.** a proverb meaning that whoever succeeds in making the last move or pulling the last trick has the most enjoyment. □ *Bill had pulled many silly tricks on Tom. Finally Tom pulled a very funny trick on Bill and said, "He who laughs last, laughs longest."* □ *Bill pulled another, even bigger trick on Tom, and said, laughing, "He laughs best who laughs last."*

head and shoulders above someone or something* to be clearly superior to someone. (A cliché. Often with *stand*, as in the examples.) □ *This wine is head and shoulders above that one.* □ *John stands head and shoulders above Bob.*

head for someone or something to aim for or move toward someone or something. □ *She waved goodbye as she headed for the door.* □ *Ann came in and headed for her mother.*

head into something to aim at or aim into something. □ *The plane headed into the cloud.* □ *The visitor headed into the worst part of town.*

head over heels in love with someone AND **head over heels in love** very much in love with someone. □ *John is head over heels in love with Mary.* □ *They are head over heels in love with each other.* □ *They are head over heels in love.*

head someone or something into someone or something AND **head someone or something at someone or something; head someone or something toward someone or something** to aim or drive someone or something in the direction of someone or something. □ *The pilot headed the plane into the storm.* □ *Please head me into the dining room. I lost my glasses.* □ *He headed the boat toward the dock.* □ *The children headed themselves at the clowns.*

head someone or something off AND **head off someone or something** to prevent someone or something from arriving. □ *The farmer headed off the herd of sheep before it ruined our picnic.* □ *The doctors worked round the clock to head the epidemic off.* □ *Bill headed his mother off so that we had time to clean up the mess before she saw it.*

head something out AND **head out something** to aim something outward, especially a boat, car, etc. □ *Jane started the engine and headed out the boat.* □ *She had landed the boat, but she had never headed it out before.*

head something up AND **head up something** to serve as leader or head of something. □ *They asked me to head up the meeting.* □ *I had already agreed to head the fund-raising campaign up.*

hear from someone to get a message from someone. □ *I haven't heard from my cousin in ten years.* □ *I just heard from Tom. He's in California.*

hear of someone or something **1.** to know of the existence of someone or something. □ *I have heard of banana ice cream, but I have never eaten any.* □ *I've heard of Mr. Smith, but I've never met him.* **2.** [with *something*] to tolerate something; to permit something. (Usually negative.) □ *No, you cannot go to the movies! I won't hear of it!* □ *My mother wouldn't hear of my marrying Bill.*

hedge one's bets* to reduce one's loss on a bet or on an investment by counterbalancing the loss in some way. (Slang.) □ *Bob bet Ann that the plane would be late. He usually hedges his bets. This time he called the airline and asked about the plane before he made the bet.* □ *John bought some stock and then bet Mary that the stock would go down in value in one year. He has hedged his bets perfectly. If the stock goes up, he sells it, pays off Mary, and still makes a profit. If it goes down, he reduces his loss by winning the bet he made with Mary.*

hellbent for leather* moving or behaving recklessly; riding a horse fast and recklessly. (Informal. Typically found in Western movies.) □ *They took off after the horse thief, riding hellbent for leather.* □ *Here comes the boss. She's not just angry; she's hellbent for leather.*

help oneself to take whatever one wants or needs. □ *Please have some candy. Help yourself.* □ *When you go to a cafeteria, you help yourself to the food.* □ *Bill helped himself to dessert.*

help someone or something out with someone or something AND **help out someone or something with someone or something; help someone or something out; help out someone or something** to assist someone or something with a person or a thing. □ *Can you help me out with my geometry?* □ *Yes, I can help you out.* □ *Please help out my son with his geometry.* □ *Please help me out around the house.* □ *We helped the school out with its fund raising.*

hem and haw around* to be uncertain about something; to be evasive; to say "ah" and "eh" when speaking—avoiding saying something meaningful. (Folksy.) □ *Stop hemming and hawing around. I want an answer.* □ *Don't just hem and haw around. Speak up. We want to hear what you think.*

hem someone or something in AND **hem in someone or something** to trap or enclose someone or something. □ *Don't hem the bird in. Let it have a way to escape.* □ *The large city buildings hem me in.* ALSO: **hemmed in** enclosed; trapped. □ *I hate to feel hemmed in.* □ *The garden wall makes our back yard seem hemmed in.*

here and there at this place and that; from place to place. □ *We find rare books in used book stores here and there.* □ *She didn't make a systematic search. She just looked here and there.*

Here goes nothing.* I am beginning to do something which will fail or be poorly done. (Informal.) □ *Sally stood on the diving board and said, "Here goes nothing."* □ *As Ann walked onto the stage, she whispered, "Here goes nothing."*

hide one's face in shame to cover one's face because of shame or embarrassment. □ *Mary was so embarrassed. She could only hide her face in shame.* □ *When Tom broke Ann's crystal vase, he wanted to hide his face in shame.*

hide one's head in the sand See *bury one's head in the sand.*

hide one's light under a bushel to con-

ceal one's good ideas or talents. (A Biblical theme.) □ *Jane has some good ideas, but she doesn't speak very often. She hides her light under a bushel.* □ *Don't hide your light under a bushel. Share your gifts with other people.*

high man on the totem pole* the person at the top of the hierarchy; the person in charge of an organization. (Informal. Compare to *low man on the totem pole.*) □ *I don't want to talk to a secretary. I demand to talk to the high man on the totem pole.* □ *Who's in charge around here? Who's high man on the totem pole?*

high on something* (Slang.) **1.** intoxicated with some drug. □ *He got thrown out of the movie because he was high on something.* □ *Bill was high on marijuana and was singing loudly.* **2.** enthusiastic about something. □ *Jane quit eating red meat. She's really high on fish, however.* □ *Bob is high on meditation. He sits and meditates for an hour each day.*

high tail it out of somewhere* to run or ride a horse away from somewhere fast. (Folksy. Typically heard in Western movies.) □ *Here comes the sheriff. We'd better high tail it out of here.* □ *Look at that guy go. He really high tailed it out of town.*

hinge on something to depend on something. □ *This all hinges on how much risk you're willing to take.* □ *Whether we have the picnic hinges on the weather.*

hire someone out AND **hire out someone** to bring about the employment of someone. □ *John hired himself out as a house painter.* □ *Mr. Smith hired out his children as clothing models.*

hit a snag* to run into a problem. (Informal.) □ *We've hit a snag with the building project.* □ *I stopped working on the roof when I hit a snag.*

hit and miss AND **hit or miss** carelessly; aimlessly; without plan or direction. □ *There was no planning. It was just hit and miss.* □ *We handed out the free tickets hit or miss. Some people got one; others got five or six.* ALSO: **hit-and-miss; hit-or-miss** careless; aimless; directionless. □ *They did it in a hit-and-miss fashion.* □ *This isn't a* *hit-or-miss operation. We are well organized.*

hit bottom* to reach the lowest or worst point. (Informal.) □ *Our profits have hit bottom. This is our worst year ever.* □ *When my life hit bottom, I began to feel much better. I knew that if there was going to be any change, it would be for the better.*

hit it off with someone AND **hit it off** to quickly become good friends with someone. □ *Look how John hit it off with Mary.* □ *Yes, they really hit it off.*

hit on something* AND **hit upon something*** to discover or think up something. (Informal.) □ *Ann hit on the idea of baking lots of bread and freezing it.* □ *John hit upon a new way of planting corn.*

hit one close to home See the following entry.

hit one where one lives* AND **hit one close to home*** to affect one personally and intimately. (Informal.) □ *Her comments really hit me where I live. Her words seemed to apply directly to me.* □ *I listened carefully and didn't think she hit close to home at all.* ALSO: **close to home*; where one lives*** affecting one personally and intimately. (Informal.) □ *Her remarks were a bit too close to home. I was afraid she was discussing me!* □ *She's got me figured out all right. She knows where I live.*

hit one's stride See *reach one's stride.*

hit pay dirt* to discover something of value. (Slang. Refers to discovering valuable ore.) □ *Sally tried a number of different jobs until she hit pay dirt.* □ *I tried to borrow money from a lot of different people. They all said no. Then when I went to the bank, I hit pay dirt.*

hit someone below the belt* AND **hit below the belt*** to do something unfair or unsporting to someone. (Informal. From boxing where a blow below the belt line is not permitted. Also used literally.) □ *You really hit me below the belt when you told the boss about my tax problems.* □ *In business Bill is difficult to deal with. He hits below the belt.*

hit someone between the eyes* to become completely apparent; to surprise or impress someone. (Informal. Also with *right,* as in the examples. Also used literally.) □ *Suddenly, it hit me right between the eyes. John and Mary were in love.* □ *Then—as he was talking—the exact nature of the evil plan hit me between the eyes.*

hit someone like a ton of bricks* AND **hit like a ton of bricks*** to surprise, startle, or shock someone. (Informal.) □ *Suddenly, the truth hit me like a ton of bricks.* □ *The sudden tax increase hit like a ton of bricks. Everyone became angry.*

hit someone up for something* AND **hit up someone for something*; hit someone up*; hit up someone*** to ask someone for something. (Informal.) □ *John hit me up for a loan.* □ *I told him to go hit up someone else.*

hit the books* to begin to study; to study. (Slang.) □ *Well, time to hit the books.* □ *John, if you don't start hitting the books, you're going to fail.*

hit the bricks* to start walking; to go out into the streets. (Slang.) □ *If you want to get a job, you had better get out there and hit the bricks.* □ *I got fired today. The boss came by and told me to hit the bricks.*

hit the bull's-eye 1. to hit the center area of a circular target. □ *The archer hit the bull's-eye three times in a row.* □ *I didn't hit the bull's-eye even once.* 2.* to achieve the goal perfectly. (Informal.) □ *Your idea really hit the bull's-eye. Thank you!* □ *Jill has a lot of insight. She knows how to hit the bull's-eye.*

hit the ceiling* to become very angry. (Informal.) □ *My father hit the ceiling when I damaged the car.* □ *Our employer hit the ceiling when we lost an important contract.*

hit the hay* AND **hit the sack*** to go to bed and get some sleep. (Slang. Compare to *sack out.*) □ *Look at the clock. It's time to hit the hay.* □ *I like to hit the sack before midnight.*

hit the high spots* to do only the important, obvious, or good things. (Informal.) □ *I won't discuss the entire report. I'll just hit the high spots.* □ *First,* *let me hit the high spots; then I'll tell you about everything.*

hit the jackpot* (Slang.) **1.** to win at gambling. (Refers to the "jack" in playing cards.) □ *Bob hit the jackpot three times in one night.* □ *I've never hit the jackpot even once.* **2.** to have a success. □ *I hit the jackpot on a business deal.* □ *I really hit the jackpot in the library. I found just what I needed.*

hit the nail on the head* to do exactly the right thing; to do something in the most effective and efficient way. (A cliché. Also with *right*, as in the examples.) □ *You've spotted the flaw, Sally. You hit the nail on the head.* □ *Bob doesn't say much, but every now and then he hits the nail right on the head.*

hit the sack See *hit the hay.*

hit the skids* to decline; to decrease in value. (Slang.) □ *Business usually hits the skids in the summer.* □ *Tom hit the skids after he lost his job.*

hit the spot* to be exactly right; to be refreshing. (Informal.) □ *This cool drink really hits the spot.* □ *That was a delicious meal, dear. It hit the spot.*

hit upon something See *hit on something.*

hitch a ride See *thumb a ride.*

hold a grudge against someone See *bear a grudge against someone.*

hold a meeting to meet; to have a meeting (of an organization). □ *We'll have to hold a meeting to make a decision.* □ *Our club held a meeting to talk about future projects.*

hold all the aces* to be in a favorable position; to be in a controlling position. (Slang. Refers to having possession of all four aces in a card game.) □ *How can I advance in my job when my enemy holds all the aces?* □ *If I held all the aces, I'd be able to do great things.*

hold forth* to speak at length. (Informal.) □ *I've never seen anyone who could hold forth so long.* □ *The professor held forth about economic theory for nearly an hour.*

Hold it!* Stop!; Stop moving! (Slang.) □ *Hold it, Tom! You're going the wrong way.* □ *You're speaking out of turn. Hold it!*

hold no brief for someone or some-

thing to not care about someone or something; to dislike someone or something. □ *I hold no brief for bad typists.* □ *My father says he holds no brief for sweet potatoes.*

hold off doing something AND **hold off on doing something; hold off** to refrain from doing something; to wait until later to do something. □ *Please hold off on painting the house until I can supervise your work.* □ *I can't hold off very long. It'll be too cold pretty soon.*

hold on 1. See *hang on to someone or something.* **2.** to stop; to wait. □ *Hold on for a minute.* □ *Now, hold on. You're talking too fast.*

hold on to someone or something See *hang on to someone or something.*

Hold on to your hat! See *Hang on to your hat!*

hold one's breath 1. to stop breathing for a short period, on purpose. □ *Do you hold your breath when you dive into the water?* □ *I can't hold my breath for very long.* **2.*** to stop breathing until something special happens. (Informal. Usually in the negative.) □ BOB: *The bus is going to come soon.* BILL: *Don't hold your breath until it does.* □ *I expect the mail to be delivered soon, but I'm not holding my breath.*

hold one's end up AND **hold one's end of the bargain up; hold up one's end; hold up one's end of the bargain** to do one's part as agreed; to attend to one's responsibilities as agreed. □ *Tom has to learn to cooperate. He must hold up his end of the bargain.* □ *If you don't hold your end up, the whole project will fail.*

hold one's fire 1. to refrain from shooting (a gun, etc.). □ *The sergeant told the soldiers to hold their fire.* □ *Please hold your fire until I get out of the way.* **2.*** to postpone one's criticism or commentary. (Informal.) □ *Now, now, hold your fire until I've had a chance to explain.* □ *Hold your fire, Bill. You're too quick to complain.*

hold one's ground See *stand one's ground.*

hold one's head up AND **hold up one's head** to have one's self-respect; to

165

retain or display one's dignity. □ *I've done nothing wrong. I can hold my head up in public.* □ *I'm so embarrassed and ashamed. I'll never be able to hold up my head again.*

hold one's own to do as well as anyone else. □ *I can hold my own in a footrace any day.* □ *She was unable to hold her own, and she had to quit.*

hold one's peace to remain silent. □ *Bill was unable to hold his peace any longer. "Don't do it!" he cried.* □ *Quiet, John. Hold your peace for a little while longer.*

hold one's temper See *keep one's temper.*

hold one's tongue to refrain from speaking; to refrain from saying something unpleasant. □ *I felt like scolding her, but I held my tongue.* □ *Hold your tongue, John. You can't talk to me that way.*

hold out 1. to last or endure. (Compare to *hold up.*) □ *I need to eat something now. I can't hold out much longer.* □ *How long can a human being hold out without water?* 2. See the following entry.

hold out for someone or something AND **hold out** to wait for someone or something; to forego everything for someone or something. □ BOB: *Would you like some of this chocolate ice cream?* BILL: *No I'll hold out for the vanilla.* □ *How long will you hold out?*

hold out the olive branch to offer to end a dispute and be friendly; to offer reconciliation. (The olive branch is a symbol of peace and reconciliation. A Biblical reference.) □ *Jill was the first to hold out the olive branch after our argument.* □ *I always try to hold out the olive branch to someone I have hurt. Life is too short for a person to bear grudges for very long.*

hold someone accountable for something AND **hold someone accountable** to consider someone responsible for something; to blame something on someone. (The *something* can be replaced with *someone* meaning "someone's welfare.") □ *I hold you accountable for John's well-being.* □ *Yes, you hold me accountable for John.* □ *I must hold you accountable for the theft.* □ *No! Please don't hold me accountable.*

hold someone down AND **hold down someone** to try to keep someone from succeeding. □ *I'm not trying to hold down my brother.* □ *I still think you're trying to hold him down.*

hold someone or something at bay See *keep someone or something at bay.*

hold someone or something back See *keep someone or something back.*

hold someone or something in check See *keep someone or something in check.*

hold someone or something off See *keep someone or something off.*

hold someone or something over to retain someone or something (for a period of time). □ *The storm held John over for another day.* □ *The manager held the movie over for another week.*

hold someone or something still See *keep someone or something still.*

hold someone or something up AND **hold up someone or something** 1. to support someone or something. (Compare to *keep someone or something up.*) □ *I don't think that table will hold you up. Please sit on a chair.* □ *It took both of us to hold up the old man.* □ *We couldn't hold up the fence, and it finally fell over.* 2. [with *someone*] to rob someone (figuratively or literally). □ *I don't eat at that restaurant anymore. The food is too expensive. They really held me up the last time I ate there.* □ *That's the one who held me up at gunpoint.* 3. to detain someone or something; to make someone or something late. (Compare to *hold up on something.*) □ *A storm in Boston held up our plane.* □ *The traffic on the expressway held me up.* 4. See the following entry.

hold someone or something up as an example AND **hold up someone or something as an example; hold someone or something up; hold up someone or something** to point out someone or something as a good example. □ *I was embarrassed when the boss held me up as an example.* □ *I don't like for anyone to hold me up like that.* □ *The teacher held up the leaf as an example of a typical compound leaf.*

hold something against someone to blame something on someone; to *bear* *a grudge against someone*; to resent someone. □ *Your brother is mean to me, but I can't hold it against you.* □ *You're holding something against me. What is it?*

hold still See *keep still.*

hold still for something See *keep still for something.*

hold the fort* to take care of a place, such as a store or one's home. (Informal. From Western movies.) □ *I'm going next door to visit Mrs. Jones. You stay here and hold the fort.* □ *You should open the store at 8:00 and hold the fort until I get there at 10:00.*

hold the line at someone or something AND **hold the line** to limit the number or degree of someone or something; to limit (something) to someone or something. □ *The room will seat fifty, but I think you should hold the line at forty.* □ *The Browns and the Smiths could be invited, but I think we ought to hold the line at the Browns.* □ *Okay, we'll hold the line.*

hold tight AND **hold on tight** to grasp (someone or something) tightly. (Compare to *Hang on!*) □ *Here we go! Hold on tight!* □ *This is a carrousel. Sit on the horse and hold tight.*

hold true (for something) to be true; (for something) to remain true. □ *Does this rule hold true all the time?* □ *Yes, it holds true no matter what.*

hold up 1. See *wait up for someone or something.* 2. to endure; to last a long time. □ *How long will this cloth hold up?* □ *I want my money back for this chair. It isn't holding up well.*

hold up on something to delay doing something. □ *Please hold up on the project. We've run out of money.* □ *I have to hold up on my reading because I broke my glasses.*

hold with something* to accept or agree with something. (Folksy. Usually in the negative.) □ *My father doesn't hold with fancy clothes.* □ *I don't hold with too many X-rays.*

Hold your horses!* Wait a minute and be reasonable.; Do not run off wildly. (Folksy. From Western movies.) □ *Now, hold your horses, John. Be reasonable for a change.* □ *Don't get so mad. Just hold your horses.*

hole in one* (Informal.) 1. an instance of hitting a golf ball into a hole in only one try. (From the game of golf.) □ *John made a hole in one yesterday.* □ *I've never gotten a hole in one.* 2. an instance of succeeding the first time. □ *It worked the first time I tried it—a hole in one.* □ *Bob got a hole in one on that sale. A lady walked in the door, and he sold her a car in five minutes.*

hole up somewhere* AND **hole up*** to hide somewhere; to live in hiding somewhere. (Slang. Typically in Western or gangster movies.) □ *The old man is holed up in the mountains, waiting for the war to end.* □ *If we are going to hole up for the winter, we'll need lots of food.*

hollow something out AND **hollow out something** to make the inside of something hollow by removing material. □ *The water hollowed out a cave in the mountain.* □ *Please take a knife and hollow this block of wood out.*

home in on someone or something AND **home in** to aim exactly at something and move toward it. □ *The sheriff walked in the room and homed in on the horse thief.* □ *The plane homed in on the beacon at the airport.* □ *First, you must set your goal and then home in.*

honest and above board See *above board.*

honest to goodness* I speak the truth. (The *goodness* can be replaced with *God* or *Pete.* Use with caution. Some people may object to the use of *God* in this phrase.) □ *Did he really say that? Honest to goodness?* □ *Honest to Pete, I've been to the moon.* □ *I've been there, too—honest to God.* ALSO: **honest-to-goodness; honest-to-God; honest-to-Pete** truthful; genuine. □ *Is that an honest-to-goodness leather jacket, or is it vinyl?*

honor someone's check to accept someone's personal check. □ *The clerk at the store wouldn't honor my check. I had to pay cash.* □ *The bank didn't honor your check when I tried to deposit it. Please give me cash.*

hook something up AND **hook up something** to attach something; to install something electrical or mechanical. □ *Have they hooked up the new furnace yet?* □ *I bought a computer, but I can't even hook it up.*

hooked on something* (Slang.) **1.** addicted to a drug or something similar. □ *Jenny is hooked on cocaine.* □ *She was not hooked on anything before that.* □ *John is hooked on coffee.* **2.** enthusiastic about something; supportive of something. □ *Mary is hooked on football. She never misses a game.* □ *Jane is so happy! She's hooked on life.*

Hop to it!* Move fast!; Get started!. (Slang.) □ *Come on, you guys, move it! Hop to it!* □ *Hop to it, Bill. You look like you're loafing.*

hope against all hope to have hope even when the situation appears to be hopeless. □ *We hope against all hope that she'll see the right thing to do and do it.* □ *There is little point in hoping against all hope, except that it makes you feel better.*

hopeless at doing something incapable of doing something. □ *Tom is hopeless at cooking.* □ *Sally is hopeless at dusting. She hates it.*

hopped up* (Slang.) **1.** intoxicated with drugs or alcohol; stimulated by drugs or alcohol. □ *The old man was hopped up again. He was addicted to opium.* □ *John usually gets hopped up on the weekends.* **2.** excited; enthusiastic. □ *What are you hopped up about now? You're certainly cheery.* □ *I always get hopped up when I think of mountain climbing.*

horn in on someone* AND **horn in*** to attempt to displace someone. (Informal.) □ *I'm going to ask Sally to the party. Don't you dare try to horn in on me!* □ *I wouldn't think of horning in.*

horse around* to play around; to waste time in frivolous activities. (Informal.) □ *Stop horsing around and get to work.* □ *The children were on the playground horsing around when the bell rang.*

horse of a different color See the following entry.

horse of another color AND **horse of a different color** another matter altogether. □ *I was talking about trees, not bushes. Bushes are a horse of another color.* □ *Gambling is not the same as investing in the stock market. It's a horse of a different color.*

horse play* physically active and frivolous play. (Informal. See also *horse around.*) □ *Stop that horse play and get to work.* □ *I won't tolerate horse play in my living room.*

hot and bothered* **1.** excited; anxious. (Informal.) □ *Now don't get hot and bothered. Take it easy.* □ *John is hot and bothered about the tax increase.* **2.** amorous; interested in romance or sex. (Informal and euphemistic. Use with caution.) □ *John gets hot and bothered whenever Mary comes into the room.* □ *The dog seems hot and bothered. I think it's that time of the year again.*

Hot enough for you?* What do you think about this heat?; Do you like this hot weather? (Folksy. Said only in very hot weather.) □ *Well, hello, Sally. Hot enough for you?* □ *Some weather, huh? Hot enough for you?*

hot foot it out of somewhere* to run away from a place. (Folksy. Compare to *high tail it out of somewhere.*) □ *Did you see Tom hot foot it out of the office when the boss came in?* □ *Things are looking bad. I think we had better hot foot it out of here.*

hot under the collar* very angry. (A cliché.) □ *The boss was really hot under the collar when you told him you lost the contract.* □ *I get hot under the collar every time I think about it.*

hover over someone or something to remain close to or above someone or something; to watch over or supervise someone or something. □ *How can I work when you're always hovering over me?* □ *The hawk hovered over the rabbit for a second and then attacked.*

hung up on someone or something* AND **hung up*** obsessed with someone or something; devoted to someone or something. (Slang. See also *hang-up* at *hang up.*) □ *John is really hung up on Mary.* □ *She's hung up, too. See how she smiles at him.*

hunt someone or something down See *track someone or something down.*

hunt someone or something up See *look someone or something up.*

hurry back* come back again. (A

cliché. A friendly way of inviting some-one to return.) □ *Thank you for shopping here. Hurry back.* □ *I'm glad you could come to my house for a visit. Hurry back.*

hurt someone's feelings to cause someone emotional pain. □ *It hurts my feelings when you talk that way.* □ *I'm sorry. I didn't mean to hurt your feel-ings.*

hush someone or something up AND **hush up someone or something 1.** [with *someone*] to make someone be quiet. □ *Please hush up the baby.* □ *The teacher asked the class to hush itself up.* **2.*** [with *someone*] to kill someone. (Slang, especially criminal slang.) □ *The gangsters hushed up the witness with a gunshot.* □ *If they hear that you know who robbed the bank, they'll hush you up.* **3.** [with *something*] to keep some-thing a secret; to try to stop a rumor from spreading. □ *Please try to hush up the rumor about my uncle.* □ *Okay, I'll try to hush it up.*

I

If the shoe fits, wear it. a proverb meaning that you should pay attention to something if it applies to you. □ *Some people here need to be quiet. If the shoe fits, wear it.* □ *This doesn't apply to everyone. If the shoe fits, wear it.*

if worst comes to worst* in the worst possible situation; if things really get bad. (A cliché.) □ *If worst comes to worst, we'll hire someone to help you.* □ *If worst comes to worst, I'll have to borrow some money.*

ill at ease uneasy; anxious. □ *I feel ill at ease about the interview.* □ *You look ill at ease. Please relax.*

impose on someone to use someone for one's own benefit; to bother someone. □ *I don't want to impose on you, but could I have a ride to the library?* □ *Jane imposes on her friends too often.*

impose something on someone to force something on someone; to make someone accept something. □ *I wish you wouldn't impose your will on all of us.* □ *She said she'd impose a solution on them if they couldn't agree among themselves.*

improve on something to make something better; to improve something. (*On* can be replaced with *upon.*) □ *It's very good the way it is, but I can improve on it.* □ *It's so beautiful that it cannot be improved upon.*

in a bad mood sad; depressed; grouchy; with low spirits. □ *He's in a bad mood. He may yell at you.* □ *Please try to cheer me up. I'm in a bad mood.*

in a bad way in a critical or bad state. (Can refer to health, finances, mood, etc.) □ *Mr. Smith is in a bad way. He may have to go to the hospital.* □ *My*

bank account is in a bad way. It needs some help from a millionaire. □ *My life is in a bad way, and I'm depressed about it.*

in a bind AND **in a jam** in a tight or difficult situation; stuck on a problem. (*In* can be replaced with *into* to show movement toward or into the state described by *bind* or *jam.* Especially *get into.* See the examples.) □ *I'm in a bind. I owe a lot of money.* □ *Whenever I get into a jam, I ask my supervisor for help.* □ *When things get busy around here, we get in a bind. We could use another helper.*

in a coon's age* AND **in a month of Sundays*** in a very long time. (Folksy. The *coon* is a *raccoon.*) □ *How are you? I haven't seen you in a coon's age.* □ *I haven't had a piece of apple pie this good in a coon's age.* □ *John hasn't seen a movie in a month of Sundays.*

in a dead heat (finishing a race) at exactly the same time; tied. □ *The two horses finished the race in a dead heat.* □ *They ended the contest in a dead heat.*

in a family way* AND **in the family way*** pregnant. (Informal.) □ *I've heard that Mrs. Smith is in a family way.* □ *Our dog is in the family way.*

in a fix* in a bad situation. (Informal. *In* can be replaced with *into.* See *in a bind* and the examples below.) □ *I really got myself into a fix. I owe a lot of money on my taxes.* □ *John is in a fix because he lost his wallet.* □ *John got into a fix.*

in a flash* quickly; immediately. (Informal.) □ *I'll be there in a flash.* □ *It happened in a flash. Suddenly my wallet was gone.*

in a fog preoccupied; not paying attention to what is going on around one; not alert. □ *Jane always seems to be in a fog.* □ *When I get up, I'm in a fog for an hour.*

in a huff* in an angry or offended manner. (Informal. *In* can be replaced with *into*. See *in a bind* and the examples below.) □ *He heard what we had to say, then left in a huff.* □ *She came in a huff and ordered us to bring her something to eat.* □ *She gets into a huff very easily.*

in a jam See *in a bind*.

in a jiffy* very fast; very soon. (Slang.) □ *Just wait a minute. I'll be there in a jiffy.* □ *I'll be finished in a jiffy.*

in a lather* flustered; excited and agitated. (Slang. *In* can be replaced with *into*. See *in a bind* and the examples below.) □ *Now, calm down. Don't be in a lather.* □ *I always get in a lather when I'm late.* □ *I get into a lather easily.*

in a mad rush* in a hurry. □ *I ran around all day today in a mad rush looking for a present for Bill.* □ *Why are you always in a mad rush?*

in a month of Sundays See *in a coon's age*.

in a nutshell* in a few words; briefly; concisely. (Informal.) □ *I don't have time for the whole explanation. Please give it to me in a nutshell.* □ *Well, in a nutshell, we have to work late.*

in a pickle* AND **in a pretty pickle*** in a mess; in trouble. (Informal. *In* can be replaced with *into*. See *in a bind* and the examples below.) □ *John has gotten himself into a pickle. He has two dates for the party.* □ *Now we are in a pretty pickle. We are out of gas.*

in a quandary uncertain about what to do; confused. (*In* can be replaced with *into*. See *in a bind* and the examples below.) □ *Mary was in a quandary about what college to go to.* □ *I couldn't decide what to do. I was in such a quandary.* □ *I got myself into a quandary.*

in a second AND **in just a second** in a very short period of time. □ *I'll be there in a second.* □ *I'll be with you in just a second. I'm on the phone.*

in a sense in a way; sort of. □ *In a sense, cars make life better.* □ *But, in a sense, they also make life worse.*

in a snit* in a fit of anger or irritation. (Slang. *In* can be replaced with *into*. See *in a bind* and the examples below.) □ *Mrs. Smith threw on her coat and left in a snit.* □ *Here comes John—in a snit again—as usual.* □ *Don't get into a snit.*

in a split second* in just an instant. (Informal.) □ *The lightning struck, and in a split second the house burst into flames.* □ *Just wait. I'll be there in a split second.*

in a spot See *in a tight spot*.

in a stage whisper in a loud whisper which everyone can hear. □ *John said in a stage whisper, "This play is boring."* □ *"When do we eat?" asked Billy in a stage whisper.*

in a stew about someone or something* AND **in a stew*** upset or bothered about someone or something. (Informal. *In* can be replaced with *into*. See *in a bind* and the examples below.) □ *I'm in such a stew about my dog. She ran away last light.* □ *Now, now. Don't be in a stew. She'll be back when she gets hungry.* □ *I hate to get into a stew about my friends.*

in a tight spot* AND **in a spot*** caught in a problem; *in a jam*. (Informal. *In* can be replaced with *into*. See *in a bind* and the examples below.) □ *Look, John, I'm in a tight spot. Can you lend me twenty dollars?* □ *I'm in a spot too. I need $300.* □ *I have never gotten into a tight spot.*

in a vicious circle in a situation in which the solution of one problem leads to a second problem, and the solution of the second problem brings back the first problem, etc. (*In* can be replaced with *into*. See *in a bind* and the examples below.) □ *Life is so strange. I seem to be in a vicious circle most of the time.* □ *I put lemon in my tea to make it sour, then sugar to make it sweet. I'm in a vicious circle.* □ *Don't let your life get into a vicious circle.*

in a word said simply; concisely said. □ *Mrs. Smith is—in a word—haughty.* □ *In a word, the play flopped.*

in a world of one's own aloof; detached; self-centered. (*In* can be replaced with *into*. See *in a bind* and the examples below.) □ *John lives in a world of his* *own. He has very few friends.* □ *Mary walks around in a world of her own, but she's very intelligent.* □ *When she's thinking, she drifts into a world of her own.*

in accordance with something following the rules of something; according to the directions. □ *I've filled out the form in accordance with your instructions.* □ *We always play the game in accordance with the rules.*

in addition to someone or something AND **in addition** added to someone or something. □ *In addition to the roast beef, I would like to have a baked potato.* □ *I invited Tom in addition to John and Ann.* □ *I think I'll invite Jane in addition.*

in advance of someone or something AND **in advance** before someone or something. (Refers to both time and space.) □ *They reached the station in advance of the 7:00 train.* □ *It's good to be there in advance.* □ *I boarded the train in advance of Mr. Jones.*

in all one's born days* ever; in all one's life. (Folksy.) □ *I've never been so angry in all my born days.* □ *Have you ever heard such a thing in all your born days?*

in all probability very likely; almost certainly. □ *He'll be here on time in all probability.* □ *In all probability, they'll finish the work today.*

in any case AND **in any event** no matter what happens. □ *I intend to be home by supper time, but in any case by 8:00.* □ *In any event, I'll see you this evening.*

in any event See the previous entry.

in apple-pie order* in very good order; very well organized. (Folksy. *In* can be replaced with *into*. See *in a bind* and the examples below.) □ *Please put everything in apple-pie order before you leave.* □ *I always put my desk in apple-pie order every evening.* □ *I've put my entire life into apple-pie order.*

in arrears overdue; late, especially in reference to bills and money. □ *This bill is three months in arrears. It must be paid immediately.* □ *I was in arrears on my car payments, so the bank threatened to take my car away.*

in awe of someone or something AND **in awe** fearful and respectful of some-

one or something. □ *Everyone in the country was in awe of the king and queen.* □ *I love my new car. In fact, I'm in awe of it.* □ *When I first saw the house, I just stood there in awe.*

in back in the back part of a building; in the back yard. □ *I don't have your size here, but perhaps I can find it in back.* □ *They have a very nice house with a garage in back.*

in back of someone or something behind someone or something. □ *Please put the box in back of the chair.* □ *There is a cat in back of the tree.* □ *John, please stand in back of Mary.*

in bad faith without sincerity; with bad or dishonest intent; with duplicity. (Compare to *in good faith*.) □ *It appears that you acted in bad faith and didn't live up to the terms of our agreement.* □ *If you do things in bad faith, you'll get a bad reputation.*

in bad sorts in a bad humor. □ *Bill is in bad sorts today. He's very grouchy.* □ *I try to be extra nice to people when I'm in bad sorts.*

in bad taste AND **in poor taste** rude; vulgar; obscene. □ *Mrs. Franklin felt that your joke was in bad taste.* □ *We found the play to be in poor taste, so we walked out in the middle of the second act.*

in bad with someone* AND **in bad*** to have someone against you; to have gotten into trouble with someone. (Informal. Compare to *in good with someone*.) □ *Sally is in bad with her parents for failing algebra.* □ *She's really in bad. She has real trouble.*

in behalf of someone AND **in someone's behalf; on behalf of someone; on someone's behalf; in someone's name** (doing something) as someone's agent; (doing something) in place of someone; for the benefit of someone. □ *I'm writing in behalf of Mr. Smith who has applied for a job with your company.* □ *I'm calling on behalf of my client who wishes to complain about your actions.* □ *I'm calling in her behalf.* □ *I'm acting on your behalf.*

in black and white official, in writing or printing. (Said of something, such as an agreement or a statement, which has been recorded in writing. *In* can be replaced with *into*. See *in a bind* and the examples below.) □ *I have it in black and white that I'm entitled to three weeks of vacation each year.* □ *It says right here in black and white that oak trees make acorns.* □ *Please put the agreement into black and white.*

in brief briefly; concisely. □ *The whole story, in brief, is that Bob failed algebra because he did not study.* □ *Please tell me in brief why you want this job.*

in broad daylight publicly visible in the daytime. □ *The thief stole the car in broad daylight.* □ *There they were, selling drugs in broad daylight.*

in cahoots with someone* AND **in cahoots*** in conspiracy with someone; in league with someone. (Folksy.) □ *The mayor is in cahoots with the construction company which got the contract for the new building.* □ *Those two have been in cahoots before.*

in care of someone (to be delivered to someone) through someone or by way of someone. (Indicates that mail is to be delivered to a person at some other person's address.) □ *Bill Jones is living at his father's house. Address the letter to Bill in care of Mr. John Jones.* □ *Bill said, "Please send me my mail in care of my father at his address."*

in case of something in the event of something; if something happens. (Compare to *in the case of someone or something*.) □ *Please leave the building at once in case of fire.* □ *Please take your raincoat in case of rain.* ALSO: **just in case** if (something happens). □ *All right. I'll take it just in case.* □ *I'll take along some aspirin, just in case.*

in character typical of someone's behavior. □ *For Tom to shout that way wasn't at all in character. He's usually quite pleasant.* □ *It was quite in character for Sally to walk away angry.*

in charge of someone or something AND **have charge of someone or something; in charge** to be in control of someone or something; to have the responsibility for someone or something. □ *Who is in charge of this office?* □ *How long have you had charge of this office?* □ *Do you like being in charge?*

in clover* with good fortune; in a very good situation, especially financially. (Slang.) □ *If I get this contract, I'll be in clover for the rest of my life.* □ *I have very little money saved, so when I retire I won't exactly be in clover.*

in cold blood* without feeling; with cruel intent. (Informal or slang. Frequently said of a crime, especially murder.) □ *The killer walked up and shot the woman in cold blood.* □ *How insulting! For a person to say something like that in cold blood is just horrible.*

in concert with someone AND **in concert** in cooperation with someone; with the aid of someone. □ *Mrs. Smith planned the party in concert with her sister.* □ *In concert they planned a lovely event.*

in condition AND **in shape** in good health; strong and healthy. (Used only with people. Compare to *in good shape. In* can be replaced with *into*. See *in a bind* and the examples below.) □ *Bob exercises frequently, so he's in condition.* □ *If I were in shape, I could run faster and farther.* □ *I'm not healthy. I have to try to get into shape.*

in conformity with something being in agreement or accordance with something. (*In* can be replaced with *into*. See *in a bind* and the examples below.) □ *Your actions aren't in conformity with our contract.* □ *Please bring your actions into conformity with our agreement.* □ *Your new garage isn't in conformity with the zoning laws of this community.*

in consequence of something AND **in consequence** as a result of something; because of something. □ *In consequence of the storm, there was no electricity.* □ *The wind blew down the wires. In consequence, we had no electricity.*

in consideration of something in return for something; as a result of something. (Compare to *out of consideration for someone or something*.) □ *In consideration of your many years of service, we are pleased to present you with this gold watch.* □ *In consideration of your efforts, here is a check for $3,000.*

in creation See *on earth*.

in deep* (Slang.) **1.** deeply involved.

really in deep. □ *Bill loves the theater. He's definitely in deep. He tries out for all the plays and gets into many of them.* **2.** deeply in debt. □ *Bill owes a lot of money to the bank. He's really in deep.* □ *John is in deep with his stock broker.*

in deep water in a dangerous or vulnerable situation; in a serious situation; in trouble. (As if one were swimming in or fell into water which is over one's head. See also *go off the deep end. In* can be replaced with *into.* See *in a bind* and the examples below.) □ *John is having trouble with his taxes. He's in deep water.* □ *Bill is in deep water in algebra class. He's almost failing.* □ *He really got himself into deep water.*

in defiance of someone or something AND **in defiance** against someone's will or against instructions; in bold resistance to someone or someone's orders. □ *Jane spent the afternoon in the park in defiance of her mother's instructions.* □ *She did it in defiance of her mother.* □ *She has done a number of things in defiance lately.*

in due course AND **in due time; in good time; in the course of time; in time** in a normal or expected amount of time. □ *The roses will bloom in due course.* □ *The vice president will become president in due course.* □ *I'll retire in due time.* □ *Just wait, my dear. All in good time.* □ *It'll all work out in the course of time.* □ *In time, things will improve.*

in due time See the previous entry.

in Dutch with someone* AND **in Dutch*** in trouble with someone. (Informal. *In* can be replaced with *into.* See *in a bind* and the examples below.) □ *I'm in Dutch with my parents for my low grades.* □ *You're in Dutch quite a bit.* □ *Don't get into Dutch with anyone.*

in earnest sincerely. □ *This time I'll try in earnest.* □ *She spoke in earnest, and many people believed her.*

in exchange for someone or something AND **in exchange** in return for someone or something. □ *They gave us two of our prisoners in exchange for two of theirs.* □ *I gave him chocolate in exchange for some licorice.* □ *John gave Mary a book and got a sweater in exchange.*

in fact in reality; really; actually. □ *I'm over forty. In fact, I'm forty-six.* □ *This is a very good computer. In fact, it's the best.*

in favor of someone or something 1. AND **in favor** approving, supporting, or endorsing someone or something. □ *Are you in favor of lower taxes?* □ *Of course, I'm in favor.* **2.** [with *someone*] See *in someone's favor.*

in fear and trembling* with anxiety or fear; with dread. (A cliché.) □ *In fear and trembling, I went into the room to take the test.* □ *The witness left the courtroom in fear and trembling.*

in fine feather* in good humor; in good health. (A cliché. *In* can be replaced with *into.* See *in a bind* and the examples below.) □ *Hello, John. You appear to be in fine feather.* □ *Of course I'm in fine feather. I get lots of sleep.* □ *Good food and lots of sleep put me into fine feather.*

in for something due to receive a surprise; due to receive punishment. (When the *something* is *it*, the *it* usually means punishment.) □ *I hope I'm not in for any surprises when I get home.* □ *Tommy, you broke my baseball bat. You're really in for it!*

in force in a very large group. (See also *out in force.*) □ *The entire group arrived in force.* □ *The mosquitoes will attack in force this evening.*

in front of someone or something AND **in front** before someone or something; ahead of someone or something. □ *We waited quietly in front of the house.* □ *John said, "Who is in front of me?"* □ *Ann said, "I'm in front."*

in full swing in progress; operating or running without restraint. (*In* can be replaced with *into.* See *in a bind* and the examples below.) □ *We can't leave now! The party is in full swing.* □ *Our program to help the starving people is in full swing. You should see results soon.* □ *Just wait until our project gets into full swing.*

in good condition See *in good shape.*

in good faith with good and honest intent; with sincerity. (Compare to *in bad faith.*) □ *We are convinced you were acting in good faith, even though you* *made a serious error.* □ *I think you didn't sign the contract in good faith. You never intended to carry out our agreement.* ALSO: **show good faith** to demonstrate good intentions or good will. □ *I'm certain that you showed good faith when you signed the contract.*

in good shape AND **in good condition** physically and functionally sound and sturdy. (Used for both people and things. Compare to *in condition. In* can be replaced with *into*. See *in a bind* and the examples below.) □ *This car isn't in good shape.* □ *I'd like to have one that's in better condition.* □ *Mary is in good condition. She works hard to keep healthy.* □ *You have to make an effort to get into good shape.*

in good time **1.** quickly; in a short amount of time. □ *We travelled from Mexico to Texas in good time.* □ *I've never been able to make that trip in good time.* **2.** See *in due course.*

in good with someone AND **in good** in someone's favor; to *have pull with someone*. (Compare to *in bad with someone*.) □ *I can ask Mary a favor. I'm in good with her.* □ *Well, I'm not in good with her.* □ *I don't know Mary. How do I go about getting in good?*

in great haste very fast; in a big hurry. □ *John always did his homework in great haste.* □ *Why not take time and do it right? Don't do everything in great haste.*

in heat in a period of sexual excitement; in estrus. (*Estrus* is the period of time in which females are most willing to breed. This expression is usually used for animals. It has been used for humans in a joking sense. *In* can be replaced with *into*. See *in a bind* and the examples below.) □ *Our dog is in heat.* □ *She goes into heat every year at this time.* □ *When my dog is in heat, I have to keep her locked in the house.*

in high gear (*In* can be replaced with *into*. See *in a bind* and the examples below.) **1.** (for a machine, such as a car) to be set in its highest gear, giving the greatest speed. □ *When my car is in high gear, it goes very fast.* □ *You can't start out in high gear. You must work up through the low ones.* □ *You don't*

go into high gear soon enough. **2.*** very fast and active. (Informal.) □ *Don't leave now. The party is just now in high gear.* □ *When Jane is in high gear, she's a superb athlete.* □ *When Jane moved into high gear, I knew she'd win the race.*

in honor of someone or something showing respect or admiration for someone or something. □ *Our club gave a party in honor of the club's president.* □ *I wrote a poem in honor of John and Mary's marriage.*

in hopes of something expecting something. (Also with *high,* as in the examples.) □ *I was in hopes of getting there early.* □ *We are in high hopes that John and Mary will have a girl.*

in hot water* in trouble. (Slang. *In* can be replaced with *into*. See *in a bind* and the examples below.) □ *John got himself into hot water by being late.* □ *I'm in hot water at home for coming in late last night.* □ *I get into hot water a lot.*

in keeping with something AND **in line with something; in keeping** in accord or harmony with something; following the rules of something. □ *In keeping with your instructions, I've cancelled your order.* □ *I'm disappointed with your behavior. It really wasn't in keeping.* □ *It was not in line with the kind of behavior we expect here.*

in kind **1.** in goods rather than in money. □ *The country doctor was usually paid in kind. He accepted two pigs as payment for an operation.* □ *Do you have to pay tax on payments made in kind?* **2.** similarly; (giving) something similar to what was received. □ *John punched Bill, and Bill gave it back in kind.* □ *She spoke rudely to me, so I spoke to her in kind.*

in league with someone AND **in league** in cooperation with someone; in a conspiracy with someone. □ *The mayor is in league with the city treasurer. They are misusing public money.* □ *Those two have been in league for years.*

in less than no time very quickly. □ *I'll be there in less than no time.* □ *Don't worry. This won't take long. It'll be over with in less than no time.*

in lieu of something in place of something; instead of something. (The word *lieu* occurs only in this phrase.) □ *They gave me roast beef in lieu of beef steak.* □ *We gave money to charity in lieu of sending flowers to the funeral.*

in light of something because of certain knowledge; considering something. (As if knowledge or information shed light on something.) □ *In light of what you have told us, I think we must abandon the project.* □ *In light of the clerk's rudeness, we didn't return to that shop.*

in limbo (*In* can be replaced with *into.* See *in a bind* and the examples below.) **1.** a region on the border of hell. (In some Christian religions, there is a *limbo* set aside for souls which do not go to either heaven or hell. This sense is used only in this religious context.) □ *The baby's soul was in limbo because she had not been baptized.* □ *Considering all things, getting into limbo is probably better than going to hell.* **2.** in a state of neglect; in a state of oblivion; in an indefinite state. □ *We'll have to leave the project in limbo for a month or two.* □ *After I got hit on the head, I was in limbo for about ten minutes.*

in line AND **on line*** standing and waiting in a line of people. (*On line* is used in the New York City area.) □ *I've been in line for an hour.* □ *Get in line if you want to buy a ticket.* □ *We waited on line to see the movie.*

in line with something See *in keeping with something.*

in love with someone or something AND **in love** feeling love for someone or something; experiencing a strong affectionate emotion for someone or something. □ *Mary was in love with her new car! It was perfect for her.* □ *John is deeply in love with Mary.* □ *Those two are really in love.*

in luck fortunate; lucky. □ *You want a red one? You're in luck. There is one red one left.* □ *I had an accident, but I was in luck. It was not serious.*

in mint condition in perfect condition. (Refers to the perfect state of a coin which has just been minted. *In* can be replaced with *into.* See *in a bind* and the examples below.) □ *This is a fine car. It runs well and is in mint condi-*

tion. □ *We went through a house in mint condition and decided to buy it.* □ *We put our house into mint condition before we sold it.*

in name only nominally; not actual, only by terminology. □ *The President is head of the country in name only. Congress makes the laws.* □ *Mr. Smith is the boss of the Smith Company in name only. Mrs. Smith handles all the business affairs.*

in no mood to do something to not feel like doing something; to wish not to do something. □ *I'm in no mood to cook dinner tonight.* □ *Mother is in no mood to put up with our arguing.*

in no time AND **in no time at all** very quickly. (Compare to *in less than no time.*) □ *I'll be there in no time.* □ *It won't take long. I'll be finished in no time at all.*

in no uncertain terms* in very specific and direct language. (A cliché. *In* can be replaced with *into.* See *in a bind* and the examples below.) □ *I was so mad. I told her in no uncertain terms to leave and never come back.* □ *I told him in no uncertain terms to stop it.* □ *He put his demands into no uncertain terms, and then they listened to him.*

in nothing flat* in exactly no time at all. (Informal.) □ *Of course I can get there in a hurry. I'll be there in nothing flat.* □ *We covered the distance between New York and Philadelphia in nothing flat.*

in on the kill* AND **in at the kill*** present at the end of some activity, usually an activity with negative results. (Literally, present when a hunted animal is put to death. Informal when used about any other activity.) □ *Congress was due to defeat the bill, and I went to Washington so I could be in on the kill.* □ *The judge will sentence the criminal today, and I'm going to be in at the kill.*

in one ear and out the other* (for something to be) ignored; (for something to be) unheard or unheeded. (A cliché. *In* can be replaced with *into.* See the explanation at *in a bind* and the examples below.) □ *Everything I say to you goes into one ear and out the other!* □ *Bill just doesn't pay attention. Everything is in one ear and out the other.*

in one's birthday suit* naked; nude. (Informal. In the "clothes" in which one was born. *In* can be replaced with *into.* See *in a bind* and the examples below.) □ *I've heard that John sleeps in his birthday suit.* □ *We used to go down to the river and swim in our birthday suits.* □ *You have to get into your birthday suit to bathe.*

in one's blood See *in the blood.*

in one's book* in one's opinion. (Informal.) □ *He's okay in my book.* □ *In my book, this is the best that money can buy.*

in one's cups drunk. (Euphemistic.) □ *She doesn't make much sense when she's in her cups.* □ *The speaker—who was in his cups—could hardly be understood.*

in one's element in a natural or comfortable situation or environment. (Compare to *out of one's element. In* can be replaced with *into.* See *in a bind* and the examples below.) □ *Sally is in her element when she's working with algebra or calculus.* □ *Bob loves to work with color and texture. When he's painting, he's in his element.* □ *He's most comfortable when he can get into his element.*

in one's glory at one's happiest or best. □ *When I go to the beach on vacation, I'm in my glory.* □ *Sally is a good teacher. She's in her glory in the classroom.*

in one's mind's eye in one's mind. (Refers to visualizing something in one's mind.) □ *In my mind's eye, I can see trouble ahead.* □ *In her mind's eye, she could see a beautiful building beside the river. She decided to design such a building.*

in one's opinion according to one's belief or judgement. □ *In my opinion, that is a very ugly picture.* □ *That isn't a good idea in my opinion.*

in one's or its prime at one's or its peak or best time. (Compare to *in the prime of life.*) □ *Our dog—which is in its prime—is very active.* □ *The program ended in its prime when we ran out of money.* □ *I could work long hours when I was in my prime.*

in one's own backyard AND **in one's backyard** (figuratively) very close to one. (Also used literally.) □ *That kind of thing is quite rare. Imagine it happening right in your backyard.* □ *You always think of something like that happening to someone else. You never expect to find it in your own backyard.*

in one's own way **1.** as the best one can do; using a different and private strategy. □ *I don't know the answer to the problem, but perhaps I can help in my own way.* □ *She couldn't go to war and carry a gun, but she helped in her own way.* **2.** in the special way that one wishes or demands. □ *I don't like doing it your way. I want to do it in my own way.* □ *I prefer to do it in my own way.*

in one's right mind sane; rational and sensible. (Often in the negative.) □ *That was a stupid thing to do. You're not in your right mind.* □ *You can't be in your right mind! That sounds crazy!*

in one's second childhood being interested in things or people which normally interest children. □ *My father bought himself a toy train, and my mother said he was in his second childhood.* □ *Whenever I go to the river and throw stones, I feel like I'm in my second childhood.*

in one's spare time in one's extra time; in the time not reserved for doing something else. □ *I write novels in my spare time.* □ *I'll try to paint the house in my spare time.*

in one's Sunday best* in one's best Sunday clothes; in the clothes one wears to church. (Folksy. See also *Sunday-go-to-meeting clothes. In* can be replaced with *into.* See *in a bind* and the examples below.) □ *All the children were dressed up in their Sunday best.* □ *I like to be in my Sunday best whenever I go out.* □ *Let's get into our Sunday best and go out for dinner.*

in opposition to someone or something AND **in opposition** against someone or something. □ *You'll find that I'm firmly in opposition to any further expenditures.* □ *The mayor stands in opposition to the county sheriff. The mayor won't let the sheriff make arrests in the city.* □ *The city and county are usually in opposition.*

in orbit (*In* can be replaced with *into*. See *in a bind* and the examples below.) **1.** (for something) to circle a heavenly body. (Planets, moons, and stars are heavenly bodies.) □ *The moon is in orbit around the earth.* □ *They put the satellite into orbit.* **2.*** ecstatic; thrilled; emotionally high. (Slang.) □ *Jane is in orbit about her new job.* □ *John went into orbit when he got the check in the mail.*

in order to do something for the purpose of doing something; as a means of doing something. □ *I went to college in order to further my education.* □ *I gave John three dollars in order to buy lunch.*

in other words* said in another, simpler way. (Usually a cliché.) □ BOB: *Cease! Desist!* BILL: *In other words you want me to stop?* □ *Our cash flow is negative, and our assets are worthless. In other words, we are broke.*

in over one's head* with more difficulties than one can manage. (Informal. See also *in deep; in deep water.*) □ *Calculus is very hard for me. I'm in over my head.* □ *Ann is too busy. She's really in over her head.*

in part partly; to a lesser degree or extent. □ *I was not there, in part because of my disagreement about the purpose of the meeting. I also had a previous appointment.* □ *I hope to win, in part because I want the prize money.*

in particular specifically; especially. □ *I'm not going anywhere in particular.* □ *Of the three ideas, there is one I like in particular.*

in passing casually; as an aside. □ *I just mentioned your name in passing. I didn't say more than that.* □ *The lecturer referred to George Washington in passing.*

in place (*In* can be replaced with *into*. See *in a bind* and the examples below.) **1.** in (someone's or something's) proper place or location. (See also *out of place.*) □ *The maid came into the room and put everything into place.* □ *It's good to see everything in place again.* **2.** appropriate; proper. □ *Your remark was not in place.* □ *The presentation was quite in place and nicely done.*

in place of someone or something instead of someone or something. □ *John went in place of Mary.* □ *We had vegetables in place of meat.*

in plain English See the following entry.

in plain language AND **in plain English** in simple, clear, and straightforward language. (*In* can be replaced with *into*. See *in a bind* and the examples below.) □ *That's too confusing. Please say it again in plain English.* □ *Tell me again in plain language.* □ *Please put it into plain language.*

in poor taste See *in bad taste.*

in practice (*In* can be replaced with *into*. See *in a bind* and the examples below.) **1.** in an application (of a principle, etc.); in the actual doing of something. □ *Our policy is to be very particular, but in practice we don't care that much.* □ *The instructions say not to set it too high. In practice I always set it as high as possible.* **2.** well-rehearsed; well-practiced; well-exercised. □ *The swimmer was not in practice and almost drowned.* □ *I play the piano for a living, and I have to keep in practice.*

in print available in printed form. (Compare to *out of print.* See also *put something into print.*) □ *I think I can get that book for you. It's still in print.* □ *This is the only book in print on this subject.*

in private privately. □ *I'd like to speak to you in private.* □ *I enjoy spending the evening in private.*

in progress happening now; taking place at this time. □ *You can't go into that room. There is a meeting in progress.* □ *Please tell me about the work you have in progress.*

in pursuit of something chasing after something. □ *Bill spends most of his time in pursuit of money.* □ *Every year Bob goes into the countryside in pursuit of butterflies.*

in quest of someone or something AND **in search of someone or something** seeking or hunting something; trying to find something. □ *They went into town in quest of a reasonably priced restaurant.* □ *Monday morning I'll go out in search of a job.*

in rags in worn-out and torn clothing. □ *Oh, look at my clothing. I can't go to the party in rags!* □ *I think the new* *casual fashions make you look like you're in rags.*

in reference to someone or something AND **in regard to someone or something; in relation to someone or something; in respect to someone or something** concerning or about someone or something; in connection with someone or something. (*In* can be replaced with *with*, as in the examples.) □ *What shall we do in reference to Bill and his problem?* □ *With reference to what problem?* □ *I'm writing this letter in regard to your recent telephone call.* □ *I mention this fact in respect to your proposed trip.* □ *With respect to my trip, I have nothing to say.* □ *Let's discuss Bill in relation to his future with this company.*

in regard to someone or something See the previous entry.

in relation to someone or something See *in reference to someone or something.*

in respect to someone or something See *in reference to someone or something.*

in return for someone or something AND **in return** in exchange for someone or something; in trade for someone or something. □ *What do they ask in return for their hostages?* □ *I'll give you four chocolate candies in return for eight mint ones.* □ *I ask nothing in return.*

in round figures See the following entry.

in round numbers AND **in round figures** as an estimated number; a figure which has been rounded off. (*In* can be replaced with *into.* See *in a bind* and the examples below.) □ *Please tell me in round numbers what it'll cost.* □ *I don't need the exact amount. Just give it to me in round figures.*

in search of someone or something See *in quest of someone or something.*

in season 1. currently available for selling. (Some foods and other things are available only at certain seasons. Compare to *out of season. In* can be replaced with *into,* especially when used with *come.* See *in a bind* and the examples below.) □ *Oysters are available in season.* □ *Strawberries aren't in season in January.* □ *When do strawberries come into season?* 2. legally able to be caught

or hunted. □ *Catfish are in season all year round.* □ *When are salmon in season?*

in seventh heaven* in a very happy state. (A cliché.) □ *Ann was really in seventh heaven when she got a car of her own.* □ *I'd be in seventh heaven if I had a million dollars.*

in shape See *in condition.*

in short stated briefly. □ *At the end of the financial report, the board president said, "In short, we are okay."* □ *My remarks, in short, indicate that we are in good financial shape.*

in short order very quickly. □ *I can straighten out this mess in short order.* □ *The people came in and cleaned the place up in short order.*

in short supply scarce. (*In* can be replaced with *into.* See *in a bind* and the examples below.) □ *Fresh vegetables are in short supply in the winter.* □ *Yellow cars are in short supply because everyone likes them and buys them.* □ *At this time of the year, fresh vegetables go into short supply.*

in single file AND **single file** lined up, one behind the other; in a line, one person or one thing wide. (*In* can be replaced with *into.* See *in a bind* and the examples below.) □ *Have you ever seen ducks walking in a single file?* □ *No, do they usually walk single file?* □ *Please march in single file.* □ *Please get into single file.*

in so many words exactly; explicitly; literally. □ *I told her in so many words to leave me alone.* □ *He said yes, but not in so many words.*

in some neck of the woods* in some remote place. (Folksy. The *some* is usually *this, that, your, their,* etc. Can be used literally to refer to some section of a forest.) □ *I think that the Smiths live in your neck of the woods.* □ *What's happening over in that neck of the woods?*

in someone else's place See the following entry.

in someone else's shoes AND **in someone else's place** seeing or experiencing something from someone else's point of view. (*In* can be replaced with *into.* See *in a bind* and the examples below.) □ *You might feel different if* *you were in her shoes.* □ *Pretend you're in Tom's place, and then try to figure out why he acts the way he does.* ALSO: **put oneself in someone else's place; put oneself in someone else's shoes** to allow oneself to see or experience something from someone else's point of view. □ *Put yourself into someone else's place, and see how it feels.*

in someone's behalf See *in behalf of someone.*

in someone's favor 1. to someone's advantage or credit. (Especially in sports scores, as in the examples.) □ *The score was ten to twelve in our favor.* □ *At the end of the second half, the score was forty to three in the other team's favor.* 2. liked by someone; approved of by someone. (*In* can be replaced with *into.* See *in a bind* and the examples below.) □ *John might be able to help me. I hope I'm currently in his favor.* □ *My mother is mad at me. I'm certainly not in her favor.* □ *I'll try to get into her favor.* 3. AND **in favor of someone** to someone, as when writing a check. (See also *honor someone's check.*) □ *Please make out a check for $300 in Tom's favor.* □ *I'm making out the check in favor of Mr. Brown.*

in someone's name 1. See *in behalf of someone.* 2. in someone's ownership; as someone's property. (*In* can be replaced with *into.* See *in a bind* and the examples below.) □ *The house is in my name. I own all of it.* □ *I put the house into my husband's name.* □ *The car is in our names.*

in spite of someone or something regardless of someone or something; in defiance of someone or something. □ *In spite of what you said, I still like you.* □ *He went to the concert in spite of his parents.*

in step with someone or something AND **in step** (*In* can be replaced with *into.* See *in a bind* and the examples below.) 1. [with *someone*] (marching or dancing) in cadence with another person. □ *Please keep in step with Jane.* □ *You two, back there. You aren't in step.* □ *Get into step!* 2. AND **in time** [with *something*] keeping in time with music. □ *John, your violin isn't in step with* the beat. *Sit up straight and try it again.* □ *I'm trying to play in time.* 3. as up to date as someone or something. □ *Bob is not in step with the times.* □ *We try to keep in step with the fashion of the day.*

in stock readily available, as with goods in a store. □ *I'm sorry, I don't have that in stock. I'll have to order it for you.* □ *We have all our Christmas merchandise in stock now.*

in style 1. in fashion; fashionable. (Compare to *out of style. In* can be replaced with *into,* especially with *come.* See *in a bind* and the examples below.) □ *This old coat isn't in style anymore.* □ *I don't care if it's not in style. It's warm.* □ *I hope this coat comes into style again.* 2. in elegance; in luxury. (Informal.) □ *If I had a million dollars, I could really live in style.* □ *If he saves his money, someday he'll be able to live in style.*

in terms of something regarding something; concerning something. □ *I don't know what to do in terms of John's problem.* □ *Now, in terms of your proposal, don't you think you're asking for too much?*

in the absence of someone or something while someone or something isn't here; without someone or something. □ *In the absence of the cook, I'll prepare dinner.* □ *In the absence of opposition, she won easily.*

in the act of doing something AND **in the act** while doing something. (See also *catch someone in the act of doing something.*) □ *There he was, in the act of opening the door.* □ *I tripped while in the act of climbing.* □ *It happened in the act, not before or after.*

in the air everywhere; all about. (Also used literally.) □ *There is such a feeling of joy in the air.* □ *We felt a sense of tension in the air.*

in the altogether* AND **in the buff*; in the raw*** naked; nude. (Informal. *In* can be replaced with *into.* See *in a bind* and the examples below.) □ *We often went swimming in the altogether down at the creek.* □ *The museum has a painting of some ladies in the buff.* □ *Mary* *felt a little shy about getting into the altogether.* □ *Bill says he sleeps in the raw.*

in the bag* **1.** assured; certain. (Slang. Compare to *tied up.* Also used literally.) □ *I've got the election in the bag. Everyone is going to vote for me.* □ *I've got the contract in the bag. They are going to sign it tomorrow.* **2.** drunk. (Slang.) □ *Is Bill in the bag again? Can he stand up?* □ *Don't drink too much or you'll be in the bag.*

in the balance in an undecided state. (See also *hang in the balance.*) □ *He stood on the edge of the cliff, his life in the balance.* □ *With his fortune in the balance, John rolled the dice.*

in the bargain in addition to what was agreed on. (*In* can be replaced with *into.* See *in a bind* and the examples below.) □ *I bought a car, and they threw an air conditioner into the bargain.* □ *When I bought a house, I asked the seller to include the furniture in the bargain.*

in the best of health very healthy. □ *Bill is in the best of health. He eats well and exercises.* □ *I haven't been in the best of health. I think I have the flu.*

in the black not in debt; in a financially profitable condition. (Compare to *in the red. In* can be replaced with *into.* See *in a bind* and the examples below.) □ *I wish my accounts were in the black.* □ *Sally moved the company into the black.*

in the blood AND **in one's blood** built into one's personality or character. □ *John's a great runner. It's in his blood.* □ *The whole family is very athletic. It's in the blood.*

in the buff See *in the altogether.*

in the bullpen (for a baseball pitcher to be) in a special place near a baseball playing field, warming up to pitch. (*In* can be replaced with *into.* See *in a bind* and the examples below.) □ *You can tell who is pitching next by seeing who is in the bullpen.* □ *Our best pitcher just went into the bullpen. He'll be pitching soon.*

in the cards* in the future. (Informal.) □ *Well, what do you think is in the cards for tomorrow?* □ *I asked the boss if there was a raise in the cards for me.*

in the care of someone AND **in the charge of someone** in the keeping of someone. (*In* can be replaced with *into.* See *in a bind* and the examples below.) □ *I left the baby in the care of my mother.* □ *I placed the house into the care of my friend.* □ *Bill left the office in charge of his assistant.*

in the case of someone or something **1.** in the matter of someone or something; in the instance of someone or something. (See also *in case of something.* Compare to *in the event of something.*) □ *In the case of John, I think we had better allow his request.* □ *In the case of this woman, we'll not grant permission.* **2.** [with *someone*] in the legal proceedings relating to someone. (The *someone* may be contained in the official name of a legal case.) □ *I recall a similar situation in the case of* The State *vs.* Jane Smith. □ *Have they found any new facts in the case of Bill Wilson?*

in the charge of someone See *in the care of someone.*

in the chips* wealthy; with much money. (Slang. *In* can be replaced with *into.* See *in a bind* and the examples below.) □ *John is a stock trader, and occasionally he's in the chips.* □ *Bill really came into the chips when his uncle died.*

in the clear (*In* can be replaced with *into.* See *in a bind* and the examples below.) **1.** not obstructed; not enclosed. □ *You're in the clear. Go ahead and back up.* □ *Once the deer got into the clear, it ran away.* **2.** innocent; not guilty. □ *Don't worry, Tom. I'm sure you're in the clear.* □ *I'll feel better when I get into the clear.*

in the course of time See *in due course.*

in the dark about someone or something AND **in the dark** uninformed about someone or something; ignorant about someone or something. □ *I'm in the dark about who is in charge around here.* □ *I can't imagine why they are keeping me in the dark.* □ *You won't be in the dark long. I'm in charge.* □ *She's in the dark about how this machine works.*

in the doghouse* in trouble; in (someone's) disfavor. (Informal. *In* can be replaced with *into*. See *in a bind* and the examples below.) □ *I'm really in the doghouse. I was late for an appointment.* □ *I hate being in the doghouse all the time. I don't know why I can't stay out of trouble.*

in the doldrums sluggish; inactive; in low spirits. (*In* can be replaced with *into*. See *in a bind* and the examples below.) □ *He's usually in the doldrums in the winter.* □ *I had some bad news yesterday which put me into the doldrums.*

in the event of something if something happens. (Compare to *in the case of someone or something*.) □ *In the event of fire, please leave quickly and quietly.* □ *The picnic will be cancelled in the event of rain.*

in the family way See *in a family way*.

in the first place initially; to begin with. (Compare to *in the second place*.) □ *In the first place, you don't have enough money to buy one. In the second place, you don't need one.* □ *In the first place, I don't have the time. In the second place, I'm not interested.*

in the flesh really present; in person. □ *I've heard that the queen is coming here in the flesh.* □ *Is she really here? In the flesh?* □ *I've wanted a color television for years, and now I've got one right here in the flesh.*

in the groove 1. in a notch or a long slit. (*In* can be replaced with *into*. See *in a bind* and the examples below.) □ *The record won't play unless the needle is in the groove.* □ *Put this part into this groove, and then screw down the other part.* 2.* AND **groovy** good and satisfying; exactly what is needed; attractive. (Slang.) □ *This music is really in the groove.* □ *What a groovy hat!*

in the gutter (for a person to be) in a low state; depraved. (*In* can be replaced with *into*. See *in a bind* and the examples below.) □ *You had better straighten out your life, or you'll end up in the gutter.* □ *His bad habits put him into the gutter.*

in the hole* in debt. (Informal. *In* can be replaced with *into*. See *in a bind* and the examples below. Also used literally.) □ *I'm $200 in the hole.* □ *Our finances end up in the hole every month.*

in the hot seat See *on the hot seat*.

in the know* knowledgeable. (Informal. *In* can be replaced with *into*. See *in a bind* and the examples below.) □ *Let's ask Bob. He's in the know.* □ *I have no knowledge of how to work this machine. I think I can get into the know very quickly though.*

in the lap of luxury* in luxurious surroundings. (A cliché. *In* can be replaced with *into*. See the explanation at *in a bind* and the examples below.) □ *John lives in the lap of luxury because his family is very wealthy.* □ *When I retire, I'd like to live in the lap of luxury.*

in the limelight AND **in the spotlight** at the center of attention. (*In* can be replaced with *into*. See *in a bind* and the examples below. The literal sense is also used. *Limelight* is an obsolete form of spotlight, and the word occurs only in this phrase.) □ *John will do almost anything to get himself into the limelight.* □ *I love being in the spotlight.* □ *All elected officials spend a lot of time in the limelight.*

in the line of duty as part of the expected (military or police) duties. □ *When soldiers fight people in a war, it's in the line of duty.* □ *Police officers have to do things they may not like in the line of duty.*

in the long run* over a long period of time; ultimately. (A cliché. Compare to *in the short run*.) □ *We'd be better off in the long run buying one instead of renting one.* □ *In the long run we'd be happier in the South.*

in the market for something AND **in the market** wanting to buy something. □ *I'm in the market for a video recorder.* □ *If you have a boat for sale, we're in the market.*

in the middle of nowhere* in a very remote place. (Informal. *In* can be replaced with *into*. See *in a bind* and the examples below.) □ *To get to my house, you have to drive into the middle of nowhere.* □ *We found a nice place to eat, but it's out in the middle of nowhere.*

in the money* (Informal. See also *on the money*.) 1. wealthy. □ *John is really in the money. He's worth millions.* □ *If I am ever in the money, I'll be gener-*

ous. **2.** in the winning position in a race or contest. (As if one had won the prize money.) □ *I knew when Jane came around the final turn that she was in the money.* □ *The horses coming in first, second, and third are said to be in the money.*

in the mood for something AND **in the mood** in an appropriate state of mind for something. (*In* can be replaced with *into.* See *in a bind* and the examples below.) □ *I'm not in the mood for joking.* □ *I can't get into the mood for dancing.* □ *Sorry, I'm just not in the mood.*

in the near future in the time immediately ahead. (*In* can be replaced with *into.* See *in a bind* and the examples below.) □ *I don't plan to go to Florida in the near future.* □ *Today's prices won't extend into the near future.* □ *What do you intend to do in the near future?*

in the nick of time* just in time; at the last possible instant; just before it's too late. (A cliché.) □ *The doctor arrived in the nick of time. The patient's life was saved.* □ *I reached the airport in the nick of time.*

in the offing happening at some time in the future. (*In* can be replaced with *into.* See *in a bind* and the examples below.) □ *There is a big investigation in the offing, but I don't know when.* □ *It's hard to tell what's in the offing if you don't keep track of things.*

in the pink of condition* AND **in the pink*** in very good health; in very good condition, physically and emotionally. (Informal. *In* can be replaced with *into.* See *in a bind* and the examples below.) □ *The garden is lovely. All the flowers are in the pink of condition.* □ *Jane has to exercise hard to get into the pink of condition.* □ *I'd like to be in the pink, but I don't have the time.*

in the prime of life in the best and most productive period of one's life. (See also *in one's or its prime. in* can be replaced with *into.* See *in a bind* and the examples below.) □ *The good health of one's youth can carry over into the prime of life.* □ *He was struck down by a heart attack in the prime of life.*

in the public eye publicly; visible to all; conspicuous. (*In* can be replaced with *into.* See *in a bind* and the examples below.) □ *Elected officials find themselves constantly in the public eye.* □ *The mayor made it a practice to get into the public eye as much as possible.*

in the raw See *in the altogether.*

in the red in debt. (Compare to *in the black* and *out of the red. In* can be replaced with *into.* See *in a bind* and the examples below.) □ *My accounts are in the red at the end of every month.* □ *It's easy to get into the red if you don't pay close attention to the amount of money you spend.*

in the right on the moral or legal side of an issue; on the right side of an issue. (Compare to *in the wrong.*) □ *I felt I was in the right, but the judge ruled against me.* □ *It's hard to argue with Jane. She always believes that she's in the right.*

in the running in competition; competing and having a chance to win. (Compare to *out of the running. In* can be replaced with *into.* See *in a bind* and the examples below.) □ *Is Tom still in the running? Does he still have a chance to be elected?* □ *I'm glad I didn't get into the running.*

in the same boat* in the same situation; having the same problem. (A cliché. *In* can be replaced with *into.* See the explanation at *in a bind* and the examples below.) □ TOM: *I'm broke. Can you lend me twenty dollars?* BILL: *Sorry. I'm in the same boat.* □ *Jane and Mary are both in the same boat. They both have been called for jury duty.*

in the same breath (stated or said) almost at the same time. □ *He told me I was lazy, but then in the same breath he said I was doing a good job.* □ *The teacher said that the students were working hard and, in the same breath, that they were not working hard enough.*

in the second place secondly; in addition. (Usually said after one has said *in the first place.*) □ *In the first place, you don't have enough money to buy one. In the second place, you don't need one.* □ *In the first place, I don't have the time. In the second place, I'm not interested.*

in the short run* for the immediate future. (A cliché. Compare to *in the long run*.) □ *In the short run, we'd be better off saving our money.* □ *We decided to rent an apartment in the short run. We can buy a house later.*

in the soup* in a bad situation. (Slang. *In* can be replaced with *into*. See *in a bind* and the examples below.) □ *Now I'm really in the soup. I broke Mrs. Franklin's window.* □ *I make a lot of mistakes. It's easy for me to get into the soup.*

in the spotlight See *in the limelight*.

in the swim of things* involved in or participating in events or happenings. (A cliché. The *in* can be replaced with *into*. See the explanation at *in a bind* and the examples below.) □ *I've been ill, but soon I'll be back in the swim of things.* □ *I can't wait to settle down and get into the swim of things.*

in the twinkling of an eye very quickly. (A Biblical reference.) □ *In the twinkling of an eye, the deer had disappeared into the forest.* □ *I gave Bill ten dollars and, in the twinkling of an eye, he spent it.*

in the unlikely event of something if something—which probably will not happen—actually happens. (Compare to *in the event of something*.) □ *In the unlikely event of my getting the job, I'll have to buy a car to get there every day.* □ *In the unlikely event of a fire, please walk quickly to an exit.*

in the wake of something 1. in the waves and turbulence which follow a boat or a ship. (*In* can be replaced with *into*. See *in a bind* and the examples below.) □ *The small boat followed in the wake of the big boat.* □ *It's dangerous to steer into the wake of a large ship or a barge.* 2. after something; as a result of some event. □ *We had no place to live in the wake of the fire.* □ *In the wake of the storm, there were many broken tree limbs.*

in the way of someone or something 1. AND **in someone's or something's way; in the way** blocking someone or something; obstructing someone or something. □ *Please don't get in the way of progress.* □ *You're in the way of*

the mayor. Make room! 2. [with *something*] kind of something; style of something. □ *What do you have in the way of leather shoes?* □ *We have nothing in the way of raincoats.* □ *I've seen nothing in the way of nice weather in this part of the country.*

in the wind about to happen. (Also used literally.) □ *There are some major changes in the wind. Expect these changes to happen soon.* □ *There is something in the wind. We'll find out what it is soon.*

in the works* being prepared; being planned; being done. (Informal.) □ *There are some new laws in the works which will affect all of us.* □ *I have some ideas in the works which you might be interested in.*

in the world See *on earth*.

in the worst way* very much. (Informal. Also used literally.) □ *I want a new car in the worst way.* □ *Bob wants to retire in the worst way.*

in the wrong on the wrong or illegal side of an issue; guilty or in error. (Compare to *in the right*.) □ *I felt she was in the wrong, but the judge ruled in her favor.* □ *It's hard to argue with Jane. She always believes that everyone else is in the wrong.*

in there pitching* trying very hard. (Informal.) □ *Bob is always in there pitching.* □ *Just stay in there pitching. You'll make some progress eventually.*

in this day and age* presently; currently; nowadays. (Folksy.) □ *You don't expect people to be polite in this day and age.* □ *Young folks don't take care of their parents in this day and age.*

in time 1. See *in due course*. 2. See *in step with someone or something*. 3. before the deadline; before the last minute. □ *Did you turn in your paper in time?* □ *I didn't go to Florida. I didn't get to the airport in time.*

in tune with someone or something (*In* can be replaced with *into*. See *in a bind* and the examples below.) 1. at the same or a harmonizing musical pitch. □ *The violin isn't in tune with the piano.* □ *Bill, please get into tune with John.* 2. [with *something*] keeping up with something. □ *Tom, your clothes are old-*

fashioned. You aren't in tune with the times. □ *Come on, Sally. Get into tune with what's going on around you.*

in turn **1.** one at a time in sequence. □ *Each of us can read the book in turn.* □ *We cut the hair of every child in turn.* **2.** in return (for something). □ *I took Sally out to lunch, and she took me out in turn.* □ *We help each other in turn with yard work.*

in two shakes of a lamb's tail* very quickly. (A cliché.) □ *I'll be there in two shakes of a lamb's tail.* □ *In two shakes of a lamb's tail, the bird flew away.*

in view of something in consideration of something; because of something. □ *In view of the high cost of gasoline, I sold my car.* □ *I won't invite John to the meeting in view of his attitude.*

in with someone friends with someone; having influence with someone. □ *Are you in with John? I need to ask him for a favor.* □ *I've heard that the mayor is in with the county treasurer.*

inch along something AND **inch along** to move slowly along something little by little. □ *The cat inched along the carpet toward the mouse.* □ *Traffic was inching along.*

inch by inch one inch at a time; little by little. □ *Traffic moved along inch by inch.* □ *Inch by inch, the snail moved across the stone.*

incumbent upon someone to do something necessary for someone to do something. (*Upon* can be replaced with *on*.) □ *It's incumbent upon you to do the work.* □ *It was incumbent on me to make the presentation of the first prize.*

inquire after someone to ask about someone. □ *Mary inquired after you. I told her you were well and looked forward to seeing her.* □ *Please inquire after Mary's father the next time you see her.*

ins and outs of something the correct and successful way to do something; the special things that one needs to know to do something. □ *I don't understand the ins and outs of politics.* □ *Jane knows the ins and outs of working with computers.*

instrumental in doing something playing an important part in doing something. □ *John was instrumental in getting the contract to build the new building.* □ *Our senator was instrumental in defeating the bill.*

into something See *be into something*.

iron something out AND **iron out something** to solve a problem; to straighten out a problem; to smooth out a difficulty. □ *I just have to iron out this little problem; then I'll be able to see you.* □ *The principal had to iron a classroom problem out.*

It behooves one to do something.* It is necessary for one to do something.; It is *incumbent upon someone to do something*. (A cliché.) □ *It behooves me to report the crime.* □ *It behooves you to pay for the window which you broke.*

It figures.* It makes sense.; It confirms what one might have guessed.; I'm not surprised. (Informal.) □ BOB: *Tom was the one who broke the window.* BILL: *It figures. He's very careless.* □ ANN: *Mary was the last one to arrive.* SALLY: *It figures. She's always late.*

It never rains but it pours. a proverb meaning that a lot of bad things tend to happen at the same time. □ *The car won't start, the stairs broke, and the dog died. It never rains but it pours.*

It's a deal.* Okay.; It is agreed. (Informal or slang.) □ *You want to sell me your stereo for $100? It's a deal.* □ BILL: *Let's go to dinner together tonight.* MARY: *It's a deal.*

It's about time!* It is almost too late!; I've been waiting a long time! (Informal.) □ *So you finally got here! It's about time!* □ *They finally paid me my money. It's about time!*

It's high time.* It is past time (for something).; (Something) is overdue. (Informal.) □ *It's high time that you got recognition for what you do.* □ *They sent me my check, and it's high time, too.*

It's no use doing something. AND **It's no use.** It is hopeless to do something.; It is pointless to do something. □ *It's no use trying to call on the telephone. The line is always busy.* □ *They tried and tried, but it was no use.*

J

jack someone or something up AND **jack up someone or something** 1.* [with *someone*] to motivate someone; to stimulate someone to do something. (Slang.) □ *I guess I'll have to jack up the carpenter again to repair my stairs.* □ *The mail is late again today. We'll have to jack those people up at the post office.* **2.** [with *something*] to raise something with a jack. □ *Ann jacked up the car to change the tire.* □ *The workers jacked the house up, put logs under it, and rolled it away.* **3.** [with *something*] to raise the price. □ *The electric company jacked up the price of electricity.* □ *The grocery store jacks the price of meat up on the weekend.*

jazz something up* AND **jazz up something*** to make something more exciting, colorful, or lively. (Slang. Said especially of music.) □ *I think we need to jazz up this room. It looks so drab.* □ *When we play the music this time, let's jazz it up a bit.*

jealous of someone or something envious and resentful of someone or something. □ *I'm jealous of the prize you won. I deserve it more than you do.* □ *John was jealous of Bob for going out with Mary.*

Johnny-come-lately someone who joins in (something) after it is underway. □ *Don't pay any attention to Sally. She's just a Johnny-come-lately and doesn't know what she's talking about.* □ *We've been here for thirty years. Why should some Johnny-come-lately tell us what to do?*

Johnny-on-the-spot someone who is in the right place at the right time. □ *Here I am, Johnny-on-the-spot. I told you I* would be here at 12:20. □ *Bill is late again. You can hardly call him Johnny-on-the-spot.*

join forces with someone AND **join forces** to join with someone. □ *We joined forces with the police to search for the lost child.* □ *The choirs joined forces to sing the song.*

judge one on one's own merits to judge or evaluate one on one's own achievements and virtues, not someone else's. (See the following entry. Also with *merit*.) □ *Please judge me on my own merits, not on those of my family.* □ *You should judge Sally on her own merit. Forget that her mother is a famous opera star.*

judge something on its own merits to judge or evaluate a thing on its own good points and usefulness. (See the previous entry. Also with *merit*.) □ *You have to judge each painting on its own merits. Not every painting by a famous painter is superior.* □ *Each rose must be judged on its own merit.*

judging by something considering something; using something as an indication (of something else). □ *Judging by your wet clothing, it must be raining.* □ *Judging by the looks of this house, I would guess there has been a party here.*

jump all over someone* AND **jump down someone's throat*; jump on someone*** to scold someone severely. (Slang.) □ *If I don't get home on time, my parents will jump all over me.* □ *Don't jump on me! I didn't do it!* □ *Please don't jump all over John. He wasn't the one who broke the window.* □ *Why are you jumping down my throat? I wasn't even in the house when it happened.*

jump at something to seize the opportunity to do something. (Usually with *it*. See *jump at the chance* from which this phrase comes.) □ *When I heard about John's chance to go to England, I knew he'd jump at it.* □ *If something you really want to do comes your way, jump at it.*

jump at the chance AND **jump at the opportunity; leap at the opportunity** to take advantage of a chance to do something. □ *John jumped at the chance to go to England.* □ *I don't know why I didn't jump at the opportunity myself.* □ *I should have leaped at the chance.*

jump at the opportunity See the previous entry.

jump bail* AND **skip bail*** to fail to appear in court for trial and give up one's bail bond. (Slang.) □ *Not only was Bob arrested for theft, he skipped bail and left town. He's in a lot of trouble.* □ *I thought only criminals jumped bail.*

jump down someone's throat See *jump all over someone.*

jump off the deep end See *go off the deep end.*

jump on someone See *jump all over someone.*

jump on the bandwagon See *get on the bandwagon.*

jump out of one's skin* to react strongly to shock or surprise. (Informal. Usually with *nearly, almost,* etc. Never used literally.) □ *Oh! You really scared me. I nearly jumped out of my skin.* □ *Bill was so startled he almost jumped out of his skin.*

jump the gun to start before the starting signal. (Originally used in sports contests which are started by firing a gun.) □ *We all had to start the race again because Jane jumped the gun.* □ *When we took the test, Tom jumped the gun and started early.*

jump the track 1. (for something) to fall or jump off the rails or guides. (Usually said about a train.) □ *The train jumped the track causing many injuries to the passengers.* □ *The engine jumped the track, but the other cars stayed on.* 2. to change suddenly from one thing, thought, plan, or activity to another. □ *The entire project jumped the track, and we finally had to give up.* □ *John's mind jumped the track while he was in the play, and he forgot his lines.*

jump through a hoop* AND **jump through hoops*** to do everything possible to obey or please someone; to *bend over backwards to do something.* (Informal. Trained animals jump through hoops.) □ *She expects us to jump through hoops for her.* □ *What do you want me to do—jump through a hoop?*

jump to conclusions AND **leap to conclusions** to judge or decide something without having all the facts; to reach unwarranted conclusions. □ *Now don't jump to conclusions. Wait until you hear what I have to say.* □ *Please find out all the facts so you won't leap to conclusions.*

just as soon do something See *had as soon do something.*

just in case See *in case of something.*

just one of those things* something which couldn't have been prevented; something caused by fate. (A cliché.) □ *I'm sorry, too. It's not your fault. It's just one of those things.* □ *I feel terrible that I didn't pass the bar exam. I guess it was just one of those things.*

just what the doctor ordered* exactly what is required, especially for health or comfort. (A cliché.) □ *That meal was delicious, Bob. Just what the doctor ordered.* □ BOB: *Would you like something to drink?* MARY: *Yes, a cold glass of water would be just what the doctor ordered.*

K

keel over (for a person) to fall over or fall down in a faint or in death. □ *Suddenly, Mr. Franklin keeled over. He had had a heart attack.* □ *It was so hot in the room that two people just keeled over.*

keen about someone or something See the following entry.

keen on someone or something AND **keen about someone or something** to be enthusiastic about someone or something. □ *I'm not too keen on going to London.* □ *Sally is fairly keen about getting a new job.* □ *Mary isn't keen on her new boss.*

keep a civil tongue in one's head AND **keep a civil tongue** to speak decently and politely. (Also with *have*. See the note at *keep a straight face*.) □ *Please, John. Don't talk like that. Keep a civil tongue in your head.* □ *John seems unable to keep a civil tongue.* □ *He'd be welcome here if he had a civil tongue in his head.*

keep a stiff upper lip to be cool and unmoved by unsettling events. (Also with *have*. See the note at *keep a straight face*.) □ *John always keeps a stiff upper lip.* □ *Now, Billy, don't cry. Keep a stiff upper lip.* □ *Bill can take it. He has a stiff upper lip.*

keep a straight face to make one's face stay free from laughter. (*Keep* can be replaced with *have*. *Keep* implies the exercise of effort, and *have* simply means to possess.) □ *It's hard to keep a straight face when someone tells a funny joke.* □ *I knew it was John who played the trick. He couldn't keep a straight face.* □ *John didn't have a straight face.*

keep abreast of something AND **keep abreast** to keep informed about some-

thing; to *keep up with the times*. (Also with *be* instead of *keep*, as in the examples.) □ *I try to keep abreast of the financial markets.* □ *I believe that I'm abreast of foreign events.* □ *Yes, I try to keep abreast by reading the papers every day.*

keep after someone See *get after someone*.

keep ahead of someone or something See *get ahead of someone or something*.

keep an account of something to keep a record of something. □ *Please keep an account of everything you spend.* □ *When you go on a vacation, carry a notebook and keep an account of what you do every day.*

keep an eye on someone or something See *have an eye on someone or something*.

keep an eye out for someone or something See *have an eye out for someone or something*.

keep at someone or something 1. [with *someone*] See *get after someone*. **2.** [with *something*] to continue doing something; to continue trying to do something. □ *John's parents have to keep at him to study.* □ *Keep at the job if you want to get it finished.*

keep away from someone or something See *get away from someone or something*.

keep body and soul together* to feed, clothe, and house oneself. (A cliché.) □ *I hardly have enough money to keep body and soul together.* □ *How the old man was able to keep body and soul together is beyond me.*

keep company with someone to spend much time with someone; to associate or consort with someone. (Compare to *keep someone company.*) □ *Bill has been keeping company with Ann for three months.* □ *Bob has been keeping company with a tough-looking bunch of boys.*

keep cool* to keep calm and undisturbed. (Informal or slang. Also used literally.) □ *Relax man, keep cool!* □ *If Sally could just keep cool before a race, she could probably win.*

keep good time (for a watch) to be accurate. □ *I have to return my watch to the store because it doesn't keep good time.* □ *Mine keeps good time.*

keep house to manage a household. □ *I hate to keep house. I'd rather live in a tent than keep house.* □ *My grandmother kept house for nearly sixty years.*

keep in touch with someone See *get in touch with someone.*

keep late hours to stay up or stay out until very late. □ *I'm always tired because I keep late hours.* □ *If I didn't keep late hours, I wouldn't sleep so late in the morning.*

keep off something AND **keep off** to stay off someone's land; to not trespass. (See also *keep someone or something off.*) □ *You had better keep off my property.* □ *The sign says "Keep off."*

keep on doing something AND **keep on** to continue to do something. □ *I have to keep on painting the house until I'm finished.* □ *Please keep on working until the bell rings.* □ *I just have to keep on.*

keep on someone See *get after someone.*

keep on the good side of someone See *get on the good side of someone.*

keep on with something AND **keep on** to continue to do something; to pursue the doing of something. (See also *get on with someone or something.*) □ *I have to keep on with my studies.* □ *I can't stop now. I have to keep on.*

keep one's chin up* to keep one's spirits high; to act brave and confident. (Informal.) □ *Keep your chin up, John. Things will get better.* □ *Just keep your chin up and tell the judge exactly what happened.*

keep one's distance from someone or something AND **keep one's distance** to maintain a respectful or cautious distance from someone or something. (The distance can be figurative or literal.) □ *Keep your distance from John. He's in a bad mood.* □ *Keep your distance from the fire.* □ *Okay. I'll tell Sally to keep her distance, too.*

keep one's ear to the ground See *have one's ear to the ground.*

keep one's eye on someone or something See *have an eye on someone or something.*

keep one's eye on the ball **1.** to watch or follow the ball carefully, especially when one is playing a game which uses a ball; to follow the details of a ball game very carefully. □ *John, if you can't keep your eye on the ball, I'll have to take you out of the game.* □ *"Keep your eye on the ball," the coach roared at the players.* **2.*** to remain alert to the events occurring around one. (Informal.) □ *If you want to get along in this office, you're going to have to keep your eye on the ball.* □ *Bill would do better in his classes if he would just keep his eye on the ball.*

keep one's eyes open for someone or something AND **keep one's eyes open; keep one's eyes peeled for someone or something*; keep one's eyes peeled** to remain alert and watchful for someone or something. (The entries with *peeled* are informal. *Peel* refers to moving the eyelids back.) □ *I'm keeping my eyes open for a sale on winter coats.* □ *Please keep your eyes peeled for Mary. She's due to arrive here any time.* □ *Okay. I'll keep my eyes open.*

keep one's eyes peeled for someone or something See the previous entry.

keep one's feet on the ground See *get one's feet on the ground.*

keep one's fingers crossed for someone or something AND **cross one's fingers; keep one's fingers crossed** to wish for luck for someone or something, often by crossing one's fingers; to hope for a good outcome for someone or something. □ *I hope you win the race Saturday. I'm keeping my fingers crossed for you.* □ *I'm trying out for a play. Keep your fingers crossed!*

keep one's hand in something AND **keep one's hand in** to retain one's control of something. (See also *take a hand in*

189

something.) □ *I want to keep my hand in the running of the business.* □ *Mrs. Johnson has retired from the library, but she still wants to keep her hand in.*

keep one's hands off someone or something See *get one's hands off someone or something.*

keep one's head above water See *get one's head above water.*

keep one's mouth shut about someone or something* AND **keep one's mouth shut*** to keep quiet about someone or something; to keep a secret about someone or something. (Informal.) □ *They told me to keep my mouth shut about the boss or I'd be in big trouble.* □ *I think I'll keep my mouth shut.*

keep one's nose clean* to keep out of trouble, especially trouble with the law. (Slang.) □ *I'm trying to keep my nose clean by staying away from those rough guys.* □ *John, if you don't learn how to keep your nose clean, you're going to end up in jail.*

keep one's nose out of someone's business See *get one's nose out of someone's business.*

keep one's nose to the grindstone See *put one's nose to the grindstone.*

keep one's own counsel to keep one's thoughts and plans to oneself; to not tell other people about one's thoughts and plans. □ *Jane is very quiet. She tends to keep her own counsel.* □ *I advise you to keep your own counsel.*

keep one's place See *know one's place.*

keep one's temper AND **hold one's temper** to not get angry; to hold back an expression of anger. □ *She should have learned to keep her temper when she was a child.* □ *Sally got thrown off the team because she couldn't hold her temper.*

keep one's weather eye open to watch for something (to happen); to be on the alert (for something); to be on guard. □ *Some trouble is brewing. Keep your weather eye open.* □ *Try to be more alert. Learn to keep your weather eye open.*

keep one's wits about one See *get one's wits about one.*

keep one's word to uphold one's prom-

ise. □ *I told her I'd be there to pick her up, and I intend to keep my word.* □ *Keeping one's word is necessary in the legal profession.*

keep out of something or someplace AND **keep out; stay out of something or someplace; stay out** to not enter something or someplace; to refrain from entering something or someplace. □ *Keep out of here!* □ *Don't you hear me? Stay out!* □ *Stay out of the cookie jar.*

keep pace with someone or something AND **keep pace** to move at the same speed as someone or something; to keep up with someone or something. □ *The black horse was having a hard time keeping pace with the brown one.* □ *Bill can't keep pace with the geometry class.* □ *You've just got to keep pace.*

keep quiet about someone or something AND **keep quiet; keep still about someone or something; keep still** to not reveal something about someone or something; to keep a secret about someone or something. □ *Please keep quiet about the missing money.* □ *Please keep still about Mr. Smith's illness.* □ *All right. I'll keep still.*

keep someone company to sit or stay with someone, especially someone who is lonely. □ *I kept my uncle company for a few hours.* □ *He was very grateful for someone to keep him company. He gets very lonely.*

keep someone from doing something to prevent someone from doing something. □ *My good sense kept me from making a total fool of myself.* □ *Her father kept her from going to the party.*

keep someone in line* to make certain that someone behaves properly. (Informal.) □ *It's very hard to keep Bill in line. He's sort of rowdy.* □ *The teacher had to struggle to keep the class in line.*

keep someone in stitches* to cause someone to laugh loud and hard, over and over. (Informal. Also with *have.* See the note at *keep a straight face.*) □ *The comedian kept us in stitches for nearly an hour.* □ *The teacher kept the class in stitches, but the students didn't learn anything.*

keep someone on tenterhooks to keep someone anxious or in suspense. (Also with *have*. See the note at *keep a straight face*.) □ *Please tell me now. Don't keep me on tenterhooks any longer!* □ *Now that we have her on tenterhooks, shall we let her worry, or shall we tell her now?*

keep someone or something at a distance AND **keep someone or something at arm's length** to keep someone or something away from one; to keep from getting acquainted with someone or something. (See also *keep one's distance from someone or something*.) □ *I used a stick to keep the angry dog at a distance.* □ *John is in a bad mood, and that tends to keep people at arm's length.*

keep someone or something at arm's length See the previous entry.

keep someone or something at bay AND **hold someone or something at bay** to keep someone or something unable either to advance or to escape. □ *The dogs managed to keep the wildcat at bay.* □ *The bear held the hunters at bay.* □ *The secretary held the reporters at bay while the mayor left by the side door.*

keep someone or something back AND **keep back someone or something; hold someone or something back; hold back someone or something** **1.** to keep someone or something from moving forward. □ *Hurry! We must set sail now. I can't keep back the tide.* □ *Run away! John is mad at you, and I can't hold him back any longer.* **2.** [with *someone*] to fail a student who then must remain another year at the same level. □ *We decided it would be best if we kept your child back for a year.* □ *Is it a good idea to hold back a child for a year?* **3.** [with *something*] to hold something in reserve. □ *We'll hold back some money for emergencies.* □ *Yes, it's a good idea to keep some back.*

keep someone or something down See *get someone or something down*.

keep someone or something hanging in midair See *leave someone or something hanging in midair*.

keep someone or something in check AND **hold someone or something in check** to keep someone or something

under control; to restrain someone or something. □ *Hang on to this rope to keep the dog in check.* □ *I was so angry I could hardly hold myself in check.*

keep someone or something in mind AND **bear someone or something in mind** to remember and think about someone or something. □ *When you're driving a car, you must bear this in mind at all times: Keep your eyes on the road.* □ *As you leave home, keep your family in mind.*

keep someone or something off AND **keep off someone or something; hold off someone or something; hold someone or something off** to make someone or something keep or stay away (from someone). (See also *keep off something*.) □ *How did you keep off the wildcat?* □ *I used a pole to hold the wildcat off.*

keep someone or something out to prevent someone or something from coming or going in. (See also *leave someone or something out*.) □ *Please close the door and keep the snow out.* □ *Keep the baby out of the room.*

keep someone or something still **1.** AND **keep someone or something quiet** to make someone or something silent or less noisy. □ *Can you please keep the baby quiet?* □ *Keep that stereo still!* **2.** [with *something*] AND **keep something quiet** to keep something a secret. (See also *keep quiet about someone or something*.) □ *I'm quitting my job, but my boss doesn't know yet. Please keep it quiet.* □ *Okay. I'll keep it still.* **3.** AND **hold someone or something still** to restrain or control someone or something so that the person or thing cannot move. (See also *keep still*.) □ *Please keep your foot still. It makes me nervous when you wiggle it.* □ *You have to hold the nail still if you want to hit it.*

keep someone or something up AND **keep up someone or something** **1.** to support someone or something; to hold someone or something up. □ *The flagpole I was carrying was so heavy, I could hardly keep it up.* □ *I could barely stand up myself, but I managed to keep up Ann until we got out of the smoke filled room.* **2.** to prevent someone from going to bed; to keep someone awake. □ *Their party kept me up all night.* □ *The noise kept up the entire household.* **3.** [with *something*] to continue doing something. □ *I don't know how long I can keep this up.* □ *I can't keep up working this way much longer.*

keep someone posted to keep someone informed (of what is happening); to keep someone up to date. □ *If the price of corn goes up, I need to know. Please keep me posted.* □ *Keep her posted about the patient's status.*

keep something to oneself to keep something a secret. (Notice the use of *but* in the examples.) □ *I'm quitting my job, but please keep that to yourself.* □ *Keep it to yourself, but I'm quitting my job.* □ *John is always gossiping. He can't keep anything to himself.*

keep something under one's hat* to keep something a secret; to keep something in one's mind (only). (Informal. If the secret stays under your hat, it stays in your mind. Note the use of *but* in the examples.) □ *Keep this under your hat, but I'm getting married.* □ *I'm getting married, but keep it under your hat.*

keep something under wraps to keep something concealed (until some future time). □ *We kept the plan under wraps until after the election.* □ *The automobile company kept the new model under wraps until most of the old models had been sold.*

keep still 1. AND **hold still** do not move. (See also *keep still for something.*) □ *Quit wiggling. Keep still!* □ *"Hold still. I can't examine your ear if you're moving," said the doctor.* **2.** See *keep quiet about someone or something.*

keep still about someone or something See *keep quiet about someone or something.*

keep still for something See *stand still for something.*

keep tabs on someone or something AND **keep track of someone or something; keep tabs; keep track** to monitor someone or something; to follow the activities of someone or something. (*Tabs* can be replaced by *tab.*) □ *I'm supposed to keep track of my books.* □

Try to keep tabs on everyone who works for you. □ *It's hard to keep tabs when you have a lot of other work to do.* □ *I can't keep track of the money I earn. Maybe someone else is spending it.*

keep the ball rolling See *get the ball rolling.*

keep the home fires burning* to keep things going at one's home or other central location. (A cliché.) □ *My uncle kept the home fires burning when my sister and I went to school.* □ *The manager stays at the office and keeps the home fires burning while I'm out selling our products.*

keep the lid on something* to restrain something; to keep something quiet. (Informal.) □ *The politician worked hard to keep the lid on the scandal.* □ *The party was noisy because they weren't trying to keep the lid on it. It got louder and louder.*

keep the wolf from the door* to maintain oneself at a minimal level; to keep from starving, freezing, etc. (A cliché.) □ *I don't make a lot of money, just enough to keep the wolf from the door.* □ *We have a small amount of money saved, hardly enough to keep the wolf from the door.*

keep time 1. to maintain a musical rhythm. □ *Bob had to drop out of the band because he couldn't keep time.* □ *Since he can't keep time, he can't march, and he can't play the drums.* **2.** to keep watch over the time in a game or an athletic contest. □ *Ann kept time at all the basketball games.* □ *Whoever keeps time has to watch the referee very carefully.* **3.** (for a clock or a watch) to keep track of time accurately. □ *This watch doesn't keep time.* □ *My other watch kept time better.*

keep to oneself to be solitary; to stay away from other people. □ *Ann tends to keep to herself. She doesn't have many friends.* □ *I try to keep to myself each morning so I can get some work done.*

keep track of someone or something See *keep tabs on someone or something.*

keep up an act AND **keep up one's act** to maintain a false front; to act in a special way which is different from one's natural behavior. □ *Most of the time John kept up an act. He was really not a friendly person.* □ *He works hard to keep up his act.*

keep up with someone or something AND **keep up** to keep pace with someone or something; to advance at the same rate as someone or something. (See the following two entries.) □ *You're running so fast that I cannot keep up with you.* □ *I don't make enough money to keep up with your spending.* □ *You don't even try to keep up.*

keep up with the Joneses AND **keep up** to stay financially even with one's peers; to work hard to get the same amount of material goods that one's friends and neighbors have. □ *Mr. and Mrs. Brown bought a new car simply to keep up with the Joneses.* □ *Keeping up with the Joneses can take all your money.*

keep up with the times AND **keep up** to stay in fashion; to keep up with the news; to be contemporary or modern. □ *I try to keep up with the times. I want to know what's going on.* □ *I bought a whole new wardrobe because I want to keep up with the times.* □ *Sally learns all the new dances. She likes to keep up.*

keep watch on someone or something AND **keep watch** to monitor someone or something; to observe someone or something. □ *Keep watch on Bill. I think he's loafing.* □ *Okay. I'll keep watch, but I think he's a good worker.*

keep watch over someone or something AND **keep watch** to guard or care for someone or something. (Also with close.) □ *I'm keeping watch over my children to make sure they have the things they need.* □ *I think that an angel is keeping watch over her to make sure nothing bad happens to her.* □ *Angels don't have much to do except to keep watch.*

Keep your shirt on!* Wait a minute!; Be patient. (Slang. Usually considered rude.) □ *Hey, keep your shirt on! I'll be with you in a minute.* □ *I'll bring you your hamburger when it's cooked. Just keep your shirt on, friend.*

keyed up* anxious; tense and expectant. (Informal.) □ *I don't know why I'm so keyed up all the time. I can't even sleep.* □ *Ann gets keyed up before a test.*

kick a habit* AND **kick the habit*** (Slang.) to break a habit. □ *It's hard to kick a habit, but it can be done. I stopped biting my nails.* □ *I used to drink coffee every morning, but I kicked the habit.* ALSO: **kick the habit*** to put an end to one's drug addiction. (Slang.) □ *John had to go to a treatment center to get help with kicking the habit.*

kick off 1. to start a football game by kicking the ball a great distance. □ *Tom kicked off in the last game. Now it's my turn.* □ *John tripped when he was kicking off.* **2.*** AND **kick the bucket** to die. (Slang. Impolite.) □ *Don't say that George Washington "kicked off." Say that he "passed away."* □ *My cat kicked off last night. She was tough as a lion.* □ *When I kick the bucket, I want a huge funeral with lots of flowers and crying.*

kick oneself for doing something* AND **kick oneself*** to regret doing something. (Informal.) □ *I could just kick myself for going off and not locking the car door. Now the car is stolen.* □ *Don't kick yourself. It's insured.*

kick over See *turn over.*

kick someone or something around* AND **kick around someone or something*** (Slang.) **1.** to treat someone or something badly. (Also used literally.) □ *I finally quit my job. My boss wouldn't stop kicking me around.* □ *Stop kicking my car around. It does everything I ask it.* **2.** [with *something*] to discuss an idea or a proposal. □ *We kicked around John's idea for a while.* □ *That sounds like a good idea to me. Let's kick it around in our meeting tomorrow.*

kick someone or something out AND **boot someone or something out; boot out someone or something; kick out someone or something** to force someone or something to leave a place. (The *something* must be a living creature.) □ *I lived at home until I was eighteen, and my father kicked me out.* □ *He kicked out his own child?* □ *Yes. He booted out my brother when he was twenty.* □ *The dog was barking, so I kicked it out.*

kick something in AND **kick in something 1.** to break in something by kicking. □ *John was so mad that he kicked the door in.* □ *Did he kick in a glass door?* **2.** to contribute some money (to a cause). (Informal.) □ *I'd be happy to kick in a dollar, but no more.* □ *John kicked five dollars in.*

kick something off AND **kick off something** to start something; to start off an event. □ *We kicked off the party by singing rowdy songs.* □ *That was a great way to kick off a weekend.* □ *They kicked the picnic off with a footrace.*

kick the bucket See *kick off.*

kick up a fuss AND **kick up a row**; **kick up a storm**; **kick up** to become a nuisance; to misbehave and disturb (someone). (Informal. *Row* rhymes with *cow.* Note the variations in the examples.) □ *The customer kicked up such a fuss about the food that the manager came to apologize.* □ *I kicked up such a row that they kicked me out.* □ *Oh what pain! My arthritis is kicking up.*

kick up a row See the previous entry.

kick up a storm See *kick up a fuss.*

kick up one's heels to act frisky; to be lively and have fun. (Informal.) □ *I like to go to an old-fashioned square dance and really kick up my heels.* □ *For an old man, your uncle is really kicking up his heels.*

kid around with someone AND **kid around** to tease and joke with someone. (Informal.) □ *I like to kid around with John. We are great friends.* □ *Yes, John and I used to kid around a lot.*

kill someone or something off AND **kill off someone or something** to put an end to someone or something. □ *We are going to have to kill off that idea very soon.* □ *The criminals tried to kill the witnesses off.*

kill the fatted calf to prepare an elaborate banquet (in someone's honor). (From the Biblical story recounting the return of the prodigal son.) □ *When Bob got back from college, his parents killed the fatted calf and threw a great party.* □ *Sorry this meal isn't much, John. We didn't have time to kill the fatted calf.*

kill the goose that laid the golden egg a proverb concerning the destruction of the source of one's good fortune. □ *If you fire your best office worker, you'll be killing the goose that laid the golden egg.* □ *He sold his computer, which was like killing the goose that laid the golden egg.*

kill time to waste time. (Informal.) □ *Stop killing time. Get to work!* □ *We went over to the record shop just to kill time.*

kill two birds with one stone to solve two problems with one solution. (A cliché.) □ *John learned the words to his part in the play while peeling potatoes. He was killing two birds with one stone.* □ *I have to cash a check and make a payment on my bank loan. I'll kill two birds with one stone by doing them both in one trip to the bank.*

kind of something See *sort of something.*

kiss and make up to forgive (someone) and be friends again. (Also used literally.) □ *They were very angry, but in the end they kissed and made up.* □ *I'm sorry. Let's kiss and make up.*

kiss of death an act that puts an end to someone or something. (Informal.) □ *The mayor's veto was the kiss of death for the new law.* □ *Fainting on stage was the kiss of death for my acting career.*

kiss something goodbye to anticipate or experience the loss of something. (Not used literally.) □ *If you leave your camera on a park bench, you can kiss it goodbye.* □ *You kissed your wallet goodbye when you left it in the store.*

kit and caboodle the entire amount; everyone; everything. (Folksy.) □ *Everybody in the family was there—the whole kit and caboodle.* □ *The sheriff came and threw the crook out of town, kit and caboodle.*

knee-high to a grasshopper not very tall; short and small, as a child. (Folksy.) □ *Hello, Billy. I haven't seen you since you were knee-high to a grasshopper.* □ *I have two grandchildren, both knee-high to a grasshopper.*

knit one's brow to wrinkle one's brow, especially by frowning. □ *The woman knit her brow and asked us what we wanted from her.* □ *While he read his book, John knitted his brow occasionally. He must not agree with what he's reading.*

knock about somewhere* AND **knock about*** to travel around; to act as a vagabond. (Informal.) □ *I'd like to take off a year and knock about Europe.* □ *If you're going to knock about, you should do it when you're young.*

knock-down-drag-out fight* a serious fight; a serious argument. (Folksy.) □ *Boy, they really had a knock-down-drag-out fight.* □ *Stop calling each other names, or you're going to end up with a real knock-down-drag-out fight.*

knock it off* to stop something; to cease something. (Slang. Also used literally.) □ *Shut up, you guys. Knock it off!* □ *Knock it off. I've heard enough of your music.*

knock off work* to quit work (for the day). (Informal.) □ *It's time to knock off work.* □ *It's too early to knock off work.*

knock on wood a phrase said to cancel out imaginary bad luck. (The same as British "touch wood.") □ *My stereo has never given me any trouble—knock on wood.* □ *We plan to be in Florida by tomorrow evening—knock on wood.*

knock one off one's feet See *sweep one off one's feet.*

knock some heads together* to scold some people; to get some people to do what they are supposed to be doing. (Slang.) □ *If you kids don't quiet down and go to sleep, I'm going to come up there and knock some heads together.* □ *The government is in a mess. We need to go to Washington and knock some heads together.*

knock someone dead* to put on a stunning performance or display for someone. (Informal. *Someone* is often replaced by *'em* from *them.*) □ *This band is going to do great tonight. We're going to knock them dead.* □ *"See how your sister is all dressed up!" said Bill. "She's going to knock 'em dead."*

knock someone down to size See *beat someone down to size.*

knock someone for a loop See *throw someone for a loop.*

knock someone or something about See the following entry.

knock someone or something around AND **knock someone or something about** to physically mistreat someone or something. □ *They knocked my baggage around on the flight to Mexico.* □ *The tough guys knocked me around a little.* □ *They knocked my brother about a bit also.*

knock someone or something down AND **knock down someone or something 1.** to knock someone or something to the floor or to the ground. □ *The tough guys knocked the old lady down and took her purse.* □ *The cat knocked the flowers down.* **2.*** [with *something*] to drink down a drink of something, especially something alcoholic. (Slang.) □ *John knocked down two beers in ten minutes.* □ *I don't see how he can knock that stuff down.*

knock someone or something off* AND **knock off someone or something*** (Slang.) **1.** [with *something*] to finish something, especially in haste or carelessly. □ *I knocked off the last chapter of my book in four hours.* □ *I knocked it off with the help of Bob.* **2.** [with *someone*] See *bump someone off.*

knock someone or something out AND **knock out someone or something 1.** [with *someone*] to strike someone unconscious. □ *I knocked out the champ.* □ *He accidentally knocked the guard out.* **2.** [with *something*] to hammer something out; to remove something from inside something. □ *Bill knocked out the glass.* □ *John knocked a tooth out.*

knock someone over with a feather* to push over a person who is stunned, surprised, or awed by something extraordinary. (Folksy. Never used literally.) □ *I was so surprised you could have knocked me over with a feather.* □ *When she heard the news, you could have knocked her over with a feather.*

knock someone's block off* to strike someone hard, especially in the head. (Slang. Used in threats, but never literally.) □ *If you touch me again, I'll knock your block off.* □ *John punched Bob so hard that he almost knocked his block off.*

know a thing or two about someone or something* AND **know a thing or two*** to be well-informed about someone or something; to know something unpleasant about someone or something. (Informal.) □ *I know a thing or two about cars.* □ *I know a thing or two about Mary that would really shock you.*

know all the tricks of the trade to possess the skills and knowledge necessary to do something. (Also without *all.*) □ *Tom can repair car engines. He knows the tricks of the trade.* □ *If I knew all the tricks of the trade, I could be a better plumber.*

know one's ABCs* to know the alphabet; to know the most basic things (about something). (Informal.) □ *Bill can't do it. He doesn't even know his ABCs.* □ *You can't expect to write novels when you don't even know your ABCs.*

know one's onions See *know one's stuff.*

know one's place to know the behavior appropriate to one's position or status in life. (See also *put one in one's place.*) □ *I know my place. I won't speak unless spoken to.* □ *People around here are expected to know their place. You have to follow all the rules.* ALSO: **keep one's place** to exhibit only the behavior appropriate to one's position or status in life. (Also used literally.) □ *When I complained about the food, they told me to keep my place!* □ *I suggest you keep your place until you're in a position to change things.*

know one's stuff* AND **know one's onions*** to know what one is expected to know. (Informal or slang. See also *know what's what.*) □ *I know my stuff. I can do my job.* □ *She can't handle the assignment. She doesn't know her onions.*

know one's way about See the following entry.

know one's way around AND **know one's way about** **1.** to know how to get from one place to another. (Compare to *get around; have been around.*) □ *John won't get lost. He knows his way about.* □ *Don't let John go into the city. He doesn't know his way around.* **2.** to know the techniques of getting something done, especially in a bureaucracy. □ *Sally can get the job done. She knows her way around.* □ *Since Sally worked*

at city hall for a year, she really knows her way about.

know someone by sight to know the name and recognize the face of someone. □ *I've never met the man, but I know him by sight.* □ BOB: *Have you ever met Mary?* JANE: *No, but I know her by sight.*

know someone or something like the back of one's hand See the following entry.

know someone or something like the palm of one's hand AND **know someone or something like the back of one's hand; know someone or something like a book** to know someone or something very well. □ *Of course I know John. I know him like the back of my hand.* □ *I know him like a book.*

know something by heart See *learn something by heart.*

know something from memory to have memorized something so that one does not have to consult a written version; to know something very well from seeing it very often. (Almost the same as *know something by heart.*) □ *Mary didn't need the script because she knew the play from memory.* □ *The conductor went through the entire concert without music. He knew it from memory.*

know something inside out* to know something thoroughly; to know about something thoroughly. (Informal.) □ *I know my geometry inside out.* □ *I studied and studied for my driver's test until I knew the rules inside out.*

know something only too well* to know something very well; to know something from unpleasant experience. (A cliché. Note the variation in the examples.) □ *I know the problem only too well.* □ *I know only too well the kind of problem you must face.*

know the ropes* to know how to do something. (Informal.) □ *I can't do the job because I don't know the ropes.* □ *Ask Sally to do it. She knows the ropes.* ALSO: **show someone the ropes** to tell or show someone how something is to be done. □ *Since this was my first day on the job, the manager spent a lot of time showing me the ropes.*

know the score* AND **know what's what***

to know the facts; to know the facts about life and its difficulties. (Informal. Also used literally.) □ *Bob is so naive. He sure doesn't know the score.* □ *I know what you're trying to do. Oh yes, I know what's what.*

know what's what See the previous entry.

know where someone stands on someone or something AND **know where someone stands** to know what someone thinks or feels about something. □ *I don't know where John stands on this issue.* □ *I don't even know where I stand.*

know which is which AND **tell which is which** to be able to distinguish one person or thing from another person or thing. □ *I have an old one and a new one, but I don't know which is which.* □ *I know that Bill and Bob are twins, but I can't tell which is which.*

know which side one's bread is buttered on* to know what is most advantageous for one. (A cliché.) □ *He'll do it if his boss tells him to. He knows which side his bread is buttered on.* □ *Since John knows which side his bread is buttered on, he'll be there on time.*

knuckle down to something* AND **knuckle down*** to get busy doing something; to get serious about one's work. (Informal.) □ *It's time you knuckled down to your studies.* □ *You must knuckle down if you want to succeed.*

knuckle under to someone or something* AND **knuckle under*** to submit to someone or something; to yield or give in to someone or something. (Informal.) □ *You have to knuckle under to your boss if you expect to keep your job.* □ *I'm too stubborn to knuckle under.*

L

lace into someone or something* AND **light into someone or something*** to attack, devour, or scold someone or something. (Informal.) □ *We laced into a big meal of pork and beans.* □ *The bully punched John once, and then John really laced into him.* □ *John lit into him with both fists.* □ *My father really lit into me when I came in late. He yelled at me for ten minutes.*

lag behind someone or something AND **lag behind** to fall behind someone or something; to linger behind someone or something. □ *John always lags behind the marcher in front of him.* □ *"Don't lag behind!" shouted the leader.*

laid back* relaxed and unperplexed by difficulties. (Slang.) □ *John is so laid back. Nothing seems to disturb him.* □ *I wish I could be more laid back. I get so tense.*

laid up immobilized for recuperation or repairs. (Said of people and things.) □ *I was laid up for two weeks after my accident.* □ *My car is laid up for repairs.*

land a blow somewhere AND **land a blow** to strike someone or something with the hand or fist. □ *Bill landed a blow on Tom's chin.* □ *When Bill wasn't looking, Tom landed a blow.*

land on both feet See the following entry.

land on one's feet* AND **land on both feet*** to recover satisfactorily from a trying situation or a setback. (Informal. Also used literally.) □ *Her first year was terrible, but she landed on both feet.* □ *It's going to be a hard day. I only hope I land on my feet.*

lap something up AND **lap up something 1.** (for an animal) to drink up something. □ *The cat lapped up all the spilled milk.* □ *I watched the cat lap it up.* **2.*** to accept or believe something. (Informal.) □ *Did she believe it? She just lapped it up.* □ *I can't imagine why she lapped up that ridiculous story.*

lash out at someone or something AND **lash out** to threaten or attack someone or something, physically or verbally. (Verbal attacks are limited to humans.) □ *The snake lashed out at the bird, but the bird never got bitten.* □ *It lashed out so fast that I hardly saw it.* □ *She has such a temper. She always lashes out at whoever is close by.*

last but not least* last in sequence, but not last in importance. (A cliché. Often said in introductions.) □ *The speaker said, "And now, last but not least, I'd like to present Bill Smith who will give us some final words."* □ *And last but not least, here is the loser of the race.*

last-ditch effort* a final effort; the last possible attempt. (A cliché.) □ *I made one last-ditch effort to get her to stay.* □ *It was a last-ditch effort. I didn't expect it to work.*

last something out AND **last out something** to endure something. □ *I hope I can last out the day. I'm so awfully tired.* □ *Yes, I hope you can last it out.*

latch onto someone or something* to get or obtain someone or something; to *get hold of someone or something.* (Informal.) □ *I'm going to try to latch onto a copy of that magazine.* □ *I tried to latch onto John before he went home, but I missed him.*

late in life when one is old. □ *She injured her hip running. She's exercising rather late in life.* □ *Isn't it rather late in life to buy a house?*

laugh out of the other side of one's mouth* to change sharply from happiness to sadness. (A cliché.) □ *Now that you know the truth, you'll laugh out of the other side of your mouth.* □ *He was so proud that he won the election. He's laughing out of the other side of his mouth since they recounted the ballots and found out that he lost.*

laugh something off AND **laugh off something** to avoid or reject a serious problem by laughing at it. □ *Tom suffered an injury to his leg, but he laughed it off and kept playing ball.* □ *Mary just laughed off her bad experience.*

laugh up one's sleeve* to laugh secretly; to laugh quietly to oneself. (Informal.) □ *Jane looked very serious, but I knew she was laughing up her sleeve.* □ *I told Sally that her dress was darling, but I was laughing up my sleeve because her dress was too small.*

launch forth on something See *set forth on something.*

law unto oneself one who makes one's own laws or rules; one who sets one's own standards of behavior. □ *You can't get Bill to follow the rules. He's a law unto himself.* □ *Jane is a law unto herself. She's totally unwilling to cooperate.*

lay a finger on someone or something to touch someone or something, even slightly. (Usually in the negative. Compare to *put one's finger on something.*) □ *Don't you dare lay a finger on my pencil. Go get your own!* □ *If you lay a finger on me, I'll scream.*

lay an egg* to give a bad performance. (Informal. Also used literally.) □ *The cast of the play really laid an egg last night.* □ *I hope I don't lay an egg when it's my turn to sing.*

lay down on the job See *lie down on the job.*

lay down one's life for someone or something AND **lay one's life down for someone or something; lay down one's life; lay one's life down** to sacrifice one's life for someone or something. □ *Would you lay down your life for your country?* □ *There aren't many things for which I'd lay down my life.*

lay down the law* 1. to state firmly what the rules are (for something). (A cliché.) □ *Before the meeting, the boss laid down the law. We all knew exactly what to do.* □ *The way she laid down the law means that I'll remember her rules.* 2. to scold someone for misbehaving. (Informal.) □ *When the teacher caught us, he really laid down the law.* □ *Poor Bob. He really got it when his mother laid down the law.*

lay eyes on someone or something See *set eyes on someone or something.*

lay for someone* to wait for and attack someone; to lie in ambush for someone. (Slang.) □ *The robbers were laying for the bank clerk.* □ *The robber said, "Okay, I've been laying for you, and now I've got you."*

lay hold of someone or something* to grasp someone or something with the hands. (Informal. Compare to *lay one's hands on someone or something; get hold of someone or something.*) □ *Just wait till I lay hold of Bill!* □ *I can't wait to lay hold of that fishing pole. I'm ready to catch a huge fish.*

lay into someone or something to attack, consume, or scold someone or something. □ *Bob laid into the big plate of fried chicken.* □ *The bear laid into the hunter.* □ *My father really laid into me when I got home.*

lay it on thick AND **pour it on thick; spread it on thick** to exaggerate praise, excuses, or blame. □ *Sally was laying it on thick when she said that Tom was the best singer she had ever heard.* □ *After Bob finished making his excuses, Sally said that he was pouring it on thick.* □ *Bob always spreads it on thick.*

lay low See *lie low.*

lay off someone or something* AND **lay off*** to leave someone or something alone; to stop bothering someone or something; to *take it easy on someone or something.* (Slang. See also *lay someone off.*) □ *Lay off Bill. He didn't mean any harm!* □ *Hey! I said lay off!* □ *Lay off the butter. Don't use it all up.*

lay one's cards on the table See *put one's cards on the table.*

lay one's hands on someone or some-

thing See *get one's hands on someone or something.*

lay over somewhere AND **lay over** to pause someplace during one's journey. □ *I had to lay over in San Antonio for a few hours before my plane left.* □ *I want a bus that goes straight through. I don't want to lay over.* ALSO: **layover** a pause in one's journey. (A noun.) □ *I want a non-stop flight. I don't want to have a layover.*

lay someone off AND **lay off someone** to put an employee out of work, possibly temporarily. □ *The computer factory laid off 2000 workers.* □ *They even laid the president off.*

lay someone or something away AND **lay away someone or something** (Also used literally. Compare to *put someone or something away.*) 1. [with *someone*] to bury someone. □ *They laid my uncle away last week.* □ *They laid him away with a quiet ceremony.* 2. [with *something*] (for a store clerk) to accept a deposit for merchandise which is held until it is paid for in full. □ *I wanted the dress, but I didn't have enough money. The clerk took ten dollars and laid the dress away for me.* □ *I never lay away anything. I always charge it.* ALSO: **layaway** (the status of merchandise) held until paid for in full. (Usually with *on* or *in.*) □ *I like this dress, but I can't afford it now. Please put it on layaway for me.*

lay someone or something out AND **lay out someone or something** 1.* [with *someone*] to scold someone. (Slang.) □ *The teacher really laid out Tom for being late.* □ *My father laid me out for coming home late.* 2. [with *someone*] to prepare a corpse for burial or for a wake. □ *They laid out their uncle for the wake.* □ *In the old West, the women of the community would lay their dead out.* 3.* [with *someone*] to knock someone down with a punch; to knock someone unconscious. (Slang.) □ *Tom laid out Bill with one punch to the chin.* □ *The cop laid the thief out.* 4. [with *something*] to spend an amount of money. (Informal.) □ *I had to lay out twenty dollars for that book.* □ *I laid thirty dollars out for this one.* 5. [with *something*] to explain or present a plan of action or a set of events. □ *The farmer laid out the plan for cleaning up the barn.* □ *If you wait until I lay the plan out, you'll know what to do.* 6. [with *something*] to spread something out. □ *The nurse laid out the instruments necessary for the operation.* □ *The valet laid out the clothing for his master.*

lay someone up AND **lay up someone** to cause someone to be ill in bed. □ *A broken leg laid me up for two months.* □ *Flu laid up everyone at work for a week or more.* ALSO: **laid up** sick in bed. □ *I was laid up with the flu for a week.*

lay something aside See *set something aside.*

lay something by See *put something by.*

lay something down AND **lay down something** to place something down (on something). (See also *lay down one's life for someone or something; lay down the law.*) □ *I laid down my pencil when I finished writing.* □ *The workers laid their tools down and went on strike.*

lay something in AND **lay in something** to get something and store it for future use. □ *We always lay in a large supply of firewood each November.* □ *They laid a lot of food in for the holidays.*

lay something on someone* to direct blame, guilt, or verbal abuse at someone. (Slang. See also *lay the blame on someone or something.*) □ *Don't lay that stuff on me! It's not my fault.* □ *The boss is in the conference room laying a lot of anger on the sales staff.*

lay something on the line See *put something on the line.*

lay something to rest See *put something to rest.*

lay something to waste AND **lay waste to something** to destroy something (literally or figuratively). □ *The invaders laid the village to waste.* □ *The kids came in and laid waste to my clean house.*

lay something up AND **lay up something; lay something in** 1. to store something for future use; to *put something up;* to *lay something in.* □ *We laid up some potatoes for use in the win-*

ter months. □ *I laid some extra pencils up for your department.* **2.** to put a ship in a shipyard for repairs or maintenance. □ *We laid our boat up for a month to repair the mast.* □ *The storm laid up our boat by causing severe damage.*

lay the blame on someone or something See *put the blame on someone or something.*

lay the finger on someone See *put the finger on someone.*

lead a dog's life AND **live a dog's life** to lead a miserable life. □ *Poor Jane really leads a dog's life.* □ *I've been working so hard. I'm tired of living a dog's life.*

lead off to begin; to start (assuming that others will follow). □ *We were waiting for someone to start dancing. Finally, Bob and Jane led off.* □ *The hunter led off, and the dogs followed.* □ *The first baseman will lead off as the first batter in the baseball game.*

lead on to continue leading, explaining, or interpreting. □ *We paused for a moment, and then the captain led on.* □ *After answering the student's question, the teacher led on.*

lead someone by the nose* to force someone to go somewhere (with you); to lead someone by coercion. (Informal.) □ *John had to lead Tom by the nose to get him to the opera.* □ *I'll go, but you'll have to lead me by the nose.*

lead someone down the garden path* to deceive someone. (A cliché.) □ *Now, be honest with me. Don't lead me down the garden path.* □ *That cheater really led her down the garden path.*

lead someone on to tempt someone (to do something); to lure someone (into something). (See also *lead on.*) □ *I didn't want to do it, but he kept leading me on.* □ *I knew she really wanted me to buy the car by the way she was leading me on.*

lead someone on a merry chase to lead someone in a purposeless pursuit. □ *What a waste of time. You really led me on a merry chase.* □ *Jane led Bill on a merry chase trying to find an antique lamp.*

lead someone to believe something

to imply something to someone; to cause someone to believe something untrue, without lying. □ *But you led me to believe that this watch was guaranteed!* □ *Did you lead her to believe that she was hired as a clerk?*

lead someone to do something to cause someone to do something. □ *This agent led me to purchase a worthless piece of land.* □ *My illness led me to quit my job.*

lead the life of Riley* to live in luxury. (Informal. No one knows who Riley is.) □ *If I had a million dollars, I could live the life of Riley.* □ *The treasurer took our money to Mexico where he lived the life of Riley until the police caught him.*

lead the way to lead (someone) along the proper pathway. □ *You lead the way, and we'll follow.* □ *I feel better when you're leading the way. I get lost easily.*

leaf through something See *thumb through something.*

leak something out AND **leak something; let something get out** to disclose special information to the press so that the resulting publicity will accomplish something. (Usually said of government disclosures. Also used for accidental disclosures. Also used literally.) □ *Don't leak that information out.* □ *I don't want to be the one to leak it.* □ *They let it get out on purpose.*

lean on someone* to try to make someone do something; to coerce someone to do something. (Informal. Also used literally.) □ *If she refuses to do it, lean on her a bit.* □ *Don't lean on me! I don't have to do it if I don't want to.*

lean over backwards to do something See *fall over backwards to do something.*

leap at the opportunity See *jump at the chance.*

leap to conclusions See *jump to conclusions.*

learn something by heart to learn something so well that it can be written or recited without thinking; to memorize something. □ *The director told me to learn my speech by heart.* □ *I had to go over it many times before I learned it by heart.* ALSO: **know something by**

heart to know something perfectly; to have memorized something perfectly. □ *I know my speech by heart.* □ *I went over and over it until I knew it by heart.*

learn something by rote to learn something without giving any thought to what is being learned. □ *I learned history by rote; then I couldn't pass the test which required me to think.* □ *If you learn things by rote, you'll never understand them.*

learn something from the bottom up* to learn something thoroughly, from the very beginning; to learn all aspects of something, even the most lowly. (Informal.) □ *I learned my business from the bottom up.* □ *I started out sweeping the floors and learned everything from the bottom up.*

learn something the hard way AND **find something out the hard way; find out something the hard way; find out the hard way** to learn something by experience, especially by an unpleasant experience. □ *She learned how to make investments the hard way.* □ *I wish I didn't have to learn things the hard way.* □ *I found out the hard way that it's difficult to work and go to school at the same time.* □ *Investing in real estate is tricky. I found that out the hard way.* ALSO: **do something the hard way** to accomplish something in the most difficult manner, rather than by an easier manner. □ *I made it to this job the hard way.* □ *She did it the hard way.*

learn the ropes* to learn how to do something; to learn how to work something. (Informal.) □ *I'll be able to do my job very well as soon as I learn the ropes.* □ *John is very slow to learn the ropes.*

least of all* least; of smallest importance. (Informal. Compare to *most of all*.) □ *There were many things wrong with the new house. Least of all, the water faucets leaked.* □ *What a bad day. Many things went wrong, but least of all, I tore my shirt.*

leave a bad taste in someone's mouth* (for someone or something) to leave a bad feeling or memory with someone. (Informal. Also used literally.) □ *The whole business about the missing money left a bad taste in his mouth.* □ *It was a very nice party, but something about it left a bad taste in my mouth.* □ *I'm sorry that Bill was there. He always leaves a bad taste in my mouth.*

leave a lot to be desired to be lacking something important; to be inadequate. (A polite way of saying that something is bad.) □ *This report leaves a lot to be desired.* □ *I'm sorry to have to fire you, Mary, but your work leaves a lot to be desired.*

leave no stone unturned* to search in all possible places. (A cliché. As if one might find something under a rock.) □ *Don't worry. We'll find your stolen car. We'll leave no stone unturned.* □ *In searching for a nice place to live, we left no stone unturned.*

leave off doing something AND **leave off; leave off something** to stop doing something, usually temporarily. □ *Tom had to leave off work for a few hours to go to the dentist.* □ *Can't you leave off smoking for even a few days?* □ *No, I can't leave off, not even for a day.*

leave one to one's fate to abandon someone to whatever may happen—possibly death or some other unpleasant event. □ *We couldn't rescue the miners and were forced to leave them to their fate.* □ *Please don't try to help. Just go away and leave me to my fate.*

leave oneself wide open for something AND **leave oneself wide open to something** to invite criticism or joking about oneself; to fail to protect oneself from criticism or ridicule. □ *Yes, that was a harsh remark, Jane, but you left yourself wide open to it.* □ *I can't complain about your joke. I left myself wide open for it.*

leave someone flat* (Informal.) **1.** to fail to entertain or stimulate someone. □ *Your joke left me flat.* □ *We listened carefully to his lecture, but it left us flat.* **2.** to leave someone without any money—*flat broke*. □ *Paying all my bills left me flat.* □ *The robber took all my money and left me flat.*

leave someone for dead to abandon someone as being dead. (The abandoned person may actually be alive.) □ *He looked so bad that they almost left* *him for dead.* □ *As the soldiers turned— leaving the enemy captain for dead, the captain fired at them.*

leave someone high and dry*
(Informal.) **1.** to leave someone unsupported and unable to maneuver; to leave someone helpless. □ *All my workers quit and left me high and dry.* □ *All the children ran away and left Billy high and dry to take the blame for the broken window.* **2.** to leave someone *flat broke.*
□ *Mrs. Franklin took all the money out of the bank and left Mr. Franklin high and dry.* □ *Paying the bills always leaves me high and dry.*

leave someone holding the bag* to leave someone to take all the blame; to leave someone appearing guilty. (Informal.) □ *They all ran off and left me holding the bag. It wasn't even my fault.* □ *It was the mayor's fault, but he wasn't left holding the bag.*

leave someone in peace to stop bothering someone; to go away and leave someone in peace. (Does not necessarily mean to go away from a person.) □ *Please go—leave me in peace.* □ *Can't you see that you're upsetting her. Leave her in peace.*

leave someone in the lurch to leave someone waiting on or anticipating your actions. □ *Where were you, John? You really left me in the lurch.* □ *I didn't mean to leave you in the lurch. I thought we had canceled our meeting.*

leave someone or something alone AND **let someone or something alone; leave someone or something be; let someone or something be** to stop bothering someone or something. □ *Don't torment the cat. Leave it alone.* □ *I don't want your help. Let me alone.*

leave someone or something behind to fail or forget to bring someone or something along. □ *John was sick, so we had to leave him behind.* □ *Oh, I left my money behind.*

leave someone or something hanging in midair to suspend dealing with someone or something; to leave someone or something waiting to be finished or continued. (Also used literally.) □ *She left her sentence hanging in midair.* □ *She left us hanging in midair when*

she paused. □ *Tell me the rest of the story. Don't leave me hanging in midair.* □ *Don't leave the story hanging in midair.* ALSO: **keep someone or something hanging in midair** to maintain someone or something waiting to be completed or continued. □ *Please don't keep us hanging in midair.*

leave someone or something out to exclude someone or something; to ignore someone or something. (Also used literally. See also the following entry.) □ *If you decide to go out after the play, please don't leave me out.* □ *They left out the last paragraph.*

leave someone out in the cold* to fail to inform someone; to exclude someone. (Informal. Compare to the previous entry. Also used literally.) □ *I don't know what's going on. They left me out in the cold.* □ *Tom wasn't invited. They left him out in the cold.* ALSO: **keep someone out in the cold** to prevent someone from coming in; to prevent someone from being informed. □ *Please don't keep me out in the cold. Tell me what's going on.*

leave something for another occasion AND **keep something for another occasion** to hold back something for later. (*Occasion* can be replaced with *time, day, person,* etc.) □ *Please leave some cake for me.* □ *Don't eat all the turkey. Leave some for another day.* □ *I have to leave some of my paycheck for next month.*

leave something on to leave something running or operating. (Also used literally in reference to wearing clothes.) □ *Please don't leave the light on.* □ *Ann went to school and left her radio on.*

leave well enough alone See *let well enough alone.*

leave word with someone AND **leave word** to leave a message with someone (who will pass the message on to someone else). □ *If you decide to go to the convention, please leave word with my secretary.* □ *Leave word before you go.* □ *I left word with your brother. Didn't he give you the message?*

lend an ear to someone AND **lend an ear** to listen to someone. (Formal or literary.) □ *Lend an ear to John. Hear what he has to say.* □ *I'd be delighted to lend an ear. I find great wisdom in everything John has to say.*

lend oneself or itself to something (for someone or something) to be adaptable to something; (for someone or something) to be useful for something. □ *This room doesn't lend itself to bright colors.* □ *John doesn't lend himself to casual conversation.*

lend someone a hand AND **lend a hand** to give someone some help, not necessarily with the hands. □ *Could you lend me a hand with this piano? I need to move it across the room.* □ *Could you lend a hand with this math assignment?* □ *I'd be happy to lend a hand.*

less than pleased displeased. □ *We were less than pleased to learn of your comments.* □ *Bill was less than pleased at the outcome of the election.*

let alone someone or something to not mention or think of someone or something; to not even take someone or something into account. □ *Do I have a dollar? I don't even have a dime, let alone a dollar.* □ *I didn't invite John, let alone the rest of his family.*

Let bygones be bygones.* a proverb meaning that one should forget the problems of the past. (Also a cliché.) □ *Okay, Sally, let bygones be bygones. Let's forgive and forget.* □ *Jane was unwilling to let bygones be bygones. She still won't speak to me.*

let go of someone or something AND **let loose of someone or something; let someone or something loose; let loose; let someone or something go; let go** to release someone or something (figuratively and literally). (Figuratively, *something* can be *guilt, horror, tension, fear,* etc.) □ *Please let go of me!* □ *Try to let your fears go.* □ *I can't let go of those horrible memories.* □ *Don't let loose of this rope.* □ *I won't let loose.*

let go with something* AND **cut loose with something*; cut loose*; let loose with something*; let loose*** to shout something out or expel something; to shout or express something wildly. (Slang.) □ *The audience cut loose with*

a loud cheer. □ *The whole team let go with a loud shout.* □ *John let loose with a horrendous belch.* □ *I wish you wouldn't let loose like that!*

let grass grow under one's feet* to do nothing; to stand still. (A cliché.) □ *Mary doesn't let the grass grow under her feet. She's always busy.* □ *Bob is too lazy. He's letting the grass grow under his feet.*

let her rip* AND **let it roll*** to go ahead and start something; let something begin. (Informal or slang. *Her* is usually *'er.*) □ *When Bill was ready for John to start the engine, he said, "Okay, John, let 'er rip."* □ *When Sally heard Bob say "Let 'er rip", she let the anchor go to the bottom of the lake.* □ *Let's go, Bill. Let it roll!*

let it all hang out* to tell or reveal everything and hold back nothing (because one is relaxed or carefree). (Slang.) □ *Sally has no secrets. She lets it all hang out all the time.* □ *Relax, John. Let it all hang out.*

let it roll See *let her rip.*

let loose with something See *let go with something.*

let off steam* AND **blow off steam*** to release excess energy or anger. (Informal. Also used literally.) □ *Whenever John gets a little angry, he blows off steam.* □ *Don't worry about John. He's just letting off steam.*

let on 1. to admit to knowing something. □ *Bill knew about the surprise, but he didn't let on.* □ *He had been told exactly what would happen, but he didn't let on.* **2.** to imply; to act like. (See also *put on.*) □ *Ann let on that she was a famous writer.* □ *She let on that she was better known than she really is.*

let one's hair down* AND **let down one's hair*** to become more intimate and begin to speak frankly. (Informal.) □ *Come on, Jane, let your hair down and tell me all about it.* □ *I have a problem. Do you mind if I let down my hair?*

let oneself go to become less constrained; to get excited and have a good time. □ *I love to dance and just let myself go.* □ *Let yourself go, John. Learn to enjoy life.*

Let sleeping dogs lie.* a proverb meaning that one should not search for trouble or that one should leave well enough alone. (A cliché.) □ *Don't mention that problem with Tom again. It's almost forgotten. Let sleeping dogs lie.* □ *You'll never be able to reform Bill. Leave him alone. Let sleeping dogs lie.*

let someone down to disappoint someone; to fail someone. □ *I'm sorry I let you down. Something came up, and I couldn't meet you.* □ *I don't want to let you down, but I can't support you in the election.*

let someone have it* AND **let someone have it with both barrels*** to strike someone or attack someone verbally. (Informal. *With both barrels* simply intensifies the phrase.) □ *I really let Tom have it with both barrels. I told him he had better not do that again if he knows what's good for him.* □ *Bob let John have it—right on the chin.*

let someone in on something to tell someone the secret. (Informal. The *something* can be a *plan, arrangements, scheme, trick,* or anything else which might be kept a secret.) □ *Should we let John in on the secret?* □ *Please let me in on the plan.*

let someone off the hook AND **let someone off** to release someone from a responsibility. □ *Please let me off the hook for Saturday. I have other plans.* □ *Okay, I'll let you off.*

let someone or something alone See *leave someone or something alone.*

let someone or something be See *leave someone or something alone.*

let someone or something go See *let go of someone or something.*

let someone or something in AND **let in someone or something** to permit or help someone or something to enter. □ *Please let in the dog.* □ *I hope they'll let me in without a ticket.*

let someone or something loose See *let go of someone or something.*

let someone or something off AND **let off someone or something** 1. [with *someone*] to release or dismiss someone without punishment. (See *get off easy.*) □ *The judge let off Mary with a warning.* □ *The judge didn't let me off.* 2. [with *someone*] to permit someone

to disembark or leave a means of transportation. □ *The driver let Mary off the bus.* □ *"I can't let you off at this corner," said the driver.* 3. [with *something*] to release something; to *give something off.* □ *The engine was letting off some kind of smoke.* □ *The flower let off a wonderful smell.*

let someone or something out AND **let out someone or something** 1. to permit or help someone or something to exit. □ *Please let out the dog.* □ *I was locked in the closet, and no one would let me out.* 2. [with *something*] to reveal something which is a secret. □ *Please don't let this out, but I'm quitting my job.* □ *John let out the secret by accident.*

let something get out See *leak something out.*

let something ride* to allow something to continue or remain as it is. (Informal.) □ *It isn't the best plan, but we'll let it ride.* □ *I disagree with you, but I'll let it ride.*

let something slide* to neglect something. (Informal.) □ *John let his lessons slide.* □ *Jane doesn't let her work slide.*

let something slip by AND **let something slide by** 1. to forget or miss an important time or date. □ *I'm sorry I just let your birthday slip by.* □ *I let it slide by accidentally.* 2. to waste a period of time. □ *You wasted the whole day by letting it slip by.* □ *We were having fun, and we let the time slide by.*

let something slip out AND **let something slip** to tell a secret by accident. □ *I didn't let it slip out on purpose. It was an accident.* □ *John let the plans slip when he was talking to Bill.*

let the cat out of the bag* AND **spill the beans*** to reveal a secret or a surprise by accident. (A cliché.) □ *When Bill glanced at the door, he let the cat out of the bag. We knew then that he was expecting someone to arrive.* □ *We are planning a surprise party for Jane. Don't let the cat out of the bag. It's a secret. Try not to spill the beans.*

let the chance slip by to lose the opportunity (to do something). □ *When I was younger, I wanted to become a doc-*

tor, but I let the chance slip by. □ *Don't let the chance slip by. Do it now!*

let up on someone or something AND **let up** to take the pressure off someone or something; to *take it easy on someone or something.* □ *Please let up on me. I can't work any faster, and you're making me nervous.* □ *Let up on the project. You're working too hard.* □ *Yes, I guess I had better let up.*

let well enough alone AND **leave well enough alone** to leave things as they are (and not try to improve them). □ *There isn't much more you can accomplish here. Why don't you just let well enough alone?* □ *This is as good as I can do. I'll stop and leave well enough alone.*

level off to even out; to move up or down to an average level. □ *After the holidays, business will level off.* □ *As soon as things level off around here, I can talk to you.*

level something off AND **level off something** to make something level or even. □ *They used machines to level off the road.* □ *I have to level the soil off in the garden before I plant seeds.*

level with someone* to be honest with someone. (Slang.) □ *Come on, Bill. Level with me. Did you do it?* □ *I'm leveling with you. I wasn't even in town. I couldn't have done it.*

lick something into shape* AND **whip something into shape*** to put something into good condition. (Informal.) □ *I have to lick this report into shape this morning.* □ *Let's all lend a hand and whip this house into shape. It's a mess.*

lie down on the job AND **lay down on the job*** to do one's job poorly or not at all. (*Lay* is a common error for *lie.*) □ *Tom was fired because he was laying down on the job.* □ *You mean he was lying down on the job, don't you?* □ *Sorry, I was lying down on the job in English class.*

lie in state (for a corpse) to be on display in a public place. □ *The dead leader lay in state for three days in the country's main city.* □ *While the king lay in state, many people walked by and paid their respects.*

lie in wait for someone or something to wait quietly in ambush for someone or something. □ *The lion lay in wait for the zebra.* □ *The robber was lying in wait for a victim.*

lie low* AND **lay low*** to keep quiet and not be noticed; to avoid being conspicuous. (Informal. *Lay* is a common error for *lie.*) □ *I suggest you lie low for a few days.* □ *The robber said that he would lay low for a short time after the robbery.*

lie through one's teeth* to lie boldly. (A cliché.) □ *I knew she was lying through her teeth, but I didn't want to say so just then.* □ *I'm not lying through my teeth! I never do!*

life of the party the type of person who is lively and helps make a party fun and exciting. □ *Bill is always the life of the party. Be sure to invite him.* □ *Bob isn't exactly the life of the party, but he's polite.*

lift a hand against someone or something AND **lift a hand; raise a hand against someone or something; raise a hand** to threaten (to strike) someone or something. (Often in the negative. The *a hand* can be replaced with *one's hand.*) □ *She's very peaceful. She wouldn't lift a hand against a fly.* □ *That's right. She wouldn't lift a hand.* □ *Would you raise your hand against your own brother?*

light into someone or something See *lace into someone or something.*

light on someone or something to land on someone or something; to come to rest on someone or something. □ *The plane lit on the runway right on time.* □ *Where did that fly light? I want to swat it.*

light out for somewhere* AND **light out*** to depart in haste for somewhere. (Informal.) □ *The bus pulled away and lit out for the next stop.* □ *It's time I lit out for home.* □ *I should have lit out ten minutes ago.*

light out of somewhere* AND **light out*** to depart somewhere in haste. (Informal.) □ *It's time I lit out of here. I'm late for my next appointment.* □ *Look at that horse go. He really lit out of the starting gate.*

like a bat out of hell* with great speed and force. (A cliché. Use caution with the word *hell*.) □ *Did you see her leave? She left like a bat out of hell.* □ *The car sped down the street like a bat out of hell.*

like a bolt out of the blue* suddenly and without warning. (A cliché. Refers to a bolt of lightning coming out of a clear blue sky. See also *out of a clear blue sky*.) □ *The news came to us like a bolt out of the blue.* □ *Like a bolt out of the blue, the boss came and fired us all.*

like a bump on a log* unresponsive; immobile. (A cliché.) □ *I spoke to him, but he just sat there like a bump on a log.* □ *Don't stand there like a bump on a log. Give me a hand!*

like a fish out of water* awkward; in a foreign or unaccustomed environment. (A cliché. Compare to *bull in a china shop*.) □ *At a formal dance, John is like a fish out of water.* □ *Mary was like a fish out of water at the bowling tournament.*

like a house on fire* AND **like a house afire*** rapidly and with force. (Folksy.) □ *The truck came roaring down the road like a house on fire.* □ *The crowd burst through the gate like a house afire.*

like a sitting duck* AND **like sitting ducks*** unguarded; unsuspecting and unaware. (A cliché. The second phrase is the plural form.) □ *He was waiting there like a sitting duck—a perfect target for a mugger.* □ *The soldiers were standing at the top of the hill like sitting ducks. It's a wonder they weren't all killed.*

like a three-ring circus* chaotic; exciting and busy. (A cliché.) □ *Our household is like a three-ring circus on Monday mornings.* □ *This meeting is like a three-ring circus. Quiet down and listen!*

like crazy* AND **like mad*** furiously; very much, fast, many, or actively. (Slang.) □ *People are coming in here like crazy. There isn't enough room for them all.* □ *We sold ice cream like crazy. It was a very hot day.* □ *When she stubbed her toe, she started screaming like mad.*

like it or lump it* either accept it or *drop dead*. (Slang and fairly rude.) □ *I don't care whether you care for my attitude or not. You can just like it or lump it.* □ *This is all the food you get. Like it or lump it!*

like looking for a needle in a haystack* engaged in a hopeless search. (A cliché.) □ *Trying to find a white dog in the snow is like looking for a needle in a haystack.* □ *I tried to find my lost contact lens on the beach, but it was like looking for a needle in a haystack.*

like mad See *like crazy*.

like one of the family* as if someone (or a pet) were a member of one's family. (Informal.) □ *We treat our dog like one of the family.* □ *We are very happy to have you stay with us, Bill. I hope you don't mind if we treat you like one of the family.*

like water off a duck's back* easily; without any apparent effect. (A cliché.) □ *Insults rolled off John like water off a duck's back.* □ *The bullets had no effect on the steel door. They fell away like water off a duck's back.*

line one's own pockets* to make money for oneself in a greedy or dishonest fashion. (Slang.) □ *When it was discovered that the sales manager was lining her own pockets with commissions, she was fired.* □ *If you line your pockets while in public office, you'll get in serious trouble.*

line someone or something up with something AND **line up someone or something with something** to position someone or something (or a group) in reference to other things. (See also *fix someone up with someone or something*.) □ *Line up this brick with the bricks below and at both sides. That's the way you lay bricks.* □ *Please line the chairs up with the floor tiles.* □ *Line up the boys with the row of trees.* ALSO: **line up with something; line up** to be in line with something. □ *That brick doesn't line up with the others. Please move it.* □ *The books line up with the edge of the bookshelf and look really nice.* □ *Yes, they line up nicely.*

line someone up for something AND **line up someone for something** to schedule someone for something; to arrange for someone to do or be something. □ *I lined up four of my best friends to serve as ushers at my wedding.* □ *I lined gardeners up for the summer work on the gardens.*

line up to get into a line; to form a line. □ *Will you all please line up?* □ *It's time to go from here to the auditorium. Please line up.*

listen in on someone or something AND **listen in** to eavesdrop on someone or something. □ *I hope you weren't listening in on their conversation.* □ *Were you listening in on John and Tom?* □ *No, I'd never listen in.*

listen to reason to yield to a reasonable argument; to take the reasonable course. □ *Please listen to reason, and don't do something you'll regret.* □ *She got into trouble because she wouldn't listen to reason.*

little by little slowly, a bit at a time. □ *Little by little, he began to understand what we were talking about.* □ *The snail crossed the stone little by little.*

live and learn* to increase one's knowledge by experience. (A cliché. Also informal and folksy. Usually said when one is surprised to learn something.) □ *I didn't know that snakes could swim. Well, live and learn!* □ *John didn't know he should water his house plants a little extra in the dry winter months. When they all died, he said, "Live and learn."*

live and let live* to not interfere with other people's business or preferences. (A cliché.) □ *I don't care what they do! Live and let live, I always say.* □ *Your parents are strict. Mine just live and let live.*

live beyond one's means to spend more money than one can afford. (Compare to *live within one's means*.) □ *The Browns are deeply in debt because they are living beyond their means.* □ *I keep a budget so that I don't live beyond my means.*

live by one's wits to survive by being clever. □ *When you're in the kind of business I'm in, you have to live by your wits.* □ *John was orphaned at the age of ten and grew up living by his wits.*

live for the moment to live without

planning for the future. □ *John has no health or life insurance. He lives only for the moment.* □ *When you're young, you tend to live for the moment and not plan for your future security.*

live from hand to mouth* to live in poor circumstances. (Informal.) □ *When both my parents were out of work, we lived from hand to mouth.* □ *We lived from hand to mouth during the war. Things were very difficult.*

live high off the hog* AND **live high on the hog*; eat high on the hog*** to live well and eat good food. (Folksy. Note the variation with *pretty*.) □ *After they discovered oil on their land, they lived pretty high on the hog.* □ *Looks like we're eating high on the hog tonight. What's the occasion?*

live high on the hog See the previous entry.

live in to live at the residence at which one works. (Said of servants.) □ *In order to be here early enough to prepare breakfast, the cook has to live in.* □ *Mrs. Simpson has a valet, but he doesn't live in.*

live in an ivory tower to be aloof from the realities of living. (*Live* can be replaced by a number of expressions meaning to dwell or spend time, as in the examples.) □ *If you didn't spend so much time in your ivory tower, you'd know what people really think!* □ *Many professors are said to live in ivory towers. They don't know what the real world is like.*

live it up to have an exciting time; to do what one pleases—regardless of cost—to please oneself. □ *At the party, John was really living it up.* □ *Come on! Have fun! Live it up!* □ *They spent a week in Mexico living it up and then came home broke.*

live next door to someone AND **live next door** to live in the house or dwelling next to someone. □ *I live next door to John.* □ *John lives next door to me.* □ *John lives next door.*

live off someone or something to get one's income from or be supported by someone or something. (Compare to *live on something*.) □ *John is thirty years old and lives off his parents.* □ *I live off* *my investments.* □ *I can hardly live off what you pay me.*

live off the fat of the land* to grow one's own food; to live on stored-up resources or abundant resources. (A cliché.) □ *If I had a million dollars, I'd invest it and live off the fat of the land.* □ *I'll be happy to retire soon and live off the fat of the land.* □ *Many farmers live off the fat of the land.*

live on borrowed time to live longer than circumstances warrant. □ *John has a terminal disease, and he's living on borrowed time.* □ *This project is living on borrowed time. It is overdue for completion.*

live on something to depend on something for sustenance. (Compare to *live off someone or something.*) □ *I can't live on bread and water.* □ *We can hardly live on $300 a week.*

live out of a suitcase to live briefly in a place, never unpacking one's luggage. □ *I hate living out of a suitcase. For my next vacation, I want to go to just one place and stay there the whole time.* □ *We were living out of suitcases in a motel while they repaired the damage the fire caused to our house.*

live something down AND **live down something** to overcome the shame or embarrassment of something. □ *I'll never be able to live down what happened at the party last night.* □ *Oh, you'll live it down someday.*

live through something to endure something. (Also used literally.) □ *I thought I'd never be able to live through the lecture. It was so boring.* □ *I just can't live through another day like this.*

live up to something to fulfill expectations; to satisfy a set of goals. (Often with *one's reputation, promise, word, standards,* etc.) □ *I hope I can live up to my reputation.* □ *The class lives up to its reputation of being exciting and interesting.* □ *He never lives up to his promises.* □ *She was unable to live up to her own high standards.*

live within one's means to spend no more money than one has. (Compare to *live beyond one's means.*) □ *We have to struggle to live within our means, but we manage.* □ *John is unable to live within his means.*

loaded for bear* (Slang and folksy.) **1.** angry. □ *He left here in a rage. He was really loaded for bear.* □ *When I got home from work, I was really loaded for bear. What a horrible day!* **2.** drunk. (An elaboration of *loaded,* which means drunk.) □ *By the end of the party, Bill was loaded for bear.* □ *The whole gang drank for an hour until they were loaded for bear.*

lock horns with someone* AND **lock horns*** to get into an argument with someone. (Informal.) □ *Let's settle this peacefully. I don't want to lock horns with the boss.* □ *The boss doesn't want to lock horns either.*

lock someone or something in something to cause someone or something to be locked within a room, car, etc., possibly accidentally. (See also *lock something in.* Compare to *lock someone or something up.*) □ *I locked my keys in the car, and I can't get them out.* □ *The robber locked us in the closet and took all our valuables.*

lock someone or something up AND **lock up someone or something** to lock someone or something (in a place) deliberately. □ *The police locked Bob up in jail.* □ *We locked up the dog in the basement during the party.*

lock something in to make something, such as a rate of interest, permanent over a period of time. (Informal.) □ *We locked in an eleven percent rate on our mortgage.* □ *You should try to lock in a high percentage rate on your bonds.*

lock, stock, and barrel everything. □ *We had to move everything out of the house—lock, stock, and barrel.* □ *We lost everything—lock, stock, and barrel—in the fire.*

Long time no see.* to not have seen someone for a long time. (Informal.) □ *Hello, John. Long time no see.* □ *When John and Mary met on the street, they both said, "Long time no see."*

look after someone or something AND **see after someone or something** to watch over and take care of someone or something. □ *Please look after my cat while I'm on vacation.* □ *I'd be happy to see after your baby while you go shopping.*

209

look as if butter wouldn't melt in one's mouth to appear to be cold and unfeeling (despite any information to the contrary). □ *Sally looks as if butter wouldn't melt in her mouth. She can be so cruel.* □ *What a sour face. He looks as if butter wouldn't melt in his mouth.*

look at someone cross-eyed* AND **look cross-eyed at someone*** to do something slightly provocative. (Informal.) □ *Bob is very excitable. He'd lose his temper if anyone so much as looked at him cross-eyed.* □ *Don't even look cross-eyed at the boss this morning unless you want trouble.*

look back on someone or something to review one's memories of someone or something. (Also used literally.) □ *When I look back on Tom and the good times we had, I realize what good friends we were.* □ *I get upset when I look back on the automobile accident.*

look daggers at someone to give someone a dirty look. (Compare to *look at someone cross-eyed*.) □ *Tom must have been mad at Ann from the way he was looking daggers at her.* □ *Don't you dare look daggers at me. Don't even look cross-eyed at me!*

look down on someone or something AND **look down one's nose at someone or something** to regard someone or something with contempt or displeasure. □ *I think that John liked Mary, although he did seem to look down on her.* □ *Don't look down your nose at my car just because it's rusty and noisy.*

look down one's nose at someone or something See the previous entry.

look for someone or something to hunt or search for someone or something. □ *I'm looking for someone to give me a ride home.* □ *I'm looking for a ride home.*

look for someone or something high and low AND **look high and low for someone or something; look high and low** to look everywhere for someone or something. □ *I've looked for our dog high and low, and I can't find him.* □ *I've looked high and low for a red jacket.* □ *I don't know where my glasses are. I've looked high and low.*

look for trouble* to try to get into trouble. (Informal.) □ *The guard asked me to leave unless I was looking for trouble.* □ *You're looking for trouble if you ask the boss for a raise.*

look forward to something to anticipate something with pleasure. □ *I'm really looking forward to your visit next week.* □ *We all look forward to your new book on gardening.*

look in on someone or something AND **check in on someone or something; check in; look in** to see to the welfare of someone or something; to visit someone or something. □ *I'll stop by your house and look in on things while you're on vacation.* □ *Yes, just look in and make sure nothing is wrong.* □ *I checked in on John yesterday. He's almost over his illness.* □ *He was glad I checked in.*

look into something AND **check into something; see into something** to investigate something. □ *I'll have to look into that matter.* □ *The police checked into her story.* □ *Don't worry about your problem. I'll see into it.*

look like a million dollars* to look very good. (A cliché.) □ *Oh, Sally, you look like a million dollars.* □ *Your new hairdo looks like a million dollars.*

look like someone or something 1. to resemble someone or something. □ *I look like my father.* □ *This box looks like my box.* **2.** to give the appearance of predicting (something). □ *The sky looks like rain.* □ *No, it looks like snow.* □ *Oh, oh. This looks like trouble. Let's go.*

look like the cat that swallowed the canary* to appear as if one had just had a great success. (A cliché.) □ *After the meeting John looked like the cat that swallowed the canary. I knew he must have been a success.* □ *What happened? You look like the cat that swallowed the canary.*

look on at something AND **look on** to be an observer of something (rather than a participant). □ *There was nothing to do but stand there and look on at the disaster.* □ *I don't like to stand there and look on.*

look on someone as something to view or think of someone as something. □ *I look on you as a very thought-*

ful person. □ *Mary looked on Jane as a good friend.*

look out for someone or something See *watch out for someone or something.*

look someone in the eye See the following entry.

look someone in the face AND **look someone in the eye; stare someone in the face** to face someone directly. (Facing someone this way should assure sincerity.) □ *I don't believe you. Look me in the eye and say that.* □ *She looked him in the face and said she never wanted to see him again.* □ *I dare you to stare him in the face and say that!*

look someone or something over AND **look over someone or something** to examine someone or something carefully. □ *Please look over this report.* □ *She looked him over and decided to hire him.*

look someone or something up AND **look up someone or something; hunt someone or something up; hunt up someone or something** to search for and find someone or something. □ *Would you please look up John? I need to talk to him.* □ *I don't know where the hammer is. I'll have to hunt it up.* □ *Ann looked the word up in the dictionary.*

look the other way to ignore (something) on purpose. (Also used literally.) □ *John could have prevented the problem, but he looked the other way.* □ *By looking the other way, he actually made the problem worse.*

look to someone or something for something AND **look to someone or something** to expect someone to supply something. □ *Children look to their parents for help.* □ *Tom looked to the bank for a loan.* □ *Most people who need to borrow money look to a bank.*

look up and down something to examine something from end to end. □ *The dog looked up and down the street, and then it went across.* □ *The man looked up and down the railroad tracks, but he didn't see a train.*

look up to someone to view someone with respect and admiration. □ *Bill really looks up to his father.* □ *Everyone in the class looked up to the teacher.*

lord it over someone to dominate someone; to direct and control someone. □ *Mr. Smith seems to lord it over his wife.* □ *The boss lords it over everyone in the office.*

lose face to lose status; to become less respectable. □ *John is more afraid of losing face than losing money.* □ *Things will go better if you can explain to him where he was wrong without making him lose face.*

lose ground to fall behind; to fall back. □ *She was recovering nicely yesterday, but she lost ground last night.* □ *We are losing ground in our fight against mosquitoes.*

lose heart to lose one's courage or confidence. □ *Now, don't lose heart. Keep trying.* □ *What a disappointment! It's enough to make one lose heart.*

lose one's cool* AND **blow one's cool*** to lose one's temper; to lose one's nerve. (Slang.) □ *Wow, he really lost his cool! What a tantrum!* □ *Whatever you do, don't blow your cool.*

lose one's grip 1. to lose one's grasp (of something). □ *I'm holding on to the rope as tightly as I can. I hope I don't lose my grip.* □ *This hammer is slippery. Try not to lose your grip.* **2.** to lose control (over something). □ *I can't seem to run things like I used to. I'm losing my grip.* □ *They replaced the board of directors because it was losing its grip.*

lose one's head over someone or something AND **lose one's head** to become confused or "crazy" about someone or something. (Refers especially to emotional attachments.) □ *Don't lose your head over John. He isn't worth it.* □ *I'm sorry. I got upset and lost my head.*

lose one's marbles* AND **lose one's mind** to go crazy; to go out of one's mind. (The first phrase is slang.) □ *What a silly thing to say! Have you lost your marbles?* □ *I can't seem to remember anything. I think I'm losing my mind.*

lose one's mind See the previous entry.

lose one's reason to lose one's power of reasoning, possibly in anger. □ *I was so confused that I almost lost my reason.* □ *Bob seems to have lost his reason when he struck John.*

lose one's shirt* to lose all of one's

assets (including one's shirt). (Slang. Never literal.) □ *I almost lost my shirt on that deal. I have to invest more wisely.* □ *No, I can't loan you $200. I just lost my shirt at the racetrack.*

lose one's temper to become angry. □ *Please don't lose your temper. It's not good for you.* □ *I'm sorry that I lost my temper.*

lose one's touch with someone or something AND **lose one's touch** to lose one's ability to handle someone or something. □ *I seem to have lost my touch with my children. They won't mind me anymore.* □ *We've both lost our touch as far as managing people.* □ *Tom said that he had lost his touch with the stock market.*

lose one's train of thought to forget what one was talking or thinking about. □ *Excuse me, I lost my train of thought. What was I talking about?* □ *You made the speaker lose her train of thought.*

lose oneself in something AND **lose oneself** to become deeply involved in something (so that everything else is forgotten). □ *Jane has a tendency to lose herself in her work.* □ *I often lose myself in thought.* □ *Excuse me, I lost myself for a moment.*

lose out on something See *miss out on something.*

lose out to someone or something to lose a competition to someone or something. □ *Our team lost out to the other team.* □ *Bill lost out to Sally in the contest.*

lose sight of someone or something AND **lose sight** to forget about the importance of someone or something. □ *We lost sight of you when we planned the party.* □ *You always lose sight of the important things too often.* □ *It's careless to lose sight that way.*

lose sleep over someone or something AND **lose sleep** to worry about someone or something. □ *I keep losing sleep over my son who is in the Army.* □ *Do you lose sleep over your investments?* □ *No, I don't lose sleep, and I never worry.*

lose touch with someone or something AND **lose touch** to lose contact with someone or something. (Compare to *keep in touch with someone.*) □ *Poor*

Sally has lost touch with reality. □ *I've lost touch with all my relatives.* □ *Jane didn't mean to lose touch, but she did.*

lose track of someone or something AND **lose track** to forget where someone or something is; to lose or misplace someone or something. □ *I've lost track of the time.* □ *The mother lost track of her child and started calling her.* □ *When I get tired, I tend to lose track.*

lost in thought busy thinking. □ *I'm sorry, I didn't hear what you said. I was lost in thought.* □ *Bill—lost in thought as always—went into the wrong room.*

louse something up* AND **louse up something*** to mess up or ruin something. (Slang.) □ *I've worked hard on this. Please don't louse it up.* □ *You've loused up all my plans.*

lousy with something* with something in abundance. (Slang.) □ *This place is lousy with cops.* □ *Our picnic table was lousy with ants.*

love at first sight* love established when two people first see one another. (A cliché.) □ *Bill was standing at the door when Ann opened it. It was love at first sight.* □ *It was love at first sight when they met, but it didn't last long.*

lovely weather for ducks* rainy weather. (A cliché.) □ BOB: *Not very nice out today, is it?* BILL: *It's lovely weather for ducks.* □ *I don't like this weather, but it's lovely weather for ducks.*

low man on the totem pole the least important person. (Compare to *high man on the totem pole.*) □ *I was the last to find out because I'm low man on the totem pole.* □ *I can't be of any help. I'm low man on the totem pole.*

lower one's sights to set one's goals lower. □ *Even though you get frustrated, don't lower your sights.* □ *I shouldn't lower my sights. If I work hard, I can do what I want.*

lower one's voice to speak more softly. □ *Please lower your voice, or you'll disturb the people who are working.* □ *He wouldn't lower his voice, so every one heard what he said.*

lower the boom on someone* to scold or punish someone severely; to crack down on someone; to *throw the book at someone.* (Informal.) □ *If Bob won't*

behave better, I'll have to lower the boom on him. □ *The teacher lowered the boom on the whole class for misbehaving.*
luck out* to get lucky (about something). (Slang.) □ *I won $100 in the lottery. I really lucked out.* □ *Bob lucked out when he got an easy teacher for geometry.*

M

mad about someone or something See *crazy about someone or something*.

made for doing something (literally or figuratively) well-suited for doing a specific task. □ *This tool is made for turning this kind of screw.* □ *Jane is very talented. She's just made for designing furniture.*

made for each other (for two people) to be very well-suited romantically. □ *Bill and Jane were made for each other.* □ *Mr. and Mrs. Smith were not exactly made for each other. They really don't get along.*

made to order See *make something to order*.

make a beeline for someone or something* to head straight toward someone or something. (Informal. Also used literally for bees in flight.) □ *Billy came into the kitchen and made a beeline for the cookies.* □ *After the game, we all made a beeline for John who was serving cold drinks.*

make a big deal about something See *make a federal case out of something*.

make a break for something or somewhere* to move or run quickly to something or somewhere. (Informal.) □ *Before we could stop her, she made a break for the door and got away.* □ *The mouse got frightened and made a break for a hole in the wall.*

make a bundle* AND **make a pile*** to make a lot of money. (Slang.) □ *John really made a bundle on that deal.* □ *I'd like to make a pile and retire.*

make a check out to someone AND **make out a check to someone; make**

a check out; make out a check to write a check naming someone as payee. □ *Please make a check out to John Jones.* □ *Do you want cash, or should I make out a check?*

make a clean breast of something to confess something; to *get something off one's chest.* □ *You'll feel better if you make a clean breast of it. Now tell us what happened.* □ *I was forced to make a clean breast of the whole affair.*

make a clean sweep* to do something completely or thoroughly, with no exceptions. (Informal.) □ *The boss decided to fire everybody, so he made a clean sweep.* □ *They made a clean sweep through the neighborhood, repairing all the sidewalks.*

make a comeback* to return to one's former (successful) career. (Informal.) □ *After ten years in retirement, the singer made a comeback.* □ *You're never too old to make a comeback.*

make a day of doing something AND **make a day of it** to spend the whole day doing something. □ *We went to the museum to see the new exhibit and then decided to make a day of it.* □ *They made a day of cleaning the attic.*

make a dent in something* to begin to consume or accomplish something. (Informal. Also used literally.) □ *Bob, you've hardly made a dent in your dinner!* □ *There is a lot of rice left. We hardly made a dent in it all week.* □ *Get busy! You haven't even made a dent in your work.*

make a face at someone AND **make a face 1.** to make a face at someone in ridicule. □ *Mother, Billy made a face at me!* □ *The teacher sent Jane to the* *principal for making a face in class.* **2.** to attempt to communicate to someone through facial gestures, usually an attempt to say "no" or "stop." □ *I started to tell John where I was last night, but Bill made a face so I didn't.* □ *John made a face at me as I was testifying, so I avoided telling everything.*

make a fast buck* AND **make a quick buck*** to make money with little effort. (Slang.) □ *Tom is always ready to make a fast buck.* □ *I made a quick buck selling used cars.*

make a federal case out of something* AND **make a big deal about something*** to exaggerate the seriousness of something. (Slang.) □ *Come on. It was nothing! Don't make a federal case out of it.* □ *I only stepped on your toe. Don't make a big deal about it.*

make a fool out of someone AND **make a monkey out of someone***; **make an ass of someone*** to make someone look foolish. (The second and third phrases are informal. Use *ass* with caution.) □ *John made a fool out of himself at the party.* □ *Are you trying to make a monkey out of me?* □ *Don't make an ass of yourself!*

make a fuss over someone or something AND **fuss over someone or something; make a fuss; make over someone or something** **1.** to worry about or make a bother about someone or something. □ *Why do you fuss over a problem like that?* □ *Please don't make a fuss. Everything will be all right.* □ *Don't make over me so much!* **2.** to be very solicitous and helpful toward a person or a pet. □ *How can anyone make a fuss over a cat?* □ *Billy was embarrassed when his mother made a fuss over him.* **3.** to argue about someone or something. □ *Please don't make a fuss over who gets the last cookie.* □ *Please discuss it. Don't fuss about it!*

make a go of it* to make something work out all right. (Informal.) □ *It's a tough situation, but Ann is trying to make a go of it.* □ *We don't like living here, but we have to make a go of it.*

make a great show of something to make something obvious; to do something in a showy fashion. □ *Ann made*

a great show of wiping up the drink that John spilled. □ *Jane displayed her irritation at our late arrival by making a great show of serving the cold dinner.*

make a hit with someone or something* AND **make a hit*** to please someone. (Informal.) □ *The singer made a hit with the audience.* □ *She was afraid she wouldn't make a hit.* □ *John made a hit with my parents last evening.*

make a killing* to have a great success, especially in making money. (Slang.) □ *John's got a job selling insurance. He's not exactly making a killing.* □ *Bill made a killing at the racetrack yesterday.*

make a living to earn enough money to live on. □ *I'll be glad when I get a job and can make a living.* □ *I can hardly make a living with the skills I have.*

make a long story short* to bring a story to an end. (A cliché. A formula which introduces a summary of a story or a joke.) □ *And—to make a long story short—I never got back the money that I lent him.* □ *If I can make a long story short, let me say that everything worked out fine.*

make a mess of something AND **make a mess** to do something badly; to mess up something. □ *You certainly have made a mess of your life!* □ *Oh, how could I make a mess like this?*

make a monkey out of someone See *make a fool out of someone.*

make a mountain out of a molehill* to make a major issue out of a minor one; to exaggerate the importance of something. (A cliché.) □ *Come on, don't make a mountain out of a molehill. It's not that important.* □ *Mary is always making mountains out of molehills.*

make a name for oneself AND **make a name** to become famous. □ *Sally wants to work hard and make a name for herself.* □ *It's hard to make a name without a lot of talent and hard work.*

make a night of doing something to do something for the entire night. □ *We partied until three in the morning and then decided to make a night of it.* □ *Once or twice in the early spring we make a night of fishing.*

make a note of something to write

something down. □ *Please make a note of this address.* □ *This is important. Make a note of it.*

make a nuisance of oneself to be a constant bother. □ *I'm sorry to make a nuisance of myself, but I do need an answer to my question.* □ *Stop making a nuisance of yourself and wait your turn.*

make a pass at someone to flirt with someone; to make a romantic advance at someone. (This often has sexual implications. Compare to *make a play for someone.*) □ *I was shocked when Ann made a pass at me.* □ *I think Bob was making a pass at me, but he did it very subtly.*

make a pile See *make a bundle.*

make a pitch for someone or something* AND **make a pitch*** to say something in support of someone or something; to attempt to promote or advance someone or something. (Informal.) □ *Bill is making a pitch for his friend's new product again.* □ *The theatrical agent came in and made a pitch for her client.* □ *Every time I turn on the television set, someone is making a pitch.*

make a play for someone* AND **make a play*** to attempt to attract the romantic interest of someone. (Informal. Compare to *make a pass at someone.*) □ *Ann made a play for Bill, but he wasn't interested in her.* □ *I knew he liked me, but I never thought he'd make a play.*

make a point 1. to score a point (in a game or contest). (The *a* can be replaced with any number. See the examples.) □ *Great! John just made a point.* □ *The team made ten points.* 2. See the following entry.

make a point of something 1. AND **make a point** to state an item of importance. □ *You made a point which we all should remember.* □ *He spoke for an hour without making a point.* 2. AND **make a point of doing something** to make an effort to do something. □ *Please make a point of mailing this letter. It's very important.* □ *The hostess made a point of thanking me for bringing flowers.* 3. AND **make an issue of someone or something** to turn someone or something into an important

matter. □ *Please don't make a point of John's comment. It wasn't that important.* □ *I hope you make an issue of Tom's success and the reasons for it.* □ *Tom has a lot of problems. Please don't make an issue of him.*

make a practice of something AND **make something a practice** to turn something into a habitual activity. □ *Jane makes a practice of planting daisies every summer.* □ *Her mother also made it a practice.*

make a quick buck See *make a fast buck.*

make a run for it* to run fast to get away or get somewhere. (Informal. Compare to *make a break for something or somewhere.*) □ *When the guard wasn't looking, the prisoner made a run for it.* □ *In the baseball game, the player on first base made a run for it, but he didn't make it to second base.*

make a scene AND **create a scene** to make a public display or disturbance. □ *When John found a fly in his drink, he started to create a scene.* □ *Oh, John, please don't make a scene. Just forget about it.*

Make a silk purse out of a sow's ear.* to create something of value out of something of no value. (A cliché. Often in the negative.) □ *Don't bother trying to fix up this old bicycle. You can't make a silk purse out of a sow's ear.* □ *My mother made a lovely jacket out of an old coat. She succeeded in making a silk purse out of a sow's ear.*

make allowance for someone or something AND **make allowance** (Also with *allowances,* the plural.) 1. to allow time, space, food, etc., for someone or something. □ *When planning the party, please make allowances for John and his family.* □ *I'm making allowance for ten extra guests.* 2. to make excuses or explanations for someone or something; to take into consideration the negative effects of someone or something. □ *You're very late even when we make allowance for the weather.* □ *We have to make allowance for the age of the house when we judge its condition.*

make an all-out effort See *all-out effort.*

make an appearance to appear; to

appear in a performance. (Compare to *put in an appearance*.) □ *We waited for thirty minutes for the professor to make an appearance, then we went home.* □ *The famous singing star made an appearance in Detroit last August.*

make an appointment with someone AND **make an appointment** to schedule a meeting with someone. □ *I made an appointment with the doctor for late today.* □ *The professor wouldn't see me unless I made an appointment.*

make an ass of someone See *make a fool out of someone.*

make an example of someone to make a public issue out of someone's bad behavior. □ *The judge decided to make an example of John, so he fined him the full amount.* □ *The teacher made an example of Mary who disturbed the class constantly with her whispering.*

make an exception for someone AND **make an exception** to suspend a rule or practice for someone in a single instance. □ *Please make an exception just this once.* □ *The rule is a good one, and I will not make an exception for anyone.*

make an impression on someone AND **make an impression** to produce a memorable effect on someone. (Often with *good, bad* or some other adjective.) □ *Tom made a bad impression on the banker.* □ *I'm afraid that you haven't made a very good impression on our visitors.* □ *You made quite an impression on my father.*

make an uproar See *create an uproar.*

make arrangements for someone or something AND **make arrangements** **1.** to make plans for someone or something. □ *I'm making arrangements for the convention.* □ *It starts next week, and I hardly have time to make arrangements.* **2.** [with *someone*] to plan accommodations for someone. □ *John is coming for a visit next week. Please make arrangements for him at the hotel.* □ *I will make arrangements for everyone when I call the hotel.*

make arrangements to do something AND **make arrangements** to make plans to do something. □ *I'm making arrangements to sell my car.* □ *I have*

to *make arrangements before I put the advertisement in the newspaper.*

make arrangements with someone AND **make arrangements** to make plans with someone. □ *I made arrangements with John to come to his house and pick him up.* □ *I called yesterday to make arrangements.*

make away with someone or something AND **make off with someone or something** to take someone or something away; to make someone or something disappear. □ *The robber made away with the jewelry.* □ *The maid quickly made off with the children. We only saw them for a moment.*

make book on something* to make or accept bets on something. (Slang.) □ *It looks like it will rain, but I wouldn't make book on it.* □ *John's making book on the football game this Saturday.*

make both ends meet See *make ends meet.*

make chin music* to talk or chatter. (Slang.) □ *We sat around all evening making chin music.* □ *You were making chin music when you should have been listening.*

make cracks about someone or something* AND **make cracks*** to ridicule or make jokes about someone or something. (Informal.) □ *Please stop making cracks about my haircut. It's the new style.* □ *Some people can't help making cracks. They are just rude.*

make do with someone or something AND **make do** to do as well as possible with someone or something. □ *You'll have to make do with less money next year. The economy is very weak.* □ *We'll have to make do with John even though he's a slow worker.* □ *Yes, we'll have to make do.*

make ends meet AND **make both ends meet** to manage to live on a small amount of money. □ *It's hard these days to make ends meet.* □ *I have to work overtime to make both ends meet.*

make eyes at someone AND **make eyes** to flirt with someone. □ *Tom spent all afternoon making eyes at Ann.* □ *How could they sit there in class making eyes?*

make for somewhere* to run or travel to somewhere. (Slang, especially criminal slang.) □ *When I got out of class, I made for the gym.* □ *When he got out of jail, he made for Toledo.*

make free with someone or something AND **make free** **1.** [with *someone*] See *take liberties with someone or something.* **2.** [with *something*] to take advantage of or use something as if it were one's own. (Compare to *take liberties with someone or something.*) □ *I wish you wouldn't come into my house and make free with my food and drink.* □ *Please make free with my car while I'm gone.*

make friends with someone AND **make friends** to become a friend of someone. □ *I tried to make friends with John, but he didn't seem to like me.* □ *I find it hard to make friends.*

make fun of someone or something AND **make fun** to ridicule someone or something. □ *Please stop making fun of me. It hurts my feelings.* □ *Billy teases and makes fun a lot, but he means no harm.*

make good as something to succeed in a particular role. □ *I hope I make good as a teacher.* □ *John made good as a football player.*

make good at something AND **make good** to succeed at something. □ *Bob worked hard to make good at selling.* □ *Jane was determined to make good.*

make good money* to earn a large amount of money. (Informal.) □ *Ann makes good money at her job.* □ *I don't know what she does, but she makes good money.*

make good on something **1.** to fulfill a promise. □ *Tom made good on his pledge to donate $1000.* □ *Bill refused to make good on his promise.* **2.** to repay a debt. (See also *make something good.*) □ *I couldn't make good on my debts, and I got in a lot of trouble.* □ *If you don't make good on this bill, I'll have to take back your car.*

make good time* to proceed at a fast or reasonable rate. (Informal.) □ *On our trip to Toledo, we made good time.* □ *I'm making good time, but I have a long way to go.*

make hamburger out of someone or something* AND **make mincemeat out**

of someone or something* to beat up or overcome someone or something. (Slang. Used literally when referring to foodstuffs. Used figuratively with people.) □ *Stop acting silly, or I'll make hamburger out of you.* □ *Our team made mincemeat out of the other team.*

Make hay while the sun is shining. a proverb meaning that you should make the most of good times. □ *There are lots of people here now. You should try to sell them soda pop. Make hay while the sun is shining.* □ *Go to school and get a good education while you're young. Make hay while the sun is shining.*

make it hot for someone* to make things difficult for someone; to put someone under pressure. (Slang.) □ *Maybe if we make it hot for them, they'll leave.* □ *John likes making it hot for people. He's sort of mean.*

Make it snappy!* Hurry up! (Slang.) □ *Come on. Make it snappy! I can't wait all day.* □ *Make it snappy! We have to leave now!*

make life miserable for someone to make someone unhappy over a long period of time. □ *My shoes are tight, and they are making life miserable for me.* □ *Jane's boss is making life miserable for her.*

make light of something to treat something as if it were unimportant or humorous. □ *I wish you wouldn't make light of his problems. They're quite serious.* □ *I make light of my problems, and that makes me feel better.*

make little of someone or something to minimize someone or something; to *play someone or something down;* to *belittle someone or something.* □ *John made little of my efforts to collect money for charity.* □ *The neighbors made little of John and thought he would amount to nothing.*

make love to someone AND **make love** to share physical or emotional love (or both) with someone. (This phrase usually has a sexual meaning.) □ *Tom and Ann turned out the lights and made love.* □ *The actress refused to make love on stage.*

make mincemeat out of someone or

something See *make hamburger out of someone or something.*

make no bones about it* without a doubt; absolutely. (Folksy.) □ *This is the greatest cake I've ever eaten. Make no bones about it.* □ *Make no bones about it, Mary is a great singer.*

make no difference to someone AND **make no difference** to not matter to someone; for someone not to care (about something). □ *It makes no difference to me what you do.* □ *Do whatever you want. It really makes no difference.*

make no mistake about it* AND **make no mistake*** without a doubt; certainly. (Informal. Compare to *make no bones about it.* Also used literally.) □ *This car is a great buy. Make no mistake about it.* □ *We support your candidacy—make no mistake.*

make nothing of it to ignore something as if it had not happened. □ *My father caught me throwing the snowball, but he made nothing of it.* □ *I saw him leave, but I made nothing of it.*

make off with someone or something See *make away with someone or something.*

make one's way through something AND **make one's way** to work or travel through something. □ *Slowly, she made her way through the forest.* □ *She found it difficult to make her way.* □ *The speaker made his way through the speech very slowly.*

make oneself at home to make oneself comfortable as if one were in one's own home. □ *Please come in and make yourself at home.* □ *I'm glad you're here. During your visit, just make yourself at home.*

make oneself conspicuous to attract attention to oneself. □ *Please don't make yourself conspicuous. It embarrasses me.* □ *Ann makes herself conspicuous by wearing brightly-colored clothing.*

make oneself miserable to do things which cause one to be unhappy. □ *You're just making yourself miserable by trying to do something you aren't qualified to do.* □ *I'm not making myself miserable! You're making me miserable.*

make oneself scarce* to go away. (Slang.) □ *Hey kid, go away. Make yourself scarce.* □ *When there is work to be done, I make myself scarce.*

make or break someone* to improve or ruin someone. (A cliché.) □ *The army will either make or break him.* □ *It's a tough assignment, and it will either make or break her.*

make out with someone or something AND **make out** **1.** to manage to do (something) with someone or something. □ *I think I can make out with this hammer.* □ *If I can't make out with John, I'll have to ask for more help.* **2.*** [with *someone*] to flirt with, kiss, or hug someone; to *make love to someone.* (Slang.) □ *Bob was trying to make out with Sally all evening.* □ *She didn't want to make out, so she left.*

make over someone or something See *make a fuss over someone or something; do someone or something over.*

make peace with someone AND **make peace** to end a quarrel with someone. (Compare to *kiss and make up.*) □ *Don't you think it's time to make peace with your brother? There is no point in arguing anymore.* □ *Yes, it's time we made peace.*

make points with someone* AND **make points*** to gain favor with someone. (Slang.) □ *Tom is trying to make points with Ann. He wants to ask her out.* □ *He's trying to make points by smiling and telling her how nice she looks.*

make sense out of someone or something to understand or interpret someone or something. (Also with *some,* as in the examples.) □ *I can hardly make sense out of John.* □ *I'm trying to make some sense out of what John is saying.* ALSO: **make sense** to be understandable. □ *John doesn't make sense.* □ *What John says makes sense.*

make short work of someone or something AND **make fast work of someone or something** to finish with someone or something quickly. □ *I made short work of Tom so I could leave the office to play golf.* □ *Billy made fast work of his dinner so he could go out and play.*

make someone eat crow* to cause

someone to retract a statement or admit an error. (Informal.) □ *Because Mary was completely wrong, we made her eat crow.* □ *They won't make me eat crow. They don't know I was wrong.*

make someone look good to cause someone to appear successful or competent (especially when this is not the case). (Also used literally.) □ *John arranges all his affairs to make himself look good.* □ *The manager didn't like the quarterly report because it didn't make her look good.*

make someone look ridiculous to make someone look foolish (not funny). □ *This hat makes me look ridiculous.* □ *Please make me look good. Don't make me look ridiculous!*

make someone or something available to someone to supply someone with someone or something. □ *I made my car available to Bob.* □ *They made their maid available to us.*

make someone or something over See *do someone or something over.*

make someone or something tick* to cause someone or something to run or function. (Informal. Usually with *what.*) □ *I don't know what makes it tick.* □ *What makes John tick? I just don't understand him.* □ *I took apart the radio to find out what made it tick.*

make someone or something up AND **make up someone or something** **1.** [with *something*] to repay or redo something. □ *Can I make up the test I missed?* □ *Please make up the payment you missed.* **2.** [with *something*] to think up something; to make and tell a lie. □ *That's not true! You just made that up!* □ *I didn't make it up!* **3.** to mix something up; to assemble something. (The *up* can be left out.) □ JOHN: *Is my prescription ready?* DRUGGIST: *No, I haven't made it up yet. I'll make up your prescription in a minute.* □ *How long does it take to make up a cheese sandwich?* **4.** [with *someone*] to put makeup on someone. □ *She made herself up before leaving the house.* □ *The crew made up the cast before the play.* ALSO: **make up** to put makeup on oneself. □ *I have to make up now. I go on stage in ten minutes.*

make someone the scapegoat for something to make someone take the blame for something. □ *They made Tom the scapegoat for the whole affair. It wasn't all his fault.* □ *Don't try to make me the scapegoat. I'll tell who really did it.*

make someone's blood boil* to make someone very angry. (Informal.) □ *It just makes my blood boil to think of the amount of food that gets wasted around here.* □ *Whenever I think of that dishonest mess, it makes my blood boil.*

make someone's blood run cold to shock or horrify someone. □ *The terrible story in the newspaper made my blood run cold.* □ *I could tell you things about prisons which would make your blood run cold.*

make someone's hair stand on end* to cause someone to be very frightened. (Informal.) □ *The horrible scream made my hair stand on end.* □ *The ghost story made our hair stand on end.*

make someone's head spin See the following entry.

make someone's head swim AND **make someone's head spin** **1.** to make someone dizzy or disoriented. □ *Riding in your car makes my head spin.* □ *Breathing the gas made my head swim.* **2.** to confuse or overwhelm someone. □ *All these numbers make my head swim.* □ *The physics lecture made my head spin.*

make someone's mind up AND **make up someone's mind** to make someone decide. □ *Please make your mind up. Which do you want?* □ *Would you help me make my mind up?*

make someone's mouth water* to make someone hungry (for something). (Informal. Also used literally.) □ *That beautiful salad makes my mouth water.* □ *Talking about food makes my mouth water.*

make someone's position clear to clarify where someone stands on an issue. □ *I don't think you understand what I said. Let me make my position clear.* □ *I can't tell whether you are in favor of or against the proposal. Please make your position clear.*

make something from scratch* to

make something by starting with the basic ingredients. (Informal.) □ *We made the cake from scratch, using no prepared ingredients.* □ *I didn't have a ladder, so I made one from scratch.*

make something good AND **make something right** to replace or restore something. (Informal.) □ *I know I owe you some money, but don't worry, I'll make it good.* □ *I'm sorry I broke your window. I'll make it right, though.*

make something of something 1. to make an interpretation of something. □ *Can you make anything out of this message? I don't understand it.* □ *I'm sorry, I can't make any sense out of it.* 2.* to interpret something negatively. (Informal. Compare to *make nothing of it.*) □ *So, I'm wrong! You want to make something of it?* □ *The hostess made too much of my absence.*

make something out AND **make out something** to read something (which is not written or printed clearly); to decipher something. □ *What does this say? I can hardly make it out.* □ *Can you make out what this says?*

make something out of nothing 1. to make an issue of something of little importance. (See also *make a mountain out of a molehill.*) □ *Relax John, you're making a big problem out of nothing.* □ *You have no evidence. You're making a case out of nothing.* 2. to create something of value from nearly worthless parts. □ *My uncle—he sells sand—made a fortune out of nothing.* □ *My model airplane won the contest even though I made it out of nothing.*

make something to order to put something together only when someone requests it. (Usually said about clothing.) □ *This store only makes suits to order.* □ *Our shirts fit perfectly because each one is made to order.* ALSO: **made to order** put together on request. (Compare to *in stock.*) □ *This suit fits so well because it's made to order.* □ *His feet are so big that all his shoes have to be made to order.*

make something up out of whole cloth* AND **make up something out of whole cloth*** to create a story or a lie from no facts at all. (A cliché.) □ *I don't believe you. I think you made that up out of whole cloth.* □ *Ann made up her explanation out of whole cloth. There was not a bit of truth in it.*

make something up to someone to repay someone; to make amends to someone. □ *I'm so sorry I've insulted you. How can I make it up to you?* □ *I'm sorry I broke our date. I'll make it up to you, I promise.*

make the bed AND **make someone's bed** to restore a bed to an unslept-in condition. □ *I make my bed every morning.* □ *The maid goes to all the rooms to make the beds.*

make the best of something to try to make a bad situation work out well. (Compare to *make the most of something.*) □ *It's not good, but we'll have to make the best of it.* □ *Ann is clever enough to make the best of a bad situation.*

make the feathers fly See the following entry.

make the fur fly* AND **make the feathers fly*** to cause a fight or an argument; to *create an uproar* (about something). (Informal.) □ *When your mother gets home and sees what you've done, she'll really make the fur fly.* □ *When those two get together, they'll make the feathers fly. They hate each other.*

make the grade* to be satisfactory; to be what is expected. (Informal.) □ *I'm sorry, but your work doesn't exactly make the grade.* □ *This meal doesn't just make the grade. It is excellent.*

make the most of something to make something appear as good as possible; to exploit something; to get as much out of something as is possible. (Compare to *make the best of something.*) □ *Mary knows how to make the most of her talents.* □ *They designed the advertisements to make the most of the product's features.*

make the scene* to appear somewhere. (Slang.) □ *I hope I can make the scene Saturday night.* □ *Man, I've got to make the scene. The whole world will be there!*

make time with someone* AND **make time*** to flirt with, date, or hang around with someone. (Informal.) □ *I* *hear that Tom's been making time with Ann.* □ *I hear they've been making time for months.*

make tracks somewhere* AND **make tracks*** to leave and travel (by foot or horse) to somewhere. (Folksy. Typical of Western movies.) □ *Come on, partner. It's time to make tracks home* □ *Yes, let's make tracks.*

make up See *make someone or something up; make up with someone.*

make up for lost time to do much of something; to do something fast. □ *Because we spent too much time eating lunch, we have to drive faster to make up for lost time. Otherwise we won't arrive on time.* □ *At the age of sixty, Bill learned to play golf. Now he plays it all the time. He's making up for lost time.*

make up for someone or something to take the place of someone or something. □ *John can't play in the game Saturday, but I think I can make up for him.* □ *Do you think that this cat can make up for the one which ran away?*

make up with someone AND **make up** to apologize and become friends with someone. □ *I'm sorry. I was wrong. I want to make up with you.* □ *I want to make up, too.*

make use of someone or something to utilize someone or something (for a specific purpose). □ *Can you make use of an extra helper?* □ *I could make use of a lot of help.* □ *I could make use of John to help me.*

make waves* to make trouble or difficulties. (Informal. Compare to *rock the boat.*) □ *I don't want to make waves, but this just isn't right.* □ *Why do you always have to make waves? Can't you be constructive?*

make way **1.** to make progress; to move ahead. (Originally nautical.) □ *Is this project making way?* □ *A sailboat can't make way if there is no wind.* **2.** See the following entry.

make way for someone or something AND **make way** to clear a path for someone or something. □ *Make way for the stretcher.* □ *Please make way for the nurse.* □ *Here comes the doctor—make way!*

many is the time* on many occasions. (A cliché.) □ *Many is the time I wanted to complain, but I just kept quiet.* □ *Many is the time that we don't have enough to eat.*

march to a different drummer* to believe in a different set of principles. (A cliché.) □ *John is marching to a different drummer, and he doesn't come to our parties anymore.* □ *Since Sally started marching to a different drummer, she has had a lot of great new ideas.*

Mark my words.* AND **Mark my word.*** Remember what I'm telling you.; Remember that I have predicted (something). (A cliché.) □ *Mark my word, you'll regret this.* □ *This whole project will fail—mark my words.*

mark someone or something down AND **mark down someone or something** **1.** [with *someone*] to make a note about someone; to note a fact about someone. □ *I'm going to the party. Please mark me down.* □ *Mark me down, too.* **2.** [with *someone*] (for a teacher) to give someone a low score. □ *He'll mark you down for misspelled words.* □ *I marked down Tom for bad spelling.* **3.** [with *something*] to lower the price of something. □ *Let's mark down this price so it'll sell faster.* □ *Okay, we'll mark it down.*

mark something up AND **mark up something** **1.** to mess something up with marks. □ *Don't mark up your book!* □ *Who marked this book up?* **2.** to grade a paper and make lots of informative marks and comments on it. □ *The teacher really marked up my term paper.* □ *Why did you mark my test up so much? I hardly made any errors.* **3.** to raise the price of something. □ *They mark up the price of turkey at Thanksgiving.* □ *The grocery store seems to mark the price of food up every week.*

matter-of-fact businesslike; unfeeling. (See also *as a matter of fact.*) □ *Don't expect a lot of sympathy from Ann. She's very matter-of-fact.* □ *Don't be so matter-of-fact. It hurts my feelings.*

mean nothing to someone AND **mean nothing** **1.** to not make sense to someone. (See also the following entry.) □ *This sentence means nothing to me. It* *isn't clearly written.* □ *I'm sorry. This message means nothing.* **2.** (for someone) to not have feeling for (someone or something). □ *Do I mean nothing to you after all these years?* □ *Do all those years mean nothing?*

mean something to someone AND **mean something** **1.** to make sense to someone. (See also the preceding entry.) □ *Does this line mean anything to you?* □ *Yes, it means something.* **2.** for someone to have feeling for (someone or something). □ *You mean a lot to me.* □ *This job means a lot to Ann.*

mean to do something AND **mean to** to intend to do something. □ *Did you mean to do that?* □ *No, it was an accident. I didn't mean to.*

measure up to someone or something AND **measure up** to be equal to someone or something. □ *Ann is good, but she doesn't measure up to Mary.* □ *This measures up to my standards quite nicely.* □ *Yes, it measures up.*

measure up to someone's expectations AND **measure up** to be as good as one expects. □ *This meal doesn't measure up to my expectations.* □ *Why doesn't it measure up?*

meet one's end to die. □ *The dog met his end under the wheels of a car.* □ *I don't intend to meet my end until I'm 100 years old.*

meet one's match to meet one's equal. □ *John played tennis with Bill yesterday, and it looks like John has finally met his match.* □ *Listen to Jane and Mary argue. I always thought that Jane was loud, but she has finally met her match.*

meet one's Waterloo* to meet one's final and insurmountable challenge. (A cliché. Refers to Napoleon at Waterloo.) □ *The boss is being very hard on Bill. It seems that Bill has finally met his Waterloo.* □ *John was more than Sally could handle. She has finally met her Waterloo.*

meet someone halfway to offer to compromise with someone. □ *No, I won't give in, but I'll meet you halfway.* □ *They settled the argument by agreeing to meet each other halfway.*

meet the requirements for something

AND **meet the requirements** to fulfill the requirements for something. □ *Sally was unable to meet the requirements for the job.* □ *Jane met the requirements and was told to report to work the next day.*

melt in one's mouth* to taste very good. (A cliché.) □ *This cake is so good it'll melt in your mouth.* □ *John said that the food didn't exactly melt in his mouth.*

mend one's fences AND **mend fences** to restore good relations (with someone). (Also used literally.) □ *I think I had better get home and mend my fences. I had an argument with my daughter this morning.* □ *Sally called up her uncle to apologize and try to mend fences.*

mention something in passing to mention something casually; to mention something while talking about something else. □ *He just happened to mention in passing that the mayor had resigned.* □ *John mentioned in passing that he was nearly eighty years old.*

mess about with someone or something See the following entry.

mess around with someone or something* AND **mess about with someone or something***; **mess about***; **mess around***; **monkey around with someone or something***; **monkey around***; **screw around with someone or something***; **screw around*** to play with or waste time with someone or something. (Slang.) □ *Will you please stop messing around with that old car!* □ *Stop messing about! Get busy!* □ *Tom wastes a lot of time messing around with Bill.* □ *Don't monkey around with my computer!* □ *John is always screwing around with his stereo.*

mess someone or something up AND **mess up someone or something** **1.*** [with *someone*] to rough someone up; to beat someone up. (Slang.) □ *The robbers threatened to mess Bob up if he didn't cooperate.* □ *John messed up Bill a little, but no real harm was done.* **2.** [with *something*] to make something disorderly. □ *You really messed this place up!* □ *Who messed up my bed?*

method in one's madness* (for there to be) purpose in what one is doing. (A cliché.) □ *What I'm doing may look* strange, but there is method in my madness. □ Wait until she finishes; then you'll see that there is method in her madness.

millstone about one's neck a continual burden or handicap. □ This huge and expensive house is a millstone about my neck. □ Bill's inability to read is a millstone about his neck.

mince one's words AND **mince words** to lessen the force of one's statement by choosing weak or polite words; to be euphemistic. (Formal.) □ I won't mince words. You did a rotten job. □ I'm not one to mince words, so I have to say that you behaved very badly.

mind one's own business to attend only to the things which concern one. □ Leave me alone, Bill. Mind your own business. □ I'd be fine if John would mind his own business.

mind one's P's and Q's to mind one's manners. □ When we go to the mayor's reception, please mind your P's and Q's. □ I always mind my P's and Q's when I eat at a restaurant with white table cloths.

mind the store* to take care of local matters. (Informal. Also used literally.) □ Please stay here in the office and mind the store while I go to the conference. □ I had to stay home and mind the store when Ann went to Boston.

miss out on something AND **lose out on something; lose out; miss out** to fail to participate in something; to fail to take part in something. □ I'm sorry I missed out on the ice cream. □ I lost out on it, too. □ We both missed out.

miss something by a mile* AND **miss by a mile*** to fail to hit something by a great distance; to land wide of the mark. (A cliché.) □ Ann shot the arrow and missed the target by a mile. □ "Good grief, you missed by a mile," shouted Sally.

miss the boat* to miss out (on something); to be ignorant (of something). (Slang. Also used literally.) □ Pay attention, John, or you'll miss the boat. □ Tom really missed the boat when it came to making friends.

miss the point to fail to understand the point. □ I'm afraid you missed the point.

Let me explain it again. □ You keep explaining, and I keep missing the point.

mistake someone for someone else AND **mix someone up with someone else** to confuse someone with someone else; to think that one person is another person. □ I'm sorry. I mistook you for John. □ Tom is always mistaking Bill for me. We don't look a thing alike, though. □ Try not to mix Bill up with Bob.

mistake something for something else AND **mix something up with something else** to confuse something with something else; to think that one thing is another thing. □ I mistook the roast chicken for turkey. □ How can anyone mix chicken up with turkey? □ Tom will probably mistake your house for mine.

mix it up* to argue or fight. (Slang. Also used literally.) □ First they were just talking, then suddenly one of them got mad and they really began to mix it up. □ Look at you, Bill! Your face is bleeding. Have you been mixing it up with John again?

mix someone or something up AND **mix up someone or something 1.** to confuse two things or two people with each other. □ Please don't mix these ideas up. They are quite distinct. □ I always mix up Bill and Bob. □ Why do you mix them up? **2.** [with someone] to cause someone to be confused or puzzled. □ I'm confused as it is. Don't mix me up anymore. □ They mixed up my uncle by giving him too many things to remember. **3.** [with something] to blend the ingredients of something; to assemble and mix the parts of something. (Usually refers to fluid matter such as paint, gasoline, or milk.) □ Now, mix up the eggs, water, and salt; then add the mixture to the flour and sugar. □ The glue will be ready to use as soon as I mix it up.

mix someone up with someone else See mistake someone for someone else.

mix something up with something else See mistake something for something else.

Money burns a hole in someone's pocket.* Someone spends as much money as possible. (Informal. See also *have money to burn*.) □ *Sally can't seem to save anything. Money burns a hole in her pocket.* □ *If money burns a hole in your pocket, you never have any for emergencies.*

Money is no object. It does not matter how much something costs. □ *Please show me your finest automobile. Money is no object.* □ *I want the finest earrings you have. Don't worry about how much it costs because money is no object.*

Money is the root of all evil. a proverb meaning that money is the basic cause of all wrongdoing. □ *Why do you work so hard to make money? It will just cause you trouble. Money is the root of all evil.* □ *Any thief in prison can tell you that money is the root of all evil.*

money talks* money gives one power and influence to help get things done or get one's own way. (Informal.) □ *Don't worry, I have a way of getting things done. Money talks.* □ *I can't compete against rich old Mrs. Jones. She'll get her way because money talks.*

monkey around with someone or something See *mess around with someone or something.*

mop up the floor with someone* AND **mop the floor up with someone*** to overwhelm and physically subdue someone; to beat someone. (Slang.) □ *Stop talking like that, or I'll mop the floor up with you!* □ *Did you hear that? He threatened to mop up the floor with me!*

mope around* to go about in a depressed state. (Informal.) □ *Since her dog ran away, Sally mopes around all day.* □ *Don't mope around. Cheer up!*

more often than not usually. □ *These flowers will live through the winter more often than not.* □ *This kind of a dog will grow up to be a good watchdog more often than not.*

more or less to some extent; approximately; sort of. □ *This one will do all right, more or less.* □ *We'll be there at eight, more or less.*

more than one can shake a stick at* AND **more someone or something than one can shake a stick at*** a lot; too many to count. (Folksy.) □ *There were*

more snakes than one can shake a stick at.* □ *There were lots of flowers in the field—more than one can shake a stick at.*

more to something than meets the eye* AND **more than meets the eye*** (there are) hidden values or facts in something. (A cliché.) □ *There is more to that problem than meets the eye.* □ *What makes you think that there is more than meets the eye?*

most of all of greatest importance; more than any other. (Compare to *least of all*.) □ *I wanted to go to that museum most of all. Why can't I go?* □ *There are many reasons why I didn't use my car today. Most of all, it's a lovely day for walking.*

move heaven and earth to do something* to make a major effort to do something. (A cliché. Not used literally.) □ *"I'll move heaven and earth to be with you, Mary," said Bill.* □ *I had to move heaven and earth to get there on time.*

move in on someone or something* AND **move in*** **1.** [with *someone*] to attempt to displace someone or take over someone's property, interests, or relationships. (Slang, especially criminal slang. Compare to *muscle in on someone or something*.) □ *Look here pal, Sally's my girl. Are you trying to move in on me?* □ *It looks like the south side gang is trying to move in. We'll have to teach them a lesson.* **2.** [with *someone*] to move into someone's household. □ *My mother-in-law moved in on us for two months.* □ *I wouldn't move in on you without an invitation.* **3.** to move closer to someone or something, especially with a camera. □ *Now, slowly move in on the cereal box. This will be a great advertisement.* □ *Hold the camera very steady and move in on the baby.*

move into something **1.** AND **move in** to move into a living or working space. □ *I hear you have a new place to live. When did you move in?* □ *We moved into our new offices last week.* **2.** to get started in a new enterprise, job, etc. □ *I moved into a new job last week. It's very exciting work.* □ *John moved into a new line of work, too.*

move on to keep moving; to move away. □ *Okay, everyone, move on now. The excitement is over.* □ *I've done all that I can do in this town. It's time to move on.*

move out 1. to move out of a living or working space. □ *We didn't like our apartment, so we moved out.* □ *We have a lease. We can't move out.* 2.* to leave; to move on. (Informal.) □ *If you guys are ready to go, let's move out.* □ *As soon as all the horses are saddled, we'll move out.*

move up in the world AND **move up** to advance (oneself) and become successful. □ *The harder I work, the more I move up in the world.* □ *Keep your eye on John. He's really moving up.*

much ado about nothing* a lot of excitement about nothing. (A cliché. This is the title of a play by Shakespeare. Do not confuse *ado* with *adieu*.) □ *All the commotion about the new tax law turned out to be much ado about nothing.* □ *Your promises always turn out to be much ado about nothing.*

much in evidence* very visible or evident. (A cliché.) □ *John was much in evidence during the conference.* □ *Your influence is much in evidence. I appreciate your efforts.*

much sought after* wanted or desired very much. (A cliché.) □ *This kind of crystal is much sought after. It's very rare.* □ *Sally is a great singer. She's much sought after.*

muff one's lines See *fluff one's lines*.

mull something over AND **mull over something** to think about something; to ponder or worry about something. □ *That's an interesting idea, but I'll have to mull it over.* □ *I'll mull over your suggestions and report to you next week.*

Mum's the word. Don't spread the secret. □ *Don't tell anyone what I told you. Remember, mum's the word.* □ *Okay, mum's the word. Your secret is safe with me.*

muscle in on something* AND **muscle in*** to try to forcefully displace someone or take over someone's property, interests, or relationships. (Slang, especially criminal slang. Compare to *move in on someone or something*.) □ *Are you trying to muscle in on my scheme?* □ *If you try to muscle in, you'll be facing big trouble.*

N

nail someone or something down AND **nail down someone or something 1.*** [with *someone*] to get a firm and final decision from someone (on something). (Informal.) □ *I want you to find Bob and get an answer from him. Nail him down one way or the other.* □ *Please nail down John on the question of signing the contract.* **2.*** [with *something*] to get a firm and final decision (from someone) on something. (Informal.) □ *Find Bob and nail down an answer.* □ *Let's get in touch with John and nail down this contract.* **3.** [with *something*] to nail (with a hammer) something which is loose. □ *Nail down this loose floor board.* □ *Please nail this thing down.*

name of the game* the goal or purpose (of something). (Slang.) □ *The name of the game is sell. You must sell, sell, sell if you want to make a living.* □ *Around here, the name of the game is look out for yourself.*

name someone after someone else AND **name someone for someone else** to give someone (usually a baby) the name of another person. □ *We named our baby after my aunt.* □ *My parents named me for my grandfather.*

near at hand close or handy (to someone). □ *Do you have a pencil near at hand?* □ *My dictionary isn't near at hand.*

neck and neck* exactly even, especially in a race or a contest. (Informal.) □ *John and Tom finished the race neck and neck.* □ *Mary and Ann were neck and neck in the spelling contest. Their scores were tied.*

neither fish nor fowl* not any recog-

nizable thing. (A cliché.) □ *The car that they drove up in was neither fish nor fowl. It must have been made out of spare parts.* □ *This proposal is neither fish nor fowl. I can't tell what you're proposing.*

neither here nor there* of no consequence or meaning; irrelevant and immaterial. (A cliché.) □ *Whether you go to the movie or stay at home is neither here nor there.* □ *Your comment—though interesting—is neither here nor there.*

neither hide nor hair* no sign or indication (of someone or something). (A cliché.) □ *We could find neither hide nor hair of him. I don't know where he is.* □ *There has been no one here—neither hide nor hair—for the last three days.*

never fear* do not worry; have confidence. (A cliché.) □ *I'll be there on time—never fear.* □ *I'll help you, never fear.*

never had it so good* (to have) never had so much good fortune. (Informal.) □ *No, I'm not complaining. I've never had it so good.* □ *Mary is pleased with her new job. She's never had it so good.*

never in one's life* not in one's experience. (A cliché.) □ *Never in my life have I been so insulted!* □ *He said that never in his life had he seen such an ugly painting.*

Never mind. Forget it!; Pay no more attention (to something). □ *I wanted to talk to you, but never mind. It wasn't important.* □ *Never mind. I'm sorry to bother you.*

new ball game* a new set of circumstances. (Slang. Originally from sports.

Often with *whole*.) □ *It's a whole new ball game since Jane took over the office.* □ *You can't do the things you used to do around here. It's a new ball game.*

new lease on life* a renewed and revitalized outlook on life. (A cliché.) □ *Getting the job offer was a new lease on life.* □ *When I got out of the hospital, I felt like I had a new lease on life.*

night and day See *day and night*.

night on the town a night of celebrating (at one or more places in a town). □ *Did you enjoy your night on the town?* □ *After we got the contract signed, we celebrated with a night on the town.*

nine-to-five job a job with regular and normal hours. □ *I wouldn't want a nine-to-five job. I like the freedom I have as my own boss.* □ *I used to work nights, but now I have a nine-to-five job.*

nip and tuck* almost even; almost tied. (Informal.) □ *The horses ran nip and tuck for the first half of the race. Then my horse pulled ahead.* □ *In the football game last Saturday, both teams were nip and tuck throughout the game.*

nip something in the bud* to put an end to something at an early stage. (A cliché.) □ *John is getting into bad habits, and it's best to nip them in the bud.* □ *There was trouble in the classroom, but the teacher nipped it in the bud.*

no buts about it See *no ifs, ands, or buts about it*.

no can do* cannot do (something). (Slang.) □ *Sorry, John. No can do. I can't sell you this one. I've promised it to Mrs. Smith.* □ BILL: *Please fix this clock today.* BOB: *No can do. It'll take a week to get the parts.*

No dice.* No, absolutely not. (Slang.) □ *As John hung up the telephone, he said, "No dice. She says she won't cooperate."* □ *No dice! I won't lie in court!*

no doubt surely; without a doubt; undoubtedly. □ *He will be here again tomorrow, no doubt.* □ *No doubt you will require a ride home?*

no end of something* lots of something. (Informal.) □ *It was a wonderful banquet. They had no end of good food.* □ *Tom is a real problem. He's no end of trouble.*

no great shakes* nothing important or worth noticing. (Slang.) □ *It's okay, but it's no great shakes.* □ *I like John, but he's no great shakes when it comes to sports.*

no hard feelings* no anger or resentment. (Informal. *No* can be replaced with *any*.) □ *I hope you don't have any hard feelings.* □ *No, I have no hard feelings.*

no holds barred* with no restraints. (Slang. From wrestling.) □ *I intend to argue it out with Mary, no holds barred.* □ *When Ann negotiates a contract, she goes in with no holds barred and comes out with a good contract.*

no ifs, ands, or buts about it* AND **no buts about it*** absolutely no discussion, dissension, or doubt about something. (A cliché.) □ *I want you there exactly at eight, no ifs, ands, or buts about it.* □ *This is the best television set available for the money, no buts about it.*

no kidding* (spoken) honestly; (someone is) not joking or lying. (Slang.) □ *No kidding, you really got an A in geometry?* □ *I really did, no kidding.*

no laughing matter* a serious matter. (A cliché.) □ *Be serious. This is no laughing matter.* □ *This disease is no laughing matter. It's quite deadly.*

no love lost between someone and someone else* AND **no love lost*** no friendship wasted between someone and someone else (because they are enemies). (A cliché.) □ *Ever since their big argument, there has been no love lost between Tom and Bill.* □ *You can tell by the way that Jane is acting toward Ann that there is no love lost.*

no matter what AND **no matter what happens** in any event; without regard to what happens (in the future). □ *We'll be there on time, no matter what.* □ *No matter what happens, we'll still be friends.*

no problem See *No sweat*.

no skin off someone's nose See the following entry.

no skin off someone's teeth* AND **no skin off someone's nose*** no difficulty for someone; no concern of someone. (A cliché.) □ *It's no skin off my nose if she wants to act that way.* □

She said it was no skin off her teeth if we wanted to sell the house.

no sooner said than done* done quickly and obediently. (Informal.) □ When Sally asked for someone to open the window, it was no sooner said than done. □ As Jane opened the window, she said, "No sooner said than done."

no spring chicken* not young (anymore). (Informal.) □ I don't get around very well anymore. I'm no spring chicken, you know. □ Even though John is no spring chicken, he still plays tennis twice a week.

No sweat.* AND **No problem.*** No difficulty, do not worry. (Slang.) □ Of course I can have your car repaired by noon. No sweat. □ You'd like a red one? No problem.

no trespassing do not enter. (Usually seen on a sign. Not usually spoken.) □ The sign on the tree said, "No Trespassing." So we didn't go in. □ The angry farmer chased us out of the field shouting, "Get out! Don't you see the no trespassing sign?"

no two ways about it* no choice about it; no other interpretation of it. (Folksy. Note the form there's rather than there are.) □ You have to go to the doctor whether you like it or not. There's no two ways about it. □ This letter means you're in trouble with the tax people. There's no two ways about it.

No way.* Absolutely not. (Slang.) □ You think I'm going to sit around here while you're having fun at the picnic? No way! □ BOB: Will you please take this to the post office for me? BILL: No way.

no wonder* (something is) not surprising. (Informal.) □ No wonder the baby is crying. She's wet. □ It's no wonder that plant died. You watered it too much.

none of someone's beeswax* none of someone's business. (Slang.) □ The answer to that question is none of your beeswax. □ It's none of your beeswax what I do with my spare time.

none the worse for wear no worse because of use or effort. □ I lent my car to John. When I got it back, it was none the worse for wear. □ I had a hard day today, but I'm none the worse for wear.

nose about See the following entry.

nose around* AND **nose about*** to investigate; to check (into something). (Informal.) □ I don't have an answer to your question, but I'll nose around and see what I can find out. □ I'll nose about, too. Who knows what we'll find out?

nose into something AND **nose in** to move into something, front end first. □ Slowly the car nosed into its parking place. □ You must nose in very carefully.

nose someone out AND **nose out someone** to push someone away; to exclude someone. □ Where I work someone is always trying to nose me out. I'd hate to lose my job. □ John nosed out Bill from the team.

Not a bit. Not at all. □ Am I unhappy? Not a bit. □ I don't want any mashed potatoes. Not a bit!

not a living soul* nobody. (Informal. See some of the possible variations in the examples.) □ I won't tell anybody—not a living soul. □ I won't tell a living soul. □ They wouldn't think of telling a living soul.

not able See the expressions listed at can't as well as those listed below.

not able to call one's time one's own* too busy; so busy as to not be in charge of one's own schedule. (Informal. Not able to is often expressed as can't.) □ It's been so busy around here that I haven't been able to call my time my own. □ She can't call her time her own these days.

not able to go on unable to continue (doing something—even living). (Not able to is often expressed as can't.) □ I just can't go on this way. □ Before her death, she left a note saying she was not able to go on.

not able to help something unable to prevent or control something. (Not able to is often expressed as can't.) □ I'm sorry about being late. I wasn't able to help it. □ Bob can't help being boring.

not able to make anything out of someone or something unable to understand someone or something. (Not able to is often expressed as can't. The anything may refer to something specific, as in the first example.) □ I can't make sense out of what you just said. □ *We were not able to make anything out of the message.*

not able to see the forest for the trees* allowing many details of a problem to obscure the problem as a whole. (A cliché. *Not able to* is often expressed as *can't*.) □ *The solution is obvious. You missed it because you can't see the forest for the trees.* □ *She suddenly realized that she hadn't been able to see the forest for the trees.*

not able to wait **1.** too anxious to wait; excited (about something in the future.) (*Not able to* is often expressed as *can't*. Also used literally.) □ *I'm so excited. I can't wait.* □ *Billy couldn't wait for his birthday.* **2.*** to have to *go to the bathroom* urgently. (Informal.) □ *Mom, I can't wait.* □ *Driver, stop the bus! My little boy can't wait.*

not all it is cracked up to be* AND **not what it is cracked up to be*** not as good as something is supposed to be. (Informal. Not always in the negative.) □ *This isn't a very good pen. It's not all it's cracked up to be.* □ *Is this one all it's cracked up to be?* □ *This restaurant isn't what it's cracked up to be.*

not all there* not mentally adequate; crazy or silly. (Informal.) □ *Sometimes I think you're not all there.* □ *Be nice to Sally. She's not all there.* ALSO: **not have all one's marbles*** to not have all one's mental capacities. (Informal.) □ *John acts like he doesn't have all his marbles.*

not at all certainly not; absolutely not. □ *No, it doesn't bother me—not at all.* □ *I'm not complaining. Not me. Not at all.* ALSO: **not in the least** not even a little bit. □ *You've been no trouble at all, no sir, not in the least.*

not born yesterday experienced; knowledgeable in the ways of the world. □ *I know what's going on. I wasn't born yesterday.* □ *Sally knows the score. She wasn't born yesterday.*

not breathe a word about someone or something AND **not breathe a word** to keep a secret about someone or something. □ *Don't worry. I won't breathe a word about it.* □ *Please don't breathe a word about Bob and his problems.*

ALSO: **not breathe a word of something; not breathe a word** to not tell something (to anyone). □ *Don't worry. I won't breathe a word of it.* □ *Tom won't breathe a word.*

not buy something* not accept something (to be true). (Slang.) □ *You may think so, but I don't buy it.* □ *The police wouldn't buy his story.*

not by a long shot* not by a great amount; not. (Informal. Not necessarily negative.) □ *Did I win the race? Not by a long shot.* □ *Not by a long shot did she complete the assignment.*

not care two hoots about someone or something* AND **not give two hoots about someone or something*; not give a hang about someone or something*; not give a hoot about someone or something*** to not care at all about someone or something. (Folksy. The *someone* and the *something* are *anyone* and *anything* in the negative.) □ *I don't care two hoots about whether you go to the picnic or not.* □ *She doesn't give a hoot about me. Why should I care?* □ *I don't give a hang about it.*

not enough room to swing a cat* not very much space. (Folksy.) □ *Their living room was very small. There wasn't enough room to swing a cat.* □ *How can you work in a small room like this? There's not enough room to swing a cat.*

not for anything in the world See *not for the world.*

not for love nor money See the following entry.

not for the world AND **not for anything in the world; not for love nor money; not on your life** not for anything (no matter what its value). (Note the variation in the examples.) □ *I won't do it for love nor money.* □ *He said he wouldn't do it—not for the world.* □ *She said no, not for anything in the world.* □ *Me, go there? Not on your life!*

not give a hang about anyone or anything See *not care two hoots about someone or something.*

not give a hoot about anyone or anything See *not care two hoots about someone or something.*

not give anyone the time of day* to ignore someone (usually out of dislike). (Informal.) □ *Mary won't speak to Sally. She won't give her the time of day.* □ *I couldn't get an appointment with Mr. Smith. He wouldn't even give me the time of day.*

not half bad* okay; pretty good. (Folksy.) □ *Say, this roast beef isn't half bad.* □ *Hey, Sally! You're not half bad!*

not have a care in the world free and casual; unworried and carefree. □ *I really feel good today—as if I didn't have a care in the world.* □ *Ann always acts like she doesn't have a care in the world.*

not have a leg to stand on* (for an argument or a case) to have no support. (Informal.) □ *You may think you're in the right, but you don't have a leg to stand on.* □ *My lawyer said I didn't have a leg to stand on, so I shouldn't sue the company.*

not have all one's marbles See *not all there.*

not have anything on to be naked. (See also *have someone or something on.*) □ *Don't come in. I don't have anything on.* □ *Of course I don't have anything on. I'm taking a bath.*

not hold a candle to someone or something See the following entry.

not hold a stick to someone or something* AND **not hold a candle to someone or something*** to not be nearly as good as someone or something. (Informal. The *someone* and the *something* are *anyone* and *anything* in the negative.) □ *Sally is much faster than Bob. Bob doesn't hold a stick to Sally.* □ *This T.V. doesn't hold a candle to that one. That one is much better.*

not hold water* to make no sense; to be illogical. (Informal. Said of ideas, arguments, etc., not people. It means that the idea has holes in it.) □ *Your argument doesn't hold water.* □ *This scheme won't work because it won't hold water.*

not in the least See *not at all.*

not in the same league with someone or something not anywhere nearly as good as someone or something. □ *John isn't in the same league with Bob and his friends.* □ *This house isn't in the same league with our old one.*

not know beans about something* AND **not know beans*** to know nothing about something. (Slang.) □ *Bill doesn't know beans about flying an airplane.* □ *When it comes to flying, I don't know beans.*

not know enough to come in out of the rain* to be very stupid. (A cliché.) □ *Bob is so stupid he doesn't know enough to come in out of the rain.* □ *You can't expect very much from somebody who doesn't know enough to come in out of the rain.*

not know from nothing* to be stupid, innocent, and naive. (Slang. This *nothing* is not replaced with *something.* Usually with *don't,* as in the examples.) □ *Old John—he don't know from nothing.* □ *What do you expect from somebody who don't know from nothing?*

not know someone from Adam* to not know someone at all. (A cliché.) □ *I wouldn't recognize John if I saw him. I don't know him from Adam.* □ *What does she look like? I don't know her from Adam.*

not know the first thing about someone or something to not know anything about someone or something. □ *I don't know the first thing about flying an airplane.* □ *She doesn't know the first thing about John.*

not know where to turn AND **not know which way to turn** to have no idea about what to do (about something). □ *I was so confused I didn't know where to turn.* □ *We needed help, but we didn't know which way to turn.*

not know whether one is coming or going* AND **not know if one is coming or going*** to be very confused. (A cliché.) □ *I'm so busy that I don't know if I'm coming or going.* □ *You look as if you don't know whether you're coming or going.*

not know which way to turn See *not know where to turn.*

not lift a finger to help someone AND **not lift a finger** to do nothing to help someone. (The *someone* is anyone in the negative.) □ *They wouldn't lift a finger to help us.* □ *Can you imagine that they wouldn't lift a finger?*

not long for this world* to be about to

die. (A cliché.) □ *Our dog is nearly twelve years old and not long for this world.* □ *I'm so tired. I think I'm not long for this world.*

not move a muscle to remain perfectly motionless. □ *Be quiet. Sit there and don't move a muscle.* □ *I was so tired I couldn't move a muscle.*

not on any account See *on no account.*

not on your life See *not for the world.*

not open one's mouth AND **not utter a word** to not say anything at all; to not tell something (to anyone). □ *Don't worry, I'll keep your secret. I won't even open my mouth.* □ *Have no fear. I won't utter a word.* □ *I don't know how they found out. I didn't even open my mouth.*

not set foot somewhere to not go somewhere. □ *I wouldn't set foot in John's room. I'm very angry at him.* □ *He never set foot here.*

not show one's face to not appear (somewhere). □ *After what she said, she had better not show her face around here again.* □ *If I don't say I'm sorry, I'll never be able to show my face again.*

not sleep a wink* to not sleep at all. (Informal.) □ *I couldn't sleep a wink last night.* □ *Ann hasn't been able to sleep a wink for a week.*

not someone's cup of tea* not something one prefers. (A cliché.) □ *Playing cards isn't her cup of tea.* □ *Sorry, that's not my cup of tea.*

not take no for an answer* to not accept someone's refusal. (Informal. A polite way of being insistent.) □ *Now, you must drop over and see us tomorrow. We won't take no for an answer.* □ *I had to go. They just wouldn't take no for an answer.*

not up to scratch* AND **not up to snuff*** not adequate. (Informal.) □ *Sorry, your paper isn't up to scratch. Please do it over again.* □ *The performance was not up to snuff.*

not utter a word See *not open one's mouth.*

not worth a dime* AND **not worth a red cent*** worthless. (Informal.) □ *This land is all swampy. It's not worth a dime.* □ *This pen I bought isn't worth a dime. It has no ink.* □ *It's not worth a red cent.*

not worth a hill of beans* worthless. (Folksy.) □ *Your advice isn't worth a hill of beans.* □ *This old cow isn't worth a hill of beans.*

not worth a red cent See *not worth a dime.*

nothing but skin and bones* AND **all skin and bones*** very thin or emaciated. (Informal.) □ *Bill has lost so much weight. He's nothing but skin and bones.* □ *That old horse is all skin and bones. I won't ride it.*

nothing doing* no. (Informal.) □ *No, I won't do that. Nothing doing.* □ BOB: *Will you help me with this?* BILL: *Nothing doing.*

nothing down requiring no down payment. □ *You can have this car for nothing down and $140 a month.* □ *I bought a winter coat for nothing down and no payments due until February.*

nothing of the kind no; absolutely not. □ *I didn't tear your jacket—nothing of the kind!* □ *That's not true. We did nothing of the kind!*

nothing to complain about* all right. (Folksy. Said in answer to the question "How are you?") □ *Bob said he has nothing to complain about.* □ BILL: *How're you doing, Bob?* BOB: *Nothing to complain about, Bill. Yourself?*

nothing to it it is easy; no difficulty involved. □ *Driving a car is easy. There's nothing to it.* □ *Geometry is fun to learn. There's nothing to it.*

nothing to sneeze at* nothing small or unimportant. (Informal.) □ *It's not a lot of money, but it's nothing to sneeze at.* □ *Our house isn't a mansion, but it's nothing to sneeze at.*

nothing to speak of* not many; not much. (Informal.) □ JOHN: *What's happening around here?* BILL: *Nothing to speak of.* □ MARY: *Has there been any rain in the last week?* SALLY: *Nothing to speak of.*

nothing to write home about* nothing exciting or interesting. (Folksy. Also used literally.) □ *I've been busy, but nothing to write home about.* □ *I had a dull week—nothing to write home about.*

Nothing ventured, nothing gained. a proverb meaning that you cannot achieve anything if you do not try. □ *Come on, John. Give it a try. Nothing ventured, nothing gained.* □ *I felt like I had to take the chance. Nothing ventured, nothing gained.*

now and again See the following entry.

now and then AND **now and again** occasionally. □ *I like to smoke a cigar now and then.* □ *Now and again we go out to dinner and a show.*

now or never at this time and no other. □ *This is your only chance, John. It's now or never.* □ *I decided that it was now or never and jumped.*

null and void cancelled; worthless. □ *I tore the contract up, and the entire agreement became null and void.* □ *The*

judge declared the whole business null and void.

nurse a grudge against someone AND **nurse a grudge** to keep resenting and disliking someone. □ *Sally is still nursing a grudge against Mary.* □ *How long can anyone nurse a grudge?*

nuts about someone or something See *crazy about someone or something.*

nutty as a fruitcake* silly; crazy. (Slang. A fruitcake usually has lots of nuts in it.) □ *Whenever John goes to a party, he gets as nutty as a fruitcake.* □ *Sally has been acting as nutty as a fruitcake lately.*

O

obligated to someone to owe someone a favor. □ *I'll help John with his homework because I'm obligated to him.* □ *Just because I gave you some advice, it doesn't mean you're obligated to me.*

occur to someone (for an idea or thought) to come into someone's mind. □ *It occurred to me that you might be hungry after your long journey.* □ *Would it ever occur to you that I want to be left alone?*

odd man out an unusual or atypical person or thing. □ *I'm odd man out because I'm not wearing a tie.* □ *You had better learn to work a computer unless you want to be odd man out.*

Of all the nerve!* How shocking, how dare (someone)! (Informal. The speaker is exclaiming that someone is being very cheeky or rude.) □ *How dare you talk to me that way! Of all the nerve!* □ *Imagine anyone coming to a formal dance in jeans. Of all the nerve!*

Of all things!* Can you imagine?; Imagine that! (Folksy.) □ *She wore jeans to the dance. Of all things!* □ *Billy, stop eating the house plant! Of all things!*

of benefit to someone AND **of benefit** serving someone well; to the good of someone. □ *I can't believe that this proposal is of benefit to anyone.* □ *Oh, I'm sure it's of benefit.*

of late lately. (Formal.) □ *Have you seen Sally of late?* □ *We haven't had an opportunity to eat out of late.*

of no avail See *to no avail.*

of one's own accord AND **of one's own free will** by one's own choice, without coercion. □ *I wish that Sally would choose to do it of her own accord.* □ *I'll have to order her to do it because she won't do it of her own free will.*

of one's own free will See the previous entry.

of the first water of the finest quality. □ *This is a very fine pearl—a pearl of the first water.* □ *Tom is of the first water—a true gentleman.*

off again, on again uncertain; indecisive. □ *I don't know about the picnic. It's off again, on again. It depends on the weather.* □ *Jane doesn't know if she's going to the picnic. She's off again, on again about it.*

off and on See *on and off.*

off base unrealistic; inexact; wrong. (Also used literally in baseball.) □ *I'm afraid you're off base when you state that this problem will take care of itself.* □ *You're way off base!*

off center not exactly in the center or middle. □ *The arrow hit the target a little off center.* □ *The picture hanging over the chair is a little off center.*

off color 1. not the exact color (which one wants). □ *The book cover used to be red, but now it's a little off color.* □ *The wall was painted off color. I think it was meant to be orange.* 2. in bad taste; rude, vulgar, or impolite. □ *That joke you told was off color and embarrassed me.* □ *The nightclub act was a bit off color.*

off duty not working at one's job. (The opposite of *on duty.*) □ *I'm sorry, I can't talk to you until I'm off duty.* □ *The police officer couldn't help me because he was off duty.*

off limits AND **out of bounds** forbidden. □ *This area is off limits. You can't go in there.* □ *Don't go there. It's out of bounds.* □ *That kind of behavior is off limits. Stop it!*

off one's nut See the following entry.

off one's rocker* AND **off one's nut*; off one's trolley*** crazy; silly. (Slang.) □ *Sometimes, Bob, I think you're off your rocker.* □ *Good grief, John. You're off your nut.* □ *About this time of the day I go off my trolley. I get so tired.*

off one's trolley See the previous entry.

off season not in the busy time of the year. □ *We don't have much to do off season.* □ *Things are very quiet around here off season.* ALSO: **the off season** the time of the year which is not busy. □ *What do you do around here in the off season?*

off someone or something goes someone or something is leaving. (Said on the departure of someone or something.) □ *It's time to leave. Off I go.* □ *Sally looked at the airplane taking off and said, "Off it goes."*

off the air not broadcasting (a radio or television program). □ *The radio audience won't hear what you say when you're off the air.* □ *When the performers were off the air, the director told them how well they had done.*

off the beaten track AND **off the track** in an unfamiliar place; on a route which is not often traveled. (See also *off the track.*) □ *Their home is in a quiet neighborhood, off the beaten track.* □ *We like to stop there and admire the scenery. It's off the track, but it's worth the trip.*

off the cuff* spontaneous; without preparation or rehearsal. (Informal.) □ *Her remarks were off the cuff, but very sensible.* □ *I'm not very good at making speeches off the cuff.* ALSO: **off-the-cuff** without any preparation; spontaneous. □ *Her off-the-cuff remarks were quite sensible.*

off the record unofficial; informal. □ *This is off the record, but I disagree with the mayor on this matter.* □ *Although her comments were off the record, the newspaper published them anyway.*

off the top of one's head* (to state something) rapidly and without having to think or remember. (Informal.) □ *I can't think of the answer off the top of my head.* □ *Jane can tell you the correct amount off the top of her head.*

off the track 1. See *off the beaten track.* 2. irrelevant and immaterial (comments). □ *I'm afraid you're off the track, John. Try again.* □ *I'm sorry. I was thinking about dinner, and I got off the track.*

off the wall* odd; silly; unusual. (Slang.) □ *Why are you so off the wall today?* □ *This book is strange. It's really off the wall.*

off to a running start with a good, fast beginning, possibly a head start. □ *I got off to a running start in math this year.* □ *The horses got off to a running start.*

off to one side beside (something); (moved) slightly away from something. □ *Our garden has roses in the middle and a spruce tree off to one side.* □ *He took me off to one side to tell me the bad news.*

oil someone's palm* to bribe someone. (Slang.) □ *The way to get things done around there is to oil someone's palm.* □ *No sense oiling her palm. She's totally honest.*

old enough to be someone's father See the following entry.

old enough to be someone's mother AND **old enough to be someone's father** as old as someone's parents. (Usually a way of saying that a person is too old. Not used literally.) □ *You can't go out with Bill. He's old enough to be your father!* □ *He married a woman who is old enough to be his mother.*

old hand at doing something someone who is experienced at doing something. □ *I'm an old hand at fixing clocks.* □ *He's an old hand at changing diapers.*

on a diet trying to lose weight by eating less food or specific foods. □ *I didn't eat any cake because I'm on a diet.* □ *I'm getting too heavy. I'll have to go on a diet.*

on a first name basis with someone AND **on a first name basis** knowing someone very well; good friends with someone. □ *I'm on a first name basis with John.* □ *John and I are on a first name basis.*

on a waiting list (with one's name) on

a list of people waiting for an opportunity to do something. (*A* can be replaced with *the*.) □ *I couldn't get a seat on the plane, but I got on a waiting list.* □ *There is no room for you, but we can put your name on the waiting list.*

on account (money paid or owed) on a debt. □ *I paid twelve dollars on account last month. Wasn't that enough?* □ *I still have $100 due on account.*

on account of someone or something because of someone or something. □ *We can't go on a picnic on account of the rain.* □ *I was late on account of John.*

on active duty in battle or ready to go into battle. (Military.) □ *The soldier was on active duty for ten months.* □ *That was a long time to be on active duty.*

on all fours on one's hands and knees. □ *I dropped a contact lens and spent an hour on all fours looking for it.* □ *The baby can walk, but is on all fours most of the time anyway.*

on and off AND **off and on** occasionally; erratically; *now and again*. □ *I feel better off and on, but I'm not well yet.* □ *He only came to class on and off.*

on any account for any purpose; for any reason; no matter what. (Compare to *on no account*.) □ *On any account, I'll be there on time.* □ *This doesn't make sense on any account.*

on approval for examination, with the privilege of return. □ *I ordered the merchandise on approval so I could send it back if I didn't like it.* □ *Sorry, you can't buy this on approval. All sales are final.*

on behalf of someone See *in behalf of someone.*

on board **1.** aboard (on or in) a ship, bus, airplane, etc. □ *Is there a doctor on board? We have a sick passenger.* □ *When everyone is on board, we will leave.* **2.*** employed by (someone); working with (someone). (Informal.) □ *Our firm has a computer specialist on board to advise us about automation.* □ *Welcome to the company, Tom. We're all glad you're on board now.*

on call ready to serve when called. □

I live a very hard life. I'm on call twenty hours a day. □ *I'm sorry, but I can't go out tonight. I'm on call at the hospital.*

on cloud nine* very happy. (Informal.) □ *When I got my promotion, I was on cloud nine.* □ *When the check came, I was on cloud nine for days.*

on dead center **1.** at the exact center of something. □ *The arrow hit the target on dead center.* □ *When you put the flowers on the table, put them on dead center.* **2.** exactly correct. □ *Mary is quite observant. Her analysis is on dead center.* □ *My view isn't on dead center, but it's sensible.*

on deck **1.** on the deck of a boat or a ship. □ *Everyone except the cook was on deck when the storm hit.* □ *Just pull up the anchor and leave it on deck.* **2.** ready (to do something); ready to be next (at something). □ *Ann, get on deck. You're next.* □ *Who's on deck now?*

on deposit deposited or stored in a safe place. □ *I have $10,000 on deposit in that bank.* □ *We have some gold coins on deposit in the bank's vault.*

on duty at work; currently doing one's work. (The opposite of *off duty*.) □ *I can't help you now, but I'll be on duty in about an hour.* □ *Who is on duty here? I need some help.*

on earth AND **in creation; in the world** how amazing!; *of all things!* (Used as an intensifier after the interrogative pronouns *who, what, when, where, how, which*.) □ *What on earth do you mean?* □ *How in creation do you expect me to do that?* □ *Who in the world do you think you are?* □ *When on earth do you expect me to do this?*

on easy street* in luxury. (Slang.) □ *If I had a million dollars, I'd be on easy street.* □ *Everyone has problems, even people who live on easy street.*

on edge **1.** on (something's own) edge. □ *Can you stand a dime on edge?* □ *You should store your records on edge, not flat.* **2.** nervous. □ *I have really been on edge lately.* □ *Why are you so on edge?*

on foot by walking. □ *My bicycle is broken, so I'll have to travel on foot.* □ *You can't expect me to get there on foot! It's twelve miles!*

on good terms with someone AND **on good terms** friendly with someone. □ *I'm on good terms with Ann. I'll ask her to help.* □ *We're on good terms now. Last week we were not.*

on guard AND **on one's guard** cautious; watchful. □ *Be on guard. There are pickpockets around here.* □ *You had better be on your guard.*

on hold (See also *put someone or something on hold.*) **1.** waiting; temporarily halted. □ *The building project is on hold while we try to find money to complete it.* □ *We put our plans on hold until we finished school.* **2.** left waiting on a telephone line. □ *I hate to call up someone and then end up on hold.* □ *I waited on hold for ten minutes when I called city hall.*

on in years See *up in years.*

on line 1. See *in line.* **2.** connected to a computer. □ *As soon as I get on line, I can check the balance of your account.* □ *I was on line for an hour before I found out what I wanted to know.*

on no account AND **not on any account** for no reason; absolutely not. □ *On no account will I lend you the money.* □ *Will I say I'm sorry? Not on any account.*

on occasion occasionally. □ *We go out for dinner on occasion.* □ *I enjoy going to a movie on occasion.*

on one hand See *on the one hand.*

on one's best behavior being as polite as possible. □ *When we went out, the children were on their best behavior.* □ *I try to be on my best behavior all the time.*

on one's feet 1. standing up. □ *Get on your feet. They are playing the national anthem.* □ *I've been on my feet all day, and they hurt.* **2.** well and healthy, especially after an illness. □ *I hope to be back on my feet next week.* □ *I can help out as soon as I'm back on my feet.*

on one's honor on one's solemn oath; promised sincerely. □ *On my honor, I'll be there on time.* □ *He promised on his honor that he'd pay me back next week.*

on one's mind occupying one's thoughts; currently being thought about. □ *You've been on my mind all day.* □ *Do you have something on your mind? You look so serious.*

on one's own by oneself. □ *Did you do this on your own, or did you have help?* □ *I have to learn to do this kind of thing on my own.*

on one's own time not while one is at work. □ *The boss made me write the report on my own time. That's not fair.* □ *Please make your personal telephone calls on your own time.*

on one's toes alert. (See also *step on someone's toes.*) □ *You have to be on your toes if you want to be in this business.* □ *My boss keeps me on my toes.*

on order ordered with delivery expected. □ *You car is on order. It'll be here in a few weeks.* □ *I don't have the part in stock, but it's on order.*

on par with someone or something AND **on par** equal to someone or something. □ *Your effort is simply not on par with what's expected from you.* □ *These two reports are right on par.*

on pins and needles* anxious; in suspense. (A cliché.) □ *I've been on pins and needles all day waiting for you to call with the news.* □ *We were on pins and needles until we heard that your plane landed safely.*

on record recorded. □ *We don't have that music on tape, but here it is on record.* □ *This is the fastest race on record.*

on sale offered for sale at a special low price. □ *I won't buy anything that's not on sale.* □ *I need a new coat, but I want to find a nice one on sale.*

on schedule at the expected or desired time. □ *The plane came in right on schedule.* □ *Things have to happen on schedule in a theatrical performance.*

on second thought having given something more thought; having reconsidered something. □ *On second thought, maybe you should sell your house and move into an apartment.* □ *On second thought, let's not go to a movie.*

on someone's account because of someone. □ *Don't do it on my account.* □ *They were late on Jane's account.*

on someone's back See *on someone's case.*

on someone's behalf See *in behalf of someone.*

on someone's case* AND **on some-**

one's back* constantly criticizing someone. (Slang. See also *Get off someone's case!*) □ *I'm tired of your being on my case all the time.* □ *It seems like someone is always on his back.*

on someone's doorstep See *at someone's doorstep.*

on someone's head on someone's own self. (Usually with *blame. On* can be replaced with *upon.*) □ *All the blame fell on their heads.* □ *I don't think that all the criticism should be on my head.*

on someone's or something's last legs* for someone or something to be almost finished. (Informal.) □ *This building is on its last legs. It should be torn down.* □ *I feel like I'm on my last legs. I'm really tired.*

on someone's say-so on someone's authority; with someone's permission. □ *I can't do it on your say-so. I'll have to get a written request.* □ BILL: *I canceled the contract with the A.B.C. Company.* BOB: *On whose say-so?*

on someone's shoulders on someone's own self. (Usually with *responsibility. On* can be replaced with *upon.*) □ *Why should all the responsibility fall on my shoulders?* □ *She carries a tremendous amount of responsibility on her shoulders.*

on someone's way AND **on the way** on the route (to somewhere). □ *I can give you a ride to the bank. It's right on my way.* □ *Is the bakery on the way, too?*

on speaking terms with someone AND **on speaking terms** on friendly terms with someone. (Often in the negative. Compare to *on good terms with someone.*) □ *I'm not on speaking terms with Mary. We had a serious disagreement.* □ *We're not on speaking terms.*

on target on schedule; exactly as predicted. □ *Your estimate of the cost was right on target.* □ *My prediction was not on target.*

on the air broadcasting (a radio or television program). □ *The radio station came back on the air shortly after the storm.* □ *We were on the air for two hours.*

on the alert for someone or something AND **on the alert** watchful and attentive for someone or something. □ *Be on the alert for pickpockets.* □ *You should be on the alert when you cross the street in heavy traffic.*

on the average generally; usually. □ *On the average, you can expect about a ten per cent failure.* □ *This report looks okay, on the average.*

on the ball* alert, effective, and efficient. (Slang.) □ *Sally has a lot on the ball.* □ *You've got to be on the ball if you want to succeed in this business.*

on the beam* exactly right; thinking along the correct lines. (Informal. Also used literally.) □ *That's the right idea. Now you're on the beam!* □ *She's not on the beam yet. Explain it to her again.*

on the bench 1. directing a session of court. (Said of a judge.) □ *I have to go to court tomorrow. Who's on the bench?* □ *It doesn't matter who's on the bench. You'll get a fair hearing.* 2. sitting, waiting for a chance to play in a game. (In sports, such as basketball, football, soccer, etc.) □ *Bill is on the bench now. I hope he gets to play.* □ *John played during the first quarter, but now he's on the bench.*

on the blink See *on the fritz.*

on the block 1. on a city block. □ *John is the biggest kid on the block.* □ *We had a party on the block last weekend.* 2. on sale at auction; on the auction block. □ *We couldn't afford to keep up the house, so it was put on the block to pay the taxes.* □ *That's the finest painting I've ever seen on the block.*

on the button* exactly right; in exactly the right place; at exactly the right time. (Informal.) □ *That's it! You're right on the button.* □ *He got here at 1:00 on the button.*

on the contrary (as the) opposite. (Compare to *to the contrary.*) □ *I'm not ill. On the contrary, I'm very healthy.* □ *She's not in a bad mood. On the contrary, she's as happy as a lark.*

on the dot* at exactly the right time. (Informal. Compare to *at sometime sharp.*) □ *I'll be there at noon on the dot.* □ *I expect to see you here at 8:00 on the dot.*

on the double* very fast. (Informal.) □ *Okay, you guys. Get over here on the* *double.* □ *Get yourself into this house on the double.*

on the eve of something just before something, possibly the evening before something. □ *John decided to leave school on the eve of his graduation.* □ *The team held a party on the eve of the tournament.*

on the face of it superficially; from the way it looks. □ *This looks like a serious problem on the face of it. It probably is minor, however.* □ *On the face of it, it seems worthless.*

on the fence about something* AND **on the fence*** undecided. (Informal. Also used literally.) □ *Ann is on the fence about going to Mexico.* □ *I wouldn't be on the fence. I'd love to go.*

on the fritz* AND **on the blink*** not operating; not operating correctly. (Slang.) □ *This vacuum cleaner is on the fritz. Let's get it fixed.* □ *How long has it been on the blink?*

on the go* busy; moving about busily. (Informal.) □ *I'm usually on the go all day long.* □ *I hate being on the go all the time.*

on the heels of something* soon after something. (Informal.) □ *There was a rainstorm on the heels of the windstorm.* □ *The team held a victory celebration on the heels of their winning season.*

on the horizon soon to happen. (Also used literally. See also *in the offing.*) □ *Do you know what's on the horizon?* □ *Who can tell what's on the horizon?*

on the horns of a dilemma having to decide between two things, people, etc. □ *Mary found herself on the horns of a dilemma. She didn't know which to choose.* □ *I make up my mind easily. I'm not on the horns of a dilemma very often.*

on the hot seat* AND **in the hot seat*** in a difficult position; subject to much criticism. (Slang.) □ *I was really in the hot seat for a while.* □ *Now that John is on the hot seat, no one is paying any attention to what I do.*

on the hour at each hour on the hour mark. □ *I have to take this medicine every hour on the hour.* □ *I expect to see you there on the hour, not one minute before and not one minute after.*

on the house* (something which is) given away free by a merchant. (Informal. Also used literally.) □ *"Here," said the waiter, "have a cup of coffee on the house."* □ *I went to a restaurant last night. I was the 10,000th customer, so my dinner was on the house.*

on the job working; doing what one is expected to do. □ *I'm always on the job when I should be.* □ *I can depend on my furnace to be on the job day and night.*

on the level* honest; dependably open and fair. (Informal. Also with *strictly.* Compare to *on the up and up.*) □ *How can I be sure you're on the level?* □ *You can trust Sally. She's on the level.*

on the lookout for someone or something AND **on the lookout** watchful for someone or something. □ *Be on the lookout for signs of a storm.* □ *I'm on the lookout for John who is due here any minute.* □ *Okay, you remain on the lookout for another hour.*

on the loose* running around free. (Informal.) □ *Look out! There is a bear on the loose from the zoo.* □ *Most kids enjoy being on the loose when they go to college.*

on the make* 1. building or developing; being made. (Informal.) □ *There is a company which is on the make.* □ *That was a very good sales strategy, John. You're a real estate agent on the make.* 2. making sexual advances; seeking sexual activities. (Slang.) □ *It seems like Bill is always on the make.* □ *He should meet Sally who is also on the make.*

on the market available for sale; offered for sale. (Compare to *on the block.*) □ *I had to put my car on the market.* □ *This is the finest home computer on the market.*

on the mend getting well; healing. □ *My cold was terrible, but I'm on the mend now.* □ *What you need is some hot chicken soup. Then you'll really be on the mend.*

on the money* AND **on the nose*** in exactly the right place; in exactly the right amount (of money). (Slang.) □ *That's a good answer, Bob. You're right on the money.* □ *This project is going to be finished right on the money.*

on the move moving; happening busily. □ *What a busy day. Things are really on the move at the store.* □ *When all the buffalo were on the move across the plains, it must have been very exciting.*

on the nose See *on the money.*

on the one hand AND **on one hand** from one point of view; as one side (of an issue). □ *On one hand, I really ought to support my team. On the other hand, I don't have the time to attend all the games.* □ *On the one hand, I need Ann's help. On the other hand, she and I don't get along very well.* ALSO: **on the other hand** from another point of view; as the other side (of an issue). See the examples for *on the one hand.*

on the other hand See the previous entry.

on the point of doing something AND **at the point of doing something** ready to start doing something. (Compare to *on the verge of doing something.*) □ *I was just on the point of going out the door.* □ *We were almost at the point of buying a new car.*

on the Q.T.* quietly; secretly. (Informal.) □ *The company president was making payments to his wife on the Q.T.* □ *The mayor accepted a bribe on the Q.T.*

on the spot* (Informal.) **1.** at exactly the right place; at exactly the right time. (See also *Johnny-on-the-spot.*) □ *It's noon, and I'm glad you're all here on the spot. Now we can begin.* □ *I expect for you to be on the spot when and where trouble arises.* **2.** in trouble; in a difficult situation. (Compare to *on the hot seat.*) □ *There is a problem in the department I manage, and I'm really on the spot.* □ *I hate to be on the spot when it's not my fault.*

on the spur of the moment suddenly; spontaneously. □ *We decided to go on the spur of the moment.* □ *I had to leave town on the spur of the moment.*

on the strength of something because of the support of something, such as a promise or evidence; due to something. □ *On the strength of your comment, I decided to give John another chance.* □ *On the strength of my testimony, my case was dismissed.*

on the take* accepting bribes. (Slang.) □ *I don't believe that the mayor is on the take.* □ *The county clerk has been on the take for years.*

on the tip of one's tongue about to be said; almost remembered. □ *I have his name right on the tip of my tongue. I'll think of it in a second.* □ *John had the answer on the tip of his tongue, but Ann said it first.*

on the track of someone or something See the following entry.

on the trail of someone or something AND **on the track of someone or something** seeking someone or something; about to find someone or something. (See also *track someone or something down.*) □ *I'm on the trail of a new can opener which is supposed to be easier to use.* □ *I spent all morning on the track of the new secretary who got lost on the way to work.*

on the up and up* AND **strictly on the up and up*** honest; fair and straight. (Slang. Compare to *on the level.*) □ *Do you think that the mayor is on the up and up?* □ *Yes, the mayor is strictly on the up and up.*

on the verge of doing something AND **on the verge** just about to do something, usually something important. (Compare to *on the point of doing something.*) □ *I'm on the verge of opening a shoe store.* □ *Tom was on the verge of quitting school when he became interested in physics.* □ *I haven't done it yet, but I'm on the verge.*

on the wagon not drinking alcohol; no longer drinking alcohol. (Also used literally.) □ *None for me, thanks. I'm on the wagon.* □ *Look at John. I don't think he's on the wagon anymore.*

on the warpath* angry and upset (at someone). (Informal.) □ *Oh, oh. Here comes Mrs. Smith. She's on the warpath again.* □ *Why are you always on the warpath? What's wrong?*

on the way somewhere AND **on one's way somewhere; on one's way; on the way** along the route to somewhere. □ *She's now on her way to San Francisco.* □ *Yes, she's on the way.*

on the way to doing something AND **on one's way to doing something** in the process of doing something. □ *You're on the way to becoming a very good carpenter.* □ *She's on her way to becoming a first-class sculptor.*

on the whole generally; considering everything. □ *On the whole, this was a very good day.* □ *Your work—on the whole—is quite good.*

on the wing while flying; while in flight. (Formal. Usually refers to birds, fowl, etc., not people or planes.) □ *There is nothing as pretty as a bird on the wing.* □ *The hawk caught the sparrow on the wing.*

on the wrong track going the wrong way; following the wrong set of assumptions. (Also used literally.) □ *You'll never get the right answer. You're on the wrong track.* □ *They won't get it figured out because they are on the wrong track.*

on thin ice in a risky situation. □ *If you try that you'll really be on thin ice. That's too risky.* □ *If you don't want to find yourself on thin ice, you must be sure of your facts.* ALSO: **skate on thin ice** to be in a risky situation. (Also used literally.) □ *I try to stay well informed so I don't end up skating on thin ice when the teacher asks me a question.*

on time at the scheduled time; at the predicted time. □ *The plane landed right on time.* □ *We'll have to hurry to get there on time.*

on tiptoe standing or walking on the front part of the feet (the balls of the feet) with no weight put on the heels. (This is done to gain height or to walk quietly.) □ *I had to stand on tiptoe in order to see over the fence.* □ *I came in late and walked on tiptoe so I wouldn't wake anybody up.*

on top 1. victorious over something; famous or notorious for something. □ *I have to study day and night to keep on top.* □ *Bill is on top in his field.* **2.** See the following entry.

on top of something 1. AND **on top** resting on the upper surface of something. □ *Please put this book on top of the piano.* □ *Where do you want it? On top?* **2.*** AND **on top** up-to-date on something; knowing about the current state of something. (Informal.) □ *Ask*

Mary. *She's on top of this issue.* □ *This issue is constantly changing. She has to pay attention to it to stay on top.* **3.** in addition to something. □ *Jane told Bill he was dull. On top of that, she said he was unfriendly.* □ *On top of being dull, he's unfriendly.*

on top of the world* AND **sitting on top of the world*** feeling wonderful; glorious; ecstatic. (A cliché.) □ *Wow, I feel on top of the world.* □ *Since he got a new job, he's on top of the world.* □ *I've been sitting on top of the world all week because I passed my exams.*

on trial being tried in court. □ *My sister is on trial today, so I have to go to court.* □ *They placed the suspected thief on trial.*

on vacation away, taking a vacation; on holiday. □ *Where are you going on vacation this year?* □ *I'll be away on vacation for three weeks.*

on view visible; on public display. □ *The painting will be on view at the museum.* □ *I'll pull the shades so that we won't be on view.*

on watch for someone or something AND **on watch** alert and watching for someone or something. □ *Please stay on watch for trouble.* □ *Okay, I'll be on watch.* □ *I'm always on watch for Ann. I want to know when she's around.*

once and for all finally and irreversibly. □ *I want to get this problem settled once and for all.* □ *I told him once and for all that he has to start studying.*

once in a blue moon* very rarely. (A cliché.) □ *I seldom go to a movie—maybe once in a blue moon.* □ *I don't go into the city except once in a blue moon.*

once-in-a-lifetime chance a chance that will never occur again in one's lifetime. □ *This is a once-in-a-lifetime chance. Don't miss it.* □ *She offered me a once-in-a-lifetime chance, but I turned it down.*

once in a while occasionally; *every now and then*. □ *I go to a movie once in a while.* □ *Once in a while we have lamb, but not very often.*

once-over-lightly 1. a quick and careless treatment. (A noun. Said of an act of cleaning, studying, examination, or appraisal.) □ *Bill gave his geometry the once-over-lightly and then quit studying.* □ *Ann, you didn't wash the dishes properly. They only got a once-over-lightly.* **2.** cursory; in a quick and careless manner. (An adverb.) □ *Tom studied geometry once-over-lightly.* □ *Ann washed the dishes once-over-lightly.*

once upon a time* once in the past. (A cliché and a formula used to begin a fairy tale.) □ *Once upon a time, there were three bears.* □ *Once upon a time, I had a puppy of my own.*

one and all* everyone. (A cliché.) □ *"Good morning to one and all," said Jane as she walked through the outer office.* □ *Let's hope that this turns out to be a wonderful party for one and all.*

one and only 1. the famous and talented (person). (Used in theatrical introductions.) □ *And now—the one and only—Jane Smith!* □ *Let's have a big hand for the one and only Bob Jones!* **2.*** one's spouse. (Informal.) □ *Look at the time. I've got to get home to my one and only.* □ *You're my one and only. There is no one else for me.*

one and the same the very same person or thing. □ *John Jones and J. Jones are one and the same.* □ *Men's socks and men's stockings are almost one and the same.*

one at a time See the following entry.

one by one AND **one at a time** the first one, then the next one, then the next one, etc. □ *I have to deal with problems one by one. I can't handle them all at once.* □ *Okay, just take things one at a time.*

one for the books See the following entry.

one for the record books AND **one for the books** a record-breaking act. □ *What a dive! That's one for the record books.* □ *I've never heard such a funny joke. That's really one for the books.*

One good turn deserves another. a proverb meaning that a good deed should be repaid with another good deed. □ *If he does you a favor, you should do him a favor. One good turn deserves another.* □ *Glad to help you out. One good turn deserves another.*

one in a hundred See the following entry.

one in a thousand AND **one in a hundred; one in a million** unique; one of a very few. □ *He's a great guy. He's one in a million.* □ *Mary's one in a hundred—such a hard worker.*

one jump ahead of someone or something AND **one jump ahead; one move ahead of someone or something; one move ahead** one step in advance of someone or something. □ *Try to stay one jump ahead of the customer.* □ *If you're one move ahead, you're well prepared to deal with problems. Then, nothing is a surprise.*

One man's meat is another man's poison. a proverb meaning that one person's preference may be disliked by another person. □ *John just loves his new fur hat, but I think it is horrible. Oh well, one man's meat is another man's poison.* □ *The neighbors are very fond of their dog even though it's ugly, loud, and smelly. I guess one man's meat is another man's poison.*

one means business* one is very serious. (Informal.) □ *Billy, get into this house and do your homework, and I mean business.* □ *We mean business when we say you must stop all this nonsense.*

one-night stand* an activity lasting one night. (Informal. Often refers to a musical performance or to sexual activity.) □ *Our band has played a lot of one-night stands.* □ *What we want is an engagement for a week, not just a one-night stand.*

one of these days someday; in some situation like this one. □ *One of these days, someone is going to steal your purse if you don't take better care of it.* □ *You're going to get in trouble one of these days.*

one up on someone AND **one up** ahead of someone; with an advantage over someone. □ *Tom is one up on Sally because he got a job and she didn't.* □ *Yes, it sounds like Tom is one up.*

one way or another somehow. □ *I'll do it one way or another.* □ *One way or another, I'll get through school.*

One's bark is worse than one's bite. a proverb meaning that one may threaten, but not do much damage. □

Don't worry about Bob. He won't hurt you. His bark is worse than his bite. □ *She may scream and yell, but have no fear. Her bark is worse than her bite.*

one's better half one's spouse. (Usually refers to a wife.) □ *I think we'd like to come for dinner, but I'll have to ask my better half.* □ *I have to go home now to my better half. We are going out tonight.*

one's days are numbered* (for someone) to face death or dismissal. (A cliché.) □ *If I don't get this contract, my days are numbered at this company.* □ *Uncle Tom has a terminal disease. His days are numbered.*

one's eyes are bigger than one's stomach (for one) to take more food than one can eat. □ *I can't eat all this. I'm afraid that my eyes were bigger than my stomach.* □ *Try to take less food. Your eyes are bigger than your stomach at every meal.* ALSO: **have eyes bigger than one's stomach** to have a desire for more food than one could possibly eat. □ *I know I have eyes bigger than my stomach, so I won't take a lot of food.*

one's heart goes out to someone for one to feel compassion toward someone. □ *My heart goes out to starving children.* □ *When I heard her story, my heart went out to her.*

one's name is mud* for one to be in trouble or humiliated. (Slang.) □ *If I can't get this contract signed, my name will be mud.* □ *His name is mud ever since he broke the crystal vase.*

one's number is up* one's time to die—or suffer some other unpleasantness—has come. (Informal.) □ *John is worried. He thinks his number is up.* □ *When my number is up, I hope it all goes fast.*

one's old stamping ground* the place where one was raised or where one has spent a lot of time. (Folksy. There are variants with *stomping* and *grounds*.) □ *Ann should know about that place. It's near her old stamping ground.* □ *I can't wait to get back to my old stomping grounds.*

one's way of life one's lifestyle; one's pattern of living. □ *That kind of thing just doesn't fit into my way of life.* □ *Our way of life includes contributing to worthy causes.*

only have eyes for someone* to be loyal to only one person, in the context of romance. (A cliché.) □ *Oh, Jane! I only have eyes for you!* □ *Don't waste any time on Tom. He only has eyes for Ann.*

onto someone or something* having discovered the truth about someone or something. (Informal.) □ *The police are onto John's plot.* □ *Yes, they are onto him, and they are onto the plot.*

open a can of worms* to uncover a set of problems; to create unnecessary complications. (Informal. *Can of worms* means mess. Also with *open up* and with various modifiers such as *new, whole, another,* as in the examples. Compare to *open Pandora's box*.) □ *Now you are opening a whole new can of worms.* □ *How about cleaning up this mess before you open up a new can of worms.*

open and above board See *above board*.

open fire on someone* AND **open fire*** to start (doing something, such as asking questions or criticizing). (Informal. Also used literally.) □ *The reporters opened fire on the mayor.* □ *When the reporters opened fire, the mayor was smiling, but not for long.*

open one's heart to someone AND **open one's heart** to reveal one's inmost thoughts to someone. □ *I always open my heart to my spouse when I have a problem.* □ *It's a good idea to open your heart every now and then.*

open Pandora's box* to uncover a lot of unsuspected problems. (A cliché.) □ *When I asked Jane about her problems, I didn't know I had opened Pandora's box.* □ *You should be cautious with people who are upset. You don't want to open Pandora's box.*

open season on someone or something AND **open season** 1. [with *something*] unrestricted hunting of a particular game animal. □ *It's always open season on rabbits around here.* □ *Is it ever open season on deer?* 2.* [with *someone*] a time when everyone is criticizing someone. (Informal. See *open* *fire.*) □ *It seems like it's always open season on politicians.* □ *At the news conference, it was open season on the mayor.*

open someone's eyes to something AND **open someone's eyes** **1.** to become aware of something. □ *He finally opened his eyes to what was going on.* □ *It was a long time before he opened his eyes and realized what had been happening.* **2.** to cause someone to be aware of something. □ *I opened his eyes to what was happening at the office.* □ *Why can't I make you understand? Why don't you open your eyes?*

open something up AND **open up something** **1.** to open something. □ *I can't wait to open up my presents.* □ *Yes, I want to open them up too.* □ *Open up this door!* **2.** to begin examining or discussing something. □ *Now is the time to open up the question of taxes.* □ *Do you really want to open it up now?* **3.** to reveal the possibilities of something; to reveal an opportunity. □ *Your comments opened up a whole new train of thought.* □ *Your letter opened new possibilities up.* **4.** to start the use of something, such as land, a building, a business, etc. □ *They opened up the coastal lands to cotton planting.* □ *We opened up a new store last March.* **5.** * to make a vehicle go as fast as possible. (Informal.) □ *We took the new car out on the highway and opened it up.* □ *I've never really opened up this truck. I don't know how fast it'll go.* **6.** to make something less congested. □ *We opened up the room by taking the piano out.* □ *They opened the yard up by cutting out a lot of old shrubbery.* ALSO: **open up** **1.** open your door. (A command.) □ *I want in. Open up!* □ *Open up! This is the police.* **2.** to become available. □ *A new job is opening up at my office.* □ *Let me know if any other opportunities open up.* **3.** to go as fast as possible. □ *I can't get this car to open up. Must be something wrong with the engine.* □ *Faster, Tom! Open up! Let's go!* **4.** to become clear, uncluttered, or open. □ *As we drove along, the forest opened up, and we entered into a grassy plain.* □ *The sky opened up, and the sun shone.*

open the door to something to permit or allow something to become a possibility. (Also used literally.) □ *Your policy opens the door to cheating.* □ *Your statement opens the door to John's candidacy.*

open up See *open something up* and the next two entries.

open up on someone or something AND **open up** to fire a gun or other weapon at someone or something. □ *The sergeant told the soldiers to open up on the enemy position.* □ *"Okay, you guys," shouted the sergeant. "Open up!"*

open up to someone AND **open up with someone; open up** to talk frankly, truthfully, or intimately. □ *Finally Sally opened up to her sister and told her what the problem was.* □ *Bill wouldn't open up with me. He's still keeping quiet.* □ *At last, Sally opened up and told everything.*

open up with someone See the previous entry.

open with something to start out with something. (Usually said of a performance of some type.) □ *We'll open with a love song and then go on to something faster.* □ *The play opened with an exciting first act, and then it became very boring.*

order someone about AND **order someone around** to give commands to someone. □ *I don't like for someone to order me about.* □ *Don't order me around!*

order something to go See *buy something to go.*

other side of the tracks the poorer part of a town, often near the railroad tracks. (Especially with *from the* or *live on the.*) □ *Who cares if she's from the other side of the tracks?* □ *I came from a poor family—we lived on the other side of the tracks.*

out and about able to go out and travel around; well enough to go out. □ *Beth has been ill, but now she's out and about.* □ *As soon as I feel better, I'll be able to get out and about.*

out-and-out something* a complete or absolute something; an indisputable something. (Informal. The *something* must always be a specific thing.) □ *If* he said that, he told you an out-and-out lie! □ You're an out-and-out liar!

out back in one's backyard. □ We have a maple tree out back and a spruce tree out front. □ Just put that stuff out back.

out cold AND **out like a light** unconscious. □ I fell and hit my head. I was out cold for about a minute. □ Tom fainted! He's out like a light!

out from under something AND **out from under** free and clear of something; no longer bearing a (figurative) burden. □ I'll feel much better when I'm out from under this project. □ Now that I'm out from under, I can relax.

out front in the front of one's house. □ Our mailbox is out front. □ We have a spruce tree out front and a maple tree in the back.

out-guess someone to guess what someone else might do; to predict what someone might do. □ I can't out-guess Bill. I just have to wait and see what happens. □ Don't try to out-guess John. He's too sharp and tricky.

out in force appearing in great numbers. (See also in force.) □ What a night! The mosquitoes are out in force. □ The police were out in force over the holiday weekend.

out in left field* offbeat; unusual and eccentric. (Informal.) □ Sally is a lot of fun, but she's sort of out in left field. □ What a strange idea. It's really out in left field.

out like a light See out cold.

out of a clear blue sky* AND **out of the blue*** suddenly; without warning. (A cliché. See also like a bolt out of the blue.) □ Then, out of a clear blue sky, he told me he was leaving. □ Mary appeared on my doorstep out of the blue.

out of all proportion of an exaggerated proportion; of an unrealistic proportion compared to something else; (figuratively) lopsided. (The all can be left out.) □ This problem has grown out of all proportion. □ Yes, this thing is way out of proportion. ALSO: **blow something out of all proportion** to cause something to be unrealistically proportioned relative to something else. (The all can be left out.) □ The press has blown this issue out of all proportion. □

Let's be reasonable. Don't blow this thing out of proportion.

out of bounds 1. outside the boundaries of the playing area. (In various sports.) □ The ball went out of bounds, but the referee didn't notice. □ The play ended when Sally ran out of bounds. **2.*** unreasonable. (Informal.) □ Your demands are totally out of bounds. □ Your request for money is out of bounds. **3.** See off limits.

out of breath breathing fast and hard. □ I ran so much that I got out of breath. □ Mary gets out of breath when she climbs stairs.

out of character 1. unlike one's usual behavior. □ Ann's remark was quite out of character. □ It was out of character for Ann to act so stubborn. **2.** inappropriate for the character which an actor is playing. □ Bill went out of character when the audience started giggling. □ Bill played the part so well that it was hard for him to get out of character after the performance.

out of circulation 1. no longer available for use or lending. (Usually said of library materials.) □ I'm sorry, but the book you want is temporarily out of circulation. □ How long will it be out of circulation? **2.*** not interacting socially with other people. (Informal.) □ I don't know what's happening because I've been out of circulation for a while. □ My cold has kept me out of circulation for a few weeks.

out of commission 1. (for a ship) to be not currently in use or under command. □ This vessel will remain out of commission for another month. □ The ship has been out of commission since repairs began. **2.** broken, unserviceable, or inoperable. (See also out of service.) □ My watch is out of commission and is running slowly. □ I can't run in the marathon because my knees are out of commission.

out of condition See out of shape.

out of consideration for someone or something AND **out of consideration** with consideration for someone or something; with kind regard for someone or something. □ Out of consideration for your past efforts, I will do what *you ask.* □ *They let me do it out of consideration. It was very thoughtful of them.*

out of control AND **out of hand** uncontrollable; wild and unruly. □ *The party got out of control about midnight, and the neighbors called the police.* □ *We tried to keep things from getting out of hand.*

out of courtesy to someone AND **out of courtesy** in order to be polite to someone; out of consideration for someone. □ *We invited Mary's brother out of courtesy to her.* □ *They invited me out of courtesy.*

out of date old fashioned; *out of style;* obsolete. □ *Isn't that suit sort of out of date?* □ *All my clothes are out of date.* ALSO: **out-of-date** old-fashioned; in an old style. □ *Please take off that out-of-date suit.* □ *You can't go out wearing that out-of-date hat!*

out of fashion See *out of style.*

out of favor with someone AND **out of favor** no longer desirable or preferred by someone. □ *I can't ask John to help. I'm out of favor with him.* □ *That kind of thing has been out of favor for years.*

out of gas 1. having no gasoline (in a car, truck, etc.). □ *We can't go any farther. We're out of gas.* □ *This car will be completely out of gas in a few more miles.* **2.*** tired; exhausted; worn out. (Informal.) □ *What a day! I've been working since morning, and I'm really out of gas.* □ *This electric clock is out of gas. I'll have to get a new one.* ALSO: **run out of gas** to use up all the gasoline available. □ *I hope we don't run out of gas.*

out of hand 1. See *out of control.* **2.** immediately and without consulting anyone; without delay. (Compare to *off hand.*) □ *I can't answer that out of hand. I'll check with the manager and call you back.* □ *The offer was so good that I accepted it out of hand.*

out of it* AND **out to lunch*** not alert; giddy; uninformed. (Slang.) □ *Bill is really out of it. Why can't he pay attention?* □ *Don't be out of it, John. Wake up!* □ *Ann is really out to lunch these days.*

out of keeping with something AND **out**

of keeping not following the rules of something; out of accord with something. (Compare to *in keeping with something.*) □ *The length of this report is out of keeping with your request.* □ *I didn't even read it because it was so much out of keeping.*

out of kilter* (Slang.) **1.** out of balance; crooked or tilted. □ *John, your tie is sort of out of kilter. Let me fix it.* □ *Please straighten the picture on the wall. It's out of kilter.* **2.** malfunctioning; *on the fritz.* □ *My furnace is out of kilter. I have to call someone to fix it.* □ *This computer is out of kilter. It doesn't work.*

out of line 1. See *out of line with something.* **2.** improper. □ *I'm afraid that your behavior was quite out of line. I do not wish to speak further about this matter.* □ *Bill, that remark was out of line. Please be more respectful.* **3.** See the following entry.

out of line with something AND **out of line 1.** not properly lined up in a line of things. □ *I told you not to get out of line. Now, get back in line.* □ *One of those books on the shelf is out of line with the others. Please fix it.* **2.** unreasonable when compared to something (else). □ *The cost of this meal is out of line with what other restaurants charge.* □ *Your request is out of line.*

out of luck* without good luck; having bad fortune. (Informal.) □ *If you wanted some ice cream, you're out of luck.* □ *I was out of luck. I got there too late to get a seat.*

out of necessity because of necessity; due to need. □ *I bought this hat out of necessity. I needed one, and this was all there was.* □ *We sold our car out of necessity.*

out of one's element not in a natural or comfortable situation. (Compare to *in one's element.*) □ *When it comes to computers, I'm out of my element.* □ *Sally's out of her element in math.*

out of one's head See the following entry.

out of one's mind AND **out of one's head; out of one's senses** silly and senseless; crazy; irrational. □ *Why did you do that? You must be out of your mind!* □ *Good grief, Tom! You have to be out* *of your head!* □ *She's acting as if she were out of her senses.*

out of one's senses See the previous entry.

out of order **1.** not in the correct order. □ *This book is out of order. Please put it in the right place on the shelf.* □ *You're out of order, John. Please get in line after Jane.* **2.** not following correct parliamentary procedure. □ *I was declared out of order by the president.* □ *Ann inquired, "Isn't a motion to table the question out of order at this time?"*

out of place **1.** not in a proper place. □ *The salt was out of place in the cupboard, so I couldn't find it.* □ *Billy, you're out of place. Please sit next to Tom.* **2.** improper and impertinent; *out of line.* □ *That kind of behavior is out of place in church.* □ *Your rude remark is quite out of place.*

out-of-pocket expenses the actual amount of money spent. (Refers to the money one person pays while doing something on someone else's behalf. One is usually paid back this money.) □ *My out-of-pocket expenses for the party were nearly $175.* □ *My employer usually pays all out-of-pocket expenses for a business trip.*

out of practice performing poorly due to a lack of practice. □ *I used to be able to play the piano extremely well, but now I'm out of practice.* □ *The baseball players lost the game because they were out of practice.*

out of print (for a book) to be no longer available for sale. □ *The book you want is out of print, but perhaps I can find a used copy for you.* □ *It was published nearly ten years ago, so it's probably out of print.*

out of reach **1.** not near enough to be reached or touched. □ *Place the cookies out of reach, or Bob will eat them all.* □ *The mouse ran behind the piano, out of reach. The cat just sat and waited for it.* **2.** unattainable. □ *I wanted to be president, but I'm afraid that such a goal is out of reach.* □ *I shall choose a goal which is not out of reach.*

out of season (The opposite of *in season.* Compare to *off season.*) **1.** not now available for sale. □ *Sorry, oysters are*

out of season. We don't have any. □ *Watermelon is out of season in the winter.* **2.** not now legally able to be hunted or caught. □ *Are salmon out of season?* □ *I caught a trout out of season and had to pay a fine.*

out of service inoperable; not now operating. (See also *out of commission.*) □ *Both elevators are out of service, so I had to use the stairs.* □ *The washroom is temporarily out of service.*

out of shape AND **out of condition** not in the best physical condition. □ *I get out of breath when I run because I'm out of shape.* □ *Keep exercising regularly, or you'll get out of condition.*

out of sight **1.** not visible. (Especially with *get, keep, stay.*) □ *The cat kept out of sight until the mouse came out.* □ *"Get out of sight, or they'll see you!" called John.* **2.*** (for a price to be) very high. (Informal.) □ *I won't pay this bill. It's out of sight.* □ *The estimate was out of sight, so I didn't accept it.* **3.*** (figuratively) stunning, unbelievable, or awesome. (Slang.) □ *Wow, this music is out of sight!* □ *What a wild party—out of sight!*

Out of sight, out of mind. a proverb meaning that if you do not see something, you will not think about it. □ *When I go home, I put my school books away so I won't worry about doing my homework. After all, out of sight, out of mind.* □ *Jane dented the fender on her car. It's on the right side so she doesn't have to look at it. Like they say, out of sight, out of mind.*

out of sorts not feeling well; grumpy and irritable. □ *I've been out of sorts for a day or two. I think I'm coming down with something.* □ *The baby is out of sorts. Maybe she's getting a tooth.*

out of step with someone or something AND **out of step** (Compare to *in step with someone or something.*) **1.** [with *someone*] AND **out of time with someone or something; out of time** (marching or dancing) out of cadence with someone else. □ *You're out of step with the music.* □ *Pay attention, Ann. You're out of time.* **2.** not as up to date as someone or something. □ *John is* *out of step with the times.* □ *Billy is out of step with the rest of the class.*

out of stock not immediately available in a store; (for goods) to be temporarily unavailable. □ *Those items are out of stock, but a new supply will be delivered on Thursday.* □ *I'm sorry, but the red ones are out of stock. Would a blue one do?*

out of style AND **out of fashion** not fashionable; old fashioned; obsolete. □ *John's clothes are really out of style.* □ *He doesn't care if his clothes are out of fashion.* ALSO: **go out of fashion; go out of style** to become unfashionable; to become obsolete. □ *That kind of furniture went out of style years ago.*

out of the blue See *out of a clear blue sky.*

out of the corner of one's eye (seeing something) at a glance; glimpsing (something). □ *I saw someone do it out of the corner of my eye. It might have been Jane who did it.* □ *I only saw the accident out of the corner of my eye. I don't know who is at fault.*

out of the frying pan, into the fire from a bad situation to a worse situation. (A cliché.) □ *When I tried to argue about my fine for a traffic violation, the judge charged me with contempt of court. I really went out of the frying pan, into the fire.* □ *I got deeply in debt. Then I really got out of the frying pan into the fire when I lost my job.*

out of the hole* out of debt. (Informal. Also used literally.) □ *I get paid next week, and then I can get out of the hole.* □ *I can't seem to get out of the hole. I keep spending more money than I earn.*

out of the ordinary unusual. □ *It was a good meal, but not out of the ordinary.* □ *Your report was nicely done, but nothing out of the ordinary.*

out of the question not possible; not permitted. □ *I'm sorry, but it's out of the question.* □ *You can't go to Florida this spring. We can't afford it. It's out of the question.*

out of the red* out of debt. (Informal.) □ *This year our firm is likely to get out of the red before fall.* □ *If we can cut down on expenses, we can get out of the red fairly soon.*

out of the running no longer being considered; eliminated from a contest. □ *After the first part of the diving meet, three of our team were out of the running.* □ *After the scandal was made public, I was no longer in the running. I pulled out of the election.*

out of the swim of things* not in the middle of activity; not involved in things. (Informal. The opposite of *in the swim of things.*) □ *While I had my cold, I was out of the swim of things.* □ *I've been out of the swim of things for a few weeks. Please bring me up to date.*

out of the way AND **out of one's way** **1.** not blocking or impeding the way. □ *Please get out of my way.* □ *Would you please get your foot out of the way?* **2.** not along the way. □ *I'm sorry, but I can't give you a ride home. It's out of the way.* □ *That route is out of my way.* ALSO: **out-of-the-way** difficult to get to. □ *They live on a quiet, out-of-the-way street.*

out of the woods* past a critical phase; out of the unknown. (Informal.) □ *When the patient got out of the woods, everyone relaxed.* □ *I can give you a better prediction for your future health when you are out of the woods.*

out of thin air* out of nowhere; out of nothing. (Informal.) □ *Suddenly—out of thin air—the messenger appeared.* □ *You just made that up out of thin air.*

out of this world* wonderful; extraordinary. (A cliché. Also used literally.) □ *This pie is just out of this world.* □ *Look at you! How lovely you look—simply out of this world.*

out of time **1.** with no more time. □ *I was out of time before I could finish.* □ *I can't be out of time! I still have a lot to do.* **2.** See *out of step with someone or something.* ALSO: **run out of time** to use up all the available time. □ *I ran out of time and couldn't finish.*

out of touch with someone or something AND **out of touch** **1.** [with *someone*] no longer talking to or writing to someone; knowing no news of someone. □ *I've been out of touch with my brother for many years.* □ *We've been out of touch for quite some time.* **2.** [with *something*] not keeping up with the developments of something. □ *I've been out of touch with automobile mechanics for many years.* □ *I couldn't go back into mechanics because I've been out of touch for too long.*

out of town temporarily not in one's own town. □ *I'll be out of town next week. I'm going to a conference.* □ *I take care of Mary's cat when she's out of town.*

out of tune with someone or something AND **out of tune** 1. in musical harmony with someone or something. □ *The oboe is out of tune with the flute.* □ *The flute is out of tune with John.* □ *They are all out of tune.* 2. not in (figurative) harmony or agreement. □ *Your proposal is out of tune with my ideas of what we should be doing.* □ *Let's get all our efforts in tune.*

out of turn not at the proper time; not in the proper order. (See also *speak out of turn*.) □ *We were permitted to be served out of turn, because we had to leave early.* □ *Bill tried to register out of turn and was sent away.*

out of whack* AND **out of wack*** (Slang.) 1. crazy; silly; irrational. □ *Why do you always act like you're out of whack?* □ *I'm not out of wack. I'm eccentric.* 2. out of adjustment; out of order. □ *I'm afraid that my watch is out of whack.* □ *The elevator is out of wack. We'll have to walk up.*

out of work unemployed, temporarily or permanently. □ *How long have you been out of work?* □ *My brother has been out of work for nearly a year.*

out on a limb in a dangerous position; taking a chance. □ *I don't want to go out on a limb, but I think I'd agree to your request.* □ *She really went out on a limb when she agreed.*

out on bail out of jail because bail bond money has been paid. (The money will be forfeited if the person who is out on bail does not appear in court at the proper time. See also *jump bail*.) □ *Bob is out on bail waiting for his trial.* □ *The robber committed another crime while out on bail.*

out on parole out of jail but still under police supervision. □ *Bob got out on parole after serving only a few years of*

his sentence. □ *He was out on parole because of good behavior.*

out on the town celebrating at one or more places in a town. (See also *night on the town*.) □ *I'm really tired. I was out on the town until dawn.* □ *We went out on the town to celebrate our wedding anniversary.*

out to lunch 1. eating lunch away from one's place of work. □ *I'm sorry, but Sally Jones is out to lunch. May I take a message?* □ *She's been out to lunch for nearly two hours. When will she be back?* 2. See *out of it*.

out West in the western part of the United States. (See also *back East, down South, up North*.) □ *We lived out West for nearly ten years.* □ *Do they really ride horses out West?*

outgrow something See *grow out of something*.

outside of something except for something; besides something. (Also used literally.) □ *Outside of the cost of my laundry, I have practically no expenses.* □ *Outside of some new shoes, I don't need any new clothing.*

over and above something* more than something; in addition to something. (Informal.) □ *I'll need another twenty dollars over and above the amount you have already given me.* □ *You've been eating too much food over and above what is required for good nutrition. That's why you're gaining weight.*

over and done with* finished. (Informal.) □ *I'm glad that's over and done with.* □ *Now that I have college over and done with, I can get a job.*

over and over AND **over and over again** repeatedly. □ *She stamped her foot over and over again.* □ *Bill whistled the same song over and over.*

over my dead body* not if I can stop you. (Slang. It means that you'll have to kill me to prevent me from keeping you from doing something.) □ *Over my dead body you'll sell this house!* □ *You want to quit college? Over my dead body!*

over the hill* overage; too old to do something. (Informal.) □ *Now that Mary's forty, she thinks she's over the hill.* □ *My grandfather was over eighty before he felt like he was over the hill.*

over the hump* over the difficult part. (Informal.) □ *This is a difficult project, but we're over the hump now.* □ *I'm halfway through—over the hump—and it looks like I may get finished after all.*

over the long haul for a relatively long period of time. □ *Over the long haul, it might be better to invest in stocks.* □ *Over the long haul, everything will turn out all right.*

over the short haul for the immediate future. □ *Over the short haul, you'd be better off to put your money in the bank.* □ *Over the short haul, you may wish* *you had done something different. But things will work out all right.*

over the top having gained more than one's goal. □ *Our fund raising campaign went over the top by $3,000.* □ *We didn't go over the top. We didn't even get half of what we set out to collect.*

own up to something AND **own up** to confess to something. □ *I know you broke the window. Come on and own up to it.* □ *The boy holding the baseball bat owned up. What else could he do?*

P

pack a punch See the following entry.

pack a wallop* AND **pack a punch*** to provide a burst of energy, power, or excitement. (Informal.) □ *Wow, this spicy food really packs a wallop.* □ *I put a special kind of gasoline in my car because I thought it would pack a punch. It didn't.*

pack someone off to somewhere AND **pack off someone to somewhere; pack off someone; pack someone off** to send someone away to somewhere. (Compare to *send someone packing*.) □ *We packed off my aunt to Boston yesterday.* □ *John has left for Florida. We packed him off last week.*

pack them in* to draw a lot of people. (Informal.) □ *It was a good night at the theater. The play really packed them in.* □ *The circus manager knew he could pack them in if he advertised the lion tamer.*

packed in like sardines* AND **packed like sardines*** packed very tightly. (A cliché. Many variations are possible, as in the examples.) □ *It was terribly crowded there. We were packed in like sardines.* □ *The bus was full. The passengers were packed like sardines.* □ *They packed us in like sardines.*

pad the bill* to put unnecessary items on a bill to make the total cost higher. (Informal.) □ *The plumber had padded the bill with things we didn't need.* □ *I was falsely accused of padding the bill.*

paddle one's own canoe* to do (something) by oneself; to be alone. (A cliché. Could also be used literally.) □ *I've been left to paddle my own canoe too many times.* □ *Sally isn't with us. She's off paddling her own canoe.*

pain in the neck* a bother; an annoyance. (Slang.) □ *This assignment is a pain in the neck.* □ *Your little brother is a pain in the neck.*

paint the town red to have a wild celebration during a *night on the town*. □ *Let's all go out and paint the town red!* □ *Oh, do I feel awful. I was out all last night painting the town red.*

pair off with someone AND **pair off; pair up with someone; pair up** (for two people) to form a pair for some purpose, possibly a romantic purpose. □ *All right. You two pair off and go to the right. The rest of us will go to the left.* □ *Tom paired off with Ann for the rest of the evening.* □ *Okay—everybody pair up and let's get this job done.*

pair up with someone See the previous entry.

pal around with someone AND **pal around** to be friends with someone; to be the companion of someone. □ *Bill likes to pal around with Mary, but it's nothing serious.* □ *Ann and Jane still like to pal around.*

pale around the gills* AND **blue around the gills*; green around the gills*** looking sick. (Informal. The *around* can be replaced with *about*.) □ *John is looking a little pale around the gills. What's wrong?* □ *Oh, I feel a little green about the gills.*

palm someone or something off on someone AND **palm off someone or something on someone; palm off someone or something; palm someone or something off** to get rid of someone or something by giving or selling it to another person. □ *My brother palmed off his old baseball bat on me.*

□ *Tom palmed Ann off on Bill. Both Ann and Bill were furious.*

pan out See *turn out all right.*

par for the course* typical; about what one could expect. (A cliché. This refers to golf courses, not school courses.) □ *So he went off and left you? Well that's about par for the course. He's no friend.* □ *I worked for days on this project, but it was rejected. That's par for the course around here.*

parcel someone or something out AND **parcel out someone or something** to give out or hand out someone or something. □ *Mr. and Mrs. Smith went on vacation and parceled out the children to various relatives.* □ *We parceled the candy out to all the visitors.*

part and parcel of something* AND **part and parcel*** part of something; an important part of something. (A cliché. See also *bag and baggage.*) □ *This point is part and parcel of my whole argument.* □ *Get every part and parcel of this machine out of my living room.* □ *Come on! Move out—part and parcel!*

part company with someone AND **part company** to leave someone; to depart from someone. □ *Tom finally parted company with his brother.* □ *They parted company, and Tom got in his car and drove away.*

part someone's hair* to come very close to someone. (Informal. Usually an exaggeration. Also used literally.) □ *That plane flew so low that it nearly parted my hair.* □ *He punched at me and missed. He only parted my hair.*

part with someone or something to separate from someone or something; to give up someone or something. □ *I hated to part with that old hat. I've had it for years.* □ *Tom was sad to part with Ann, but that's the way it had to be.*

partake of something to take something; to eat or drink something. (Formal.) □ *I don't usually partake of rich foods, but in this instance I'll make an exception.* □ *Good afternoon, Judge Smith, would you care to partake of some wine?*

parting of the ways a point at which people separate and go their own ways.

(Often with *come to a, arrive at a, reach a*, etc.) □ *Jane and Bob finally came to a parting of the ways.* □ *Bill and his parents reached a parting of the ways.*

pass as someone or something to succeed in being accepted as someone or something. □ *The spy was able to pass as a regular citizen.* □ *The thief was arrested when he tried to pass as a priest.*

pass away AND **pass on** to die. (A euphemism.) □ *My aunt passed away last month.* □ *When I pass away, I want to have lots of flowers and a big funeral.* □ *When I pass on, I won't care about the funeral.*

pass muster* to measure up to the required standards. (Folksy.) □ *I tried, but my efforts didn't pass muster.* □ *If you don't wear a suit, you won't pass muster at that fancy restaurant. They won't let you in.*

pass on See *pass away.*

pass out to faint; to lose consciousness. □ *Oh, look! Tom has passed out.* □ *When he got the news, he passed out.*

pass over someone or something See *pass someone or something over.*

pass someone or something by AND **pass by someone or something** to miss someone or something; to overlook someone or something. (Refers specifically to moving beside someone or something. Compare to *pass someone or something up* and *pass someone or something over.*) □ *The storm passed the town by.* □ *The teacher passed me by and chose the next person in line.* □ *We passed by John. We didn't even see him standing there.*

pass someone or something over AND **pass over someone or something** **1.** to move over without affecting someone or something. (Refers specifically to moving above.) □ *The storm passed over us.* □ *The cloud passed over the mountain.* **2.** to skip over someone or something. (Compare to *pass someone or something by* and *pass someone or something up.*) □ *They passed over John and chose Ann.* □ *Please don't pass me over again.*

pass someone or something up AND **pass up someone or something** to ignore or avoid someone or something; to overlook someone or something. (Compare to *pass someone or something by* and *pass someone or something over*.) □ *Yes, I'd love some chocolate cake, but I'll have to pass it up. I'm on a diet.* □ *They passed up John in favor of Mary.*

pass something off as something
1. See *pawn something off on someone as something.* **2.** See *shrug something off as something.*

pass something off on someone as something See *pawn something off on someone as something.*

pass something on AND **pass on something** **1.** to hand or give something (to another person). □ *Have a piece of candy and pass the box on.* □ *Please pass on this book to the next person on the list.* **2.** to tell someone something; to spread news or gossip. □ *Don't pass this on, but Bill isn't living at home anymore.* □ *I refuse to pass on rumors.*

pass something out AND **pass out something** to distribute or hand out something. □ *Please pass out one paper to each person.* □ *Please pass these out for me.*

pass the buck* to pass the blame (to someone else); to give the responsibility (to someone else). (Informal.) □ *Don't try to pass the buck! It's your fault, and everybody knows it.* □ *Some people try to pass the buck whenever they can.*

pass the hat to attempt to collect money for some (charitable) project. □ *Bob is passing the hat to collect money to buy flowers for Ann.* □ *He's always passing the hat for something.*

pass the time to fill up time (by doing something). □ *I never know how to pass the time when I'm on vacation.* □ *What do you do to pass the time?*

pass the time of day with someone AND **pass the time of day** to chat or talk informally with someone. □ *I saw Mr. Brown in town yesterday. I stopped and passed the time of day with him.* □ *No, we didn't have a serious talk; we just passed the time of day.*

pass through someone's mind AND **cross someone's mind** to come to mind briefly; for an idea to occur to someone. (Compare to *come to*

mind.) □ *Let me tell you what just crossed my mind.* □ *As you were speaking, something passed through my mind which I'd like to discuss.*

pat someone on the back AND **give someone a pat on the back** to congratulate someone; to encourage someone. (Also used literally.) □ *We patted Ann on the back for a good performance.* □ *When people do a good job, you should give them a pat on the back.* ALSO: **get a pat on the back** to receive congratulations. □ *Ann was glad to get a pat on the back.*

patch someone or something up AND **patch up someone or something** **1.*** to doctor someone; to dress someone's wounds. (Informal.) □ *I patched up Ann's cuts with bandages and sent her home.* □ *They patched John up in the emergency room.* **2.** [with *something*] to repair something temporarily, often literally, with patches. □ *I tried to patch the lawn mower up so I could use it for the rest of the summer.* □ *See if you can patch up this tire for me.* **3.** [with *something*] to (figuratively) repair the damage done by an argument or disagreement. □ *Mr. and Mrs. Smith are trying to patch things up.* □ *We patched up our argument, then kissed and made up.*

path of least resistance to do the easiest thing; to take the easiest route. (Often with *follow the* or *take the*.) □ *John will follow the path of least resistance.* □ *I like challenges. I won't usually take the path of least resistance.*

pave the way for someone or something AND **pave the way** to prepare (someone or something) for someone or something. □ *The public doesn't understand the metric system. We need to pave the way for its introduction.* □ *They are paving the way in the schools.*

pawn something off on someone as something* AND **pass off something as something; pass off something on someone as something; pass off something on someone; pass something off as something; pass something off on someone as something; pass something off on someone; pawn off something as something*; pawn**

off something on someone*; **pawn something off as something***; **pawn something off on someone as something***; **pawn something off on someone*** to get rid of something deceptively by giving or selling it to someone as something else. (The expressions with *pawn* are informal or slang.) □ *I passed the rhinestone off on John as a diamond.* □ *Don't pawn that fake off on me!* □ *Don't pawn it off at all!*

pay an arm and a leg for something* AND **pay an arm and a leg***; **pay through the nose for something***; **pay through the nose*** to pay too much money for something. (Informal.) □ *I hate to have to pay an arm and a leg for a tank of gas.* □ *If you shop around, you won't have to pay an arm and a leg.* □ *Why should you pay through the nose?* ALSO: **cost an arm and a leg** to cost too much. □ *It cost an arm and a leg, so I didn't buy it.*

pay as you go to pay costs as they occur; to pay for goods as they are bought (rather than charging them). □ *You ought to pay as you go. Then you won't be in debt.* □ *If you pay as you go, you'll never spend too much money.* ALSO: **pay-as-you-go** paying costs as they occur. □ *There is no charging allowed here. This store is strictly pay-as-you-go.* □ *I can't buy this then. I didn't know your policy was pay-as-you-go.*

pay attention to someone or something AND **pay attention** to be attentive to someone or something; to give one's attention or concentration to someone or something. □ *Pay attention to me!* □ *I'm paying attention!*

pay for something 1. to pay out money for something. □ *Did you pay for the magazine, or shall I?* □ *No, I'll pay for it.* **2.** to be punished for something. □ *The criminal will pay for his crimes.* □ *I don't like what you did to me, and I'm going to see that you pay for it.*

pay in advance to pay (for something) before it is received or delivered. □ *I want to make a special order. Will I have to pay in advance?* □ *Yes, please pay in advance.*

pay lip service to something AND **pay lip service** to express loyalty, respect, or support for something insincerely. □ *You don't really care about politics. You're just paying lip service to the candidate.* □ *Don't sit here and pay lip service. Get busy!*

pay one's debt to society AND **pay one's debt** to serve a sentence for a crime, usually in prison. □ *The judge said that Mr. Simpson had to pay his debt to society.* □ *Mr. Brown paid his debt in state prison.*

pay one's dues 1. to pay the fees required to belong to an organization. □ *If you haven't paid your dues, you can't come to the club picnic.* □ *How many people have paid their dues?* **2.*** to have earned one's right to something through hard work or suffering. (Informal.) □ *He worked hard to get to where he is today. He paid his dues and did what he was told.* □ *I have every right to be here. I paid my dues!*

pay someone a compliment to compliment someone. □ *Sally thanked me for paying her a compliment.* □ *When Tom did his job well, I paid him a compliment.*

pay someone a left-handed compliment to give someone a false compliment which is really an insult. □ *John said that he had never seen me looking better. I think he was paying me a left-handed compliment.* □ *I'd prefer that someone insult me directly. I hate it when someone pays me a left-handed compliment—unless it's a joke.*

pay someone a visit AND **pay a visit** to visit someone. □ *I think I'll pay Mary a visit.* □ *We'd like to see you. When would be a good time to pay a visit?*

pay someone or something off AND **pay off someone or something 1.** [with *someone*] to pay someone a bribe (for a favor already done). (Compare to *buy someone off*.) □ *The lawyer paid off the judge for deciding the case in the lawyer's favor.* □ *The lawyer was put in prison for paying the judge off. The judge was imprisoned also.* **2.** to pay a debt; to pay a debtor; to pay the final payment for something bought on credit. □ *Did you pay off the plumber yet?* □ *This month I'll pay off the car.*

pay someone's way AND **pay one's own way** to pay the costs (of something) for a person. □ *I wanted to go to Florida this spring, but my parents say I have to pay my own way.* □ *My aunt is going to pay my way to Florida—only if I take her with me!*

pay the piper* to face the results of one's actions; to receive punishment for something. (A cliché.) □ *You can put off paying your debts only so long. Eventually you'll have to pay the piper.* □ *You can't get away with that forever. You'll have to pay the piper someday.*

pay through the nose for something See *pay an arm and a leg for something.*

pay up* Pay me now! (Slang.) □ *You owe me $200. Come on, pay up!* □ *If you don't pay up, I'll take you to court.*

peel something off something AND **peel off something from something; peel off something; peel something off** to pull something from the surface of something (else). □ *Peel the label off the jar and put a plant in it.* □ *Peel off the label from the box.* □ *Okay, I peeled it off. What do I do now?*

peg away at something See *plug away at something.*

penny wise and pound foolish* a proverb meaning that it is foolish to lose a lot of money to save a little money. (A cliché.) □ *Sally shops very carefully to save a few cents on food, then charges the food to a charge card that costs a lot in annual interest. That's being penny wise and pound foolish.* □ *John drives thirty miles to buy gas for three cents a gallon less than it costs here. He's really penny wise and pound foolish.*

Perish the thought. Do not even consider thinking of something. (Formal.) □ *If you should become ill—perish the thought—I'd take care of you.* □ *I'm afraid that we need a new car. Perish the thought.*

perk someone or something up AND **perk up someone or something** to make someone or something more cheery. □ *Don't you think that new curtains would perk up this room?* □ *A nice cup of coffee would really perk me up.*

peter out* to die away; to dwindle away; to become exhausted gradually. (Informal.) □ *When the fire petered out, I went to bed.* □ *My money finally petered out, and I had to come home.*

phase someone or something out AND **phase out someone or something** to plan the gradual removal of someone or something. □ *They are phasing out dial telephones. Only button telephones will be available.* □ *There is a new boss at work. I hope they won't phase me out, too.*

pick a quarrel with someone AND **pick a quarrel** to start an argument with someone. □ *Are you trying to pick a quarrel with me?* □ *No, I'm not trying to pick a quarrel.*

pick at someone or something 1.* to be very critical of someone or something; to *pick on someone or something.* (Informal.) □ *Why are you always picking at me?* □ *You always seem to be picking at your car.* **2.** [with *something*] to eat only little bits of something. □ *You're only picking at your food. Don't you feel well?* □ *Billy is only picking at his peas, and he usually eats all of them.* **3.** [with *something*] to pull, scratch, or pry at something. □ *If you pick at that sore, it'll get infected.* □ *Don't pick at the label. It'll come off.*

pick holes in something AND **pick something to pieces** to criticize something severely; to find all the flaws or fallacies in an argument. □ *The lawyer picked holes in the witness's story.* □ *They will pick holes in your argument.* □ *She picked my story to pieces.*

pick on someone or something to criticize someone or something; to abuse someone or something. □ *Stop picking on me!* □ *Why are you always picking on your dog?* □ *Don't pick on our house. It's old, but we love it.* ALSO: **pick on someone your own size** to abuse someone who is big enough to fight back. □ *Go pick on somebody your own size!*

pick one's way through something 1. to work slowly and meticulously through something. □ *My teacher said he couldn't even pick his way through my report. It was just too confusing.* □ *I spent an hour picking my way through the state tax forms.* **2.** to move along a

255

route full of obstacles. □ *When the grandchildren visit, I have to pick my way through the toys on the floor.* □ *We slowly picked our way through the thorny bushes to get to the ripe raspberries.*

pick someone or something off AND **pick off someone or something 1.** [with *something*] to remove something by picking, scratching, or plucking. □ *Don't pick the scab off. You'll get an infection.* □ *Pick off all the feathers before you cook the duck.* **2.** to kill someone or something with a carefully aimed gunshot. □ *The hunter picked the deer off with great skill.* □ *The killer tried to pick off the police officer.*

pick someone or something out AND **pick out someone or something** to choose someone or something. □ *I don't know which one to choose. You pick one out for me.* □ *I used the telephone book to pick out a plumber.* □ *The store picked out John as the winner of the contest.*

pick someone or something up AND **pick up someone or something 1.** to lift up someone or something. □ *Please pick up the stone.* □ *Don't pick me up!* **2.** [with *someone*] to go to a place in a car, bus, etc., and take on a person as a passenger. □ *Please come to my office and pick me up at noon.* □ *I have to pick up Billy at school.* **3.** [with *someone*] to stop one's car, bus, etc., and offer someone a ride. □ *I picked up a hitchhiker today, and we had a nice chat.* □ *Don't ever pick a stranger up when you're out driving!* **4.*** [with *someone*] to attempt to become acquainted with someone for romantic or sexual purposes. (Informal.) □ *Who are you anyway? Are you trying to pick me up?* □ *No, I never picked up anybody in my life!* **5.** [with *someone*] (for the police) to find and bring someone to the police station for questioning or arrest. □ *Sergeant Jones, go pick up Sally Franklin and bring her in to be questioned about the jewel robbery.* □ *I tried to pick her up, but she heard me coming and got away.* **6.** [with *something*] to tidy up or clean up a room or some other place. □ *Let's pick this room up in a hurry.* □ *I want you to*

pick up the entire house. **7.** [with *something*] to find or acquire casually. □ *I picked up this tool at the hardware store.* □ *Where did you pick that up?* **8.** [with *something*] to learn something. □ *I picked up a lot of knowledge about music from my brother.* □ *I picked up an interesting melody from a movie.* **9.** [with *something*] to cause something to go faster, especially music. □ *All right, let's pick this piece up and get it moving faster.* □ *Okay, get moving. Pick it up!* **10.** [with *something*] to resume something. □ *I'll have to pick up my work where I left off.* □ *Pick it up right where you stopped.* **11.** [with *something*] to receive radio signals; to bring something into view. □ *I can hardly pick up a signal.* □ *We can pick up a pretty good television picture where we live.* □ *I can just pick it up with a powerful telescope.* **12.** [with *something*] to find a trail or route. □ *The dogs finally picked up the scent.* □ *You should pick up highway 80 in a few miles.* ALSO: **pick up 1.** to tidy up. □ *When you finish playing, you have to pick up.* **2.** to get busy; to go faster. □ *Things usually pick up around here about 8:00.*

pick something over AND **pick over something** to sort through something; to rummage through something. □ *The shoppers quickly picked over the sale merchandise.* □ *They picked all the records over.* ALSO: **picked over** rejected; worn, dirty, or undesirable. □ *This merchandise looks worn and picked over. I don't want any of it.*

pick something to pieces See *pick holes in something.*

pick up See *pick someone or something up.*

pick up the tab* to pay the bill. (Informal.) □ *Whenever we go out, my father picks up the tab.* □ *Order whatever you want. The company is picking up the tab.*

pie in the sky* a future reward, especially after death. (A cliché.) □ *Are you nice to people just because of pie in the sky, or do you really like them?* □ *Don't hold out for a big reward, you know— pie in the sky.*

piece of cake* very easy. (Slang.) □

No, it won't be any trouble. It's a piece of cake. □ *It's easy! Look here—piece of cake.*

piece of the action* a share in a scheme or project; a degree of involvement. (Slang.) □ *If you guys are going to bet on the football game, I want a piece of the action, too.* □ *My brother wants in on it. Give him a piece of the action.*

piece something out See *piece something together.*

piece something together AND **piece together something; piece something out; piece out something 1.** to assemble something from pieces. □ *We were able to piece out a simple meal from the stuff we found in the cupboard.* □ *We pieced the puzzle together in about an hour.* **2.** to extend or repair something with pieces. □ *I pieced the hose together with tape.* □ *We used scraps of cloth to piece the tent out into a much larger tent.*

pile into something AND **pile in** to climb in or get in roughly. □ *Okay, kids, pile in!* □ *The children piled into the car and slammed the door.*

pile out of something AND **pile out** to get out of something roughly. □ *Okay, kids, pile out!* □ *The car door burst open, and the children piled out.*

pile something on someone or something AND **pile something on; pile on something** to put a lot of something on someone or something; to provide a lot of something for someone or something. □ *The teacher really piled the homework on us this week.* □ *Bill piled a lot of mashed potatoes on his plate.* □ *He really piled on the potatoes.*

pile something up AND **pile up something** (See also the following entry.) **1.** to make a heap or pile of something. □ *John piled up the rocks.* □ *They chopped the wood and piled it up.* **2.** to crash or wreck something. □ *The driver piled up the car against a tree.* □ *Drive carefully if you don't want to pile the car up.*

pile up (See also the previous entry.) **1.** to accumulate; to grow into a pile. □ *My work is piling up. I have to work faster and harder.* □ *The newspapers are piling up. It's time to get rid of them.*

2. to crash or wreck. □ *The car piled up against the tree.* □ *The bus piled up on the curve.*

pin one's faith on someone or something to put one's hope, trust, or faith in someone or something. □ *I'm pinning my faith on your efforts.* □ *Don't pin your faith on Tom. He's not dependable.*

pin someone or something down on something AND **pin down someone or something on something; pin someone or something down; pin down someone or something 1.** to hold someone or something down on something. □ *Bob pinned down Tom on the mat.* □ *We pinned the calf down on the ground so it couldn't get away.* **2.*** [with *someone*] to force someone to explain or clarify something. (Informal.) □ *Try to pin her down on the time.* □ *Please find out exactly how much it costs. Pin them down on the price.*

pin someone's ears back* to scold someone severely; to beat someone. (Slang.) □ *Tom pinned my ears back because I insulted him.* □ *I got very mad at John and wanted to pin his ears back, but I didn't.*

pin something on someone or something 1. to attach something to someone or something with pins. □ *Would you please pin this name label on my jacket?* □ *No, don't pin it on me! Pin it on my jacket!* **2.*** [with *someone*] to place the blame for something on someone. (Slang.) □ *I didn't take the money. Don't try to pin it on me. I wasn't even there.* □ *The police managed to pin the crime on Bob.*

pinch-hit for someone AND **pinch-hit** to substitute for someone. (Originally from baseball where it refers to a substitute batter.) □ *Will you pinch-hit for me at band practice?* □ *Sorry, I can't pinch-hit. I don't have the time.*

pipe down* to be quiet; to get quiet. (Slang.) □ *Okay, you guys, pipe down!* □ *I've heard enough out of you. Pipe down!*

pipe up with something to speak up and say something, especially with a high-pitched voice. □ *Billy piped up with a silly remark.* □ *Did I hear somebody pipe up with an insult?*

pit someone or something against someone or something to set someone or something in opposition to someone or something. □ *The rules of the tournament pit their team against ours.* □ *John pitted Mary against Sally in the tennis match.* □ *In an interesting plowing match, Bill pitted himself against a small tractor.*

pitch in and help AND **pitch in** to get busy and help (with something). □ *Pick up a paint brush and pitch in and help.* □ *Why don't some of you pitch in? We need all the help we can get.*

pitch someone a curve ball* AND **pitch someone a curve*** to surprise someone with an unexpected act or event. (Informal. Also used literally referring to a curve ball in baseball.) □ *You really pitched me a curve ball when you said I had done a poor job. I did my best.* □ *You asked Tom a hard question. You certainly pitched him a curve.*

place the blame on someone or something See *put the blame on someone or something.*

plan on something to make arrangements for something; to anticipate something. □ *I didn't plan on so much trouble.* □ *I'm planning on four people for dinner.*

play around with someone or something AND **play about with someone or something; play about; play around** to engage in some amusing activity with someone or something; to tease someone or something. □ *Please don't play around with that vase. You'll break it.* □ *Don't play around with the parrot. It'll bite you.* □ *Bill and I were just playing around when we heard the sound of breaking glass.*

play ball with someone AND **play ball**
1. to play a ball game with someone. (Note the special baseball use in the second example.) □ *When will our team play ball with yours?* □ *Suddenly, the umpire shouted, "Play ball!" and the game began.* 2.* to cooperate with someone. (Informal.) □ *Look, friend, if you play ball with me, everything will work out all right.* □ *Things would go better for you if you'd learn to play ball.*

play both ends against the middle* AND

play both ends* (for one) to scheme in a way that pits two sides against each other (for one's own gain). (Informal.) □ *I told my brother that Mary doesn't like him. Then I told Mary that my brother doesn't like her. They broke up, so now I can have the car this weekend. I succeeded in playing both ends against the middle.* □ *If you try to play both ends, you're likely to get in trouble with both sides.*

play by ear See *play something by ear.*

play-by-play description a description of an event given as the event is taking place. (Usually in reference to a sporting event.) □ *And now here is Bill Jones with a play-by-play description of the baseball game.* □ *John was giving me a play-by-play description of the argument going on next door.*

play cat and mouse with someone AND **play cat and mouse** to (literally or figuratively) capture and release someone over and over. (A cliché.) □ *The police played cat and mouse with the suspect until they had sufficient evidence to make an arrest.* □ *Tom has been playing cat and mouse with Ann. Finally she got tired of it and broke up with him.*

play fair to do something by the rules; to play something in a fair and just manner. □ *John won't play with Bill anymore because Bill doesn't play fair.* □ *You moved the golf ball with your foot! That's not playing fair!*

play fast and loose with someone or something AND **play fast and loose** to act carelessly, thoughtlessly, and irresponsibly (Informal.) □ *I'm tired of your playing fast and loose with me. Leave me alone.* □ *Bob got fired for playing fast and loose with the company's money.* □ *If you play fast and loose like that, you can get into a lot of trouble.*

play first chair 1. to be the leader of a section of instruments in an orchestra or a band. □ *Sally learned to play the violin so well that she now plays first chair in the orchestra.* □ *I'm going to practice my flute so I can play first chair.* 2. to act as a leader. □ *I need to get this job done. Who plays first chair around here?* □ *You're not the boss! You don't play first chair.*

play footsie with someone* AND **play footsie*** (Informal.) **1.** to attract someone's attention by touching feet under the table; to flirt with someone. □ *Bill was trying to play footsie with Sally at the dinner table. The hostess was appalled.* □ *They shouldn't play footsie at a formal dinner.* **2.*** to get involved with someone; to collaborate with someone. (Informal.) □ *The treasurer got fired for playing footsie with the vice president.* □ *When politicians play footsie, there is usually something illegal going on.*

play for keeps* to take an action which is permanent or final. (Slang.) □ *Mary told me that Tom wants to marry me. I didn't know he wanted to play for keeps.* □ *I like to play cards and make money, but I don't like to play for keeps.*

play hard to get to be coy, shy, and fickle. (Usually refers to someone of the opposite sex.) □ *Why can't we go out? Why do you play hard to get?* □ *Sally annoys all the boys because she plays hard to get.*

play havoc with someone or something See *raise havoc with someone or something.*

play hob with someone or something See *raise hob with someone or something.*

play hooky* to not go to school or to some important meeting. (Slang.) □ *Why aren't you in school? Are you playing hooky?* □ *I don't have time for the sales meeting today, so I think I'll just play hooky.*

play into someone's hands (for a person one is scheming against) to assist one on one's scheming without realizing it. □ *John is doing exactly what I hoped he would. He's playing into my hands.* □ *John played into my hands by taking the coins he found in my desk. I caught him and had him arrested.*

play it cool* to act calm and unconcerned. (Slang.) □ *No one will suspect anything if you play it cool.* □ *Don't get angry, Bob. Play it cool.*

play it safe to be or act safe; to do something safely. □ *You should play it safe and take your umbrella.* □ *If you have a cold or the flu, play it safe and go to bed.*

play on something to have an effect on something; to manage something for a desired effect. (The *on* can be replaced by *upon.*) □ *The clerk played on my sense of responsibility in trying to get me to buy the book.* □ *See if you can get her to confess by playing on her sense of guilt.*

play one's cards close to the chest AND **play one's cards close to one's vest** (for someone) to work or negotiate in a careful and private manner. □ *It's hard to figure out what John is up to because he plays his cards close to his chest.* □ *Don't let them know what you're up to. Play your cards close to your vest.*

play one's cards right* AND **play one's cards well*** to work or negotiate correctly and skillfully. (Informal.) □ *If you play your cards right, you can get whatever you want.* □ *She didn't play her cards well, and she ended up with something less than what she wanted.*

play one's trump card* to use a special trick; to use one's most powerful or effective strategy or device. (Informal.) □ *I won't play my trump card until I have tried everything else.* □ *I thought that the whole situation was hopeless until Mary played her trump card and solved the whole problem.*

play politics **1.** to negotiate politically. □ *Everybody at city hall is playing politics as usual.* □ *If you're elected as a member of a political party, you'll have to play politics.* **2.** to allow politics to dominate in matters where principle should prevail. □ *Look, I came here to discuss this trial, not play politics.* □ *They're not making reasonable decisions. They're playing politics.*

play possum* to pretend to be inactive, unobservant, asleep, or dead. (Folksy. The *possum* is an *opossum.*) □ *I knew that Bob wasn't asleep. He was just playing possum.* □ *I can't tell if this animal is dead or just playing possum.*

play second fiddle to someone AND **play second fiddle** to be in a subordinate position to someone. □ *I'm tired of playing second fiddle to John.* □ *I'm better trained than he, and I have more experience. I shouldn't play second fiddle.*

play someone for something* to treat

259

someone like (a) something. (Slang. Compare to *take someone for someone or something.*) □ *Don't play me for a fool! I know what's going on.* □ *They played her for a jerk, but were they surprised!*

play someone off against someone else to scheme in a manner that pits two of your adversaries against one another. □ *Bill wanted to beat me up and so did Bob. I did some fast talking, and they ended up fighting with each other. I really played Bill off against Bob.* □ *The President played Congress off against the Senate and ended up getting his own way.*

play someone or something down AND **play down someone or something** to lessen the effect or importance of someone or something. □ *They tried to play down her earlier arrest.* □ *John is a famous actor, but the director tried to play John down as just another member of the cast.*

play someone or something up AND **play up someone or something** to make someone or something seem to be more important. □ *The director tried to play up Ann, but she was not really a star.* □ *Try to play up the good qualities of our product.*

play something 1. to participate in a game. □ *I want to play baseball when I grow up.* □ *Let's play a game!* 2. to play music; to play a musical instrument. □ *I practice every day so I can play the piano like a real musician.* □ *I'm learning to play Bach on the organ.* 3. to pretend to be something. □ *Ann played Carmen in the New York performance of the opera.* □ *She played the title role in the opera.*

play something by ear 1. to be able to play a piece of music after just listening to it a few times, without looking at the notes. □ *I can play* Stardust *by ear.* □ *Some people can play Chopin's music by ear.* 2. AND **play by ear** to play a musical instrument well, without formal training. □ *John can play the piano by ear.* □ *If I could play by ear, I wouldn't have to take lessons—or practice!*

play the field* to date many different

people rather than going steady. (Informal. See *go steady with someone.*) □ *When Tom told Ann goodbye, he said he wanted to play the field.* □ *He said he wanted to play the field while he was still young.*

play the market* to invest in the stock market. (Informal. As if it were a game or as if it were gambling.) □ *Would you rather put your money in the bank or play the market?* □ *I've learned my lesson playing the market. I lost a fortune.*

play to the gallery to perform in a manner that will get the strong approval of the audience; to perform in a manner that will get the approval of the lower elements in the audience. □ *John is a competent actor, but he has a tendency to play to the gallery.* □ *When he made the rude remark, he was just playing to the gallery.*

play tricks on someone AND **play tricks** to trick or confuse someone. □ *I thought I saw a camel over there. I guess that my eyes are playing tricks on me.* □ *Please don't play tricks on your little brother. It makes him cry.*

play up to someone to try to gain someone's favor. □ *Bill is always playing up to the teacher.* □ *Ann played up to Bill as if she wanted him to marry her.*

play with fire* to take a big risk. (Informal. Also used literally.) □ *If you accuse her of stealing, you'll be playing with fire.* □ *I wouldn't try that if I were you—unless you like playing with fire.*

played out worn out; spent; exhausted. □ *This charcoal is just about played out.* □ *The batteries in this flashlight are almost played out.*

plow into someone or something to crash or push into someone or something. □ *The car plowed into the ditch.* □ *The runner plowed into another player.*

pluck up someone's courage AND **pluck up** to increase one's courage a bit. □ *Come on, Ann, make the dive. Pluck up your courage and do it.* □ *Pluck up, Ann! You can do it!*

plug away at something AND **peg away at something; peg away; plug away** to keep trying something; to keep working at something. □ *John kept pegging* away at the trumpet until he became pretty good at it. □ *I'm not very good at it, but I keep plugging away.* □ *If you keep plugging away at your biology, you can't help but succeed.*

plug something in AND **plug in something** to place a plug into a receptacle. (*In* can be replaced with *into*.) □ *Please plug in this lamp.* □ *This television set won't work unless you plug it in!*

plug something up AND **plug up something** to stop or fill up a hole, crack, or gap. □ *You have to plug up the cracks to keep out the cold.* □ *Take out the nail and plug the hole up with something.*

plunk someone or something down* AND **plunk down someone or something*** to toss, place, or drop something. (Informal.) □ *He plunked down a quarter for the newspaper.* □ *The wrestler plunked his opponent down with great force.*

point someone or something out AND **point out someone or something** to select or indicate someone or something (from a group). □ *She pointed out the boy who took her purse.* □ *Everyone pointed out the error.* □ *I'd like to point out to you that this is the second time you have been late this week.*

point something up AND **point up something** to emphasize something; to demonstrate a fact. □ *This kind of incident points up the flaws in your system.* □ *I'd like to point your approach up by citing some authorities who agree with you.*

poke about See the following entry.

poke around AND **poke about** to look or search around. □ *I've been poking around in the library looking for some statistics.* □ *I don't mind if you look in my drawer for a paper clip, but please don't poke about.*

poke fun at someone AND **poke fun** to make fun of someone; to ridicule someone. □ *Stop poking fun at me! It's not nice.* □ *Bob is always poking fun.*

poke one's nose into something AND **poke one's nose in; stick one's nose into something; stick one's nose in** to interfere with something; to be nosy about something. □ *I wish you'd stop poking your nose into my business.* □ *She was too upset for me to stick my nose in and ask what was wrong.*

polish something off AND **polish off something** to finish something off. □ *Bob polished off the rest of the pie.* □ *There is just a little bit of work left. It won't take any time to polish it off.*

poop out* to quit; to wear out and stop. (Slang.) □ *I'm so tired I could poop out right here.* □ *My car sounded like it was going to poop out.* ALSO: **pooped out*** (for a person or animal) to be exhausted. (Slang.) □ *The horse was pooped out and could run no more.* □ *I can't go on. I'm pooped out.*

pop off* to make a wisecrack or smart aleck remark. (Informal.) □ *If you pop off one more time, you'll have to stay after school.* □ *Bob keeps popping off at the worst times.*

pop one's cork* (Slang.) **1.** to suddenly become mentally disturbed; to go crazy. □ *I was so upset that I nearly popped my cork.* □ *They put him away because he popped his cork.* **2.** to become very angry. □ *My mother popped her cork when she heard about my grades.* □ *Calm down! Don't pop your cork.*

pop the question* to ask someone to marry you. (Informal.) □ *I was surprised when he popped the question.* □ *I've been waiting for years for someone to pop the question.*

pop up* (Informal.) **1.** (for a baseball batter) to hit a baseball which goes upward rather than outward. □ *The catcher came to bat and popped up.* □ *I hope I don't pop up this time.* **2.** (for a baseball) to fly upward rather than outward. □ *The ball popped up and went foul.* □ *The ball will always pop up if you hit it in a certain way.* **3.** to arise suddenly; to appear without warning. □ *New problems keep popping up all the time.* □ *Billy popped up out of nowhere and scared his mother.*

possessed by something under the control of something; obsessed with something. □ *She acted as if she were possessed by evil spirits.* □ *He was possessed by a powerful sense of guilt.*

possessed of something having something. (Formal.) □ *Bill was possessed of* *an enormous sense of self worth.* □ *The Smiths were possessed of a great deal of fine ranch land.*

pound a beat* to walk a route. (Informal. Usually said of a police patrol officer.) □ *The patrolman pounded the same beat for years and years.* □ *Pounding a beat will wreck your feet.*

pound something out AND **pound out something** 1. to make something flat or smooth by pounding. □ *They used hammers to pound out the dents.* □ *Please pound this out until it's flat.* 2.* to play something loudly on the piano. (Slang. Compare to *belt something out.*) □ *Listen to her pound out that song.* □ *Don't pound the music out! Just play it.* 3.* to type something on a typewriter. (Slang.) □ *It'll take just a few hours to pound out this letter.* □ *Please pound it out again. There are six errors.*

pound the pavement* to walk through the streets looking for a job. (Informal.) □ *I spent two months pounding the pavement after the factory I worked for closed.* □ *Hey, Bob. You'd better get busy pounding those nails unless you want to be out pounding the pavement.*

pour cold water on something AND **dash cold water on something; throw cold water on something** to discourage doing something; to reduce enthusiasm for something. □ *When my father said I couldn't have the car, he poured cold water on my plans.* □ *John threw cold water on the whole project by refusing to participate.*

pour it on thick See *lay it on thick.*

pour money down the drain* to waste money; to throw money away. (Informal.) □ *What a waste! You're just pouring money down the drain.* □ *Don't buy any more of that low quality merchandise. That's just throwing money down the drain.*

pour oil on troubled water* to calm things down. (A cliché. If oil is poured onto rough seas during a storm, the water will become more calm.) □ *That was a good thing to say to John. It helped pour oil on troubled water. Now he looks happy.* □ *Bob is the kind of person who pours oil on troubled water.*

pour one's heart out to someone AND

pour one's heart out; pour out one's heart to someone; pour out one's heart to tell all one's hopes, fears, and feelings to someone. □ *She was so upset. She poured her heart out to Sally.* □ *She sat there for over an hour talking—pouring out her heart.*

pour something out AND **pour out something** to empty (a container) of something. □ *John poured the rice out of the jar.* □ *Ann poured the cider out of the bottle.* □ *Sally poured out the glass of water.*

power behind the throne* the person who controls the person who is apparently in charge. (A cliché.) □ *Mr. Smith appears to run the shop, but his brother is the power behind the throne.* □ *They say that the vice president is the power behind the throne.*

practice what you preach* to do what you advise other people to do. (A cliché.) □ *If you'd practice what you preach, you'd be better off.* □ *You give good advice. Why not practice what you preach?*

praise someone or something to the skies* to give someone much praise. (A cliché.) □ *He wasn't very good, but his friends praised him to the skies.* □ *They liked your pie. Everyone praised it to the skies.*

press one's luck See *push one's luck.*

Pretty is as pretty does.* You should do pleasant things if you wish to be considered pleasant. (A cliché.) □ *Now, Sally. Let's be nice. Pretty is as pretty does.* □ *My great aunt always used to say "pretty is as pretty does" to my sister.*

pretty state of affairs AND **fine state of affairs** an unpleasant state of affairs. (See also *fine kettle of fish.*) □ *This is a pretty state of affairs, and it's all your fault.* □ *What a fine state of affairs you've got us into.*

prevail upon someone AND **prevail on someone** to ask or beg someone (for a favor). □ *Can I prevail upon you to give me some help?* □ *Perhaps you could prevail on my brother for a loan.*

prey upon someone or something AND **prey on someone or something** 1. [with *someone*] to make a practice of cheating or swindling someone. □ *The crooks preyed upon widows.* □ *Watch out for swindlers who prey on elderly people.* **2.** [with *something*] to exploit someone's fears or weakness. □ *They were unable to prey on our fears.* □ *Please don't prey upon the fact that they aren't well educated.* **3.** [with *something*] to use something for food. (Said of animals.) □ *Cats prey on mice.* □ *Hawks prey upon small birds.*

prick up one's ears* to listen more closely. (Informal.) □ *At the sound of my voice, my dog pricked up her ears.* □ *I pricked up my ears when I heard my name mentioned.*

pride oneself on something AND **pride oneself in something** to take special pride in something. □ *Ann prides herself on her apple pies.* □ *John prides himself in his ability to make people feel at ease.*

promise the moon to someone AND **promise someone the moon; promise the moon** to make extravagant promises to someone. □ *Bill will promise you the moon, but he won't live up to his promises.* □ *My boss promised the moon, but only paid the minimum wage.*

psyche someone out* AND **psyche out someone*** (Slang. Pronounced as if it were spelled *sike*.) **1.** to figure out someone psychologically. □ *I think I've psyched out my opponent so I can beat him.* □ *Don't try to psyche me out. Just be my friend.* **2.** to confuse someone; to cause someone to go crazy. □ *All that bright light psyched me out. I couldn't think straight.* □ *They psyched out the enemy causing them to jump into the river.* ALSO: **psyche out*** to go crazy. (Slang.) □ *I don't know what happened to me. Suddenly I psyched out and started yelling.* ALSO: **psyched out*** confused and disoriented. (Slang.) □ *What an upsetting day! I'm really psyched out.*

psyche someone up* AND **psyche up someone*** to cause someone to be enthusiastic about doing something. (Slang.) □ *The coach psyched up the team before the game.* □ *I need someone to psyche me up before I go on stage.* ALSO: **psyched up*** excited and

enthusiastic. (Slang.) □ *I can play a great tennis game if I'm psyched up.*

pull a boner* to do something stupid or silly. (Slang.) □ *Boy, I really pulled a boner! I'm so dumb.* □ *If you pull a boner like that again, you're fired!*

pull a fast one* to succeed in an act of deception. (Slang.) □ *She was pulling a fast one when she said she had a headache and went home.* □ *Don't try to pull a fast one with me! I know what you're doing.*

pull a stunt on someone AND **pull a stunt; pull a trick on someone; pull a trick** to deceive someone. □ *Let's pull a trick on the teacher.* □ *Don't you dare pull a stunt like that!*

pull a trick on someone See the previous entry.

pull ahead of someone or something AND **pull ahead** to pass or surpass someone or something. □ *I pulled ahead of everyone in my math class.* □ *Our car pulled ahead of theirs.*

pull in somewhere AND **pull in** to drive into a place and stop. □ *Please pull in at this service station.* □ *Okay, I'll pull in and get some gas.*

pull one's punches* (Slang.) **1.** (for a boxer) to strike with light blows to enable the other boxer to win. □ *Bill has been barred from the boxing ring for pulling his punches.* □ *"I never pulled my punches in my life!" cried Tom.* **2.** to hold back in one's criticism. (Usually in the negative. The *one's* can be replaced with *any*.) □ *I didn't pull any punches. I told her just what I thought of her.* □ *The teacher doesn't pull any punches when it comes to discipline.*

pull one's weight See *carry one's own weight*.

pull oneself together to become emotionally stabilized; to *regain one's composure*. □ *Now, calm down. Pull yourself together.* □ *I'll be all right as soon as I can pull myself together.*

pull oneself up by one's own bootstraps* AND **pull oneself up*** to achieve (something) through one's own efforts. (A cliché.) □ *They simply don't have the resources to pull themselves up by their own bootstraps.* □ *If I could have pulled myself up, I'd have done it by now.*

pull over to drive to the side of the road and stop. □ *Okay, pull over right here. I'll get out here.* □ *I'll pull over up ahead where there is a sidewalk.*

pull rank on someone AND **pull rank** to assert one's rank, authority, or position over someone when making a request or giving an order. □ *Don't pull rank on me! I don't have to do what you say!* □ *When she couldn't get her way politely, she pulled rank and really got some action.*

pull someone or something down AND **pull down someone or something** **1.** to lower or haul down someone or something. □ *The boy was on the roof, so we pulled him down.* □ *There is a kite in the tree. Let's pull it down.* **2.** [with *someone*] to degrade someone; to humiliate someone. □ *I'm afraid that your friends are pulling you down. Your manners used to be much better.* □ *My bad habits are pulling me down.* **3.*** [with *something*] to earn a certain amount of money. (Slang.) □ *She's able to pull down $400 a week.* □ *I wish I could pull down a salary like that.* **4.** [with *something*] to demolish something; to raze something. □ *They are going to pull down the old building today.* □ *Why do they want to pull it down? Why not remodel it?* **5.** [with *something*] to lower or reduce the amount of something. □ *Let's see if we can pull down your temperature.* □ *That last test pulled down my grade.*

pull someone or something through something AND **pull someone or something through** (See also *pull through.*) **1.** to help someone or something pass through something. □ *I pulled her through the window.* □ *We pulled the rope through the hole.* **2.** [with *someone*] to help someone survive something. (See also *pull through.*) □ *With the help of the doctor, we pulled her through her illness.* □ *With lots of encouragement, we pulled her through.*

pull someone's leg* to kid, fool, or trick someone. (Informal.) □ *You don't mean that. You're just pulling my leg.* □ *Don't believe him. He's just pulling your leg.*

pull someone's or something's teeth* to reduce the power of someone or something. (Informal. Also used literally.) □ *The mayor tried to pull the teeth of the new law.* □ *The city council pulled the teeth of the new mayor.*

pull something off AND **pull off something** **1.** to tear something away. □ *I don't want to pull off the bandage. It'll hurt.* □ *Go ahead. Pull it off.* **2.*** to manage to make something happen. (Slang.) □ *Do you think you can pull this project off?* □ *Yes, I can pull it off.*

pull something on someone **1.** to surprise someone with a weapon. □ *He pulled a knife on me!* □ *The robber pulled a gun on the bank teller.* **2.** to play a trick on someone; to deceive someone with a trick. □ *You wouldn't pull a trick on me, would you?* □ *Who would play a trick like that on an old lady?*

pull something out of a hat AND **pull something out of thin air** to produce something as if by magic. □ *This is a serious problem, and we just can't pull a solution out of a hat.* □ *I'm sorry, but I don't have a pen. What do you want me to do, pull one out of thin air?*

pull something out of thin air See the previous entry.

pull something together to organize something; to arrange something. (Compare to *scrape something together.*) □ *How about a party? I'll see if I can pull something together for Friday night.* □ *This place is a mess. Please pull things together.*

pull strings to use influence (with someone to get something done). □ *I can get it done easily by pulling strings.* □ *Is it possible to get anything done around here without pulling strings?*

pull the plug on someone or something* AND **pull the plug*** to cause someone or something to end; to reduce the power or effectiveness of someone or something. (Informal.) □ *Jane pulled the plug on the whole project.* □ *The mayor was doing a fine job until the treasurer pulled the plug because there was no more money.*

pull the rug out from under someone AND **pull the rug out** to make someone ineffective. □ *The treasurer pulled the rug out from under the mayor.* □ *Things were going along fine until the treasurer pulled the rug out.*

pull the wool over someone's eyes* to deceive someone. (A cliché.) □ *You can't pull the wool over my eyes. I know what's going on.* □ *Don't try to pull the wool over her eyes. She's too smart.*

pull through to get better; to recover from a serious illness or other problem. □ *She's very ill, but I think she'll pull through.* □ *Oh, I hope she pulls through.*

pull up See *haul up somewhere.*

pull up stakes to move to another place. (As if one were pulling up tent stakes.) □ *I've been here long enough. It's time to pull up stakes.* □ *I hate the thought of having to pull up stakes.*

push one's luck AND **press one's luck** to expect continued good fortune; to expect to continue to escape bad luck. □ *You're okay so far, but don't push your luck.* □ *Bob pressed his luck too much and got into a lot of trouble.*

push someone to the wall AND **press someone to the wall** to force someone into a position where there is only one choice to make; to put someone in a defensive position. (Also used literally. See also *have one's back to the wall.*) □ *There was little else I could do. They pushed me to the wall.* □ *When we pressed him to the wall, he told us where the cookies were hidden.*

push the panic button* AND **press the panic button*** to panic; to become anxious or panicky. (Slang.) □ *I do okay taking tests as long as I don't push the panic button.* □ *Whatever you do, don't press the panic button.*

pushing up daisies* dead. (Folksy.) □ *If you don't drive safely, you'll be pushing up daisies.* □ *We'll all be pushing up daisies in the long run.*

put a bee in someone's bonnet See *have a bee in one's bonnet.*

put a stop to something AND **put an end to something** to bring something to an end. □ *I want you to put a stop to all this bad behavior.* □ *Please put an end to this conversation.*

put all one's eggs in one basket* to risk everything at once. (A cliché. Often negative.) □ *Don't put all your eggs in one basket. Then everything won't be lost if there is a catastrophe.* □ *John only applied to the one college he wanted to go to. He put all his eggs in one basket.*

put an end to something See *put a stop to something.*

put ideas into someone's head to suggest something—usually something bad—to someone (who would not have thought of it otherwise). □ *Bill keeps getting into trouble. Please don't put ideas into his head.* □ *Bob would get along all right if other kids didn't put ideas into his head.*

put in a good word for someone AND **put in a good word** to say something (to someone) in support of someone. □ *I hope you get the job. I'll put in a good word for you.* □ *Yes, I want the job. If you see the boss, please put in a good word.*

put in an appearance to appear (somewhere) for just a little while. (Compare to *make an appearance.*) □ *I couldn't stay for the whole party, so I just put in an appearance and left.* □ *Even if you can't stay for the whole thing, at least put in an appearance.*

put in one's two cents worth* AND **put in one's two cents***; **put one's two cents in*** to add one's comments (to something). (Informal.) □ *Can I put in my two cents worth?* □ *Sure, go ahead—put your two cents in.*

put off by someone or something See *put someone or something off.*

put on to pretend; to act as if something were true. (Compare to *let on.* See also *put someone or something on.*) □ *Ann wasn't really angry. She was just putting on.* □ *I can't believe she was just putting on. She really looked mad.*

put on airs to act superior. □ *Stop putting on airs. You're just human like the rest of us.* □ *Ann is always putting on airs. You'd think she was a queen.*

put on an act to pretend that one is something other than what one is. (See also *put on* at *let on.*) □ *Be yourself, Ann. Stop putting on an act.* □ *You don't have to put on an act. We accept you the way you are.*

put on one's thinking cap* to start thinking in a serious manner. (A cliché. Usually used with children.) □

265

All right now, let's put on our thinking caps and do some arithmetic. □ *It's time to put on our thinking caps, children.*

put on the dog* to dress or entertain in an extravagant or showy manner. (Informal.) □ *The Smiths really put on the dog at their party last Saturday.* □ *They're always putting on the dog.*

put on the feed bag* to eat a meal. (Folksy and slang.) □ *It's noon—time to put on the feed bag.* □ *I didn't put on the feed bag until about 8:00 last night.*

put on weight to gain weight; to grow fat. □ *I have to go on a diet because I've been putting on a little weight lately.* □ *The doctor says I need to put on some weight.*

put one in one's place to rebuke someone; to remind one of one's (lower) rank or station. □ *The boss put me in my place for criticizing her.* □ *Then her boss put her in her place for being rude.*

put one through one's paces to make one demonstrate what one can do; to make one do one's job thoroughly. (See also *put something through its paces*.) □ *The boss really put me through my paces today. I'm tired.* □ *I tried out for a part in the play, and the director really put me through my paces.*

put one's back to something 1. to apply great physical effort to lift or move something. □ *All right, you guys. Put your backs into moving this piano.* □ *You can lift it if you put your back into it.* **2.** to apply a lot of mental or creative effort to doing something. □ *If we put our backs to it, we can bake twelve dozen cookies today.* □ *The artist put his back to finishing the picture on time.*

put one's best foot forward* to act or appear at one's best; to try to make a good impression. (A cliché.) □ *When you apply for a job, you should always put your best foot forward.* □ *I try to put my best foot forward whenever I meet someone for the first time.*

put one's cards on the table* AND **lay one's cards on the table*** to reveal everything; to be open and honest with someone. (Informal.) □ *Come on, John, lay your cards on the table. Tell me what you really think.* □ *Why don't we both put our cards on the table?*

put one's dibs on something See *have dibs on something*.

put one's finger on something* to identify something as very important. (Informal.) □ *Ann put her finger on the cause of the problem.* □ *Yes, she really put her finger on it.*

put one's foot down about something* AND **put one's foot down*** to become adamant about something. (Informal.) □ *Ann put her foot down about what kind of car she wanted.* □ *She doesn't put her foot down very often, but when she does, she really means it.*

put one's foot in one's mouth AND **put one's foot in it; stick one's foot in one's mouth** to say something which you regret; to say something stupid, insulting, or hurtful. □ *When I told Ann that her hair was more beautiful than I had ever seen it, I really put my foot in my mouth. It was a wig.* □ *I put my foot in it by telling John's secret.*

put one's hand to the plow* to begin to do a big and important task; to undertake a major effort. (A cliché.) □ *If John would only put his hand to the plow, he could do an excellent job.* □ *You'll never accomplish anything if you don't put your hand to the plow.*

put one's hands on something AND **put one's hand on something** to locate and acquire something. (Compare to *get one's hands on someone or something*.) □ *I wish I could put my hands on a 1954 Chevrolet.* □ *If I could put my hands on that book, I could find the information I need.*

put one's house in order to put one's business or personal affairs into good order. (Not used literally.) □ *There was some trouble at work and the manager was told to put his house in order.* □ *Every now and then, I have to put my house in order. Then life becomes more manageable.*

put one's nose to the grindstone to keep busy doing one's work. (Also with *have* and *get*, as in the examples.) □ *The boss told me to put my nose to the grindstone.* □ *I've had my nose to the grindstone ever since I started working here.* □ *If the other people in this office would get their noses to the grind-*

stone, more work would get done. ALSO:
keep one's nose to the grindstone to
keep busy continuously over a period
of time. □ *The manager told me to
keep my nose to the grindstone or be
fired.*

put one's oar in AND **put in one's oar**
to give help; to interfere by giving
advice; to *put in one's two cents worth.*
□ *You don't need to put your oar in. I
don't need your advice.* □ *I'm sorry. I
shouldn't have put in my oar.*

put one's shoulder to the wheel to get
busy. (Not used literally.) □ *You won't
accomplish anything unless you put your
shoulder to the wheel.* □ *I put my shoulder to the wheel and finished the job
quickly.*

put oneself in someone else's place
See *in someone else's shoes.*

put out See *put someone or something out.*

put out feelers AND **put out some feelers** to attempt to find out something
without being too obvious. □ *I wanted
to get a new job, so I put out some feelers.* □ *The manager was mean to everyone in the office, so everyone put out
feelers in an attempt to find new jobs.*

put someone down as something
to assume that someone is something.
(See also *put someone or something
down.*) □ *He was so rude that I put him
down as someone to be avoided.* □ *If
you act silly all the time, people will put
you down as a fool.*

put someone down for something AND
put someone down to put someone's
name on a list of people who volunteer
to do something or give an amount of
money. □ *Can I put you down for ten
dollars?* □ *We're having a picnic, and
you're invited. Everyone is bringing
something. Can I put you down for potato salad?*

put someone on a pedestal* to respect,
admire, or worship a person. (A
cliché.) □ *He has put her on a pedestal
and thinks she can do no wrong.* □ *Don't
put me on a pedestal. I'm only human.*

put someone on the spot to ask someone embarrassing questions; to demand
that someone produce as expected. □
Don't put me on the spot. I can't give

you an answer. □ *The boss put Bob on
the spot and demanded that he do everything he had promised.*

put someone or something across AND
get someone or something across
1. [with *someone*] to present someone
in a good way or a good light. □ *I don't
want Tom to make the speech. He
doesn't put himself across well.* □ *I get
myself across in situations like this. I'll
do it.* **2.** to make a clear explanation of
something; to explain oneself clearly.
□ *The teacher got the idea across with
the help of pictures.* □ *I'm taking a
course in public speaking to help put
myself across better.* **3.** [with
something] to convince someone of
something; to get a plan accepted. □
*After many weeks of trying, we were
unable to put our plan across. They
refused to accept it.* □ *We just couldn't
get it across.*

**put someone or something at some-
one's disposal** to make someone or
something available to someone; to offer
someone or something to someone. □
*I'd be glad to help you if you need me.
I put myself at your disposal.* □ *I put
my car at my neighbor's disposal.*

put someone or something away AND
put away someone or something
(Compare to *lay someone or something away.*) **1.** [with *something*] to put
something into a safe place; to put something where it belongs. □ *Billy, please
put away your toys.* □ *No! I won't put
them away.* **2.*** [with *someone*] to kill
someone. (Slang.) □ *The gangster
threatened to put me away if I told the
police.* □ *They've put away witnesses in
the past.* **3.** [with *someone*] to bury someone. □ *My uncle died last week. They
put him away on Saturday.* **4.** [with
someone] to have someone put into a
mental institution. □ *My uncle became
irrational, and they put him away.* □
They put away my aunt the year before.

put someone or something down AND
put down someone or something
1.* to belittle or degrade someone or
something. (Slang.) □ *It's an old car,
but that's no reason to put it down.* □
*Please stop putting me down all the time.
It hurts my feelings.* **2.** [with

something] to repress or (figuratively) crush something. □ *The army was called to put down the rebellion.* □ *The police used tear gas to put the riot down.* **3.** [with *something*] to write something down. □ *I'll give you the address. Please put it down.* □ *I'll put it down in my address book.* **4.** [with *something*] to land an aircraft. □ *The pilot put the plane down exactly on time.* □ *I can't put the plane down in the rain.* **5.** [with *something*] to take the life of an animal, such as a pet which is suffering. (This is usually done by a veterinarian.) □ *We had to put our dog down. She was suffering so.* □ *It's very difficult to put one's pet down.*

put someone or something off AND **put off someone or something 1.** [with *someone*] to divert or avoid someone. □ *I don't wish to see Mr. Brown now. Please put him off.* □ *I won't talk to reporters. Tell them something which will put them off.* **2.** [with *someone*] to upset or distress someone. □ *She always puts me off. She's so rude.* □ *I try not to put off people.* **3.** [with *something*] to delay something; to postpone something. □ *I had to put off my appointment with the doctor.* □ *It's raining, so we'll have to put the picnic off.* ALSO: **put off by someone or something** distressed or repelled by someone or something. □ *I was really put off by your behavior.* □ *We were all put off by the unfairness of the rules.*

put someone or something on 1. [with *someone*] AND **put on something** to dress in something; to put on and wear clothing. □ *Here, put on this hat.* □ *I don't want to put that hat on!* **2.*** [with *someone*] to tease or deceive someone. (Slang.) □ *Oh, you're not serious. You're putting me on.* □ *Stop putting me on!*

put someone or something on hold (See also *on hold*.) **1.** [with *someone*] to stop all activity or communication with someone. □ *John put Ann on hold and started dating Mary.* □ *"You can't just put me on hold!" cried Ann.* **2.** [with *someone*] to leave someone waiting on a telephone call. □ *Please don't put me on hold. I'll call back later when you*

aren't so busy. □ *I'll have to put you on hold while I look up the information.* **3.** [with *something*] to postpone something; to stop the progress of something. □ *They put the project on hold until they got enough money to finish it.* □ *Sorry, but we must put your plan on hold.*

put someone or something out AND **put out someone or something 1.** to make someone or something go outside. □ *Please put the dog out.* □ *The boys were being a disturbance so the usher put them out.* **2.** [with *something*] to extinguish something. □ *Put out the fire before you go to bed.* □ *My grandfather told me to put out the light and go to bed.* **3.** [with *someone*] to distress or inconvenience someone. □ *I'd like to have a ride home, but not if it puts you out.* □ *Don't worry. It won't put out anybody.* **4.** [with *something*] to publish something. □ *They are putting the book out next month.* □ *When did you put the article out?* **5.** [with *someone*] to make someone "out" in baseball. □ *The pitcher put the runner out.* □ *I thought the catcher put him out.* ALSO: **put out** irritated; bothered. □ *John behaved rudely at the party, and the hostess was quite put out.*

put someone or something out of one's mind to forget someone or something; to make an effort to stop thinking about someone or something. (Almost the same as *get someone or something out of one's mind*.) □ *Try to put it out of your mind.* □ *I can't seem to put him out of my mind.*

put someone or something out of the way (Compare to *get someone or something out of the way*.) **1.** [with *something*] to remove something from the pathway. □ *Please put that pile of magazines out of the way.* □ *Put those out of the way, too.* **2.*** [with *someone*] to remove someone from the scene; to kill someone. (Slang.) □ *The robber threatened to put me out of the way.* □ *Are you threatening to put him out of the way?*

put someone or something out to pasture* to retire someone or something.

(Informal. Originally said of a horse which was too old to work.) □ *Please don't put me out to pasture. I have lots of good years left.* □ *This car has reached the end of the line. It's time to put it out to pasture.*

put someone or something to bed
1. [with *someone*] to help someone—usually a child—get into a bed. □ *Come on, Billy, it's time for me to put you to bed.* □ *I want grandpa to put me to bed.* **2.** [with *something*] to complete work on something and send it on to the next step in production, especially in publishing. □ *This edition is finished. Let's put it to bed.* □ *Finish the editing of this book and put it to bed.*

put someone or something to sleep
1. to kill someone or something. (Euphemistic.) □ *We had to put our dog to sleep.* □ *The robber said he'd put us to sleep forever if we didn't cooperate.* **2.** to cause someone or something to sleep, perhaps through drugs or anesthesia. □ *The doctor put the patient to sleep before the operation.* □ *I put the cat to sleep by stroking its tummy.* **3.** [with *someone*] to bore someone. □ *That dull lecture put me to sleep.* □ *Her long story almost put me to sleep.*

put someone or something up AND **put up someone or something 1.** [with *something*] to raise up something; to put something up (onto something). □ *Please put the window up.* □ *It's time to put the decorations up.* **2.** [with *someone*] to provide lodging for someone. □ *They were able to put up John for the night.* □ *I hope I can find someone to put me up.* **3.** [with *something*] to preserve and store food by canning or freezing. □ *This year we'll put some strawberries up.* □ *We put up a lot of food every year.* **4.** [with *something*] to offer something, such as an idea. □ *Let me put up a different idea.* □ *We need a better idea. Who'll put one up?* **5.** [with *someone*] to run someone as a candidate. □ *We're putting up Ann for treasurer.* □ *I think you should put someone else up.* **6.** [with *something*] to prepare portions of food—usually a lunch—to be eaten during the day. □ *The cook put up a sack*

lunch for me. □ *I put my own lunch up.* **7.** [with *something*] to build a building, a sign, a fence, a wall, etc. □ *The city put up a fence next to our house.* □ *We'll put a garage up next month.* **8.** [with *something*] to provide the money for something. □ *Who will put up the money for my education?* □ *The government put the money up for the cost of construction.* **9.** [with *something*] to shape and arrange one's hair (with curlers, hairpins, etc.). □ *I can't go out because I just put my hair up.* □ *I put up my hair every night.* **10.** [with *something*] to make a struggle, a fight, etc. (Usually *put up something*, and not *put something up*.) □ *Did he put up a fight?* □ *No, he only put up a bit of a struggle.* **11.*** [with *something*] to put something away. (Folksy or old fashioned.) □ *Put up your toys and go to bed.* □ *I don't want to put them up.*

put someone through the wringer* to give someone a difficult time. (Informal.) □ *They are really putting me through the wringer at school.* □ *The boss put Bob through the wringer over this contract.*

put someone to shame to show someone up; to embarrass someone; to make someone ashamed. □ *Your excellent efforts put us all to shame.* □ *I put him to shame by telling everyone about his bad behavior.*

put someone to the test to test someone; to see what someone can achieve. □ *I think I can jump that far, but no one has ever put me to the test.* □ *I'm going to put you to the test right now!*

put someone up to something to cause someone to do something; to bribe someone to do something; to give someone the idea of doing something. □ *Who put you up to it?* □ *Nobody put me up to it. I thought it up myself.*

put someone wise to someone or something* to inform someone about someone or something. (Informal.) □ *I put her wise to the way we do things around here.* □ *I didn't know she was taking money. Mary put me wise to her.*

put someone's nose out of joint* to offend someone; to cause someone to feel slighted or insulted. (Informal.)

□ *I'm afraid I put his nose out of joint by not inviting him to the picnic.* □ *There is no reason to put your nose out of joint. I meant no harm.*

put something aside See *set something aside.*

put something by* AND **lay something by*** to reserve a portion of something; to preserve and store something, such as food. (Folksy.) □ *I put some money by for a rainy day.* □ *I laid some eggs by for our use tomorrow.*

put something down to something AND **set something down to something** to explain something as being caused by something else. □ *I put his bad humor down to his illness.* □ *We set your failure down to your emotional upset.*

put something forward to state an idea; to advance an idea. (Also used literally.) □ *Toward the end of the meeting, Sally put an idea forward.* □ *Now, I'd like to put something forward.*

put something in AND **put in something** (Also used literally.) **1.** to submit something. □ *I put in a request for a new typewriter.* □ *In fact, I put it in some time ago.* **2.** to spend an amount of time (doing something). □ *I put in four months on that project.* □ *You put how much time in?*

put something in the way of someone AND **put something in the way** to put a (figurative or literal) barrier in someone's way. □ *I hate to put something in the way of your happiness, but I'm afraid that your husband is gravely ill.* □ *You certainly have put something in the way.*

put something into order AND **get something into order** to make something orderly. □ *I'll put your papers into order as soon as possible.* □ *I'll be able to get my office into order only when I get free from other things.*

put something into practice to start using a scheme or plan. □ *I hope we can put your idea into practice soon.* □ *The mayor hopes to put the new plan into practice after the next election.*

put something into print to have something printed and published. □ *It's true, but I never believed you'd put it into print.* □ *This is a very interesting story. I can't wait to put it into print.*

put something into words to state or utter a thought; to find a way to express a feeling with words. □ *I can hardly put my gratitude into words.* □ *John has a hard time putting his feelings into words.*

put something on ice* AND **put something on the back burner*** to delay or postpone something; to put something on hold. (Informal. Both phrases are also used literally.) □ *I'm afraid that we'll have to put your project on ice for a while.* □ *Just put your idea on ice and keep it there till we get some money.*

put something on paper to write something down. □ *You have a great idea for a novel. Now put it on paper.* □ *I'm sorry, I can't discuss your offer until I see something in writing. Put it on paper, and then we'll talk.*

put something on the back burner See *put something on ice.*

put something on the cuff to buy something on credit; to add to one's credit balance. □ *I'll take two of those, and please put them on the cuff.* □ *I'm sorry, Tom. We can't put anything more on the cuff.*

put something on the line AND **lay something on the line** to speak very firmly and directly about something. □ *She was very mad. She put it on the line, and we have no doubt about what she meant.* □ *All right, you kids. I'm going to lay it on the line. Don't ever do that again if you know what's good for you.*

put something over **1.** to accomplish something; to put something across. □ *This is a very hard thing to explain to a large audience. I hope I can put it over.* □ *This is a big request for money. I go before the board of directors this afternoon, and I hope I can put it over.* **2.** See the following entry.

put something over on someone AND **put something over** to manage to trick or deceive someone. □ *They really put one over on me.* □ *It's easy to put something over if you plan carefully.*

put something plainly to state something firmly and explicitly. □ *To put it plainly, I want you out of this house immediately.* □ *Thank you. I think you've put your feelings quite plainly.*

put something straight AND **set something straight** to clarify something; to straighten something out. □ *He has made such a mess of this report. It'll take hours to put it straight.* □ *I'm sorry I confused you. Let me set it straight.*

put something through its paces to demonstrate how well something operates; to demonstrate all the things something can do. (Compare to *put one through one's paces*.) □ *I was down by the barn watching Sally put her horse through its paces.* □ *This is an excellent can opener. Watch me put it through its paces.*

put something to good use AND **put something to use** to use something. □ *This is a very nice present. I'm sure I'll put it to good use.* □ *I hope you can put these old clothes to use.*

put something to rest AND **lay something to rest** to put an end to a rumor; to finish dealing with something and forget about it. □ *I've heard enough about Ann and her illness. I'd like to put the whole matter to rest.* □ *I'm happy to lay it to rest, but will Jane?*

put something together AND **put together something** 1. to assemble something. □ *I bought a model airplane, but I couldn't put it together.* □ *I need some help to put this thing together.* 2. to consider some facts and arrive at a conclusion. (See also *put two and two together*.) □ *When I put together all the facts, I found the answer.* □ *I couldn't put everything together to figure out the answer in time.*

Put that in your pipe and smoke it!* See how you like that!; It is final, and you have to live with it. (A cliché.) □ *Well, I'm not going to do it, so put that in your pipe and smoke it!* □ *I'm sick of you, and I'm leaving. Put that in your pipe and smoke it!*

put the arm on someone* to apply pressure to someone. (Slang.) □ *John's been putting the arm on Mary to get her to go out with him.* □ *John has been putting the arm on Bill to get him to cooperate.*

put the bite on someone* AND **put the touch on someone*** to try to get money from someone. (Slang.) □ *Tom put the bite on me for ten dollars.* □ *Bill put the touch on me, but I told him to drop dead.*

put the blame on someone or something AND **lay the blame on someone or something; place the blame on someone or something** to blame someone or something. □ *Don't put the blame on me. I didn't do it.* □ *We'll have to place the blame for the damage on the storm.*

put the cart before the horse* to have things in the wrong order; to have things confused and mixed up. (A cliché. Also with *have*.) □ *You're eating your dessert! You've put the cart before the horse.* □ *Slow down and get organized. Don't put the cart before the horse!* □ *John has the cart before the horse in most of his projects.*

put the clamps on someone* AND **put on the clamps*; put the clamps on*** to restrain or restrict someone. (Slang.) □ *Tom's parents put the clamps on him. They decided he was getting out of hand.* □ *They got mad and put the clamps on.*

put the finger on someone* AND **lay the finger on someone*** to accuse someone; to identify someone as the one who did something. (Slang.) □ *Tom put the finger on John, and John is really mad.* □ *He'd better not lay the finger on me. I didn't do it.*

put the heat on someone* AND **put the heat on*; put the screws on someone*; put the screws on*; put the screws to someone*; put the squeeze on someone*; put the squeeze on*** to put pressure on someone (to do something); to coerce someone. (Slang.) □ *John wouldn't talk, so the police were putting the heat on him to confess.* □ *When they put the screws on, they can be very unpleasant.* □ *The police know how to put the squeeze on.*

put the kibosh on something* to put an end to something; to veto something. (Slang.) □ *The mayor put the kibosh on the project.* □ *It's a great idea, and I'm sorry that I had to put the kibosh on it.*

put the screws on someone See *put the heat on someone.*

put the skids on something* AND **put**

the skids on* to cause something to fail. (Slang.) □ *They put the skids on the project when they refused to give us any more money.* □ *That's the end of our great idea! Somebody put the skids on.*

put the squeeze on someone See *put the heat on someone.*

put to bed with a shovel* to kill someone; to kill and bury someone. (Slang.) □ *That guy'd better be careful, or somebody's going to put him to bed with a shovel.* □ *"Watch out, wise guy," said the robber, "or I'll put you to bed with a shovel."*

put to it* in trouble or difficulty; hard up (for something such as money). (Slang.) □ *I'm in big trouble. I'm really put to it.* □ *John was put to it to get there on time.*

put two and two together* to figure something out from the information available. (A cliché.) □ *Well, I put two and two together and came up with an idea of who did it.* □ *Don't worry. John won't figure it out. He can't put two and two together.*

put up a brave front AND **put up a front** to appear to be brave (even if one is not). □ *Mary is frightened, but she's putting up a brave front.* □ *If she weren't putting up a front, I'd be more frightened than I am.*

Put up or shut up!* **1.** Prove something or stop talking about it.; Do something or stop promising to do it. (Slang.) □ *I'm tired of your telling everyone how fast you can run. Now, do it! Put up or shut up!* □ *Now's your chance to show us that you can run as fast as you can talk. Put up or shut up!* **2.** You should bet your money on what you advocate. (See also *Put your money where your mouth is!*) □ *If you think that your horse is faster than mine, then make a bet. Put up or shut up!* □ *You think you can beat me at cards? Twenty bucks says you're wrong. Put up or shut up!*

put up with someone or something to endure someone or something. □ *I can't put up with you anymore. I'm leaving.* □ *She couldn't put up with the smell, so she opened the window.*

put words into someone's mouth to speak for another person without permission. □ *Stop putting words into my mouth. I can speak for myself.* □ *The lawyer was scolded for putting words into the witness's mouth.*

Put your money where your mouth is!* Stop talking big and make a bet. (A cliché.) □ *I'm tired of your bragging about your skill at betting. Put your money where your mouth is!* □ *You talk about betting, but you don't bet. Put your money where your mouth is!*

Q

quake in one's boots See *shake in one's boots.*

quick on the draw See the following entry.

quick on the trigger* AND **quick on the draw*** (Informal.) **1.** quick to draw a gun and shoot. □ *Some of the old cowboys were known to be quick on the trigger.* □ *Wyatt Earp was particularly quick on the draw.* **2.** quick to respond to anything. □ *John gets the right answer before anyone else. He's really quick on the trigger.* □ *Sally will probably win the quiz game. She's really quick on the draw.*

quick on the uptake quick to understand (something). □ *Just because I'm not quick on the uptake, it doesn't mean I'm stupid.* □ *Mary understands jokes before anyone else because she's so quick on the uptake.*

quite a bit AND **quite a few; quite a little; quite a lot; quite a number** much or many. □ *Do you need one? I have quite a few.* □ *I have quite a little—enough to spare some.* □ *How many? Oh, quite a number.*

R

race against time to hurry to beat a deadline. □ *We had to race against time to finish before the deadline.* □ *You don't need to race against time. Take all the time you want.* ALSO: **race against time** a task which must be finished within a certain time. (A noun phrase.) □ *It was a race against time to finish before the deadline.*

rack one's brains* AND **rack one's brain*** to try very hard to think of something. (Informal.) □ *I racked my brains all afternoon, but couldn't remember where I put the book.* □ *Don't waste any more time racking your brain. Go borrow the book from the library.*

rain cats and dogs* to rain very hard. (A cliché.) □ *It's raining cats and dogs. Look at it pour!* □ *I'm not going out in that storm. It's raining cats and dogs.*

rain or shine* no matter whether it rains or the sun shines. (A cliché.) □ *Don't worry. I'll be there rain or shine.* □ *We'll hold the picnic—rain or shine.*

rain something out AND **rain out something** (for the weather) to spoil something by raining. □ *Oh, the weather looks awful. I hope it doesn't rain the picnic out.* □ *It's starting to sprinkle now. Do you think it will rain out the ball game?*

raise a hand against someone or something See *lift a hand against someone or something.*

raise a stink about something See *create a stink about something.*

raise an objection to someone or something AND **raise an objection** to mention an objection about someone or something. (Also without *an*, as in the examples.) □ *I hope your family won't*

raise an objection to my staying for dinner. □ *I'm certain no one will raise an objection. We are delighted to have you.*

raise havoc with someone or something AND **play havoc with someone or something; play havoc; raise havoc** to cause chaos with someone or something. (*Raise* can be replaced with *create.*) □ *Your announcement raised havoc with the students.* □ *I didn't mean to play havoc with them.* □ *I think you did mean to create havoc.*

raise hob with someone or something AND **play hob with someone or something** to do something devilish to someone or something; to cause trouble for someone or something. (A *hob* is a hobgoblin, a wicked little elf.) □ *Your sudden arrival is going to play hob with my dinner plans.* □ *Sorry, I didn't mean to raise hob with you.*

raise one's sights to set higher goals for oneself. □ *When you're young, you tend to raise your sights too high.* □ *On the other hand, some people need to raise their sights.*

raise one's voice to someone AND **raise one's voice** to speak loudly or shout at someone in anger. □ *Don't you dare raise your voice to me!* □ *I'm sorry. I didn't mean to raise my voice.*

raise some eyebrows to mildly shock or surprise people (by doing or saying something). (*Some* can be replaced with *a few, someone's, a lot of,* etc.) □ *What you just said may raise some eyebrows, but it shouldn't make anyone really angry.* □ *John's sudden marriage to Ann raised a few eyebrows.*

raise the devil with someone or something* AND **raise the devil*; raise hell**

with someone or something*; raise hell*; raise cain with someone or something*; raise cain*; raise the dickens with someone or something*; raise the dickens* to act in some extreme manner; to make trouble; to behave wildly; to be very angry. (Informal. Use *hell* with caution.) □ *John was out all night raising the devil.* □ *Don't come around here and raise hell with everybody.* □ *That cheap gas I bought really raised the dickens with my car's engine.*

rake someone over the coals AND **haul someone over the coals** to give someone a severe scolding. □ *My mother hauled me over the coals for coming in late last night.* □ *The manager raked me over the coals for being late again.*

rake something off* AND **rake off something*** to steal or embezzle a portion of a payment. (Slang.) □ *The county treasurer was caught raking off some of the tax money.* □ *They claimed that no one was raking anything off and that the money was only mislaid.*

ram someone or something down someone's throat See *shove someone or something down someone's throat.*

ramble on about something AND **ramble on** to talk aimlessly about something. □ *John is so talkative. He's always rambling on about something.* □ *You're rambling on yourself.*

rank and file 1. regular soldiers, not the officers. □ *I think there is some trouble with the rank and file, sir.* □ *The rank and file usually do exactly as they are told.* 2. the members of a group, not the leaders. □ *The rank and file will vote on the proposed contract tomorrow.* □ *The last contract was turned down by the rank and file last year.*

rap someone's knuckles to punish someone slightly. □ *She rapped his knuckles for whispering too much.* □ *Don't rap my knuckles. I didn't do it.* ALSO: **get one's knuckles rapped; have one's knuckles rapped** to receive punishment. □ *I got my knuckles rapped for whispering too much.*

rat on someone* to report someone's bad behavior; to tattle on someone. (Slang.) □ *John ratted on me, and I got in trouble.* □ *If he rats on me, I'll hit him!*

rate with someone to be in someone's favor; to be thought of highly by someone. □ *Ann is great. She really rates with me.* □ *She doesn't rate with me at all.*

rattle something off AND **rattle off something; reel something off; reel off something** to recite something quickly and accurately. □ *Listen to Mary rattle off those numbers.* □ *She can really reel them off.*

rave about someone or something 1. to shout and carry on about someone or something in great anger. □ *From the way Bill was raving about Sally, I knew he was angry.* □ *There is a man in the office raving about his gas bill.* 2. to praise someone or something with great enthusiasm. □ *The audience just raved about Mary's performance.* □ *The critics raved about her, too.*

reach an accord with someone See the following entry.

reach an agreement with someone AND **reach an agreement; reach an accord with someone; reach an accord** to agree on something, especially after much discussion. (The *accord* or *agreement* may refer to a contract or other written agreement.) □ *We were unable to reach an accord with them.* □ *After three weeks, we were finally able to reach an agreement.*

reach an understanding with someone AND **reach an understanding** to reach a compromise with someone; (for people) to discuss something until they understand one another. □ *I spent an hour trying to reach an understanding with Tom.* □ *We argued for a long time, but we were unable to reach an understanding.*

reach first base with someone or something See *get to first base with someone or something.*

reach for the sky 1. to aspire to something; to set one's goals high. □ *It's a good idea to set high goals, but there is no point in reaching for the sky.* □ *Go ahead, you can do it! Reach for the sky!* 2.* a command to put one's hands up, as in a robbery. (Slang.) □ *Reach for the sky! This is a stick up!* □ *The sheriff told the bank robbers to reach for the sky.*

reach one's stride AND **hit one's stride** to do something at one's best level of ability. □ *When I reach my stride, things will go faster, and I'll be more efficient.* □ *Now that I've hit my stride, I can work more efficiently.*

read between the lines to infer something (from something). (Usually figurative. Does not necessarily refer to written or printed information.) □ *After listening to what she said, if you read between the lines, you can begin to see what she really means.* □ *Don't believe everything you hear. Learn to read between the lines.*

read one one's rights to make the required statement of legal rights to a person who has been arrested. □ *All right, read this guy his rights and book him on a charge of theft.* □ *You have to read them their rights before putting them in jail.*

read someone like a book to understand someone very well. □ *I've got John figured out. I can read him like a book.* □ *Of course I understand you. I read you like a book.*

read someone out of something to expel someone from an organization, such as a political party. □ *Because of her statement, they read her out of the party.* □ *The officers tried to read me out of the society, but didn't succeed.*

read someone the riot act to give someone a severe scolding. □ *The manager read me the riot act for coming in late.* □ *The teacher read the students the riot act for their failure to do their assignments.*

read someone's mind to guess what someone is thinking. □ *You'll have to tell me what you want. I can't read your mind, you know.* □ *If I could read your mind, I'd know what you expect of me.*

read something into something to attach or attribute a new or different meaning to something. □ *This statement means exactly what it says. Don't try to read anything else into it.* □ *Am I reading too much into your comments?*

read something over AND **read over something** to read something. □ *When you have a chance, read this over.* □ *Also, read over this report.*

read something through AND **read through something** to read all of something. □ *Take this home and read it through.* □ *Read through this report and see if you can find any errors.*

read up on someone or something AND **read up** to find and read some information about someone or something. □ *Please go to the library and read up on George Washington.* □ *I don't know anything about that. I guess I need to read up.*

receive someone with open arms AND **welcome someone with open arms** to welcome someone eagerly. (Used literally or figuratively.) □ *I'm sure they wanted us to stay for dinner. They received us with open arms.* □ *When I came home from school, the whole family welcomed me with open arms.*

reckon with someone or something to deal with someone or something; confront someone or something. □ *Eventually you will have to reckon with getting a job.* □ *I really don't want to have to reckon with the manager when she's mad.*

red in the face embarrassed. □ *After we found Ann hiding in the closet, she became red in the face.* □ *The speaker kept making errors and became red in the face.*

reel something off See *rattle something off.*

regain one's composure to become calm and composed. □ *I found it difficult to regain my composure after the argument.* □ *Here, sit down and relax so that you can regain your composure.*

regain one's feet **1.** to stand up again after falling or stumbling. □ *I fell on the ice and almost couldn't regain my feet.* □ *I helped my uncle regain his feet as he tried to get up from the chair.* **2.** to become independent after financial difficulties. □ *I lent Bill $400 to help him regain his feet.* □ *I'll be able to pay my bills when I regain my feet.*

relative to someone or something **1.** concerning someone or something. □ *I have something to say relative to Bill.* □ *Do you have any information relative to the situation in South Ameri-*

ca? **2.** in proportion to someone or something. □ *My happiness is relative to yours.* □ *I can spend an amount of money relative to the amount of money I earn.*

rent something out AND **rent out something** to rent something to someone. □ *We rented out our house when we went to Europe for a year.* □ *We rented our spare room out to get some extra money.*

report on someone or something to give a report about someone or something. □ *The manager called me in to report on my work.* □ *My mother asked me to report on my brother and what he was doing.*

resign oneself to something to accept something reluctantly. □ *I finally resigned myself to going to Mexico even though I didn't want to.* □ *Mary resigned herself to her fate.*

rest assured to be assured; to be certain. □ *Rest assured that you'll receive the best of care.* □ *Please rest assured that we will do everything possible to help.*

rest on one's laurels* to enjoy one's success and not try to achieve more. (A cliché.) □ *Don't rest on your laurels. Try to continue to do great things!* □ *I think I'll rest on my laurels for a time before attempting anything new.*

result in something to cause something to happen. □ *The storm resulted in a lot of flooding.* □ *Her fall resulted in a broken leg.*

return the compliment AND **return someone's compliment** to pay a compliment to someone who has paid you a compliment. (See *pay someone a compliment*.) □ *Mary told me that my hair looked nice, so I returned her compliment and told her that her hair was lovely.* □ *When someone says something nice, it is polite to return the compliment.*

return the favor to do a good deed for someone who has done a good deed for you. □ *You helped me last week, so I'll return the favor and help you this week.* □ *There is no point in helping Bill. He'll never return the favor.*

rev something up AND **rev up something** to make an idling engine run very fast, in short bursts of speed. □ *I wish that Tom wouldn't sit out in front of our house in his car and rev up his engine.* □ *Hey! Stop revving it up!*

ride herd on someone or something* to supervise someone or something. (Informal. Refers to a cowboy supervising cattle.) □ *I'm tired of having to ride herd on my kids all the time.* □ *My job is to ride herd on this project and make sure everything is done right.*

ride off in all directions* to behave in a totally confused manner; to try to do everything at once. (Folksy.) □ *Bill has a tendency to ride off in all directions. He's not organized enough.* □ *Now, calm down. There is no sense in riding off in all directions.*

ride on someone's coattails AND **hang on someone's coattails** to make one's good fortune or success depend on another person. (Also with *else*, as in the examples.) □ *Bill isn't very creative, so he rides on John's coattails.* □ *Some people just have to hang on somebody else's coattails.*

ride roughshod over someone or something to treat someone or something with disdain or scorn. □ *Tom seems to ride roughshod over his friends.* □ *You shouldn't have come into our town to ride roughshod over our laws and our traditions.*

ride something out AND **ride out something** to endure something unpleasant. (Originally referred to ships lasting out a storm.) □ *It was a nasty situation, but the mayor tried to ride it out.* □ *The mayor decided to ride out the scandal.*

ride the gravy train* to live in luxury. (Informal.) □ *If I had a million dollars, I sure could ride the gravy train.* □ *I wouldn't like loafing. I don't want to ride the gravy train.*

riding for a fall risking failure or an accident, usually due to overconfidence. □ *Tom drives too fast, and he seems too sure of himself. He's riding for a fall.* □ *Bill needs to eat better and get more sleep. He's riding for a fall.*

right and left to both sides; on all sides; everywhere. □ *I dropped the tennis balls,* and they rolled right and left. □ *There were children everywhere—running right and left.*

right away immediately. □ *Please do it right away! □ I'll be there right away. I'm leaving this instant.*

right down someone's alley* AND **right up someone's alley*** ideally suited to one's interests or abilities. (Informal.) □ *Skiing is right down my alley. I love it. □ This kind of thing is right up John's alley.*

right off the bat* immediately; first thing. (Informal.) □ *When he was learning to ride a bicycle, he fell on his head right off the bat. □ The new manager demanded new office furniture right off the bat.*

Right on!* Exactly!; That is exactly right! (Slang.) □ *After the speaker finished, many people in the audience shouted, "Right on!" □ One member of the crowd called out, "Right on!"*

right on time at the correct time; no later than the specified time. □ *Bill always shows up right on time. □ If you get there right on time, you'll get one of the free tickets.*

right side up with the correct side upwards, as with a box or some other container. □ *Keep this box right side up, or the contents will become crushed. □ Please set your coffee cup right side up so I can fill it.*

right up someone's alley See *right down someone's alley.*

ring a bell* (for something) to cause someone to remember something or to seem familiar. (Informal.) □ *I've never met John Franklin, but his name rings a bell. □ Whenever I see a bee, it rings a bell. I remember when I was stung by one.*

ring in the new year to celebrate the beginning of the new year at midnight on December 31. □ *We are planning a big party to ring in the new year. □ How did you ring in the new year?*

ring someone or something up AND **ring up someone or something 1.** [with *something*] to record the cost of an item on a cash register. □ *The cashier rang up each item and told me how much money I owed. □ Please ring this chew-*

ing gum up first, and I'll put it in my purse. **2.** [with *someone*] to call someone on the telephone. □ *Please ring up Ann and ask her if she wants to come over. □ Just ring me up any time.*

rinse someone or something off AND **rinse off someone or something** to wash someone or something lightly with water. □ *The mother rinsed off the baby in the sink. □ Please rinse the vegetables off before you cook them.*

rinse something out AND **rinse out something** to wash something lightly, usually by hand. □ *I'm busy this afternoon. I have to rinse a few things out. □ Rinse out the sink when you're finished.*

rip into someone or something* to attack someone or something, physically or verbally. (Informal.) □ *The bear ripped into the deer. □ The angry teacher ripped into the student.*

rip someone or something off* AND **rip off someone or something*** (Slang.) **1.** [with *someone*] to cheat or deceive someone; to steal from someone. □ *That store operator ripped me off. □ They shouldn't rip off people like that.* **2.** [with *something*] to steal something. □ *The crooks ripped off a car in broad daylight. □ I bought it! I didn't rip it off!*

rise to the occasion to meet the challenge of an event; to try extra hard to do a task. □ *John was able to rise to the occasion and make the conference a success. □ It was a big challenge, but he rose to the occasion.*

risk one's neck to do something* AND **risk one's neck*** to risk physical harm in order to accomplish something. (Informal.) □ *Look at that traffic! I refuse to risk my neck just to cross the street to buy a paper. □ I refuse to risk my neck at all.*

rob Peter to pay Paul* to take from one in order to give to another. (A cliché.) □ *Why borrow money to pay your bills? That's just robbing Peter to pay Paul. □ There's no point in robbing Peter to pay Paul. You still will be in debt.*

rob the cradle* to marry or date someone who is much younger than you are. (Informal.) □ *I hear that Bill is dating*

Ann. Isn't that sort of robbing the cradle? She's much younger than he is. □ *Uncle Bill—who is nearly eighty—married a thirty year old woman. That is really robbing the cradle.*

rock the boat to cause trouble where none is welcome; to disturb a situation which is otherwise stable and satisfactory. (Often negative.) □ *Look Tom, everything is going fine here. Don't rock the boat!* □ *You can depend on Tom to mess things up by rocking the boat.*

roll one's sleeves up AND **roll up one's sleeves** to get ready to do some work. □ *Come on, you guys, get busy. Roll up your sleeves and go to work.* □ *Roll your sleeves up and get busy. This isn't a picnic. This is work!*

roll out the red carpet for someone See *get the red carpet treatment.*

roll something back AND **roll back something** to reduce a price to a previous amount. (Also used literally.) □ *The government forced the company to roll its prices back.* □ *It wouldn't have rolled back its prices if the government hadn't forced it.*

roll something out AND **roll out something** 1. to bring something forward by rolling it. □ *They pushed and pushed and finally rolled the car out.* □ *Bill rolled out his old lawn mower and tried to repair it.* 2. to flatten something (by rolling something over it). □ *The factory used a powerful machine to roll out the sheet of metal.* □ *The worker used a special tool to roll the bump out of the fender.*

Rome wasn't built in a day.*
Important things do not happen overnight. (A cliché.) □ *Don't expect a lot to happen right away. Rome wasn't built in a day, you know.* □ *Don't be anxious about how fast you are growing. Rome wasn't built in a day.*

room and board food to eat and a place to live; the cost of food and lodging. □ *That college charges too much for room and board.* □ *How much is your room and board?*

room with someone to share a room with someone, for a short or long time. □ *Do you room with someone, or do you live alone?* □ *I don't room with anyone. I don't have a roommate.*

root for someone or something* to cheer and encourage someone or something. (Informal.) □ *Are you rooting for anyone in particular, or are you just shouting because you're excited?* □ *I'm rooting for the home team.*

rope someone into doing something* to persuade or trick someone into doing something. (Informal.) □ *I don't know who roped me into this, but I don't want to do it.* □ *See if you can rope somebody into taking this to the post office.*

rough someone up* AND **rough up someone*** to beat or physically harass someone. (Slang.) □ *The police roughed up the suspect, and they got in trouble for it.* □ *The gangsters roughed their victim up.*

round something off AND **round off something** 1. to make something rounded or curved. □ *I rounded off the sharp corner with sandpaper.* □ *Please try to round off that sharp place.* 2. to change a number to the next higher or lower whole number. □ *I rounded off 8.789 to 9.* □ *You should round off 8.122 to 8.* 3. AND **round out something; round something out** to finish something (in a special way; by doing something). □ *She rounded her schooling off with a trip to Europe.* □ *I like to round out the day with a period of meditation.*

round something out See the previous entry.

round something up AND **round up something** to collect something; to organize something into a group. □ *The cowboys rounded up the cattle for market.* □ *See if you can round some helpers up.*

round-trip ticket a ticket (for a plane, train, bus, etc.) which allows one to go to a destination and return. □ *A round-trip ticket is usually cheaper than a one-way ticket.* □ *How much is a round-trip ticket to San Francisco?*

rub elbows with someone AND **rub elbows; rub shoulders with someone** to associate with someone; to work closely with someone. □ *I don't care to rub elbows with someone who acts like that!* □ *I rub shoulders with John at work. We are good friends.*

rub off on someone AND **rub off**

279

(for a characteristic of one person) to seem to transfer to someone else. □ *I'll sit by Ann. She has been lucky all evening. Maybe it'll rub off on me.* □ *Sorry. I don't think that luck rubs off.*

rub shoulders with someone See *rub elbows with someone.*

rub someone or something down AND **rub down someone or something 1.** to dry someone or something. □ *I like to rub myself down after a cold shower.* □ *The trainer rubbed down the horse after running it through the stream.* **2.** to massage or knead the muscles of someone or something. □ *The trainer rubbed down the horse after the race.* □ *The coach rubbed down the boxer before and after the fight.*

rub someone out* AND **rub out someone*** to kill someone. (Slang.) □ *The gangsters tried to rub out the witness.* □ *The crook said, "Bill is getting to be a problem. We're going to have to rub him out."*

rub someone the wrong way See the following entry.

rub someone's fur the wrong way AND **rub someone the wrong way** to irritate someone. □ *I'm sorry I rubbed your fur the wrong way. I didn't mean to upset you.* □ *Don't rub her the wrong way!*

rub something in AND **rub in something 1.** to work something into something by rubbing. □ *If your sunburn hurts, take this lotion and rub it in.* □ *Should I rub in all of it?* **2.*** to keep reminding one of one's failures; to nag someone about something. (Informal.) □ *Why do you have to rub in everything I do wrong?* □ *I like to rub it in. You deserve it!*

rub something off AND **rub off something** to remove something by rubbing; to erase something by rubbing. □ *There's some dust on your shoes. You should rub it off.* □ *Please rub off that dirty place so that the wall looks clean.*

rule someone or something out AND **rule out someone or something** to prevent, disqualify, overrule, or cancel someone or something. □ *John's bad temper rules him out for the job.* □ *The weather ruled out a picnic for the weekend.*

rule the roost* to be the boss or manager, especially at home. (Informal.) □ *Who rules the roost at your house?* □ *Our new office manager really rules the roost.*

run a fever AND **run a temperature** to have a body temperature higher than normal; to have a fever. □ *I ran a fever when I had the flu.* □ *The baby is running a temperature and is grouchy.*

run a risk of something AND **run a risk; run the risk of something; run the risk** to take a chance that something (bad) will happen. □ *I don't want to run the risk of losing my job.* □ *Don't worry. You won't have to run a risk.*

run a taut ship See *run a tight ship.*

run a temperature See *run a fever.*

run a tight ship* AND **run a taut ship** to run a ship or an organization in an orderly and disciplined manner. (*Taut* and *tight* mean the same thing. *Taut* is correct nautical use.) □ *The new office manager really runs a tight ship.* □ *Captain Jones is known for running a taut ship.*

run across someone or something See *come across someone or something.*

run afoul of someone or something to get in trouble with someone or something; to conflict with someone or something. □ *I hope I don't run afoul of your sister. She doesn't like me.* □ *John ran afoul of the law.*

run after someone or something 1. to chase (by running) someone or something. □ *The dog ran after the car.* □ *Bill ran after Tom.* **2.** [with *someone*] to chase someone of the opposite sex hoping for a date or some attention. □ *Is John still running after Ann?* □ *No, Ann is running after John.*

run an errand AND **go on an errand** to take a short trip to do a specific thing. □ *I've got to run an errand. I'll be back in a minute.* □ *John has gone on an errand. He'll be back shortly.*

run around See *chase after someone or something.*

run around after someone or something See *chase after someone or something.*

run around like a chicken with its head

cut off* AND **run in circles; run around in circles*** to run around frantically and aimlessly; to be in a state of chaos. (A cliché.) □ *I spent all afternoon running around like a chicken with its head cut off.* □ *If you run around in circles, you'll never get anything done.* □ *Get organized and stop running in circles.*

run around with someone AND **go around with someone** to be friends with someone; to go places with regular friends. □ *John and I were great friends. We used to run around with each other all the time.* □ *Mary went around with Jane for about a year.*

run away from someone or something AND **run away** to flee from someone or something. □ *The cat ran away from the dog.* □ *It ran away because it was frightened.* □ *Ann ran away from Tom.*

run away with someone or something AND **run away** to flee (from someplace) with someone, as in an elopement. (See *run off with someone or something*.) □ *Tom ran away with Ann and got married.* □ *They ran away because her parents opposed the marriage.*

run circles around someone* AND **run rings around someone*** to outrun or outdo someone. (Informal.) □ *John is a much better racer than Mary. He can run circles around her.* □ *Mary can run rings around Sally.*

run counter to something to be in opposition to something; to run against something. (This has nothing to do with running.) □ *Your proposal runs counter to what is required by the manager.* □ *His idea runs counter to good sense.*

run down to run out of power or energy. (Said especially of batteries and clock springs.) □ *My watch has run down. I need new batteries.* □ *It used to be that when a watch ran down, you just wound it up again.*

run for one's life to run away to save one's life. □ *The dam has burst! Run for your life!* □ *The captain told us all to run for our lives.*

run in circles See *run around like a chicken with its head cut off.*

run in the family for a characteristic to appear in all (or most) members of a family. □ *My grandparents lived well into their nineties, and it runs in the family.* □ *My brothers and I have red hair. It runs in the family.*

run into a stone wall* to come to a barrier against further progress. (Informal. Also used literally.) □ *We've run into a stone wall in our investigation.* □ *Algebra was hard for Tom, but he really ran into a stone wall with geometry.*

run into someone or something See *bump into someone or something.*

run-of-the-mill* common or average; typical. (A cliché.) □ *The restaurant we went to was nothing special—just run-of-the-mill.* □ *The service was good, but the food was run-of-the-mill or worse.*

run off at the mouth* to talk excessively. (Slang.) □ *Shut up, John. You're always running off at the mouth.* □ *There is no need to run off at the mouth. Stop talking so much for so long.*

run off with someone or something 1. to take something or someone away; to steal something or kidnap someone. □ *The thief ran off with the lady's purse.* □ *The kidnapper ran off with the baby.* 2. [with *someone*] AND **run off** to run away with someone, as in an elopement. □ *Tom ran off with Ann.* □ *Tom and Ann ran off and got married.*

run out of gas See *out of gas.*

run out of something AND **run out** 1. to use up the last of something and have no more. □ *I ran out of eggs while I was baking the cakes. I had to buy more right then.* □ *What a horrible time to run out.* 2. to exit from someplace running. □ *The cat ran out of the house.* □ *The cat ran out because the dog was chasing it.*

run out of time See *out of time.*

run over someone or something (for a car, bus, etc.) to drive over someone or something; to drive (a car, bus, etc.) over someone or something. □ *Be careful when you cross the street so that a car doesn't run over you.* □ *The car ran over the bicycle left in the driveway.*

run rings around someone See *run circles around someone.*

run riot AND **run wild** to get out of control. □ *The dandelions have run riot in our lawn.* □ *The children ran wild at* *the birthday party and had to be taken home.*

run scared* to behave as if one were going to fail. (Informal. Typically said of someone running for election.) □ *The mayor was running scared, but won anyway.* □ *When we lost that big contract, everyone in the office was running scared. We thought we'd be fired.*

run short of something AND **run short** to use up almost all of something; to have too little or few of something left. □ *We are running short of milk. Please buy some on the way home.* □ *When it comes to money, we are always running short.*

run someone in AND **run in someone** to take someone to the police station and make an arrest. □ *The police officer got angry and ran in the motorist.* □ *"Don't run me in," cried the driver. "I'm innocent."*

run someone or something down AND **run down someone or something** 1. to chase and run over someone or something (with a car, bus, etc.); to chase and catch someone or something. □ *The hunters ran down the deer.* □ *The murderer ran the man down with a car.* 2. to physically degrade or put wear on someone or something. □ *Our neighbors ran their house down before they sold it.* □ *All these years of hard work have run Mrs. Brown down severely.* 3. to say bad things about someone or something. □ *Why are you always running your friends down?* □ *Don't run down my paintings! You just don't understand art!*

run someone or something off AND **run off someone or something** to chase someone or something away. □ *The man went out and ran the rabbits off. They were eating his vegetable garden.* □ *When I went to visit Mary, her father ran me off.*

run someone ragged* to run someone hard and fast; to keep someone or something very busy. (Informal.) □ *This busy season is running us all ragged at the store.* □ *What a busy day. I ran myself ragged.*

run something into the ground* AND **drive something into the ground*** □ to carry something too far. (Informal.) □ *It was a good joke at first, Tom, but you've run it into the ground.* □ *Just because everyone laughed once, you don't have to drive it into the ground.*

run something up AND **run up something** 1. to raise a flag. □ *We run up the flag every day.* □ *I run it up every day except when it's raining.* 2. to add to a bill; to add many charges to one's account. □ *Tom ran up a big bill at the hotel.* □ *He ran the bill up until they asked him to pay part of it.*

Run that by again.* Say that again. (Slang.) □ *I didn't hear you. Could you run that by again?* □ *Run that by again. I don't believe my ears.*

run through something to waste something; to use up something rapidly. (Also used literally.) □ *Have you run through all those eggs already?* □ *I ran through my allowance in one day.*

run to seed AND **go to seed** to become worn out and uncared for. (Said especially of a lawn which needs care.) □ *Look at that lawn. The whole thing has run to seed.* □ *Pick things up around here. This place is going to seed. What a mess!*

run wild See *run riot*.

rustle something up* AND **rustle up something*** to find and prepare some food. (Folksy.) □ *Just go out into the kitchen and ask Bill to rustle up some food.* □ *I'm sure he can rustle something up.*

S

sack out* to go to bed; to go to sleep. (Slang. Compare to *hit the sack* at *hit the hay*.) □ *Look at the clock. It's time to sack out.* □ *John sacks out at about 9:00.*

safe and sound* safe and whole or healthy. (A cliché.) □ *It was a rough trip, but we got there safe and sound.* □ *I'm glad to see you here safe and sound.*

sail through something* AND **sail right through something*** to finish something quickly and easily. (Informal.) □ *The test was not difficult. I sailed right through it.* □ *Bob sailed through his homework in a short amount of time.*

sail under false colors to pretend to be something that one is not. (Originally nautical, referring to a pirate ship disguised as an innocent merchant ship.) □ *John has been sailing under false colors. He's really a spy.* □ *I thought you were wearing that uniform because you worked here. You are sailing under false colors.*

salt something away AND **salt away something** to store something. (Originally referred to preserving food and storing it.) □ *I salted away about $1,000 when I worked as a clerk in the grocery store.* □ *Mary salted away some extra candy for use during the holidays.*

Same here.* Me too.; I agree. (Informal.) □ BOB: *I'll have chocolate ice cream!* BILL: *Same here.* □ MARY: *I'll vote for the best candidate.* TOM: *Same here!*

save one's breath to refrain from talking, explaining, or arguing. □ *There is no sense in trying to convince her. Save your breath.* □ *Tell her to save her breath. He won't listen to her.*

save one's face AND **save face** to preserve one's good standing or high position (after a failure). □ *The ambassador was more interested in saving his face than winning the argument.* □ *Most diplomats are concerned with saving face.*

save someone's neck See the following entry.

save someone's skin* AND **save someone's neck*** to save someone from injury, embarrassment, or punishment. (Informal.) □ *I saved my skin by getting the job done on time.* □ *Thanks for saving my neck! I would have fallen down the stairs if you hadn't held my arm.*

save something for a rainy day* to reserve something—usually money—for some future need. (A cliché. Also used literally. *Save something* can be replaced with *put something aside, hold something back, keep something,* etc.) □ *I've saved a little money for a rainy day.* □ *Keep some extra candy for a rainy day.*

save something up AND **save up something** to save something; to accumulate something. (*Up* can also be left out.) □ *I'm saving up coupons to get a prize.* □ *If you'd only save your money up, you could buy anything you want.*

save the day to produce a good result when a bad result was expected. □ *The team was expected to lose, but Sally made many points and saved the day.* □ *Your excellent speech saved the day.*

save up for something AND **save up** to save money for something. □ *I'm saving up for a bicycle.* □ *I'll have to save up for a long time. It costs a lot of money.*

say a mouthful* to say a lot; to say something very important or meaningful. (Folksy.) □ *When you said things were busy around here, you said a mouthful. It is terribly busy.* □ *You sure said a mouthful, Bob. Things are really busy.*

say something in a roundabout way to imply something without saying it; to say something indirectly; to speak using circumlocution. □ *Why don't you say what you mean? Why do you always say something in a roundabout way?* □ *What did she mean? Why did she say it in a roundabout way?*

say something out loud to say something so that people can hear it; to say something aloud. □ *If you know the answer, say it out loud.* □ *Don't mumble. Say it out loud.*

say something right to someone's face AND **say something to one's face** to say something (unpleasant) directly to someone. □ *She knew I thought she was rude because I said it right to her face.* □ *I thought she felt that way about me, but I never thought she'd say it to my face.*

say something under one's breath to say something so softly that almost no one can hear it. □ *John was saying something under his breath, and I don't think it was very pleasant.* □ *I'm glad he said it under his breath. If he had said it out loud, it would have caused an argument.*

say the word to give a signal to begin; to say yes or okay. □ *I'm ready to start any time you say the word.* □ *We'll all shout "Happy birthday!" when I say the word.*

say uncle* to surrender; to give in. (Informal.) □ *Ann held Bobby down on the ground until he said uncle.* □ *Why isn't it enough to win the argument? Why do you demand that I say uncle?*

scale something down AND **scale down something** to make something smaller. □ *Your plan is much too grand. We'll have to scale it down.* □ *We can't afford to build a building that big. Please scale down the size and the cost.*

scarcer than hen's teeth See *as scarce as hen's teeth.*

scare one out of one's wits See *frighten one out of one's wits.*

scare someone or something up* AND **scare up someone or something*** to search for and find someone or something. (Slang.) □ *I'll see if I can scare up somebody to fix the broken chair.* □ *Go out in the kitchen and scare some food up.*

scare someone stiff to scare someone severely; to *frighten someone to death.* (*Stiff* means dead.) □ *That loud noise scared me stiff.* □ *The robber jumped out and scared us stiff.* ALSO: **scared stiff** badly frightened. (See also *scared to death* at *frighten someone to death.*) □ *We were scared stiff by the robber.*

scare someone to death See *frighten someone to death.*

scare the daylights out of someone See *frighten the wits out of someone.*

scare the wits out of someone See *frighten the wits out of someone.*

scared to death See *frighten someone to death.*

scrape something together AND **scrape together something** to assemble something quickly, usually from a small supply of components. (Compare to *pull something together.*) □ *I'll try to scrape something together for dinner.* □ *We really should try to have a party to celebrate the boss's birthday. Let's try to scrape something together.*

scrape the bottom of the barrel* to select from among the worst; to choose from what is left over. (A cliché.) □ *You've bought a bad looking car. You really scraped the bottom of the barrel to get that one.* □ *The worker you sent over was the worst I've ever seen. Send me another—and don't scrape the bottom of the barrel.*

scratch around for something* AND **scratch around*** to look here and there for something. (Informal.) □ *Let me scratch around for a better bargain. Maybe I can come up with something you like.* □ *I'll scratch around for a week or two and see what I come up with.*

scratch someone's back* to do a favor for someone in return for a favor done for you. (Informal.) □ *You scratch my* *back, and I'll scratch yours.* □ *We believe that the mayor has been scratching the treasurer's back.*

scratch the surface to just begin to find out about something; to examine only the superficial aspects of something. □ *The investigation of the governor's staff revealed some suspicious dealing. It is thought that the investigators have just scratched the surface.* □ *We don't know how bad the problem is. We've only scratched the surface.*

scream bloody murder* to complain bitterly; to complain unduly. (Slang.) □ *When we put him in an office without a window, he screamed bloody murder.* □ *There is something wrong next door. Everyone is screaming bloody murder.*

screw around with someone or something See *mess around with someone or something.*

screw someone or something up* AND **screw up someone or something*** (Slang.) **1.** to cause trouble for someone or something. □ *Your advice about making a lot of money really screwed me up. Now I'm broke.* □ *Your efforts screwed up the entire project.* **2.** [with *someone*] to drive someone crazy. □ *Bob screwed himself up with drugs.* □ *All the trouble at home really screwed up the two brothers.*

screw up one's courage to build up one's courage. □ *I guess I have to screw up my courage and go to the dentist.* □ *I spent all morning screwing up my courage to take my driver's test.*

Search me.* I do not know.; You will not find the answer with me. (Informal.) □ BILL: *Where is the screwdriver?* BOB: *Search me.* □ *When I asked Mary what time it was, she only said, "Search me."*

search someone or something out AND **search out someone or something** to search for and find someone or something in particular. □ *I searched out John and asked him about the party.* □ *I searched the right sized hammer out and took it with me.*

second nature to someone easy and natural for someone. □ *Swimming is second nature to Jane.* □ *Driving is no problem for Bob. It's second nature to him.*

second to none better than anything else. □ *This is an excellent car—second to none.* □ *Her suggestion was second to none, and the manager accepted it eagerly.*

see a man about a dog* to leave for some unmentioned purpose. (Informal. Often refers to going to the restroom.) □ *I don't know where Tom went. He said he had to see a man abut a dog.* □ *When John said he was going to see a man about a dog, I thought he would be gone for only a minute.*

see about something to ask about something; to check on something. □ *I'll have to see about your request to leave early.* □ *I must see about the cake I have in the oven.*

see after someone or something See *look after someone or something.*

see eye to eye about something AND **see eye to eye on something; see eye to eye** to view something in the same way (as someone else). □ *John and Ann see eye to eye about the new law. Neither of them likes it.* □ *That's interesting because they rarely see eye to eye.*

see fit to do something AND **see fit** to decide to do something. □ *If I see fit to return, I'll bring Bill with me.* □ *She'll do it if she sees fit.*

see into something See *look into something.*

see no objection to something AND **see no objection** to not think of any objection to something. (The *no* is *any* in the affirmative.) □ *I see no objection to your idea.* □ *Do you see any objection?*

see one's way clear to do something AND **see one's way clear** to find it possible to do something. □ *I'd be happy if you could see your way clear to attend our meeting.* □ *I wanted to be there, but I couldn't see my way clear.*

see red* to be angry. (Informal.) □ *Whenever I think of the needless destruction of trees, I see red.* □ *Bill really saw red when the tax bill arrived.*

see someone home to accompany someone home. □ *Bill agreed to see his aunt home after the movie.* □ *You don't need to see me home. It's perfectly safe, and I can get there on my own.*

see someone off AND **see off someone**

to bid someone goodbye at an airport, train station, bus station, etc. □ *John left for Mexico, and his whole family turned out at the bus station to see him off.* □ *We saw off the children who were going to summer camp.*

see someone out See *show someone out.*

see someone to the door See *show someone to the door.*

see something through to follow through on something until it is completed. (Compare to *see through someone or something.*) □ *Mary is prepared to see the project through.* □ *It's going to be an unpleasant experience, and I hope you'll see it through.*

see the color of someone's money* to verify that someone has money or has enough money. (Slang.) □ *So, you want to make a bet? Not until I see the color of your money.* □ *I want to see the color of your money before we go any further with this business deal.*

see the handwriting on the wall* AND **see the writing on the wall*** to know that something is certain to happen. (A cliché.) □ *If you don't improve your performance, they'll fire you. Can't you see the writing on the wall?* □ *I know I'll get fired. I can see the handwriting on the wall.*

see the last of someone or something to see someone or something for the last time. □ *I'm glad to see the last of that old car. It has a lot of problems.* □ *The people at my office were happy to see the last of John. He caused a lot of trouble before he left.*

see the light 1. to understand something clearly at last. □ *After a lot of studying and asking many questions, I finally saw the light.* □ *I know that geometry is difficult. Keep working at it. You'll see the light pretty soon.* **2.** See *see the light at the end of the tunnel.* **3.** See *see the light of day.*

see the light at the end of the tunnel AND **see the light** to foresee an end to one's problems after a long period of time. □ *I had been horribly ill for two months before I began to see the light at the end of the tunnel.* □ *I began to see the light one day in early spring. At that moment, I knew I'd get well.*

see the light of day AND **see the light** to come to the end of a very busy time. □ *Finally, when the holiday season was over, we could see the light of day. We had been so busy!* □ *When business lets up for a while, we'll be able to see the light.*

see the sights to see the important things in a place; to see what tourists usually see. □ *We plan to visit Paris and see the sights.* □ *Everyone left the hotel early in the morning to see the sights.*

see through someone or something to understand or detect the true nature of someone or something. (Compare to *see something through.*) □ *You can't fool me anymore. I can see through you and all your tricks.* □ *This plan is designed to make money for you, not to help people. I can see through it! I'm not a fool!*

see to someone or something to take care of someone or something. □ *Tom will see to the horses. Come to the house and freshen up.* □ *I hear the doorbell. Will someone please see to the door?* □ *This paper needs filling out. Will you please see to it?*

Seeing is believing.* One must believe something that one sees. (A cliché.) □ *I never would have thought that a cow could swim, but seeing is believing.* □ *I can hardly believe we are in Paris, but there's the Eiffel tower, and seeing is believing.*

seize on something to (figuratively) take hold of something and make an issue of it. (*On* can be replaced with *upon.* Also used literally.) □ *Whenever I mention money, you seize on it and turn it into an argument!* □ *The lawyer seized upon one point and asked many questions about it.*

seize the opportunity to take advantage of an opportunity. □ *My uncle offered me a trip to Europe, so I seized the opportunity.* □ *Whenever you have a chance, you should seize the opportunity.*

sell out See *sell someone or something out.*

sell someone a bill of goods* to get someone to believe something which isn't true; to deceive someone. (Informal.) □ *Don't pay any attention to what John says. He's just trying to sell you a bill of goods.* □ *I'm not selling you a bill of goods. What I say is true.*

sell someone down the river See *sell someone or something out.*

sell someone on something* to convince someone of something. (Informal.) □ *You don't have to sell me on the value of an education.* □ *Try to sell John on going to Mexico for a vacation.*

sell someone or something out AND **sell out someone or something; sell out** 1. [with *someone*] AND **sell someone down the river** to betray someone; to reveal damaging information about someone. (Slang, especially criminal slang.) □ *Bill told everything he knew about Bob, and that sold Bob down the river.* □ *You'll be sorry if you sell me out.* □ *Lefty sold out, and we'll all soon be arrested.* 2. to sell all of something. □ *We sold out all our red ones yesterday.* □ *You've sold them all out?*

sell someone or something short to underestimate someone or something; to fail to see the good qualities of someone or something. □ *This is a very good restaurant. Don't sell it short.* □ *When you say that John isn't interested in music, you're selling him short. Did you know he plays the violin quite well?*

sell something off AND **sell off something** to sell much or all of something. □ *I sold off all my books.* □ *Please try to sell these items off. We have too many of them.*

sell something on credit to sell something now and let the purchaser pay for it later. (Compare to *buy something on credit.*) □ *I'm sorry, we don't sell groceries on credit. It's strictly cash and carry.* □ *There is a shop around the corner which sells clothing on credit.*

send away for something AND **send away** to order or request something by mail. □ *I sent away for a record catalog from a small company in Montana.* □ *I can't find what I want locally, so I'll have to send away.*

send for someone or something to request that someone or something be

brought (to where one is). (The request can be made by mail, telephone, or in person. Compare to *send out for someone or something.*) □ *Ann is quite ill. Please send for the doctor.* □ *We are out of ice. Please send for some.*

send in for something AND **write in for something** to request something by mail, often in response to a radio or television advertisement. (Similar to *send away for something.*) □ *I sent in for a record album which I saw advertised on television.* □ *I liked it so well, I decided to write in for one.*

send off for something AND **write off for something** to request something by mail, presumably from a great distance. □ *I couldn't find the one I wanted in a store, so I had to send off for it.* □ *No one here could answer my questions, so I had to write off for more information.*

send one about one's business to send someone away, usually in an unfriendly way. □ *Is that annoying man on the telephone again? Please send him about his business.* □ *Ann, I can't clean up the house with you running around. I'm going to have to send you about your business.*

send out for someone or something AND **send out** to request that something be brought (to where one is). (The request can be made by telephone or in person. Compare to *send for someone or something.*) □ *Let's send out for pizza!* □ *We sent out for John because we needed his advice.* □ *We have no more food, so we'll have to send out.*

send someone away to ask someone to leave; to make someone go away. □ *When I asked for money, they sent me away.* □ *I don't want to see Bill. Send him away!*

send someone on an errand AND **send someone out on an errand** to send someone out to do a specific task. □ *Mother sent Billy out on an errand.* □ *I'm late because Bill sent me on an errand.*

send someone or something off AND **send off someone or something** to dispatch someone or something; to send someone or something on its way.

☐ *John was home from college for the holidays, and we sent him off again last week.*

send someone out for someone or something AND **send someone out** to send someone out to bring back someone or something. ☐ *Let's send John out for pizza.* ☐ *First we have to send out somebody for John. He hasn't arrived yet.*

send someone packing to send someone away; to dismiss someone, possibly rudely. ☐ *I couldn't stand him any more, so I sent him packing.* ☐ *The maid proved to be so incompetent that I had to send her packing.*

send someone to the showers* to send a player out of the game and off the field, court, etc. (From sports.) ☐ *John played so badly that the coach sent him to the showers after the third quarter.* ☐ *After the fist fight, the coaches sent both players to the showers.*

send someone up the river* to send someone to prison. (Slang.) ☐ *The judge sent Bill up the river for ten years.* ☐ *The same judge sent him up the river the last time.*

send something C.O.D. to send merchandise to someone who will pay for it when it is delivered. (*C.O.D.* means cash on delivery or collect on delivery.) ☐ *I sent away for a record album and asked them to send it C.O.D.* ☐ *This person has ordered a copy of our record. Send the record C.O.D.*

send up a trial balloon* to suggest something and see how people respond to it; to test public opinion. (Slang.) ☐ *Mary had an excellent idea, but when we sent up a trial balloon, the response was very negative.* ☐ *Don't start the whole project without sending up a trial balloon.*

send word to someone AND **send word** to send a message to someone. ☐ *Send word to Sally that her essay won first place.* ☐ *If you need any help, please send word.*

separate the men from the boys* to separate the competent from those who are less competent. (A cliché.) ☐ *This is the kind of task that separates the men from the boys.* ☐ *This project*

requires a lot of thinking. *It'll separate the men from the boys.*

separate the sheep from the goats* to divide people into two groups. (A cliché.) ☐ *Working in a place like this really separates the sheep from the goats.* ☐ *We can't go on with the game until we separate the sheep from the goats. Let's see who can jump the furthest.*

serve as a guinea pig* (for someone) to be experimented on; to allow some sort of test to be performed on someone. (A cliché.) ☐ *Try it on someone else! I don't want to serve as a guinea pig!* ☐ *Jane agreed to serve as a guinea pig. She'll be the one to try out the new flavor of ice cream.*

serve notice to announce (something). ☐ *John served notice that he wouldn't prepare the coffee anymore.* ☐ *I'm serving notice that I'll resign as secretary next month.*

serve someone right (for an act or event) to punish someone fairly (for doing something). ☐ *John copied off my test paper. It would serve him right if he fails the test.* ☐ *It'd serve John right if he got arrested.*

serve someone's purpose See *answer someone's purpose.*

serve something up AND **serve up something 1.** to serve food. ☐ *The cook served up a fine soup for lunch.* ☐ *Please don't serve so much meat up. We can get along on less.* **2.*** to present an idea or an opinion. (Informal.) ☐ *You can't go on serving up nonsense if you expect people to trust you.* ☐ *The president served a promising idea up at the last board meeting.*

set a precedent to establish a pattern; to set a policy which must be followed in future cases. ☐ *I'll do what you ask this time, but it doesn't set a precedent.* ☐ *We've already set a precedent in matters such as these.*

set eyes on someone or something AND **lay eyes on someone or something** to see someone or something for the first time. ☐ *I knew when I set eyes on that car that it was the car for me.* ☐ *Have you ever laid eyes on such a beautiful flower?*

set fire to someone or something AND

set someone or something on fire to ignite someone or something; to put someone or something to flames. □ *The thief set fire to the building.* □ *The poor man accidentally set himself on fire.*

set foot somewhere to go or enter somewhere. (Often in the negative.) □ *If I were you, I wouldn't set foot in that town.* □ *I wouldn't set foot in her house! Not after the way she spoke to me.*

set forth on something AND **launch forth on something; launch forth; set forth** **1.** to start out on something. □ *We intend to set forth on our journey very early in the morning.* □ *What time will you launch forth?* **2.** to begin presenting a speech or an explanation. □ *As soon as John set forth on his speech, three people walked out.* □ *Every time he launches forth, somebody walks out.*

set great store by someone or something to have positive expectations for someone or something; to have high hopes for someone or something. □ *I set great store by my computer and its ability to help me in my work.* □ *We set great store by John because of his quick mind.*

set in to begin. (Often said of weather or climatic conditions.) □ *Winter set in very early this year.* □ *We got the windows closed before the storm set in.*

set off for somewhere AND **set off; set out for somewhere; set out** to begin a journey to a place. (See also *set forth on something*.) □ *We set off for the seaside late in the afternoon.* □ *We couldn't set off then because the dog was lost.* □ *The children set out for school even though the snow was two feet deep.*

set one back on one's heels to surprise, shock, or overwhelm someone. □ *Her sudden announcement set us all back on our heels.* □ *The manager scolded me, and that really set me back on my heels.*

set one's sights on something to select something as on goal. □ *I set my sights on a master's degree from the state university.* □ *Don't set your sights on something you cannot possibly do.*

set out for somewhere See *set off for somewhere*.

set sail for somewhere AND **set sail** to depart in a boat for somewhere. (In a sail boat or power boat.) □ *This ship sets sail for Japan in two days.* □ *When do you set sail?*

set someone or something back AND **set back someone or something** (Also used literally.) **1.** to delay someone or something; to undo the progress of someone or something. □ *The storm set back the work on the new building.* □ *A serious illness set Ann back in school.* **2.*** [with *someone*] to cost someone (an amount of money). (Informal.) □ *This coat set me back about $250.* □ *That dinner at the restaurant last night really set us back.*

set someone or something free to free someone or something. □ *I found a bird caught in the fence, and I set it free.* □ *I was locked in the closet for an hour before someone opened the door and set me free.*

set someone or something off AND **set off someone or something** **1.** [with *someone*] to get someone very excited and angry. □ *Whenever I see someone mistreating an animal, it really sets me off.* □ *The tax bill set off Bob. He raved for an hour!* **2.** [with *something*] to start something. □ *The question of taxes set off an argument.* □ *Don't set another discussion off, please!*

set someone or something on fire See *set fire to someone or something*.

set someone or something straight **1.** [with *someone*] to explain (something) to someone. □ *I don't think you understand about taxation. Let me set you straight.* □ *Ann was confused, so I set her straight.* **2.** [with *something*] to explain something (to someone). □ *This is very confusing, but with a little explaining I can set it straight.* □ *We'll set this matter straight in a short time.* **3.** See *put something straight*.

set someone or something up AND **set up someone or something** **1.*** [with *someone*] to lead—by deception—a person to play a particular role in an event; to arrange an event—usually by deception—so that a specific person takes the consequences for the event; to frame someone. (Informal or slang.) □ *John isn't the one who started the fight. Some-*

body set up the poor guy. □ *I had nothing to do with the robbery! I was just standing there. Somebody must have set me up!* **2.** [with *someone*] See the following two entries. **3.** [with *something*] to place something in an upright position. □ *Set up your glass so I can fill it.* □ *The candle is beginning to tilt. Please set it up again.* **4.** [with *something*] to put something together; to erect something. □ *My parents bought me a doll house, but I had to set it up myself.* □ *It took nearly an hour to set up the tent.* **5.** [with *something*] to establish or found something. □ *We set up a fund to buy food for the needy.* □ *The business owners set a bank up in the small town.* **6.** [with *something*] to make plans for something. □ *Sally and Tom set up a party for Saturday night.* □ *John and Mary are hard at work setting something up for the meeting.* **7.*** [with *something*] (for a bartender) to serve drinks to a customer. (Slang. Usually *something* is *'em.*) □ *The mean looking man walked into the bar, looked at the bartender, and said, "Set 'em up."* □ *The bartender set up a drink for the man. He wanted no trouble.*

set someone up as something AND **set up someone as something; set someone up** to establish someone as something. (Compare to the following entry.) □ *Bill set himself up as boss.* □ *When Mary got her degree, she set herself up as a consultant.* □ *My father set up my sisters as co-owners of the family business.* □ *He set them up with the help of a lawyer.*

set someone up in business AND **set someone up** to help establish someone in business; to provide the money someone needs to start a business. (Compare to the previous entry.) □ *My father set my sisters up in business.* □ *He helped set them up so he could keep the business in the family.*

set someone's teeth on edge **1.** (for a sour or bitter taste) to irritate one's mouth and make it feel funny. □ *Have you ever eaten a lemon? It'll set your teeth on edge.* □ *I can't stand food that sets my teeth on edge.* **2.** (for a person or a noise) to be irritating or get on

one's nerves. □ *Please don't scrape your fingernails on the blackboard! It sets my teeth on edge!* □ *Here comes Bob. He's so annoying. He really sets my teeth on edge.*

set something aside **1.** to discard or reject something. □ *The judge set the ruling aside and released the prisoner.* □ *I have to set aside your opinion. I think you're wrong.* **2.** AND **lay something aside; put something aside** to put something apart or to the side. □ *Take part of the cooking juices and set them aside for later use.* □ *Lay that glass aside because it's cracked.*

set something down to something See *put something down to something.*

set something out AND **set out something** **1.** to plant small plants out of doors. □ *We set some tomatoes out early in the spring.* □ *Don't set out your plants until after the last freeze.* **2.** to remove something (from something) and leave it out (of something). (Often said of removing frozen food from a freezer to thaw.) □ *Please set some lamb chops out to thaw.* □ *When you find the file on Tom Smith, please set it out so I can look at it later.*

set something right AND **put something right** to correct something; to alter a situation to make it more fair. □ *This is a very unfortunate situation. I'll ask the people responsible to set this matter right.* □ *I'm sorry that we overcharged you. We'll try to put it right.*

set the ball rolling See *get the ball rolling.*

set the table to place plates, glasses, napkins, etc. on the table before a meal. □ *Jane, would you please set the table?* □ *I'm tired of setting the table. Ask someone else to do it.*

set the world on fire to do exciting things that bring fame and glory. (Frequently negative.) □ *I'm not very ambitious. I don't want to set the world on fire.* □ *You don't have to set the world on fire. Just do a good job.*

set to do something AND **all set to do something; all set** prepared or ready to do something. □ *Are you set to cook the steaks?* □ *Yes, the fire is ready, and I'm all set to start.*

set up shop somewhere* to establish one's place of work somewhere. (Informal.) □ *Mary set up shop in a small office building on Oak Street.* □ *The police officer said, "You can't set up shop right here on the sidewalk!"*

set upon someone or something to attack someone or something violently. □ *The dogs set upon the bear and chased it up a tree.* □ *Bill set upon Tom and struck him hard in the face.*

settle a score with someone* AND **settle a score*; settle the score with someone*; settle the score*** to clear up a problem with someone; to get even with someone. (Slang.) □ *John wants to settle a score with his neighbor.* □ *Tom, it's time you and I settled the score.* ALSO: **have a score to settle with someone** to have a problem to clear up with someone; to have to get even with someone about something. □ *I have a score to settle with John.*

settle down 1. to calm down. □ *Now, children, it's time to settle down and start class.* □ *If you don't settle down, I'll send you all home.* 2. to settle into a stable way of life; to get married and settle into a stable way of life. □ *Tom, don't you think it's about time you settled down and stopped all of this running around?* □ *Bill and Ann decided to settle down and raise some children.*

settle for something to agree to accept something (even though something else would be better). □ *We wanted a red one, but settled for a blue one.* □ *Ask your grocer for Wilson's canned corn— the best corn in cans. Don't settle for less.*

settle on something to decide on something. □ *We've discussed the merits of all of them, and we've settled on this one.* □ *I can't settle on one or the other, so I'll buy both.*

settle someone's affairs to deal with one's business matters; to manage the business affairs of someone who can't. □ *When my uncle died, I had to settle his affairs.* □ *I have to settle my affairs before going to Mexico for a year.*

sew something up AND **sew up something** (See also *get something sewed up*.) 1. to sew something; to stitch closed a tear or hole. □ *I had better sew this rip up before it tears more.* □ *Please sew up this hole in my sock. My toe keeps coming out.* 2.* to finalize something; to secure something. (Informal.) □ *The manager told me to sew the contract up, or else.* □ *Let's sew this contract up today.*

shack up with someone See *sleep with someone*.

shake hands on something AND **shake on something** to clasp and shake the hand of someone as a sign of agreement about something. □ *The two people didn't sign a contract; they just shook hands on the terms of the agreement.* □ *I think it would be better to sign an agreement and shake on it.*

shake hands with someone AND **shake hands** to clasp and shake the hand of someone as a greeting. □ *His hands were full, and I didn't know whether to try to shake hands with him or not.* □ *He put down his packages, and we shook hands.*

shake in one's boots AND **quake in one's boots** to be afraid; to shake from fear. □ *I was shaking in my boots because I had to go see the manager.* □ *Stop quaking in your boots, Bob. I'm not going to fire you.*

shake someone or something down AND **shake down someone or something** 1.* [with *someone*] to extort money from someone; to blackmail someone. (Slang, especially criminal slang.) □ *Lefty was trying to shake down the store keeper.* □ *The gang of criminals made a living from shaking people down.* 2. [with *something*] to make something settle by shaking it. □ *We shook down the box of rice so that it'd hold more.* □ *The olives wouldn't fit back in the jar, so I put some in and shook them down to make room for more.* 3.* [with *something*] to try something out; to test something and give the flaws a chance to appear. (Informal.) □ *We took the new car out for a trip to shake it down.* □ *You need to shake down a complicated piece of machinery when you first get it. Then any problems will show up while the guarantee is still in effect.*

shake someone or something off AND

291

shake off someone or something
1.* [with *someone*] to get rid of someone; to get free of someone who is bothering you. (Slang.) □ *I wish I could shake off John. He's such a pest!* □ *Stop bothering me! What do I have to do to shake you off?* **2.*** [with *something*] to avoid getting a disease, such as a cold; to fight something off. (Informal.) □ *I hope I can shake off this cold pretty soon.* □ *I thought I was catching a cold, but I guess I shook it off.*

shake someone or something up AND **shake up someone or something**
1.* [with *someone*] to shock or upset someone. (Slang. See also *shook up*.) □ *The sight of the injured man shook me up.* □ *Your rude remark really shook up Tom.* **2.** [with *someone*] to jostle or knock someone around. □ *The accident shook up John quite a bit.* □ *We rode over a rough road, and that shook us up.* **3.** [with *something*] to mix one or more substances by shaking. □ *I shook up the can of spray paint before I used it.* □ *I had to shake it up a lot to mix the paint well.*

shake the lead out See *get the lead out.*

Shame on someone. What a shameful thing!; Someone should be ashamed. □ *You've torn your shirt again, Billy! Shame on you!* □ *When Billy tore his shirt, his mother said, "Shame on you!"* ALSO: **For shame!** That is naughty or shameful. □ *What a terrible thing to do. For shame!*

shape someone up AND **shape up someone** to get someone into good physical shape; to make someone behave or perform better. (See also *shape up.*) □ *The trainer was told that he'd have to shape up the boxer before the fight.* □ *I've got to shape myself up to improve my health.*

shape up to improve one's behavior or performance; to improve one's physical shape. □ *Look at this, John! What a poor job you've done! It's time you shaped up!* □ *If I'm going to run in the marathon, I'm going to have to shape up.*

Shape up or ship out.* to either improve one's performance (or behavior) or leave or quit. (A cliché.) □ *Okay, Tom. That's the end. Shape up or ship out!* □ *John was late again, so I told him to shape up or ship out.*

share and share alike* with equal shares. (A cliché.) □ *I kept five and gave the other five to Mary—share and share alike.* □ *The two roommates agreed that they would divide expenses—share and share alike.*

shed crocodile tears to shed false tears; to pretend that one is weeping. □ *The child wasn't hurt, but shed crocodile tears anyway.* □ *He thought he could get his way if he shed crocodile tears.*

shed light on something AND **shed some light on something** to reveal something about something; to clarify something. □ *This discussion has shed some light on the problem.* □ *Let's see if Ann can shed light on this question.*

shell something out* AND **shell out something*** to pay money (out). (Slang.) □ *The traffic ticket turned out to be very expensive. I had to shell out $150.* □ *You'll have to shell plenty out to settle this bill.*

shift for oneself AND **fend for oneself** to get along by oneself; to support oneself. □ *I'm sorry, I can't pay your rent anymore. You'll just have to shift for yourself.* □ *When I became twenty years old, I left home and began to fend for myself.*

shine up to someone to try to gain someone's favor by being extra nice. □ *John is a nice guy, except that he's always trying to shine up to the professor.* □ *Mary never tries to shine up to the manager.*

ship someone or something out AND **ship out someone or something**
1. [with *someone*] to send a sailor off on a ship; to send someone away (from a place). □ *I just got my orders. The Navy is shipping me out next week.* □ *The cook wasn't doing well, so we shipped him out.* **2.** [with *something*] to send out a parcel or a similar item. □ *Your order has been filled. We shipped it out yesterday.* □ *I'll ship out the part you ordered tomorrow.*

shirk one's duty to neglect one's job or task. □ *The guard was fired for shirking* *his duty.* □ *You cannot expect to continue shirking your duty without someone noticing.*

shook up* upset; shocked. (Slang. See also *shake someone or something up*.) □ *Relax man! Don't get shook up!* □ *I always get shook up when I see something like that.*

shoot from the hip 1. to fire a gun which is held at one's side, against one's hip. (This increases one's speed in firing a gun.) □ *When I lived at home on the farm, my father taught me to shoot from the hip.* □ *I quickly shot the snake before it bit my horse. I'm glad I learned to shoot from the hip.* 2.* to speak directly and frankly. (Informal.) □ *John has a tendency to shoot from the hip, but he generally speaks the truth.* □ *Don't pay any attention to John. He means no harm. It's just his nature to shoot from the hip.*

shoot one's mouth off* AND **shoot off one's mouth*** to boast or talk too much; to tell someone's secrets. (Slang.) □ *Don't pay any attention to Bob. He's always shooting his mouth off.* □ *Oh. Sally! Stop shooting off your mouth! You don't know what you're talking about.*

shoot something out AND **shoot out something** 1. to stick, throw, or thrust something outward. □ *The little girl shot out her tongue at the teacher.* □ *The diamond shot bright shafts of light out when the sun fell on it.* 2.* to settle a matter by the use of guns. (Slang. Typical of gangster or Western movies.) □ *Bill and the cowboy—with whom he had been arguing—went out in the street and shot it out.* □ *Don't they know they can settle a problem by talking? They don't need to shoot out the problem when they can talk it over.*

shoot the breeze* to spend time chatting. (Slang. See the following entry.) □ *I went over to Bob's place and shot the breeze for about an hour.* □ *Don't spend so much time shooting the breeze. Get to work!*

shoot the bull* to tell exaggerated tales of one's accomplishments, especially with others who are doing the same. (Slang. See the previous entry.) □ *Those guys out in the back yard are just sitting around shooting the bull.* □ *It was raining, so everybody spent the day indoors drinking beer and shooting the bull.*

shoot the works* to do everything; to use up everything; to bet everything. (Slang.) □ *Shall I bet half our money, or shall I shoot the works?* □ *We shot the works at the carnival—spent every cent we brought with us.*

shop around for something AND **shop around** to shop at different stores to find what you want at the best price. □ *I've been shopping around for a new car, but they are all priced too high.* □ *You can find a bargain, but you'll have to shop around.*

shore someone or something up AND **shore up someone or something** 1. [with *someone*] to (figuratively) prop up or support someone. □ *Everyone cooperated to shore up John when his mother died.* □ *Mary's solid character and personality helped shore her up during her recent problems with the law.* 2. [with *something*] to prop up or support something. □ *The storm weakened the foundation of our house, and we had to have workers shore up the house.* □ *The fence fell over, so we shored it up.*

short and sweet* brief (and pleasant because of briefness). (A cliché.) □ *That was a good sermon—short and sweet.* □ *I don't care what you say, as long as you make it short and sweet.*

short of something not having enough of something. □ *I wanted to bake a cake, but I was short of eggs.* □ *Usually at the end of the month, I'm short of money.*

shot in the arm* a boost; something that gives someone energy. (Informal.) □ *Thank you for cheering me up. It was a real shot in the arm.* □ *Your friendly greeting card was just what I needed—a real shot in the arm.*

shot in the dark* a random or wild guess or try. (Slang.) □ *I don't know how I guessed the right answer. It was just a shot in the dark.* □ *I was lucky to hire such a good worker as Sally. When I hired her, it was just a shot in the dark.*

shot through with something containing something; interwoven, intermixed, or filled with something. □ *The* rose was a lovely pink shot through with streaks of white. □ *John's comments are often shot through with sarcasm.* □ *I want a well-marbled steak—one shot through with fat.*

should have stood in bed should have stayed in bed. □ *What a horrible day! I should have stood in bed.* □ *The minute I got up and heard the news this morning, I knew I should have stood in bed.*

shout someone or something down AND **shout down someone or something** to overwhelm someone or something by shouting. □ *Mary was trying to speak, but Sally shouted her down.* □ *Ann brought up a very important suggestion, but Bob shouted it down.*

shove off for somewhere* AND **shove off*** to depart for somewhere. (Informal. As if one were pushing a boat away from the shore.) □ *Well, it's time for me to shove off for home.* □ *Yes, I have to shove off, too.*

shove someone or something down someone's throat* AND **ram someone or something down someone's throat*** to force someone or something on someone. (Slang and a little rude.) □ *I don't want any more insurance, and I don't want anyone to shove any insurance down my throat.* □ *Mary isn't invited to my party, and I don't wish for anyone to ram her down my throat!*

show good faith See *in good faith.*

show off to behave in a way that will draw attention to oneself. □ *Bob is always showing off. He needs lots of attention.* □ *Why do you show off so much?* ALSO: **showoff** a person who shows off. □ *Ann is such a showoff!*

show one's colors AND **show one's true colors** to show what one is really like or what one is really thinking. □ *Whose side are you on, John? Come on. Show your colors.* □ *It's hard to tell what Mary is thinking. She never shows her true colors.*

show signs of something to show hints or indications of something. □ *I let the horse run at full speed until it began to show signs of tiring.* □ *Sally is showing signs of going to sleep.*

show someone around to give someone a tour of somewhere. □ *I'm very glad you've come to work here. Let me show you around so you'll know where things are.* □ *Welcome to our town. As soon as you unpack, I'll have someone show you around. You'll find our town quite charming.*

show someone into someplace to lead or usher someone into someplace. □ *The butler showed me into the sitting room and asked me to wait.* □ *The car dealer showed me into the sales office and asked me to sign some papers.*

show someone or something off AND **show off someone or something** to display someone or something so that the best features are apparent. □ *Mrs. Williams was showing off her baby to the neighbors.* □ *Bill drove around all afternoon showing his new car off.*

show someone out AND **see someone out** to lead or take someone to the way out (of a place). □ *Thank you for coming. John will show you out.* □ *There is no need to show me out. I can find the way.* □ *I'm so glad you came. I'll see you out.*

show someone the door See *show someone to the door.*

show someone the ropes See *know the ropes.*

show someone to the door AND **see someone to the door; show someone the door** to lead or take someone to the door or exit. □ *After we finished our talk, she showed me to the door.* □ *Bill and I finished our chat as he saw me to the door.*

show someone up AND **show someone up** to make someone's faults or shortcomings apparent. □ *John's excellent effort really showed up Bill who didn't try very hard at all.* □ *John is always trying to show someone up to make himself look better.*

show someone up as something to reveal that someone is really something (else). □ *The investigation showed her up as a fraud.* □ *The test showed the banker up as unqualified.*

show something to good advantage to display the best features of something; to display something so that its best features are apparent. □ *Put the* *vase in the center of the table and show it to good advantage.* □ *Having and using a large vocabulary shows your intelligence to good advantage.*

show up to appear; to arrive. □ *Where is John? I hope he shows up soon.* □ *When will the bus show up?* □ *As I grew older, a few aches and pains began to show up.*

shrivel up to shrink or diminish; to become withered and shrunken. (Also without *up*.) □ *The flower shriveled up after a day or two.* □ *We couldn't eat all the apples that grew on our tree, so most of them shriveled up.*

shrug something off as something AND **pass off something as something; pass something off as something; pass off something; pass something off; shrug off something; shrug something off** to ignore something unpleasant or offensive as if it meant something else. □ *She shrugged off the criticism as harmless.* □ *I passed off the remark as misinformed.* □ *Bill scolded me, but I just passed it off.*

shut someone or something off AND **shut off someone or something 1.*** [with *someone*] to silence someone; to obstruct someone. (Slang.) □ *Please shut off John and his friends. They are making too much noise.* □ *Don't try to shut me off! I have more to say.* □ *I hate to shut you off, but I have to leave.* **2.** [with *something*] to end the flow of something; to disconnect a utility. □ *The members voted to shut off debate.* □ *If you don't pay your water bill, they will shut your water off.*

shut someone or something out AND **shut out someone or something 1.** to exclude someone or something; to refuse entrance to someone or something. □ *We tried to get into the stadium, but they shut us out because there was no more room.* □ *Your actions have shut out the hope of ever making things better.* **2.** to prevent the opposing team from scoring. (From sports.) □ *The Bears shut out nearly every other team.* □ *They shut us out—we never scored a point.*

shut someone or something up AND **shut up someone or something 1.** [with

someone] to silence someone. □ *Will you please shut up that crying baby!* □ *Oh, shut yourself up!* **2.** [with *something*] to close something. (Also without *up*.) □ *Please shut the cabinet up when you're finished.* □ *I always shut up all the windows before going to bed.*

shut someone or something up in something AND **shut up someone or something in something** to put someone or something inside something; to lock someone or something up in something. □ *The dog was barking, so I shut it up in the basement.* □ *Bill shut up Bob in the closet when they were playing hide and seek.*

shut something down See *close something down.*

shut the door on someone or something AND **close the door on someone or something 1.** to close the door in order to keep someone or something out. □ *Bob opened the door, and when he saw it was Mary, he closed the door on her.* □ *"Don't shut the door on me!" screamed Mary.* **2.** [with *something*] to terminate, exclude, or obstruct something. □ *Your bad attitude shuts the door on any future cooperation from me.* □ *The bad service at that store closes the door on any more business from my company.*

shy away from someone or something AND **shy away** to avoid someone or something. □ *The dog shies away from John since John kicked it.* □ *I can understand why the dog would shy away.* □ *I shy away from eating onions. I think I'm allergic to them.*

sick and tired of someone or something* disgusted and annoyed with someone or something. (A cliché.) □ *I'm sick and tired of Ann and her whistling.* □ *We are all sick and tired of this old car.*

sick in bed remaining in bed while (one is) ill. □ *Tom is sick in bed with the flu.* □ *He's been sick in bed for nearly a week.*

side against someone to be against someone; to take sides against someone. □ *I thought you were my friend! I never thought you would side against me!* □ *The two brothers were always siding against their sister.*

side with someone to join with someone; to take someone else's part; to be on someone's side. □ *Why is it that you always side with him when he and I argue?* □ *I never side with anybody. I form my own opinions.*

sight for sore eyes* a welcome sight. (Folksy.) □ *Oh, am I glad to see you here! You're a sight for sore eyes.* □ *I'm sure hungry. This meal is a sight for sore eyes.*

sign in to register; to sign one's name or have one's name signed on a list which shows that one has arrived. □ *Please sign in as soon as you arrive so that we'll know you're here.* □ *Go over to that table and sign in. Then you'll be told what to do next.*

sign off to stop radio or television transmission. □ *The announcer said, "This is radio station WONH signing off for Thursday, the nineteenth of December."* □ *This television station broadcasts from dawn until it signs off at midnight.*

sign on **1.** to begin radio or television transmission. □ *What time does the station sign on?* □ *The station broadcasts twenty-four hours a day, so it never signs on and it never signs off.* **2.** See *sign on with someone.*

sign on the dotted line* to place one's signature on a contract or other important paper. (A cliché.) □ *This agreement isn't properly concluded until we both sign on the dotted line.* □ *Here are the papers for the purchase of your car. As soon as you sign on the dotted line, that beautiful, shiny automobile will be all yours!*

sign on with someone AND **sign on** to sign an agreement to work with or for someone, especially on a ship. □ *The sailor signed on with Captain Smith.* □ *Hardly any other sailor was willing to sign on.*

sign one's own death warrant* to (figuratively) sign a paper which calls for one's death. (A cliché.) □ *I wouldn't ever gamble a large sum of money. That would be signing my own death warrant.* □ *The killer signed his own death warrant when he walked into the police station and gave himself up.*

sign someone or something in AND **sign in someone or something** **1.** [with *someone*] to register someone; to write someone's name on a registration list. □ *Please go over to the table where the secretary will sign you in.* □ *The secretary is signing in everyone at that table.* **2.** [with *someone*] to return an object (to someone) and have the fact of the return recorded on a list. □ *The coach told the players to sign their uniforms in.* □ *"Where should I sign in my uniform?" asked Bob.*

sign someone or something out AND **sign out someone or something** **1.** [with *someone*] to supervise the checking out of a person; to make a record of someone's departure. □ *The campers are due to leave in the morning, and I have to sign out each person.* □ *Can I help you sign them out?* **2.** [with *something*] to record the removal or loan of an object. □ *Go over to the office and sign out a helmet to wear until you can buy your own.* □ *I'm going to the coach's office to sign a uniform out.*

sign someone up AND **sign up someone** to put someone's name on a list for something. (See also *sign up for something.*) □ *I want a ride to the game Friday. Please sign me up.* □ *I'm sorry, but the car is full. I can't sign up anybody else.*

sign something over to someone AND **sign something over** to transfer ownership of something to someone. □ *The seller signed the house over to the buyer when everyone was satisfied with the sale.* □ *I'm ready to purchase your car from you any time you're ready to sign it over.*

sign up for something AND **sign up** to put one's name on a list for something. □ *I was too late to sign up for the class. I had to enroll in a different one.* □ *I should have signed up yesterday.*

signed, sealed, and delivered* formally and officially signed; (for a formal document to be) executed. (A cliché.) □ *Here is the deed to the property—signed, sealed, and delivered.* □ *I can't begin work on this project until I have the contract signed, sealed, and delivered.*

simmer down* to get quiet or calm. (Informal.) □ *Hey, you guys! Simmer down! Stop all the noise and go to sleep!* □ *I'm very busy now. Please come back in a few hours when things have simmered down a bit.*

sing a different tune See *change someone's tune.*

single someone or something out AND **single out someone or something** to select or refer to a particular person or thing. □ *I'm not the only one who is late. Don't single me out!* □ *Why did you single out that book to criticize?* □ *John singled out Mary for a special award.*

sink in **1.** to submerge slowly into something; to soak in (to something). □ *The road was very muddy, and my car's tires kept sinking in.* □ *I couldn't serve myself any stew because the spoon had sunk in.* **2.*** (for knowledge) to be understood. (Informal.) □ *I heard what you said, but it took a while for it to sink in.* □ *I pay careful attention to everything I hear in class, but it usually doesn't sink in.*

sink into despair (for someone) to grieve or become depressed. □ *After losing all my money, I sank into despair.* □ *There is no need to sink into despair. Everything is going to be all right.*

sink one's teeth into something* (A cliché.) **1.** to take a bite of some kind of food, usually a special kind of food. □ *I can't wait to sink my teeth into a nice, juicy steak.* □ *Look at that chocolate cake! Don't you want to sink your teeth into that?* **2.** to get a chance to do, learn, or control something. □ *That appears to be a very challenging assignment. I can't wait to sink my teeth into it.* □ *Being the manager of this department is a big task. I'm very eager to sink my teeth into it.*

sink or swim* fail or succeed. (A cliché.) □ *After I've studied and learned all I can, I have to take the test and sink or swim.* □ *It's too late to help John now. It's sink or swim for him.*

sit back and let something happen to relax and not interfere with something; to let something happen without playing a part in it. □ *I can't just sit back and let you waste all our money!* □ *Don't worry. Just sit back and let things take care of themselves.*

sit idly by* AND **sit by*** to remain inactive when other people are doing something; to ignore a situation which calls for help. (A cliché.) □ *Bob sat idly by even though everyone else was hard at work.* □ *I can't sit by while all those people need food.*

sit in for someone to take someone else's place in a specific activity. (The activity usually involves being seated.) □ *I can't be at the meeting Thursday. Will you sit in for me?* □ *Sorry, I can't sit in for you. John is also going to be absent, and I am sitting in for him.*

sit in on something AND **sit in** to witness or observe something without participating. (Usually involves being seated.) □ *I can't sign up for the history class, but I have permission to sit in on it.* □ *I asked the professor if I could sit in.*

sit on its hands See the following entry.

sit on one's hands to do nothing; to fail to help. □ *When we needed help from Mary, she just sat on her hands.* □ *We need the cooperation of everyone. You can't sit on your hands!* ALSO: **sit on its hands** (for an audience) to refuse to applaud. □ *We saw a very poor performance of the play. The audience sat on its hands for the entire play.*

sit on someone or something* to hold someone or something back; to delay someone or something. (Informal. Also used literally.) □ *The project cannot be finished because the city council is sitting on the final approval.* □ *Ann deserves to be promoted, but the manager is sitting on her because of a disagreement.*

sit something out AND **sit out something** to not participate in something; to wait until something is over before participating. □ *I'm tired of playing cards, so I think I'll sit out this game.* □ *Oh, please play with us. Don't sit it out.*

sit through something to witness or endure all of something. □ *The performance was so bad that I could hardly sit through it.* □ *You can't expect small children to sit through a long movie.*

sit tight* to wait; to wait patiently. (Informal. Does not necessarily refer to sitting.) □ *Just relax and sit tight. I'll* be right with you. □ *We were waiting in line for the gates to open when someone came out and told us to sit tight because it wouldn't be much longer before we could go in.*

sit up and take notice to become alert and pay attention. □ *A loud noise from the front of the room caused everyone to sit up and take notice.* □ *The company wouldn't pay any attention to my complaints. When I had my lawyer write them a letter, they sat up and took notice.*

sit up with someone to stay with someone through the night, especially with a sick or troubled person or with someone who is waiting for something. □ *I had to sit up with my younger sister when she was ill.* □ *I sat up with Bill while he waited for an overseas telephone call.*

sit with someone 1. to stay with someone; to *sit up with someone.* □ *Sally was upset, so I sat with her for a while.* □ *My uncle sat with me my first day in the hospital.* 2. to stay with and care for one or more children; to baby-sit with someone. □ *I hired Mrs. Wilson to sit with the children.* □ *We couldn't go out for dinner because we couldn't find anyone to sit with the kids.*

sitting on a powder keg* in a risky or explosive situation; in a situation where something serious or dangerous may happen at any time. (Informal. A powder keg is a keg of gunpowder.) □ *Things are very tense at work. The whole office is sitting on a powder keg.* □ *The fire at the oil field seems to be under control for now, but all the workers there are sitting on a powder keg.*

sitting on top of the world See *on top of the world.*

sitting pretty* living in comfort or luxury; in a good situation. (Informal.) □ *My uncle died and left enough money for me to be sitting pretty for the rest of my life.* □ *Now that I have a good-paying job, I'm sitting pretty.*

six of one and half a dozen of the other* about the same one way or another. (A cliché.) □ *It doesn't matter to me which way you do it. It's six of one and half a dozen of the other.* □ *What difference does it make? They're both the same— six of one and half a dozen of the other.*

size someone or something up AND **size up someone or something** to observe someone or something to get information; to *check someone or something out.* □ *The comedian sized the audience up and decided not to use his new material.* □ *I like to size up a situation before I act.*

skate on thin ice See *on thin ice.*

skeleton in the closet a hidden and shocking secret. (Often in the plural.) □ *You can ask anyone about how reliable I am. I don't mind. I don't have any skeletons in the closet.* □ *My uncle was in jail for a day once. That's our family's skeleton in the closet.*

skin someone alive* to be very angry with someone; to scold someone severely. (Folksy.) □ *I was so mad at Jane that I could have skinned her alive.* □ *If I don't get home on time, my parents will skin me alive.*

skip bail See *jump bail.*

Skip it!* Forget it! (Informal.) □ BILL: *What did you say?* BOB: *Oh, skip it!* □ *It's not important. Just skip it!*

skip out on someone or something* AND **skip out*** to sneak away from someone; to leave someone in secret. (Slang.) □ *I heard that Bill skipped out on his wife.* □ *I'm not surprised. I thought he should have skipped out long ago.*

slack off 1. to taper off; to reduce gradually. □ *Business tends to slack off during the winter months.* □ *The storms begin to slack off in April.* 2. to become less active; to become lazy or inefficient. □ *Near the end of the school year, Sally began to slack off, and her grades showed it.* □ *John got fired for slacking off during the busy season.*

slap someone down AND **smack someone down** to rebuke or rebuff someone. (Also used literally.) □ *You may disagree with her, but you needn't slap her down like that.* □ *I only asked you what time it was! There's no need to smack me down! What a rotten humor you're in.*

slap someone's wrist See *get a slap on the wrist.*

slap something together See *throw something together.*

slated for something scheduled for

something. (As if a schedule had been written on a slate.) □ *John was slated for Friday's game, but he couldn't play with the team.* □ *Ann is slated for promotion next year.* ALSO: **slated to do something** scheduled to do something. □ *John was slated to play ball Friday.*

slated to do something See the previous entry.

sleep like a log* to sleep very soundly. (A cliché.) □ *Nothing can wake me up. I usually sleep like a log.* □ *Everyone in our family sleeps like a log, so no one heard the fire engines in the middle of the night.*

sleep on something to think about something overnight; to weigh a decision overnight. □ *I don't know whether I agree to do it. Let me sleep on it.* □ *I slept on it, and I've decided to accept your offer.*

sleep something off AND **sleep off something** to sleep while the effects of liquor or drugs pass away. □ *John drank too much and went home to sleep it off.* □ *Bill is at home sleeping off the effects of the drug they gave him.*

sleep with someone AND **shack up with someone*; shack up*** to have sex with someone; to copulate with someone. (Euphemistic. This may not involve sleep. The expressions with *shack* are slang, and they are not used to refer to marital sex.) □ *Everyone assumes that Mr. Franklin doesn't sleep with Mrs. Franklin.* □ *Somebody said he shacks up with a girlfriend downtown. They've been shacking up for years now.*

slip away AND **slip off; slip out** to go away or escape quietly or in secret. □ *I slipped away when no one was looking.* □ *Let's slip off somewhere and have a little talk.* □ *I'll try to slip out for an hour or two when Tom is asleep.*

slip of the tongue an error in speaking where a word is pronounced incorrectly, or where something which the speaker did not mean to say is said. □ *I didn't mean to tell her that. It was a slip of the tongue.* □ *I failed to understand the instructions because the speaker made a slip of the tongue at an important point.*

slip off 1. to slide off (something). □ *I had a fish on the hook, but it slipped off.* □ *The soap was on a shelf by the sink. If it's not there, it must have slipped off.* 2. See *slip away*.

slip one's mind (for something which was to be remembered) to be forgotten. □ *I meant to go to the grocery store on the way home, but it slipped my mind.* □ *My birthday slipped my mind. I guess I wanted to forget it.*

slip out 1. to come out or get out by accident. □ *John got stuck in a narrow passage in the cave, but he finally managed to slip out.* □ *I put the car in gear, but it slipped out and caused me to lose control.* 2. (for secret information) to be revealed. □ *I asked her to keep our engagement secret, but she let it slip out.* □ *I didn't mean to tell. It just slipped out.* 3. See *slip away*.

slip through someone's fingers to get away from someone; for someone to lose track (of something or someone). □ *I had a copy of the book you want, but somehow it slipped through my fingers.* □ *There was a detective following me, but I managed to slip through his fingers.*

slip up* to make an error. (Informal. Also without *up*.) □ *Try as hard as you can to do it right and not slip up.* □ *Everything was going fine until the last minute when I slipped up.* ALSO: **slip-up*** an error. (Informal.) □ *See if you can get through this game without another slip-up.*

slough something off AND **slough off something** to shed something; to get rid of something; to throw off or repel something. (See also *shrug something off as something*.) □ *The snake spent about an hour sloughing off its old skin.* □ *Sally sloughed her dirty clothes off and took a shower.* □ *Ann made an insulting remark to me, but I just sloughed it off.*

Slow and steady wins the race. a proverb meaning that deliberateness and determination will lead to success, or (literally) a reasonable pace will win a race. □ *I worked my way through college in six years. Now I know what they mean when they say, "Slow and steady* *wins the race."* □ *Ann won the race because she started off slowly and established a good pace. The other runners tried to sprint the whole distance, and they tired out before the final lap. Ann's trainer said, "You see! I told you! Slow and steady wins the race."*

slow on the draw* (Slang. Compare to *quick on the draw*.) **1.** slow in drawing a gun. (Cowboy and gangster talk.) □ *Bill got shot because he's so slow on the draw.* □ *The gunslinger said, "I have to be fast. If I'm slow on the draw, I'm dead."* **2.** AND **slow on the uptake** slow to figure something out; slow-thinking. □ *Sally didn't get the joke because she's sort of slow on the draw.* □ *Bill—who's slow on the uptake—didn't get the joke until it was explained to him.*

slow on the uptake See *slow on the draw.*

slow someone or something down See the following entry.

slow someone or something up* AND **slow down; slow up*; slow someone or something down** to cause someone or something to reduce speed. (The phrases with *up* are informal.) □ *I'm in a hurry. Don't try to slow me down.* □ *Please slow up the train. There are sheep near the track.* □ *Slow up! I can't keep up with you.* □ *Okay, I'll slow down.*

smack dab in the middle* right in the middle. (Informal.) □ *I want a big helping of mashed potatoes with a glob of butter smack dab in the middle.* □ *Tom and Sally were having a terrible argument, and I was trapped—smack dab in the middle.*

smack someone down See *slap someone down.*

smell a rat* to suspect that something is wrong; to sense that someone has caused something wrong. (Slang.) □ *I don't think this was an accident. I smell a rat. Bob had something to do with this.* □ *The minute I came in, I smelled a rat. Sure enough, I had been robbed.*

smoke someone or something out AND **smoke out someone or something** to force someone or something out (of something), perhaps with smoke. (In cowboy or gangster talk this refers to

the smoke from gunfire.) □ *There was a mouse in the attic, but I smoked it out.* □ *The sheriff and the deputies smoked out the bank robbers.*

smooth something out AND **smooth out something** **1.** to make something flat, neat, and smooth. □ *The sheet of paper was wrinkled, so I smoothed it out.* □ *The workers used a huge roller to smooth out the gravel road.* **2.** See the following entry.

smooth something over AND **smooth something out; smooth out something; smooth over something** to reduce the intensity of an argument or a misunderstanding; to try to make people feel better about something that has happened. □ *Mary and John had a terrible argument, and they are both trying to smooth it over.* □ *Let's get everyone together and try to smooth things out. We can't keep on arguing with one another.*

snake-in-the-grass a low and deceitful person. □ *Sally said that Bob couldn't be trusted because he was a snake-in-the-grass.* □ *"You snake-in-the-grass!" cried Sally. "You cheated me."*

snap out of something* to become suddenly freed from a state. (Informal. The state can be a depression, an illness, unconsciousness, etc.) □ *I was very depressed for a week, but this morning I snapped out of it.* □ *It isn't often that a cold gets me down. Usually I can snap out of it quickly.*

snap something up* AND **snap up something*** (Informal.) **1.** to grab and buy something. □ *I went to the store, and they had soup on sale, so I snapped up plenty.* □ *I always snap bargains up whenever I go shopping.* **2.** to make something go faster. □ *You're playing this music too slowly. Snap it up!* □ *This performance is getting slow and dull. Let's snap up the whole thing!*

Snap to it!* Get busy!; Hurry up! (Informal.) □ *Stop wasting time! Snap to it!* □ *I asked you to wash the dishes an hour ago. Now, snap to it!*

sneak up on someone or something to move up on someone or something quietly or secretly. □ *Jane sneaked up on John and startled him.* □ *The date* *when tax payments are due sneaks up on us before we know it.*

sniff someone or something out AND **sniff out someone or something** to locate someone or something. □ *I'll see if I can sniff out the correct stylus for your stereo.* □ *Billy was lost, but by looking around, we were able to sniff him out.*

snowed in trapped somewhere because of too much snow. □ *The snow was so deep that we were snowed in for three days.* □ *Being snowed in is no problem if you have enough food.*

snowed under having too much work to do. □ *I had to stay downtown and work late last night because we were snowed under at the office.* □ *If I keep up with my work, I won't get snowed under.*

snuff something out AND **snuff out something** to extinguish something, especially a candle. □ *Before I went to bed, I snuffed all the candles out.* □ *Ann licks her fingers and snuffs out a candle by pinching the wick.*

so-and-so* a despised person. (Informal. This expression is used in place of other very insulting terms. Often modified, as in the examples.) □ *You dirty so-and-so! I can't stand you!* □ *Don't you call me a so-and-so, you creep!*

So be it. This is the way it will be. □ *If you insist on running off and marrying her, so be it. Only don't say I didn't warn you!* □ *Mary had decided that this is what she wants. So be it.*

So far, so good. All is going well so far. □ *We are half finished with our project. So far, so good.* □ *The operation is proceeding quite nicely—so far, so good.*

So it goes.* That is the kind of thing that happens.; That is life. (A cliché.) □ *Too bad about John and his problems. So it goes.* □ *I just lost a twenty-dollar bill, and I can't find it anywhere. So it goes.*

so long* goodbye. (Informal.) □ *So long, see you later.* □ *As John got out of the car, he said, "Thanks for the ride. So long."*

so much for someone or something that is the last of someone or something; there is no need to consider someone or something anymore. □ *It just started raining. So much for our picnic this afternoon.* □ *So much for John. He just called in sick and can't come to work today.*

so much the better* even better; all to the better. (Informal.) □ *Please come to the picnic. If you can bring a salad, so much the better.* □ *The flowers look lovely on the shelf. It would be so much the better if you put them on the table.*

so-so* not good and not bad; mediocre. (Informal.) □ *I didn't have a bad day. It was just so-so.* □ *The players put on a so-so performance.*

so still you could hear a pin drop* AND **so quiet you could hear a pin drop*** very quiet. (A cliché. Also with *can*.) □ *When I came into the room, it was so still you could hear a pin drop. Then everyone shouted, "Happy birthday!"* □ *Please be quiet. Be so quiet you can hear a pin drop.*

so to speak as one might say; said a certain way, even though the words are not exactly accurate. □ *John helps me with my taxes. He's my accountant, so to speak.* □ *I just love my little poodle. She's my baby, so to speak.*

soak in (for moisture) to penetrate paper, cloth, soil, etc. (Compare to *sink in*.) □ *I have to rinse the ink off my shirt before it soaks in.* □ *It rained a little yesterday, but not enough to soak in.*

soak something up AND **soak up something; take something up; take up something** to absorb something such as liquid, knowledge, sunshine, etc. □ *Billy spilled a glass of water and used a paper towel to soak it up.* □ *The lecture was great. I sat there and soaked up the whole thing.* □ *The sponge didn't take up all the spilled water.*

soaked to the skin with one's clothing wet clear through to the skin. □ *I was caught in the rain and got soaked to the skin.* □ *Oh, come in and dry off! You must be soaked to the skin.*

sock something away* AND **sock away something*** to store something in a safe place. (Informal.) □ *While I worked in the city, I was able to sock $100 away every month.* □ *At the present time, I can't sock away that much.*

soil one's hands See *get one's hands dirty.*

someone or something checks out* someone or something is verified or authenticated. (Informal. See also *check someone or something out.*) □ *I spent all afternoon working with my checkbook, trying to get the figures to check out.* □ *The police wouldn't believe that I am who I say I am until they made a few telephone calls to see if my story checked out.*

something about someone or something something strange or curious about someone or something. □ *There is something about Jane. I just can't figure her out.* □ *I love Mexican food. There's just something about it.*

something else* **1.** something wonderful; something extra special. (Informal.) □ *Did you see her new car? That's really something else!* □ *John hit a ball yesterday that went out of the stadium and kept on going. He's something else!* **2.** See the following entry.

something else again* AND **something else*** something entirely different. (Informal.) □ *Borrowing is one thing, but stealing is something else.* □ *Skindiving is easy and fun, but scuba diving is something else again.*

something of the sort something of the kind just mentioned. □ *The tree isn't exactly a spruce tree, just something of the sort.* □ *Jane has a cold or something of the sort.*

something or other* something; one thing or another. (Informal.) □ *I can't remember what Ann said—something or other.* □ *A messenger came by and dropped off something or other at the front desk.*

something to that effect* meaning something like that. (Informal.) □ *She said she wouldn't be available until after three, or something to that effect.* □ *I was told to keep out of the house—or something to that effect.*

something's up* something is going to happen; something is going on. (Slang. See also *What's up?*) □ *Everybody looks very nervous. I think something's up.* □ *From the looks of all the activity around here, I think something's up.*

son of a bitch* (Informal.) **1.** a very horrible person. (Usually intended as a strong insult. Never used casually.) □ *Bill called Bob a son of a bitch, and Bob punched Bill in the face.* □ *This guy's a son of a bitch. He treats everybody rotten.* **2.** a useless thing. (Use with caution.) □ *This car is a son of a bitch. It won't ever start when it's cold.* □ *This bumpy old road needs paving. It's a real son of a bitch.* **3.** a difficult task. (Informal. Use with caution.) □ *This job is a son of a bitch.* □ *I can't do this kind of thing. It's too hard—a real son of a bitch.*

son of a gun* (Informal.) **1.** a horrible person. (A euphemism for *son of a bitch.* Use with caution.) □ *When is that plumber going to show up and fix this leak? The stupid son of a gun!* □ *Bob is a rotten son of a gun if he thinks he can get away with that.* **2.** old (male) friend. (A friendly—male to male—way of referring to a friend. Use with caution.) □ *Why Bill, you old son of a gun, I haven't seen you in three or four years.* □ *When is that son of a gun John going to come visit us? He's neglecting his friends.*

sooner or later eventually; in the short term or in the long term. □ *He'll have to pay the bill sooner or later.* □ *She'll get what she deserves sooner or later.*

sort of something* AND **kind of something***; **kind of***; **sort of*** almost something; somewhat; somehow. (Informal.) □ *Isn't it sort of cold out?* □ *Yes, sort of.* □ *That was kind of a stupid thing to do, wasn't it?* □ *Kind of, yes.*

sort something out AND **sort out something** **1.** to arrange something in numerical or alphabetical order; to arrange or classify something according to some order. □ *I have to sort out this box of note cards.* □ *As soon as I sort out these files and put them away, I can help you.* **2.** to clear up confusion; to straighten out something disorderly. □ *Now that things are settled down, I can sort out my life.* □ *This place is a mess. Let's sort things out before we do anything else.*

sound someone out AND **sound out someone** to try to find out what someone thinks (about something). □ *I don't know what Jane thinks about your suggestion, but I'll sound her out.* □ *Please sound out everyone in your department.*

soup something up* AND **soup up something*** to make something (especially a car) more powerful. (Slang.) □ *Bill spent all summer souping up that old car he bought.* □ *I wish someone would soup up my car. It'll hardly run.*

sow one's wild oats to do wild and foolish things in one's youth. (Often assumed to have some sort of a sexual meaning.) □ *Dale was out sowing his wild oats last night, and he's in jail this morning.* □ *Mrs. Smith told Mr. Smith that he was too old to be sowing his wild oats.*

spaced out* dopey; giddy. (Slang.) □ *I don't see how Sally can accomplish anything. She's so spaced out!* □ *She's not really spaced out. She acts that way on purpose.*

speak highly of someone or something to say good things about someone or something. (Note the variations in the examples.) □ *Ann speaks quite highly of Jane's work.* □ *Everyone speaks very highly of Jane.*

speak of the devil* said when someone whose name has just been mentioned appears or is heard from. (A cliché.) □ *Well, speak of the devil! Hello, Tom. We were just talking about you.* □ *I had just mentioned Sally when—speak of the devil—she walked in the door.*

speak off the cuff to speak in public without preparation. □ *I'm not too good at speaking off the cuff.* □ *I need to prepare a speech for Friday, although I speak off the cuff quite well.*

speak one's mind See the following entry.

speak one's piece AND **speak one's mind** to say frankly what one thinks (about something). (Compare to *speak out on something.*) □ *Please let me speak my piece, and then you can do whatever you wish.* □ *You can always depend on John to speak his mind. He'll let you know what he really thinks.*

speak out of turn to say something unwise or imprudent; to say the right thing at the wrong time. □ *Excuse me if I'm speaking out of turn, but what you are proposing is quite wrong.* □ *Bob was quite honest, even if he was speaking out of turn.*

speak out on something AND **speak out** to say something frankly and directly; to *speak one's piece.* (See also *speak up.*) □ *This law is wrong, and I intend to speak out on it until it is repealed.* □ *You must speak out. People need to know what you think.*

speak up 1. to speak more loudly. □ *They can't hear you in the back of the room. Please speak up.* □ *What? Speak up, please. I'm hard of hearing.* **2.** to *speak out on something*; to *speak out.* (See the previous entry.) □ *If you think that this is wrong, you must speak up and say so.* □ *I'm too shy to speak up.*

speak up for someone or something to speak in favor of someone or something. □ *If anybody says bad things about me, I hope you speak up for me.* □ *I want to speak up for the rights of students.*

speed someone or something up AND **speed up someone or something** to make someone or something go faster. □ *Bill is going too slow. See if you can speed him up.* □ *We have to speed up the election process so that we can have officers by the end of the month.*

spell something out AND **spell out something 1.** to spell something (in letters). (Also without *out.*) □ *I can't understand your name. Can you spell it out?* □ *Please spell out all the strange words so I can write them down correctly.* **2.** to give all the details of something. □ *I want you to understand this completely, so I'm going to spell all this out very carefully.* □ *The instruction book for my computer spells out everything very carefully.*

spell trouble* to signify future trouble; to mean trouble. (Informal.) □ *This letter that came today spells trouble.* □ *The sky looks angry and dark. That spells trouble.*

spick-and-span* very clean. (Informal.) □ *I have to clean up the house and get it spick-and-span for the party Friday night.* □ *I love to have everything around me spick-and-span.*

spill the beans See *let the cat out of the bag.*

spin one's wheels* to be in motion, but get nowhere. (Slang.) □ *This is a terrible job. I'm just spinning my wheels and not getting anywhere.* □ *Get organized and try to accomplish something. Stop spinning your wheels!*

spin something off AND **spin off something** to create something as a byproduct of something else. □ *When the company reorganized, it spun off its banking division.* □ *By spinning off part of its assets, a company gets needed capital.*

spin something out AND **spin out** to cause a car, bus, truck, etc. to lose control and swerve or spin. □ *Bill spun his car out on a curve and wrecked it.* □ *It's very easy to spin out on icy roads.*

spit and image AND **spitting image** the perfect likeness (of a person). (Folksy. *Spitting image* is a misunderstanding of *spit and image.*) □ *Jane is the spit and image of her mother.* □ *John is his brother's spitting image.*

spit something up AND **spit up something; spit up** to throw something up; to vomit something. (Compare to *throw up.*) □ *I guess that the food didn't agree with the dog, because he spit it up.* □ *The baby has been spitting up all morning.* □ *Bob spit up his whole dinner.*

split hairs to quibble; to try to make petty distinctions. □ *They don't have any serious differences. They are just splitting hairs.* □ *Don't waste time splitting hairs. Accept it the way it is.*

split people up AND **split up people** to separate two or more people (from one another). (See also *split up.*) □ *If you two don't stop chattering, I'll have to split you up.* □ *The group of people grew too large, so we had to split them up.*

split something fifty-fifty See *divide something fifty-fifty.*

split the difference to divide the difference (with someone else). □ *You want to sell for $120, and I want to buy for $100. Let's split the difference and close the deal at $110.* □ *I don't want to split the difference. I want $120.*

split up* (for people) to separate or leave one another. (Informal. Can refer to divorce or separation.) □ *I heard that Mr. and Mrs. Brown have split up.* □ *Our little club had to split up because everyone was too busy.*

spoken for taken; reserved (for someone). □ *I'm sorry, but this one is already spoken for.* □ *Pardon me. Can I sit here, or is this seat spoken for?*

spook someone or something* to startle or disorient someone or something. (Folksy.) □ *A snake spooked my horse, and I nearly fell off.* □ *Your warning spooked me, and I was upset for the rest of the day.*

spout off about someone or something* AND **spout off*** to talk too much about someone or something. (Informal.) □ *Why do you always have to spout off about things that don't concern you?* □ *Everyone in our office spouts off about the boss.* □ *There is no need to spout off like that. Calm down and think about what you're saying.*

spread it on thick See *lay it on thick.*

spread like wildfire* to spread rapidly and without control. (A cliché.) □ *The epidemic is spreading like wildfire. Everyone is getting sick.* □ *John told a joke that was so funny it spread like wildfire.*

spread oneself too thin to do so many things that you can do none of them well. □ *It's a good idea to get involved in a lot of activities, but don't spread yourself too thin.* □ *I'm too busy these days. I'm afraid I've spread myself too thin.*

spring for something* to treat (someone) to something. (Slang.) □ *John and I went out last night, and he sprang for dinner.* □ *At the park Bill usually springs for ice cream.*

spring something on someone* to surprise someone with something. (Informal.) □ *I'm glad you told me now, rather than springing it on me at the last minute.* □ *I sprang the news on my parents last night. They were not glad to hear it.*

spruce someone or something up AND **spruce up someone or something** to make someone or something clean and orderly. □ *I'll be ready to go as soon as I spruce myself up a bit.* □ *I have to spruce up the house for the party.*

square accounts with someone AND **square accounts 1.** to settle one's financial accounts with someone. □ *I have to square accounts with the bank this week, or it'll take back my car.* □ *I called the bank and said I needed to come in and square accounts.* **2.*** to get even with someone; to straighten out a misunderstanding with someone. (Informal.) □ *I'm going to square accounts with Tom. He insulted me in public, and he owes me an apology.* □ *Tom, you and I are going to have to square accounts.*

square off for something AND **square off** to get ready for an argument or a fight. □ *John was angry and appeared to be squaring off for a fight.* □ *When those two square off, everyone gets out of the way.*

square peg in a round hole* a misfit. (A cliché.) □ *John just can't seem to get along with the people he works with. He's just a square peg in a round hole.* □ *I'm not a square peg in a round hole. It's just that no one understands me.*

square someone or something away AND **square away someone or something** to get someone or something arranged or properly taken care of. □ *Please square away the problems we discussed earlier.* □ *See if you can square Bob away in his new office.* ALSO: **squared away** arranged or properly taken care of. □ *Is Ann squared away yet?*

squeak by someone or something* AND **squeak by*** to just get by someone or something. (Informal.) □ *The guard was almost asleep, so I squeaked by him.* □ *I wasn't very well prepared for the test, and I just squeaked by.*

squirrel something away* AND **squirrel away something*** to hide or store something. (Folksy.) □ *I've been squirreling away a little money each week for years.* □ *Billy has been squirreling candy away in his top drawer.*

stab someone in the back* to betray someone. (Informal. Also used literally.) □ *I thought we were friends! Why did you stab me in the back?* □ *You don't expect a person whom you trust to stab you in the back.*

stack something up AND **stack up something** to make a stack of things. (Also without the *up*.) □ *Please stack up these boxes.* □ *Where should I stack them up?*

stack the cards against someone or something See the following entry.

stack the deck against someone or something* AND **stack the cards against someone or something***; **stack the cards***; **stack the deck*** to arrange things against someone or something. (Slang. Originally from card playing.) □ *I can't get ahead at my office. The cards are stacked against me.* □ *It's hard to succeed when the deck is stacked against success.* □ *Do you really think that someone has stacked the cards? Isn't it just fate?*

stake a claim to something* AND **stake a claim*** to lay or make a claim for something. (Informal.) □ *I want to stake a claim to that last piece of pie.* □ *You don't need to stake a claim. Just ask politely.*

stall someone or something off AND **stall off someone or something** to put off or delay someone or something. □ *The sheriff is at the door. I'll stall him off while you get out the back door.* □ *You can stall off the sheriff, but you can't stall off justice.*

stamp someone or something out AND **stamp out someone or something 1.*** [with *someone*] to get rid of or kill someone. (Slang.) □ *The victim wanted to stamp out the robbers without a trial.* □ *You just can't stamp somebody out on your own.* **2.** [with *something*] to extinguish something. □ *Tom stamped out the sparks before they started a fire.* □ *Quick, stamp that fire out before it spreads.* **3.** [with *something*] to eliminate something. □ *Many people think that they can stamp out evil.* □ *The doctors hope they can stamp out cancer.*

stand a chance to have a chance. □ *Do you think I stand a chance of winning first place?* □ *Everyone stands a chance of catching the disease.*

stand back of someone or something See the following entry.

stand behind someone or something AND **stand back of someone or some-**

thing 1. to place oneself in back of someone or something. □ *Please stand behind your grandmother in case she falls.* □ *John is standing behind the tree where you can't see him.* **2.** to endorse or guarantee something or the actions of a person. □ *Our company stands behind this product 100%.* □ *I stand behind Bill and everything he does.*

stand by to wait and remain ready. (Generally heard in communication, such as broadcasting, telephones, etc.) □ *Your transatlantic telephone call is almost ready. Please stand by.* □ *Is everyone ready for the telecast? Only ten seconds—stand by.*

stand by someone to support someone; to continue supporting someone even when things are bad. (Compare to *stick by someone or something.* Also used literally.) □ *Don't worry. I'll stand by you no matter what.* □ *I feel like I have to stand by my brother even if he goes to jail.*

stand for something 1. to endure something. □ *The teacher won't stand for any whispering in class.* □ *We just can't stand for that kind of behavior.* **2.** to signify something. □ *In a traffic signal, the red light stands for "stop."* □ *The abbreviation "Dr." stands for "doctor."* **3.** to endorse or support an ideal. □ *The mayor claims to stand for honesty in government and jobs for everyone.* □ *Every candidate for public office stands for all the good things in life.*

stand in awe of someone or something AND **stand in awe** to be overwhelmed with respect for someone or something. □ *Many people stand in awe of the President.* □ *Bob says he stands in awe of a big juicy steak. I think he's exaggerating.* □ *When it comes to food, you can say that it's delicious, but one hardly stands in awe.*

stand in for someone AND **stand in** to substitute for someone; to serve in someone's place. □ *The famous opera singer was ill, and an inexperienced singer had to stand in for her.* □ *The new singer was grateful for the opportunity to stand in.* ALSO: **stand-in** a person who substitutes for another person. □ *We had hoped to hear a famous opera star, but the stand-in was absolutely superb.*

stand in someone's way 1. to block someone's pathway. □ *Please don't stand in my way. I have to get out of here fast.* □ *I tried to grab her before she fell, but someone was standing in my way.* **2.** to be a barrier to someone's desires or intentions. □ *I know you want a divorce so you can marry Ann. Well I won't stand in your way. You can have the divorce.* □ *I know you want to leave home, and I don't want to stand in your way. You're free to go.*

stand on ceremony to hold rigidly to protocol or formal manners. (Often in the negative.) □ *Please help yourself to more. Don't stand on ceremony.* □ *We are very informal around here. Hardly anyone stands on ceremony.*

stand on one's own two feet* to be independent and self-sufficient. (Informal. Compare to *get back on one's feet.*) □ *I'll be glad when I have a good job and can stand on my own two feet.* □ *When Jane gets out of debt, she'll be able to stand on her own two feet again.*

stand one's ground AND **hold one's ground** to stand up for one's rights; to resist an attack. □ *The lawyer tried to confuse me when I was giving testimony, but I managed to stand my ground.* □ *Some people were trying to crowd us off the beach, but we held our ground.*

stand out to be uniquely visible or conspicuous. □ *This computer stands out as one of the best available.* □ *Because John is so tall, he really stands out in a crowd.*

stand over someone to monitor or watch over someone. □ *You don't have to stand over me. I can do it by myself.* □ *I know from previous experience that if I don't stand over you, you'll never finish.*

stand pat* to remain as is; to preserve the status quo. (Informal.) □ *We can't just stand pat! We have to keep making progress!* □ *This company isn't increasing sales. It's just standing pat.*

stand someone in good stead to be useful or beneficial to someone. □ *This is a fine overcoat. I'm sure it'll stand* *you in good stead for many years.* □ *I did the mayor a favor which I'm sure will stand me in good stead.*

stand someone to a treat to pay for food or drink for someone as a special favor. □ *We went to the zoo, and my father stood us all to a treat. We had ice cream and soft drinks.* □ *We went to a nice restaurant and had a fine meal. It was even better when Mr. Williams told us he'd stand us to a treat, and he picked up the bill.*

stand someone up AND **stand up someone** to fail to meet someone for a date or an appointment. □ *John and Jane were supposed to go out last night, but she stood him up.* □ *If you stand up people very often, you'll find that you have no friends at all.*

stand still for someone or something AND **hold still for someone or something** 1. AND **hold still; keep still for someone or something; keep still; stand still** to remain motionless while something is happening (to oneself). □ *Please hold still for the barber.* □ *Please keep still for the picture.* □ *If you don't stand still, you'll fall off the stool.* **2.** [with *something*] to tolerate or endure something. (Often in the negative.) □ *I won't stand still for that kind of behavior!* □ *She won't hold still for that kind of talk.*

stand to reason to seem reasonable; (for a fact or conclusion) to survive careful or logical evaluation. □ *It stands to reason that it'll be colder in January than it is in November.* □ *It stands to reason than Bill left in a hurry, although no one saw him go.*

stand up to rise to a standing position. □ *Please stand up so everyone can see you.* □ *I'm too tired to stand up.*

stand up against someone or something See *stand up to someone or something.*

stand up and be counted to state one's support (for someone or something); to *come out for someone or something.* □ *If you believe in more government help for farmers, write your representative—stand up and be counted.* □ *I'm generally in favor of what you propose, but not enough to stand up and be counted.*

stand up for someone or something to support or defend someone or something. □ *You must stand up for your own ideals!* □ *They were saying bad things about you after you left, but I stood up for you.*

stand up to someone or something AND **stand up against someone or something** to endure or resist someone or something. □ *After I learned to stand up to the manager, I found that my job was more pleasant and less threatening.* □ *I was glad that the fence I built was able to stand up against the storm.*

stand up with someone to serve as an attendant at someone's wedding. (Also used literally.) □ *Of course I know, John. He stood up with me at my wedding.* □ *He had to come from out of town, but he really wanted to stand up with me.*

stare someone in the face See *look someone in the face.*

start from scratch* to start from the beginning; to start from nothing. (Informal. Compare to *make something from scratch.*) □ *Whenever I bake a cake, I start from scratch. I never use a cake mix in a box.* □ *I built every bit of my own house. I started from scratch and did everything with my own hands.*

start out to begin; to set forth. □ *I'm going to bed early before my journey. I plan to start out before dawn.* □ *Why start out so early?*

start out as something AND **start out** to begin as something. □ *How did you start out in this business?* □ *I started out as a cook, and now I own the restaurant.*

start someone in as something AND **start someone in; start someone out as something; start someone out** to start someone on a job as a certain kind of worker. □ *I got a job in a restaurant today. They started me in as a dishwasher.* □ *I now work for the telephone company. They started me out as a local operator.*

start someone out as something See the previous entry.

start something to start a fight or an argument. (Also used literally. *Something* is *anything* or *nothing* in the negative.) □ *Hey, you! Better be careful* *unless you want to start something.* □ *I don't want to start anything. I'm just leaving.*

start something up AND **start up something** to start something, such as a car, or some procedure. (Also without *up*.) □ *It was cold, but I managed to start up the car without any difficulty.* □ *We can't start the project up until we have more money.*

start the ball rolling See *get the ball rolling.*

start with a clean slate AND **start off with a clean slate; start over with a clean slate** to start out again afresh; to ignore the past and start over again. □ *I plowed under all last year's flowers so I could start with a clean slate next spring.* □ *If I start off with a clean slate, then I'll know exactly what each plant is.* □ *When Bob got out of jail, he started over with a clean slate.*

stay after someone See *get after someone.*

stay ahead of someone or something See *get ahead of someone or something.*

stay away from someone or something See *keep away from someone or something.*

stay in touch with someone See *keep in touch with someone.*

stay out See *keep out of something or someplace.*

stay up late AND **stay up** to remain awake later than usual. □ *If I stay up late, I'm sleepy all the next day.* □ *Don't stay up if you don't want to be sleepy the next day.*

steal a base to sneak from one base to another in baseball. □ *The runner stole second base, but he nearly got put out on the way.* □ *Tom runs so slowly that he never tries to steal a base.*

steal a march on someone AND **steal a march** to get some sort of an advantage over someone without being noticed. □ *I got the contract because I was able to steal a march on my competitor.* □ *You have to be clever and fast—not dishonest—to steal a march.*

steal someone's thunder to lessen someone's force or authority. □ *What do you mean by coming in here and*

stealing my thunder? I'm in charge here! □ *Someone stole my thunder by leaking my announcement to the press.*

steal the show See the following entry.

steal the spotlight AND **steal the show** to give the best performance in a show, play, or some other event; to get attention for oneself. □ *The lead in the play was very good, but the butler stole the show.* □ *Ann always tries to steal the spotlight when she and I make a presentation.*

steamed up* angry. (Informal.) □ *What Bob said really got me steamed up.* □ *Why do you get so steamed up about nothing?*

steer clear of someone or something AND **steer clear** to avoid someone or something. □ *John is mad at me, so I've been steering clear of him.* □ *Steer clear of that book. It has many errors in it.* □ *Good advice. I'll steer clear.*

step by step little by little, one step at a time. □ *Just follow the instructions step by step, and everything will be fine.* □ *The old man slowly moved across the lawn step by step.* ALSO: **step-by-step** (listed) one after the other; gradual and orderly. □ *Just follow the step-by-step instructions, and everything will be okay.*

step down from something AND **step down** 1. to come down from something by taking one or more steps. □ *The host stepped down from the platform.* □ *We must step down carefully to avoid falling.* 2. to resign a job or a responsibility. □ *The mayor stepped down from office last week.* □ *It's unusual for a mayor to step down.*

step into the breach AND **step in** to move into a space or vacancy. □ *When Ann resigned as president, I stepped into the breach.* □ *A number of people asked me to step in and take her place.*

step on it See *step on the gas.*

step on someone's toes AND **tread on someone's toes** to interfere with or offend someone. (Also used literally. Note examples with *anyone.*) □ *When you're in public office, you have to avoid stepping on anyone's toes.* □ *Ann tread on someone's toes during the last campaign and lost the election.*

step on the gas* AND **step on it*** to hurry up. (Informal.) □ *I'm in a hurry,* *driver. Step on it!* □ *I can't step on the gas, mister. There's too much traffic.*

step out of line 1. to move briefly out of a line where one was standing. □ *I stepped out of line for a minute and lost my place.* □ *It's better not to step out of line if you aren't sure you can get back in again.* 2. to misbehave; to do something offensive. □ *I'm terribly sorry. I hope I didn't step out of line.* □ *John is a lot of fun to go out with, but he has a tendency to step out of line.*

step something up AND **step up something** to cause something to go faster. □ *The factory was not making enough cars, so they stepped up production.* □ *The music was not fast enough, so the conductor told everyone to step it up.*

step up 1. to go up one step. □ *Step up one more step, and then you'll be high enough.* □ *Step up carefully. The stair is slippery.* 2. AND **step right up** to move forward, toward someone. □ *Step right up and get your mail when I call your name.* □ *Come on, everybody. Step right up and help yourself to supper.*

stew in one's own juice* to be left alone to suffer one's anger or disappointment. (Informal.) □ *John has such a terrible temper. When he got mad at us, we just let him go away and stew in his own juice.* □ *After John stewed in his own juice for a while, he decided to come back and apologize to us.*

Stick 'em up! See *Hands up!*

stick around* (for a person) to remain in a place. (Informal.) □ *The kids stuck around for a time after the party was over.* □ *Oh, Ann. Please stick around for a while. I want to talk to you later.*

stick by someone or something AND **stick with someone or something** to support someone or something; to continue supporting someone or something when things are bad. (Informal. Compare to *stand by someone.*) □ *Don't worry. I'll stick by you no matter what.* □ *I feel like I have to stick by my brother even if he goes to jail.* □ *I'll stick by my ideas whether you like them or not.*

stick-in-the-mud someone who is stubbornly old-fashioned. □ *Come on to the party with us and have some fun.*

Don't be an old stick-in-the-mud! □ *Tom is no stick-in-the-mud. He's really up to date.*

stick one's foot in one's mouth See *put one's foot in one's mouth.*

stick one's neck out* to take a risk. (Informal.) □ *Why should I stick my neck out to do something for her? What's she ever done for me?* □ *He made a risky investment. He stuck his neck out because he thought he could make some money.*

stick one's nose into something* AND **stick one's nose in*** to interfere in something that doesn't concern one. (Informal.) □ *Will you please stop sticking your nose into my business!* □ *There are a lot of people around here who can't mind their own business. If you're doing something interesting, you'll find some of them sticking their noses in.*

stick out like a sore thumb* to be very prominent or unsightly; to be obvious and visible. (Informal.) □ *Bob is so tall that he sticks out like a sore thumb in a crowd.* □ *The house next door needs painting. It sticks out like a sore thumb.*

stick someone or something up AND **stick up someone or something** 1. [with *something*] to affix or attach something onto a wall, post, etc. □ *This notice ought to be on the bulletin board. Please stick it up.* □ *I'm going to stick up this poster near the entrance.* 2. to rob someone or something. □ *The robbers came in and tried to stick up the bank, but they got caught first.* □ *One robber stuck the cashier up first, but someone sounded the alarm before any money was taken.*

stick someone with someone or something* to burden someone with someone or something. (Informal.) □ *The dishonest merchant stuck me with a faulty television set.* □ *John stuck me with his talkative uncle and went off with his friends.* ALSO: **stuck with someone or something** burdened with someone or something. □ *I don't like to be stuck with someone else's problems.*

stick something out to endure something. (Also used literally.) □ *The play was terribly boring, but I managed to* *stick it out.* □ *College was very difficult for Bill, but he decided to stick it out.*

stick to one's guns* to remain firm in one's convictions; to stand up for one's rights. (Informal. Compare to *stand one's ground*.) □ *I'll stick to my guns on this matter. I'm sure I'm right.* □ *Bob can be persuaded to do it our way. He probably won't stick to his guns on this point.*

stick together* to remain together as a group. (Informal. Also used literally.) □ *Come on, you guys. Let's stick together. Otherwise somebody will get lost.* □ *Our group of friends has managed to stick together for almost twenty years.*

stick up for someone or something to support someone or something; to stand up for someone or something. □ *Everyone was making unpleasant remarks about John, but I stuck up for him.* □ *Our team was losing, but I stuck up for it anyway.*

stick with someone or something See *stick by someone or something.*

Still waters run deep. a proverb meaning that a quiet person is probably thinking deep or important thoughts. □ *Jane is so quiet. She's probably thinking. Still waters run deep, you know.* □ *It's true that still waters run deep, but I think that Jane is really half asleep.*

stir someone or something up AND **stir up someone or something 1.** [with *someone*] to make someone angry or excited; to make someone get active. □ *Reading the newspaper always stirs up my father.* □ *I need a cup of hot coffee to stir me up in the morning.* **2.** [with *something*] to mix something by stirring. (Also without *up*.) □ *I put the instant coffee into hot water and stirred it up.* □ *Stir the orange juice up before you pour it.*

stir up a hornet's nest* to create trouble or difficulties. (Informal.) □ *What a mess you have made of things. You've really stirred up a hornet's nest.* □ *Bill stirred up a hornet's nest when he discovered the theft.*

stock up on something AND **stock up** to build up a supply of something. □ *Before the first snow, we always stock up on firewood.* □ *John drinks a lot of milk,* so we stock up when we know he's coming.

stoop to doing something AND **stoop to something** to degrade oneself or condescend to doing something; to do something which is beneath one. □ *Whoever thought that the manager of the department would stoop to typing?* □ *I never dreamed that Bill would stoop to stealing.*

stop at nothing to do everything possible (to accomplish something); to be unscrupulous. □ *Bill would stop at nothing to get his way.* □ *Bob is completely determined to get promoted. He'll stop at nothing.*

stop by someplace AND **stop by; stop in someplace; stop in** to visit someplace, usually briefly. □ *I was coming home, but I decided to stop by my aunt's on the way.* □ *She was very glad that I stopped in.*

stop in someplace See *stop by someplace.*

stop off someplace AND **stop off** to stop somewhere on the way to some other place. □ *I stopped off at the store to buy milk on the way home.* □ *We stopped off for a few minutes and chatted with my uncle.*

stop over someplace AND **stop over** to break one's journey, usually overnight or even longer. □ *On our way to New York, we stopped over in Philadelphia for the night.* □ *That's a good place to stop over. There are some nice hotels in Philadelphia.* ALSO: **stopover** a place where one breaks one's journey. □ *We went to New York with a stopover in Philadelphia.*

stow away to hide away on a ship or an airplane in order to get free transportation. □ *I once read about a man who made a journey around the world by stowing away.* □ *You can get arrested if you stow away.* ALSO: **stowaway** someone who stows away. □ *The crew found two stowaways aboard and locked them in a cabin.*

straight from the horse's mouth* from an authoritative or dependable source. (A cliché.) □ *I know it's true! I heard it straight from the horse's mouth!* □ *This comes straight from the horse's mouth, so it has to be believed.*

straight from the shoulder* sincerely; frankly; holding nothing back. (A cliché.) □ *Sally always speaks straight from the shoulder. You never have to guess what she really means.* □ *Bill gave a good presentation—straight from the shoulder and brief.*

straighten someone or something out AND **straighten out someone or something 1.** [with *someone*] to make someone understand something. □ *Jane was confused about the date, so I straightened her out.* □ *I took a few minutes and straightened out everyone.* **2.** [with *someone*] to reform someone. □ *The judge felt that a few years at hard labor would straighten out the thief.* □ *Most people think that jail never straightens anybody out.* **3.** [with *something*] to make a situation less confused. □ *John made a mess of the contract, so I helped him straighten it out.* □ *Please straighten out your checking account. It's all messed up.* **4.** to make someone or something straight. □ *Tom stood up and straightened himself out.* □ *I straightened out the row of chairs.*

straighten someone or something up AND **straighten up someone or something 1.** to put someone or something into an upright position. □ *The post is tilted. Please straighten it up.* □ *Bill, you're slouching again. Straighten yourself up.* **2.** to tidy up someone or something. □ *This room is a mess. Let's straighten it up.* □ *John straightened himself up a little before going on stage.*

straighten up 1. to sit or stand more straight. □ *Billy's mother told him to straighten up or he'd fall out of his chair.* □ *John straightened up so he'd look taller.* **2.** to behave better. □ *Bill was acting badly for a while; then he straightened up.* □ *Sally, straighten up, or I will punish you!*

strapped for something* AND **strapped*** (Informal.) very much in need of money. □ *I'm strapped for a few bucks. Can you loan me five dollars?* □ *Sorry, I'm strapped, too.*

stretch a point AND **stretch the point** to interpret a point flexibly and with great latitude. □ *Would it be stretching a point to suggest that everyone is invited*

to your picnic? □ *To say that everyone is invited is stretching the point.*

strictly on the up and up See *on the up and up.*

strike a bargain to reach an agreement on a price (for something). □ *They argued for a while and finally struck a bargain.* □ *They were unable to strike a bargain, so they left.*

strike a happy medium AND **hit a happy medium** to find a compromise position; to arrive at a position halfway between two unacceptable extremes. □ *Ann likes very spicy food, but Bob doesn't care for spicy food at all. We are trying to find a restaurant which strikes a happy medium.* □ *Tom is either very happy or very sad. He can't seem to hit a happy medium.*

strike a match to light a match. □ *Mary struck a match and lit a candle.* □ *When Sally struck a match to light a cigarette, Jane said quickly, "No smoking, please."*

strike a sour note* AND **hit a sour note*** to signify something unpleasant. (Informal.) □ *Jane's sad announcement struck a sour note at the annual banquet.* □ *News of the crime hit a sour note in our holiday celebration.*

strike it rich* to acquire wealth suddenly. (Informal.) □ *If I could strike it rich, I wouldn't have to work anymore.* □ *Sally ordered a dozen oysters and found a huge pearl in one of them. She struck it rich!*

strike out 1. (for a baseball batter) to be declared "out" after three strikes. (See also *strike someone out.*) □ *Bill almost never strikes out.* □ *John struck out at least once in every game this season.* **2.*** to fail. (Slang.) □ *Ann did her best, but she struck out anyway.* □ *Give it another try. Just because you struck out once, it doesn't mean you can't do better now.*

strike out at someone or something to (figuratively or literally) hit at or attack someone or something. □ *She was so angry she struck out at the person she was arguing with.* □ *I was frantic. I wanted to strike out at everything and everybody.*

strike someone funny to seem funny to someone. □ *Sally has a great sense* *of humor. Everything she says strikes me funny.* □ *Why are you laughing? Did something I say strike you funny?*

strike someone out AND **strike out someone** (for a baseball pitcher) to get a batter declared "out" after three strikes. □ *Bill struck out all our best players.* □ *I never thought he'd strike Tom out.*

strike someone's fancy to appeal to someone. □ *I'll have some ice cream, please. Chocolate strikes my fancy right now.* □ *Why don't you go to the store and buy a record album that strikes your fancy?*

strike up a conversation to start a conversation (with someone). □ *I struck up an interesting conversation with someone on the bus yesterday.* □ *It's easy to strike up a conversation with someone when you're traveling.*

strike up a friendship to become friends (with someone). □ *I struck up a friendship with John while were we on a business trip together.* □ *If you're lonely, you should go out and try to strike up a friendship with someone you like.*

strike while the iron is hot* to do something at the best possible time; to do something when the time is ripe. (A cliché.) □ *He was in a good mood, so I asked for a loan of $200. I thought I'd better strike while the iron was hot.* □ *Please go to the bank and settle this matter now! They are willing to be reasonable. You've got to strike while the iron is hot.*

string along with someone AND **string along** to accompany someone; to *run around with someone.* □ *Sally seemed to know where she was going, so I decided to string along with her.* □ *She said it was okay if I strung along.*

string something out AND **string out something** to draw something out (in time); to make something last a long time. (See also *strung out.*) □ *The meeting was long enough. There was no need to string it out further with all those speeches.* □ *They tried to string out the meeting to make things seem more important.*

stroke of luck a bit of luck; a lucky happening. □ *I had a stroke of luck and found Tom at home when I called. He's*

not usually there. □ *Unless I have a stroke of luck, I'm not going to finish this report by tomorrow.*

struggle to the death* **1.** a bitter struggle to the end. (A cliché. Literal and figurative uses.) □ *The wolf and the elk fought in a struggle to the death.* □ *I had a terrible time getting my car started. It was a struggle to the death, but it finally started.* **2.** to struggle or fight to the end or to death. □ *The wolf and the elk struggled to the death.* □ *I struggled to the death to get my report done on time.*

strung out **1.** extended in time; overly long. □ *Why was that lecture so strung out? She talked and talked.* □ *It was strung out because there was very little to be said.* **2.*** doped or drugged. (Slang.) □ *Bob acted very strangely—as if he were strung out or something.* □ *I've never seen Bob or any of his friends strung out.*

stuck on someone or something **1.** [with *someone*] to be fond of or in love with someone; to *have a crush on someone.* □ *John was stuck on Sally, but she didn't know it.* □ *He always gets stuck on the wrong person.* **2.** [with *something*] to be locked into an idea, cause, or purpose. □ *Mary is really stuck on the idea of going to France this spring.* □ *You've proposed a good plan, Jane, but don't get stuck on it. We may have to make some changes.*

stuck with someone or something* burdened with someone or something; left having to care for someone or something. (Informal.) □ *Please don't leave me stuck with your aunt. She talks too much.* □ *My roommate quit school and left me stuck with the telephone bill.*

stuff and nonsense* nonsense. (Informal.) □ *Come on! Don't give me all that stuff and nonsense!* □ *I don't understand this book. It's all stuff and nonsense as far as I am concerned.*

stuff the ballot box to put fraudulent ballots into a ballot box; to cheat in counting the votes in an election. □ *The election judge was caught stuffing the ballot box in the election yesterday.* □ *Election officials are supposed to guard against stuffing the ballot box.*

stumble across someone or something AND **stumble into someone or something; stumble on someone or something** to find someone or something, usually by accident. (See also the following entry.) □ *I stumbled across an interesting book yesterday when I was shopping.* □ *Guess who I stumbled into at the library yesterday?* □ *I stumbled on a real bargain at the bookstore last week.*

stumble into someone or something 1. to bump into someone or something accidentally. □ *I stumbled into John, and I apologized. It was my fault.* □ *I stumbled into a post and hurt my arm.* 2. See the previous entry. 3. [with *something*] to enter something or a place by stumbling. □ *I tripped on the curb and stumbled into the car.* □ *I stumbled into the house, exhausted and in need of a cool drink.*

stumble on someone or something 1. See *stumble across someone or something.* 2. to trip over someone or something. □ *There were three of us sleeping in the small tent. Each of us would stumble on the others whenever we went out or came in.* □ *I stumbled on the curb and twisted my ankle.*

subject to something likely to have or get something, usually a disease or ailment. □ *Bill is subject to fainting spells.* □ *Bob says he's subject to colds and the flu.*

subscribe to something to have a standing order for a magazine or something similar. □ *I usually buy my monthly magazines at the newsstand. I don't subscribe to them.* □ *I subscribe to all the magazines I read because it's nice to have them delivered by mail.*

such-and-such* someone or something whose name has been forgotten or should not be said. (Informal.) □ *Mary said that such-and-such was coming to her party, but I forgot their names.* □ *If you walk into a store and ask for such-and-such and they don't have it, you go to a different store.*

such as it is* in the imperfect state that one sees it; in the less-than-perfect condition in which one sees it. (A cliché.) □ *This is where I live. This is my glori-*ous home—such as it is.* □ *I've worked for days on this report, and I've done the best that I can do. It's my supreme effort—such as it is.*

Such is life!* That is the way things happen. (A cliché.) □ *Oh well. Everything can't be perfect. Such is life!* □ *So I failed my test. Such is life! I can take it again some time.*

suck someone in* AND **suck in someone***; **take in someone; take someone in** to deceive someone. (The expressions with *suck* are slang.) □ *I think that someone sucked in John. I don't know why he bought this car.* □ *I try to shop carefully so that no one can take me in.*

suit someone to a T AND **fit someone to a T** to be very appropriate for someone. □ *This kind of job suits me to a T.* □ *This is Sally's kind of house. It fits her to a T.*

suit up* to put on one's sports clothing or uniform. (Informal.) □ *The team has to get there early so the players can suit up.* □ *I was late and almost didn't have time to suit up.*

suit yourself to do something one's own way; to do something to please oneself. □ *Okay, if you don't want to do it my way, suit yourself.* □ *Take either of the books that you like. Suit yourself. I'll read the other one.*

sum something up AND **sum up something** to summarize something. □ *At the end of the lecture, Dr. Williams summed the important points up for us.* □ *He said when he finished, "Well, that about sums it up."*

Sunday-go-to-meeting clothes* one's best clothes. (Folksy. See also *in one's Sunday best.*) □ *John was all dressed up in his Sunday-go-to-meeting clothes.* □ *I hate to be wearing my Sunday-go-to-meeting clothes when everyone else is casually dressed.*

survival of the fittest* the idea that the most able or fit will survive (while the less able and less fit will perish). (A cliché. This is used literally as a part of the theory of evolution.) □ *In college, it's the survival of the fittest. You have to keep working in order to survive and graduate.* □ *I don't give my house plants* *very good care, but the ones I have are really flourishing. It's the survival of the fittest, I guess.*

swallow one's pride to forget one's pride and accept something humiliating. □ *I had to swallow my pride and admit that I was wrong.* □ *When you're a student, you find yourself swallowing your pride quite often.*

swallow something hook, line, and sinker* to believe something completely. (Slang. These terms refer to fishing and fooling a fish into being caught.) □ *I made up a story about why I was so late. The boss believed it hook, line, and sinker.* □ *I feel like a fool. I fell for the trick, hook, line, and sinker.*

swear by someone or something 1. to take an oath on someone or something. □ *My uncle is sort of old fashioned. He makes promises by swearing by his "sainted mother."* □ *He sometimes swears by his foot!* **2.** to have complete faith and confidence in someone or something. □ *I'm willing to swear by John. He's completely dependable.* □ *This is an excellent brand of detergent. My sister swears by it.*

swear someone in AND **swear in someone** to give someone an oath of office. (Said of public officials, members of a jury, etc.) □ *The judge swore in the members of the jury without much ceremony.* □ *The mayor swore in the treasurer at the first city council meeting.*

swear something off AND **swear off something** to pledge to give something up. □ *Swearing habits off is very difficult for someone.* □ *I decided to swear off smoking once and for all.*

sweat blood* to be very anxious and tense. (Slang.) □ *What a terrible test! I was really sweating blood at the last.* □ *Bob is such a bad driver. I sweat blood every time I ride with him.*

sweat something out* AND **sweat out something*** to endure or wait for

something which causes tension or boredom. (Informal.) □ *I had to wait for her in the reception area. It was a long wait, but I managed to sweat it out.* □ *I took the test and then spent a week sweating out the results.*

sweep one off one's feet AND **knock one off one's feet 1.** to knock someone down. □ *The wind swept me off my feet.* □ *Bill punched Bob playfully, and knocked him off his feet.* **2.*** to overwhelm someone (figuratively). (Informal.) □ *Mary is madly in love with Bill. He swept her off her feet.* □ *The news was so exciting that it knocked me off my feet.*

sweep something up AND **sweep up something** to clean by sweeping something away. □ *I broke a glass and had to sweep up the pieces.* □ *This floor is a mess. There is stuff all over it. Please sweep it up.*

sweet on someone* fond of someone. (Folksy.) □ *Tom is sweet on Mary. He may ask her to marry him.* □ *Mary's sweet on him, too.*

sweet talk someone* to talk convincingly to someone with much flattery. (Folksy.) □ *I didn't want to help her, but she sweet talked me into it.* □ *He sweet talked her for a while, and she finally agreed to go to the dance with him.*

swim against the current See the following entry.

swim against the tide AND **swim against the current** to do the opposite of everyone else; to go against the trend. □ *Bob tends to do what everybody else does. He isn't likely to swim against the tide.* □ *Mary always swims against the current. She's a very contrary person.*

swing into action See *go into action.*

swing something* to make something happen. (Slang.) □ *I hope I can swing a deal that will make us all a lot of money.* □ *We all hope you can swing it.*

T

tail wagging the dog a situation where a small part is controlling the whole thing. □ *John was just hired yesterday, and today he's bossing everyone around. It's a case of the tail wagging the dog.* □ *Why is this small matter so important? Now the tail is wagging the dog!*

take a back seat to someone AND **take a back seat** to defer to someone; to give control to someone. □ *I decided to take a back seat to Mary and let her manage the project.* □ *I had done the best I could, but it was time to take a back seat and let someone else run things.*

take a bath on something* AND **take a bath*** to have large financial losses on an investment. (Slang.) □ *I took a bath on all my oil stock. I should have sold it sooner.* □ *I don't mind losing a little money now and then, but I really took a bath this time.*

take a bow to bow and receive credit for a good performance. □ *At the end of the concerto, the pianist rose and took a bow.* □ *The audience applauded wildly and demanded that the conductor come out and take a bow again.*

take a break AND **take one's break** to have a short rest period in one's work. □ *It's 10:00—time to take a break.* □ *I don't usually take my break until 10:30.*

take a chance AND **take a risk** to try something where failure or bad fortune is likely. □ *Come on, take a chance. You may lose, but it's worth trying.* □ *I'm not reckless, but I don't mind taking a risk now and then.*

take a crack at something* to give something a try. (Informal.) □ *I don't think I can convince her to leave, but I'll take a crack at it.* □ *Someone had to try to rescue the child. Bill said he'd take a crack at it.*

take a dig at someone* AND **take digs at someone*** to insult someone; to say something which will irritate a person. (Slang.) □ *Jane took a dig at Bob for being late all the time.* □ *Jane is always taking digs at Bob, but she never really means any harm.*

take a dim view of something to regard something skeptically or pessimistically. □ *My aunt takes a dim view of most things that young people do.* □ *The manager took a dim view of my efforts on the project. I guess I didn't try hard enough.*

take a fancy to someone or something* AND **take a liking to someone or something*; take a shine to someone or something*** to develop a fondness or a preference for someone or something. (Folksy.) □ *John began to take a fancy to Sally late last August at the picnic.* □ *I've never taken a liking to cooked carrots.* □ *I think my teacher has taken a shine to me.*

take a gander at someone or something* AND **take a gander*** to examine someone or something; to *take a look at someone or something.* (Slang.) □ *Hey, will you take a gander at that fancy car!* □ *Drive it over here so I can take a gander.*

take a hand in something to help planning or doing something. □ *I was glad to take a hand in planning the picnic.* □ *Jane refused to take a hand in any of the work.* ALSO: **have a hand in something** to play a part in (doing) something. □ *I had a hand in the picnic plans.*

take a hard line with someone AND **take a hard line** to be firm with someone; to have a firm policy for dealing with someone. □ *The manager takes a hard line with people who show up late.* □ *This is a serious matter. The police are likely to take a hard line.*

take a hint to understand a hint and behave accordingly. □ *I said I didn't want to see you anymore. Can't you take a hint? I don't like you.* □ *Sure I can take a hint, but I'd rather be told directly.*

take a leaf out of someone's book to behave or to do something in the way that someone else would. □ *When you act like that, you're taking a leaf out of your sister's book, and I don't like it!* □ *You had better do it your way. Don't take a leaf out of my book. I don't do it well.*

take a licking See *get a licking.*

take a liking to someone or something See *take a fancy to someone or something.*

take a load off one's feet See *get a load off one's feet.*

take a look at someone or something AND **take a look** to examine (briefly) someone or something. (Also with *have*, as in the examples.) □ *I asked the doctor to take a look at my ankle which has been hurting.* □ *"So your ankle's hurting," said the doctor. "Let's take a look."* □ *Please have a look at my car. It's not running well.*

take a new turn (for something) to begin a new course or direction. □ *When I received the telegram with the exciting news, my life took a new turn.* □ *I began taking the medicine at noon, and by evening the disease had begun to take a new turn. I was getting better!*

take a nose dive See *go into a nose dive.*

take a powder* to leave (a place); to sneak out or run out (of a place). (Slang.) □ *When the police came to the door, Tom decided it was time to take a powder. He left by the back door.* □ *When the party got a little dull, Bill and his friend took a powder.*

take a punch at someone* to strike or strike at someone. (Informal.) □ *Mary got so angry at Bob that she took a punch at him.* □ *She took a punch at him, but she missed.*

take a rain check on something See *get a rain check on something.*

take a risk See *take a chance.*

take a shellacking See *get a shellacking.*

take a shine to someone or something See *take a fancy to someone or something.*

take a shot at something (Also with *have* as in the example.) **1.** to shoot at something, as with a gun. □ *I aimed carefully and took a shot at the target.* □ *Be careful when you're in the woods during hunting season, or a hunter might have a shot at you.* **2.** See *take a try at something.*

take a spill to have a fall; to tip over. (Also with *bad, nasty, quite,* etc. Also with *have*.) □ *Ann tripped on the curb and took a nasty spill.* □ *John had quite a spill when he fell off his bicycle.*

take a stab at something* to make a try at something, sometimes without much hope of success. (Informal. Also with *have*.) □ *I don't know if I can do it, but I'll take a stab at it.* □ *Come on, Mary. Take a stab at catching a fish. You might end up liking to fish.* □ *Would you like to have a stab at this problem?*

take a stand against someone or something AND **take a stand** to take a position in opposition to someone or something; to oppose or resist someone or something. □ *The treasurer was forced to take a stand against the board because of its wasteful spending.* □ *The treasurer took a stand, and others agreed.*

take a try at something AND **take a shot at something*** to give something a try. (The expression with *shot* is informal. Also with *have*.) □ *I don't know if I can eat a whole pizza, but I'll be happy to take a shot at it.* □ *I can't seem to get this computer to work right. Would you like to take a try at it?* □ *I like your new bike. Can I have a try at riding it?*

take a turn for the better to start to improve; to start to get well. (The opposite of the following entry.) □ *She was very sick for a month; then suddenly she took a turn for the better.* □ *Things are* *taking a turn for the better at my store. I may make a profit this year.*

take a turn for the worse to start to get worse. (The opposite of the previous entry.) □ *It appeared that she was going to get well; then, unfortunately, she took a turn for the worse.* □ *My job was going quite well; then last week things took a turn for the worse.*

take a walk* AND **take a hike*** to leave somewhere. (Slang. Also used literally.) □ *He was rude to me, so I just took a walk and left him standing there.* □ *He was getting on my nerves, so I told him to take a hike.*

take a whack at someone or something* (Slang. *Whack* is sometimes spelled *wack*. Also with *have*, as in the examples.) **1.** [with *someone*] to hit at someone; to hit someone. □ *He took a whack at me, so I punched him.* □ *Don't try to take a whack at me again!* □ *I'll have a wack at you!* **2.** [with *something*] to take a try at (doing) something. □ *I don't know if I can do it or not, but I'll take a whack at it.* □ *You can have a whack at it when it's your turn.*

take action against someone or something AND **take action** to do something against someone or something; to use the law—as in a law suit—against someone or something. □ *If you don't stop bothering me, I'll take action against you.* □ *We'll all have to take action against this threat.* □ *All of us will take action.*

take advantage of someone or something 1. [with *someone*] to cheat or deceive someone. □ *The store owner took advantage of me, and I'm angry.* □ *You must be alert when you shop to make sure that someone doesn't take advantage of you.* **2.** to utilize someone or something to one's own benefit. □ *Jane can be of great help to me, and I intend to take advantage of her.* □ *Try to take advantage of every opportunity which comes your way.*

take after someone to resemble a close, older relative. □ *Don't you think that Sally takes after her mother?* □ *No, Sally takes after her Aunt Ann.*

take aim at someone or something AND

take aim 1. to aim (something) at someone or something. □ *The hunter took aim at the deer and pulled the trigger.* □ *You must take aim carefully before you shoot.* **2.** to prepare to deal with someone or something. □ *Now we have to take aim at the problem and try to get it solved.* □ *He turned to me and took aim. I knew he was going to scold me severely.*

take an interest in something AND **take an interest** to develop an interest in something. □ *I wish John would take an interest in his school work.* □ *We hoped you'd take an interest and join our club.*

take care of someone or something 1. to care for or keep someone or something. □ *I have to take care of my little brother this evening.* □ *I'm taking care of my mother's house plants while she's away.* **2.*** [with *someone*] to beat or kill someone. (Slang, especially criminal slang.) □ *The crook threatened to take care of the witness.* □ *"If you breathe a word of what you saw, my gang will take care of you," said the thief.*

take charge of someone or something AND **take charge** to take (over) control of someone or something. □ *The president came in late and took charge of the meeting.* □ *When the new manager took charge, things really began to happen.*

take cold See *catch cold.*

take effect See *go into effect.*

take exception to something AND **take exception** to disagree with something (which someone has said). □ *I take exception to your remarks, and I would like to discuss them with you.* □ *I'm sorry you take exception. Let's discuss the matter.*

take five* to take a five-minute rest period. (Slang.) □ *Okay, everybody. Take five!* □ *Hey, Bob. I'm tired. Can we take five?*

take forty winks* to take a nap; to go to sleep. (Informal.) □ *I think I'll go to bed and take forty winks. See you in the morning.* □ *Why don't you go take forty winks and call me in about an hour?*

take heart to be brave; to have courage. □ *Take heart, John. Things could* be worse! □ *I told her to take heart and try again next time.*

take heed to be cautious. □ *Take heed, and don't get involved with the wrong kind of people.* □ *Just take heed, and you'll be safe.*

take hold of someone or something AND **get hold of someone or something; take hold** 1. to grasp someone or something. □ *Take hold of the bat and swing it against the ball when it's pitched.* □ *Billy's mother got hold of him and dragged him away.* 2. to get in control of someone or something. □ *Take hold of yourself! Calm down and relax.* □ *She took a few minutes to get hold of herself, and then she spoke.*

take ill See *take sick.*

take issue with someone AND **take issue** to argue with someone; to dispute a point with someone. □ *I hate to take issue with you on such a minor point, but I'm quite sure you're wrong.* □ *I don't mind if you take issue, but I'm sure I'm right.*

take it away* to start up a performance. (Slang. Typically a public announcement of the beginning of a musical performance. Also used literally.) □ *And now, here is the band playing "Song of Songs." Take it away!* □ *Sally will now sing us a song. Take it away, Sally!*

take it easy on someone or something 1. to be gentle with someone or something. □ *Take it easy on Mary. She's been sick.* □ *Please take it easy on the furniture. It has to last us many years.* 2.* [with *something*] to use less of something (rather than more). (Informal.) □ *Take it easy on the soup. There's just enough for one serving for each person.* □ *Please take it easy on the pencils. There are hardly any left.*

Take it or leave it.* to accept it (the way it is) or forget it. (Informal.) □ *This is my last offer. Take it or leave it.* □ *It's not much, but it's the only food we have. You can take it or leave it.*

take it slow* to move or go slowly. (Informal.) □ *The road is rough, so take it slow.* □ *This book is very hard to read, and I have to take it slow.*

take kindly to something to be agreea-

ble to something. □ *My father doesn't take kindly to anyone using his tools.* □ *I hope they'll take kindly to our request.*

take leave of one's senses to become irrational. (Often verbatim with *one's*, as in the main entry form.) □ *What are you doing? Have you taken leave of your senses?* □ *What a terrible situation! It's enough to make one take leave of one's senses.*

take leave of someone See *take one's leave of someone.*

take liberties with someone or something AND **make free with someone or something** to use or abuse someone or something. □ *You are overly familiar with me, Mr. Jones. One might think you were taking liberties with me.* □ *I don't like it when you make free with my lawn mower. You should at least ask when you want to borrow it.*

take no stock in something AND **not take stock in something** to pay no attention to someone; to not believe or accept something. □ *I take no stock in anything John has to say.* □ *He doesn't take stock in your opinions either.*

take note of something AND **take note** to observe and remember something. □ *Please take note of the point I'm about to make.* □ *Here is something else about which you should take note.*

take notice of something AND **take notice** to observe something. □ *I didn't take notice of when he came in.* □ *They say he came in late, but I didn't take notice.*

take off after someone or something AND **take off; take out after someone or something** to begin to chase someone or something. □ *The bank guard took off after the robber.* □ *Did you see that police car take off?* □ *It took out after the bank robber's car.*

take off from work AND **take off** to not go to work (for a period of time). □ *I had to take off from work in order to renew my driver's license.* □ *I hate to take off for something like that.*

take off on something AND **launch forth on something; launch forth** to start out a lecture on something; to begin a discussion of something. □ *My father took off on the subject of taxes and talked* *for an hour.* □ *My uncle is always launching forth on the state of the economy.* □ *When he launches forth, I leave the room.*

take off one's hat to someone AND **take off one's hat** to offer praise for someone's good accomplishments. □ *I have to take off my hat to Mayor Johnson. She has done an excellent job.* □ *Yes, we all ought to take off our hats. She is our best mayor ever.*

take offense at someone or something AND **take offense** to become resentful at someone or something. □ *Bill took offense at Mary for her thoughtless remarks.* □ *Almost everyone took offense at Bill's new book.* □ *I'm sorry you took offense. I meant no harm.*

take office to begin serving as an elected or appointed official. □ *When did the mayor take office?* □ *All the elected officials took office just after the election.*

take one at one's word to believe what someone says and act accordingly. □ *She told me to go jump in the lake, and I took her at her word.* □ *You shouldn't take her at her word. She frequently says things she doesn't really mean.*

take one's death of cold See *catch one's death of cold.*

take one's hands off someone or something See *get one's hands off someone or something.*

take one's leave of someone AND **take one's leave; take leave of someone** to say goodbye to someone and leave. □ *I took leave of the hostess at an early hour.* □ *One by one, the guests took their leave.*

take one's medicine* to accept the punishment or the bad fortune which one deserves. (Informal. Also used literally.) □ *I know I did wrong, and I know I have to take my medicine.* □ *Billy knew he was going to get spanked, and he didn't want to take his medicine.*

take one's own life to kill oneself; to commit suicide. □ *Bob tried to take his own life, but he was rescued in time.* □ *Later, he was sorry that he had tried to take his own life.*

take one's time to use as much time (to do something) as one wants. □ *There*

is no hurry. Please take your time. □ *If you take your time, you'll be late.*

take out after someone or something See *take off after someone or something.*

take pains to do something AND **take pains** to make a great effort to do something. □ *Tom took pains to decorate the room exactly right.* □ *We took pains to get there on time.*

take part in something AND **take part** to participate in something. □ *They invited me to take part in their celebration.* □ *I was quite pleased to take part.*

take pity on someone or something AND **take pity** to feel sorry for someone or something. □ *We took pity on the hungry people and gave them some warm food.* □ *She took pity on the little dog and brought it in to get warm.* □ *Please take pity! Please help us!*

take place to happen. □ *When will this party take place?* □ *It's taking place right now.*

take root to begin to take hold or have effect. (Also used literally referring to plants.) □ *Things will begin to change when my new policies take root.* □ *My ideas began to take root and influence other people.*

take sick* AND **take ill*** to become ill. (Folksy.) □ *I took sick with a bad cold last week.* □ *I hope I don't take ill before final exams.*

take sides to choose one side of an argument. □ *They were arguing, but I didn't want to take sides, so I left.* □ *I don't mind taking sides on important issues.*

take someone down a notch or two See the following entry.

take someone down a peg or two AND **take someone down a notch; take someone down a notch or two** to reprimand someone who is acting too arrogant. □ *The teacher's scolding took Bob down a notch or two.* □ *He was so rude that someone was bound to take him down a peg or two.*

take someone down to size See *cut someone down to size.*

take someone for an idiot AND **take someone for a fool** to assume that someone is stupid. □ *I wouldn't do any-*

thing like that! Do you take me for an idiot? □ *I don't take you for a fool. I think you're very clever.*

take someone for someone or something to mistake someone for someone or something. □ *I took Bill for his brother, Bob. They look so much alike!* □ *I took Mr. Brown for the gardener, and he was a little bit insulted.*

take someone in to deceive someone. □ *Don't let John and his smooth manner take you in.* □ *The crook took us in, and we lost nearly $400 in the deal.*

take someone or something apart AND **take apart someone or something** **1.*** [with *someone*] to beat someone up. (Slang.) □ *Don't talk to me that way, or I'll take you apart.* □ *He was so mad that I thought he was going to take apart all of us.* **2.** [with *something*] to disassemble something; to remove or disconnect the parts of something, one by one. □ *Bill took his radio apart to try to fix it.* □ *He takes apart everything he can so he can learn how things work.*

take someone or something away AND **take away someone or something** to remove someone or something. □ *I don't want any more soup. Please take it away.* □ *Take away Bill and John. They are bothering me.*

take someone or something back AND **take back someone or something** **1.** to retrieve someone or something; to accept the return of someone or something. □ *Please take back your money. I'll pay for the meal.* □ *Jane got mad and ran away from home, but we took her back.* **2.** [with *something*] to withdraw or cancel one's statement. □ *I heard what you said, and I'm very insulted. Please take it back.* □ *Take back your words, or I'll never speak to you again!*

take someone or something by storm* to overwhelm someone or something; to attract a great deal of attention from someone or something. (A cliché.) □ *Jane is madly in love with Tom. He took her by storm at the office party, and they've been together ever since.* □ *The singer took the world of opera by storm with her performance in* La Boheme.

take someone or something by sur-

prise to startle or surprise someone or something. □ *She came into the room and took them by surprise.* □ *I took the little bird by surprise, and it flew away.*

take someone or something for granted to accept someone or something—without gratitude—as a matter of course. □ *We tend to take a lot of things for granted.* □ *Mrs. Franklin complained that Mr. Franklin takes her for granted.*

take someone or something in AND **take in someone or something** **1.** to observe someone or something. □ *The zoo is too big to take the whole thing in during one day.* □ *It takes two days to take in the museum.* **2.** to provide shelter for someone or something. □ *When I needed a place to live, my uncle took me in.* □ *Mrs. Wilson took in the lonely little dog and gave it a warm home.* **3.** [with *something*] to inhale, drink, or eat something. □ *I think I'll go for a walk and take in some fresh air.* □ *Jane was very ill, but she managed to take in a little broth.* **4.** See *suck someone in.*

take someone or something into account AND **take into account someone or something** to remember to consider someone or something. □ *I hope you'll take Bill and Bob into account when you plan the party.* □ *I'll try to take into account all the things that are important in a situation like this.*

take someone or something on AND **take on someone or something** to undertake to deal with someone or something. □ *Mrs. Smith is such a problem. I don't feel like taking her on just now.* □ *I'm too busy to take on any new problems.*

take someone or something out AND **take out someone or something** **1.** [with *someone*] to take someone out on the town on a date. □ *I hear that Tom has been taking Ann out.* □ *No, Tom has been taking out Mary.* **2.*** [with *someone*] to remove someone who is acting as a barrier, especially in football. (Informal.) □ *Our player ran fast and took out the player of the opposing team before he could tackle our runner.* □ *Okay, Bill. Get in there and take out* the quarterback. **3.*** [with *someone*] to kill someone. (Criminal slang.) □ *The crooks took out the witness to the crime.* □ *The thief who drove the car was afraid that the other thieves were going to take him out, too.* **4.** to remove someone or something (from someplace). □ *Billy is getting to be a pest. Please take him out.* □ *Please take out the frozen chicken for dinner tonight.*

take someone or something over AND **take over someone or something** to *take charge of someone or something*; to assume control of someone or something. □ *The new manager will take the office over next week.* □ *Will you please take over your children? I can't seem to control them.*

take someone or something wrong to misunderstand someone or something. □ *Please don't take me wrong, but I believe that your socks don't match.* □ *You'll probably take this wrong, but I have to say that I've never seen you looking better.*

take someone to task to scold or reprimand someone. □ *The teacher took John to task for his bad behavior.* □ *I lost a big contract, and the boss took me to task in front of everyone.*

take someone to the cleaners* to abuse or damage someone. (Slang.) □ *There was a real rough guy there who threatened to take me to the cleaners if I didn't cooperate.* □ *The crook said he'd take anybody who interfered to the cleaners.*

take someone under one's wing AND **take someone under one's wings** to take over and care for a person. □ *John wasn't doing well in geometry until the teacher took him under her wing.* □ *I took the new workers under my wings, and they learned the job in no time.*

take someone up on something* AND **take up someone on something*** to take advantage of someone's offer of something. (Informal.) □ *I'd like to take you up on your offer to help.* □ *We took up the Browns on their invitation to come to dinner.*

take someone's breath away 1. to cause someone to be out of breath due to a shock or hard exercise. □ *Walking*

this fast takes my breath away. □ *Mary frightened me and took my breath away.* **2.** to overwhelm someone with beauty or grandeur. □ *The magnificent painting took my breath away.* □ *Ann looked so beautiful that she took my breath away.*

take something to endure something; to survive something. (Also used literally.) □ *I don't think I can take any more scolding today. I've been in trouble since I got up this morning.* □ *Mary was very insulting to Tom, but he can take it.*

take something amiss AND **take something the wrong way** to understand something as wrong or insulting. (Compare to *take someone or something wrong*.) □ *Would you take it amiss if I told you I thought you look lovely?* □ *Why would anyone take such a nice compliment amiss?* □ *I was afraid you'd take it the wrong way.*

take something at face value to accept something just as it is presented. □ *John said he wanted to come to the party, and I took that at face value. I'm sure he'll arrive soon.* □ *He made us a promise, and we took his word at face value.*

take something in stride to accept something as natural or expected. □ *The argument surprised him, but he took it in stride.* □ *It was a very rude remark, but Mary took it in stride.*

take something lying down to endure something unpleasant without fighting back. □ *He insulted me publicly. You don't expect me to take that lying down, do you?* □ *I'm not the kind of person who'll take something like that lying down.*

take something off AND **take off something** to remove something. □ *Please take your coat off and stay a while.* □ *Take off the things from the table, please.*

take something on faith to accept or believe something on the basis of little or no evidence. □ *Please try to believe what I'm telling you. Just take it on faith.* □ *Surely you can't expect me to take a story like that on faith.*

take something on the chin to experience and endure a direct (figurative or literal) blow or assault. □ *The bad news* was a real shock, and John took it on the chin. □ The worst luck comes my way, and I always end up taking it on the chin.

take something out on someone or something to direct (or redirect) one's anger or fear onto someone or something. □ I don't care if you're mad at your brother. Don't take it out on me! □ John took his anger out on the wall by kicking it.

take something the wrong way See take something amiss.

take something to heart to take something very seriously. □ John took the criticism to heart and made an honest effort to improve. □ I know Bob said a lot of cruel things to you, but he was angry. You shouldn't take those things to heart.

take something up AND **take up something 1.** to begin to deal with an issue. □ That's too big a job for today. I'll take it up tomorrow. □ Now we'll take up the task of the election of officers. **2.** to make the bottom of a skirt or pants cuffs higher from the floor. □ I'll have to take this skirt up. It's too long for me. □ Please take up my pants cuffs. They are an inch too long. **3.** See soak something up.

take something up with someone AND **take up something with someone** to raise and discuss a matter with someone. □ This is a very complicated problem. I'll have to take it up with the office manager. □ She'll take up this problem with the owner in the morning.

take something upon oneself AND **take something on oneself** to make something one's responsibility. □ I took it upon myself to order more pencils since we were running out of them. □ I'm glad that you took it on yourself to do that.

take something with a grain of salt See the following entry.

take something with a pinch of salt AND **take something with a grain of salt** to listen to a story or an explanation with considerable doubt. □ You must take anything she says with a grain of salt. She doesn't always tell the truth. □ They took my explanation with a pinch of salt. I was sure they didn't believe me.

take steps to prevent something AND **take steps** to do what is necessary to prevent something. □ I took steps to prevent John from learning what we were talking about. □ I have to keep John from knowing what I've been doing. I can prevent it if I take steps.

take stock of something AND **take stock** to make an appraisal of resources and potentialities. □ I spent some time yesterday taking stock of my good and bad qualities. □ We all need to take stock now and then.

take the bit in one's teeth* to put oneself in charge. (A cliché.) □ Someone needed to direct the project, so I took the bit in my teeth. □ If you want to get something done, you've got to put the bit in your teeth and get to work.

take the bitter with the sweet* to accept the bad things along with the good things. (A cliché.) □ We all have disappointments. You have to learn to take the bitter with the sweet. □ There are good days and bad days, but everyday you take the bitter with the sweet. That's life.

take the bull by the horns* to meet a challenge directly. (A cliché.) □ If we are going to solve this problem, someone is going to have to take the bull by the horns. □ This threat isn't going to go away by itself. We are going to take the bull by the horns and settle this matter once and for all.

take the cake* to win the prize; to be most remarkable. (Folksy.) □ Look at those fireworks. If they don't take the cake, I don't know what does. □ Well, Jane, this dinner really takes the cake! It's delicious.

take the day off to choose not to go to work for one day. (Compare to get the day off.) □ The sun was shining, and it was warm, so I took the day off and went fishing. □ Jane wasn't feeling well, so she took the day off.

take the edge off something AND **take the edge off** to remove the essence, power, or "bite" of something. □ I had to tell her some very sad things, so I spoke slowly and softly to take the edge off the news. □ I put sugar in my coffee to take the edge off.

take the law into one's own hands to attempt to administer the law; to act as a judge and jury for someone who has done something wrong. □ *Citizens don't have the right to take the law into their own hands.* □ *The shopkeeper took the law into his own hands when he tried to arrest the thief.*

take the liberty of doing something to assume the right to do something. □ *Since I knew you were arriving late, I took the liberty of securing a hotel room for you.* □ *May I take the liberty of addressing you by your first name?*

take the lid off something* to begin to deal with a problem. (Informal. Also used literally.) □ *Now that you've taken the lid off that problem, we'll have to deal with it.* □ *I have this matter settled for now. Please don't take the lid off it again.*

take the rap for someone or something* AND **take the rap*** (Slang, especially criminal slang.) **1.** [with *someone*] to take the blame (for something) for someone else. □ *I don't want to take the rap for you.* □ *John robbed the bank, but Tom took the rap for him.* **2.** [with *something*] to take the blame for (doing) something. □ *I won't take the rap for the crime. I wasn't even in town.* □ *Who'll take the rap for it? Who did it?*

take the stand to go to and sit in the witness chair in a courtroom. □ *I was in court all day waiting to take the stand.* □ *The lawyer asked the witness to take the stand.*

take the starch out of someone* (Informal.) **1.** to make someone less arrogant or stiff. □ *I told a joke that made Mr. Jones laugh very hard. It really took the starch out of him.* □ *John is so arrogant. I'd really like to take the starch out of him!* **2.** to make someone tired and weak. □ *This hot weather really takes the starch out of me.* □ *What a long day! It sure took the starch out of me.*

take the trouble to do something AND **take the trouble** to make an effort to do something (which one might not otherwise do). □ *I wish I had taken the trouble to study this matter more care-*

fully. □ *I just didn't have enough time to take the trouble.*

take the wind out of someone's sails* to challenge someone's boasting or arrogance. (Informal.) □ *John was bragging about how much money he earned until he learned that most of us make more. That took the wind out of his sails.* □ *Learning that one has been totally wrong about something can really take the wind out of one's sails.*

take the words out of one's mouth* (for someone else) to say what you were going to say. (Informal. Also with *right*, as in the example below.) □ *John said exactly what I was going to say. He took the words out of my mouth.* □ *I agree with you, and I wanted to say the same thing. You took the words right out of my mouth.*

take time off to not work for a period of time—a few minutes or a longer period. (Compare to *get time off*.) □ *I had to take time off to go to the dentist.* □ *Mary took time off to have a cup of coffee.*

take to one's heels to run away. □ *The little boy said hello and then took to his heels.* □ *The man took to his heels to try to get to the bus stop before the bus left.*

take to someone or something* to become fond of or attracted to someone or something. (Informal.) □ *Mary didn't take to her new job, and she quit after two weeks.* □ *Mary seemed to take to John right away.*

take too much on AND **take on too much** to undertake to do too much work or too many tasks. (See *take too much on*.) □ *Don't take too much on, or you won't be able to do any of it well.* □ *Ann tends to take on too much and get exhausted.*

take turns at doing something AND **take turns; take turns doing something** to do something, one (person) at a time, (rather than everyone all at once). □ *Please take turns at reading the book.* □ *Everyone is taking turns looking at the picture.* □ *It's more orderly when everyone takes turns.*

take up a collection to collect some money for a specific project. □ *We* wanted to send Bill some flowers, so we took up a collection. □ The office staff took up a collection to pay for the office party.

take up arms against someone or something AND **take up arms** to prepare to fight against someone or something. □ Everyone in the town took up arms against the enemy. □ They were all so angry that the leader convinced them to take up arms.

take up one's abode somewhere to settle down and live somewhere. (Formal.) □ I took up my abode downtown near my office. □ We decided to take up our abode in a warmer climate.

take up room See take up space.

take up someone's time to require too much of someone else's time; to waste someone's time. (Also with so much of or too much of, as in the examples.) □ You're taking up my time. Please go away. □ I'm sorry. I didn't mean to take up so much of your time. □ This problem is taking up too much of my time.

take up space AND **take up room** to fill or occupy space. (Note the variations in the examples.) □ The piano is taking up too much room in our living room. □ John, you're not being any help at all. You're just taking up space.

take up time to require or fill time. (Note the variations in the examples. Also without up.) □ This project is taking up too much time. □ This kind of thing always takes up time.

take up with someone to become a friend or companion to someone. □ Billy's mother was afraid that he was taking up with the wrong kind of people. □ John and Bob took up with each other and became close friends.

taken aback surprised and confused. □ When Mary told me the news, I was taken aback for a moment. □ When I told my parents I was married, they were completely taken aback.

taken for dead appearing to be dead; assumed to be dead. □ I was so ill with the flu that I was almost taken for dead. □ The accident victims were so seriously injured that they were taken for dead at first.

talk a blue streak* to talk very much and very rapidly. (Informal.) □ Billy didn't talk until he was six, and then he started talking a blue streak. □ I can't understand anything Bob says. He talks a blue streak, and I can't follow his thinking.

talk back to someone AND **talk back** to respond (to a rebuke) rudely or impertinently. □ John got in trouble for talking back to the teacher. □ A student never gains anything by talking back.

talk big* to brag or boast; to talk in an intimidating manner. (Slang.) □ John is always talking big, but he hasn't really accomplished a lot in life. □ She talks big, but she's harmless.

talk down to someone to speak to someone in a patronizing manner; to speak to someone in the simplest way. □ The manager insulted everyone in the office by talking down to them. □ Please don't talk down to me. I can understand almost anything you have to say.

talk in circles to talk in a confusing or round-about manner. □ I couldn't understand a thing he said. All he did was talk in circles. □ We argued for a long time and finally decided that we were talking in circles.

talk oneself out to talk until one can talk no more. □ After nearly an hour, he had talked himself out. Then we began to ask questions. □ I talked myself out in the meeting, but no one would support my position.

talk shop* to talk about business matters at a social event (where business talk is out of place). (Informal.) □ All right everyone, we're not here to talk shop. Let's have a good time. □ Mary and Jane stood by the punch bowl talking shop.

talk someone down 1. to win out over someone in an argument; to convince someone by arguing. □ She loves to argue. She takes pleasure in talking someone down. □ She tried to talk me down, but I held my ground. 2. to convince someone to lower the price. □ She wanted $2,000 for the car, but I talked her down. □ This is my final offer. Don't try to talk me down.

talk someone into doing something to overcome someone's objections to doing something; to convince someone to do something. □ *They talked me into going to the meeting, even though I didn't really have the time.* □ *No one can talk me into doing something illegal.*

talk someone or something up* AND **talk up someone or something*** to promote or speak in support of something. (Informal.) □ *I've been talking the party up all day, trying to get people to come.* □ *The mayor is running for re-election, and everyone at city hall is talking her up.*

talk someone out of doing something to convince someone not to do something. □ *I tried to talk her out of going, but she insisted.* □ *Don't try to talk me out of quitting school. My mind is made up.*

talk someone out of something to convince someone to give something up. □ *This is my candy, and you can't talk me out of it.* □ *I tried to talk her out of her property, but she didn't want to sell.*

talk someone's ear off See the following entry.

talk someone's head off* (Slang.) **1.** (for someone) to speak too much. □ *Why does John always talk his head off? Doesn't he know he bores people?* □ *She talks her head off and doesn't seem to know what she's saying.* **2.** AND **talk someone's ear off** to talk to and bore someone. □ *John is very friendly, but watch out or he'll talk your head off.* □ *My uncle always talked my ear off whenever I went to visit him.*

talk something out AND **talk out something** to talk about all aspects of a problem or disagreement. □ *Ann and Sally had a problem, so they agreed to talk it out.* □ *It's better to talk out a disagreement than to stay mad.*

talk something over AND **talk over something** to discuss something. □ *Come into my office so we can talk this over.* □ *We talked over the plans for nearly an hour.*

talk through one's hat* to talk nonsense; to brag and boast. (Informal.) □ *John isn't really as good as he says. He's just talking through his hat.* □ *Stop talking through your hat and start being sincere!*

talk turkey* to talk business; to talk frankly. (Slang.) □ *Okay, Bob, we have business to discuss. Let's talk turkey.* □ *John wanted to talk turkey, but Jane just wanted to joke around.*

talk until one is blue in the face* to talk until one is exhausted. (Informal.) □ *I talked until I was blue in the face, but I couldn't change her mind.* □ *She had to talk until she was blue in the face in order to convince him.*

tamper with something to attempt to alter or change something; to meddle with or damage something. □ *Someone has tampered with my door lock.* □ *Please don't tamper with my stereo.*

tan someone's hide* to spank someone. (Folksy.) □ *Billy's mother said she'd tan Billy's hide if he ever did that again.* □ *"I'll tan your hide if you're late!" said Tom's father.*

taper off doing something AND **taper off** to stop doing something gradually. □ *My doctor told me to taper off smoking cigarettes.* □ *I have to taper off because I can't stop all at once.*

tar and feather someone to chastise someone severely. (Also used literally at one time.) □ *They threatened to tar and feather me if I ever came back into their town.* □ *I don't believe that they'd really tar and feather me, but they could be very unpleasant.*

teach someone a lesson to get even with someone for bad behavior. (Also used literally.) □ *John tripped me, so I punched him. That ought to teach him a lesson.* □ *That taught me a lesson. I won't do it again.*

team up with someone to join with someone. □ *I teamed up with Jane to write the report.* □ *I had never teamed up with anyone else before. I had always worked alone.*

tear into someone or something 1. [with *someone*] to criticize and scold someone. □ *Tom tore into John and yelled at him for an hour.* □ *Don't tear into me like that. You have no right to speak to me that way.* **2.** to attack or fight with someone or something. □

The boxer tore into his opponent. □ *The lion tore into the herd of zebras.*

tear off* to leave or depart in a great hurry. (Informal.) □ *Well, excuse me. I have to tear off.* □ *Bob tore off down the street chasing the fire engine.*

tear one's hair to be anxious, frustrated, or angry. (Not used literally.) □ *I was so nervous, I was about to tear my hair.* □ *I had better get home. My parents will be tearing their hair.*

tear someone or something down AND **tear down someone or something** 1. [with *someone*] to criticize or degrade someone. □ *Tom is always tearing Jane down. I guess he doesn't like her.* □ *It's not nice to tear down the people who work in your office.* 2. [with *something*] to dismantle or destroy something. □ *They plan to tear the old building down and build a new one there.* □ *They'll tear down the building in about two weeks.*

tear someone or something up AND **tear up something** 1.* [with *someone*] to cause someone much grief. (Slang.) □ *The news of Tom's death really tore up Bill.* □ *Bad news tears up some people. Other people can take it calmly.* 2. [with *something*] to rip something up into pieces. □ *Jane got mad and tore the papers up and threw them away.* □ *Don't tear up your receipt until you know you want to keep what you bought.* ALSO: **torn up*** upset; grieving. (Slang.) □ *Bill was badly torn up by the news of Tom's death.*

tear something off AND **to tear off something** to tear something free (from something). □ *I found a pad of paper, and I tore a piece of paper off.* □ *Please tear off a piece of paper for me, too.*

tee someone off* to make someone angry. (Slang.) □ *That kind of talk really tees me off!* □ *Don't let him tee you off. He doesn't mean any harm.*

Tell it to the marines.* I do not believe you—maybe the marines will. (Informal.) □ *That's silly. Tell it to the marines.* □ *I don't care how good you think your reason is. Tell it to the marines!*

tell on someone to report someone's bad behavior; to tattle on someone. (See

also *tell someone on someone.*) □ *If you do that again, I'll tell on you!* □ *Please don't tell on me. I'm in enough trouble as it is.*

tell one to one's face to tell (something) to someone directly. □ *I'm sorry that Sally feels that way about me. I wish she had told me to my face.* □ *I won't tell Tom that you're mad at him. You should tell him to his face.*

tell people apart to distinguish one person or a group of people from another person or group of people. □ *Tom and John are brothers, and you can hardly tell them apart.* □ *Our team is wearing red, and the other team is wearing orange. I can't tell them apart.*

tell someone a thing or two* AND **tell someone where to get off*** to scold someone; to express one's anger to someone; to *tell someone off.* (Informal.) □ *Wait till I see Sally. I'll tell her a thing or two!* □ *She told me where to get off and then started in scolding Tom.*

tell someone off AND **tell off someone** to scold someone; to attack someone verbally. (This has a sense of finality about it.) □ *I was so mad at Bob that I told him off.* □ *By the end of the day, I had told off everyone else, too.*

tell someone on someone to report someone's bad behavior to someone else. (See also *tell on someone.*) □ *Stop it, or I'll tell the teacher on you.* □ *Please don't tell the teacher on me! I'll have to stand in the corner.*

tell someone where to get off See *tell someone a thing or two.*

tell tales out of school to tell secrets or spread rumors. □ *I wish that John would keep quiet. He's telling tales out of school again.* □ *If you tell tales out of school a lot, people won't know when to believe you.*

tell things apart to distinguish one thing or a group of things from another thing or group of things. □ *This one is gold, and the others are brass. Can you tell them apart?* □ *Without their labels, I can't tell them apart.*

tell time 1. to keep or report the correct time. □ *This clock doesn't tell time very accurately.* □ *My watch stopped telling time, so I had to have it repaired.* 2. to be able to read time from a clock or watch. □ *Billy is only four. He can't tell time yet.* □ *They are teaching the children to tell time at school.*

tell which is which See *know which is which.*

tempest in a teapot* an uproar about practically nothing. (A cliché.) □ *This isn't a serious problem—just a tempest in a teapot.* □ *Even a tempest in a teapot can take a lot of time to get settled.*

thank one's lucky stars* to be thankful for one's luck. (A cliché.) □ *You can thank your lucky stars that I was there to help you.* □ *I thank my lucky stars that I studied the right things for the test.*

thanks to someone or something due to someone or something; because of someone or something. (This does not refer to gratitude.) □ *Thanks to the storm, we have no electricity.* □ *Thanks to Mary, we have tickets to the game. She bought them early before they were sold out.*

That ain't hay.* That is not a small amount of money. (Folksy.) □ *I paid forty dollars for it, and that ain't hay!* □ *Bob lost his wallet with $200 in it—and that ain't hay.*

That makes two of us.* The same goes for me.; I, too. (A cliché.) □ *So, you're going to the football game? That makes two of us.* □ BILL: *I just passed my biology test.* BOB: *That makes two of us!*

That takes care of that.* That is settled. (A cliché.) □ *That takes care of that, and I'm glad it's over.* □ *I spent all morning dealing with this matter, and that takes care of that.*

That will do. That is enough.; Do no more. □ *That'll do, Billy. Stop your crying.* □ *"That will do," said Mr. Jones when he had heard enough of our arguing.*

That'll be the day.* I don't believe that the day will ever come (when something will happen). (A cliché.) □ *Do you really think that John will pass geometry? That'll be the day.* □ *John graduate? That'll be the day!*

That's about the size of it.* It is final and correct. (Slang.) □ MARY: *Do you mean that you aren't going?* TOM: *That's about the size of it.* □ *At the end of his speech Bob said, "That's about the size of it."*

That's all for someone. Someone will get no more chances to do things correctly. □ *That's all for you, Tom. I've had all I can take from you. One disappointment after another.* □ *You've gone too far, Mary. That's all for you. Goodbye!*

That's all she wrote.* That is all. (Slang.) □ *At the end of his informal talk, Tom said, "That's all she wrote."* □ *Sally looked at the empty catsup bottle and said, "That's all she wrote."*

That's that. It is permanently settled and need not be dealt with again. □ *I said no, and that's that.* □ *You can't come back. I told you to leave, and that's that.*

That's the last straw.* AND **That's the straw that broke the camel's back.*** That is the final thing. (A cliché.) □ *Now it's raining! That's the last straw. The picnic is cancelled!* □ *When Sally came down sick, that was the straw that broke the camel's back.*

That's the ticket.* That is exactly what is needed. (A cliché.) □ *That's the ticket, John. You're doing it just the way it should be done.* □ *That's the ticket! I knew you could do it.*

That's the way the ball bounces.* AND **That's the way the cookie crumbles.*** That is too bad.; Those things happen. (Slang.) □ *Sorry to hear about your problems. That's the way the ball bounces.* □ *John wrecked his car and then lost his job. That's the way the cookie crumbles.*

That's the way the cookie crumbles. See the previous entry.

the bottom line* (Slang.) **1.** the last figure on a financial balance sheet. □ *What's the bottom line? How much do I owe you?* □ *Don't tell me all those figures! Just tell me the bottom line.* **2.** the result; the final outcome. □ *I know about all the problems, but what is the bottom line? What will happen?* □ *The bottom line is that you have to go to the meeting because no one else can.*

The coast is clear. There is no visible

danger. □ *I'm going to stay hidden here until the coast is clear.* □ *You can come out of your hiding place now. The coast is clear.*

the daily grind* (someone's) everyday work routine. (Informal.) □ *I'm getting very tired of the daily grind.* □ *When my vacation was over, I had to go back to the daily grind.*

The early bird gets the worm. a proverb meaning that the early person will get the reward. □ *Don't be late again! Don't you know that the early bird gets the worm?* □ *I'll be there before the sun is up. After all, the early bird gets the worm.*

The fat is in the fire. a proverb meaning that serious trouble has broken out. □ *Now that Mary is leaving, the fat is in the fire. How can we get along without her?* □ *The fat's in the fire! There's $3,000 missing from the office safe.*

the here and now the present, as opposed to the past or the future. □ *I don't care what's happening tomorrow or next week! I care about the here and now.* □ *The past is dead. Let's worry about the here and now.*

The honeymoon is over.* The early pleasant beginning has ended. (A cliché.) □ *Okay, the honeymoon is over. It's time to settle down and do some hard work.* □ *I knew the honeymoon was over when they started yelling at me to work faster.*

the in thing to do AND **the in thing** the fashionable thing to do. □ *Eating low-fat food is the in thing to do.* □ *Bob is very old-fashioned. He never does the in thing.*

The jig is up.* The scheme or plot has been discovered, and it is finished. (Slang, especially criminal slang.) □ *"All right, you boys," said the teacher. "The jig is up. Get back into class."* □ *Hold it right there. The jig is up. You're under arrest.*

the likes of someone* someone; anyone like someone. (Informal. Almost always in a negative sense.) □ *I don't like Bob. I wouldn't do anything for the likes of him.* □ *Nobody wants the likes of him around.*

the more the merrier* the more people

there are, the happier they will be. (A cliché.) □ *Of course you can have a ride with us! The more the merrier.* □ *The manager hired a new employee even though there's not enough work for all of us now. Oh well, the more the merrier.*

the opposite sex (from the point of view of a female) males; (from the point of view of a male) females. (Also with *member of,* as in the examples.) □ *Ann is crazy about the opposite sex.* □ *Bill is very shy when he's introduced to the opposite sex.* □ *Do members of the opposite sex make you nervous?*

the other way round the reverse; the opposite. □ *No, it won't fit that way. Try it the other way round.* □ *It doesn't make any sense like that. It belongs the other way around.*

the pits* the worst possible. (Slang.) □ *John is such a boring person. He's the pits.* □ *This restaurant isn't the best, but it's not the pits either.*

the pot calling the kettle black* (an instance of) someone with a fault accusing someone else of having the same fault. (A cliché.) □ *Ann is always late, but she was rude enough to tell everyone when I was late. Now that's the pot calling the kettle black!* □ *You're calling me thoughtless? That's really a case of the pot calling the kettle black.*

The same to you.* The same comment applies to you. (Informal. Can be a polite or a rude comment.) □ BILL: *Have a pleasant evening.* BOB: *Thank you. The same to you.* □ MARY: *You're the most horrible person I've ever met!* JOHN: *The same to you!*

The shoe is on the other foot. a proverb meaning that one is experiencing the same things that one caused another person to experience. (Note the variations in the examples.) □ *The teacher is taking a course in summer school and is finding out what it's like when the shoe is on the other foot.* □ *When the policeman was arrested, he learned what it was like to have the shoe on the other foot.*

the upshot of something the result or outcome of something. □ *The upshot of my criticism was a change in policy.*

□ *The upshot of the argument was an agreement to hire a new secretary.*

the wrong side of the tracks the poor part of a town. (Often with *come from, be from,* or *live on,* as in the examples.) □ *They said that Bob was from the wrong side of the tracks, but that it didn't matter.* □ *We went to a school which was on the wrong side of the tracks, and we all got a fine education.*

Them's fighting words.* Those are words which will start a fight. (Folksy. Note that *them is* is permissible in this expression.) □ *Better not talk like that around here. Them's fighting words.* □ *Them's fighting words, and you'd better be quiet unless you want trouble.*

then and there right then. □ *I asked him right then and there exactly what he meant.* □ *I decided to settle the matter then and there and not wait until Monday.*

There are plenty of other fish in the sea.* There are many other choices. (A cliché. Used to refer to persons.) □ *When John broke up with Ann, I told her not to worry. There are plenty of other fish in the sea.* □ *It's too bad that your secretary quit, but there are plenty of other fish in the sea.*

there is no doing something* one is not permitted to do something. (Informal.) □ *There is no arguing with Bill.* □ *There is no cigarette smoking here.*

There will be the devil to pay.* There will be lots of trouble. (Informal. See *have the devil to pay.*) □ *If you damage my car, there will be the devil to pay.* □ *Bill broke a window, and now there will be the devil to pay.*

There's more than one way to skin a cat. a proverb meaning that there is more than one way to do something. □ *If that way won't work, try another way. There's more than one way to skin a cat.* □ *Don't worry, I'll figure out a way to get it done. There's more than one way to skin a cat.*

There's no accounting for taste. a proverb meaning that there is no explanation for people's preferences. □ *Look at that purple and orange car! There's no accounting for taste.* □ *Some people seemed to like the music, although I*

thought it was worse than noise. *There's no accounting for taste.*

thin out to disperse; to become sparse. (See also *thin something out.*) □ *As Tom grew older, his hair began to thin out.* □ *Soon after the accident, the crowd began to thin out.*

thin something out AND **thin out something** to dilute something; to make something sparse. □ *Please thin out this paint. It's too thick.* □ *The flowers are planted too close together. Please thin the plants out.*

Things are looking up. Conditions are looking better. □ *Since I got a salary increase, things are looking up.* □ *Things are looking up at school. I'm doing better in all my classes.*

think a great deal of someone or something See the following entry.

think a lot of someone or something AND **think a great deal of someone or something; think highly of someone or something; think much of someone or something** to think well of someone or something. □ *The teacher thinks a lot of Mary and her talents.* □ *No one really thinks a great deal of the new policies.* □ *I think highly of John.* □ *The manager doesn't think much of John and says so to everyone.*

think back on someone or something AND **think back** to remember and think about someone or something. □ *When I think back on Sally and the good times we had together, I get very sad.* □ *I like to think back on my childhood and try to remember what it was like.*

think highly of someone or something See *think a lot of someone or something.*

think little of someone or something AND **think nothing of someone or something** to have a low opinion of someone or something. □ *Most experts think little of Jane's theory.* □ *People may think nothing of it now, but in a few years everyone will praise it.* □ *No one thinks little of her latest book.*

think much of someone or something See *think a lot of someone or something.*

think nothing of someone or some-

thing See *think little of someone or something*.

think on one's feet to think while one is talking. □ *If you want to be a successful teacher, you must be able to think on your feet.* □ *I have to write out everything I'm going to say, because I can't think on my feet too well.*

think out loud to say one's thoughts aloud. □ *Excuse me. I didn't really mean to say that. I was just thinking out loud.* □ *Mr. Johnson didn't prepare a speech. He just stood there and thought out loud. It was a terrible presentation.*

think someone or something fit for something to believe that someone or something is suitable for something. □ *I don't think John fit for the job.* □ *Do you think this car fit for a long trip?*

think something out AND think out something to think through something; to *think something over*. □ *This is an interesting problem. I'll have to take some time and think it out.* □ *We spent all morning thinking out our plan.*

think something over AND think over something to consider something; to think about something (before giving a decision). □ *Please think it over and give me your decision in the morning.* □ *I need more time to think over your offer.*

think something up AND think up something to contrive or invent something. □ *Don't worry. I'll find a way to do it. I can think something up in time to get it done.* □ *John thought up a way to solve our problem.*

think twice before doing something AND think twice to consider carefully whether one should do something; to be cautious about doing something. □ *You should think twice before quitting your job.* □ *That's a serious decision, and you should certainly think twice.*

thrill someone to death See the following entry.

thrill someone to pieces* AND thrill someone to death* to please or excite someone very much. (Informal. Not used literally.) □ *John sent flowers to Ann and thrilled her to pieces.* □ *Your wonderful comments thrilled me to death.* ALSO: **thrilled to death; thrilled**

to pieces very excited; very pleased. □ *She was thrilled to death to get the flowers.* □ *I'm just thrilled to pieces to have you visit me.*

thrilled to death See the previous entry.

thrilled to pieces See *thrill someone to pieces*.

through and through thoroughly; completely. □ *I've studied this report through and through trying to find the facts you've mentioned.* □ *I was angry through and through, and I had to sit down and recover before I could talk to anyone.*

through hell and high water* through all sorts of severe difficulties. (A cliché.) □ *I came through hell and high water to get to this meeting on time. Why don't you start on time?* □ *You'll have to go through hell and high water to accomplish your goal, but it'll be worth it.*

through thick and thin* through good times and bad times. (A cliché.) □ *We've been together through thick and thin and we won't desert each other now.* □ *Over the years, we went through thick and thin and enjoyed every minute of it.*

through with someone or something finished with someone or something. □ *I'm through with John. We had a big argument and said goodbye to each other.* □ *Where shall I put the paint brush when I'm through with it?*

throw a fit* to become very angry; to put on a display of anger. (Folksy.) □ *Sally threw a fit when I showed up without the things she asked me to buy.* □ *My dad threw a fit when I got home three hours late.*

throw a monkey wrench in the works* to cause problems for someone's plans. (Informal.) □ *I don't want to throw a monkey wrench in the works, but have you checked your plans with a lawyer?* □ *When John refused to help us, he really threw a monkey wrench in the works.*

throw a party for someone AND throw a party to give or hold a party for someone. □ *Mary was leaving town, so we threw a party for her.* □ *Do you know a place where we could throw a party?*

throw caution to the wind* to become

very careless. (A cliché.) □ *Jane, who is usually cautious, threw caution to the wind and went windsurfing.* □ *I don't mind taking a little chance now and then, but I'm not the type of person who throws caution to the wind.*

throw cold water on something See *pour cold water on something.*

throw down the gauntlet to challenge (someone) to an argument or (figurative) combat. □ *When Bob challenged my conclusions, he threw down the gauntlet. I was ready for an argument.* □ *Frowning at Bob is the same as throwing down the gauntlet. He loves to get into a fight about something.*

throw good money after bad* to waste additional money after wasting money once. (A cliché.) □ *I bought a used car and then had to spend $300 on repairs. That was throwing good money after bad.* □ *The Browns are always throwing good money after bad. They bought an acre of land which turned out to be swamp, and then had to pay to have it filled in.*

throw in the sponge See the following entry.

throw in the towel* AND **throw in the sponge*** to quit (doing something). (Informal.) □ *When John could stand no more of Mary's bad temper, he threw in the towel and left.* □ *Don't give up now! It's too soon to throw in the sponge.*

throw one's weight around* to attempt to boss people around; to give orders. (Informal.) □ *The district manager came to our office and tried to throw his weight around, but no one paid any attention to him.* □ *Don't try to throw your weight around in this office. We know who our boss is.*

throw oneself at someone AND **fling oneself at someone** to give oneself willingly to someone else for romance. □ *I guess that Mary really likes John. She practically threw herself at him when he came into the room.* □ *Everyone could see by the way Tom flung himself at Jane that he was going to ask her for a date.*

throw oneself at someone's feet to bow down humbly at someone's feet. (Used both figuratively and literally).

□ *Do I have to throw myself at your feet in order to convince you that I'm sorry?* □ *I love you sincerely, Jane. I'll throw myself at your feet and await your command. I'm your slave!*

throw oneself on the mercy of the court AND **throw oneself at the mercy of the court** to plead for mercy from a judge in a courtroom. □ *Your honor, please believe me, I didn't do it on purpose. I throw myself on the mercy of the court and beg for a light sentence.* □ *Jane threw herself at the mercy of the court and hoped for the best.*

throw someone to confuse someone. □ *You threw me for a minute when you asked for my identification. I thought you recognized me.* □ *The question the teacher asked was so hard that it threw me, and I became very nervous.*

throw someone a curve 1. to pitch a curve ball to someone in baseball. □ *The pitcher threw John a curve, and John swung wildly against thin air.* □ *During that game, the pitcher threw everyone a curve at least once.* 2. to confuse someone by doing something unexpected. □ *When you said "house" you threw me a curve. The password was supposed to be "home."* □ *John threw me a curve when we were making our presentation, and I forgot my speech.*

throw someone for a loop* AND **knock someone for a loop*** to confuse or shock someone. (Informal. This is more severe and upsetting than *throw someone a curve.*) □ *When Bill heard the news, it threw him for a loop.* □ *The manager knocked Bob for a loop by firing him on the spot.*

throw someone for a loss to cause someone to be uncertain or confused. □ *The stress of being in front of so many people threw Ann for a loss. She forgot her speech.* □ *It was a difficult problem. I was thrown for a loss for an answer.*

throw someone off the track 1. to cause one to lose one's place in the sequence of things. □ *The interruption threw me off the track for a moment, but I soon got started again with my presentation.* □ *Don't let little things throw you off the track. Concentrate on what you're doing.* 2. AND **throw someone off the**

trail   to cause someone to lose the trail (when following someone or something). □ *The raccoon threw us off the track by running through the creek.* □ *The robber threw the police off the trail by leaving town.*

throw someone or something off AND **throw off someone or something** 1. [with *someone*] to confuse someone; to mislead someone. □ *The interruption threw me off, and I lost my place in the speech.* □ *Little noises throw me off. Please try to be quiet.* 2. [with *something*] to push or pull something off. □ *It was so warm that the child threw the blanket off.* □ *I threw off my coat and ran into the room.* 3. [with *something*] to resist or recover from a disease. □ *It was a bad cold, but I managed to throw it off in a few days.* □ *I can't seem to throw off my cold. I've had it for weeks.* 4. [with *something*] to emit or give off an odor. □ *The flowers threw off a heavy perfume.* □ *The small animal threw off an amazingly strong odor.*

throw someone out of something AND **throw someone out**   to force a person to leave a place. (Also used literally.) □ *John behaved so badly that they threw him out of the party.* □ *I was very loud, but they didn't throw me out.*

throw someone over   to end a romance with someone. □ *Jane threw Bill over. I think she met someone she likes better.* □ *Bill was about ready to throw her over, so it's just as well.*

throw someone to the wolves*   to (figuratively) sacrifice someone. (A cliché. Not used literally.) □ *The press was demanding an explanation, so the mayor blamed the mess on John and threw him to the wolves.* □ *I wouldn't let them throw me to the wolves! I did nothing wrong, and I won't take the blame for their errors.*

throw someone's name around*   to impress people by saying you know a famous or influential person. (Informal.) □ *You won't get anywhere around here by throwing the mayor's name around.* □ *When you get to the meeting, just throw my name around a bit, and people will pay attention to you.*

throw something away AND **throw away**

something   to discard something; to get rid of something. □ *Please throw this pile of papers away.* □ *Don't throw away anything you might be able to use later.*

throw something into the bargain   to include something in a deal. □ *To encourage me to buy a new car, the car dealer threw a free radio into the bargain.* □ *If you purchase three pounds of chocolates, I'll throw one pound of salted nuts into the bargain.*

throw something together AND **slap something together; slap together something; throw together something**   to assemble or arrange something in haste. □ *John went into the kitchen to throw something together for dinner.* □ *Don't just slap something together! Use care and do it right.* □ *You assembled this device very badly. It seems that you just slapped it together.*

throw something up AND **throw up something; throw up**   to vomit something. □ *The meat was bad, and I threw it up.* □ *Billy threw up his dinner.* □ *I hate throwing up.*

throw something up to someone   to mention a shortcoming to someone repeatedly. □ *I know I'm thoughtless. Why do you keep throwing it up to me?* □ *Bill was always throwing Jane's faults up to her.*

throw the book at someone*   to charge or convict someone with as many crimes as is possible. (Slang.) □ *I made the police officer angry, so he took me to the station and threw the book at me.* □ *The judge threatened to throw the book at me if I didn't stop insulting the police officer.*

throw up   See *throw something up.*

throw up one's hands in despair   to give up; to raise one's hands making a sign of giving up. □ *There was nothing I could do to help. I threw up my hands in despair and left.* □ *John threw up his hands in despair because they wouldn't let him see his brother in the hospital.*

throw up one's hands in horror   to be shocked; to raise one's hands as if one had been frightened. □ *When Bill heard the bad news, he threw up his hands in horror.* □ *I could do no more. I had* *seen more than I could stand. I just threw up my hands in horror and screamed.*

thumb a ride AND **hitch a ride** to get a ride from a passing motorist; to make a sign with one's thumb that indicates to passing drivers that one is begging for a ride. □ *My car broke down on the highway, and I had to thumb a ride to get back to town.* □ *Sometimes it's dangerous to hitch a ride with a stranger.*

thumb one's nose at someone or something to (figuratively or literally) make a rude gesture of disgust with one's thumb and nose at someone or something. □ *The tramp thumbed his nose at the lady and walked away.* □ *You can't just thumb your nose at people who give you trouble. You've got to learn to get along.*

thumb through something AND **leaf through something** to look through a book, magazine, or newspaper, without reading it carefully. □ *I've only thumbed through this book, but it looks very interesting.* □ *I leafed through a magazine while waiting to see the doctor.*

thumbs down on someone or something AND **thumbs down** opposed to someone or something. (Often with *turn*, as in the example.) □ *Bob is thumbs down on hiring anyone else.* □ *I had hoped that she'd agree with our plan, but she turned thumbs down.*

tickle someone pink* AND **tickle someone to death*** to please or entertain someone very much. (Informal. Never used literally.) □ *Bill told a joke that really tickled us all pink.* □ *I know that these flowers will tickle her to death.* ALSO: **tickled pink*; tickled to death*** very much pleased or entertained. (Informal.) □ *I was tickled to death to have you visit us.* □ *We were tickled pink when your flowers arrived.*

tickle someone to death See the previous entry.

tickle someone's fancy to interest someone; to make someone curious. □ *I have an interesting problem here which I think will tickle your fancy.* □ *This doesn't tickle my fancy at all. This is dull and boring.*

tide someone over (for a portion of

something) to last until someone can get some more. □ *I don't get paid until next Wednesday. Could you lend me thirty dollars to tide me over?* □ *Could I borrow some coffee to tide me over until I can get to the store tomorrow?*

tie into something to connect to something. □ *I'm trying to get my home computer to tie in with the big one at the university.* □ *Could I tie into your water line while I'm waiting for mine to be repaired?*

tie someone down to restrict or encumber someone. □ *I'd like to go fishing every weekend, but my family ties me down.* □ *I don't want to tie you down, but you do have responsibilities here at home.* ALSO: **tied down** restricted by responsibilities at home. □ *I love my home, but sometimes I don't like being tied down.*

tie someone in knots* to become anxious or upset. (Informal.) □ *John tied himself in knots worrying about his wife during the operation.* □ *This waiting and worrying really ties me in knots.*

tie someone or something up AND **tie up someone something 1.** [with *someone*] to keep someone busy or occupied. □ *Sorry, this matter will tie me up for about an hour.* □ *The same matter will tie up almost everyone in the office.* **2.*** [with *something*] to conclude and finalize something. (Informal.) □ *Let's try to tie up this deal by Thursday.* □ *We'll manage to tie our business up by Wednesday at the latest.* **3.** to bind someone or something. □ *They tied up the prisoner with heavy rope.* □ *I tied up the horse near the gate.* ALSO: **tied up 1.** busy. □ *How long will you be tied up?* **2.** completed. □ *When will this matter be tied up?*

tie someone's hands to prevent someone from doing something. (Also used literally.) □ *I'd like to help you, but my boss has tied my hands.* □ *Please don't tie my hands with unnecessary restrictions. I'd like the freedom to do whatever is necessary.*

tie the knot* to get married. (Informal.) □ *Well, I hear that you and John are going to tie the knot.* □ *My parents tied the knot almost forty years ago.*

tie traffic up AND **tie up traffic**   to cause road traffic to stop. □ *If you tie traffic up for too long, you'll get a traffic ticket.* □ *Please don't stop on the roadway. It'll tie up traffic.*

tied down   See *tie someone down.*

tied to one's mother's apron strings   dominated by one's mother; dependent on one's mother. □ *Tom is still tied to his mother's apron strings.* □ *Isn't he a little old to be tied to his mother's apron strings?*

tied up   See *tie someone or something up.*

tighten one's belt   to manage to spend less money. □ *Things are beginning to cost more and more. It looks like we'll all have to tighten our belts.* □ *Times are hard, and prices are high. I can tighten my belt for only so long.*

till the cows come home*   until the last; until the end of the day. (Cows are returned to the barn at the end of the day.) (Folksy or informal.) □ *We were having so much fun that we decided to stay away till the cows came home.* □ *Where've you been? Who said you could stay away till the cows come home?*

tilt at windmills   to fight battle with imaginary enemies; to fight against unimportant enemies or issues. (As with the fictional character Don Quixote who attacked windmills.) □ *Aren't you too smart to go around tilting at windmills?* □ *I'm not going to fight this issue. I've wasted too much of my life tilting at windmills.*

time after time AND **time and again; time and time again**   repeatedly. □ *You've made the same error time after time! Please try to be more careful!* □ *I've told you time and again not to do that.* □ *You keep saying the same thing over and over, time and time again. Stop it!*

time and again   See the previous entry.

time and time again   See *time after time.*

Time hangs heavy on someone's hands.   Time seems to go slowly when one has nothing to do. (Note the variations in the examples.) □ *I don't like it when time hangs so heavily on my hands.* □ *John looks so bored. Time hangs heavy on his hands.*

Time is money.   (My) time is valuable, so don't waste it. □ *I can't afford to spend a lot of time standing here talking. Time is money, you know!* □ *People who keep saying time is money may be working too hard.*

Time is up.   The allotted time has run out. □ *You must stop now. Your time is up.* □ *Time's up! Turn in your tests whether you're finished or not.*

time out   (a call to) stop the clock (in a sporting event which is played in a fixed time period). □ *The coach made a sign for time out, and the clock stopped and a buzzer sounded.* □ *After someone called time out, the players gathered around the coach.*

Time will tell.   a proverb meaning that something will become known in the course of time. □ *I don't know if things will improve. Time will tell.* □ *Who knows what the future will bring? Only time will tell.*

tip someone off* AND **tip off someone***   to give someone a hint; to warn someone. (Slang.) □ *I tipped John off that there would be a test in his algebra class.* □ *I didn't want to tip off everyone, so I only told John.*

tip something over AND **tip over something**   to push or knock something over. (Refers to something which is standing up.) □ *Billy tipped his milk glass over.* □ *Please don't tip over the vase.*

tip the scales at something   to weigh some amount. □ *Tom tips the scales at nearly 200 pounds.* □ *I'll be glad when I tip the scales at a few pounds less.*

tire someone out AND **tire out someone**   to make someone tired; to exhaust someone. □ *Too much arguing tires me out.* □ *The manager tired out everyone in the office today.*

to a great extent   mainly; largely. □ *To a great extent, Mary is the cause of her own problems.* □ *I've finished my work to a great extent. There is nothing important left to do.*

to and fro   toward and away from (something). (Compare to *back and forth.*) □ *The puppy was very active—running to and fro—wagging its tail.* □ *The lion in the cage moved to and fro, watching the people in front of the cage.*

to boot* in addition; besides. (Informal.) □ *For breakfast I had my usual two eggs and a slice of ham to boot.* □ *When I left for school, my parents gave me an airplane ticket and fifty dollars to boot.*

to date up to the present time. □ *How much have you accomplished to date?* □ *I've done everything I'm supposed to have done to date.*

to no avail AND **of no avail** with no effect; unsuccessful. □ *All of my efforts were to no avail.* □ *Everything I did to help was of no avail. Nothing worked.*

to one's heart's content as much as one wants. □ *John wanted a week's vacation so he could go to the lake and fish to his heart's content.* □ *I just sat there eating chocolate to my heart's content.*

to put it mildly* to understate something; to say something politely. (A cliché. Note the variation in the examples.) □ *She was angry at almost everyone—to put it mildly.* □ *To say she was angry is putting it mildly.* □ *To put it mildly, she was enraged.*

to say nothing of someone or something to not even mention the importance of someone or something. □ *John and Mary had to be taken care of, to say nothing of Bill, who would require even more attention.* □ *I'm having enough difficulty painting the house, to say nothing of the garage which is very much in need of paint.*

to say the least* at the very least; without dwelling on the subject; *to put it mildly.* (A cliché.) □ *We were not at all pleased with her work—to say the least.* □ *When they had an accident, they were upset to say the least.*

to some extent to some degree; in some amount; partly. □ *I've solved this problem to some extent.* □ *I can help you understand this to some extent.*

to someone's liking in a way which pleases someone. □ *I hope I've done the work to your liking.* □ *Sally didn't find the meal to her liking and didn't eat any of it.*

to someone's way of thinking in someone's opinion. □ *This isn't satisfactory to my way of thinking.* □ *To my way of*
thinking, this is the perfect kind of vacation.

to the best of one's ability as well as one is able. □ *I did the work to the best of my ability.* □ *You should always work to the best of your ability.*

to the best of one's knowledge* as far as one knows; from one's knowledge. (A cliché.) □ *This is the true story to the best of my knowledge.* □ *To the best of my knowledge, John is the only person who can answer that question.*

to the bitter end to the very end. (Originally nautical. This originally had nothing to do with bitterness.) □ *I kept trying to the bitter end.* □ *It took me a long time to get through school, but I worked hard at it all the way to the bitter end.*

to the contrary as the opposite of what has been stated; contrary to what has been stated. (Compare to *on the contrary.*) □ *The brown horse didn't beat the black horse. To the contrary, the black one won.* □ *Among spiders, the male is not the larger one. To the contrary, the female is larger.*

to the core all the way through; basically and essentially. (Usually with some negative sense, such as *evil, rotten,* etc.) □ *Bill said that John is evil to the core.* □ *This organization is rotten to the core.*

to the ends of the earth to the remotest and most inaccessible points on the earth. □ *I'll pursue him to the ends of the earth.* □ *We've almost explored the whole world. We've traveled to the ends of the earth trying to learn about our world.*

to the last to the end; to the conclusion. □ *All of us kept trying to the last.* □ *It was a very boring play, but I sat through it to the last.*

to the letter exactly as instructed; exactly as written. □ *I didn't make an error. I followed your instruction to the letter.* □ *We didn't prepare the recipe to the letter, but the cake still turned out very well.*

to the nth degree* to the maximum amount. (Informal.) □ *Jane is a perfectionist and tries to be careful to the nth degree.* □ *This scientific instrument is accurate to the nth degree.*

to the tune of some amount of money* a certain amount of money. (Informal.) □ *My checking account is overdrawn to the tune of $340.* □ *My wallet was stolen, and I'm short of money to the tune of seventy dollars.*

To the victors belong the spoils. a proverb meaning that the winners achieve power over people and property. □ *The mayor took office and immediately fired many workers and hired new ones. Everyone said, "To the victors belong the spoils."* □ *The office of President includes the right to live in the White House and at Camp David. To the victors belong the spoils.*

to whom it may concern to the person to whom this applies. (A form of address used when you do not know the name of the person who handles the kind of business you are writing about.) □ *The letter started out, "To Whom it May Concern."* □ *When you don't know who to write to, just say, "To Whom it May Concern."*

toe the line See the following entry.

toe the mark AND **toe the line** to do what one is expected to do; to follow the rules. □ *You'll get ahead, Sally. Don't worry. Just toe the mark, and everything will be okay.* □ *John finally got fired. He just couldn't learn to toe the line.*

tone something down AND **tone down something** to make something less extreme. □ *That yellow is too bright. Please try to tone it down.* □ *Can you tone down your remarks? They seem quite strong for this situation.*

tongue-in-cheek insincere; joking. □ *Ann made a tongue-in-cheek remark to John, and he got mad because he thought she was serious.* □ *The play seemed very serious at first, but then everyone saw that it was tongue-in-cheek, and they began laughing.*

too big for one's britches* too haughty for one's status or age. (Folksy or informal.) □ *Bill's getting a little too big for his britches, and somebody's going to straighten him out.* □ *You're too big for your britches, young man! You had better be more respectful.*

too close for comfort* (for a misfortune or a threat) to be dangerously close. (A cliché. See also *close to home*.) □ *That car nearly hit me! That was too close for comfort.* □ *When I was in the hospital, I nearly died from pneumonia. Believe me, that was too close for comfort.*

too good to be true* almost unbelievable; so good as to be unbelievable. (A cliché.) □ *The news was too good to be true.* □ *When I finally got a big raise, it was too good to be true.*

Too many cooks spoil the broth. See the following entry.

Too many cooks spoil the stew. AND **Too many cooks spoil the broth.** a proverb meaning that too many people trying to manage something simply spoil it. □ *Let's decide who is in charge around here. Too many cooks spoil the stew.* □ *Everyone is giving orders, but no one is following them! Too many cooks spoil the broth.*

too much of a good thing* more of a thing than is good or useful. (A cliché.) □ *I usually take short vacations. I can't stand too much of a good thing.* □ *Too much of a good thing can make you sick, especially if the good thing is chocolate.*

toot one's own horn AND **blow one's own horn** to boast or praise oneself. □ *Tom is always tooting his own horn. Is he really as good as he says he is?* □ *I find it hard to blow my own horn, but I manage.*

top someone or something* to do or be better than someone or something. (Informal.) □ *Ann has done very well, but I don't think she can top Jane.* □ *Do you think your car tops mine when it comes to gas mileage?*

top something off 1. to add to the difficulty of something. □ *Jane lost her job, and to top that off, she caught the flu.* □ *I had a bad day, and to top it off, I have to go to a meeting tonight.* 2. See the following entry.

top something off with something AND **top off something; top something off; top off something with something** to end or terminate something with something; to put something on the top of something. □ *He topped off each piece*

of pie with a heap of whipped cream. □
That's the way to top off a piece of pie!
□ *They topped the building off with a
tall flagpole.*

toss one's cookies* to vomit. (Slang.)
□ *Don't run too fast after you eat or
you'll toss your cookies.* □ *Oh, I feel
terrible. I think I'm going to toss my
cookies.*

toss one's hat into the ring* to state
that one is running for an elective office.
(Informal.) □ *Jane wanted to run for
treasurer, so she tossed her hat into the
ring.* □ *The mayor never tossed his hat
into the ring. Instead he announced his
retirement.*

toss someone or something out AND
toss out someone or something
to throw someone or something out; to
get rid of someone or something. □
*John was behaving badly, so they threw
him out.* □ *This meat looks bad. I think
we should toss it out.*

toss something off AND **shake off something; shake something off; toss off
something** **1.** to throw something off
(of oneself). □ *Tom tossed off his jacket
and sat down to watch television.* □ *Bob
coughed so hard he shook his blanket
off.* **2.** to ignore or resist the bad effects
of something. □ *John insulted Bob, but
Bob just tossed it off.* □ *If I couldn't
shake off insults, I'd be miserable.*

total something up See *add something up.*

touch a sore point See the following
entry.

touch a sore spot AND **touch a sore point**
to refer to a sensitive matter which will
upset someone. (Also used literally.) □
*I seem to have touched a sore spot. I'm
sorry. I didn't mean to upset you.* □
*When you talk to him, avoid talking
about money. It's best not to touch a
sore point if possible.*

touch and go* very uncertain or critical. (A cliché.) □ *Things were touch and
go at the office until a new manager was
hired.* □ *Jane had a serious operation,
and everything was touch and go for two
days after her surgery.*

touch base with someone* AND **touch
base*** to talk to someone; to confer
with someone. (Slang.) □ *I need to touch*

base with John on this matter. □ *John
and I touched base on this question yesterday, and we are in agreement.*

touch on something to mention something; to talk about something briefly.
□ *In tomorrow's lecture I'd like to touch
on the matter of taxation.* □ *The teacher
only touched on the subject. There wasn't
time to do more than that.*

touch someone or something off AND
touch off someone or something
1. [with *someone*] to make someone very
angry. □ *Your rude comments touched
Mary off. She's very angry at you.* □ *I
didn't mean to touch off anyone. I was
only being honest.* **2.** [with
something] to ignite something; to start
something. □ *The argument touched
off a serious fight.* □ *A few sparks touched all the fireworks off at once.*

touch something up AND **touch up something** to repair a paint job on something. □ *We don't need to paint the
whole room. We can just touch the walls
up.* □ *You should touch up scratches on
your car as soon as they occur.*

touched by someone or something
emotionally affected or moved by someone or something. □ *Sally was very nice
to me. I was very touched by her.* □ *I
was really touched by your kind letter.*

touched in the head* AND **touched***
crazy. (Folksy or slang.) □ *Sometimes
Bob acts like he's touched in the head.*
□ *In fact, I thought he was touched.*

tough act to follow* a difficult presentation or performance to follow with
one's own performance. (A cliché.) □
*Bill's speech was excellent. It was a tough
act to follow, but my speech was good
also.* □ *In spite of the fact that I had a
tough act to follow, I did my best.*

tough break* a bit of bad fortune.
(Slang.) □ *I'm sorry to hear about your
accident. Tough break.* □ *John had a
lot of tough breaks when he was a kid,
but he's doing okay now.*

tough it out* to endure a difficult situation. (Slang.) □ *Geometry is very hard
for John, but he managed to tough it out
until the end of the year.* □ *This was a
very bad day at the office. A few times,
I was afraid I wouldn't be able to tough
it out.*

Tough luck!* That is too bad! (Slang. Usually an insincere expression.) □ *So you were late and missed the bus. Tough luck!* □ *Tough luck, kid! Try again next time.*

tough nut to crack See *hard nut to crack.*

tough row to hoe* a difficult task to undertake. (A cliché.) □ *It was a tough row to hoe, but I finally got a college degree.* □ *Getting the contract signed is going to be a tough row to hoe, but I'm sure I can do it.*

toy with someone or something 1. [with *someone*] to tease someone; to deal lightly with someone's emotions. □ *Ann broke up with Tom because he was just toying with her. He was not serious at all.* □ *Don't toy with me! I won't have it!* **2.** [with *something*] to play or fiddle with something. □ *Stop toying with the radio, or you'll break it.* □ *John sat there toying with a pencil all through the meeting.*

track someone or something down AND **hunt down someone or something; hunt someone or something down; track down someone or something** to search for or pursue someone or something. □ *See if you can track Tom down for me. I need to talk to him.* □ *Please hunt down a red pencil for me.* □ *I can't seem to track down the file you want. Give me another few minutes.*

trade on something to use a fact or a situation to one's advantage. □ *Tom was able to trade on the fact that he had once been in the Army.* □ *John traded on his poor eyesight to get a seat closer to the stage.*

trade something in on something AND **trade in something on something; trade in something; trade something in** to trade a used thing as part payment for a new thing. □ *I traded my old car in on a new one.* □ *Did you trade in the red one or the green one?*

tread on someone's toes See *step on someone's toes.*

trial and error trying repeatedly for success. □ *I finally found the right key after lots of trial and error.* □ *Sometimes trial and error is the only way to get something done.*

trip someone up AND **trip up someone 1.** to trip someone. □ *Bob tripped himself up on his own feet.* □ *The loose gravel beside the track tripped up Bob, and he fell.* **2.** to cause difficulty for someone; to cause someone to fail. □ *Bill tripped Tom up during the spelling contest, and Tom lost.* □ *I didn't mean to trip up anyone. I'm sorry I caused trouble.*

Trouble is brewing. AND **There is trouble brewing.** Trouble is developing. □ *Trouble's brewing at the office. I have to get there early tomorrow.* □ *There is trouble brewing in the government. The prime minister may resign.*

trouble one's head about someone or something* to worry about someone or something; to *trouble oneself about someone or something* which is none of one's business. (Folksy. Usually in the negative. Also with *pretty*, as in the examples. Usually in the negative meaning to mind one's own business.) □ *Now, now, don't trouble your pretty head about all these things.* □ *You needn't trouble your head about Sally.*

trouble oneself about someone or something to worry oneself about someone or something. (Usually in the negative.) □ *Please don't trouble yourself about me. I'm doing fine.* □ *I can't take time to trouble myself about this matter. Do it yourself.*

trouble oneself to do something AND **trouble oneself** to bother doing something. (Usually in the negative.) □ *He didn't even trouble himself to turn off the light when he left.* □ *No thank you. I don't need any help. Please don't trouble yourself.*

true to form exactly as expected; following the usual pattern. (Often with *running*, as in the examples.) □ *As usual, John is late. At least he's true to form.* □ *And true to form, Mary left before the meeting was adjourned.* □ *This winter season is running true to form—miserable!*

true to one's word keeping one's promise. □ *True to his word, Tom showed up at exactly eight o'clock.* □ *We'll soon know if Jane is true to her word. We'll see if she does what she promised.*

trumped-up false; fraudulently devised. □ *They tried to have Tom arrested on a trumped-up charge.* □ *Bob gave some trumped-up excuse for not being at the meeting.*

try one's hand at something AND **try one's hand** to take a try at something. □ *Someday I'd like to try my hand at flying a plane.* □ *Give me a chance. Let me try my hand!*

try one's luck at something AND **try one's luck** to attempt to do something (where success requires luck). □ *My great grandfather came to California to try his luck at finding gold.* □ *I went into a gambling casino to try my luck.*

try one's wings to try to do something one has recently become qualified to do. (Like a young bird uses its wings to try to fly.) □ *John just got his driver's license and wants to borrow the car to try out his wings.* □ *I learned to skin dive, and I want to go to the seaside to try out my wings.*

try out for something AND **try out** to test one's fitness for a role in a play, a position on a sports team, etc. □ *I sing pretty well, so I thought I'd try out for the chorus.* □ *Hardly anyone else showed up to try out.*

try someone or something out AND **try out someone or something** to test someone or something for suitability (for some particular purpose). □ *John thought he could handle the job, so I thought I'd try him out.* □ *I'd like to try out that tool to see if it suits my purposes.*

try someone's patience to do something annoying which may cause someone to lose patience; to cause someone to be annoyed. □ *Stop whistling. You're trying my patience. Very soon I'm going to lose my temper.* □ *Some students think it's fun to try the teacher's patience.*

try something on AND **try on something** to put on a piece of clothing (or something else what fits on the body) to see if it fits. □ *Here, try this shirt on. I think it's your size.* □ *I tried on seven pairs of shoes before I found some that I liked.*

try something out on someone AND **try out something on someone** 1. to test something on someone (to see how it works or if it is liked). □ *I found a recipe for oyster stew and tried it out on my roommate.* □ *I'm glad you didn't try out that stuff on me!* 2.* to tell about a plan or an idea and ask someone for an opinion about it. (Informal.) □ *I have a tremendous idea! Let me try it out on you.* □ *I want to try out my plan on you. Please give me your honest opinion.*

tune someone or something out AND **tune out someone or something** to ignore someone or something; to become unaware of someone or something. □ *Sally annoys me sometimes, so I just tune her out.* □ *Your radio doesn't bother me. I just tune out the noise.*

tune something in AND **tune in something; tune in** to set a radio or television control so as to receive something. □ *Why don't you try to tune the ball game in?* □ *This is a cheap radio, and I can't tune in distant stations.* □ *Please try to tune in.*

tune something up AND **tune up something** to adjust an engine so that it runs the way it was meant to. (In the examples, *car* means car engine.) □ *I need to find someone to tune my car up.* □ *I have a friend who tunes up cars.*

turn a blind eye to someone or something to ignore something and pretend you do not see it. □ *The usher turned a blind eye to the little boy who sneaked into the theater.* □ *How can you turn a blind eye to all those starving children?*

turn a deaf ear to something AND **turn a deaf ear** to ignore what someone says; to ignore a cry for help. □ *How can you just turn a deaf ear to their cries for food and shelter?* □ *The government has turned a deaf ear.*

turn against someone or something to become opposed to someone or something (after once supporting someone or something). □ *Bob turned against Mary after years of being her friend.* □ *I used to like small cars, but lately I've turned against them.*

turn around AND **turn about** **1.** to rotate. □ *How fast does the earth turn around?* □ *Billy turned about as fast as he could until he got dizzy and fell down.* **2.** to reverse direction. □ *Public opinion has finally turned around. Now people are in favor of the law.* □ *The car turned about and headed straight for us.*

turn in to go to bed. □ *It's late. I think I'll turn in.* □ *We usually turn in at about midnight.*

turn into something to become something. □ *The caterpillar turned into a butterfly.* □ *When the big lights came on, night turned into day.*

turn of the century the end of one century and the beginning of another. □ *It's just a few years until the turn of the century.* □ *People like to celebrate the turn of the century.*

turn on a dime* to turn in a very tight turn. (Informal.) □ *This car handles very well. It can turn on a dime.* □ *The speeding car turned on a dime and headed the other direction.*

turn on someone **1.** to attack someone. □ *I thought the strange dog was friendly, but suddenly it turned on me and bit me.* □ *Bob knows a lot about lions, and he says that no matter how well they are trained, there is always the danger that they'll turn on you.* **2.** See *turn someone or something on.*

turn on the waterworks* to begin to cry. (Slang.) □ *Every time Billy got homesick, he turned on the waterworks.* □ *Sally hurt her knee and turned on the waterworks for about twenty minutes.*

turn one's back on someone or something AND **turn one's back** to abandon or ignore someone or something. □ *Don't turn your back on your old friends.* □ *Bob has a tendency to turn his back on serious problems.* □ *This matter needs your attention. Please don't just turn your back.*

turn one's nose up at someone or something AND **turn up one's nose at someone or something** to sneer at someone or something; to reject someone or something. □ *John turned his nose up at Ann, and that hurt her feelings.* □ *I never turn up my nose at dessert, no matter what it is.*

turn out See the following entry.

turn out all right AND **pan out; turn out; work out all right; work out** to end satisfactorily. (Compare to *work out for the best.*) □ *I hope everything turns out all right.* □ *Oh, yes. It'll all pan out.* □ *Things usually work out, no matter how bad they seem.*

turn out to be someone or something to end up being someone or something; to be shown to be someone or something. □ *The most helpful person turned out to be Tom.* □ *The real cause of the frightening noise turned out to be the wind.*

turn over **1.** (for someone in a bed) to turn to one's other side. □ *I slept very restlessly last night. I turned over about forty times.* □ *I had to turn over to get out of a draft.* **2.** AND **kick over** (for an engine) to start or to rotate. □ *My car engine was so cold that it wouldn't even turn over.* □ *The engine turned over a few times and then stopped for good.* **3.** (for goods) to be stocked and sold (at a certain rate). □ *Don't order any more of those items. They turn over too slowly.* □ *Most of our items turn over very well, and this means that our business is good.*

turn over a new leaf* to start again with the intention of doing better; to begin again ignoring past errors. (A cliché.) □ *Tom promised to turn over a new leaf and do better from now on.* □ *After a minor accident, Sally decided to turn over a new leaf and drive more carefully.*

turn over in one's grave* (for a dead person) to be shocked or horrified. (A cliché. Never used literally.) □ *If Beethoven heard Mary play one of his sonatas, he'd turn over in his grave.* □ *If Aunt Jane knew what you were doing with her favorite chair, she would turn over in her grave.*

turn someone or something down AND **turn down someone or something** **1.** [with *someone*] to refuse or deny someone. □ *I applied for a job with the city, but they turned me down.* □ *They turned down Mary who also applied.* **2.** [with *something*] to deny someone's request. □ *I offered her some help, but* she turned it down. □ She had turned down John's offer of help, too. **3.** [with something] to fold part of something downward. □ The hotel maid turned down the bed while I was at dinner. □ In the mail-order catalog, I always turn down a page which interests me. **4.** [with something] to lower the volume or amount of something, such as heat, sound, water, air pressure, etc. □ It's hot in here. Please turn down the heat. □ Turn the stereo down. It's too loud.

turn someone or something in AND **turn in someone or something 1.** [with someone] to give someone over to the authorities; to report someone's bad behavior. □ I knew who stole the money, so I turned him in. □ I know that Mr. Johnson cheated on his income tax, so I turned him in. **2.** [with something] to give something back; to take something to the proper place. □ I found a pair of gloves in the hallway, and I turned them in. □ I earned over five dollars when I turned in a lot of soft drink bottles.

turn someone or something into something to make someone or something become something. □ My teachers tried to turn me into a scholar, but they failed. □ I can turn these vegetables into a delicious soup.

turn someone or something off AND **turn off someone or something 1.*** [with someone] to discourage or disgust someone. (Informal.) □ His manner really turns me off. □ That man has a way of turning off everyone he comes in contact with. **2.** to switch off lights, a radio, a television, a stereo, etc. □ Please turn that radio off and pay attention. □ John Johnson is talking on the television again. Please turn him off. I'm tired of hearing him.

turn someone or something on AND **turn on someone or something 1.*** [with someone] to excite someone; to excite someone sexually. (Informal.) □ The lecture was very good. It turned on the whole class. □ Sally said she preferred not to watch movies that attempted to turn people on. **2.** [with something] to switch on lights, a radio, television, stereo, etc. □ Turn on the radio so we

can listen to the news. □ Let's turn the television on and watch a movie.

turn someone or something out AND **turn out someone or something 1.** [with someone] to send someone out of somewhere. □ I didn't pay my rent, so the manager turned me out. □ I'm glad it's not winter. I'd hate to be turned out in the snow. **2.** [with something] to manufacture something; to produce something. □ This machine can turn out 2,000 items a day. □ John wasn't turning enough work out, so the manager had a talk with him.

turn someone or something over AND **turn over someone or something 1.** to roll someone or something over; to turn someone or something from one side to the other. □ The man was unconscious when we arrived. We turned him over to see if we could tell who he was. □ Turn over the box and read what is written on the bottom. **2.** See the following entry.

turn someone or something over to someone AND **turn someone or something over** to hand over someone or something to someone. □ The teacher turned over the student to the principal. □ Please turn over the extra money to me. □ I'll take care of the extra money. Please turn it over as soon as possible.

turn someone or something up AND **turn up someone or something 1.** to search for and find someone or something. □ Let me try to see if I can turn someone up who knows how to do the job. □ I turned up a number of interesting items when I went through Aunt Jane's attic. **2.** [with something] to increase the volume or amount of something, such as a light, heat, a radio, etc. □ Don't turn your stereo up. It's too loud already. □ I'm going to turn up the heat. It's too cold in here. ALSO: **turn up** to appear. □ We'll send out invitations and see who turns up.

turn someone's head (for flattery or success) to distract someone; to cause someone to not be sensible. (Also used literally.) □ Don't let our praise turn your head. You're not perfect! □ Her successes had turned her head. She was now quite arrogant.

turn someone's stomach to make someone (figuratively or literally) ill. □ *This milk is spoiled. The smell of it turns my stomach.* □ *The play was so bad that it turned my stomach.*

turn something around to reverse the direction of something. □ *They turned the car around and headed in the other direction.* □ *The new manager took over and turned the business around. Suddenly we were making a profit.*

turn something to one's advantage to make an advantage for oneself out of something (which might otherwise be a disadvantage). □ *Sally found a way to turn the problem to her advantage.* □ *The ice cream store manager was able to turn the hot weather to her advantage.*

turn the other cheek to ignore abuse or an insult. □ *When Bob got mad at Mary and yelled at her, she just turned the other cheek.* □ *Usually I turn the other cheek when someone is rude to me.*

turn the tables on someone AND **turn the tables** to cause a reversal in someone's plans; to make one's plans turn back on one. □ *I went to Jane's house to help get ready for a surprise party for Bob. It turned out that the surprise party was for me! Jane really turned the tables on me!* □ *Turning the tables like that requires a lot of planning and a lot of secrecy.*

turn the tide to cause a reversal in the direction of events; to cause a reversal in public opinion. □ *It looked like the team was going to lose, but near the end of the game, our star player turned the tide.* □ *At first, people were opposed to our plan. After a lot of discussion, we were able to turn the tide.*

turn to to begin to get busy. □ *Come on, you guys! Turn to! Let's get to work.* □ *If you people will turn to, we can finish this work in no time at all.*

turn to someone or something for something AND **turn to someone or something** 1. to seek something from someone or something. □ *I turned to Ann for help.* □ *Bill turned to aspirin for relief from his headache.* 2. [with *something*] to turn (pages) to find a par-

ticular thing. □ *I opened the book and turned to chapter seven.* □ *Please turn to the index. You can use it to find what you want.*

turn turtle* to turn upside down. (Slang.) □ *The sailboat turned turtle, but the sailors only got wet.* □ *The car ran off the road and turned turtle in the ditch.*

turn up See *turn someone or something up.*

turn up one's toes* to die. (Slang.) □ *When I turn up my toes, I want a big funeral with lots of flowers.* □ *Our cat turned up his toes during the night. He was nearly ten years old.*

twiddle one's thumbs to fill up time by playing with one's fingers. □ *What am I supposed to do while waiting for you? Sit here and twiddle my thumbs?* □ *Don't sit around twiddling your thumbs. Get busy!*

twist someone around one's little finger* to manipulate and control someone. (A cliché.) □ *Bob really fell for Jane. She can twist him around her little finger.* □ *Billy's mother has twisted him around her little finger. He's very dependent on her.*

twist someone's arm to force or persuade someone. □ *At first she refused, but after I twisted her arm a little, she agreed to help.* □ *I didn't want to run for mayor, but everyone twisted my arm.*

two-time someone* to cheat on or betray one's spouse or lover by dating or seeing someone else. (Slang.) □ *When Mrs. Franklin learned that Mr. Franklin was two-timing her, she left him.* □ *Ann told Bob that if he ever two-timed her, she would cause him a lot of trouble.*

U

under a cloud of suspicion AND **under a cloud** to be suspected of (doing) something. □ *Someone stole some money at work, and now everyone is under a cloud of suspicion.* □ *Even the manager is under a cloud.*

under construction being built or repaired. □ *We cannot travel on this road because it's under construction.* □ *Our new home has been under construction all summer. We hope to move in next month.*

under fire during an attack. □ *There was a scandal in city hall, and the mayor was forced to resign under fire.* □ *John is a good lawyer because he can think under fire.*

under one's own steam* by one's own power or effort. (Informal.) □ *I missed my ride to class, so I had to get there under my own steam.* □ *John will need some help with this project. He can't do it under his own steam.*

under the circumstances in a particular situation; because of the circumstances. □ *I'm sorry to hear that you're ill. Under the circumstances, you may take the day off.* □ *We won't expect you to come to work for a few days, under the circumstances.*

under the counter (bought or sold) in secret or illegally. (Also used literally.) □ *The drugstore owner was arrested for selling liquor under the counter.* □ *This owner was also selling dirty books under the counter.*

under the table* in secret, as with the giving of a bribe. (Informal. Also used literally.) □ *The mayor had been paying money to the construction company under the table.* □ *Tom transferred the deed to the property to his wife under the table.*

under the weather ill. □ *I'm a bit under the weather today, so I can't go to the office.* □ *My head is aching, and I feel a little under the weather.*

under the wire* just barely in time or on time. (Informal.) □ *I turned in my report just under the wire.* □ *Bill was the last person to get in the door. He got in under the wire.*

until all hours until very late. □ *Mary is out until all hours night after night.* □ *If I'm up until all hours two nights in a row, I'm just exhausted.*

up a blind alley* at a dead end; on a route that leads nowhere. (Informal.) □ *I have been trying to find out something about my ancestors, but I'm up a blind alley. I can't find anything.* □ *The police are up a blind alley in their investigation of the crime.*

up a creek See *up the creek without a paddle.*

up a tree* in a difficult situation and unable to get out; stymied and confused. (Slang.) □ *I'm really up a tree on this problem.* □ *Geometry is too hard for me. It's got me up a tree.*

up against something having trouble with something. (The *something* is often *it*, meaning facing trouble in general.) □ *Jane is up against a serious problem.* □ *Yes, she really looks like she's up against it.*

up and about healthy and moving about—not sick in bed. □ *Mary is getting better. She should be up and about in a few days.* □ *She can't wait until she's up and about. She's tired of being in bed.*

up and at them* to get up and go at people or things; to get active and get busy. (Informal. Usually *them* is *'em*.) □ *Come on, Bob—up and at 'em!* □ *There is a lot of work to be done around here. Up and at 'em, everybody!* ALSO: **up and Adam*** an incorrect way of spelling *up and at them*. (Informal. Do not use in writing.) □ *Come on, Bob—up and Adam!*

up-and-coming enterprising and alert. □ *Jane is a hard worker—really up-and-coming.* □ *Bob is also an up-and-coming youngster who is going to become well known.*

up for grabs* available to anyone. (Slang.) □ *Mary quit yesterday, and her job is up for grabs.* □ *Who's in charge around here? This whole organization is up for grabs.*

up front* (Slang.) **1.** sincere and open. □ *Ann is a very up front kind of person. Everyone feels easy around her.* □ *It's hard to tell what Tom is really thinking. He's not very up front.* **2.** in advance. □ *I ordered a new car, and they wanted 20% up front.* □ *I couldn't afford to pay that much up front. I'd have to make a smaller deposit.*

up in arms rising up in anger; (figuratively or literally) armed with weapons. □ *My father was really up in arms when he got his tax bill this year.* □ *The citizens were up in arms, pounding on the gates of the palace, demanding justice.*

up in the air undecided; uncertain. (Also used literally.) □ *I don't know what Sally plans to do. Things were sort of up in the air the last time we talked.* □ *Let's leave this question up in the air until next week.*

up in years AND **advanced in years; along in years; on in years** old; elderly. □ *My uncle is up in years, and can't hear too well.* □ *Many people lose their hearing somewhat when they are along in years.*

up North to or at the northern part of the country or the world. (See also *back East, down South,* and *out West.*) □ *I don't like living up North. I want to move down South where it's warm.* □ *When you say "up North", do you mean where the polar bears live, or just in the northern states?*

up the creek without a paddle* AND **up a creek; up the creek*** in a bad situation. (Slang. Use with caution. There is a taboo version of this phrase.) □ *What a mess I'm in. I'm really up the creek without a paddle.* □ *I tried to prevent it, but I seem to be up a creek, too.*

up to date up to the current standards of fashion. □ *I'm having my living room redecorated to bring it up to date.* □ *I don't care if my rooms are up to date. I just want them to be comfortable.* ALSO: **up-to-date** modern; contemporary. □ *I'd like to see a more up-to-date report on Mr. Smith.*

up to no good* doing something bad. (Informal.) □ *I could tell from the look on Tom's face that he was up to no good.* □ *There are three boys in the front yard. I don't know what they are doing, but I think they are up to no good.*

up to one to be one's own choice. □ *She said I didn't have to go if I didn't want to. It's entirely up to me.* □ *It's up to Mary whether she takes the job or tries to find another one.*

up to one's ears in something See the following entry.

up to one's neck in something* AND **up to one's ears in something*; up to one's ears*; up to one's neck*** very much involved in something. (Informal.) □ *I can't come to the meeting. I'm up to my neck in these reports.* □ *Mary is up to her ears in her work.*

up to par as good as the standard or average; up to standard. □ *I'm just not feeling up to par today. I must be coming down with something.* □ *The manager said that the report was not up to par and gave it back to Mary to do over again.*

up to snuff* as good as is required; meeting the minimum requirements. (Slang. Compare to *up to par.*) □ *Sorry, Tom. Your performance isn't up to snuff. You'll have to improve or find another job.* □ *My paper wasn't up to snuff, so I got an F.*

up-to-the-minute the very latest or most recent. □ *I want to hear some up-to-the-minute news on the hostage situation.* □ *I just got an up-to-the-minute report on Tom's health.*

ups and downs good fortune and bad fortune. □ *I've had my ups and downs, but in general life has been good to me.* □ *All people have their ups and downs.*

upset someone's plans to ruin someone's plans. □ *I hope it doesn't upset your plans if I'm late for the meeting.* □ *No, it won't upset my plans at all.*

upset the apple cart to mess up or ruin something. □ *Tom really upset the apple cart by telling Mary the truth about Jane.* □ *I always knew he'd upset the apple cart.*

upside down turned over with the top on the bottom. □ *The turtle was upside down and couldn't go anywhere.* □ *The book was upside down, and I couldn't see what the title was.*

use every trick in the book* to use every method possible. (Informal.) □ *I used every trick in the book, but I still couldn't manage to get a ticket to the game Saturday.* □ *Bob tried to use every trick in the book, but he still failed.*

use one's head AND **use one's noggin*; use one's noodle*** to use one's own intelligence. (The words *noggin* and *noodle* are slang terms for head.) □ *You can do better in math if you'll just use your head.* □ *Jane uses her noggin and gets things done correctly and on time.* □ *Yes, she sure knows how to use her noodle.*

use some elbow grease* use some effort. (Slang. As if lubricating one's elbow would make one more efficient. Note the variations in the examples.) □ *Come on, Bill. You can do it. Just use some elbow grease.* □ *I tried elbow grease, but it doesn't help get the job done.*

use someone or something as an excuse to blame someone or something (for a failure). □ *John used his old car as an excuse for not going to the meeting.* □ *My husband was sick in bed, and I used him as an excuse.*

use something up AND **use up something** to use all of something. □ *Who used up the last of the toothpaste?* □ *I used it all up. Should I buy some more?*

use strong language to swear, threaten, or use abusive language. □ *I wish you wouldn't use strong language in front of the children.* □ *If you feel like you have to use strong language with the manager, perhaps you had better let me do the talking.*

used to someone or something accustomed to someone or something. □ *I'm not used to Jane yet. She's a bit hard to get along with.* □ *How long does it take to get used to this weather?*

V

vanish into thin air to disappear without leaving a trace. □ *My money gets spent so fast. It seems to vanish into thin air.* □ *When I came back, my car was gone. I had locked it, and it couldn't have vanished in thin air!*

Variety is the spice of life. a proverb meaning that differences and changes make life interesting. □ *Mary reads all kinds of books. She says variety is the spice of life.* □ *The Franklins travel all over the world so they can learn how different people live. After all, variety is the spice of life.*

verge on something to be almost something. □ *Your blouse is a lovely color. It seems to be blue verging on purple.* □ *Sally has a terrible case of the flu, and they are afraid it's verging on pneumonia.*

vote a straight ticket to cast a ballot with all the votes for members of the same political party. □ *I'm not a member of any political party, so I never vote* a straight ticket. □ *I usually vote a straight ticket because I believe in the principles of one party and not in the other.*

vote someone in AND **vote in someone** to elect someone. □ *The village voted in the same mayor year after year.* □ *I didn't really want to hold public office, but everyone voted me in, so I had to serve.*

vote someone out AND **vote out someone** to send someone out of elective office (by voting someone else into office). □ *Mr. Williams was a poor mayor, so they voted him out in the following election.* □ *They voted out the mayor.*

vote something down AND **vote down something** to vote against something. □ *The voters were against spending money to build a new park, so they voted it down.* □ *The mayor proposed an increase in taxes, but everyone voted down the increase.*

W

wade into something AND **wade in** to start into (doing) something immediately. □ *I need some preparation. I can't just wade into the job and start doing things correctly.* □ *We don't expect you to wade in. We'll tell you what to do.*

wag one's chin* to chatter or chat with someone. (Slang.) □ *We stood around and wagged our chins for almost an hour.* □ *Don't just wag your chin. Stop talking and get to work!*

wait-and-see attitude a skeptical attitude; an uncertain attitude where someone will just wait and see what happens. □ *John thought that Mary couldn't do it, but he took a wait-and-see attitude.* □ *His wait-and-see attitude didn't influence me at all.*

wait on someone hand and foot to serve someone very well, attending to all personal needs. □ *I don't mind bringing you your coffee, but I don't intend to wait on you hand and foot.* □ *I don't want anyone to wait on me hand and foot. I can take care of myself.*

wait one's turn to keep from doing something until everyone ahead of you has done it. □ *You can't cross the intersection yet. You must wait your turn.* □ *I can't wait my turn. I'm in a big hurry.*

wait up for someone or something AND **wait up** **1.** to stay up late waiting for someone to arrive or something to happen. □ *I'll be home late. Don't wait up for me.* □ *We waited up for the coming of the new year, and then we went to bed.* **2.** AND **hold up for someone or something; hold up** to wait for someone or something to catch up. □ *Hey! Don't go so fast. Wait up for me.* □ *Hold up! You're going too fast.*

wake someone or something up AND **wake up someone or something** to cause someone or something to stop sleeping. □ *Ann is sleeping. Don't wake her up.* □ *I came home late and woke up the dog which then started barking at me.*

walk a tightrope to be in a situation where one must be very cautious. (Also used literally.) □ *I've been walking a tightrope all day. I need to relax.* □ *Our business is about to fail. We've been walking a tightrope for three months.*

walk all over someone to treat someone badly. □ *She's so mean to her children. She walks all over them.* □ *The manager had walked all over Ann for months. Finally she quit.*

walk away with something* to win something easily. (Informal.) □ *John won the tennis match with no difficulty. He walked away with it.* □ *Our team walked away with first place.*

walk off with something to take or steal something. □ *I think somebody just walked off with my purse!* □ *Somebody walked off with my daughter's bicycle.*

walk on air to be very happy; to be euphoric. (Never used literally.) □ *Ann was walking on air when she got the job.* □ *On the last day of school, all the children are walking on air.*

walk on eggs* to be very cautious. (Informal. Never used literally.) □ *The manager is very hard to deal with. You really have to walk on eggs.* □ *I've been walking on eggs ever since I started working here.*

walk out on someone or something AND **walk out** **1.** [with *someone*] to abandon someone; to leave one's spouse. □

Mr. Franklin walked out on Mrs. Franklin last week. □ *Bob walked out on Jane without saying goodbye.* **2.** to leave a performance (of something by someone). □ *We didn't like the play at all, so we walked out.* □ *John was giving a very dull speech, and a few people even walked out on him.*

walk the floor to pace nervously while waiting. □ *While Bill waited for news of the operation, he walked the floor for hours on end.* □ *Walking the floor won't help. You might as well sit down and relax.*

Walls have ears.* We may be overheard. (A cliché.) □ *Let's not discuss this matter here. Walls have ears, you know.* □ *Shhh. Walls have ears. Someone may be listening.*

want out of something AND **want out** to want to remove oneself from a place or a situation. □ *The children want out of the house so they can play. Please let them go out.* □ *I took this job because I liked the work. Now I want out.*

warm someone or something up AND **warm up someone or something** to heat up someone or something. (Also without *up.*) □ *Why don't you warm up some soup for dinner?* □ *Come over here and warm yourself up by the fire.*

warm the bench (for a player) to remain out of play during a game—seated on a bench. □ *John spent the whole game warming the bench.* □ *Mary never warms the bench. She plays from the beginning to the end.*

warm the cockles of someone's heart* to make someone warm and happy. (A cliché.) □ *It warms the cockles of my heart to hear you say that.* □ *Hearing that old song again warmed the cockles of her heart.*

warm up to someone to become friendly with someone; to get used to a person and become friends. □ *It took a while before John warmed up to me, but then we became good friends.* □ *It's hard to warm up to Sally. She's very quiet and shy.*

wash a few things out AND **wash out a few things** to do a little bit of laundry, such as socks and underclothing. □ *I'm sorry I can't go out tonight. I've*

got to wash a few things out. □ *I'll be ready to leave in just a minute. I've just got to wash out a few things.*

wash one's hands of someone or something to end one's association with someone or something. □ *I washed my hands of Tom. I wanted no more to do with him.* □ *That car was a real headache. I washed my hands of it long ago.*

wash someone or something off AND **wash off someone or something 1.** [with *something*] to rinse or wash something off (of something else). □ *I got honey on my hands, so I washed it off.* □ *There is dirt on the tomatoes. Please wash it off.* **2.** to rinse or wash someone or something. □ *Let me wash off my hands, and I'll be ready to go with you.* □ *Please wash off the lettuce before you serve it.*

wash someone or something up AND **wash up someone or something 1.** to clean up someone or something by washing. □ *Please wash up the dishes when you finish eating.* □ *I've got to wash the baby up. He spilled his milk.* **2.** (for waves, wind, etc.) to carry someone or something to the shore. □ *A man drowned, and the waves washed him up.* □ *The storm washed up a lot of seaweed.* **3.*** [with *someone*] to put an end to someone's career. (Informal.) □ *That poor performance washed Tom up as a clerk.* □ *"Well, that washes me up," said Tom.* ALSO: **washed up*** finished. (Informal.) □ *"You're through, Tom," said the manager, "fired—washed up!"*

wash something down AND **wash down something 1.** to rinse or wash something. □ *The car was dusty, so I washed it down.* □ *I used the hose to wash the driveway down.* **2.** to drink a liquid to aid in the swallowing of something. □ *I took a drink of milk to wash down my cookie.* □ *John washed the pizza down with a beer.*

wash something out AND **wash out something 1.** to wash the inside of something. □ *Please wash out the tub when you finish bathing.* □ *Wash out the glass before you use it.* **2.** (for a liquid) to erode or wash something away. □ *The storm washed out the bridge over* the river. □ *The rain washed the wall out after a few years.*

waste away to decline gradually; to wither; to become weak and feeble. □ *Our cat was very old, and she just wasted away over the last few years.* □ *I can't seem to hold onto my money. It just wastes away.*

waste one's breath* to waste one's time talking; to talk in vain. (Informal.) □ *Don't waste your breath talking to her. She won't listen.* □ *You can't persuade me. You're just wasting your breath.*

waste someone* to kill someone. (Slang, especially criminal slang.) □ *The thief tried to waste the bank guard after the bank robbery.* □ *The crook said, "Try that again, and I'll waste you!"*

watch out for someone or something AND **look out for someone or something** **1.** [with *someone*] to watch over and care for someone. □ *When I was a kid, my older brother always watched out for me.* □ *I really needed someone to look out for me then.* **2.** to be on guard for someone or something; to be on watch for someone or something. □ *Watch out for someone wearing a white carnation.* □ *Look out for John and his friends. They'll be coming this way very soon.* **3.** AND **look out; watch out** to try to avoid a confrontation with someone or something. □ *Watch out for that car! It nearly hit you!* □ *Look out for John. He's looking for you, and he's really mad.* □ *Thanks. I'd better look out.*

water something down AND **water down something** to dilute something; to thin something out and make it lighter. (Used figuratively and literally.) □ *The punch was good until someone watered it down.* □ *Professor Jones sometimes waters down his lectures so people can understand them better.*

water under the bridge (something) past and forgotten. (A cliché.) □ *Please don't worry about it anymore. It's all water under the bridge.* □ *I can't change the past. It's water under the bridge.*

wear and tear on something AND **wear and tear** the process of wearing down or breaking down something. □ *Driving in freezing weather means lots of*

wear and tear on your car. □ *I drive carefully and sensibly to avoid wear and tear.*

wear more than one hat to have more than one set of responsibilities; to hold more than one office. □ *The mayor is also the police chief. She wears more than one hat.* □ *I have too much to do to wear more than one hat.*

wear on someone to bother or annoy someone. □ *We stayed with them only a short time because my children seemed to wear on them.* □ *Always being short of money wears on a person after a while.*

wear one's heart on one's sleeve AND **have one's heart on one's sleeve** to habitually display one's feelings openly, rather than keep them private. □ *John always has his heart on his sleeve so that everyone knows how he feels.* □ *Because she wears her heart on her sleeve, it's easy to hurt her feelings.* ALSO: **one's heart is on one's sleeve** (for one) to display one's feelings openly. □ *Because his heart is on his sleeve, we know how he feels.*

wear out (for a thing) to become useless or break down because of over-use or wear. □ *My coat finally wore out, so I got a new one.* □ *I hope this car doesn't wear out before spring.* ALSO: **worn-out 1.** unusable or unserviceable because of wear. □ *This coat is worn-out.* □ *My car is almost worn-out.* **2.** tired; exhausted. □ *I had a busy day, and I'm completely worn-out.* □ *Everyone on the team was completely worn-out.*

wear out one's welcome* to stay too long (at an event to which one has been invited); to visit somewhere too often. (A cliché.) □ *Tom visited the Smiths so often that he wore out his welcome.* □ *At about midnight, I decided that I had worn out my welcome, so I went home.*

wear someone or something down AND **wear down someone or something 1.** [with *someone*] to overcome someone's objections; to persist until someone has been persuaded. □ *John didn't want to go, but we finally wore him down.* □ *We were unable to wear down John, and when we left, he was still insisting on running away from home.* **2.** [with *something*] to reduce something by wear or use; to erode something. □ *A lot of foot traffic in the hallway wore down the carpet.* □ *The mountain used to be taller, but the wind and rain have worn it down.*

wear someone or something out AND **wear out someone or something 1.** [with *someone*] to exhaust someone; to make someone tired. (See *worn-out* at *wear out*.) □ *The coach made the team practice until he wore them out.* □ *If he wears out everybody on the team, nobody will be left to play in the game.* **2.** [with *something*] to make something useless or unserviceable through wear or over-use. (See also *wear out*.) □ *Tom wore his car's tires out by driving on bumpy roads.* □ *I wore out my favorite record by playing it too much.*

weasel out of something* AND **weasel out*** to (figuratively or literally) get out or sneak out of something. (Informal.) □ *I don't want to go to the meeting. I think I'll try to weasel out of it.* □ *You had better be there! Don't try to weasel out!*

weave in and out of something AND **weave in and out** to move, drive, or walk in and out of something, such as traffic, a line, etc. □ *The car was dangerously weaving in and out of traffic.* □ *The deer ran rapidly through the forest, weaving in and out of the trees.*

week in, week out* every week, week after week. (Informal.) □ *We have the same old food, week in, week out.* □ *I'm tired of this job. I've done the same thing—week in, week out—for three years.*

weigh on someone's mind (for something) to be in a person's thoughts; (for something) to be bothering someone's thinking. □ *This problem has been weighing on my mind for many days now.* □ *I hate to have things weighing on my mind. I can't sleep when I'm worried.*

weigh someone down AND **weigh down someone** (for a thought) to worry or depress someone. (Also used literally.) □ *All these problems really weigh me down.* □ *Financial problems have been weighing down our entire family.*

weigh someone's words 1. to consider carefully what someone says. □ *I listened to what he said, and I weighed his words very carefully.* □ *Everyone was weighing his words. None of us knew exactly what he meant.* **2.** to consider one's own words carefully when speaking. □ *I always weigh my words when I speak in public.* □ *John was weighing his words carefully because he didn't want to be misunderstood.*

welcome someone with open arms See *receive someone with open arms*.

welcome to do something to be free to do something. □ *You're welcome to leave whenever you wish.* □ *He's welcome to join the club whenever he feels he's ready.*

well and good* AND **all well and good*** good; desirable. (A cliché.) □ *It's well and good that you're here on time. I was afraid you'd be late again.* □ *It's all well and good that you're passing English, but what about math and science?*

well-fixed See the following entry.

well-heeled AND **well-fixed; well-off** wealthy; with sufficient money. □ *My uncle can afford a new car. He's well-heeled.* □ *Everyone in his family is well-off.*

well-off See the previous entry.

well-to-do wealthy and of good social position. (Often with *quite*, as in the examples.) □ *The Jones family is quite well-to-do.* □ *There is a gentleman waiting for you at the door. He appears quite well-to-do.*

wet behind the ears young and inexperienced. □ *John's too young to take on a job like this! He's still wet behind the ears!* □ *He may be wet behind the ears, but he's well-trained and totally competent.*

wet someone's whistle* to take a drink of something. (Folksy.) □ *Wow, am I thirsty. I need something to wet my whistle.* □ *Hey, Sally! Give her something to wet her whistle.*

whale the tar out of someone* to spank or beat someone. (Folksy.) □ *If you're not home in time, I'll whale the tar out of you!* □ *Bill's dad was really mad. He whaled the tar out of Bill.*

What are you driving at?* What are

you implying?; What do you mean? (Informal.) □ *What are you driving at? What are you trying to say?* □ *Why are you asking me all these questions? What are you driving at?*

What difference does it make? Does it really matter?; Does it cause any trouble? □ *What if I choose to leave home? What difference does it make?* □ *So Jane dropped out of the club. What difference does it make?*

What gives?* AND **What goes?*** What is happening? (Slang.) □ *What's going on here? What gives?* □ *There's a strange car in my driveway. What goes?*

What goes? See the previous entry.

What is sauce for the goose is sauce for the gander. a proverb meaning that what is appropriate for one is appropriate for the other. □ *If John gets a new coat, I should get one, too. After all, what is sauce for the goose is sauce for the gander.* □ *If I get punished for breaking the window, so should Mary. What is sauce for the goose is sauce for the gander.*

what makes someone tick* what motivates someone; what makes someone behave in a certain way. (Informal.) □ *William is sort of strange. I don't know what makes him tick.* □ *When you get to know people, you find out what makes them tick.*

What of it?* Why does it matter?; So what? (Informal.) □ *So I'm a few minutes late. What of it?* □ BILL: *Your hands are dirty.* BOB: *What of it?*

What's cooking?* AND **What's up?*** What is happening? (Slang.) □ *What's going on around here? What's cooking?* □ *Are there any plans for this evening? What's up?*

What's done is done. It is final and in the past. □ *It's too late to change it now. What's done is done.* □ *What's done is done. The past cannot be altered.*

What's eating you?* What is bothering you? (Slang.) □ *What's wrong, Bob? What's eating you?* □ *You seem upset, Mary. What's eating you?*

What's going on? What is happening? □ *Things seem very busy here. What's going on?* □ *What's going on? Is someone causing trouble?*

What's gotten into someone? What has caused someone to behave in some way? □ *Why are you doing that? What's gotten into you?* □ *What's gotten into Bob? He's acting so strangely.*

What's the good of something? What is the point of something?; Why bother with something? □ *What's the good of my going at all if I'll be late?* □ *There is no need to get there early. What's the good of that?*

What's the idea?* AND **What's the big idea?*** Why did you do that? (Informal. Usually said in anger.) □ *Hey, don't do that! What's the idea?* □ *Why did you shove me? What's the big idea?*

What's up? See *What's cooking?*

What's with someone?* What is bothering or affecting someone? (Slang.) □ *John seems upset. What's with him?* □ *There's nothing wrong with me. What's with you?*

when all is said and done* when everything is finished and settled; when everything is considered. (A cliché.) □ *When all is said and done, this isn't such a bad part of the country to live in after all.* □ *When all is said and done, I believe I had a very enjoyable time on my vacation.*

When in Rome do as the Romans do. a proverb meaning that one should behave in the same way that the local people behave. □ *I don't usually eat lamb, but I did when I went to Australia. When in Rome do as the Romans do.* □ *I always carry an umbrella when I visit London. When in Rome do as the Romans do.*

when it comes right down to it* all things considered; when one really thinks about something. (A cliché.) □ *When it comes right down to it, I'd like to find a new job.* □ *When it comes right down to it, he can't really afford a new car.*

when it comes to something* as for something; speaking about something. (Informal.) □ *When it comes to fishing, John is an expert.* □ *When it comes to trouble, Mary really knows how to cause it.*

when least expected when one does not expect (something). □ *An old car is* likely to give you trouble when least expected. □ *My pencil usually breaks when least expected.*

when one is good and ready* when one is completely ready. (Informal.) □ *I'll be there when I'm good and ready.* □ *Ann will finish the job when she's good and ready and not a minute sooner.*

When the cat's away the mice will play.* Some people will get into mischief when they are not being watched. (A cliché.) □ *The student behaved very badly for the substitute teacher. When the cat's away the mice will play.* □ *John had a wild party at his house when his parents were out of town. When the cat's away the mice will play.*

when the time is ripe at exactly the right time. □ *I'll tell her the good news when the time is ripe.* □ *When the time is ripe, I'll bring up the subject again.*

where one is coming from* one's point of view. (Slang.) □ *I think I know what you mean. I know where you're coming from.* □ *Man, you don't know where I'm coming from! You don't understand a single word I say.*

where one lives See *hit one where one lives.*

Where there's a will there's a way. a proverb meaning that one can do something if one really wants to. □ *Don't give up, Ann. You can do it. Where there's a will there's a way.* □ *They told John he'd never walk again after his accident. He worked at it, and he was able to walk again! Where there's a will there's a way.*

Where there's smoke there's fire. a proverb meaning that some evidence of a problem probably indicates that there really is a problem. □ *There is a lot of noise coming from the classroom. There is probably something wrong. Where there's smoke there's fire.* □ *I think there is something wrong at the Franklins' house. The police are there again. Where there's smoke there's fire.*

while away the time AND **while the time away** to spend or waste time. □ *I like to read to while away the time.* □ *Jane whiles the time away by daydreaming.*

whip something up* AND **whip up something*** to prepare, create, or put some-

thing together. (Informal.) □ *I haven't written my report yet, but I'll whip one up before the deadline.* □ *Come in and sit down. I'll go whip up something to eat.*

wide awake completely awake. □ *After the telephone rang, I was wide awake for an hour.* □ *I'm not very wide awake at 6:00 in the morning.*

wide of the mark 1. far from the target. □ *Tom's shot was wide of the mark.* □ *The pitch was quite fast, but wide of the mark.* 2. inadequate; far from what is required or expected. □ *Jane's efforts were sincere, but wide of the mark.* □ *He failed the course because everything he did was wide of the mark.*

wild about someone or something enthusiastic about someone or something. □ *Bill is wild about chocolate ice cream.* □ *Sally is wild about Tom and his new car.*

wild-goose chase a worthless hunt or chase; a futile pursuit. □ *I wasted all afternoon on a wild-goose chase.* □ *John was angry because he was sent out on a wild-goose chase.*

Wild horses couldn't drag someone.* Nothing could force someone (to go somewhere). (Informal.) □ *I refuse to go to that meeting! Wild horses couldn't drag me.* □ *Wild horses couldn't drag her to that game.*

will not hear of something to refuse to tolerate or permit something. □ *You mustn't drive home alone. I won't hear of it.* □ *My parents won't hear of my staying out that late.*

win by a nose* to win by the slightest amount of difference. (Informal. As in a horse race where one horse wins with only its nose ahead of the horse which comes in second.) □ *I ran the fastest race I could, but I only won by a nose.* □ *Sally won the race, but she only won by a nose.*

win out over someone or something AND **win out** to beat someone or something in a race or a contest. □ *My horse won out over yours, so you lose your bet.* □ *I knew I could win out if I just kept trying.*

wind down to decrease or diminish. □ *Things are very busy now, but they'll* *wind down in about an hour.* □ *I hope business winds down soon. I'm exhausted.*

wind something up AND **wind up something** **1.** to tighten up the spring of something such as a clock. □ *I have to wind my grandfather clock up once a week.* □ *If I don't wind up my watch every day, it stops.* **2.** to conclude something. □ *I have a few items of business to wind up; then I'll be with you.* □ *Today we'll wind up that deal with the bank.*

wind up by doing something See *end up by doing something.*

wind up somewhere See *end up somewhere.*

wink at something* to ignore something. (Informal.) □ *Billy caused me a little trouble, but I just winked at it.* □ *This is a serious matter, and you can't expect me just to wink at it.*

wipe someone or something out* AND **wipe out someone or something*** (Slang.) **1.** to cause someone to be broke. □ *They wiped me out in the poker game.* □ *The crop failure wiped out all the farmers.* **2.** to exterminate someone or something. □ *The hunters came and wiped out all the deer.* □ *The crooks wiped out the two witnesses.*

wipe someone's slate clean to (figuratively) erase someone's (bad) record. □ *I'd like to wipe my slate clean and start all over again.* □ *Bob did badly in high school, but he wiped his slate clean and did a good job in college.*

wipe something off AND **wipe off something** **1.** to remove something (from something else) by wiping or rubbing. □ *There is mud on your shirt. Please wipe it off.* □ *My shirt has catsup on it. I must wipe off the catsup.* **2.** to tidy or clean something by wiping (something else) off. □ *Please wipe the table off. There's water on it.* □ *Wipe off your shirt. There's catsup on it.*

wipe up the floor with someone* to beat or physically abuse someone. (Slang. Usually said as a threat.) □ *You say that to me one more time, and I'll wipe up the floor with you.* □ *Oh, yeah! You're not big enough to wipe up the floor with anybody!*

wise up to someone or something* AND **wise up*** to begin to understand the truth about someone or something. (Slang.) □ *It was almost a week before I began to wise up to John. He's a total phony.* □ *You had better stay hidden for a while. The police are beginning to wise up.*

wish something off on someone* AND **wish off something on someone*** to pass something off onto someone else. (Informal.) □ *I don't want to have to deal with your problems. Don't wish them off on me.* □ *The storekeeper wished off the defective watch on the very next customer who came in.*

with a heavy heart* sadly. (A cliché.) □ *With a heavy heart, she said goodbye.* □ *We left school on the last day with a heavy heart.*

with a view to doing something AND **with an eye to doing something** with the intention of doing something. □ *I came to this school with a view to getting a degree.* □ *The mayor took office with an eye to improving the town.*

with all one's heart and soul* very sincerely. (A cliché.) □ *Oh Bill, I love you with all my heart and soul, and I always will!* □ *She thanked us with all her heart and soul for the gift.*

with an eye to doing something See *with a view to doing something.*

with bells on* AND **with bells on one's toes*** eagerly, willingly, and on time. (A cliché.) □ *Oh, yes! I'll meet you at the restaurant. I'll be there with bells on.* □ *All the smiling children were there waiting for me with bells on their toes.*

with every other breath AND **with every breath** (saying something) repeatedly or continually. □ *Bob was out in the yard raking leaves, and cursing with every other breath.* □ *The child was so grateful that she was thanking me with every breath.*

with flying colors easily and excellently. □ *John passed his geometry test with flying colors.* □ *Sally qualified for the race with flying colors.*

with it See *get with something.*

with no strings attached AND **without any strings attached** unconditionally; with no obligations attached. □ *My parents gave me a computer without any strings attached.* □ *I want this only if there are no strings attached.*

with one hand tied behind one's back* AND **with both hands tied behind one's back*** under a handicap; easily. (A cliché.) □ *I could put an end to this argument with one hand tied behind my back.* □ *John could do this job with both hands tied behind his back.*

with reference to someone or something See *in reference to someone or something.*

with regard to someone or something See *in regard to someone or something.*

with respect to someone or something See *in respect to someone or something.*

wither on the vine AND **die on the vine** (for something) to decline or fade away at an early stage of development. (Also used literally in reference to grapes or other fruit.) □ *You have a great plan, Tom. Let's keep it alive. Don't let it wither on the vine.* □ *The whole project died on the vine when the contract was canceled.*

within an inch of one's life* very close to taking one's life; almost to death. (A cliché.) □ *The accident frightened me within an inch of my life.* □ *When Mary was seriously ill in the hospital, she came within an inch of her life.*

within bounds See *within limits.*

within calling distance See the following entry.

within hailing distance AND **within calling distance** close enough to hear someone call out. □ *When the boat came within hailing distance, I asked if I could borrow some gasoline.* □ *We weren't within calling distance, so I couldn't hear what you said to me.*

within limits AND **within bounds** up to a certain point; with certain restrictions. □ *You're free to do what you want—within limits, of course.* □ *You must try to keep behavior at the party within bounds.*

within reason reasonable; reasonably. □ *You can do anything you want within reason.* □ *I'll pay any sum you ask—within reason.*

within someone's reach AND **within someone's grasp** almost in the possession of someone. □ *My goals are almost within my reach, so I know I'll succeed.* □ *We almost had the contract within our grasp, but the deal fell through at the last minute.*

without batting an eye* without showing alarm or response; without blinking an eye. (A cliché.) □ *I knew I had insulted her, but she turned to me and asked me to leave without batting an eye.* □ *Right in the middle of the speech—without batting an eye—the speaker walked off the stage.*

without fail for certain; absolutely. □ *I'll be there at noon without fail.* □ *The plane leaves on time every day without fail.*

without further ado* without further talk. (A cliché. An overworked phrase usually heard in public announcements.) □ *And without further ado, I would like to introduce Mr. Bill Franklin!* □ *The time has come to leave, so without further ado, good evening and goodbye.*

without question absolutely; certainly. □ *She agreed to help without question.* □ *She said, "I stand ready to support you without question."*

without rhyme or reason* without purpose, order, or reason. (A cliché. See variations in the examples.) □ *The teacher said my report was disorganized. My paragraphs seemed to be without rhyme or reason.* □ *Everything you do seems to be without rhyme or reason.* □ *This procedure seems to have no rhyme or reason.*

wolf in sheep's clothing* something threatening disguised as something kind. (A cliché.) □ *Beware of the police chief. He seems polite, but he's a wolf in sheep's clothing.* □ *This proposal seems harmless enough, but I think it's a wolf in sheep's clothing.*

won't hold water* to be inadequate, insubstantial, or ill-conceived. (Informal.) □ *Sorry, your ideas won't hold water. Nice try, though.* □ *The lawyer's case wouldn't hold water, so the defendant was released.*

word by word See the following entry.

word for word 1. in the exact words; verbatim. □ *I memorized the speech, word for word.* □ *I can't recall word for word what she told us.* **2.** AND **word by word** one word at a time. □ *We examined the contract word by word to make sure everything was the way we wanted.* □ *We compared the stories word for word to see what made them different.*

words to that effect (other) words which have about the same meaning. □ *She told me I ought to read more carefully—or words to that effect.* □ *I was instructed to go to the devil, or words to that effect.*

work like a horse* to work very hard. (A cliché.) □ *I've been working like a horse all day, and I'm tired.* □ *I'm too old to work like a horse. I'd prefer to relax more.*

work on someone or something 1.* [with *someone*] to try to convince someone about something. (Informal.) □ *We worked on Tom for nearly an hour, but we couldn't get him to change his mind.* □ *I'll work on him for a while, and I'll change his mind.* **2.** [with *someone*] to give medical treatment to someone. □ *The dentist was working on Mary while I waited for her in the other room.* □ *The surgeon worked on the patient, trying to stop the bleeding.* **3.** [with *something*] to repair, build, or adjust something. □ *The carpenter worked on the fence for three hours.* □ *Bill is out working on his car engine.*

work one's fingers to the bone* to work very hard. (A cliché.) □ *I worked my fingers to the bone so you children could have everything you needed. Now look at the way you treat me!* □ *I spent the day working my fingers to the bone, and now I want to relax.*

work one's way into something AND **work into something** to (literally or figuratively) squeeze into something. □ *Ann worked her way into the club, and now she's a member in good standing.* □ *The skunk worked its way into the hollow log.*

work one's way through college to hold a job which pays part of one's college expenses. □ *Tom couldn't get a loan, so he had to work his way through college.* □ *I worked my way through college, and that made college seem more valuable to me.*

work one's way up to advance in one's job or position, from the beginning level to a higher level. □ *I haven't always been president of this bank. I started as a teller and worked my way up.* □ *If I work my way up, can I be president of the bank?*

work out 1. to exercise. □ *I have to work out every day in order to keep healthy.* □ *Working out a lot gives me a big appetite.* **2.** See *turn out all right.*

work out for the best to end up in the best possible way. □ *Don't worry. Things will work out for the best.* □ *It seems bad now, but it'll work out for the best.*

work someone or something in AND **work in someone or something** to insert someone or something (into something). □ *The doctor's schedule was very busy, but the nurse agreed to try to work me in.* □ *The mechanic had many cars to fix, but he said he'd work my car in.* □ *I'm glad he could work in my car.* □ *The rabbit found an opening in the pile of branches and managed to work itself in.*

work someone or something up AND **work up someone or something 1.** [with *someone*] to get someone ready for something, especially medical treatment. □ *The coach worked up the whole team before the game.* □ *The doctor told the nurse to work Mr. Franklin up for surgery.* **2.** [with *something*] to create, cook, or arrange something. □ *Bob is in the kitchen working up dinner.* □ *Is there something planned for Friday night, or should we work something up?*

work someone over* AND **work over someone*** to threaten, intimidate, or beat someone. (Slang, especially criminal slang.) □ *I thought they were really going to work me over, but they only asked a few questions.* □ *The police worked over Bill until he told where the money was hidden.*

work something into something to rub or knead something into something else. □ *You should work more butter into the dough before baking the bread.* □ *Work* *this lotion into your skin to make your sunburn stop hurting.*

work something out AND **work out something 1.** to settle a problem. □ *It was a serious problem, but we managed to work it out.* □ *I'm glad we can work out our problems without fighting.* **2.** to get something out (of something else). □ *I have a splinter in my finger, and I can't work it out.* □ *I tried to work the nail out of the board.*

work through channels to try to get something done by going through the proper procedures and persons. □ *You can't accomplish anything around here if you don't work through channels.* □ *I tried working through channels, but it takes too long. This is an emergency.*

worm one's way out of something* to squeeze or wiggle out of a problem or a responsibility. (Informal.) □ *This is your job, and you can't worm your way out of it!* □ *I'm not trying to worm my way out of anything!*

worm something out of someone* to get some kind of information out of someone. (Informal.) □ *He didn't want to tell me the truth, but I finally wormed it out of him.* □ *She succeeded in worming the secret out of me. I didn't mean to tell it.*

worn-out See *wear out.*

worth its weight in gold* very valuable. (A cliché.) □ *This book is worth its weight in gold.* □ *Oh, Bill. You're wonderful. You're worth your weight in gold.*

worth one's salt* worth one's salary. (A cliché.) □ *Tom doesn't work very hard, and he's just barely worth his salt, but he's very easy to get along with.* □ *I think he's more than worth his salt. He's a good worker.*

would as soon do something See *had as soon do something.*

wouldn't dream of doing something* would not even consider doing something. (Informal.) □ *I wouldn't dream of taking your money!* □ *I'm sure that John wouldn't dream of complaining to the manager.*

wrap something up AND **wrap up something 1.** to wrap something in paper, cloth, etc. □ *Please wrap this package*

up for me. □ *Be sure to wrap up the present well before you mail it.* **2.*** to terminate something. (Informal. See also *get something sewed up.*) □ *It's time to wrap this project up and move on to something else.* □ *Let's wrap up this discussion. It's time to go home.*

wrapped up in someone or something 1. [with *something*] wrapped in something, such as paper, cloth, etc. □ *The gift was wrapped up in colorful paper.* □ *The old lady was wrapped up in a blanket to keep warm.* **2.** concerned and involved with someone or something. □ *Sally is wrapped up in her work.* □ *Ann is all wrapped up in her children and their activities.*

wreak havoc with something to cause a lot of trouble with something; to ruin or damage something. □ *Your attitude will wreak havoc with my project.* □ *The weather wreaked havoc with our picnic plans.*

write in for something See *send in for something.*

write off for something See *send off for something.*

write someone or something off AND **write off someone or something 1.** [with *something*] to absorb a debt or a loss in accounting. □ *The bill couldn't be collected, so we had to write it off.* □ *The bill was too large, and we couldn't write off the amount. We decided to sue.* **2.** to drop someone or something from consideration. □ *The manager wrote Tom off for a promotion.* □ *I wrote off that piece of land as worthless. It can't be used for anything.*

write someone or something up AND **write up someone or something 1.** [with *something*] to prepare a bill, order, or statement. □ *Please write the order up and send me a copy.* □ *As soon as I finish writing up your check, I'll bring you some more coffee.* **2.** to write an article about someone or something. □ *A reporter wrote me up for the Sunday paper.* □ *I wrote up a local factory and sent the story to a magazine, but they didn't buy the story.*

write something down AND **write down something** to write something; to make a note of something. (Also without *down*.) □ *If I write it down, I won't forget it.* □ *I wrote down everything she said.*

write something out AND **write out something** to spell or write a number or an abbreviation. □ *Don't just write "7", write it out.* □ *Please write out all abbreviations, such as Doctor for Dr.*

X

X marks the spot* this is the exact spot. (A cliché. Can be used literally when someone draws an X to mark an exact spot.) □ *This is where the rock struck my car—X marks the spot.* □ *Now, please move that table over here. Yes, right here—X marks the spot.*

Y

year in, year out year after year, all year long. □ *I seem to have hay fever year in, year out. I never get over it.* □ *John wears the same old suit, year in, year out.*

yield the right-of-way to give the right to turn or move forward to another person or vehicle. □ *When you're driving, it's better to yield the right-of-way than to have a wreck.* □ *You must always yield the right-of-way when you're making a left turn.*

you all* two or more of you. (Folksy. Considered Southern American English. Often *y'all* in the South.) □ *We hope you all will come and see us when you have a chance.* □ *Oh, yes. We'd just love to. We haven't seen you all in such a long time!*

You bet!* AND **You bet your boots!***; **You can bet on it!*** Surely!; Absolutely! (Informal.) □ BILL: *Coming to the meeting next Saturday?* BOB: *You bet!* □ *You bet your boots I'll be there!*

You bet your boots! See the previous entry.

You can say that again!* AND **You said it!*** That is true.; You are correct. (Informal. The word *that* is emphasized.) □ MARY: *It sure is hot today.* JANE: *You can say that again!* □ BILL: *This cake is yummy!* BOB: *You said it!*

You can't take it with you.* You should enjoy your money now, because it is no good when you're dead. (A cliché.) □ *My uncle is a wealthy miser. I keep tell-ing him, "You can't take it with you."* □ *If you have money, you should make out a will. You can't take it with you, you know!*

You can't teach an old dog new tricks. a proverb meaning that old people cannot learn anything new. (Also used literally of dogs.) □ *"Of course I can learn,"* bellowed uncle John. *"Who says you can't teach an old dog new tricks?"* □ *I'm sorry. I can't seem to learn to do it right. Oh, well. You can't teach an old dog new tricks.*

you know* as you are aware, or should be aware. (Informal. This should not be overused.) □ *This is a very valuable book, you know.* □ *Goldfish can be overfed, you know.*

You said it! See *You can say that again!*

Your guess is as good as mine.* Your answer is likely to be as correct as mine. (Informal.) □ *I don't know where the scissors are. Your guess is as good as mine.* □ *Your guess is as good as mine as to when the train will arrive.*

yours truly 1. a closing phrase at the end of a letter, just before the signature. □ *Yours truly, Tom Jones* □ *Best wishes from yours truly, Bill Smith* **2.*** oneself; I; me. (Informal.) □ *There's nobody here right now but yours truly.* □ *Everyone else got up and left the table leaving yours truly to pay the bill.*

Z

zero in on something* to aim or focus directly on something. (Informal.) □ *"Now," said Mr. Smith, "I would like to zero in on another important point."* □ *Mary is very good about zeroing in on the most important and helpful ideas.*

zonk out* to pass out; to fall asleep. (Slang.) □ *I was so tired after playing football that I almost zonked out on the floor.* □ *I had a cup of coffee before the test to keep from zonking out in the middle of it.*

zoom in on someone or something AND **zoom in 1.*** to fly or move rapidly at someone or something. (Slang.) □ *The hawk zoomed in on the sparrow.* □ *The angry bees zoomed in on Jane and stung her.* □ *When the door opened, the cat zoomed in.* **2.** (for a photographer) to use a zoom lens to get a closer view of someone or something. □ *Bill zoomed in on Sally's face just as she grinned.* □ *On the next shot I'll zoom in for a close-up.*

PHRASE-FINDER INDEX

Use this Index to find the form of a phrase that you want to look up in the **Dictionary.** First, pick out any major word in the phrase you are seeking. Second, look that word up in this Index to find the form of the phrase used in the **Dictionary.** Third, look up the phrase in the **Dictionary.** See the **Examples** and **Hints** below.

Some of the words found as entries in the **Dictionary** do not occur as entries in the Index. They have been omitted because they occur so frequently that each of their lists of phrases is many pages long. In these instances it is better to find the entry by looking up some other word. The following words and personal pronouns do not occur as entries in the Index:

a	or
an	out
and	someone
at	someone's
do	something
for	that
get	the
have	these
in	this
of	those
off	to
on	up
one's	with

Examples

If you are trying to find a saying that includes something about a "bird" and a "hand," look up *bird* or *hand* in the Index. You will find—listed at both words—the proverb "A bird in the hand is worth two in the bush." Then go to the **A** section in the **Dictionary** where you will find the meaning of the saying and examples of its use. In fact this phrase is listed at *bird, hand, worth, two,* and *bush.* There are no Index entries for the remaining, very common words *a, in,* and *the.*

If you are trying to figure out the meaning of the sentence "Bill's parents always come down hard on him," you would first try to isolate the idiomatic phrase from the rest of the sentence. Use the Index to help you find a phrase that matches most closely the confusing part of the sentence. Look up *come,* for instance. You will find **come down hard on someone or something**, which matches most closely the confusing part of the sentence. Look this phrase up in the **Dictionary**. The phrase **come down hard on someone or something** is also listed at *down* and *hard* in the Phrase-Finder Index.

Imagine that you are trying to remember the correct form of a phrase to use in a letter you are writing. You want to say something about a bad or troublesome situation someone is in, but you are not sure of the idiomatic way of expressing the situation in American English. Simply look up *bad* in the Index. You might select the phrases "in a bad way" and "in bad sorts" as possibilities. Look them each up in the **Dictionary** and see which is best for your purposes.

If you are trying to remember the correct combination of verb and preposition in a phrasal verb combination, just look up the verb in the Index to find the possible phrasal verb combinations, and then look up the most promising ones in the **Dictionary**.

Hints

1. When you are trying to find a phrase in the Index, look up the verb first, if there is one.

2. When you are looking for a verb, try first to find the present tense form of the verb.

3. When you are looking for a noun, try first to find the singular form of the noun.

4. In most phrases where a noun or pronoun is part of an idiom, it will be represented by the word "someone" or the word "something" in the form of the phrase used in the **Dictionary**.

5. This is an Index of form, not of meaning. The phrases in an index entry do not usually have any meanings in common. Consult the **Dictionary** for information about meaning.

ABACK
☐ taken aback
ABANDON
☐ abandon oneself to someone or something
ABCs
☐ know one's ABCs
ABET
☐ aid and abet someone
ABIDE
☐ abide by something
ABILITY
☐ to the best of one's ability
ABLE
(See also *CAN.*)☐ able to breathe again ☐ able to do something blindfolded ☐ able to do something standing on one's head ☐ able to make something ☐ able to take a joke ☐ able to take something ☐ not able to call one's time one's own ☐ not able to go on ☐ not able to help something ☐ not able to make anything out of someone or something ☐ not able to see the forest for the trees ☐ not able to wait
ABODE
☐ take up one's abode somewhere
ABOUND
☐ abound with something
ABOUT
☐ about to do something ☐ ask about someone or something ☐ at sea about something ☐ bandy something about ☐ be about something ☐ be about to do something ☐ be careful about someone or something ☐ be half-hearted about someone or something ☐ beat about the bush ☐ bother oneself about someone or something ☐ brag about someone or something ☐ bring something about ☐ care about someone or something ☐ care nothing about someone or something ☐ carry on about someone or something ☐ come about ☐ crazy about someone or something ☐ create a stink about something ☐ do an about-face ☐ dream about someone or something ☐ find out about someone or something ☐ get a rough idea about something ☐ get about ☐ get one's wits about one ☐ get second thoughts about someone or something ☐ give someone a rough idea about something ☐ go about doing some-

thing ☐ go about one's business ☐ go into one's song and dance about something ☐ have a clean conscience about someone or something ☐ have a clear conscience about someone or something ☐ have a rough idea about something ☐ have a thing about someone or something ☐ have mixed feelings about someone or something ☐ have one's wits about one ☐ have second thoughts about someone or something ☐ in a stew about someone or something ☐ in the dark about someone or something ☐ It's about time! ☐ keen about someone or something ☐ keep one's mouth shut about someone or something ☐ keep one's wits about one ☐ keep quiet about someone or something ☐ keep still about someone or something ☐ knock about somewhere ☐ knock someone or something about ☐ know a thing or two about someone or something ☐ know one's way about ☐ mad about someone or something ☐ make a big deal about something ☐ make cracks about someone or something ☐ make no bones about it ☐ make no mistake about it ☐ mess about with someone or something ☐ millstone about one's neck ☐ much ado about nothing ☐ no buts about it ☐ no ifs, ands, or buts about it ☐ no two ways about it ☐ nose about ☐ not breathe a word about someone or something ☐ not care two hoots about someone or something ☐ not give a hang about anyone or anything ☐ not give a hoot about anyone or anything ☐ not know beans about something ☐ not know the first thing about someone or something ☐ nothing to complain about ☐ nothing to write home about ☐ nuts about someone or something ☐ on the fence about something ☐ order someone about ☐ out and about ☐ poke about ☐ put one's foot down about something ☐ raise a stink about something ☐ ramble on about something ☐ rave about someone or something ☐ see a man about a dog ☐ see about something ☐ see eye to eye about something ☐ send one about one's business ☐ something about someone or something ☐ spout off about someone or something ☐ That's about the size of it. □ trouble one's head about someone or something □ trouble oneself about someone or something □ up and about □ wild about someone or something

ABOVE
□ a cut above someone or something □ above and beyond the call of duty □ above board □ above suspicion □ get one's head above water □ head and shoulders above someone or something □ honest and above board □ keep one's head above water □ open and above board □ over and above something

ABREAST
□ keep abreast of something

ABSENCE
□ conspicuous by one's absence □ in the absence of someone or something

ABSENT
□ absent without leave

ACCIDENT
□ have an accident

ACCORD
□ of one's own accord □ reach an accord with someone

ACCORDANCE
□ in accordance with something

ACCORDING
□ according to all accounts □ according to Hoyle □ according to one's own lights □ according to someone or something

ACCOUNT
□ according to all accounts □ account for someone or something □ balance the accounts □ blow-by-blow account □ bring someone to account □ by all accounts □ call someone to account □ cook the accounts □ give a good account of oneself □ give an account of someone or something □ keep an account of something □ not on any account □ on account of someone or something □ on account □ on any account □ on no account □ on someone's account □ square accounts with someone □ take someone or something into account □ There's no accounting for taste.

ACCOUNTABLE
□ hold someone accountable for something

ACCUSTOMED
□ accustomed to someone or something

ACE
□ ace in the hole □ come within an ace of doing something □ hold all the aces

ACKNOWLEDGE
□ acknowledge receipt of something □ acknowledge someone to be right

ACQUAINTED
□ acquainted with someone or something

ACQUIRE
□ acquire a taste for something

ACROSS
□ across from someone or something □ across the board □ come across someone or something □ cut across something □ get someone or something across □ get something across to someone □ put someone or something across □ run across someone or something □ stumble across someone or something

ACT
□ act as someone □ act high and mighty □ act of faith □ act of God □ act of war □ act on something □ act one's age □ act something out □ act up □ catch someone in the act of doing something □ caught in the act □ clean up one's act □ get one's act together □ in the act of doing something □ keep up an act □ put on an act □ read someone the riot act □ tough act to follow

ACTION
□ Actions speak louder than words. □ all talk and no action □ go into action □ piece of the action □ swing into action □ take action against someone or something

ACTIVE
□ on active duty

ADAM
□ not know someone from Adam

ADD
□ add fuel to the fire □ add insult to injury □ add something up □ add up to something

ADDITION
□ in addition to someone or something

ADDRESS
□ address someone as something

ADIEU
 □ bid adieu to someone or something
ADO
 □ much ado about nothing □ without further ado
ADVANCE
 □ advanced in years □ in advance of someone or something □ pay in advance
ADVANTAGE
 □ get the advantage of someone □ have the advantage of someone □ show something to good advantage □ take advantage of someone or something □ turn something to one's advantage
AFFAIRS
 □ pretty state of affairs □ settle someone's affairs
AFOUL
 □ run afoul of someone or something
AFRAID
 □ afraid of one's own shadow
AFTER
 □ after a fashion □ after all is said and done □ after all □ after hours □ after the fact □ after the fashion of someone or something □ chase after someone or something □ chase around after someone or something □ day after day □ get after someone □ go after someone or something □ inquire after someone □ keep after someone □ look after someone or something □ much sought after □ name someone after someone else □ run after someone or something □ run around after someone or something □ see after someone or something □ stay after someone □ take after someone □ take off after someone or something □ take out after someone or something □ throw good money after bad □ time after time
AGAIN
 □ able to breathe again □ at it again □ be oneself again □ Come again? □ do something over again □ every now and again □ now and again □ off again, on again □ Run that by again. □ something else again □ time and again □ time and time again □ You can say that again!
AGAINST
 □ against someone's will □ against the clock □ bang one's head against a brick

wall □ be against someone □ bear a grudge against someone □ beat one's head against the wall □ dead set against someone or something □ fight against time □ for the odds to be against one □ get two strikes against one □ go against the grain □ guard against someone or something □ have a case against someone □ have a grudge against someone □ have one's heart set against something □ have something against someone or something □ have the cards stacked against one □ have two strikes against one □ hold a grudge against someone □ hold something against someone □ hope against all hope □ lift a hand against someone or something □ nurse a grudge against someone □ pit someone or something against someone or something □ play both ends against the middle □ play someone off against someone else □ race against time □ raise a hand against someone or something □ side against someone □ stack the cards against someone or something □ stack the deck against someone or something □ stand up against someone or something □ swim against the current □ swim against the tide □ take a stand against someone or something □ take action against someone or something □ take up arms against someone or something □ turn against someone or something □ up against something
AGE
 □ act one's age □ be of age □ come of age □ in a coon's age □ in this day and age
AGREE
 □ agree on someone or something □ agree to something □ agree with someone or something
AGREEMENT
 □ reach an agreement with someone
AHEAD
 □ ahead of someone or something □ ahead of the game □ ahead of time □ come out ahead □ dead ahead □ get ahead of someone or something □ get the go-ahead □ give someone the go-ahead □ go ahead with something □ keep ahead of someone or something □ one jump ahead of someone or some-

thing □ pull ahead of someone or something □ stay ahead of someone or something

AID

□ aid and abet someone

AIM

□ aim at someone or something □ aim to do something □ take aim at someone or something

AIN'T

□ That ain't hay.

AIR

□ air one's grievances □ air someone's dirty linen in public □ air something out □ breath of fresh air □ build castles in the air □ clear the air □ full of hot air □ get the air □ give oneself airs □ give someone the air □ have one's nose in the air □ in the air □ off the air □ on the air □ out of thin air □ pull something out of thin air □ put on airs □ up in the air □ vanish into thin air □ walk on air

AISLES

□ have them rolling in the aisles

ALERT

□ on the alert for someone or something

ALIKE

□ share and share alike

ALIVE

□ alive and kicking □ alive with someone or something □ skin someone alive

ALL

□ according to all accounts □ after all is said and done □ after all □ all and sundry □ all at once □ all balled up □ all better now □ all day long □ all dressed up □ all for something □ all for the best □ all gone □ all hours of the day and night □ all in a day's work □ all in all □ all in good time □ all in one breath □ all in one piece □ all in the family □ all in □ all kinds of someone or something □ all manner of someone or something □ all night long □ all of a sudden □ all over but the shouting □ all over the earth □ all over the place □ all over town □ all over with □ all over □ All right for you! □ all right with someone □ all right □ All roads lead to Rome. □ all set □ all systems are go □ all talk and no action □ All that glitters is not gold. □ all the live-

long day □ all the rage □ all the same to someone □ all the same □ all the time □ all the way □ all thumbs □ all to the good □ all told □ all tuckered out □ all walks of life □ all wet □ all wool and a yard wide □ All work and no play makes Jack a dull boy. □ all worked up over something □ all year round □ All's well that ends well. □ all-out effort □ all-out war □ as bad as all that □ as big as all outdoors □ at all costs □ at all times □ at all □ be all ears □ be all eyes □ blow something out of all proportion □ by all accounts □ by all appearances □ by all means of something □ by all means □ downhill all the way □ fall all over oneself □ fall all over someone □ first of all □ for all I care □ for all I know □ for all it's worth □ for all practical purposes □ for all something □ for all the world □ free-for-all □ get away from it all □ get it all together □ go all out □ go all the way to somewhere □ go all the way with someone □ have it all over someone or something □ hold all the aces □ hope against all hope □ in all one's born days □ in all probability □ jump all over someone □ know all the tricks of the trade □ least of all □ let it all hang out □ make an all-out effort □ Money is the root of all evil. □ most of all □ not all it is cracked up to be □ not all there □ not at all □ not have all one's marbles □ Of all the nerve! □ Of all things! □ on all fours □ once and for all □ one and all □ out of all proportion □ put all one's eggs in one basket □ ride off in all directions □ That's all for someone. □ That's all she wrote. □ turn out all right □ until all hours □ walk all over someone □ when all is said and done □ with all one's heart and soul □ you all

ALLEY

□ right down someone's alley □ right up someone's alley □ up a blind alley

ALLOW

□ allow for someone or something

ALLOWANCE

□ make allowance for someone or something

ALONE
☐ go it alone ☐ leave someone or something alone ☐ leave well enough alone ☐ let alone someone or something ☐ let someone or something alone ☐ let well enough alone

ALONG
☐ along in years ☐ come along with one ☐ get along in years ☐ get along on a shoestring ☐ get along with someone ☐ get along without someone or something ☐ get along ☐ go along for the ride ☐ go along with someone or something ☐ inch along something ☐ string along with someone

ALONGSIDE
☐ alongside of someone or something

ALTOGETHER
☐ in the altogether

AMISS
☐ take something amiss

AMOUNT
☐ amount to something ☐ to the tune of some amount of money

ANDS
☐ no ifs, ands, or buts about it

ANOTHER
☐ another country heard from ☐ dance to another tune ☐ have another guess coming ☐ have another think coming ☐ horse of another color ☐ leave something for another occasion ☐ One good turn deserves another. ☐ One man's meat is another man's poison. ☐ one way or another

ANSWER
☐ answer for someone or something ☐ answer someone's purpose ☐ answer to someone ☐ not take no for an answer

ANTS
☐ get ants in one's pants ☐ have ants in one's pants

ANY
☐ any number of someone or something ☐ at any cost ☐ at any rate ☐ by any means ☐ go to any length ☐ in any case ☐ in any event ☐ not on any account ☐ on any account

ANYONE
☐ as far as anyone knows ☐ not give a hang about anyone or anything ☐ not give a hoot about anyone or anything ☐ not give anyone the time of day

ANYTHING
☐ can't do anything with someone or something ☐ not able to make anything out of someone or something ☐ not for anything in the world ☐ not give a hang about anyone or anything ☐ not give a hoot about anyone or anything ☐ not have anything on

APART
☐ be poles apart ☐ come apart at the seams ☐ fall apart at the seams ☐ fall apart ☐ take someone or something apart ☐ tell people apart ☐ tell things apart

APE
☐ go ape over someone or something

APPEAR
☐ appear as something

APPEARANCE
☐ by all appearances ☐ make an appearance ☐ put in an appearance

APPLE
☐ apple of someone's eye ☐ as easy as apple pie ☐ in apple-pie order ☐ upset the apple cart

APPOINTED
☐ at the appointed time

APPOINTMENT
☐ make an appointment with someone

APPROVAL
☐ on approval

APRON
☐ tied to one's mother's apron strings

ARGUMENT
☐ get into an argument with someone ☐ have an argument

ARISE
☐ arise from something

ARM
☐ arm in arm ☐ armed to the teeth ☐ cost an arm and a leg ☐ give one's right arm for someone or something ☐ keep someone or something at arm's length ☐ pay an arm and a leg for something ☐ put the arm on someone ☐ receive someone with open arms ☐ shot in the arm ☐ take up arms against someone or something ☐ twist someone's arm ☐ up in arms ☐ welcome someone with open arms

AROUND
☐ around the clock ☐ beat around the bush ☐ blue around the gills ☐ boss someone around ☐ bring someone around ☐ bring something crashing down around one ☐ cast around for

someone or something □ chase around after someone or something □ chase someone or something around □ come around □ drop around sometime □ enough to go around □ every time one turns around □ fiddle around with someone or something □ find one's way around □ fool around with someone or something □ get around to something □ get around □ go around in circles □ go around with someone □ green around the gills □ hang around with someone □ have been around □ hem and haw around □ horse around □ kick someone or something around □ kid around with someone □ knock someone or something around □ know one's way around □ mess around with someone or something □ monkey around with someone or something □ mope around □ nose around □ pal around with someone □ pale around the gills □ play around with someone or something □ poke around □ run around after someone or something □ run around like a chicken with its head cut off □ run around with someone □ run around □ run circles around someone □ run rings around someone □ scratch around for something □ screw around with someone or something □ shop around for something □ show someone around □ stick around □ throw one's weight around □ throw someone's name around □ turn around □ turn something around □ twist someone around one's little finger

ARRANGE
□ arrange something with someone

ARRANGEMENTS
□ make arrangements for someone or something □ make arrangements to do something □ make arrangements with someone

ARREARS
□ in arrears

AS
□ act as someone □ address someone as something □ appear as something □ as a duck takes to water □ as a general rule □ as a last resort □ as a matter of course □ as a matter of fact □ as a result of something □ as a rule □ as a token of something □ as an aside □ as bad as all that   □ as big as all

outdoors □ as big as life □ as blind as a bat □ as busy as a beaver □ as busy as a bee □ as busy as Grand Central Station □ as clear as mud □ as comfortable as an old shoe □ as cool as a cucumber □ as crazy as a loon □ as dead as a dodo □ as dead as a doornail □ as different as night and day □ as easy as apple pie □ as easy as duck soup □ as easy as falling off a log □ as easy as pie □ as far as anyone knows □ as far as I'm concerned □ as far as it goes □ as far as possible □ as fit as a fiddle □ as flat as a pancake □ as for someone or something □ as free as a bird □ as full as a tick □ as funny as a crutch □ as good as done □ as good as gold □ as happy as a clam □ as happy as a lark □ as hard as nails □ as high as a kite □ as high as the sky □ as hot as hell □ as hungry as a bear □ as innocent as a lamb □ as it were □ as light as a feather □ as likely as not □ as long as □ as luck would have it □ as mad as a hatter □ as mad as a hornet □ as mad as a March hare □ as mad as a wet hen □ as mad as hell □ as naked as a jaybird □ as one □ as plain as day □ as plain as the nose on one's face □ as poor as a church mouse □ as pretty as a picture □ as proud as a peacock □ as quick as a wink □ as quick as greased lightning □ as quiet as a mouse □ as regular as clockwork □ as right as rain □ as scarce as hen's teeth □ as sick as a dog □ as slick as a whistle □ as slippery as an eel □ as smart as a fox □ as snug as a bug in a rug □ as sober as a judge □ as soft as a baby's bottom □ as soon as possible □ as strong as an ox □ as stubborn as a mule □ as the crow flies □ as thick as pea soup □ as thick as thieves □ as tight as a tick □ as tight as Dick's hatband □ as to someone or something □ as weak as a kitten □ as white as the driven snow □ as wise as an owl □ catch-as-catch-can □ get a reputation as a something □ give as good as one gets □ give someone a reputation as a something □ go so far as to say something □ had as soon do something □ have a reputation as a something □ hold someone or something up as an example □ just as soon do something □ look as if butter wouldn't melt in one's mouth □ look on someone as something □ make good as something □ nutty as a fruitcake □ pass as someone or something □ pass something off as something □ pass something off on someone as something □ pawn something off on someone as something □ pay as you go □ Pretty is as pretty does. □ put someone down as something □ serve as a guinea pig □ set someone up as something □ show someone up as something □ shrug something off as something □ start out as something □ start someone in as something □ start someone out as something □ such as it is □ use someone or something as an excuse □ When in Rome do as the Romans do. □ would as soon do something □ Your guess is as good as mine.

ASHAMED
□ ashamed of someone or something

ASIDE
□ as an aside □ aside from someone or something □ lay something aside □ put something aside □ set something aside

ASK
□ ask about someone or something □ ask for someone or something □ ask for the moon □ ask for trouble □ ask someone for something □ ask someone out □ for the asking

ASLEEP
□ asleep at the switch □ fall asleep

ASS
□ make an ass of someone

ASSURED
□ rest assured

ASTONISHED
□ astonished at someone or something

ASTRAY
□ go astray

ATTACHED
□ with no strings attached

ATTEND
□ attend to someone or something

ATTENTION
□ attract someone's attention □ call someone's attention to something □ pay attention to someone or something

ATTITUDE
□ devil-may-care attitude □ wait-and-see attitude

ATTRACT
□ attract someone's attention

AVAIL
□ avail oneself of something □ of no avail □ to no avail

AVAILABLE
□ make someone or something available to someone

AVERAGE
□ on the average

AVOID
□ avoid someone or something like the plague

AWAKE
□ wide awake

AWARE
□ aware of someone or something

AWAY
□ a stone's throw away □ away from one's desk □ blow someone or something away □ break away from someone or something □ break something away □ carried away □ carry someone or something away □ come away empty-handed □ die away □ do away with someone or something □ draw fire away from someone or something □ eat away at someone or something □ eat something away □ explain something away □ far and away the best □ fire away at someone or something □ fritter something away □ get away from it all □ get away from someone or something □ get away with something □ get carried away □ give someone or something away □ give the bride away □ give the game away □ go away empty-handed □ hammer away at someone or something □ keep away from someone or something □ lay someone or something away □ make away with someone or something □ pass away □ peg away at something □ plug away at something □ put someone or something away □ right away □ run away from someone or something □ run away with someone or something □ salt something away □ send away for something □ send someone away □ shy away from someone or something □ slip away □ sock something away □ square some-

one or something away □ squirrel something away □ stay away from someone or something □ stow away □ take it away □ take someone or something away □ take someone's breath away □ throw something away □ walk away with something □ waste away □ When the cat's away the mice will play. □ while away the time

AWE

□ in awe of someone or something □ stand in awe of someone or something

AWOL

□ go AWOL

AX

□ get the ax □ give someone the ax □ have an ax to grind

BABE

□ babe-in-the-woods

BABY

□ as soft as a baby's bottom

BACK

□ back and forth □ back down from someone or something □ back East □ back in circulation □ back off from someone or something □ back order something □ back out of something □ back someone or something up □ back something out □ back to the drawing board □ back to the salt mines □ back-to-back □ behind someone's back □ break one's back to do something □ break the back of something □ bring someone or something back □ call someone back □ come back □ cut back on something □ cut back □ date back to sometime □ double back on someone or something □ drive someone or something back □ drop back □ fall back from something □ fall back on someone or something □ from way back □ get a pat on the back □ get back at someone □ get back on one's feet □ get back to someone □ get back □ Get off someone's back! □ get someone's back up □ get something back □ give someone a pat on the back □ give someone the shirt off one's back □ go back on one's word □ go back □ hang back □ hark back to something □ have back at someone □ have eyes in the back of one's head □ have one's back to the wall □ hold someone or something back □ hurry back □ in back of someone or

something □ in back □ keep someone or something back □ know someone or something like the back of one's hand □ laid back □ like water off a duck's back □ look back on someone or something □ on someone's back □ out back □ pat someone on the back □ pin someone's ears back □ put one's back to something □ put something on the back burner □ roll something back □ scratch someone's back □ set one back on one's heels □ set someone or something back □ sit back and let something happen □ stab someone in the back □ stand back of someone or something □ take a back seat to someone □ take someone or something back □ talk back to someone □ think back on someone or something □ turn one's back on someone or something □ with one hand tied behind one's back

BACKWARDS

□ bend over backwards to do something □ fall over backwards to do something □ lean over backwards to do something

BACKYARD

□ in one's own backyard

BACON

□ bring home the bacon

BAD

(See also *WORSE, WORST.*)□ as bad as all that □ bad-mouth someone or something □ come to a bad end □ get off to a bad start □ go bad □ go from bad to worse □ have a bad effect on someone or something □ in a bad mood □ in a bad way □ in bad faith □ in bad sorts □ in bad taste □ in bad with someone □ leave a bad taste in someone's mouth □ not half bad □ throw good money after bad

BAG

□ bag and baggage □ bag of tricks □ in the bag □ leave someone holding the bag □ let the cat out of the bag □ put on the feed bag

BAGGAGE

□ bag and baggage

BAIL

□ bail out of something □ bail someone or something out □ jump bail □ out on bail □ skip bail

BAIT

□ fish or cut bait

BALANCE
☐ balance the accounts ☐ catch someone off balance ☐ hang in the balance ☐ in the balance

BALL
☐ all balled up ☐ ball and chain ☐ ball of fire ☐ ball someone or something up ☐ behind the eight ball ☐ carry the ball ☐ drop the ball ☐ get the ball rolling ☐ have a ball ☐ have something on the ball ☐ keep one's eye on the ball ☐ keep the ball rolling ☐ new ball game ☐ on the ball ☐ pitch someone a curve ball ☐ play ball with someone ☐ set the ball rolling ☐ start the ball rolling ☐ That's the way the ball bounces.

BALLOON
☐ go over like a lead balloon ☐ send up a trial balloon

BALLOT
☐ stuff the ballot box

BANANAS
☐ go bananas

BAND
☐ beat the band

BANDWAGON
☐ climb on the bandwagon ☐ get on the bandwagon ☐ jump on the bandwagon

BANDY
☐ bandy something about

BANG
☐ bang one's head against a brick wall ☐ get a bang out of someone or something ☐ give someone a bang ☐ go over with a bang

BANK
☐ bank on something

BARGAIN
☐ bargain for something ☐ drive a hard bargain ☐ in the bargain ☐ strike a bargain ☐ throw something into the bargain

BARGE
☐ barge in on someone or something

BARK
☐ bark up the wrong tree ☐ One's bark is worse than one's bite.

BARRED
☐ no holds barred

BARREL
☐ get someone over a barrel ☐ have someone over a barrel ☐ lock, stock, and barrel ☐ scrape the bottom of the barrel

BARRELHEAD
☐ cash on the barrelhead

BASE
☐ base one's opinion on something ☐ get to first base with someone or something ☐ off base ☐ reach first base with someone or something ☐ steal a base ☐ touch base with someone

BASIS
☐ on a first name basis with someone

BASKET
☐ put all one's eggs in one basket

BAT
☐ as blind as a bat ☐ go to bat for someone ☐ have bats in one's belfry ☐ like a bat out of hell ☐ right off the bat ☐ without batting an eye

BATH
☐ take a bath on something

BATHROOM
☐ go to the bathroom

BAWL
☐ bawl someone out

BAY
☐ hold someone or something at bay ☐ keep someone or something at bay

BE
(See also *BEING, IS.*)☐ acknowledge someone to be right ☐ as it were ☐ be a cold fish ☐ be a copy-cat ☐ be a dead duck ☐ be a drag on someone ☐ be a fan of someone ☐ be a goner ☐ be a must ☐ be a thorn in someone's side ☐ be about something ☐ be about to do something ☐ be against someone ☐ be all ears ☐ be all eyes ☐ be an unknown quantity ☐ be at someone's service ☐ be bushed ☐ be careful about someone or something ☐ be careful not to do something ☐ be certain of someone or something ☐ be death on something ☐ be done with someone or something ☐ be even-steven ☐ be for someone or something ☐ be friends with someone ☐ be from Missouri ☐ be half-hearted about someone or something ☐ be into something ☐ be of age ☐ be of service to someone ☐ be off ☐ be old hat ☐ be oneself again ☐ be poles apart ☐ be sick ☐ be talked out ☐ be the spit and image of someone ☐ be the teacher's pet ☐ be too ☐ be with someone ☐ Beggars can't be choosers. ☐ cut out to be something ☐ far be it from me to do

something □ fit to be tied □ for the odds to be against one □ leave a lot to be desired □ Let bygones be bygones. □ let someone or something be □ not all it is cracked up to be □ old enough to be someone's father □ old enough to be someone's mother □ So be it. □ stand up and be counted □ That'll be the day. □ There will be the devil to pay. □ too good to be true □ turn out to be someone or something

BEAD
□ draw a bead on someone or something

BEAM
□ on the beam

BEANS
□ full of beans □ not know beans about something □ not worth a hill of beans □ spill the beans

BEAR
(See also *BORN*.)□ as hungry as a bear □ bear a grudge against someone □ bear down on someone or something □ bear fruit □ bear one's cross □ bear someone or something in mind □ bear someone or something up □ bear something out □ bear the brunt of something □ bear up □ bear watching □ bear with someone or something □ grin and bear it □ loaded for bear

BEARD
□ beard the lion in his den

BEAT
□ beat a dead horse □ beat a path to someone's door □ beat a retreat □ beat about the bush □ beat around the bush □ beat one's gums □ beat one's head against the wall □ beat someone down to size □ beat someone to the draw □ beat someone to the punch □ beat someone up □ beat someone's brains out □ beat something into someone's head □ beat the band □ beat the gun □ beat the living daylights out of someone □ beat the pants off someone □ beat the rap □ beat the stuffing out of someone □ beat the tar out of someone □ have one's heart miss a beat □ have one's heart skip a beat □ off the beaten track □ pound a beat

BEAUTY
□ Beauty is only skin deep.

BEAVER
□ as busy as a beaver

BECK
□ at someone's beck and call

BECOMING
□ becoming to someone

BED
□ Early to bed, early to rise, makes a man healthy, wealthy, and wise. □ get out of the wrong side of the bed □ get up on the wrong side of the bed □ go to bed with someone □ go to bed with the chickens □ make the bed □ put someone or something to bed □ put to bed with a shovel □ should have stood in bed □ sick in bed

BEE
□ as busy as a bee □ birds and the bees □ have a bee in one's bonnet □ put a bee in someone's bonnet

BEEF
□ beef something up

BEELINE
□ make a beeline for someone or something

BEESWAX
□ none of someone's beeswax

BEFORE
□ before long □ before you can say Jack Robinson □ before you know it □ cast pearls before swine □ count one's chickens before they hatch □ cross a bridge before one comes to it □ cry before one is hurt □ put the cart before the horse □ think twice before doing something

BEG
□ beg something off □ beg the question □ go begging

BEGGARS
□ Beggars can't be choosers.

BEGIN
□ begin to see daylight □ begin to see the light □ Charity begins at home.

BEHALF
□ in behalf of someone □ in someone's behalf □ on behalf of someone □ on someone's behalf

BEHAVIOR
□ on one's best behavior

BEHIND
□ behind someone's back □ behind the eight ball □ behind the scenes □ burn one's bridges behind one □ come up from behind □ driving force behind someone or something □ dry behind

the ears □ fall behind in something □ fall behind on something □ fall behind □ get behind in something □ lag behind someone or something □ leave someone or something behind □ power behind the throne □ stand behind someone or something □ wet behind the ears □ with one hand tied behind one's back

BEHOOVES
□ It behooves one to do something.

BEING
□ for the time being

BELFRY
□ have bats in one's belfry

BELIEVE
□ believe in someone or something □ believe it or not □ lead someone to believe something □ Seeing is believing.

BELL
□ ring a bell □ with bells on

BELONG
□ belong to someone □ To the victors belong the spoils.

BELOW
□ hit someone below the belt

BELT
□ belt something out □ get something under one's belt □ hit someone below the belt □ tighten one's belt

BENCH
□ on the bench □ warm the bench

BEND
□ bend over backwards to do something □ bend someone's ear □ bent on doing something □ go round the bend

BENEATH
□ feel it beneath one to do something

BENEFIT
□ get the benefit of the doubt □ give someone the benefit of the doubt □ of benefit to someone

BERTH
□ give someone or something a wide berth

BESIDE
□ beside oneself □ beside the point □ beside the question

BEST
(See also *BETTER, GOOD.*)□ all for the best □ at best □ at one's best □ at the best □ best bib and tucker □ come off second best □ do one's best □ far

and away the best □ for the best □ get one's best shot □ get the best of someone □ give something one's best shot □ had best do something □ He laughs best who laughs last. □ in one's Sunday best □ in the best of health □ make the best of something □ on one's best behavior □ put one's best foot forward □ to the best of one's ability □ to the best of one's knowledge □ work out for the best

BET
□ bet one's bottom dollar □ bet one's life □ hedge one's bets □ You bet your boots! □ You bet!

BETTER
(See also *BEST.*)□ all better now □ better late than never □ better off doing something □ better off somewhere □ better off □ better to do something □ do someone one better □ for better or for worse □ for the better □ get better □ get the better of someone □ go someone one better □ had better do something □ Half a loaf is better than none. □ have seen better days □ one's better half □ so much the better □ take a turn for the better

BETWEEN
□ between a rock and a hard place □ between life and death □ between the devil and the deep blue sea □ betwixt and between □ come between someone and someone else □ draw a line between something and something else □ few and far between □ have one's tail between one's legs □ hit someone between the eyes □ no love lost between someone and someone else □ read between the lines

BETWIXT
□ betwixt and between

BEYOND
□ above and beyond the call of duty □ beyond a reasonable doubt □ beyond measure □ beyond one's depth □ beyond one's means □ beyond the pale □ beyond the shadow of a doubt □ beyond words □ can't see beyond the end of one's nose □ live beyond one's means

BIB
□ best bib and tucker

BID
□ bid adieu to someone or something

BIDE
☐ bide one's time

BIG
☐ as big as all outdoors ☐ as big as life ☐ big frog in a small pond ☐ get a big send-off ☐ give someone a big send-off ☐ have a big mouth ☐ have eyes bigger than one's stomach ☐ make a big deal about something ☐ one's eyes are bigger than one's stomach ☐ talk big ☐ too big for one's britches

BILL
☐ fill the bill ☐ foot the bill ☐ get a clean bill of health ☐ give someone a clean bill of health ☐ pad the bill ☐ sell someone a bill of goods

BIND
(See also *BOUND*.)☐ in a bind

BINGE
☐ go on a binge

BIRD
☐ A bird in the hand is worth two in the bush. ☐ a little bird told me ☐ as free as a bird ☐ birds and the bees ☐ Birds of a feather flock together. ☐ eat like a bird ☐ for the birds ☐ kill two birds with one stone ☐ The early bird gets the worm.

BIRTH
☐ give birth to someone or something

BIRTHDAY
☐ in one's birthday suit

BIT
☐ champ at the bit ☐ do one's bit ☐ hair of the dog that bit one ☐ Not a bit. ☐ quite a bit ☐ take the bit in one's teeth

BITCH
☐ son of a bitch

BITE
☐ bite off more than one can chew ☐ bite one's nails ☐ bite one's tongue ☐ bite something off ☐ bite the bullet ☐ bite the dust ☐ bite the hand that feeds one ☐ One's bark is worse than one's bite. ☐ put the bite on someone

BITTER
☐ take the bitter with the sweet ☐ to the bitter end

BLACK
☐ black out ☐ black sheep of the family ☐ get a black eye ☐ give someone a black eye ☐ in black and white ☐ in the black ☐ the pot calling the kettle black

BLAME
☐ blame someone for something ☐ blame something on someone ☐ lay the blame on someone or something ☐ place the blame on someone or something ☐ put the blame on someone or something

BLANK
☐ draw a blank

BLAST
☐ blast off

BLAZE
☐ blaze a trail

BLEEP
☐ bleep something out

BLIND
☐ as blind as a bat ☐ blind leading the blind ☐ turn a blind eye to someone or something ☐ up a blind alley

BLINDFOLDED
☐ able to do something blindfolded

BLINK
☐ on the blink

BLOCK
☐ a chip off the old block ☐ knock someone's block off ☐ on the block

BLOOD
☐ draw blood ☐ flesh and blood ☐ in cold blood ☐ in one's blood ☐ in the blood ☐ make someone's blood boil ☐ make someone's blood run cold ☐ sweat blood

BLOODY
☐ cry bloody murder ☐ scream bloody murder

BLOW
☐ blow a fuse ☐ blow a gasket ☐ blow hot and cold ☐ blow off steam ☐ blow one's cookies ☐ blow one's cool ☐ blow one's cork ☐ blow one's lines ☐ blow one's lunch ☐ blow one's own horn ☐ blow one's stack ☐ blow one's top ☐ blow over ☐ blow someone or something away ☐ blow someone or something off ☐ blow someone's brains out ☐ blow someone's cover ☐ blow someone's mind ☐ blow something down ☐ blow something out of all proportion ☐ blow something up ☐ blow the lid off something ☐ blow the whistle on someone ☐ blow up in someone's face ☐ blow up ☐ blow-by-blow account ☐ come to blows over something ☐ land a blow somewhere

BLOWOUT
- have a blowout

BLUE
- between the devil and the deep blue sea - blue around the gills - burn with a low blue flame - like a bolt out of the blue - once in a blue moon - out of a clear blue sky - out of the blue - talk a blue streak - talk until one is blue in the face

BLUES
- get the blues - have the blues

BLUFF
- call someone's bluff

BLURT
- blurt something out

BLUSH
- at first blush

BOARD
- above board - across the board - back to the drawing board - go by the board - honest and above board - on board - open and above board - room and board

BOAST
- boast of someone or something

BOAT
- in the same boat - miss the boat - rock the boat

BODY
- come in a body - go in a body - keep body and soul together - over my dead body

BOG
- bog down

BOGGLE
- boggle someone's mind

BOIL
- A watched pot never boils. - boil down to something - have a low boiling point - make someone's blood boil

BOLT
- like a bolt out of the blue

BOMBSHELL
- drop a bombshell - explode a bombshell

BONE
- bone of contention - bone up on something - cut someone or something to the bone - feel something in one's bones - have a bone to pick with someone - make no bones about it - nothing but skin and bones - work one's fingers to the bone

BONER
- pull a boner

BONNET
- have a bee in one's bonnet - put a bee in someone's bonnet

BOOK
- by the book - close the books on someone or something - crack a book - have one's nose in a book - hit the books - in one's book - make book on something - one for the books - one for the record books - read someone like a book - take a leaf out of someone's book - throw the book at someone - use every trick in the book

BOOM
- lower the boom on someone

BOOT
- boot someone or something out - die in one's boots - die with one's boots on - get the boot - give someone the boot - quake in one's boots - shake in one's boots - to boot - You bet your boots!

BOOTSTRAPS
- pull oneself up by one's own bootstraps

BORE
- bore someone stiff - bore someone to death

BOREDOM
- die of boredom

BORN
- born out of wedlock - born with a silver spoon in one's mouth - in all one's born days - not born yesterday

BORROW
- borrow trouble - live on borrowed time

BOSS
- boss someone around

BOTCH
- botch something up

BOTH
- burn the candle at both ends - have it both ways - land on both feet - make both ends meet - play both ends against the middle

BOTHER
- bother oneself about someone or something - bother with someone or something - hot and bothered

BOTTLE
- bottle something up

BOTTOM

☐ as soft as a baby's bottom ☐ at the bottom of the ladder ☐ bet one's bottom dollar ☐ bottom out ☐ from the bottom of one's heart ☐ from top to bottom ☐ get to the bottom of something ☐ hit bottom ☐ learn something from the bottom up ☐ scrape the bottom of the barrel ☐ the bottom line

BOUNCES

☐ That's the way the ball bounces.

BOUND

☐ bound and determined ☐ bound for somewhere ☐ bound hand and foot ☐ bound to do something ☐ by leaps and bounds ☐ duty bound to do something ☐ out of bounds ☐ within bounds

BOW

☐ bow and scrape ☐ bow out ☐ take a bow

BOWL

☐ bowl someone over

BOX

☐ open Pandora's box ☐ stuff the ballot box

BOY

☐ All work and no play makes Jack a dull boy. ☐ separate the men from the boys

BRAG

☐ brag about someone or something

BRAIN

☐ beat someone's brains out ☐ blow someone's brains out ☐ have something on the brain ☐ rack one's brains

BRANCH

☐ branch off ☐ branch out ☐ hold out the olive branch

BRASS

☐ double in brass ☐ get down to brass tacks

BRAVE

☐ put up a brave front

BREACH

☐ step into the breach

BREAD

☐ bread and butter ☐ know which side one's bread is buttered on

BREADTH

☐ by a hair's breadth

BREAK

(See also *BROKE*.)☐ at the break of dawn ☐ Break a leg! ☐ break away from someone or something ☐ break camp ☐ break down ☐ break even ☐ break ground for something ☐ break in on someone or something ☐ break into something ☐ break loose from someone or something ☐ break new ground ☐ break off with someone ☐ break one's back to do something ☐ break one's neck to do something ☐ break out in a cold sweat ☐ break out in something ☐ break out into tears ☐ break out of something ☐ break out ☐ break someone or something down ☐ break someone or something in ☐ break someone or something up ☐ break someone's fall ☐ break someone's heart ☐ break something away ☐ break something loose ☐ break something off ☐ break something to pieces ☐ break the back of something ☐ break the ice ☐ break the news to someone ☐ break through something ☐ break up with someone ☐ die of a broken heart ☐ get a break ☐ give someone a break ☐ have a break ☐ make a break for something or somewhere ☐ make or break someone ☐ take a break ☐ tough break

BREAST

☐ make a clean breast of something

BREATH

☐ all in one breath ☐ breath of fresh air ☐ catch one's breath ☐ Don't hold your breath. ☐ get time to catch one's breath ☐ have time to catch one's breath ☐ hold one's breath ☐ in the same breath ☐ out of breath ☐ save one's breath ☐ say something under one's breath ☐ take someone's breath away ☐ waste one's breath ☐ with every other breath

BREATHE

☐ able to breathe again ☐ breathe down someone's neck ☐ breathe one's last ☐ hardly have time to breathe ☐ not breathe a word about someone or something

BREEDS

☐ Familiarity breeds contempt.

BREEZE

☐ shoot the breeze

BREWING

☐ Trouble is brewing.

BRICK

☐ bang one's head against a brick wall ☐ drop a brick ☐ hit someone like a ton of bricks ☐ hit the bricks

BRIDE
□ give the bride away
BRIDGE
□ burn one's bridges behind one □ cross a bridge before one comes to it □ cross a bridge when one comes to it □ water under the bridge
BRIEF
□ hold no brief for someone or something □ in brief
BRIGHT
□ bright and early □ get a bright idea □ have a bright idea
BRING
□ bring home the bacon □ bring someone around □ bring someone or something back □ bring someone or something out □ bring someone or something up to date □ bring someone or something up □ bring someone to account □ bring someone to □ bring someone up to date on someone or something □ bring something about □ bring something crashing down around one □ bring something into question □ bring something off □ bring something to a close □ bring something to a halt □ bring something to an end □ bring something to light □ bring the house down □ bring up the rear
BRITCHES
□ too big for one's britches
BROAD
□ in broad daylight
BROKE
□ flat broke □ go broke □ go for broke
BROTH
□ Too many cooks spoil the broth.
BROW
□ by the sweat of one's brow □ knit one's brow
BROWN
□ do something up brown
BRUNT
□ bear the brunt of something
BRUSH
□ brush up on something □ have a brush with something
BRUSHOFF
□ get the brushoff □ give someone the brushoff
BUCK
□ buck for something □ buck up □ make a fast buck □ make a quick buck □ pass the buck

BUCKET
□ a drop in the bucket □ kick the bucket
BUCKLE
□ buckle down to something
BUD
□ nip something in the bud
BUFF
□ in the buff
BUG
□ as snug as a bug in a rug □ bug out □ bug someone
BUILD
□ build a fire under someone □ build castles in Spain □ build castles in the air □ build someone or something up □ build something to order □ build up to something □ Rome wasn't built in a day.
BULL
□ bull in a china shop □ cock-and-bull story □ full of bull □ hit the bull's-eye □ shoot the bull □ take the bull by the horns
BULLET
□ bite the bullet
BULLPEN
□ in the bullpen
BUMP
□ bump into someone or something □ bump someone off □ get goose bumps □ have goose bumps □ like a bump on a log
BUNDLE
□ bundle someone up □ make a bundle
BURN
□ burn one's bridges behind one □ burn oneself out □ burn someone at the stake □ burn someone in effigy □ burn someone or something to a crisp □ burn someone or something up □ burn something down □ burn something out □ burn the candle at both ends □ burn the midnight oil □ burn with a low blue flame □ burned up □ get one's fingers burned □ have money to burn □ keep the home fires burning □ Money burns a hole in someone's pocket.
BURNER
□ put something on the back burner
BURST
□ burst at the seams □ burst in on

someone or something ☐ burst into flames ☐ burst into tears ☐ burst out crying ☐ burst out laughing ☐ burst with joy ☐ burst with pride

BURY

☐ bury one's head in the sand ☐ bury the hatchet ☐ dead and buried

BUSH

☐ A bird in the hand is worth two in the bush. ☐ be bushed ☐ beat about the bush ☐ beat around the bush

BUSHEL

☐ hide one's light under a bushel

BUSINESS

☐ do a land office business ☐ drum some business up ☐ get down to business ☐ get one's nose out of someone's business ☐ get the business ☐ give someone the business ☐ go about one's business ☐ have no business doing something ☐ keep one's nose out of someone's business ☐ mind one's own business ☐ one means business ☐ send one about one's business ☐ set someone up in business

BUST

☐ bust a gut

BUSY

☐ as busy as a beaver ☐ as busy as a bee ☐ as busy as Grand Central Station ☐ get busy

BUT

☐ all over but the shouting ☐ but for someone or something ☐ can't help but do something ☐ everything but the kitchen sink ☐ It never rains but it pours. ☐ last but not least ☐ no buts about it ☐ no ifs, ands, or buts about it ☐ nothing but skin and bones

BUTT

☐ butt in on someone or something

BUTTER

☐ bread and butter ☐ butter someone up ☐ know which side one's bread is buttered on ☐ look as if butter wouldn't melt in one's mouth

BUTTERFLIES

☐ get butterflies in one's stomach ☐ give one butterflies in one's stomach ☐ have butterflies in one's stomach

BUTTON

☐ button one's lip ☐ on the button ☐ push the panic button

BUY

☐ buy a pig in a poke ☐ buy someone

☐ buy someone off ☐ buy someone or something out ☐ buy something for a song ☐ buy something on credit ☐ buy something sight unseen ☐ buy something to go ☐ buy something up ☐ buy something ☐ not buy something

BUZZ

☐ give someone a buzz

BY

☐ abide by something ☐ blow-by-blow account ☐ by a great deal ☐ by a hair's breadth ☐ by a mile ☐ by a whisker ☐ by all accounts ☐ by all appearances ☐ by all means of something ☐ by all means ☐ by and by ☐ by and large ☐ by any means ☐ by chance ☐ by choice ☐ by coincidence ☐ by dint of something ☐ by fits and starts ☐ by guess and by golly ☐ by hook or by crook ☐ by leaps and bounds ☐ by means of something ☐ by mistake ☐ by no means ☐ by return mail ☐ by shank's mare ☐ by the book ☐ by the day ☐ by the dozen ☐ by the dozens ☐ by the handful ☐ by the hour ☐ by the month ☐ by the nape of the neck ☐ by the numbers ☐ by the same token ☐ by the seat of one's pants ☐ by the skin of one's teeth ☐ by the sweat of one's brow ☐ by the way ☐ by the week ☐ by the year ☐ by virtue of something ☐ by way of something ☐ by word of mouth ☐ come by something honestly ☐ come by something ☐ conspicuous by one's absence ☐ crushed by something ☐ do somehow by someone ☐ do something by hand ☐ drop by the wayside ☐ drop by ☐ easy to come by ☐ end up by doing something ☐ fall by the wayside ☐ fly-by-night ☐ get by on something ☐ get by someone or something ☐ get by with something ☐ get by ☐ get the go-by ☐ give someone the go-by ☐ go by the board ☐ hang by a hair ☐ inch by inch ☐ judging by something ☐ know someone by sight ☐ know something by heart ☐ lay something by ☐ lead someone by the nose ☐ learn something by heart ☐ learn something by rote ☐ let something slip by ☐ let the chance slip by ☐ little by little ☐ live by one's wits ☐ miss something by a mile ☐ not by a long shot ☐ one by one ☐ pass someone or something by ☐

play by ear □ play something by ear □ play-by-play description □ possessed by something □ pull oneself up by one's own bootstraps □ put off by someone or something □ put something by □ Run that by again. □ set great store by someone or something □ sit idly by □ squeak by someone or something □ stand by someone □ stand by □ step by step □ stick by someone or something □ stop by someplace □ swear by someone or something □ take someone or something by storm □ take someone or something by surprise □ take the bull by the horns □ touched by someone or something □ win by a nose □ wind up by doing something □ word by word

BYGONES
□ Let bygones be bygones.

CABOODLE
□ kit and caboodle

CAHOOTS
□ in cahoots with someone

CAKE
□ eat one's cake and have it too □ have one's cake and eat it too □ piece of cake □ take the cake

CALF
□ kill the fatted calf

CALL
□ above and beyond the call of duty □ at someone's beck and call □ call a halt to something □ call a meeting □ call a spade a spade □ call for someone or something □ call it a day □ call it quits □ call on someone □ call someone back □ call someone down □ call someone names □ call someone on the carpet □ call someone or something in □ call someone or something into question □ call someone or something off □ call someone or something up □ call someone to account □ call someone's attention to something □ call someone's bluff □ call the dogs off □ call the meeting to order □ call the shots □ call the tune □ call upon someone □ have a close call □ not able to call one's time one's own □ on call □ the pot calling the kettle black □ within calling distance

CAMP
□ break camp

CAN
(See also *ABLE, CAN'T, COULD.*)□ before you can say Jack Robinson □ bite off more than one can chew □ Can it! □ catch-as-catch-can □ game at which two can play □ more than one can shake a stick at □ no can do □ open a can of worms □ You can say that again!

CAN'T
(See also *NOT.*)□ Beggars can't be choosers. □ can't carry a tune □ can't do anything with someone or something □ can't help but do something □ can't hold a candle to someone □ can't make heads or tails of someone or something □ can't see beyond the end of one's nose □ can't see one's hand in front of one's face □ can't stand someone or something □ can't stand the sight of someone or something □ can't stomach someone or something □ can't □ You can't take it with you. □ You can't teach an old dog new tricks.

CANARY
□ look like the cat that swallowed the canary

CANCEL
□ cancel something out

CANDLE
□ burn the candle at both ends □ can't hold a candle to someone □ not hold a candle to someone or something

CANOE
□ paddle one's own canoe

CAP
□ feather in one's cap □ put on one's thinking cap

CARD
□ have the cards stacked against one □ in the cards □ lay one's cards on the table □ play one's cards close to the chest □ play one's cards right □ play one's trump card □ put one's cards on the table □ stack the cards against someone or something

CARE
□ care about someone or something □ care for someone or something □ care nothing about someone or something □ couldn't care less □ devil-may-care attitude □ for all I care □ in care of someone □ in the care of someone □ not care two hoots about someone or

something □ not have a care in the world □ take care of someone or something □ That takes care of that.

CAREFUL

□ be careful about someone or something □ be careful not to do something

CARPET

□ call someone on the carpet □ get the red carpet treatment □ give someone the red carpet treatment □ roll out the red carpet for someone

CARRY

□ can't carry a tune □ carried away □ carry a torch for someone □ carry coals to Newcastle □ carry on about someone or something □ carry on with someone or something □ carry one's cross □ carry one's own weight □ carry someone or something away □ carry someone or something off □ carry someone or something out □ carry something over □ carry the ball □ carry the torch □ carry the weight of the world on one's shoulders □ carry through on something □ carry weight with someone □ cash-and-carry □ get carried away

CART

□ put the cart before the horse □ upset the apple cart

CASE

□ case in point □ get down to cases □ Get off someone's case! □ have a case against someone □ in any case □ in case of something □ in the case of someone or something □ just in case □ make a federal case out of something □ on someone's case

CASH

□ cash in on something □ cash in one's chips □ cash on the barrelhead □ cash something in □ cash-and-carry □ cold, hard cash

CAST

□ cast around for someone or something □ cast doubt on someone or something □ cast one's lot in with someone □ cast pearls before swine □ cast someone or something out □ cast the first stone

CASTLES

□ build castles in Spain □ build castles in the air

CAT

□ be a copy-cat □ Cat got your tongue?

□ let the cat out of the bag □ look like the cat that swallowed the canary □ not enough room to swing a cat □ play cat and mouse with someone □ rain cats and dogs □ There's more than one way to skin a cat. □ When the cat's away the mice will play.

CATCH

□ catch cold □ catch fire □ catch forty winks □ catch hell □ catch hold of someone or something □ catch it □ catch on fire □ catch on to someone or something □ catch one with one's pants down □ catch one's breath □ catch one's death of cold □ catch sight of someone or something □ catch some Zs □ catch someone in the act of doing something □ catch someone off balance □ catch someone off guard □ catch someone red-handed □ catch someone's eye □ catch the devil □ catch up to someone or something □ catch up with someone or something □ catch-as-catch-can □ caught in the act □ caught in the cross-fire □ caught in the middle □ caught short □ get time to catch one's breath □ have time to catch one's breath

CAUGHT

(See *CATCH.*)

CAUSE

□ cause a commotion □ cause a stir □ cause eyebrows to raise □ cause tongues to wag

CAUTION

□ throw caution to the wind

CAVE

□ cave in to someone or something □ cave in

CEILING

□ hit the ceiling

CENT

□ not worth a red cent □ put in one's two cents worth

CENTER

□ off center □ on dead center

CENTRAL

□ as busy as Grand Central Station

CENTURY

□ turn of the century

CEREMONY

□ stand on ceremony

CERTAIN

□ be certain of someone or something

CHAIN
☐ ball and chain

CHAIR
☐ play first chair

CHALK
☐ chalk something up to something

CHAMP
☐ champ at the bit

CHANCE
☐ by chance ☐ chance on someone or something ☐ chance something ☐ ghost of a chance ☐ have a snowball's chance in hell ☐ jump at the chance ☐ let the chance slip by ☐ once-in-a-lifetime chance ☐ stand a chance ☐ take a chance

CHANGE
☐ change horses in midstream ☐ change someone's mind ☐ change someone's tune ☐ for something to change hands ☐ go through the changes

CHANNELS
☐ go through channels ☐ work through channels

CHARACTER
☐ in character ☐ out of character

CHARGE
☐ charge off ☐ charge someone or something up ☐ charge something to someone or something ☐ charge something up to someone or something ☐ get a charge out of someone or something ☐ have charge of someone or something ☐ in charge of someone or something ☐ in the charge of someone ☐ take charge of someone or something

CHARITY
☐ Charity begins at home.

CHARLEY
☐ get a Charley horse ☐ have a Charley horse

CHASE
☐ chase after someone or something ☐ chase around after someone or something ☐ chase someone or something around ☐ give chase to someone or something ☐ go chase oneself ☐ lead someone on a merry chase ☐ wild-goose chase

CHEAT
☐ cheat on someone

CHECK
☐ check in on someone or something ☐ check into something ☐ check on someone or something ☐ check out of something ☐ check someone in ☐ check someone or something off ☐ check someone or something out ☐ check up on someone or something ☐ check with someone ☐ get a check-up ☐ get a rain check on something ☐ give someone a check-up ☐ give someone a rain check ☐ hold someone or something in check ☐ honor someone's check ☐ keep someone or something in check ☐ make a check out to someone ☐ someone or something checks out ☐ take a rain check on something

CHEEK
☐ tongue-in-cheek ☐ turn the other cheek

CHEER
☐ cheer someone on ☐ cheer someone up ☐ cheer up

CHEST
☐ get something off one's chest ☐ play one's cards close to the chest

CHEW
☐ bite off more than one can chew ☐ chew someone or something up ☐ chew someone out ☐ chew something off ☐ chew the fat ☐ chew the rag

CHICKEN
☐ chicken out of something ☐ count one's chickens before they hatch ☐ for chicken feed ☐ go to bed with the chickens ☐ no spring chicken ☐ run around like a chicken with its head cut off

CHILD
☐ expecting a child

CHILDHOOD
☐ in one's second childhood

CHIME
☐ chime in with something

CHIN
☐ keep one's chin up ☐ make chin music ☐ take something on the chin ☐ wag one's chin

CHINA
☐ bull in a china shop

CHIP
☐ a chip off the old block ☐ cash in one's chips ☐ chip in on something ☐ chip something in on something ☐ have a chip on one's shoulder ☐ in the chips

CHOICE
☐ by choice

CHOKE

□ choke someone up □ choke something off

CHOOSE

□ choose up sides

CHOOSERS

□ Beggars can't be choosers.

CHOP

□ chop someone or something up

CHURCH

□ as poor as a church mouse

CIRCLE

□ go around in circles □ in a vicious circle □ run circles around someone □ run in circles □ talk in circles

CIRCULATION

□ back in circulation □ out of circulation

CIRCUMSTANCES

□ extenuating circumstances □ under the circumstances

CIRCUS

□ like a three-ring circus

CIVIL

□ keep a civil tongue in one's head

CLAIM

□ stake a claim to something

CLAM

□ as happy as a clam □ clam up

CLAMP

□ clamp down on someone or something □ put the clamps on someone

CLASS

□ cut class

CLAY

□ have feet of clay

CLEAN

□ clean out of something □ clean someone or something out □ clean someone or something up □ clean up one's act □ clean up □ come clean with someone □ get a clean bill of health □ give someone a clean bill of health □ have a clean conscience about someone or something □ have clean hands □ keep one's nose clean □ make a clean breast of something □ make a clean sweep □ start with a clean slate □ wipe someone's slate clean

CLEANERS

□ take someone to the cleaners

CLEAR

□ as clear as mud □ clear out □ clear something off □ clear something out □ clear something up □ clear the air □ clear the table □ clear up □ have a clear conscience about someone or something □ in the clear □ make someone's position clear □ out of a clear blue sky □ see one's way clear to do something □ steer clear of someone or something □ The coast is clear.

CLIMB

□ climb on the bandwagon □ climb the wall

CLIP

□ clip someone's wings □ clip something out

CLOCK

□ against the clock □ around the clock

CLOCKWORK

□ as regular as clockwork □ go like clockwork

CLOG

□ clog someone or something up

CLOSE

□ at close range □ bring something to a close □ close at hand □ close in on someone or something □ close one's eyes to something □ close ranks □ close someone out of something □ close something down □ close something out □ close the books on someone or something □ close the door on someone or something □ close to home □ close to someone □ close up shop □ draw something to a close □ draw to a close □ get close to someone or something □ have a close call □ have a close shave □ hit one close to home □ play one's cards close to the chest □ too close for comfort

CLOSET

□ come out of the closet □ skeleton in the closet

CLOTH

□ make something up out of whole cloth

CLOTHES

□ Sunday-go-to-meeting clothes

CLOTHING

□ wolf in sheep's clothing

CLOUD

□ cloud up □ Every cloud has a silver lining. □ have one's head in the clouds □ on cloud nine □ under a cloud of suspicion

CLOVER

□ in clover

CLUE
- clue someone in on something

COALS
- carry coals to Newcastle □ haul someone over the coals □ rake someone over the coals

COAST
- coast-to-coast □ The coast is clear.

COATTAILS
- hang on someone's coattails □ ride on someone's coattails

COCK
- cock-and-bull story

COCKED
- go off half-cocked

COCKLES
- warm the cockles of someone's heart

COINCIDENCE
- by coincidence

COLD
- be a cold fish □ blow hot and cold □ break out in a cold sweat □ catch cold □ catch one's death of cold □ cold, hard cash □ dash cold water on something □ get cold feet □ get the cold shoulder □ give someone the cold shoulder □ go cold turkey □ have cold feet □ in cold blood □ leave someone out in the cold □ make someone's blood run cold □ out cold □ pour cold water on something □ take cold □ take one's death of cold □ throw cold water on something

COLLAR
- hot under the collar

COLLECTION
- take up a collection

COLLEGE
- work one's way through college

COLOR
- horse of a different color □ horse of another color □ off color □ sail under false colors □ see the color of someone's money □ show one's colors □ with flying colors

COMB
- go over something with a fine-tooth comb

COME
- come a cropper □ come about □ come across someone or something □ Come again? □ come along with one □ Come and get it! □ come apart at the seams □ come around □ come at someone or something □ come away empty-handed □ come back □ come between someone and someone else □ come by something honestly □ come by something □ come clean with someone □ come down hard on someone or something □ come down in the world □ come down to earth □ come down to something □ come down with something □ come down □ come from far and wide □ come hell or high water □ come home to roost □ come home □ come in a body □ come in for something □ come in handy □ come in out of the rain □ come in □ come into one's or its own □ come into something □ come of age □ Come off it! □ come off second best □ come off □ come on somehow □ come on □ come out ahead □ come out for someone or something □ come out in the wash □ come out of nowhere □ come out of one's shell □ come out of the closet □ come out with something □ come out □ come over □ come round □ come someone's way □ come through □ come to a bad end □ come to a dead end □ come to a head □ come to a standstill □ come to an end □ come to an untimely end □ come to blows over something □ come to grief □ come to grips with something □ come to life □ come to light □ come to mind □ come to naught □ come to nothing □ come to one's senses □ come to pass □ come to rest □ come to terms with someone or something □ come to the fore □ come to the point □ come to think of it □ come to □ come true □ come unglued □ come up from behind □ come up in the world □ come up with someone or something □ come up □ come upon someone or something □ come what may □ come with someone or something □ come with □ come within an ace of doing something □ come within an inch of doing something □ cross a bridge before one comes to it □ cross a bridge when one comes to it □ dream come true □ easy come, easy go □ easy to come by □ First come, first served. □ get what's coming to one □ have another guess coming □ have another think coming □

have come a long way □ have something coming □ if worst comes to worst □ Johnny-come-lately □ not know enough to come in out of the rain □ not know whether one is coming or going □ till the cows come home □ up-and-coming □ when it comes right down to it □ when it comes to something □ where one is coming from

COMEBACK
□ make a comeback

COMEUPPANCE
□ get one's comeuppance

COMFORT
□ too close for comfort

COMFORTABLE
□ as comfortable as an old shoe

COMMAND
□ have a good command of something

COMMISSION
□ out of commission

COMMIT
□ commit something to memory

COMMON
□ have something in common with someone or something

COMMOTION
□ cause a commotion

COMPANY
□ keep company with someone □ keep someone company □ part company with someone

COMPARE
□ compare someone to someone □ compare someone with someone □ compare something to something □ compare something with something

COMPEL
□ compel someone to do something □ feel compelled to do something

COMPLAIN
□ nothing to complain about

COMPLIMENT
□ fish for a compliment □ pay someone a compliment □ pay someone a left-handed compliment □ return the compliment

COMPOSURE
□ regain one's composure

CONCERN
□ as far as I'm concerned □ to whom it may concern

CONCERT
□ in concert with someone

CONCLUSIONS
□ jump to conclusions □ leap to conclusions

CONDITION
□ in condition □ in good condition □ in mint condition □ in the pink of condition □ out of condition

CONFIDE
□ confide in someone

CONFORMITY
□ in conformity with something

CONK
□ conk out

CONNIPTION
□ have a conniption

CONSCIENCE
□ have a clean conscience about someone or something □ have a clear conscience about someone or something

CONSEQUENCE
□ in consequence of something

CONSIDERATION
□ in consideration of something □ out of consideration for someone or something

CONSPICUOUS
□ conspicuous by one's absence □ make oneself conspicuous

CONSTRUCTION
□ under construction

CONTEMPT
□ Familiarity breeds contempt.

CONTEND
□ contend with someone or something

CONTENT
□ to one's heart's content

CONTENTION
□ bone of contention

CONTRARY
□ on the contrary □ to the contrary

CONTROL
□ control the purse strings □ get someone or something under control □ have someone or something under control □ out of control

CONVENIENCE
□ at someone's earliest convenience

CONVERSATION
□ strike up a conversation

CONVICTIONS
□ have the courage of one's convictions

CONVINCE
□ convince someone of something

COOK
☐ cook someone's goose ☐ cook something up ☐ cook the accounts ☐ Too many cooks spoil the broth. ☐ Too many cooks spoil the stew. ☐ What's cooking?

COOKIE
☐ blow one's cookies ☐ That's the way the cookie crumbles. ☐ toss one's cookies

COOL
☐ as cool as a cucumber ☐ blow one's cool ☐ Cool it! ☐ cool off ☐ cool one's heels ☐ cool someone or something down ☐ cool someone or something off ☐ keep cool ☐ lose one's cool ☐ play it cool

COON
☐ in a coon's age

COOP
☐ fly the coop

COP
☐ cop a plea ☐ cop out

COPY
☐ be a copy-cat

CORE
☐ to the core

CORK
☐ blow one's cork ☐ pop one's cork

CORNER
☐ cut corners ☐ have turned the corner ☐ out of the corner of one's eye

COST
☐ at all costs ☐ at any cost ☐ cost a pretty penny ☐ cost an arm and a leg

COUGH
☐ cough something up

COULD
(See also *CAN*.)☐ could do with someone or something ☐ couldn't care less ☐ so still you could hear a pin drop ☐ Wild horses couldn't drag someone.

COUNSEL
☐ keep one's own counsel

COUNT
☐ count noses ☐ count off ☐ count on someone or something ☐ count one's chickens before they hatch ☐ count someone in for something ☐ count someone or something off ☐ count someone out for something ☐ count something up ☐ Every minute counts. ☐ stand up and be counted

COUNTER
☐ run counter to something ☐ under the counter

COUNTRY
☐ another country heard from

COURAGE
☐ have the courage of one's convictions ☐ pluck up someone's courage ☐ screw up one's courage

COURSE
☐ as a matter of course ☐ in due course ☐ in the course of time ☐ par for the course

COURT
☐ throw oneself on the mercy of the court

COURTESY
☐ out of courtesy to someone

COVER
☐ blow someone's cover ☐ cover a lot of ground ☐ cover for someone ☐ cover someone or something up ☐ cover someone's tracks up ☐ cover the territory ☐ cover the waterfront

COW
☐ till the cows come home

COZY
☐ cozy up to someone

CRACK
☐ at the crack of dawn ☐ crack a book ☐ crack a joke ☐ crack a smile ☐ crack down on someone or something ☐ crack someone or something up ☐ crack something wide open ☐ crack up ☐ get cracking ☐ hard nut to crack ☐ make cracks about someone or something ☐ not all it is cracked up to be ☐ take a crack at something ☐ tough nut to crack

CRADLE
☐ rob the cradle

CRAMP
☐ cramp someone's style

CRANK
☐ crank something out

CRASH
☐ bring something crashing down around one

CRAW
☐ have something stick in one's craw

CRAZY
☐ as crazy as a loon ☐ crazy about someone or something ☐ drive someone crazy ☐ go stir crazy ☐ like crazy

CREAM
☐ cream of the crop

CREATE
☐ create a stink about something ☐ create an uproar

someone or something to the bone ☐ cut someone or something up ☐ cut someone to the quick ☐ cut someone's losses ☐ cut someone's throat ☐ cut teeth ☐ cut the ground out from under someone ☐ cut up ☐ cuts no ice ☐ fish or cut bait ☐ have one's work cut out for one ☐ run around like a chicken with its head cut off

DAB
☐ smack dab in the middle

DAGGERS
☐ look daggers at someone

DAILY
☐ the daily grind

DAISIES
☐ pushing up daisies

DAMAGE
☐ do someone damage

DANCE
☐ dance to another tune ☐ go into one's song and dance about something

DANDER
☐ get someone's dander up

DANGEROUS
☐ A little knowledge is a dangerous thing.

DARE
☐ dare someone to do something

DARK
☐ in the dark about someone or something ☐ shot in the dark

DARKEN
☐ darken someone's door

DASH
☐ dash cold water on something ☐ dash off ☐ dash something off

DATE
☐ at an early date ☐ bring someone or something up to date ☐ bring someone up to date on someone or something ☐ date back to sometime ☐ out of date ☐ to date ☐ up to date

DAVY
☐ go to Davy Jones's locker

DAWN
☐ at the break of dawn ☐ at the crack of dawn ☐ dawn on someone

DAY
☐ all day long ☐ all hours of the day and night ☐ all in a day's work ☐ all the live-long day ☐ as different as night and day ☐ as plain as day ☐ by the day ☐ call it a day ☐ day after day ☐ day

and night ☐ day in and day out ☐ day-to-day ☐ Every dog has its day. ☐ for days on end ☐ forever and a day ☐ from day to day ☐ from this day on ☐ get the day off ☐ have seen better days ☐ have the day off ☐ in all one's born days ☐ in this day and age ☐ make a day of doing something ☐ night and day ☐ not give anyone the time of day ☐ one of these days ☐ one's days are numbered ☐ pass the time of day with someone ☐ Rome wasn't built in a day. ☐ save something for a rainy day ☐ save the day ☐ see the light of day ☐ take the day off ☐ That'll be the day.

DAYLIGHT
☐ beat the living daylights out of someone ☐ begin to see daylight ☐ in broad daylight ☐ scare the daylights out of someone

DEAD
☐ as dead as a dodo ☐ as dead as a doornail ☐ be a dead duck ☐ beat a dead horse ☐ come to a dead end ☐ dead ahead ☐ dead and buried ☐ dead in someone's or something's tracks ☐ dead loss ☐ dead on one's or its feet ☐ dead set against someone or something ☐ dead to the world ☐ drop dead ☐ have someone dead to rights ☐ in a dead heat ☐ knock someone dead ☐ leave someone for dead ☐ on dead center ☐ over my dead body ☐ taken for dead

DEAF
☐ turn a deaf ear to something

DEAL
☐ by a great deal ☐ deal in something ☐ deal someone in ☐ deal something out ☐ deal with someone or something ☐ get a raw deal ☐ give someone a raw deal ☐ It's a deal. ☐ make a big deal about something ☐ think a great deal of someone or something

DEATH
☐ at death's door ☐ be death on something ☐ between life and death ☐ bore someone to death ☐ catch one's death of cold ☐ death on someone or something ☐ die a natural death ☐ frighten someone to death ☐ frightened to death ☐ kiss of death ☐ scare someone to death ☐ scared to death ☐ sign one's own death warrant ☐ struggle to the

death □ take one's death of cold □
thrill someone to death □ thrilled to
death □ tickle someone to death

DEBT
□ pay one's debt to society

DECIDE
□ decide in favor of someone or something

DECISION
□ eleventh-hour decision

DECK
□ on deck □ stack the deck against someone or something

DEEP
□ Beauty is only skin deep. □ between the devil and the deep blue sea □ deep-six someone or something □ go off the deep end □ in deep water □ in deep □ jump off the deep end □ Still waters run deep.

DEFIANCE
□ in defiance of someone or something

DEGREE
□ get the third degree □ give someone the third degree □ to the nth degree

DELIVERED
□ signed, sealed, and delivered

DEN
□ beard the lion in his den

DENT
□ make a dent in something

DEPEND
□ depend on someone or something

DEPOSIT
□ on deposit

DEPTH
□ beyond one's depth

DESCRIPTION
□ play-by-play description

DESERT
□ desert a sinking ship

DESERVE
□ One good turn deserves another.

DESIGNS
□ have designs on someone or something

DESIRED
□ leave a lot to be desired

DESK
□ away from one's desk

DESPAIR
□ sink into despair □ throw up one's hands in despair

DESSERTS
□ get one's just desserts

DETERMINED
□ bound and determined

DEVIL
□ between the devil and the deep blue sea □ catch the devil □ devil-may-care attitude □ for the devil of it □ full of the devil □ get the devil □ give the devil his due □ go to the devil □ have the devil to pay □ raise the devil with someone or something □ speak of the devil □ There will be the devil to pay.

DIAMOND
□ diamond in the rough

DIBS
□ have dibs on something □ put one's dibs on something

DICE
□ No dice.

DICK
□ as tight as Dick's hatband

DIE
□ cross one's heart and hope to die □ curl up and die □ die a natural death □ die away □ die down □ die in one's boots □ die laughing □ die of a broken heart □ die of boredom □ die off □ die on the vine □ die out □ die with one's boots on □ dying to do something

DIET
□ on a diet

DIFFERENCE
□ make no difference to someone □ split the difference □ What difference does it make?

DIFFERENT
□ as different as night and day □ horse of a different color □ march to a different drummer □ sing a different tune

DIG
□ dig in □ dig some dirt up on someone □ dig someone or something out □ dig someone or something up □ dig someone or something □ take a dig at someone

DILEMMA
□ on the horns of a dilemma

DIM
□ take a dim view of something

DIME
□ dime a dozen □ not worth a dime □ turn on a dime

DINE
□ dine out

DINT
- [ ] by dint of something

DIP
- [ ] dip into something

DIRECTIONS
- [ ] ride off in all directions

DIRT
- [ ] dig some dirt up on someone [ ] hit pay dirt

DIRTY
- [ ] air someone's dirty linen in public [ ] dirty one's hands [ ] get a dirty look from someone [ ] get one's hands dirty [ ] give someone a dirty look

DISAGREE
- [ ] disagree with someone

DISEASE
- [ ] down with a disease [ ] have foot-in-mouth disease

DISH
- [ ] dish something out [ ] dish something up [ ] do the dishes

DISPOSAL
- [ ] put someone or something at someone's disposal

DISPOSE
- [ ] dispose of someone or something

DISTANCE
- [ ] go the distance [ ] keep one's distance from someone or something [ ] keep someone or something at a distance [ ] within calling distance [ ] within hailing distance

DITCH
- [ ] last-ditch effort

DIVE
- [ ] go into a nose dive [ ] take a nose dive

DIVIDE
- [ ] divide something fifty-fifty [ ] divide something in two [ ] divide something into something

DOCTOR
- [ ] just what the doctor ordered

DODO
- [ ] as dead as a dodo

DOG
- [ ] as sick as a dog [ ] call the dogs off [ ] Every dog has its day. [ ] go to the dogs [ ] hair of the dog that bit one [ ] lead a dog's life [ ] Let sleeping dogs lie. [ ] put on the dog [ ] rain cats and dogs [ ] see a man about a dog [ ] tail wagging the dog [ ] You can't teach an old dog new tricks.

DOGHOUSE
- [ ] in the doghouse

DOLDRUMS
- [ ] in the doldrums

DOLLAR
- [ ] bet one's bottom dollar [ ] dollar for dollar [ ] feel like a million dollars [ ] look like a million dollars

DOLLED
- [ ] get dolled up

DON'T
- [ ] Don't hold your breath. [ ] Don't let someone or something get you down. [ ] Don't look a gift horse in the mouth.

DOOR
- [ ] at death's door [ ] beat a path to someone's door [ ] close the door on someone or something [ ] darken someone's door [ ] door to door [ ] get one's foot in the door [ ] have one's foot in the door [ ] keep the wolf from the door [ ] live next door to someone [ ] open the door to something [ ] see someone to the door [ ] show someone the door [ ] show someone to the door [ ] shut the door on someone or something

DOORNAIL
- [ ] as dead as a doornail

DOORSTEP
- [ ] at someone's doorstep [ ] on someone's doorstep

DOSE
- [ ] dose of one's own medicine

DOT
- [ ] on the dot

DOTTED
- [ ] sign on the dotted line

DOUBLE
- [ ] do a double take [ ] double back on someone or something [ ] double in brass [ ] double up with someone [ ] double-cross someone [ ] on the double

DOUBT
- [ ] beyond a reasonable doubt [ ] beyond the shadow of a doubt [ ] cast doubt on someone or something [ ] get the benefit of the doubt [ ] give someone the benefit of the doubt [ ] no doubt

DOWN
(See also *DOWNS*.) [ ] back down from someone or something [ ] bear down on someone or something [ ] beat someone down to size [ ] blow something down [ ] bog down [ ] boil down to

389

something □ break down □ break someone or something down □ breathe down someone's neck □ bring something crashing down around one □ bring the house down □ buckle down to something □ burn something down □ call someone down □ catch one with one's pants down □ clamp down on someone or something □ close something down □ come down hard on someone or something □ come down in the world □ come down to earth □ come down to something □ come down with something □ come down □ cool someone or something down □ crack down on someone or something □ cut down on something □ cut someone down to size □ die down □ do something hands down □ Don't let someone or something get you down. □ down at the heels □ down in the dumps □ down in the mouth □ down on one's luck □ down on someone or something □ down South □ down the drain □ down the hatch □ down the street □ down to earth □ down to the wire □ down with a disease □ dress someone down □ face someone down □ fall down on the job □ flag someone or something down □ get down to brass tacks □ get down to business □ get down to cases □ get down to something □ get down to the facts □ get down to the nitty-gritty □ get down to work □ get someone or something down □ get the low-down on someone or something □ give someone the low-down on someone or something □ go down fighting □ go down in history □ hand something down to someone □ hand-me-down □ hold someone down □ hunt someone or something down □ jump down someone's throat □ keep someone or something down □ knock someone down to size □ knock someone or something down □ knock-down-drag-out fight □ knuckle down to something □ lay down on the job □ lay down one's life for someone or something □ lay down the law □ lay something down □ lead someone down the garden path □ let one's hair down □ let someone down □ lie down on the job □ live something down □ look down on someone or something □ look down one's nose at someone or something □ look up and down something □ mark someone or something down □ nail someone or something down □ nothing down □ pin someone or something down on something □ pipe down □ play someone or something down □ plunk someone or something down □ pour money down the drain □ pull someone or something down □ put one's foot down about something □ put someone down as something □ put someone down for something □ put someone or something down □ put something down to something □ ram someone or something down someone's throat □ right down someone's alley □ rub someone or something down □ run down □ run someone or something down □ scale something down □ sell someone down the river □ set something down to something □ settle down □ shake someone or something down □ shout someone or something down □ shove someone or something down someone's throat □ shut something down □ simmer down □ slap someone down □ slow someone or something down □ smack someone down □ step down from something □ take someone down a notch or two □ take someone down a peg or two □ take someone down to size □ take something lying down □ talk down to someone □ talk someone down □ tear someone or something down □ throw down the gauntlet □ thumbs down on someone or something □ tie someone down □ tied down □ tone something down □ track someone or something down □ turn someone or something down □ upside down □ vote something down □ wash something down □ water something down □ wear someone or something down □ weigh someone down □ when it comes right down to it □ wind down □ write something down

DOWNHILL
□ downhill all the way □ downhill from here on □ go downhill

DOWNS
□ ups and downs

DOZE
□ doze off to sleep

DOZEN
□ by the dozen □ by the dozens □ dime a dozen □ six of one and half a dozen of the other

DRAG
□ be a drag on someone □ drag on □ drag out □ drag someone or something in □ drag someone or something off □ drag something on □ drag something out □ feel dragged out □ knock-down-drag-out fight □ Wild horses couldn't drag someone.

DRAIN
□ down the drain □ pour money down the drain

DRAW
□ back to the drawing board □ beat someone to the draw □ draw a bead on someone or something □ draw a blank □ draw a line between something and something else □ draw blood □ draw fire away from someone or something □ draw interest □ draw near □ draw oneself up □ draw someone or something out □ draw something to a close □ draw something up □ draw the line at something □ draw to a close □ draw up □ quick on the draw □ slow on the draw

DREAM
□ dream about someone or something □ dream come true □ dream of someone or something □ dream something up □ wouldn't dream of doing something

DRESS
□ all dressed up □ dress someone down □ dress someone or something up □ dress up □ dressed to kill

DRIED
(See DRY.)

DRIFT
□ drift off to sleep

DRINK
□ drink something up □ drink to excess

DRIVE
□ as white as the driven snow □ drive a hard bargain □ drive someone crazy □ drive someone mad □ drive someone or something back □ drive someone or something home □ drive someone to the wall □ drive someone

up the wall □ drive something into the ground □ drive up to something □ driving force behind someone or something □ What are you driving at?

DROP
□ a drop in the bucket □ a drop in the ocean □ at the drop of a hat □ drop a bombshell □ drop a brick □ drop around sometime □ drop back □ drop by the wayside □ drop by □ drop dead □ drop in on someone □ drop in one's tracks □ drop in to say hello □ drop off to sleep □ drop out of something □ drop someone a line □ drop someone or something off □ drop someone □ drop the ball □ drop the other shoe □ so still you could hear a pin drop

DROWN
□ drown one's sorrows □ drown one's troubles □ drown someone or something out

DRUG
□ drug on the market

DRUM
□ drum some business up □ drum something into someone □ drum something up

DRUMMER
□ march to a different drummer

DRUTHERS
□ have one's druthers

DRY
□ cut and dried □ dry behind the ears □ dry someone or something off □ dry someone or something out □ dry something up □ dry up □ leave someone high and dry

DUCK
□ as a duck takes to water □ as easy as duck soup □ be a dead duck □ get one's ducks in a row □ like a sitting duck □ like water off a duck's back □ lovely weather for ducks

DUE
□ due to someone or something □ give credit where credit is due □ give the devil his due □ in due course □ in due time

DUES
□ pay one's dues

DULL
□ All work and no play makes Jack a dull boy.

DUMPS
□ down in the dumps

DUST
□ bite the dust □ dust someone or something off

DUTCH
□ go Dutch □ in Dutch with someone

DUTY
□ above and beyond the call of duty □ do one's duty □ duty bound to do something □ in the line of duty □ off duty □ on active duty □ on duty □ shirk one's duty

DWELL
□ dwell on something

DYED
□ dyed-in-the-wool

EACH
□ made for each other

EAR
□ be all ears □ bend someone's ear □ dry behind the ears □ get someone's ear □ give an ear to someone or something □ go in one ear and out the other □ have one's ear to the ground □ have someone's ear □ in one ear and out the other □ keep one's ear to the ground □ lend an ear to someone □ Make a silk purse out of a sow's ear. □ pin someone's ears back □ play by ear □ play something by ear □ prick up one's ears □ talk someone's ear off □ turn a deaf ear to something □ up to one's ears in something □ Walls have ears. □ wet behind the ears

EARLY
□ at an early date □ at someone's earliest convenience □ bright and early □ early on □ Early to bed, early to rise, makes a man healthy, wealthy, and wise. □ The early bird gets the worm.

EARN
□ A penny saved is a penny earned. □ earn one's keep

EARNEST
□ in earnest

EARTH
□ all over the earth □ come down to earth □ down to earth □ move heaven and earth to do something □ on earth □ to the ends of the earth

EASE
□ at ease □ ease off on someone or something □ ease someone out □ ease up on someone or something □ ill at ease

EAST
□ back East

EASY
□ as easy as apple pie □ as easy as duck soup □ as easy as falling off a log □ as easy as pie □ easier said than done □ easy come, easy go □ Easy does it. □ easy to come by □ free and easy □ get off easy □ go easy on someone or something □ on easy street □ take it easy on someone or something

EAT
□ eat a meal out □ eat away at someone or something □ eat high on the hog □ eat humble pie □ eat like a bird □ eat like a horse □ eat one's cake and have it too □ eat one's hat □ eat one's heart out □ eat one's words □ eat out of someone's hands □ eat out □ eat someone out of house and home □ eat someone out □ eat something away □ eat something up □ have one's cake and eat it too □ make someone eat crow □ What's eating you?

EDGE
□ edge someone out □ get the edge on someone □ have the edge on someone □ on edge □ set someone's teeth on edge □ take the edge off something

EDGEWAYS
□ get a word in edgeways

EDGEWISE
□ get a word in edgewise

EEL
□ as slippery as an eel

EFFECT
□ go into effect □ have a bad effect on someone or something □ something to that effect □ take effect □ words to that effect

EFFIGY
□ burn someone in effigy □ hang someone in effigy

EFFORT
□ all-out effort □ last-ditch effort □ make an all-out effort

EGG
□ egg someone on □ have egg on one's face □ kill the goose that laid the golden egg □ lay an egg □ put all one's eggs in one basket □ walk on eggs

EIGHT
□ behind the eight ball

EITHER
□ either feast or famine

ELBOW
☐ rub elbows with someone ☐ use some elbow grease

ELEMENT
☐ in one's element ☐ out of one's element

ELEVENTH
☐ at the eleventh hour ☐ eleventh-hour decision

ELSE
☐ come between someone and someone else ☐ draw a line between something and something else ☐ in someone else's place ☐ in someone else's shoes ☐ mistake someone for someone else ☐ mistake something for something else ☐ mix someone up with someone else ☐ mix something up with something else ☐ name someone after someone else ☐ no love lost between someone and someone else ☐ play someone off against someone else ☐ put oneself in someone else's place ☐ something else again ☐ something else

EMPTY
☐ come away empty-handed ☐ go away empty-handed

END
☐ All's well that ends well. ☐ at loose ends ☐ at one's wits' end ☐ at the end of nowhere ☐ at the end of one's rope ☐ at the end of one's tether ☐ bring something to an end ☐ burn the candle at both ends ☐ can't see beyond the end of one's nose ☐ come to a bad end ☐ come to a dead end ☐ come to an end ☐ come to an untimely end ☐ end in itself ☐ end of the line ☐ end of the road ☐ end something up ☐ end up by doing something ☐ end up somehow ☐ end up somewhere ☐ end up ☐ for days on end ☐ for hours on end ☐ get the short end of the stick ☐ go off the deep end ☐ hold one's end up ☐ jump off the deep end ☐ make both ends meet ☐ make ends meet ☐ make someone's hair stand on end ☐ meet one's end ☐ no end of something ☐ play both ends against the middle ☐ put an end to something ☐ see the light at the end of the tunnel ☐ to the bitter end ☐ to the ends of the earth

ENGAGE
☐ engage in small talk

ENGLISH
☐ in plain English

ENLARGE
☐ enlarge on something

ENOUGH
☐ Enough is enough. ☐ enough to go around ☐ get up enough nerve to do something ☐ good enough for someone or something ☐ have had enough ☐ Hot enough for you? ☐ leave well enough alone ☐ let well enough alone ☐ not enough room to swing a cat ☐ not know enough to come in out of the rain ☐ old enough to be someone's father ☐ old enough to be someone's mother

ENTER
☐ enter one's mind

ENVY
☐ green with envy

EQUAL
☐ equal to someone or something

ERRAND
☐ go on an errand ☐ run an errand ☐ send someone on an errand

ERROR
☐ trial and error

ESCAPE
☐ escape someone's notice

EVE
☐ on the eve of something

EVEN
☐ be even-steven ☐ break even ☐ get even with someone

EVENT
☐ in any event ☐ in the event of something ☐ in the unlikely event of something

EVER
☐ forever and ever

EVERY
☐ at every turn ☐ Every cloud has a silver lining. ☐ Every dog has its day. ☐ every last one ☐ every living soul ☐ Every minute counts. ☐ every now and again ☐ every now and then ☐ every once in a while ☐ every time one turns around ☐ every which way ☐ hang on someone's every word ☐ use every trick in the book ☐ with every other breath

EVERYTHING
☐ everything but the kitchen sink ☐ everything from A to Z ☐ everything from soup to nuts

EVIDENCE
□ much in evidence
EVIL
□ Money is the root of all evil.
EXAMINE
□ cross-examine someone
EXAMPLE
□ hold someone or something up as an example □ make an example of someone
EXCEPT
□ except for someone or something
EXCEPTION
□ make an exception for someone □ take exception to something
EXCESS
□ drink to excess
EXCHANGE
□ in exchange for someone or something
EXCUSE
□ excuse someone □ use someone or something as an excuse
EXPAND
□ expand on something
EXPECT
□ expecting a child □ when least expected
EXPECTATIONS
□ measure up to someone's expectations
EXPEDITION
□ go on a fishing expedition
EXPENSE
□ at the expense of someone or something □ go to the expense of doing something □ out-of-pocket expenses
EXPLAIN
□ explain oneself □ explain something away
EXPLODE
□ explode a bombshell
EXTEND
□ extend credit to someone □ extend one's sympathy to someone
EXTENT
□ to a great extent □ to some extent
EXTENUATING
□ extenuating circumstances
EYE
□ An eye for an eye, a tooth for a tooth. □ apple of someone's eye □ be all eyes □ catch someone's eye □ close one's eyes to something □ cry one's eyes out

□ get a black eye □ get someone's eye □ get stars in one's eyes □ give someone a black eye □ give someone the eye □ have an eye for someone or something □ have an eye on someone or something □ have an eye out for someone or something □ have eyes bigger than one's stomach □ have eyes in the back of one's head □ have one's eye on someone or something □ have stars in one's eyes □ hit someone between the eyes □ hit the bull's-eye □ in one's mind's eye □ in the public eye □ in the twinkling of an eye □ keep an eye on someone or something □ keep an eye out for someone or something □ keep one's eye on someone or something □ keep one's eye on the ball □ keep one's eyes open for someone or something □ keep one's eyes peeled for someone or something □ keep one's weather eye open □ lay eyes on someone or something □ look at someone cross-eyed □ look someone in the eye □ make eyes at someone □ more to something than meets the eye □ one's eyes are bigger than one's stomach □ only have eyes for someone □ open someone's eyes to something □ out of the corner of one's eye □ pull the wool over someone's eyes □ see eye to eye about something □ set eyes on someone or something □ sight for sore eyes □ turn a blind eye to someone or something □ with an eye to doing something □ without batting an eye
EYEBROWS
□ cause eyebrows to raise □ raise some eyebrows
EYETEETH
□ cut one's eyeteeth on something
FACE
□ as plain as the nose on one's face □ blow up in someone's face □ can't see one's hand in front of one's face □ cut off one's nose to spite one's face □ do an about-face □ face someone down □ face someone or something □ face the music □ face to face □ face up to someone or something □ fall flat on one's face □ feed one's face □ fly in the face of someone or something □ get a red face □ give someone a red face □ have a red face □ have egg on one's face □

hide one's face in shame □ keep a straight face □ look someone in the face □ lose face □ make a face at someone □ not show one's face □ on the face of it □ red in the face □ save one's face □ say something right to someone's face □ stare someone in the face □ take something at face value □ talk until one is blue in the face □ tell one to one's face

FACT
□ after the fact □ as a matter of fact □ facts of life □ get down to the facts □ in fact □ matter-of-fact

FAIL
□ fail to do something □ without fail

FAIR
□ do something fair and square □ fair to middling □ fair-weather friend □ get a fair shake from someone □ give someone a fair shake □ play fair

FAITH
□ act of faith □ in bad faith □ in good faith □ pin one's faith on someone or something □ show good faith □ take something on faith

FAKE
□ fake someone out

FALL
(See also *FELL*.)□ as easy as falling off a log □ break someone's fall □ fall all over oneself □ fall all over someone □ fall apart at the seams □ fall apart □ fall asleep □ fall back from something □ fall back on someone or something □ fall behind in something □ fall behind on something □ fall behind □ fall by the wayside □ fall down on the job □ fall flat on one's face □ fall for someone or something □ fall in for something □ fall in line □ fall in love with someone □ fall in place □ fall in with someone or something □ fall in □ fall into a trap □ fall off something □ fall off □ fall on someone or something □ fall out with someone over something □ fall out □ fall over backwards to do something □ fall over someone or something □ fall over □ fall short of something □ fall through □ fall to pieces □ fall to □ fall upon someone or something □ have a falling-out with someone over something □ riding for a fall

FALSE
□ sail under false colors

FAMILIAR
□ have a familiar ring

FAMILIARITY
□ Familiarity breeds contempt.

FAMILY
□ all in the family □ black sheep of the family □ in a family way □ in the family way □ like one of the family □ run in the family

FAMINE
□ either feast or famine

FAN
□ be a fan of someone

FANCY
□ strike someone's fancy □ take a fancy to someone or something □ tickle someone's fancy

FAR
□ as far as anyone knows □ as far as I'm concerned □ as far as it goes □ as far as possible □ come from far and wide □ far and away the best □ far be it from me to do something □ far cry from something □ Far from it. □ far into the night □ far out □ few and far between □ go so far as to say something □ go too far □ So far, so good.

FARM
□ farm someone or something out

FASHION
□ after a fashion □ after the fashion of someone or something □ go out of fashion □ out of fashion

FAST
□ get nowhere fast □ hard-and-fast rule □ make a fast buck □ play fast and loose with someone or something □ pull a fast one

FAT
□ chew the fat □ live off the fat of the land □ The fat is in the fire.

FATE
□ leave one to one's fate

FATHER
□ old enough to be someone's father

FATTED
□ kill the fatted calf

FAULT
□ find fault with someone or something □ generous to a fault

FAVOR
□ curry favor with someone □ decide

in favor of someone or something ☐ in favor of someone or something ☐ in someone's favor ☐ out of favor with someone ☐ return the favor

FEAR
☐ for fear of something ☐ in fear and trembling ☐ never fear

FEAST
☐ either feast or famine ☐ feast one's eyes on someone or something

FEATHER
☐ as light as a feather ☐ Birds of a feather flock together. ☐ feather in one's cap ☐ feather one's nest ☐ in fine feather ☐ knock someone over with a feather ☐ make the feathers fly ☐ tar and feather someone

FEDERAL
☐ make a federal case out of something

FEED
☐ bite the hand that feeds one ☐ fed up with someone or something ☐ feed one's face ☐ feed someone a line ☐ feed the kitty ☐ for chicken feed ☐ put on the feed bag

FEEL
☐ feel compelled to do something ☐ feel dragged out ☐ feel fit ☐ feel free to do something ☐ feel it beneath one to do something ☐ feel like a million dollars ☐ feel like a new person ☐ feel like something ☐ feel out of place ☐ feel put upon ☐ feel someone out ☐ feel something in one's bones ☐ feel up to something ☐ get the feel of something ☐ have the feel of something

FEELERS
☐ put out feelers

FEELINGS
☐ have mixed feelings about someone or something ☐ hurt someone's feelings ☐ no hard feelings

FEET
(See also *FOOT.*)☐ dead on one's or its feet ☐ get a load off one's feet ☐ get back on one's feet ☐ get cold feet ☐ get one's feet on the ground ☐ get one's feet wet ☐ get to one's feet ☐ have cold feet ☐ have feet of clay ☐ have one's feet on the ground ☐ keep one's feet on the ground ☐ knock one off one's feet ☐ land on both feet ☐ land on one's feet ☐ let grass grow under one's feet

☐ regain one's feet ☐ stand on one's own two feet ☐ sweep one off one's feet ☐ take a load off one's feet ☐ think on one's feet ☐ throw oneself at someone's feet

FELL
☐ at one fell swoop

FELLOW
☐ hail fellow well met

FENCE
☐ fence someone in ☐ fenced in ☐ mend one's fences ☐ on the fence about something

FEND
☐ fend for oneself

FERRET
☐ ferret something out of someone or something

FEVER
☐ run a fever

FEW
☐ few and far between ☐ wash a few things out

FIDDLE
☐ as fit as a fiddle ☐ fiddle around with someone or something ☐ play second fiddle to someone

FIELD
☐ out in left field ☐ play the field

FIFTY
☐ divide something fifty-fifty ☐ split something fifty-fifty

FIGHT
☐ fight against time ☐ fight someone or something hammer and tongs ☐ fight someone or something off ☐ fight someone or something tooth and nail ☐ go down fighting ☐ knock-down-drag-out fight ☐ Them's fighting words.

FIGURE
☐ cut a fine figure ☐ figure in something ☐ figure on something ☐ figure someone or something in ☐ figure someone or something out ☐ figure something up ☐ in round figures ☐ It figures.

FILE
☐ have something on file ☐ in single file ☐ rank and file

FILL
☐ fill in for someone ☐ fill out ☐ fill someone in on someone or something ☐ fill someone or something in ☐ fill someone or something up ☐ fill someone's shoes ☐ fill something out ☐ fill

the bill □ fill the gap □ get one's fill of someone or something □ have one's fill of someone or something

FIND
□ find fault with someone or something □ find it in one's heart to do something □ find one's or something's way somewhere □ find one's tongue □ find one's way around □ find oneself □ find out about someone or something □ find someone or something out □ find something out the hard way

FINDERS
□ Finders keepers, losers weepers.

FINE
□ cut a fine figure □ fine kettle of fish □ go over something with a fine-tooth comb □ in fine feather

FINGER
□ cross one's fingers □ get one's fingers burned □ have one's finger in the pie □ have sticky fingers □ keep one's fingers crossed for someone or something □ lay a finger on someone or something □ lay the finger on someone □ not lift a finger to help someone □ put one's finger on something □ put the finger on someone □ slip through someone's fingers □ twist someone around one's little finger □ work one's fingers to the bone

FINGERTIPS
□ have something at one's fingertips

FINISH
□ finish something up □ finish up □ from start to finish

FIRE
□ add fuel to the fire □ ball of fire □ build a fire under someone □ catch fire □ catch on fire □ caught in the crossfire □ draw fire away from someone or something □ fire away at someone or something □ have too many irons in the fire □ hold one's fire □ keep the home fires burning □ like a house on fire □ open fire on someone □ out of the frying pan, into the fire □ play with fire □ set fire to someone or something □ set someone or something on fire □ set the world on fire □ The fat is in the fire. □ under fire □ Where there's smoke there's fire.

FIRST
□ at first blush □ at first glance □ at first □ cast the first stone □ first and foremost □ First come, first served. □ first of all □ first off □ first thing in the morning □ First things first. □ get to first base with someone or something □ in the first place □ love at first sight □ not know the first thing about someone or something □ of the first water □ on a first name basis with someone □ play first chair □ reach first base with someone or something

FISH
□ be a cold fish □ fine kettle of fish □ fish for a compliment □ fish for something □ fish or cut bait □ go on a fishing expedition □ have other fish to fry □ like a fish out of water □ neither fish nor fowl □ There are plenty of other fish in the sea

FIST
□ hand over fist

FIT
□ as fit as a fiddle □ by fits and starts □ feel fit □ fit for a king □ fit in with someone or something □ fit like a glove □ fit someone or something into something □ fit someone or something out with something □ fit someone to a T □ fit to be tied □ fit to kill □ have a fit □ If the shoe fits, wear it. □ see fit to do something □ survival of the fittest □ think someone or something fit for something □ throw a fit

FIVE
□ nine-to-five job □ take five

FIX
□ fix someone or something up □ fix someone up with someone or something □ fix someone's wagon □ get a fix on something □ have a fix on something □ in a fix □ well-fixed

FIZZLE
□ fizzle out

FLAG
□ flag someone or something down

FLAME
□ burn with a low blue flame □ burst into flames □ go up in flames

FLARE
□ flare up

FLASH
□ flash in the pan □ in a flash

FLAT
□ as flat as a pancake □ fall flat on

one's face ☐ flat broke ☐ flat out ☐ in nothing flat ☐ leave someone flat
FLESH
☐ flesh and blood ☐ flesh out ☐ flesh something out ☐ in the flesh
FLING
☐ fling oneself at someone
FLIP
☐ do a flip-flop on something ☐ flip one's lid ☐ flip one's wig
FLOAT
☐ float a loan
FLOCK
☐ Birds of a feather flock together.
FLOOR
☐ get in on the ground floor ☐ get the floor ☐ have the floor ☐ mop up the floor with someone ☐ walk the floor ☐ wipe up the floor with someone
FLOP
☐ do a flip-flop on something
FLUFF
☐ fluff one's lines
FLUNK
☐ flunk out ☐ flunk someone out
FLY
☐ as the crow flies ☐ do something on the fly ☐ fly in the face of someone or something ☐ fly in the ointment ☐ fly in the teeth of someone or something ☐ fly off the handle ☐ fly the coop ☐ fly-by-night ☐ Go fly a kite! ☐ make the feathers fly ☐ make the fur fly ☐ with flying colors
FOAM
☐ foam at the mouth
FOB
☐ fob something off on someone
FOG
☐ in a fog
FOLD
☐ fold something up
FOLLOW
☐ follow in someone's footsteps ☐ follow in someone's tracks ☐ follow one's heart ☐ follow one's nose ☐ follow someone or something up ☐ follow suit ☐ follow through on something ☐ follow up on someone or something ☐ tough act to follow
FOND
☐ fond of someone or something
FOOD
☐ food for thought

FOOL
☐ A fool and his money are soon parted. ☐ fool around with someone or something ☐ make a fool out of someone
FOOLISH
☐ penny wise and pound foolish
FOOT
(See also *FEET*.)☐ bound hand and foot ☐ foot the bill ☐ get off on the wrong foot ☐ get one's foot in the door ☐ have foot-in-mouth disease ☐ have one's foot in the door ☐ have the shoe on the other foot ☐ hot foot it out of somewhere ☐ not set foot somewhere ☐ on foot ☐ put one's best foot forward ☐ put one's foot down about something ☐ put one's foot in one's mouth ☐ set foot somewhere ☐ stick one's foot in one's mouth ☐ The shoe is on the other foot. ☐ wait on someone hand and foot
FOOTSIE
☐ play footsie with someone
FOOTSTEPS
☐ follow in someone's footsteps
FORCE
☐ driving force behind someone or something ☐ force someone out of something ☐ force someone to the wall ☐ force someone's hand ☐ in force ☐ join forces with someone ☐ out in force
FORE
☐ come to the fore
FOREMOST
☐ first and foremost
FOREST
☐ not able to see the forest for the trees
FOREVER
☐ forever and a day ☐ forever and ever
FORGET
☐ forget oneself ☐ forgive and forget
FORGIVE
☐ forgive and forget
FORK
☐ fork money out for something ☐ fork something over
FORM
☐ form an opinion ☐ true to form
FORT
☐ hold the fort
FORTH
☐ back and forth ☐ hold forth ☐ launch forth on something ☐ set forth on something

FORTY
□ catch forty winks □ take forty winks
FORWARD
□ look forward to something □ put one's best foot forward □ put something forward
FOUL
□ foul play □ foul someone or something up □ foul up
FOURS
□ on all fours
FOWL
□ neither fish nor fowl
FOX
□ as smart as a fox
FREE
□ as free as a bird □ feel free to do something □ free and easy □ free-for-all □ get a free hand with something □ give free rein to someone □ give someone a free hand with something □ go scot-free □ make free with someone or something □ of one's own free will □ set someone or something free
FREEDOM
□ give one one's freedom
FRESH
□ breath of fresh air □ fresh out of something □ get fresh with someone
FRIEND
□ A friend in need is a friend indeed. □ be friends with someone □ fair-weather friend □ make friends with someone
FRIENDSHIP
□ strike up a friendship
FRIGHTEN
□ frighten one out of one's wits □ frighten someone to death □ frighten the wits out of someone □ frightened to death
FRITTER
□ fritter something away
FRITZ
□ on the fritz
FRO
□ to and fro
FROG
□ big frog in a small pond
FROM
□ across from someone or something □ another country heard from □ arise from something □ aside from someone or something □ away from one's

desk □ back down from someone or something □ back off from someone or something □ be from Missouri □ break away from someone or something □ break loose from someone or something □ come from far and wide □ come up from behind □ cut loose from someone or something □ cut the ground out from under someone □ downhill from here on □ draw fire away from someone or something □ everything from A to Z □ everything from soup to nuts □ fall back from something □ far be it from me to do something □ far cry from something □ Far from it. □ from day to day □ from hand to hand □ from pillar to post □ from rags to riches □ from start to finish □ from stem to stern □ from the bottom of one's heart □ from the ground up □ from the heart □ from the outset □ from the word go □ from this day on □ from time to time □ from top to bottom □ from way back □ get a dirty look from someone □ get a fair shake from someone □ get away from it all □ get away from someone or something □ get out from under someone or something □ go from bad to worse □ hail from somewhere □ hear from someone □ keep away from someone or something □ keep one's distance from someone or something □ keep someone from doing something □ keep the wolf from the door □ know something from memory □ learn something from the bottom up □ live from hand to mouth □ make something from scratch □ not know from nothing □ not know someone from Adam □ out from under something □ pull the rug out from under someone □ run away from someone or something □ separate the men from the boys □ separate the sheep from the goats □ shoot from the hip □ shy away from someone or something □ start from scratch □ stay away from someone or something □ step down from something □ straight from the horse's mouth □ straight from the shoulder □ take off from work □ where one is coming from
FRONT
□ can't see one's hand in front of one's

399

face ☐ in front of someone or something ☐ out front ☐ put up a brave front ☐ up front
FRUIT
☐ bear fruit
FRUITCAKE
☐ nutty as a fruitcake
FRY
☐ have other fish to fry ☐ out of the frying pan, into the fire
FUEL
☐ add fuel to the fire
FULL
☐ as full as a tick ☐ at full speed ☐ at full tilt ☐ full of beans ☐ full of bull ☐ full of hot air ☐ full of Old Nick ☐ full of prunes ☐ full of the devil ☐ get into full swing ☐ have one's hands full with someone or something ☐ in full swing
FUN
☐ fun and games ☐ make fun of someone or something ☐ poke fun at someone
FUNNY
☐ as funny as a crutch ☐ strike someone funny
FUR
☐ make the fur fly ☐ rub someone's fur the wrong way
FURTHER
☐ without further ado
FUSE
☐ blow a fuse
FUSS
☐ fuss over someone or something ☐ kick up a fuss ☐ make a fuss over someone or something
FUTURE
☐ in the near future
GAB
☐ have the gift of gab
GAIN
☐ gain on someone or something ☐ Nothing ventured, nothing gained.
GALLERY
☐ play to the gallery
GAME
☐ ahead of the game ☐ at this stage of the game ☐ fun and games ☐ game at which two can play ☐ give the game away ☐ name of the game ☐ new ball game
GANDER
☐ take a gander at someone or some-

thing ☐ What is sauce for the goose is sauce for the gander.
GANG
☐ gang up on someone
GAP
☐ fill the gap
GARDEN
☐ lead someone down the garden path
GAS
☐ gas up ☐ out of gas ☐ run out of gas ☐ step on the gas
GASKET
☐ blow a gasket
GATE
☐ get the gate ☐ give someone the gate
GATHER
☐ A rolling stone gathers no moss.
GAUNTLET
☐ throw down the gauntlet
GEAR
☐ get into high gear ☐ in high gear
GENERAL
☐ as a general rule
GENEROUS
☐ generous to a fault
GHOST
☐ ghost of a chance ☐ give up the ghost
GIFT
☐ Don't look a gift horse in the mouth. ☐ have the gift of gab
GILD
☐ gild the lily
GILLS
☐ blue around the gills ☐ green around the gills ☐ pale around the gills
GIRD
☐ gird one's loins
GIVE
☐ give a good account of oneself ☐ give an account of someone or something ☐ give an ear to someone or something ☐ give as good as one gets ☐ give birth to someone or something ☐ give chase to someone or something ☐ give credence to something ☐ give credit where credit is due ☐ give free rein to someone ☐ give ground ☐ give in to someone or something ☐ give it the gun ☐ give it to someone ☐ give of oneself ☐ give one a run for one's money ☐ Give one an inch, and one will take a mile. ☐ give one butterflies in one's stomach ☐ give one one's freedom ☐ give one one's walking papers

☐ give oneself airs ☐ give oneself up to someone or something ☐ give out with something ☐ give out ☐ give rise to something ☐ give someone a bang ☐ give someone a big send-off ☐ give someone a black eye ☐ give someone a break ☐ give someone a buzz ☐ give someone a check-up ☐ give someone a clean bill of health ☐ give someone a dirty look ☐ give someone a fair shake ☐ give someone a free hand with something ☐ give someone a grasp of something ☐ give someone a hand for something ☐ give someone a hand with something ☐ give someone a hard time ☐ give someone a head start on someone or something ☐ give someone a licking ☐ give someone a line ☐ give someone a pain ☐ give someone a pat on the back ☐ give someone a piece of one's mind ☐ give someone a rain check ☐ give someone a raw deal ☐ give someone a red face ☐ give someone a reputation as a something ☐ give someone a reputation for doing something ☐ give someone a ring ☐ give someone a rough idea about something ☐ give someone a shellacking ☐ give someone a slap on the wrist ☐ give someone a start ☐ give someone a swelled head ☐ give someone a tongue-lashing ☐ give someone credit for something ☐ give someone gray hair ☐ give someone hell ☐ give someone or something a wide berth ☐ give someone or something away ☐ give someone or something the once-over ☐ give someone or something up ☐ give someone pause ☐ give someone some skin ☐ give someone the air ☐ give someone the ax ☐ give someone the benefit of the doubt ☐ give someone the boot ☐ give someone the brushoff ☐ give someone the business ☐ give someone the cold shoulder ☐ give someone the creeps ☐ give someone the eye ☐ give someone the gate ☐ give someone the glad hand ☐ give someone the go-ahead ☐ give someone the go-by ☐ give someone the green light ☐ give someone the hard sell ☐ give someone the high sign ☐ give someone the low-down on someone or something ☐ give someone the old heave-ho ☐ give some-

one the red carpet treatment ☐ give someone the runaround ☐ give someone the sack ☐ give someone the shirt off one's back ☐ give someone the slip ☐ give someone the third degree ☐ give someone the willies ☐ give someone the works ☐ give someone tit for tat ☐ give someone to understand something ☐ give someone what for ☐ give something a lick and a promise ☐ give something off ☐ give something one's best shot ☐ give something out ☐ give the bride away ☐ give the devil his due ☐ give the game away ☐ give up the ghost ☐ give up ☐ give vent to something ☐ give voice to something ☐ give way to someone or something ☐ given to understand ☐ not give a hang about anyone or anything ☐ not give a hoot about anyone or anything ☐ not give anyone the time of day ☐ What gives?

GLAD

☐ get the glad hand ☐ give someone the glad hand

GLANCE

☐ at first glance ☐ glance at someone or something ☐ glance something over

GLASS

☐ have a glass jaw

GLITTER

☐ All that glitters is not gold.

GLORY

☐ in one's glory

GLOSS

☐ gloss something over

GLOVE

☐ fit like a glove ☐ hand in glove with someone ☐ handle someone with kid gloves

GO

☐ all gone ☐ all systems are go ☐ as far as it goes ☐ buy something to go ☐ easy come, easy go ☐ enough to go around ☐ from the word go ☐ get something to go ☐ get the go-ahead ☐ get the go-by ☐ get-up-and-go ☐ give someone the go-ahead ☐ give someone the go-by ☐ go a long way toward doing something ☐ go about doing something ☐ go about one's business ☐ go after someone or something ☐ go against the grain ☐ go ahead with something ☐ go all out ☐ go all the way to somewhere ☐ go all the way with someone ☐ go along for the ride ☐ go along with someone or something ☐ go ape over someone or something ☐ go around in circles ☐ go around with someone ☐ go astray ☐ go at it hammer and tongs ☐ go at it tooth and nail ☐ go at someone or something ☐ go away empty-handed ☐ go AWOL ☐ go back on one's word ☐ go back ☐ go bad ☐ go bananas ☐ go begging ☐ go broke ☐ go by the board ☐ go chase oneself ☐ go cold turkey ☐ go down fighting ☐ go down in history ☐ go downhill ☐ go Dutch ☐ go easy on someone or something ☐ Go fly a kite! ☐ go for broke ☐ go for it ☐ go for someone or something ☐ go from bad to worse ☐ go great guns ☐ go haywire ☐ go hog wild ☐ go in a body ☐ go in for something ☐ go in one ear and out the other ☐ go into a nose dive ☐ go into a tailspin ☐ go into action ☐ go into effect ☐ go into one's song and dance about something ☐ go into orbit ☐ go into something ☐ go it alone ☐ go like clockwork ☐ go off half-cocked ☐ go off the deep end ☐ go off ☐ go on a binge ☐ go on a fishing expedition ☐ go on an errand ☐ go on and on ☐ go on doing something ☐ go on strike ☐ go on with something ☐ go on ☐ go out for something ☐ go out in search of someone or something ☐ go out of fashion ☐ go out of one's way to do something ☐ go out of style ☐ go out with someone ☐ go over like a lead balloon ☐ go over someone's head ☐ go over something with a fine-tooth comb ☐ go over something ☐ go over with a bang ☐ go overboard ☐ go places ☐ go right through someone ☐ go round the bend ☐ go scot-free ☐ go sky high ☐ go so far as to say something ☐ go someone one better ☐ go stag ☐ go steady with someone ☐ go stir crazy ☐ go straight ☐ go the distance ☐ go the limit ☐ go through channels ☐ go through something ☐ go through the changes ☐ go through the motions ☐ go through the roof ☐ go through with something ☐ go through ☐ go to any length ☐ go to bat for someone ☐ go to bed with someone ☐ go to bed with the chickens ☐ go to Davy Jones's

locker ☐ go to hell in a handbasket ☐ go to hell ☐ go to pieces ☐ go to pot ☐ go to rack and ruin ☐ go to seed ☐ go to someone's head ☐ go to the bathroom ☐ go to the devil ☐ go to the dogs ☐ go to the expense of doing something ☐ go to the limit ☐ go to the trouble of doing something ☐ go to the trouble to do something ☐ go to the wall ☐ go to town ☐ go to waste ☐ go to ☐ go together ☐ go too far ☐ go under the knife ☐ go under ☐ go up in flames ☐ go up in smoke ☐ go whole hog ☐ go with someone or something ☐ go without something ☐ go wrong ☐ goes to show you ☐ goes without saying ☐ gone on ☐ have a go at something ☐ have a good thing going ☐ have a lot going for one ☐ have a thing going with someone ☐ have one's heart go out to someone ☐ have something going for oneself ☐ have something going with someone ☐ have something to go ☐ Here goes nothing. ☐ let go of someone or something ☐ let go with something ☐ let oneself go ☐ let someone or something go ☐ make a go of it ☐ not able to go on ☐ not know whether one is coming or going ☐ off someone or something goes ☐ on the go ☐ one's heart goes out to someone ☐ order something to go ☐ pay as you go ☐ So it goes. ☐ Sunday-go-to-meeting clothes ☐ touch and go ☐ What goes? ☐ What's going on?

GOAT
☐ get someone's goat ☐ separate the sheep from the goats

GOD
☐ act of God

GOLD
☐ All that glitters is not gold. ☐ as good as gold ☐ have a heart of gold ☐ worth its weight in gold

GOLDEN
☐ kill the goose that laid the golden egg

GOLLY
☐ by guess and by golly

GONE
(See GO.)

GONER
☐ be a goner

GOOD
(See also BEST, BETTER.)☐ all in good

time ☐ all to the good ☐ as good as done ☐ as good as gold ☐ do someone good ☐ do someone's heart good ☐ for good measure ☐ for good ☐ get on the good side of someone ☐ get the goods on someone ☐ give a good account of oneself ☐ give as good as one gets ☐ good and something ☐ good enough for someone or something ☐ good riddance ☐ good-for-nothing ☐ have a good command of something ☐ have a good head on one's shoulders ☐ have a good thing going ☐ in good condition ☐ in good faith ☐ in good shape ☐ in good time ☐ in good with someone ☐ keep good time ☐ keep on the good side of someone ☐ make good as something ☐ make good at something ☐ make good money ☐ make good on something ☐ make good time ☐ make someone look good ☐ make something good ☐ never had it so good ☐ on good terms with someone ☐ One good turn deserves another. ☐ put in a good word for someone ☐ put something to good use ☐ sell someone a bill of goods ☐ show good faith ☐ show something to good advantage ☐ So far, so good. ☐ stand someone in good stead ☐ throw good money after bad ☐ too good to be true ☐ too much of a good thing ☐ up to no good ☐ well and good ☐ What's the good of something? ☐ when one is good and ready ☐ Your guess is as good as mine.

GOODBYE
☐ kiss something goodbye

GOODNESS
☐ honest to goodness

GOOF
☐ goof off

GOOSE
☐ cook someone's goose ☐ get goose bumps ☐ have goose bumps ☐ kill the goose that laid the golden egg ☐ What is sauce for the goose is sauce for the gander. ☐ wild-goose chase

GOT
☐ Cat got your tongue? ☐ have got to do something ☐ What's gotten into someone?

GRABS
☐ up for grabs

GRADE
☐ make the grade

GRAIN
☐ go against the grain ☐ take something with a grain of salt

GRAND
☐ as busy as Grand Central Station

GRANTED
☐ take someone or something for granted

GRASP
☐ get a grasp of something ☐ give someone a grasp of something ☐ grasp at straws ☐ have a grasp of something

GRASS
☐ let grass grow under one's feet ☐ snake-in-the-grass

GRASSHOPPER
☐ knee-high to a grasshopper

GRAVE
☐ turn over in one's grave

GRAVY
☐ ride the gravy train

GRAY
☐ get gray hair ☐ give someone gray hair

GREASE
☐ as quick as greased lightning ☐ grease someone's palm ☐ use some elbow grease

GREAT
☐ by a great deal ☐ go great guns ☐ in great haste ☐ make a great show of something ☐ no great shakes ☐ set great store by someone or something ☐ think a great deal of someone or something ☐ to a great extent

GREEK
☐ Greek to me

GREEN
☐ get the green light ☐ give someone the green light ☐ green around the gills ☐ green with envy ☐ have a green thumb

GRIEF
☐ come to grief

GRIEVANCE
☐ air one's grievances

GRIN
☐ grin and bear it

GRIND
(See also *GROUND*.)☐ grind to a halt ☐ have an ax to grind ☐ the daily grind

GRINDSTONE
☐ keep one's nose to the grindstone ☐ put one's nose to the grindstone

GRIP
□ come to grips with something □ lose one's grip

GRIT
□ grit one's teeth

GRITTY
□ get down to the nitty-gritty

GROOVE
□ in the groove

GROSS
□ gross someone out

GROUND
□ break ground for something □ break new ground □ cover a lot of ground □ cut the ground out from under someone □ drive something into the ground □ from the ground up □ get in on the ground floor □ get one's feet on the ground □ get something off the ground □ give ground □ ground someone □ have one's ear to the ground □ have one's feet on the ground □ hold one's ground □ keep one's ear to the ground □ keep one's feet on the ground □ lose ground □ one's old stamping ground □ run something into the ground □ stand one's ground

GROW
□ grow on someone □ grow out of something □ grow up □ have growing pains □ let grass grow under one's feet

GRUDGE
□ bear a grudge against someone □ have a grudge against someone □ hold a grudge against someone □ nurse a grudge against someone

GUARD
□ catch someone off guard □ guard against someone or something □ on guard

GUESS
□ by guess and by golly □ guess at something □ have another guess coming □ out-guess someone □ Your guess is as good as mine.

GUINEA
□ serve as a guinea pig

GUM
□ beat one's gums □ gum something up □ gum up the works

GUN
□ beat the gun □ give it the gun □ go great guns □ gun for someone □ jump the gun □ son of a gun □ stick to one's guns

GUT
□ bust a gut □ hate someone's guts

GUTTER
□ in the gutter

HABIT
□ kick a habit

HACK
□ hack something up □ hack something

HACKLES
□ get someone's hackles up

HAIL
□ hail fellow well met □ hail from somewhere □ within hailing distance

HAIR
□ by a hair's breadth □ curl someone's hair □ get gray hair □ get in someone's hair □ give someone gray hair □ hair of the dog that bit one □ hang by a hair □ let one's hair down □ make someone's hair stand on end □ neither hide nor hair □ part someone's hair □ split hairs □ tear one's hair

HALE
□ hale and hearty

HALF
□ at half mast □ be half-hearted about someone or something □ go off half-cocked □ Half a loaf is better than none. □ have half a mind to do something □ have half a notion to do something □ not half bad □ one's better half □ six of one and half a dozen of the other

HALFWAY
□ meet someone halfway

HALT
□ bring something to a halt □ call a halt to something □ grind to a halt

HAM
□ ham something up

HAMBURGER
□ make hamburger out of someone or something

HAMMER
□ fight someone or something hammer and tongs □ go at it hammer and tongs □ hammer away at someone or something □ hammer something out

HAND
□ A bird in the hand is worth two in the bush. □ at hand □ bite the hand that feeds one □ bound hand and foot □ can't see one's hand in front of one's face □ catch someone red-handed □

close at hand □ come away empty-handed □ dirty one's hands □ do something by hand □ do something hands down □ eat out of someone's hands □ for something to change hands □ force someone's hand □ from hand to hand □ get a free hand with something □ get a hand for something □ get a hand with something □ get one's hands dirty □ get one's hands off someone or something □ get one's hands on someone or something □ get the glad hand □ get the upper hand on someone □ give someone a free hand with something □ give someone a hand for something □ give someone a hand with something □ give someone the glad hand □ go away empty-handed □ hand in glove with someone □ hand in hand □ hand it to someone □ hand over fist □ hand over hand □ hand something down to someone □ hand something in □ hand something on to someone □ hand something out to someone □ hand something over □ hand-me-down □ Hands off! □ Hands up! □ have a hand in something □ have clean hands □ have one's hand in the till □ have one's hands full with someone or something □ have one's hands tied □ have someone or something in one's hands □ have someone or something on one's hands □ have something at hand □ have something in hand □ have the upper hand on someone □ keep one's hand in something □ keep one's hands off someone or something □ know someone or something like the back of one's hand □ know someone or something like the palm of one's hand □ lay one's hands on someone or something □ lend someone a hand □ lift a hand against someone or something □ live from hand to mouth □ near at hand □ old hand at doing something □ on one hand □ on the one hand □ on the other hand □ out of hand □ pay someone a left-handed compliment □ play into someone's hands □ put one's hand to the plow □ put one's hands on something □ raise a hand against someone or something □ shake hands on something □ shake hands with someone □ sit on its hands □ sit on one's hands □

soil one's hands □ take a hand in something □ take one's hands off someone or something □ take the law into one's own hands □ throw up one's hands in despair □ throw up one's hands in horror □ tie someone's hands □ Time hangs heavy on someone's hands. □ try one's hand at something □ wait on someone hand and foot □ wash one's hands of someone or something □ with one hand tied behind one's back

HANDBASKET
□ go to hell in a handbasket

HANDFUL
□ by the handful

HANDLE
□ fly off the handle □ get a handle on something □ handle someone with kid gloves □ have a handle on something

HANDWRITING
□ see the handwriting on the wall

HANDY
□ come in handy

HANG
(See also *HUNG*.)□ get the hang of something □ hang a left □ hang a right □ hang around with someone □ hang back □ hang by a hair □ hang in the balance □ hang in there □ hang loose □ hang on someone's coattails □ hang on someone's every word □ hang on to someone or something □ Hang on to your hat! □ Hang on! □ hang out somewhere □ hang out with someone □ hang someone in effigy □ hang something out □ hang something up □ hang together □ hang tough □ hang up □ have something hanging over one's head □ keep someone or something hanging in midair □ leave someone or something hanging in midair □ let it all hang out □ not give a hang about anyone or anything □ Time hangs heavy on someone's hands.

HAPPEN
□ happen on someone or something □ sit back and let something happen

HAPPY
□ as happy as a clam □ as happy as a lark □ strike a happy medium

HARD
□ as hard as nails □ between a rock and a hard place □ cold, hard cash □ come down hard on someone or some-

thing □ do something the hard way □ drive a hard bargain □ find something out the hard way □ get a hard time □ get the hard sell □ give someone a hard time □ give someone the hard sell □ hard nut to crack □ hard on someone's heels □ hard pressed to do something □ hard put to do something □ hard up for something □ hard-and-fast rule □ learn something the hard way □ no hard feelings □ play hard to get □ take a hard line with someone

HARDLY
□ hardly have time to breathe

HARE
□ as mad as a March hare

HARK
□ hark back to something

HASH
□ hash something over

HASTE
□ Haste makes waste. □ in great haste

HAT
□ at the drop of a hat □ be old hat □ eat one's hat □ Hang on to your hat! □ Hold on to your hat! □ keep something under one's hat □ pass the hat □ pull something out of a hat □ take off one's hat to someone □ talk through one's hat □ toss one's hat into the ring □ wear more than one hat

HATBAND
□ as tight as Dick's hatband

HATCH
□ count one's chickens before they hatch □ down the hatch

HATCHET
□ bury the hatchet

HATE
□ hate someone's guts

HATTER
□ as mad as a hatter

HAUL
□ haul someone or something in □ haul someone over the coals □ haul up somewhere □ over the long haul □ over the short haul

HAVOC
□ play havoc with someone or something □ raise havoc with someone or something □ wreak havoc with something

HAW
□ hem and haw around

HAY
□ hit the hay □ Make hay while the sun is shining. □ That ain't hay.

HAYSTACK
□ like looking for a needle in a haystack

HAYWIRE
□ go haywire

HEAD
□ able to do something standing on one's head □ bang one's head against a brick wall □ beat one's head against the wall □ beat something into someone's head □ bury one's head in the sand □ can't make heads or tails of someone or something □ come to a head □ get a head start on someone or something □ get a swelled head □ get one's head above water □ get something into someone's thick head □ give someone a head start on someone or something □ give someone a swelled head □ go over someone's head □ go to someone's head □ have a good head on one's shoulders □ have a head start on someone or something □ have a price on one's head □ have a swelled head □ have eyes in the back of one's head □ have one's head in the clouds □ have rocks in one's head □ have something hanging over one's head □ head and shoulders above someone or something □ head for someone or something □ head into something □ head over heels in love with someone □ head someone or something into someone or something □ head someone or something off □ head something out □ head something up □ hide one's head in the sand □ hit the nail on the head □ hold one's head up □ in over one's head □ keep a civil tongue in one's head □ keep one's head above water □ knock some heads together □ lose one's head over someone or something □ make someone's head spin □ make someone's head swim □ off the top of one's head □ on someone's head □ out of one's head □ put ideas into someone's head □ run around like a chicken with its head cut off □ talk someone's head off □ touched in the head □ trouble one's head about someone or something □ turn someone's head □ use one's head

HEALTH
□ get a clean bill of health □ give someone a clean bill of health □ in the best of health
HEALTHY
□ Early to bed, early to rise, makes a man healthy, wealthy, and wise.
HEAR
□ another country heard from □ hear from someone □ hear of someone or something □ so still you could hear a pin drop □ will not hear of something
HEART
□ be half-hearted about someone or something □ break someone's heart □ cross one's heart and hope to die □ die of a broken heart □ do someone's heart good □ eat one's heart out □ find it in one's heart to do something □ follow one's heart □ from the bottom of one's heart □ from the heart □ get to the heart of the matter □ have a heart of gold □ have a heart of stone □ have a heart □ have a heart-to-heart talk □ have a soft spot in one's heart for someone or something □ have one's heart go out to someone □ have one's heart in one's mouth □ have one's heart in the right place □ have one's heart miss a beat □ have one's heart on one's sleeve □ have one's heart set against something □ have one's heart set on something □ have one's heart skip a beat □ have one's heart stand still □ know something by heart □ learn something by heart □ lose heart □ one's heart goes out to someone □ open one's heart to someone □ pour one's heart out to someone □ take heart □ take something to heart □ to one's heart's content □ warm the cockles of someone's heart □ wear one's heart on one's sleeve □ with a heavy heart □ with all one's heart and soul
HEARTY
□ hale and hearty
HEAT
□ in a dead heat □ in heat □ put the heat on someone
HEAVE
□ get the old heave-ho □ give someone the old heave-ho
HEAVEN
□ in seventh heaven □ move heaven and earth to do something

HEAVY
□ Time hangs heavy on someone's hands. □ with a heavy heart
HECK
□ for the heck of it
HEDGE
□ hedge one's bets
HEED
□ take heed
HEELED
□ well-heeled
HEELS
□ cool one's heels □ down at the heels □ hard on someone's heels □ head over heels in love with someone □ kick up one's heels □ on the heels of something □ set one back on one's heels □ take to one's heels
HELL
□ as hot as hell □ as mad as hell □ catch hell □ come hell or high water □ for the hell of it □ give someone hell □ go to hell in a handbasket □ go to hell □ have a snowball's chance in hell □ like a bat out of hell □ through hell and high water
HELLBENT
□ hellbent for leather
HELLO
□ drop in to say hello
HELP
□ can't help but do something □ help oneself □ help someone or something out with someone or something □ not able to help something □ not lift a finger to help someone □ pitch in and help
HEM
□ hem and haw around □ hem someone or something in
HEN
□ as mad as a wet hen □ as scarce as hen's teeth □ scarcer than hen's teeth
HERD
□ ride herd on someone or something
HERE
□ downhill from here on □ have had it up to here □ here and there □ Here goes nothing. □ neither here nor there □ Same here. □ the here and now
HIDE
□ have someone's hide □ hide one's face in shame □ hide one's head in the sand □ hide one's light under a bushel □ neither hide nor hair □ tan someone's hide

HIGH

□ act high and mighty □ as high as a kite □ as high as the sky □ come hell or high water □ eat high on the hog □ get into high gear □ get the high sign □ give someone the high sign □ go sky high □ high man on the totem pole □ high on something □ high tail it out of somewhere □ hit the high spots □ in high gear □ It's high time. □ knee-high to a grasshopper □ leave someone high and dry □ live high off the hog □ live high on the hog □ look for someone or something high and low □ through hell and high water

HIGHLY

□ speak highly of someone or something □ think highly of someone or something

HILL

□ not worth a hill of beans □ over the hill

HINGE

□ hinge on something

HINT

□ take a hint

HIP

□ shoot from the hip

HIRE

□ hire someone out

HISTORY

□ go down in history

HIT

□ hit a snag □ hit and miss □ hit bottom □ hit it off with someone □ hit on something □ hit one close to home □ hit one where one lives □ hit one's stride □ hit pay dirt □ hit someone below the belt □ hit someone between the eyes □ hit someone like a ton of bricks □ hit someone up for something □ hit the books □ hit the bricks □ hit the bull's-eye □ hit the ceiling □ hit the hay □ hit the high spots □ hit the jackpot □ hit the nail on the head □ hit the sack □ hit the skids □ hit the spot □ hit upon something □ make a hit with someone or something □ pinch-hit for someone

HITCH

□ hitch a ride

HO

□ get the old heave-ho □ give someone the old heave-ho

HOB

□ play hob with someone or something □ raise hob with someone or something

HOE

□ tough row to hoe

HOG

□ eat high on the hog □ go hog wild □ go whole hog □ live high off the hog □ live high on the hog

HOLD

□ can't hold a candle to someone □ catch hold of someone or something □ Don't hold your breath. □ get hold of someone or something □ have hold of someone or something □ hold a grudge against someone □ hold a meeting □ hold all the aces □ hold forth □ Hold it! □ hold no brief for someone or something □ hold off doing something □ hold on to someone or something □ Hold on to your hat! □ hold on □ hold one's breath □ hold one's end up □ hold one's fire □ hold one's ground □ hold one's head up □ hold one's own □ hold one's peace □ hold one's temper □ hold one's tongue □ hold out for someone or something □ hold out the olive branch □ hold out □ hold someone accountable for something □ hold someone down □ hold someone or something at bay □ hold someone or something back □ hold someone or something in check □ hold someone or something off □ hold someone or something over □ hold someone or something still □ hold someone or something up as an example □ hold someone or something up □ hold something against someone □ hold still for something □ hold still □ hold the fort □ hold the line at someone or something □ hold tight □ hold true □ hold up on something □ hold up □ hold with something □ Hold your horses! □ lay hold of someone or something □ leave someone holding the bag □ no holds barred □ not hold a candle to someone or something □ not hold a stick to someone or something □ not hold water □ on hold □ put someone or something on hold □ take hold of someone or something □ won't hold water

HOLE

□ ace in the hole □ hole in one □ hole

up somewhere □ in the hole □ Money burns a hole in someone's pocket. □ out of the hole □ pick holes in something □ square peg in a round hole

HOLLOW
□ hollow something out

HOME
□ at home with someone or something □ at home □ bring home the bacon □ Charity begins at home. □ close to home □ come home to roost □ come home □ drive someone or something home □ eat someone out of house and home □ hit one close to home □ home in on someone or something □ keep the home fires burning □ make oneself at home □ nothing to write home about □ see someone home □ till the cows come home

HONEST
□ honest and above board □ honest to goodness

HONESTLY
□ come by something honestly

HONEYMOON
□ The honeymoon is over.

HONOR
□ do the honors □ honor someone's check □ in honor of someone or something □ on one's honor

HOOK
□ by hook or by crook □ get someone off the hook □ hook something up □ hooked on something □ let someone off the hook □ swallow something hook, line, and sinker

HOOKY
□ play hooky

HOOP
□ jump through a hoop

HOOT
□ not care two hoots about someone or something □ not give a hoot about anyone or anything

HOP
□ Hop to it! □ hopped up

HOPE
□ cross one's heart and hope to die □ hope against all hope □ in hopes of something

HOPELESS
□ hopeless at doing something

HORIZON
□ on the horizon

HORN
□ blow one's own horn □ horn in on someone □ lock horns with someone □ on the horns of a dilemma □ take the bull by the horns □ toot one's own horn

HORNET
□ as mad as a hornet □ stir up a hornet's nest

HORROR
□ throw up one's hands in horror

HORSE
□ beat a dead horse □ change horses in midstream □ Don't look a gift horse in the mouth. □ eat like a horse □ get a Charley horse □ have a Charley horse □ Hold your horses! □ horse around □ horse of a different color □ horse of another color □ horse play □ put the cart before the horse □ straight from the horse's mouth □ Wild horses couldn't drag someone. □ work like a horse

HOT
□ as hot as hell □ blow hot and cold □ full of hot air □ hot and bothered □ Hot enough for you? □ hot foot it out of somewhere □ hot under the collar □ in hot water □ in the hot seat □ make it hot for someone □ on the hot seat □ strike while the iron is hot

HOTCAKES
□ for something to sell like hotcakes

HOUR
□ after hours □ all hours of the day and night □ at the eleventh hour □ by the hour □ eleventh-hour decision □ for hours on end □ keep late hours □ on the hour □ until all hours

HOUSE
□ bring the house down □ eat someone out of house and home □ keep house □ like a house on fire □ on the house □ put one's house in order

HOVER
□ hover over someone or something

HOYLE
□ according to Hoyle

HUFF
□ in a huff

HUMBLE
□ eat humble pie

HUMP
□ over the hump

HUNDRED
☐ one in a hundred
HUNG
☐ hung up on someone or something
HUNGRY
☐ as hungry as a bear
HUNT
☐ hunt someone or something down ☐ hunt someone or something up
HURRY
☐ get a hurry on ☐ hurry back
HURT
☐ cry before one is hurt ☐ hurt someone's feelings
HUSH
☐ hush someone or something up
ICE
☐ break the ice ☐ cuts no ice ☐ on thin ice ☐ put something on ice ☐ skate on thin ice
IDEA
☐ get a bright idea ☐ get a rough idea about something ☐ give someone a rough idea about something ☐ have a bright idea ☐ have a rough idea about something ☐ put ideas into someone's head ☐ What's the idea?
IDIOT
☐ take someone for an idiot
IDLY
☐ sit idly by
IF
☐ If the shoe fits, wear it. ☐ if worst comes to worst ☐ look as if butter wouldn't melt in one's mouth ☐ no ifs, ands, or buts about it
ILL
☐ ill at ease ☐ take ill
IMAGE
☐ be the spit and image of someone ☐ spit and image
IMPOSE
☐ impose on someone ☐ impose something on someone
IMPRESSION
☐ make an impression on someone
IMPROVE
☐ improve on something
INCH
☐ come within an inch of doing something ☐ Give one an inch, and one will take a mile. ☐ inch along something ☐ inch by inch ☐ within an inch of one's life

INCUMBENT
☐ incumbent upon someone to do something
INDEED
☐ A friend in need is a friend indeed.
INJURY
☐ add insult to injury
INNOCENT
☐ as innocent as a lamb
INQUIRE
☐ inquire after someone
INSIDE
☐ get the inside track ☐ have the inside track ☐ know something inside out
INSTRUMENTAL
☐ instrumental in doing something
INSULT
☐ add insult to injury
INTEREST
☐ draw interest ☐ take an interest in something
INTO
☐ be into something ☐ beat something into someone's head ☐ break into something ☐ break out into tears ☐ bring something into question ☐ bump into someone or something ☐ burst into flames ☐ burst into tears ☐ call someone or something into question ☐ check into something ☐ come into one's or its own ☐ come into something ☐ cut into something ☐ dip into something ☐ divide something into something ☐ drive something into the ground ☐ drum something into someone ☐ fall into a trap ☐ far into the night ☐ fit someone or something into something ☐ get into a mess ☐ get into an argument with someone ☐ get into full swing ☐ get into high gear ☐ get into something ☐ get into the swing of things ☐ get one's teeth into something ☐ get something into someone's thick head ☐ go into a nose dive ☐ go into a tailspin ☐ go into action ☐ go into effect ☐ go into one's song and dance about something ☐ go into orbit ☐ go into something ☐ head into something ☐ head someone or something into someone or something ☐ into something ☐ lace into someone or something ☐ lay into someone or something ☐ lick something into shape ☐ light into someone or something ☐ look into something ☐ move into some-

thing □ nose into something □ out of the frying pan, into the fire □ pile into something □ play into someone's hands □ plow into someone or something □ poke one's nose into something □ put ideas into someone's head □ put something into order □ put something into practice □ put something into print □ put something into words □ put words into someone's mouth □ read something into something □ rip into someone or something □ rope someone into doing something □ run into a stone wall □ run into someone or something □ run something into the ground □ see into something □ show someone into someplace □ sink into despair □ sink one's teeth into something □ step into the breach □ stick one's nose into something □ stumble into someone or something □ swing into action □ take someone or something into account □ take the law into one's own hands □ talk someone into doing something □ tear into someone or something □ throw something into the bargain □ tie into something □ toss one's hat into the ring □ turn into something □ turn someone or something into something □ vanish into thin air □ wade into something □ What's gotten into someone? □ work one's way into something □ work something into something

INVOLVED

□ get involved with someone or something

IRISH

□ get someone's Irish up

IRON

□ have too many irons in the fire □ iron something out □ strike while the iron is hot

IS

(See also *BE.*)□ A bird in the hand is worth two in the bush. □ A friend in need is a friend indeed. □ A little knowledge is a dangerous thing. □ A penny saved is a penny earned. □ after all is said and done □ All that glitters is not gold. □ An ounce of prevention is worth a pound of cure. □ as it were □ Beauty is only skin deep. □ cry before one is hurt □ Enough is enough. □ give credit where credit is due □ Half a loaf is

better than none. □ know which is which □ know which side one's bread is buttered on □ make hay while the sun is shining □ many is the time □ Money is no object. □ Money is the root of all evil. □ not all it is cracked up to be □ not know whether one is coming or going □ One man's meat is another man's poison. □ One's bark is worse than one's bite. □ one's name is mud □ one's number is up □ Pretty is as pretty does. □ Put your money where your mouth is! □ Seeing is believing. □ strike while the iron is hot □ such as it is □ Such is life! □ talk until one is blue in the face □ tell which is which □ The coast is clear. □ The fat is in the fire. □ The honeymoon is over. □ The jig is up. □ The shoe is on the other foot. □ there is no doing something □ Time is money. □ Time is up. □ Trouble is brewing. □ Variety is the spice of life. □ What is sauce for the goose is sauce for the gander. □ What's done is done. □ when all is said and done □ when one is good and ready □ when the time is ripe □ where one is coming from □ Your guess is as good as mine.

ISSUE

□ take issue with someone

IT

□ as far as it goes □ as it were □ as luck would have it □ at it again □ before you know it □ believe it or not □ call it a day □ call it quits □ Can it! □ catch it □ Come and get it! □ come into one's or its own □ Come off it! □ come to think of it □ Cool it! □ cross a bridge before one comes to it □ cross a bridge when one comes to it □ Cut it out! □ dead on one's or its feet □ Easy does it. □ eat one's cake and have it too □ Every dog has its day. □ far be it from me to do something □ Far from it. □ feel it beneath one to do something □ find it in one's heart to do something □ for all it's worth □ for the devil of it □ for the heck of it □ for the hell of it □ for whatever it's worth □ get away from it all □ get it all together □ get it in the neck □ get it together □ get it □ Get off it! □ give it the gun □ give it to someone □ go at it hammer and tongs □ go at it tooth and nail □ go for

it ☐ go it alone ☐ grin and bear it ☐
hand it to someone ☐ have a rough
time of it ☐ have had it up to here ☐
have had it ☐ have it all over someone
or something ☐ have it both ways ☐
have it in for someone ☐ have one's
cake and eat it too ☐ have what it takes
☐ high tail it out of somewhere ☐ hit
it off with someone ☐ Hold it! ☐ Hop
to it! ☐ hot foot it out of somewhere ☐
If the shoe fits, wear it. ☐ in one's or its
prime ☐ It behooves one to do something. ☐ It figures. ☐ It never rains but
it pours. ☐ It's a deal. ☐ It's about
time! ☐ It's high time. ☐ It's no use
doing something. ☐ judge something
on its own merits ☐ knock it off ☐ lay
it on thick ☐ let it all hang out ☐ let it
roll ☐ let someone have it ☐ like it or
lump it ☐ live it up ☐ lord it over
someone ☐ make a go of it ☐ make a
run for it ☐ make it hot for someone ☐
Make it snappy! ☐ make no bones about
it ☐ make no mistake about it ☐ make
nothing of it ☐ mix it up ☐ never had
it so good ☐ no buts about it ☐ no ifs,
ands, or buts about it ☐ no two ways
about it ☐ not all it is cracked up to be
☐ nothing to it ☐ on the face of it ☐
out of it ☐ play it cool ☐ play it safe ☐
pour it on thick ☐ put something
through its paces ☐ Put that in your
pipe and smoke it! ☐ put to it ☐ run
around like a chicken with its head cut
off ☐ sit on its hands ☐ Skip it! ☐ Snap
to it! ☐ So be it. ☐ So it goes. ☐ spread
it on thick ☐ step on it ☐ strike it rich
☐ such as it is ☐ take it away ☐ take
it easy on someone or something ☐ take
it or leave it ☐ take it slow ☐ Tell it to
the marines. ☐ That's about the size of
it. ☐ to put it mildly ☐ to whom it may
concern ☐ tough it out ☐ What
difference does it make? ☐ What of it?
☐ when it comes right down to it ☐
when it comes to something ☐ with it
☐ worth its weight in gold ☐ You can't
take it with you. ☐ You said it!
ITCHY
☐ have an itchy palm
IVORY
☐ live in an ivory tower
JACK
☐ All work and no play makes Jack a

dull boy. ☐ before you can say Jack
Robinson ☐ jack someone or something up
JACKPOT
☐ hit the jackpot
JAM
☐ get someone out of a jam ☐ in a jam
JAW
☐ have a glass jaw
JAYBIRD
☐ as naked as a jaybird
JAZZ
☐ jazz something up
JEALOUS
☐ jealous of someone or something
JIFFY
☐ in a jiffy
JIG
☐ The jig is up.
JOB
☐ do a job on someone or something
☐ do a snow job on someone ☐ fall
down on the job ☐ lay down on the job
☐ lie down on the job ☐ nine-to-five
job ☐ on the job
JOHNNY
☐ Johnny-come-lately ☐ Johnny-on-
the-spot
JOIN
☐ join forces with someone
JOINT
☐ put someone's nose out of joint
JOKE
☐ able to take a joke ☐ crack a joke
JONES
☐ go to Davy Jones's locker ☐ keep up
with the Joneses
JOY
☐ burst with joy
JUDGE
☐ as sober as a judge ☐ judge one on
one's own merits ☐ judge something
on its own merits ☐ judging by something
JUICE
☐ stew in one's own juice
JUMP
☐ get the jump on someone ☐ jump all
over someone ☐ jump at something ☐
jump at the chance ☐ jump at the opportunity ☐ jump bail ☐ jump down someone's throat ☐ jump off the deep end ☐
jump on someone ☐ jump on the bandwagon ☐ jump out of one's skin ☐ jump

the gun □ jump the track □ jump through a hoop □ jump to conclusions □ one jump ahead of someone or something

JUST

□ get one's just desserts □ just as soon do something □ just in case □ just one of those things □ just what the doctor ordered

JUSTICE

□ do justice to something

KEEL

□ keel over

KEEN

□ keen about someone or something □ keen on someone or something

KEEP

□ earn one's keep □ for keeps □ in keeping with something □ keep a civil tongue in one's head □ keep a stiff upper lip □ keep a straight face □ keep abreast of something □ keep after someone □ keep ahead of someone or something □ keep an account of something □ keep an eye on someone or something □ keep an eye out for someone or something □ keep at someone or something □ keep away from someone or something □ keep body and soul together □ keep company with someone □ keep cool □ keep good time □ keep house □ keep in touch with someone □ keep late hours □ keep off something □ keep on doing something □ keep on someone □ keep on the good side of someone □ keep on with something □ keep one's chin up □ keep one's distance from someone or something □ keep one's ear to the ground □ keep one's eye on someone or something □ keep one's eye on the ball □ keep one's eyes open for someone or something □ keep one's eyes peeled for someone or something □ keep one's feet on the ground □ keep one's fingers crossed for someone or something □ keep one's hand in something □ keep one's hands off someone or something □ keep one's head above water □ keep one's mouth shut about someone or something □ keep one's nose clean □ keep one's nose out of someone's business □ keep one's nose to the grindstone □ keep one's own counsel □ keep one's place □ keep one's

□ keep one's temper □ keep one's weather eye open □ keep one's wits about one □ keep one's word □ keep out of something or someplace □ keep pace with someone or something □ keep quiet about someone or something □ keep someone company □ keep someone from doing something □ keep someone in line □ keep someone in stitches □ keep someone on tenterhooks □ keep someone or something at a distance □ keep someone or something at arm's length □ keep someone or something at bay □ keep someone or something back □ keep someone or something down □ keep someone or something hanging in midair □ keep someone or something in check □ keep someone or something in mind □ keep someone or something off □ keep someone or something out □ keep someone or something still □ keep someone or something up □ keep someone posted □ keep something to oneself □ keep something under one's hat □ keep something under wraps □ keep still about someone or something □ keep still for something □ keep still □ keep tabs on someone or something □ keep the ball rolling □ keep the home fires burning □ keep the lid on something □ keep the wolf from the door □ keep time □ keep to oneself □ keep track of someone or something □ keep up an act □ keep up with someone or something □ keep up with the Joneses □ keep up with the times □ keep watch on someone or something □ keep watch over someone or something □ Keep your shirt on! □ out of keeping with something □ play for keeps

KEEPERS

□ Finders keepers, losers weepers.

KEG

□ sitting on a powder keg

KETTLE

□ fine kettle of fish □ the pot calling the kettle black

KEYED

□ keyed up

KIBOSH

□ put the kibosh on something

KICK

☐ alive and kicking ☐ for kicks ☐ get a kick out of someone or something ☐ kick a habit ☐ kick off ☐ kick oneself for doing something ☐ kick over ☐ kick someone or something around ☐ kick someone or something out ☐ kick something in ☐ kick something off ☐ kick the bucket ☐ kick up a fuss ☐ kick up a row ☐ kick up a storm ☐ kick up one's heels

KID

☐ handle someone with kid gloves ☐ kid around with someone ☐ no kidding

KILL

☐ Curiosity killed the cat. ☐ dressed to kill ☐ fit to kill ☐ in on the kill ☐ kill someone or something off ☐ kill the fatted calf ☐ kill the goose that laid the golden egg ☐ kill time ☐ kill two birds with one stone ☐ make a killing

KILTER

☐ out of kilter

KIND

☐ all kinds of someone or something ☐ in kind ☐ kind of something ☐ nothing of the kind

KINDLY

☐ take kindly to something

KING

☐ fit for a king

KISS

☐ kiss and make up ☐ kiss of death ☐ kiss something goodbye

KIT

☐ kit and caboodle

KITCHEN

☐ everything but the kitchen sink

KITE

☐ as high as a kite ☐ Go fly a kite!

KITTEN

☐ as weak as a kitten

KITTY

☐ feed the kitty

KNEE

☐ knee-high to a grasshopper

KNIFE

☐ go under the knife

KNIT

☐ knit one's brow

KNOCK

☐ knock about somewhere ☐ knock it off ☐ knock off work ☐ knock on wood

☐ knock some heads together ☐ knock someone dead ☐ knock someone down to size ☐ knock someone for a loop ☐ knock someone or something about ☐ knock someone or something around ☐ knock someone or something down ☐ knock someone or something off ☐ knock someone or something out ☐ knock someone over with a feather ☐ knock someone's block off ☐ knock-down-drag-out fight

KNOT

☐ tie someone in knots ☐ tie the knot

KNOW

☐ as far as anyone knows ☐ before you know it ☐ for all I know ☐ in the know ☐ know a thing or two about someone or something ☐ know all the tricks of the trade ☐ know one's ABCs ☐ know one's onions ☐ know one's place ☐ know one's stuff ☐ know one's way about ☐ know one's way around ☐ know someone by sight ☐ know someone or something like the back of one's hand ☐ know someone or something like the palm of one's hand ☐ know something by heart ☐ know something from memory ☐ know something inside out ☐ know something only too well ☐ know the ropes ☐ know the score ☐ know what's what ☐ know where someone stands on someone or something ☐ know which is which ☐ know which side one's bread is buttered on ☐ not know beans about something ☐ not know enough to come in out of the rain ☐ not know from nothing ☐ not know someone from Adam ☐ not know the first thing about someone or something ☐ not know where to turn ☐ not know whether one is coming or going ☐ not know which way to turn ☐ you know

KNOWLEDGE

☐ A little knowledge is a dangerous thing. ☐ to the best of one's knowledge

KNUCKLE

☐ knuckle down to something ☐ knuckle under to someone or something ☐ rap someone's knuckles

LACE

☐ lace into someone or something

LADDER

☐ at the bottom of the ladder

LAG

☐ lag behind someone or something

LAID
(See *LAY*.)

LAMB
□ as innocent as a lamb □ in two shakes of a lamb's tail

LAND
□ do a land office business □ land a blow somewhere □ land on both feet □ land on one's feet □ live off the fat of the land

LANGUAGE
□ in plain language □ use strong language

LAP
□ in the lap of luxury □ lap something up

LARGE
□ at large □ by and large

LARK
□ as happy as a lark

LASH
□ get a tongue-lashing □ give someone a tongue-lashing □ lash out at someone or something

LAST
□ as a last resort □ at last □ at long last □ at the last minute □ breathe one's last □ every last one □ get the last laugh □ get the last word □ have the last laugh □ have the last word □ He laughs best who laughs last. □ He who laughs last, laughs longest. □ last but not least □ last something out □ last-ditch effort □ on someone's or something's last legs □ see the last of someone or something □ That's the last straw. □ to the last

LATCH
□ latch onto someone or something

LATE
□ at the latest □ better late than never □ keep late hours □ late in life □ of late □ sooner or later □ stay up late

LATELY
□ Johnny-come-lately

LATHER
□ in a lather

LAUGH
□ burst out laughing □ die laughing □ get the last laugh □ have the last laugh □ He laughs best who laughs last. □ He who laughs last, laughs longest. □ laugh out of the other side of one's mouth □ laugh something off □ laugh up one's sleeve □ no laughing matter

LAUNCH
□ launch forth on something

LAURELS
□ rest on one's laurels

LAW
□ law unto oneself □ lay down the law □ take the law into one's own hands

LAY
(See also *LIE*.)□ kill the goose that laid the golden egg □ laid back □ laid up □ lay a finger on someone or something □ lay an egg □ lay down on the job □ lay down one's life for someone or something □ lay down the law □ lay eyes on someone or something □ lay for someone □ lay hold of someone or something □ lay into someone or something □ lay it on thick □ lay low □ lay off someone or something □ lay one's cards on the table □ lay one's hands on someone or something □ lay over somewhere □ lay someone off □ lay someone or something away □ lay someone or something out □ lay someone up □ lay something aside □ lay something by □ lay something down □ lay something in □ lay something on someone □ lay something on the line □ lay something to rest □ lay something to waste □ lay something up □ lay the blame on someone or something □ lay the finger on someone

LEAD
□ All roads lead to Rome. □ blind leading the blind □ get the lead out □ go over like a lead balloon □ lead a dog's life □ lead off □ lead on □ lead someone by the nose □ lead someone down the garden path □ lead someone on a merry chase □ lead someone on □ lead someone to believe something □ lead someone to do something □ lead the life of Riley □ lead the way □ shake the lead out

LEAF
□ leaf through something □ take a leaf out of someone's book □ turn over a new leaf

LEAGUE
□ in league with someone □ not in the same league with someone or something

LEAK
□ leak something out

415

LEAN

☐ lean on someone ☐ lean over backwards to do something

LEAP

☐ by leaps and bounds ☐ leap at the opportunity ☐ leap to conclusions

LEARN

☐ learn something by heart ☐ learn something by rote ☐ learn something from the bottom up ☐ learn something the hard way ☐ learn the ropes ☐ live and learn

LEASE

☐ new lease on life

LEAST

☐ at least ☐ last but not least ☐ least of all ☐ not in the least ☐ path of least resistance ☐ to say the least ☐ when least expected

LEATHER

☐ hellbent for leather

LEAVE

☐ absent without leave ☐ leave a bad taste in someone's mouth ☐ leave a lot to be desired ☐ leave no stone unturned ☐ leave off doing something ☐ leave one to one's fate ☐ leave oneself wide open for something ☐ leave someone flat ☐ leave someone for dead ☐ leave someone high and dry ☐ leave someone holding the bag ☐ leave someone in peace ☐ leave someone in the lurch ☐ leave someone or something alone ☐ leave someone or something behind ☐ leave someone or something hanging in midair ☐ leave someone or something out ☐ leave someone out in the cold ☐ leave something for another occasion ☐ leave something on ☐ leave well enough alone ☐ leave word with someone ☐ take it or leave it ☐ take leave of one's senses ☐ take leave of someone ☐ take one's leave of someone

LEFT

☐ hang a left ☐ have something left ☐ out in left field ☐ pay someone a left-handed compliment ☐ right and left

LEG

☐ Break a leg! ☐ cost an arm and a leg ☐ have one's tail between one's legs ☐ not have a leg to stand on ☐ on someone's or something's last legs ☐ pay an arm and a leg for something ☐ pull someone's leg

LEISURE

☐ at leisure

LEND

☐ lend an ear to someone ☐ lend oneself or itself to something ☐ lend someone a hand

LENGTH

☐ at length ☐ go to any length ☐ keep someone or something at arm's length

LESS

☐ couldn't care less ☐ in less than no time ☐ less than pleased ☐ more or less

LESSON

☐ teach someone a lesson

LET

☐ Don't let someone or something get you down. ☐ let alone someone or something ☐ Let bygones be bygones. ☐ let go of someone or something ☐ let go with something ☐ let grass grow under one's feet ☐ let her rip ☐ let it all hang out ☐ let it roll ☐ let loose with something ☐ let off steam ☐ let on ☐ let one's hair down ☐ let oneself go ☐ Let sleeping dogs lie. ☐ let someone down ☐ let someone have it ☐ let someone in on something ☐ let someone off the hook ☐ let someone or something alone ☐ let someone or something be ☐ let someone or something go ☐ let someone or something in ☐ let someone or something loose ☐ let someone or something off ☐ let someone or something out ☐ let something get out ☐ let something ride ☐ let something slide ☐ let something slip by ☐ let something slip out ☐ let the cat out of the bag ☐ let the chance slip by ☐ let up on someone or something ☐ let well enough alone ☐ live and let live ☐ sit back and let something happen

LETTER

☐ to the letter

LEVEL

☐ level off ☐ level something off ☐ level with someone ☐ on the level

LIBERTY

☐ at liberty ☐ take liberties with someone or something ☐ take the liberty of doing something

LICK

☐ get a licking ☐ give someone a licking ☐ give something a lick and a promise □ lick something into shape □ take a licking

LID
□ blow the lid off something □ flip one's lid □ keep the lid on something □ take the lid off something

LIE
□ Let sleeping dogs lie. □ lie down on the job □ lie in state □ lie in wait for someone or something □ lie low □ lie through one's teeth □ take something lying down

LIEU
□ in lieu of something

LIFE
□ all walks of life □ as big as life □ bet one's life □ between life and death □ come to life □ facts of life □ for the life of one □ Get a life! □ get the shock of one's life □ have the time of one's life □ in the prime of life □ late in life □ lay down one's life for someone or something □ lead a dog's life □ lead the life of Riley □ life of the party □ make life miserable for someone □ never in one's life □ new lease on life □ not on your life □ one's way of life □ run for one's life □ Such is life! □ take one's own life □ Variety is the spice of life. □ within an inch of one's life

LIFETIME
□ once-in-a-lifetime chance

LIFT
□ lift a hand against someone or something □ not lift a finger to help someone

LIGHT
□ according to one's own lights □ as light as a feather □ begin to see the light □ bring something to light □ come to light □ get the green light □ give someone the green light □ hide one's light under a bushel □ in light of something □ light into someone or something □ light on someone or something □ light out for somewhere □ light out of somewhere □ make light of something □ out like a light □ see the light at the end of the tunnel □ see the light of day □ see the light □ shed light on something

LIGHTLY
□ get off lightly □ once-over-lightly

LIGHTNING
□ as quick as greased lightning

LIKE
□ and the like □ avoid someone or something like the plague □ eat like a bird □ eat like a horse □ feel like a million dollars □ feel like a new person □ feel like something □ fit like a glove □ for something to sell like hotcakes □ go like clockwork □ go over like a lead balloon □ hit someone like a ton of bricks □ know someone or something like the back of one's hand □ know someone or something like the palm of one's hand □ like a bat out of hell □ like a bolt out of the blue □ like a bump on a log □ like a fish out of water □ like a house on fire □ like a sitting duck □ like a three-ring circus □ like crazy □ like it or lump it □ like looking for a needle in a haystack □ like mad □ like one of the family □ like water off a duck's back □ look like a million dollars □ look like someone or something □ look like the cat that swallowed the canary □ out like a light □ packed in like sardines □ read someone like a book □ run around like a chicken with its head cut off □ sleep like a log □ spread like wildfire □ stick out like a sore thumb □ take a liking to someone or something □ the likes of someone □ to someone's liking □ work like a horse

LIKELY
□ as likely as not

LILY
□ gild the lily

LIMB
□ out on a limb

LIMBO
□ in limbo

LIMELIGHT
□ in the limelight

LIMIT
□ go the limit □ go to the limit □ off limits □ within limits

LINE
□ blow one's lines □ draw a line between something and something else □ draw the line at something □ drop someone a line □ end of the line □ fall in line □ feed someone a line □ fluff one's lines □ give someone a line □

☐ hold the line at someone or something ☐ in line with something ☐ in line ☐ in the line of duty ☐ keep someone in line ☐ lay something on the line ☐ line one's own pockets ☐ line someone or something up with something ☐ line someone up for something ☐ line up ☐ muff one's lines ☐ on line ☐ out of line with something ☐ out of line ☐ put something on the line ☐ read between the lines ☐ sign on the dotted line ☐ step out of line ☐ swallow something hook, line, and sinker ☐ take a hard line with someone ☐ the bottom line ☐ toe the line

LINEN
☐ air someone's dirty linen in public

LINING
☐ Every cloud has a silver lining.

LION
☐ beard the lion in his den

LIP
☐ button one's lip ☐ keep a stiff upper lip ☐ pay lip service to something

LIST
☐ on a waiting list

LISTEN
☐ listen in on someone or something ☐ listen to reason

LITTLE
(See also *LEAST, LESS.*)☐ a little bird told me ☐ A little knowledge is a dangerous thing. ☐ little by little ☐ make little of someone or something ☐ think little of someone or something ☐ twist someone around one's little finger

LIVE
☐ all the live-long day ☐ beat the living daylights out of someone ☐ every living soul ☐ have to live with something ☐ hit one where one lives ☐ live and learn ☐ live and let live ☐ live beyond one's means ☐ live by one's wits ☐ live for the moment ☐ live from hand to mouth ☐ live high off the hog ☐ live high on the hog ☐ live in an ivory tower ☐ live in ☐ live it up ☐ live next door to someone ☐ live off someone or something ☐ live off the fat of the land ☐ live on borrowed time ☐ live on something ☐ live out of a suitcase ☐ live something down ☐ live through something ☐ live up to something ☐ live within one's means ☐ make

a living ☐ not a living soul ☐ where one lives

LOAD
☐ Get a load of someone or something. ☐ get a load off one's feet ☐ get a load off one's mind ☐ loaded for bear ☐ take a load off one's feet

LOAF
☐ Half a loaf is better than none.

LOAN
☐ float a loan

LOCK
☐ lock horns with someone ☐ lock someone or something in something ☐ lock someone or something up ☐ lock something in ☐ lock, stock, and barrel

LOCKER
☐ go to Davy Jones's locker

LOG
☐ as easy as falling off a log ☐ like a bump on a log ☐ sleep like a log

LOGGERHEADS
☐ at loggerheads

LOINS
☐ gird one's loins

LONG
☐ all day long ☐ all night long ☐ all the live-long day ☐ as long as ☐ at long last ☐ before long ☐ go a long way toward doing something ☐ have come a long way ☐ He who laughs last, laughs longest. ☐ in the long run ☐ Long time no see. ☐ make a long story short ☐ not by a long shot ☐ not long for this world ☐ over the long haul ☐ so long

LOOK
☐ Don't look a gift horse in the mouth. ☐ get a dirty look from someone ☐ give someone a dirty look ☐ like looking for a needle in a haystack ☐ look after someone or something ☐ look as if butter wouldn't melt in one's mouth ☐ look at someone cross-eyed ☐ look back on someone or something ☐ look daggers at someone ☐ look down on someone or something ☐ look down one's nose at someone or something ☐ look for someone or something high and low ☐ look for someone or something ☐ look for trouble ☐ look forward to something ☐ look in on someone or something ☐ look into something ☐ look like a million dollars ☐ look like someone or something ☐

look like the cat that swallowed the canary □ look on at something □ look on someone as something □ look out for someone or something □ look someone in the eye □ look someone in the face □ look someone or something over □ look someone or something up □ look the other way □ look to someone or something for something □ look up and down something □ look up to someone □ make someone look good □ make someone look ridiculous □ take a look at someone or something □ Things are looking up.

LOOKOUT
□ on the lookout for someone or something

LOON
□ as crazy as a loon

LOOP
□ knock someone for a loop □ throw someone for a loop

LOOSE
□ at loose ends □ break loose from someone or something □ break something loose □ cut loose from someone or something □ cut loose with something □ cut someone or something loose □ hang loose □ have a screw loose □ let loose with something □ let someone or something loose □ on the loose □ play fast and loose with someone or something

LORD
□ lord it over someone

LOSE
□ get lost □ lose face □ lose ground □ lose heart □ lose one's cool □ lose one's grip □ lose one's head over someone or something □ lose one's marbles □ lose one's mind □ lose one's reason □ lose one's shirt □ lose one's temper □ lose one's touch with someone or something □ lose one's train of thought □ lose oneself in something □ lose out on something □ lose out to someone or something □ lose sight of someone or something □ lose sleep over someone or something □ lose touch with someone or something □ lose track of someone or something □ lost in thought □ make up for lost time □ no love lost between someone and someone else

LOSERS
□ Finders keepers, losers weepers.

LOSS
□ at a loss for words □ cut someone's losses □ dead loss □ throw someone for a loss

LOST
(See *LOSE*.)

LOT
□ cast one's lot in with someone □ cover a lot of ground □ have a lot going for one □ have a lot of promise □ have a lot on one's mind □ leave a lot to be desired □ think a lot of someone or something

LOUD
□ Actions speak louder than words. □ say something out loud □ think out loud

LOUSE
□ louse something up

LOUSY
□ lousy with something

LOVE
□ fall in love with someone □ head over heels in love with someone □ in love with someone or something □ love at first sight □ make love to someone □ no love lost between someone and someone else □ not for love nor money

LOVELY
□ lovely weather for ducks

LOW
□ burn with a low blue flame □ get the low-down on someone or something □ give someone the low-down on someone or something □ have a low boiling point □ lay low □ lie low □ look for someone or something high and low □ low man on the totem pole

LOWER
□ lower one's sights □ lower one's voice □ lower the boom on someone

LUCK
□ as luck would have it □ down on one's luck □ have one's luck run out □ in luck □ luck out □ out of luck □ press one's luck □ push one's luck □ stroke of luck □ Tough luck! □ try one's luck at something

LUCKY
□ thank one's lucky stars

LUMP
□ get a lump in one's throat □ have a lump in one's throat □ like it or lump it

thing □ make short work of someone or something □ make someone eat crow □ make someone look good □ make someone look ridiculous □ make someone or something available to someone □ make someone or something over □ make someone or something tick □ make someone or something up □ make someone the scapegoat for something □ make someone's blood boil □ make someone's blood run cold □ make someone's hair stand on end □ make someone's head spin □ make someone's head swim □ make someone's mind up □ make someone's mouth water □ make someone's position clear □ make something from scratch □ make something good □ make something of something □ make something out of nothing □ make something out □ make something to order □ make something up out of whole cloth □ make something up to someone □ make the bed □ make the best of something □ make the feathers fly □ make the fur fly □ make the grade □ make the most of something □ make the scene □ make time with someone □ make tracks somewhere □ make up for lost time □ make up for someone or something □ make up with someone □ make up □ make use of someone or something □ make waves □ make way for someone or something □ make way □ not able to make anything out of someone or something □ on the make □ That makes two of us. □ What difference does it make? □ what makes someone tick

MAN
□ Early to bed, early to rise, makes a man healthy, wealthy, and wise. □ high man on the totem pole □ low man on the totem pole □ odd man out □ One man's meat is another man's poison. □ see a man about a dog □ separate the men from the boys

MANNER
□ all manner of someone or something

MANY
□ have too many irons in the fire □ in so many words □ many is the time □ Too many cooks spoil the broth. □ Too many cooks spoil the stew.

MARBLES
□ lose one's marbles □ not have all one's marbles

MARCH
□ as mad as a March hare □ march to a different drummer □ steal a march on someone

MARE
□ by shank's mare

MARINES
□ Tell it to the marines.

MARK
□ Mark my words. □ mark someone or something down □ mark something up □ toe the mark □ wide of the mark □ X marks the spot

MARKET
□ drug on the market □ in the market for something □ on the market □ play the market

MAST
□ at half mast

MATCH
□ meet one's match □ strike a match

MATTER
□ as a matter of course □ as a matter of fact □ crux of the matter □ for that matter □ get to the heart of the matter □ matter-of-fact □ no laughing matter □ no matter what

MAY
□ come what may □ devil-may-care attitude □ to whom it may concern

MEAL
□ eat a meal out

MEAN
□ mean nothing to someone □ mean something to someone □ mean to do something □ one means business

MEANS
□ beyond one's means □ by all means of something □ by all means □ by any means □ by means of something □ by no means □ live beyond one's means □ live within one's means

MEASURE
□ beyond measure □ for good measure □ measure up to someone or something □ measure up to someone's expectations

MEAT
□ One man's meat is another man's poison.

MEDICINE
□ dose of one's own medicine □ take one's medicine

MEDIUM
□ strike a happy medium
MEET
(See also *MET*.)□ make both ends meet □ make ends meet □ meet one's end □ meet one's match □ meet one's Waterloo □ meet someone halfway □ meet the requirements for something □ more to something than meets the eye
MEETING
□ call a meeting □ call the meeting to order □ hold a meeting □ Sunday-go-to-meeting clothes
MELT
□ look as if butter wouldn't melt in one's mouth □ melt in one's mouth
MEMORY
□ commit something to memory □ know something from memory
MEND
□ mend one's fences □ on the mend
MENTION
□ mention something in passing
MERCY
□ at the mercy of someone □ throw oneself on the mercy of the court
MERITS
□ judge one on one's own merits □ judge something on its own merits
MERRY
□ lead someone on a merry chase □ the more the merrier
MESS
□ get into a mess □ get out of a mess □ make a mess of something □ mess about with someone or something □ mess around with someone or something □ mess someone or something up
MESSAGE
□ get the message
MET
□ hail fellow well met
METHOD
□ method in one's madness
MICE
□ When the cat's away the mice will play.
MIDAIR
□ keep someone or something hanging in midair □ leave someone or something hanging in midair
MIDDLE
□ caught in the middle □ in the mid-

dle of nowhere □ play both ends against the middle □ smack dab in the middle
MIDDLING
□ fair to middling
MIDNIGHT
□ burn the midnight oil
MIDSTREAM
□ change horses in midstream
MIGHTY
□ act high and mighty
MILDLY
□ to put it mildly
MILE
□ by a mile □ Give one an inch, and one will take a mile. □ miss something by a mile
MILK
□ cry over spilled milk.
MILL
□ been through the mill □ run-of-the-mill
MILLION
□ feel like a million dollars □ look like a million dollars
MILLSTONE
□ millstone about one's neck
MINCE
□ mince one's words
MINCEMEAT
□ make mincemeat out of someone or something
MIND
□ bear someone or something in mind □ blow someone's mind □ boggle someone's mind □ change someone's mind □ come to mind □ cross someone's mind □ enter one's mind □ get a load off one's mind □ get someone or something out of one's mind □ give someone a piece of one's mind □ have a lot on one's mind □ have half a mind to do something □ have someone or something on one's mind □ have something in mind □ in one's mind's eye □ in one's right mind □ keep someone or something in mind □ lose one's mind □ make someone's mind up □ mind one's own business □ mind one's P's and Q's □ mind the store □ Never mind. □ on one's mind □ out of one's mind □ Out of sight, out of mind. □ pass through someone's mind □ put someone or something out of one's mind □ read someone's mind □ slip one's

mind □ speak one's mind □ weigh on someone's mind

MINES
□ back to the salt mines

MINT
□ in mint condition

MINUTE
□ at the last minute □ Every minute counts. □ up-to-the-minute

MISERABLE
□ make life miserable for someone □ make oneself miserable

MISS
□ have a near miss □ have one's heart miss a beat □ hit and miss □ miss out on something □ miss something by a mile □ miss the boat □ miss the point

MISSOURI
□ be from Missouri

MISTAKE
□ by mistake □ make no mistake about it □ mistake someone for someone else □ mistake something for something else

MIX
□ get mixed up □ have mixed feelings about someone or something □ mix it up □ mix someone or something up □ mix someone up with someone else □ mix something up with something else

MOLEHILL
□ make a mountain out of a molehill

MOMENT
□ for the moment □ live for the moment □ on the spur of the moment

MONEY
□ A fool and his money are soon parted. □ fork money out for something □ get a run for one's money □ get one's money's worth □ give one a run for one's money □ have money to burn □ in the money □ make good money □ Money burns a hole in someone's pocket. □ Money is no object. □ Money is the root of all evil. □ money talks □ not for love nor money □ on the money □ pour money down the drain □ Put your money where your mouth is! □ see the color of someone's money □ throw good money after bad □ Time is money. □ to the tune of some amount of money

MONKEY
□ make a monkey out of someone □ monkey around with someone or some-thing □ throw a monkey wrench in the works

MONTH
□ by the month □ in a month of Sun-days

MOOD
□ in a bad mood □ in no mood to do something □ in the mood for some-thing

MOON
□ ask for the moon □ once in a blue moon □ promise the moon to some-one

MOP
□ mop up the floor with someone

MOPE
□ mope around

MORE
□ bite off more than one can chew □ more often than not □ more or less □ more than one can shake a stick at □ more to something than meets the eye □ the more the merrier □ There's more than one way to skin a cat. □ wear more than one hat

MORNING
□ first thing in the morning

MOSS
□ A rolling stone gathers no moss.

MOST
□ at most □ at the most □ for the most part □ make the most of some-thing □ most of all

MOTHER
□ old enough to be someone's mother □ tied to one's mother's apron strings

MOTIONS
□ go through the motions

MOUNTAIN
□ make a mountain out of a molehill

MOUSE
□ as poor as a church mouse □ as quiet as a mouse □ play cat and mouse with someone

MOUTH
□ bad-mouth someone or something □ born with a silver spoon in one's mouth □ by word of mouth □ Don't look a gift horse in the mouth. □ down in the mouth □ foam at the mouth □ have a big mouth □ have foot-in-mouth disease □ have one's heart in one's mouth □ keep one's mouth shut about someone or something □ laugh

out of the other side of one's mouth □ leave a bad taste in someone's mouth □ live from hand to mouth □ look as if butter wouldn't melt in one's mouth □ make someone's mouth water □ melt in one's mouth □ not open one's mouth □ put one's foot in one's mouth □ put words into someone's mouth □ Put your money where your mouth is! □ run off at the mouth □ shoot one's mouth off □ stick one's foot in one's mouth □ straight from the horse's mouth □ take the words out of one's mouth

MOUTHFUL
□ say a mouthful

MOVE
□ get a move on □ get moving □ move heaven and earth to do something □ move in on someone or something □ move into something □ move on □ move out □ move up in the world □ not move a muscle □ on the move

MUCH
□ much ado about nothing □ much in evidence □ much sought after □ so much for someone or something □ so much the better □ take too much on □ think much of someone or something □ too much of a good thing

MUD
□ as clear as mud □ one's name is mud □ stick-in-the-mud

MUFF
□ muff one's lines

MULE
□ as stubborn as a mule

MULL
□ mull something over

MUM
□ Mum's the word.

MURDER
□ cry bloody murder □ scream bloody murder

MUSCLE
□ muscle in on something □ not move a muscle

MUSIC
□ face the music □ make chin music

MUST
□ be a must

MUSTER
□ pass muster

NAIL
□ as hard as nails □ bite one's nails □ fight someone or something tooth and nail □ go at it tooth and nail □ hit the nail on the head □ nail someone or something down

NAKED
□ as naked as a jaybird

NAME
□ call someone names □ in name only □ in someone's name □ make a name for oneself □ name of the game □ name someone after someone else □ on a first name basis with someone □ one's name is mud □ throw someone's name around

NAPE
□ by the nape of the neck

NATURAL
□ die a natural death

NATURE
□ second nature to someone

NAUGHT
□ come to naught

NEAR
□ draw near □ have a near miss □ in the near future □ near at hand

NECESSITY
□ out of necessity

NECK
□ break one's neck to do something □ breathe down someone's neck □ by the nape of the neck □ get it in the neck □ in some neck of the woods □ millstone about one's neck □ neck and neck □ pain in the neck □ risk one's neck to do something □ save someone's neck □ stick one's neck out □ up to one's neck in something

NEED
□ A friend in need is a friend indeed.

NEEDLE
□ like looking for a needle in a haystack □ on pins and needles

NEITHER
□ neither fish nor fowl □ neither here nor there □ neither hide nor hair

NERVE
□ get on someone's nerves □ get up enough nerve to do something □ Of all the nerve!

NEST
□ feather one's nest □ stir up a hornet's nest

NEVER
□ A watched pot never boils. □ better

late than never ☐ It never rains but it pours. ☐ never fear ☐ never had it so good ☐ never in one's life ☐ Never mind. ☐ now or never

NEW

☐ break new ground ☐ feel like a new person ☐ new ball game ☐ new lease on life ☐ ring in the new year ☐ take a new turn ☐ turn over a new leaf ☐ You can't teach an old dog new tricks.

NEWCASTLE

☐ carry coals to Newcastle

NEWS

☐ break the news to someone

NEXT

☐ get next to someone ☐ live next door to someone

NICK

☐ full of Old Nick ☐ in the nick of time

NIGHT

☐ all hours of the day and night ☐ all night long ☐ as different as night and day ☐ day and night ☐ far into the night ☐ fly-by-night ☐ make a night of doing something ☐ night and day ☐ night on the town ☐ one-night stand

NINE

☐ nine-to-five job ☐ on cloud nine

NIP

☐ nip and tuck ☐ nip something in the bud

NITTY

☐ get down to the nitty-gritty

NO

☐ A rolling stone gathers no moss. ☐ all talk and no action ☐ All work and no play makes Jack a dull boy. ☐ by no means ☐ cuts no ice ☐ have no business doing something ☐ have no staying power ☐ have no time for someone or something ☐ have no use for someone or something ☐ hold no brief for someone or something ☐ in less than no time ☐ in no mood to do something ☐ in no time ☐ in no uncertain terms ☐ It's no use doing something. ☐ leave no stone unturned ☐ Long time no see. ☐ make no bones about it ☐ make no difference to someone ☐ make no mistake about it ☐ Money is no object. ☐ no buts about it ☐ no can do ☐ No dice. ☐ no doubt ☐ no end of something ☐ no great shakes ☐ no hard

feelings ☐ no holds barred ☐ no ifs, ands, or buts about it ☐ no kidding ☐ no laughing matter ☐ no love lost between someone and someone else ☐ no matter what ☐ No problem. ☐ no skin off someone's nose ☐ no skin off someone's teeth ☐ no sooner said than done ☐ no spring chicken ☐ No sweat. ☐ no trespassing ☐ no two ways about it ☐ No way. ☐ no wonder ☐ not take no for an answer ☐ of no avail ☐ on no account ☐ see no objection to something ☐ take no stock in something ☐ there is no doing something ☐ There's no accounting for taste. ☐ to no avail ☐ up to no good ☐ with no strings attached

NOD

☐ get the nod

NONE

☐ Half a loaf is better than none. ☐ have none of something ☐ none of someone's beeswax ☐ none the worse for wear ☐ second to none

NONSENSE

☐ stuff and nonsense

NOR

☐ neither fish nor fowl ☐ neither here nor there ☐ neither hide nor hair ☐ not for love nor money

NORTH

☐ up North

NOSE

☐ as plain as the nose on one's face ☐ can't see beyond the end of one's nose ☐ count noses ☐ cut off one's nose to spite one's face ☐ follow one's nose ☐ get one's nose out of someone's business ☐ go into a nose dive ☐ have one's nose in a book ☐ have one's nose in the air ☐ keep one's nose clean ☐ keep one's nose out of someone's business ☐ keep one's nose to the grindstone ☐ lead someone by the nose ☐ look down one's nose at someone or something ☐ no skin off someone's nose ☐ nose about ☐ nose around ☐ nose into something ☐ nose someone out ☐ on the nose ☐ pay through the nose for something ☐ poke one's nose into something ☐ put one's nose to the grindstone ☐ put someone's nose out of joint ☐ stick one's nose into something ☐ take a nose dive ☐ thumb one's nose

at someone or something □ turn one's
nose up at someone or something □
win by a nose
NOT
□ All that glitters is not gold. □ as
likely as not □ be careful not to do
something □ believe it or not □ last
but not least □ more often than not □
Not a bit. □ not a living soul □ not
able to call one's time one's own □ not
able to go on □ not able to help something □ not able to make anything out
of someone or something □ not able to
see the forest for the trees □ not able
to wait □ not able □ not all it is cracked
up to be □ not all there □ not at all □
not born yesterday □ not breathe a
word about someone or something □
not buy something □ not by a long
shot □ not care two hoots about someone or something □ not enough room
to swing a cat □ not for anything in the
world □ not for love nor money □ not
for the world □ not give a hang about
anyone or anything □ not give a hoot
about anyone or anything □ not give
anyone the time of day □ not half bad
□ not have a care in the world □ not
have a leg to stand on □ not have all
one's marbles □ not have anything on
□ not hold a candle to someone or
something □ not hold a stick to someone or something □ not hold water □
not in the least □ not in the same league
with someone or something □ not know
beans about something □ not know
enough to come in out of the rain □
not know from nothing □ not know
someone from Adam □ not know the
first thing about someone or something
□ not know where to turn □ not know
whether one is coming or going □ not
know which way to turn □ not lift a
finger to help someone □ not long for
this world □ not move a muscle □ not
on any account □ not on your life □
not open one's mouth □ not set foot
somewhere □ not show one's face □
not sleep a wink □ not someone's cup
of tea □ not take no for an answer □
not up to scratch □ not utter a word □
not worth a dime □ not worth a hill of
beans □ not worth a red cent □ will
not hear of something

NOTCH
□ take someone down a notch or two
NOTE
□ make a note of something □ strike
a sour note □ take note of something
NOTHING
□ care nothing about someone or something □ come to nothing □ good-for-
nothing □ have nothing on someone
or something □ have nothing to do with
someone or something □ Here goes
nothing. □ in nothing flat □ make nothing of it □ make something out of nothing □ mean nothing to someone □
much ado about nothing □ not know
from nothing □ nothing but skin and
bones □ nothing doing □ nothing down
□ nothing of the kind □ nothing to
complain about □ nothing to it □ nothing to sneeze at □ nothing to speak of
□ nothing to write home about □ Nothing ventured, nothing gained. □ stop
at nothing □ think nothing of someone
or something □ to say nothing of someone or something
NOTICE
□ escape someone's notice □ serve
notice □ sit up and take notice □ take
notice of something
NOTION
□ have half a notion to do something
NOW
□ all better now □ every now and again
□ every now and then □ now and again
□ now and then □ now or never □ the
here and now
NOWHERE
□ at the end of nowhere □ come out
of nowhere □ get nowhere fast □ in
the middle of nowhere
NTH
□ to the nth degree
NUISANCE
□ make a nuisance of oneself
NULL
□ null and void
NUMBER
□ any number of someone or something □ by the numbers □ do a number on someone or something □ get
someone's number □ have someone's
number □ in round numbers □ one's
days are numbered □ one's number is
up

NURSE
- □ nurse a grudge against someone

NUT
- □ everything from soup to nuts □ hard nut to crack □ nuts about someone or something □ off one's nut □ tough nut to crack

NUTSHELL
- □ in a nutshell

NUTTY
- □ nutty as a fruitcake

OAR
- □ put one's oar in

OATS
- □ sow one's wild oats

OBJECT
- □ Money is no object.

OBJECTION
- □ raise an objection to someone or something □ see no objection to something

OBLIGATED
- □ obligated to someone

OCCASION
- □ leave something for another occasion □ on occasion □ rise to the occasion

OCCUR
- □ occur to someone

OCEAN
- □ a drop in the ocean

ODD
- □ at odds with someone □ for the odds to be against one □ odd man out

OFFENSE
- □ take offense at someone or something

OFFICE
- □ do a land office business □ take office

OFFING
- □ in the offing

OFTEN
- □ more often than not

OIL
- □ burn the midnight oil □ oil someone's palm □ pour oil on troubled water

OINTMENT
- □ fly in the ointment

OLD
- □ a chip off the old block □ as comfortable as an old shoe □ be old hat □ full of Old Nick □ get the old heave-ho □ give someone the old heave-ho □ old enough to be someone's father □ old enough to be someone's mother □ old hand at doing something □ one's old stamping ground □ You can't teach an old dog new tricks.

OLIVE
- □ hold out the olive branch

ONCE
- □ all at once □ at once □ every once in a while □ get the once-over □ give someone or something the once-over □ once and for all □ once in a blue moon □ once in a while □ once upon a time □ once-in-a-lifetime chance □ once-over-lightly

ONE
- □ all in one breath □ all in one piece □ as one □ at one fell swoop □ do someone one better □ every last one □ go in one ear and out the other □ go someone one better □ hole in one □ in one ear and out the other □ just one of those things □ kill two birds with one stone □ like one of the family □ off to one side □ on one hand □ on the one hand □ one and all □ one and only □ one and the same □ one at a time □ one by one □ one for the books □ one for the record books □ One good turn deserves another. □ one in a hundred □ one in a thousand □ one jump ahead of someone or something □ One man's meat is another man's poison. □ one of these days □ one up on someone □ one way or another □ one-night stand □ pull a fast one □ six of one and half a dozen of the other □ There's more than one way to skin a cat. □ wear more than one hat □ with one hand tied behind one's back

ONIONS
- □ know one's onions

ONLY
- □ Beauty is only skin deep. □ in name only □ know something only too well □ one and only □ only have eyes for someone

ONTO
- □ latch onto someone or something □ onto someone or something

OPEN
- □ crack something wide open □ get something out in the open □ keep one's eyes open for someone or something □ keep one's weather eye open □ leave

someone or something over □ hover over someone or something □ in over one's head □ jump all over someone □ keel over □ keep watch over someone or something □ kick over □ knock someone over with a feather □ lay over somewhere □ lean over backwards to do something □ look someone or something over □ lord it over someone □ lose one's head over someone or something □ lose sleep over someone or something □ make a fuss over someone or something □ make over someone or something □ make someone or something over □ mull something over □ once-over-lightly □ over and above something □ over and done with □ over and over □ over my dead body □ over the hill □ over the hump □ over the long haul □ over the short haul □ over the top □ pass over someone or something □ pass someone or something over □ pick something over □ pull over □ pull the wool over someone's eyes □ put something over on someone □ put something over □ rake someone over the coals □ read something over □ ride roughshod over someone or something □ run over someone or something □ sign something over to someone □ smooth something over □ stand over someone □ stop over someplace □ take someone or something over □ talk something over □ The honeymoon is over. □ think something over □ throw someone over □ tide someone over □ tip something over □ turn over a new leaf □ turn over in one's grave □ turn over □ turn someone or something over to someone □ turn someone or something over □ walk all over someone □ win out over someone or something □ work someone over

OVERBOARD
□ go overboard

OWL
□ as wise as an owl

OWN
□ according to one's own lights □ afraid of one's own shadow □ blow one's own horn □ carry one's own weight □ come into one's or its own □ do one's own thing □ dose of one's own medicine □ for one's own part □

□ for one's own sake □ hold one's own □ in a world of one's own □ in one's own backyard □ in one's own way □ judge one on one's own merits □ judge something on its own merits □ keep one's own counsel □ line one's own pockets □ mind one's own business □ not able to call one's time one's own □ of one's own accord □ of one's own free will □ on one's own time □ on one's own □ own up to something □ paddle one's own canoe □ pull oneself up by one's own bootstraps □ sign one's own death warrant □ stand on one's own two feet □ stew in one's own juice □ take one's own life □ take the law into one's own hands □ toot one's own horn □ under one's own steam

OX
□ as strong as an ox

P's
□ mind one's P's and Q's

PACE
□ at a snail's pace □ keep pace with someone or something □ put one through one's paces □ put something through its paces

PACK
□ pack a punch □ pack a wallop □ pack someone off to somewhere □ pack them in □ packed in like sardines □ send someone packing

PAD
□ pad the bill

PADDLE
□ paddle one's own canoe □ up the creek without a paddle

PAIN
□ give someone a pain □ have growing pains □ pain in the neck □ take pains to do something

PAINT
□ paint the town red

PAIR
□ pair off with someone □ pair up with someone

PAL
□ pal around with someone

PALE
□ beyond the pale □ pale around the gills

PALM
□ grease someone's palm □ have an itchy palm □ know someone or some-

thing like the palm of one's hand ☐ oil someone's palm ☐ palm someone or something off on someone

PAN
☐ flash in the pan ☐ out of the frying pan, into the fire ☐ pan out

PANCAKE
☐ as flat as a pancake

PANDORA
☐ open Pandora's box

PANIC
☐ push the panic button

PANTS
☐ beat the pants off someone ☐ by the seat of one's pants ☐ catch one with one's pants down ☐ get ants in one's pants ☐ have ants in one's pants

PAPER
☐ get one's walking papers ☐ give one one's walking papers ☐ put something on paper

PAR
☐ on par with someone or something ☐ par for the course ☐ up to par

PARCEL
☐ parcel someone or something out ☐ part and parcel of something

PAROLE
☐ out on parole

PART
☐ A fool and his money are soon parted. ☐ do one's part ☐ for one's own part ☐ for the most part ☐ in part ☐ part and parcel of something ☐ part company with someone ☐ part someone's hair ☐ part with someone or something ☐ parting of the ways ☐ take part in something

PARTAKE
☐ partake of something

PARTICULAR
☐ in particular

PARTY
☐ life of the party ☐ throw a party for someone

PASS
☐ come to pass ☐ in passing ☐ make a pass at someone ☐ mention something in passing ☐ pass as someone or something ☐ pass away ☐ pass muster ☐ pass on ☐ pass out ☐ pass over someone or something ☐ pass someone or something by ☐ pass someone or something over ☐ pass someone or

something up ☐ pass something off as something ☐ pass something off on someone as something ☐ pass something on ☐ pass something out ☐ pass the buck ☐ pass the hat ☐ pass the time of day with someone ☐ pass the time ☐ pass through someone's mind

PASTURE
☐ put someone or something out to pasture

PAT
☐ get a pat on the back ☐ give someone a pat on the back ☐ pat someone on the back ☐ stand pat

PATCH
☐ patch someone or something up

PATH
☐ beat a path to someone's door ☐ lead someone down the garden path ☐ path of least resistance

PATIENCE
☐ try someone's patience

PAUL
☐ rob Peter to pay Paul

PAUSE
☐ give someone pause

PAVE
☐ pave the way for someone or something

PAVEMENT
☐ pound the pavement

PAWN
☐ pawn something off on someone as something

PAY
☐ Crime doesn't pay. ☐ have the devil to pay ☐ hit pay dirt ☐ pay an arm and a leg for something ☐ pay as you go ☐ pay attention to someone or something ☐ pay for something ☐ pay in advance ☐ pay lip service to something ☐ pay one's debt to society ☐ pay one's dues ☐ pay someone a compliment ☐ pay someone a left-handed compliment ☐ pay someone a visit ☐ pay someone or something off ☐ pay someone's way ☐ pay the piper ☐ pay through the nose for something ☐ pay up ☐ rob Peter to pay Paul ☐ There will be the devil to pay.

PEA
☐ as thick as pea soup

PEACE
☐ hold one's peace ☐ leave someone in peace ☐ make peace with someone

PEACOCK
□ as proud as a peacock
PEANUTS
□ for peanuts
PEARLS
□ cast pearls before swine
PEDESTAL
□ put someone on a pedestal
PEEL
□ keep one's eyes peeled for someone or something □ peel something off something
PEG
□ peg away at something □ square peg in a round hole □ take someone down a peg or two
PENCHANT
□ have a penchant for doing something
PENNY
□ A penny saved is a penny earned. □ cost a pretty penny □ penny wise and pound foolish
PEOPLE
□ split people up □ tell people apart
PERISH
□ Perish the thought.
PERK
□ perk someone or something up
PERSON
□ do something in person □ feel like a new person
PET
□ be the teacher's pet
PETER
□ peter out □ rob Peter to pay Paul
PHASE
□ phase someone or something out
PHYSICAL
□ get physical with someone
PICK
□ have a bone to pick with someone □ have a pick-me-up □ pick a quarrel with someone □ pick at someone or something □ pick holes in something □ pick on someone or something □ pick one's way through something □ pick someone or something off □ pick someone or something out □ pick someone or something up □ pick something over □ pick something to pieces □ pick up the tab □ pick up
PICKLE
□ in a pickle

PICTURE
□ as pretty as a picture □ get the picture
PIE
□ as easy as apple pie □ as easy as pie □ eat humble pie □ have one's finger in the pie □ in apple-pie order □ pie in the sky
PIECE
□ all in one piece □ break something to pieces □ cut someone or something to pieces □ fall to pieces □ give someone a piece of one's mind □ go to pieces □ pick something to pieces □ piece of cake □ piece of the action □ piece something out □ piece something together □ speak one's piece □ thrill someone to pieces □ thrilled to pieces
PIG
□ buy a pig in a poke □ serve as a guinea pig
PILE
□ make a pile □ pile into something □ pile out of something □ pile something on someone or something □ pile something up □ pile up
PILLAR
□ from pillar to post
PIN
□ on pins and needles □ pin one's faith on someone or something □ pin someone or something down on something □ pin someone's ears back □ pin something on someone or something □ so still you could hear a pin drop
PINCH
□ pinch-hit for someone □ take something with a pinch of salt
PINK
□ in the pink of condition □ tickle someone pink
PIPE
□ pipe down □ pipe up with something □ Put that in your pipe and smoke it!
PIPER
□ pay the piper
PIT
□ pit someone or something against someone or something □ the pits
PITCH
□ in there pitching □ make a pitch for someone or something □ pitch in and help □ pitch someone a curve ball

PITY
- □ take pity on someone or something

PLACE
- □ all over the place □ between a rock and a hard place □ fall in place □ feel out of place □ go places □ have one's heart in the right place □ in place of someone or something □ in place □ in someone else's place □ in the first place □ in the second place □ keep one's place □ know one's place □ out of place □ place the blame on someone or something □ put one in one's place □ put oneself in someone else's place □ take place

PLAGUE
- □ avoid someone or something like the plague

PLAIN
- □ as plain as day □ as plain as the nose on one's face □ in plain English □ in plain language

PLAINLY
- □ put something plainly

PLAN
- □ plan on something □ upset someone's plans

PLAY
- □ All work and no play makes Jack a dull boy. □ foul play □ game at which two can play □ horse play □ make a play for someone □ play around with someone or something □ play ball with someone □ play both ends against the middle □ play by ear □ play cat and mouse with someone □ play fair □ play fast and loose with someone or something □ play first chair □ play footsie with someone □ play for keeps □ play hard to get □ play havoc with someone or something □ play hob with someone or something □ play hooky □ play into someone's hands □ play it cool □ play it safe □ play on something □ play one's cards close to the chest □ play one's cards right □ play one's trump card □ play politics □ play possum □ play second fiddle to someone □ play someone for something □ play someone off against someone else □ play someone or something down □ play someone or something up □ play something by ear □ play something □ play the field □ play the market □ play

□ play to the gallery □ play tricks on someone □ play up to someone □ play with fire □ play-by-play description □ played out □ When the cat's away the mice will play.

PLEA
- □ cop a plea

PLEASE
- □ less than pleased

PLENTY
- □ There are plenty of other fish in the sea

PLOW
- □ plow into someone or something □ put one's hand to the plow

PLUCK
- □ pluck up someone's courage

PLUG
- □ plug away at something □ plug something in □ plug something up □ pull the plug on someone or something

PLUNK
- □ plunk someone or something down

POCKET
- □ have someone in one's pocket □ line one's own pockets □ Money burns a hole in someone's pocket. □ out-of-pocket expenses

POINT
- □ at the point of doing something □ at this point in time □ beside the point □ case in point □ come to the point □ get to the point □ have a low boiling point □ make a point of something □ make a point □ make points with someone □ miss the point □ on the point of doing something □ point someone or something out □ point something up □ stretch a point □ touch a sore point

POISON
- □ One man's meat is another man's poison.

POKE
- □ buy a pig in a poke □ poke about □ poke around □ poke fun at someone □ poke one's nose into something

POLE
- □ be poles apart □ high man on the totem pole □ low man on the totem pole

POLISH
- □ polish something off

POLITICS
- □ play politics

POND
□ big frog in a small pond
POOP
□ poop out
POOR
□ as poor as a church mouse □ in poor taste
POP
□ pop off □ pop one's cork □ pop the question □ pop up
POSITION
□ make someone's position clear
POSSESSED
□ possessed by something □ possessed of something
POSSIBLE
□ as far as possible □ as soon as possible
POSSUM
□ play possum
POST
□ from pillar to post □ keep someone posted
POT
□ A watched pot never boils. □ go to pot □ the pot calling the kettle black
POUND
□ An ounce of prevention is worth a pound of cure. □ penny wise and pound foolish □ pound a beat □ pound something out □ pound the pavement
POUR
□ It never rains but it pours. □ pour cold water on something □ pour it on thick □ pour money down the drain □ pour oil on troubled water □ pour one's heart out to someone □ pour something out
POWDER
□ sitting on a powder keg □ take a powder
POWER
□ have no staying power □ power behind the throne
PRACTICAL
□ for all practical purposes
PRACTICE
□ in practice □ make a practice of something □ out of practice □ practice what you preach □ put something into practice
PRAISE
□ praise someone or something to the skies

PREACH
□ practice what you preach
PRECEDENT
□ set a precedent
PREMIUM
□ at a premium
PRESENT
□ at present □ at the present time
PRESS
□ hard pressed to do something □ press one's luck
PRETTY
□ as pretty as a picture □ cost a pretty penny □ Pretty is as pretty does. □ pretty state of affairs □ sitting pretty
PREVAIL
□ prevail upon someone
PREVENT
□ take steps to prevent something
PREVENTION
□ An ounce of prevention is worth a pound of cure.
PREY
□ prey upon someone or something
PRICE
□ have a price on one's head
PRICK
□ prick up one's ears
PRIDE
□ burst with pride □ pride oneself on something □ swallow one's pride
PRIME
□ in one's or its prime □ in the prime of life
PRINT
□ in print □ out of print □ put something into print
PRIVATE
□ in private
PROBABILITY
□ in all probability
PROBLEM
□ no problem
PROGRESS
□ in progress
PROMISE
□ give something a lick and a promise □ have a lot of promise □ promise the moon to someone
PROPORTION
□ blow something out of all proportion □ out of all proportion
PROUD
□ as proud as a peacock □ do someone proud

433

PRUNES
□ full of prunes

PSYCHE
□ psyche someone out □ psyche someone up

PUBLIC
□ air someone's dirty linen in public □ do something in public □ in the public eye

PULL
□ have pull with someone □ pull a boner □ pull a fast one □ pull a stunt on someone □ pull a trick on someone □ pull ahead of someone or something □ pull in somewhere □ pull one's punches □ pull one's weight □ pull oneself together □ pull oneself up by one's own bootstraps □ pull over □ pull rank on someone □ pull someone or something down □ pull someone or something through something □ pull someone's leg □ pull someone's or something's teeth □ pull something off □ pull something on someone □ pull something out of a hat □ pull something out of thin air □ pull something together □ pull strings □ pull the plug on someone or something □ pull the rug out from under someone □ pull the wool over someone's eyes □ pull through □ pull up stakes □ pull up

PUNCH
□ beat someone to the punch □ pack a punch □ pull one's punches □ take a punch at someone

PURPOSE
□ answer someone's purpose □ at cross purposes □ do something on purpose □ for all practical purposes □ serve someone's purpose

PURSE
□ control the purse strings □ Make a silk purse out of a sow's ear.

PURSUIT
□ in pursuit of something

PUSH
□ push one's luck □ push someone to the wall □ push the panic button □ pushing up daisies

PUT
□ feel put upon □ hard put to do something □ put a bee in someone's bonnet □ put a stop to something □ put all one's eggs in one basket □ put an end to something □ put ideas into someone's head □ put in a good word for someone □ put in an appearance □ put in one's two cents worth □ put off by someone or something □ put on airs □ put on an act □ put on one's thinking cap □ put on the dog □ put on the feed bag □ put on weight □ put on □ put one in one's place □ put one through one's paces □ put one's back to something □ put one's best foot forward □ put one's cards on the table □ put one's dibs on something □ put one's finger on something □ put one's foot down about something □ put one's foot in one's mouth □ put one's hand to the plow □ put one's hands on something □ put one's house in order □ put one's nose to the grindstone □ put one's oar in □ put one's shoulder to the wheel □ put oneself in someone else's place □ put out feelers □ put out □ put someone down as something □ put someone down for something □ put someone on a pedestal □ put someone on the spot □ put someone or something across □ put someone or something at someone's disposal □ put someone or something away □ put someone or something down □ put someone or something off □ put someone or something on hold □ put someone or something on □ put someone or something out of one's mind □ put someone or something out of the way □ put someone or something out to pasture □ put someone or something out □ put someone or something to bed □ put someone or something to sleep □ put someone or something up □ put someone through the wringer □ put someone to shame □ put someone to the test □ put someone up to something □ put someone wise to someone or something □ put someone's nose out of joint □ put something aside □ put something by □ put something down to something □ put something forward □ put something in the way of someone □ put something in □ put something into order □ put something into practice □ put something into print □ put something into words □ put something on ice □ put something on paper

□ put something on the cuff □ put something on the line □ put something over on someone □ put something over □ put something plainly □ put something straight □ put something through its paces □ put something to good use □ put something to rest □ put something together □ Put that in your pipe and smoke it! □ put the arm on someone □ put the bite on someone □ put the blame on someone or something □ put the cart before the horse □ put the clamps on someone □ put the finger on someone □ put the heat on someone □ put the kibosh on something □ put the screws on someone □ put the skids on something □ put the squeeze on someone □ put to bed with a shovel □ put to it □ put two and two together □ put up a brave front □ Put up or shut up! □ put up with someone or something □ put words into someone's mouth □ Put your money where your mouth is! □ to put it mildly

Q's
□ mind one's P's and Q's

QUAKE
□ quake in one's boots

QUANDARY
□ in a quandary

QUANTITY
□ be an unknown quantity

QUARREL
□ pick a quarrel with someone

QUEST
□ in quest of someone or something

QUESTION
□ beg the question □ beside the question □ bring something into question □ call someone or something into question □ out of the question □ pop the question □ without question

QUICK
□ as quick as a wink □ as quick as greased lightning □ cut someone to the quick □ make a quick buck □ quick on the draw □ quick on the trigger □ quick on the uptake

QUIET
□ as quiet as a mouse □ keep quiet about someone or something

QUITE
□ quite a bit

QUITS
□ call it quits

RACE
□ race against time □ Slow and steady wins the race.

RACK
□ go to rack and ruin □ rack one's brains

RAG
□ chew the rag □ from rags to riches □ in rags

RAGE
□ all the rage

RAGGED
□ run someone ragged

RAIN
□ as right as rain □ come in out of the rain □ get a rain check on something □ give someone a rain check □ It never rains but it pours. □ not know enough to come in out of the rain □ rain cats and dogs □ rain or shine □ rain something out □ save something for a rainy day □ take a rain check on something

RAISE
□ cause eyebrows to raise □ raise a hand against someone or something □ raise a stink about something □ raise an objection to someone or something □ raise havoc with someone or something □ raise hob with someone or something □ raise one's sights □ raise one's voice to someone □ raise some eyebrows □ raise the devil with someone or something

RAKE
□ rake someone over the coals □ rake something off

RAM
□ ram someone or something down someone's throat

RAMBLE
□ ramble on about something

RANDOM
□ at random

RANGE
□ at close range

RANK
□ close ranks □ pull rank on someone □ rank and file

RAP
□ beat the rap □ rap someone's knuckles □ take the rap for someone or something

RAT
□ rat on someone □ smell a rat

435

RATE
☐ at any rate ☐ at that rate ☐ at this rate ☐ rate with someone
RATHER
☐ had rather do something
RATTLE
☐ rattle something off
RAVE
☐ rave about someone or something
RAW
☐ get a raw deal ☐ give someone a raw deal ☐ in the raw
REACH
☐ out of reach ☐ reach an accord with someone ☐ reach an agreement with someone ☐ reach an understanding with someone ☐ reach first base with someone or something ☐ reach for the sky ☐ reach one's stride ☐ within someone's reach
READ
☐ read between the lines ☐ read one one's rights ☐ read someone like a book ☐ read someone out of something ☐ read someone the riot act ☐ read someone's mind ☐ read something into something ☐ read something over ☐ read something through ☐ read up on someone or something
READY
☐ get ready to do something ☐ when one is good and ready
REAL
☐ for real
REAR
☐ bring up the rear
REASON
☐ have reason to do something ☐ listen to reason ☐ lose one's reason ☐ stand to reason ☐ within reason ☐ without rhyme or reason
REASONABLE
☐ beyond a reasonable doubt
RECEIPT
☐ acknowledge receipt of something
RECEIVE
☐ receive someone with open arms
RECKON
☐ reckon with someone or something
RECORD
☐ for the record ☐ off the record ☐ on record ☐ one for the record books
RED
☐ catch someone red-handed ☐ get a

☐ get a red face ☐ get the red carpet treatment ☐ give someone a red face ☐ give someone the red carpet treatment ☐ have a red face ☐ in the red ☐ not worth a red cent ☐ out of the red ☐ paint the town red ☐ red in the face ☐ roll out the red carpet for someone ☐ see red
REEL
☐ reel something off
REFERENCE
☐ in reference to someone or something ☐ with reference to someone or something
REGAIN
☐ regain one's composure ☐ regain one's feet
REGARD
☐ in regard to someone or something ☐ with regard to someone or something
REGULAR
☐ as regular as clockwork
REIN
☐ give free rein to someone
RELATION
☐ in relation to someone or something
RELATIVE
☐ relative to someone or something
RELIGION
☐ get religion
RENT
☐ rent something out
REPORT
☐ report on someone or something
REPUTATION
☐ get a reputation as a something ☐ get a reputation for doing something ☐ give someone a reputation as a something ☐ give someone a reputation for doing something ☐ have a reputation as a something ☐ have a reputation for doing something
REQUEST
☐ at someone's request
REQUIREMENTS
☐ meet the requirements for something
RESIGN
☐ resign oneself to something
RESISTANCE
☐ path of least resistance
RESORT
☐ as a last resort

RESPECT
☐ in respect to someone or something
☐ with respect to someone or something

REST
☐ come to rest ☐ lay something to rest
☐ put something to rest ☐ rest assured
☐ rest on one's laurels

RESULT
☐ as a result of something ☐ result in something

RETREAT
☐ beat a retreat

RETURN
☐ by return mail ☐ in return for someone or something ☐ return the compliment ☐ return the favor

REV
☐ rev something up

RHYME
☐ without rhyme or reason

RICH
☐ from rags to riches ☐ strike it rich

RID
☐ get rid of someone or something

RIDDANCE
☐ good riddance

RIDE
☐ go along for the ride ☐ hitch a ride
☐ let something ride ☐ ride herd on someone or something ☐ ride off in all directions ☐ ride on someone's coattails ☐ ride roughshod over someone or something ☐ ride something out ☐ ride the gravy train ☐ riding for a fall ☐ thumb a ride

RIDICULOUS
☐ make someone look ridiculous

RIGHT
☐ acknowledge someone to be right ☐ All right for you! ☐ all right with someone ☐ all right ☐ as right as rain ☐ give one's right arm for someone or something ☐ go right through someone ☐ hang a right ☐ have a right to do something ☐ have one's heart in the right place ☐ have someone dead to rights ☐ have the right-of-way ☐ in one's right mind ☐ in the right ☐ play one's cards right ☐ read one one's rights ☐ right and left ☐ right away ☐ right down someone's alley ☐ right off the bat ☐ right on time ☐ Right on! ☐ right side up ☐ right up someone's alley

☐ say something right to someone's face
☐ serve someone right ☐ set something right ☐ turn out all right ☐ when it comes right down to it ☐ yield the right-of-way

RILEY
☐ lead the life of Riley

RING
☐ give someone a ring ☐ have a familiar ring ☐ like a three-ring circus ☐ ring a bell ☐ ring in the new year ☐ ring someone or something up ☐ run rings around someone ☐ toss one's hat into the ring

RINSE
☐ rinse someone or something off ☐ rinse something out

RIOT
☐ read someone the riot act ☐ run riot

RIP
☐ let her rip ☐ rip into someone or something ☐ rip someone or something off

RIPE
☐ when the time is ripe

RISE
☐ Early to bed, early to rise, makes a man healthy, wealthy, and wise. ☐ get a rise out of someone ☐ give rise to something ☐ rise to the occasion

RISK
☐ risk one's neck to do something ☐ run a risk of something ☐ take a risk

RIVER
☐ sell someone down the river ☐ send someone up the river

ROAD
☐ All roads lead to Rome. ☐ end of the road ☐ get the show on the road

ROB
☐ rob Peter to pay Paul ☐ rob the cradle

ROBINSON
☐ before you can say Jack Robinson

ROCK
☐ between a rock and a hard place ☐ have rocks in one's head ☐ rock the boat

ROCKER
☐ off one's rocker

ROLL
☐ A rolling stone gathers no moss. ☐ get rolling ☐ get the ball rolling ☐ have them rolling in the aisles ☐ keep the

ball rolling □ let it roll □ roll one's sleeves up □ roll out the red carpet for someone □ roll something back □ roll something out □ set the ball rolling □ start the ball rolling

ROMANS

□ When in Rome do as the Romans do.

ROME

□ All roads lead to Rome. □ Rome wasn't built in a day. □ When in Rome do as the Romans do.

ROOF

□ go through the roof

ROOM

□ not enough room to swing a cat □ room and board □ room with someone □ take up room

ROOST

□ come home to roost □ rule the roost

ROOT

□ Money is the root of all evil. □ root for someone or something □ take root

ROPE

□ at the end of one's rope □ know the ropes □ learn the ropes □ rope someone into doing something □ show someone the ropes

ROTE

□ learn something by rote

ROUGH

□ diamond in the rough □ get a rough idea about something □ give someone a rough idea about something □ have a rough idea about something □ have a rough time of it □ rough someone up

ROUGHSHOD

□ ride roughshod over someone or something

ROUND

□ all year round □ come round □ go round the bend □ in round figures □ in round numbers □ round something off □ round something out □ round something up □ round-trip ticket □ square peg in a round hole □ the other way round

ROUNDABOUT

□ say something in a roundabout way

ROW

□ get one's ducks in a row □ kick up a row □ tough row to hoe

RUB

□ rub elbows with someone □ rub off

on someone □ rub shoulders with someone □ rub someone or something down □ rub someone out □ rub someone the wrong way □ rub someone's fur the wrong way □ rub something in □ rub something off

RUG

□ as snug as a bug in a rug □ pull the rug out from under someone

RUIN

□ go to rack and ruin

RULE

□ as a general rule □ as a rule □ hard-and-fast rule □ rule someone or something out □ rule the roost

RUN

□ do something on the run □ get a run for one's money □ give one a run for one's money □ have one's luck run out □ in the long run □ in the running □ in the short run □ make a run for it □ make someone's blood run cold □ off to a running start □ out of the running □ run a fever □ run a risk of something □ run a taut ship □ run a temperature □ run a tight ship □ run across someone or something □ run afoul of someone or something □ run after someone or something □ run an errand □ run around after someone or something □ run around like a chicken with its head cut off □ run around with someone □ run around □ run away from someone or something □ run away with someone or something □ run circles around someone □ run counter to something □ run down □ run for one's life □ run in circles □ run in the family □ run into a stone wall □ run into someone or something □ run off at the mouth □ run off with someone or something □ run out of gas □ run out of something □ run out of time □ run over someone or something □ run rings around someone □ run riot □ run scared □ run short of something □ run someone in □ run someone or something down □ run someone or something off □ run someone ragged □ run something into the ground □ run something up □ Run that by again. □ run through something □ run to seed □ run wild □ run-of-the-mill □ Still waters run deep.

RUNAROUND
☐ get the runaround ☐ give someone the runaround

RUSH
☐ in a mad rush

RUSTLE
☐ rustle something up

SACK
☐ get the sack ☐ give someone the sack ☐ hit the sack ☐ sack out

SAFE
☐ play it safe ☐ safe and sound

SAID
☐ (See *SAY*.)

SAIL
☐ sail through something ☐ sail under false colors ☐ set sail for somewhere ☐ take the wind out of someone's sails

SAKE
☐ for one's own sake ☐ for the sake of someone or something

SALE
☐ for sale ☐ on sale

SALT
☐ back to the salt mines ☐ salt something away ☐ take something with a grain of salt ☐ take something with a pinch of salt ☐ worth one's salt

SAME
☐ all the same to someone ☐ all the same ☐ at the same time ☐ by the same token ☐ in the same boat ☐ in the same breath ☐ not in the same league with someone or something ☐ one and the same ☐ Same here. ☐ The same to you.

SAND
☐ bury one's head in the sand ☐ hide one's head in the sand

SARDINES
☐ packed in like sardines

SAUCE
☐ What is sauce for the goose is sauce for the gander.

SAVE
☐ A penny saved is a penny earned. ☐ save one's breath ☐ save one's face ☐ save someone's neck ☐ save someone's skin ☐ save something for a rainy day ☐ save something up ☐ save the day ☐ save up for something

SAY
☐ after all is said and done ☐ before you can say Jack Robinson ☐ drop in to say hello ☐ easier said than done ☐ get one's say ☐ go so far as to say something ☐ goes without saying ☐ have a say in something ☐ have one's say ☐ no sooner said than done ☐ on someone's say-so ☐ say a mouthful ☐ say something in a roundabout way ☐ say something out loud ☐ say something right to someone's face ☐ say something under one's breath ☐ say the word ☐ say uncle ☐ to say nothing of someone or something ☐ to say the least ☐ when all is said and done ☐ You can say that again! ☐ You said it!

SCALE
☐ scale something down ☐ tip the scales at something

SCAPEGOAT
☐ make someone the scapegoat for something

SCARCE
☐ as scarce as hen's teeth ☐ make oneself scarce ☐ scarcer than hen's teeth

SCARE
☐ run scared ☐ scare one out of one's wits ☐ scare someone or something up ☐ scare someone stiff ☐ scare someone to death ☐ scare the daylights out of someone ☐ scare the wits out of someone ☐ scared to death

SCENE
☐ behind the scenes ☐ make a scene ☐ make the scene

SCHEDULE
☐ on schedule

SCHOOL
☐ tell tales out of school

SCORE
☐ have a score to settle with someone ☐ know the score ☐ settle a score with someone

SCOT
☐ go scot-free

SCRAPE
☐ bow and scrape ☐ have a scrape with someone or something ☐ scrape something together ☐ scrape the bottom of the barrel

SCRATCH
☐ make something from scratch ☐ not up to scratch ☐ scratch around for something ☐ scratch someone's back ☐ scratch the surface ☐ start from scratch

SCREAM
☐ scream bloody murder

SCREW
☐ have a screw loose ☐ put the screws on someone ☐ screw around with someone or something ☐ screw someone or something up ☐ screw up one's courage

SEA
☐ at sea about something ☐ between the devil and the deep blue sea ☐ There are plenty of other fish in the sea

SEALED
☐ signed, sealed, and delivered

SEAMS
☐ burst at the seams ☐ come apart at the seams ☐ fall apart at the seams

SEARCH
☐ go out in search of someone or something ☐ in search of someone or something ☐ Search me. ☐ search someone or something out

SEASON
☐ in season ☐ off season ☐ open season on someone or something ☐ out of season

SEAT
☐ by the seat of one's pants ☐ in the hot seat ☐ on the hot seat ☐ take a back seat to someone

SECOND
☐ come off second best ☐ get one's second wind ☐ get second thoughts about someone or something ☐ have second thoughts about someone or something ☐ in a second ☐ in a split second ☐ in one's second childhood ☐ in the second place ☐ on second thought ☐ play second fiddle to someone ☐ second nature to someone ☐ second to none

SECRET
☐ do something in secret

SEE
☐ begin to see daylight ☐ begin to see the light ☐ can't see beyond the end of one's nose ☐ can't see one's hand in front of one's face ☐ have seen better days ☐ Long time no see. ☐ not able to see the forest for the trees ☐ see a man about a dog ☐ see about something ☐ see after someone or something ☐ see eye to eye about something ☐ see fit to do something ☐ see into

something ☐ see no objection to something ☐ see one's way clear to do something ☐ see red ☐ see someone home ☐ see someone off ☐ see someone out ☐ see someone to the door ☐ see something through ☐ see the color of someone's money ☐ see the handwriting on the wall ☐ see the last of someone or something ☐ see the light at the end of the tunnel ☐ see the light of day ☐ see the light ☐ see the sights ☐ see through someone or something ☐ see to someone or something ☐ Seeing is believing. ☐ wait-and-see attitude

SEED
☐ go to seed ☐ run to seed

SEIZE
☐ seize on something ☐ seize the opportunity

SELL
☐ for something to sell like hotcakes ☐ get the hard sell ☐ give someone the hard sell ☐ sell out ☐ sell someone a bill of goods ☐ sell someone down the river ☐ sell someone on something ☐ sell someone or something out ☐ sell someone or something short ☐ sell something off ☐ sell something on credit

SEND
☐ get a big send-off ☐ give someone a big send-off ☐ send away for something ☐ send for someone or something ☐ send in for something ☐ send off for something ☐ send one about one's business ☐ send out for someone or something ☐ send someone away ☐ send someone on an errand ☐ send someone or something off ☐ send someone out for someone or something ☐ send someone packing ☐ send someone to the showers ☐ send someone up the river ☐ send something C.O.D. ☐ send up a trial balloon ☐ send word to someone

SENSE
☐ in a sense ☐ make sense out of someone or something

SENSES
☐ come to one's senses ☐ out of one's senses ☐ take leave of one's senses

SEPARATE
☐ separate the men from the boys ☐ separate the sheep from the goats

SERVE
☐ First come, first served. ☐ serve as a guinea pig ☐ serve notice ☐ serve someone right ☐ serve someone's purpose ☐ serve something up

SERVICE
☐ be at someone's service ☐ be of service to someone ☐ out of service ☐ pay lip service to something

SET
☐ all set ☐ at a set time ☐ dead set against someone or something ☐ get set ☐ have one's heart set against something ☐ have one's heart set on something ☐ not set foot somewhere ☐ set a precedent ☐ set eyes on someone or something ☐ set fire to someone or something ☐ set foot somewhere ☐ set forth on something ☐ set great store by someone or something ☐ set in ☐ set off for somewhere ☐ set one back on one's heels ☐ set one's sights on something ☐ set out for somewhere ☐ set sail for somewhere ☐ set someone or something back ☐ set someone or something free ☐ set someone or something off ☐ set someone or something on fire ☐ set someone or something straight ☐ set someone or something up ☐ set someone up as something ☐ set someone up in business ☐ set someone's teeth on edge ☐ set something aside ☐ set something down to something ☐ set something out ☐ set something right ☐ set the ball rolling ☐ set the table ☐ set the world on fire ☐ set to do something ☐ set up shop somewhere ☐ set upon someone or something

SETTLE
☐ have a score to settle with someone ☐ settle a score with someone ☐ settle down ☐ settle for something ☐ settle on something ☐ settle someone's affairs

SEVENS
☐ at sixes and sevens

SEVENTH
☐ in seventh heaven

SEW
☐ get something sewed up ☐ have something sewed up ☐ sew something up

SEX
☐ the opposite sex

SHACK
☐ shack up with someone

SHADOW
☐ afraid of one's own shadow ☐ beyond the shadow of a doubt

SHAKE
☐ get a fair shake from someone ☐ give someone a fair shake ☐ in two shakes of a lamb's tail ☐ more than one can shake a stick at ☐ no great shakes ☐ shake hands on something ☐ shake hands with someone ☐ shake in one's boots ☐ shake someone or something down ☐ shake someone or something off ☐ shake someone or something up ☐ shake the lead out ☐ shook up

SHAME
☐ For shame! ☐ hide one's face in shame ☐ put someone to shame ☐ Shame on someone.

SHANK
☐ by shank's mare

SHAPE
☐ in good shape ☐ in shape ☐ lick something into shape ☐ out of shape ☐ shape someone up ☐ Shape up or ship out. ☐ shape up

SHARE
☐ share and share alike

SHARP
☐ at sometime sharp

SHAVE
☐ have a close shave

SHED
☐ shed crocodile tears ☐ shed light on something

SHEEP
☐ black sheep of the family ☐ separate the sheep from the goats ☐ wolf in sheep's clothing

SHELL
☐ come out of one's shell ☐ shell something out

SHELLACKING
☐ get a shellacking ☐ give someone a shellacking ☐ take a shellacking

SHIFT
☐ shift for oneself

SHINE
☐ Make hay while the sun is shining. ☐ rain or shine ☐ shine up to someone ☐ take a shine to someone or something

SHIP
☐ desert a sinking ship ☐ run a taut ship ☐ run a tight ship ☐ Shape up or ship out. ☐ ship someone or something out

SIDE

□ be a thorn in someone's side □ choose up sides □ get on the good side of someone □ get out of the wrong side of the bed □ get up on the wrong side of the bed □ keep on the good side of someone □ know which side one's bread is buttered on □ laugh out of the other side of one's mouth □ off to one side □ other side of the tracks □ right side up □ side against someone □ side with someone □ take sides □ the wrong side of the tracks

SIGHT

□ buy something sight unseen □ can't stand the sight of someone or something □ catch sight of someone or something □ know someone by sight □ lose sight of someone or something □ love at first sight □ lower one's sights □ out of sight □ Out of sight, out of mind. □ raise one's sights □ see the sights □ set one's sights on something □ sight for sore eyes

SIGN

□ get the high sign □ give someone the high sign □ show signs of something □ sign in □ sign off □ sign on the dotted line □ sign on with someone □ sign on □ sign one's own death warrant □ sign someone or something in □ sign someone or something out □ sign someone up □ sign something over to someone □ sign up for something □ signed, sealed, and delivered

SILK

□ Make a silk purse out of a sow's ear.

SILVER

□ born with a silver spoon in one's mouth □ Every cloud has a silver lining.

SIMMER

□ simmer down

SING

□ sing a different tune

SINGLE

□ in single file □ single someone or something out

SINK

□ desert a sinking ship □ everything but the kitchen sink □ sink in □ sink into despair □ sink one's teeth into something □ sink or swim

SINKER

□ swallow something hook, line, and sinker

SIT

□ at a sitting □ like a sitting duck □ sit back and let something happen □ sit idly by □ sit in for someone □ sit in on something □ sit on its hands □ sit on one's hands □ sit on someone or something □ sit something out □ sit through something □ sit tight □ sit up and take notice □ sit up with someone □ sit with someone □ sitting on a powder keg □ sitting on top of the world □ sitting pretty

SIX

□ deep-six someone or something □ six of one and half a dozen of the other

SIXES

□ at sixes and sevens

SIZE

□ beat someone down to size □ cut someone down to size □ knock someone down to size □ size someone or something up □ take someone down to size □ That's about the size of it.

SKATE

□ skate on thin ice

SKELETON

□ skeleton in the closet

SKIDS

□ hit the skids □ put the skids on something

SKIN

□ Beauty is only skin deep. □ by the skin of one's teeth □ get under someone's skin □ give someone some skin □ jump out of one's skin □ no skin off someone's nose □ no skin off someone's teeth □ nothing but skin and bones □ save someone's skin □ skin someone alive □ soaked to the skin □ There's more than one way to skin a cat.

SKIP

□ have one's heart skip a beat □ skip bail □ Skip it! □ skip out on someone or something

SKULL

□ get something through someone's thick skull

SKY

□ as high as the sky □ go sky high □ out of a clear blue sky □ pie in the sky □ praise someone or something to the skies □ reach for the sky

SLACK

□ slack off

SLAP
□ get a slap on the wrist □ give someone a slap on the wrist □ slap someone down □ slap someone's wrist □ slap something together

SLATE
□ slated for something □ slated to do something □ start with a clean slate □ wipe someone's slate clean

SLEEP
□ doze off to sleep □ drift off to sleep □ drop off to sleep □ Let sleeping dogs lie. □ lose sleep over someone or something □ not sleep a wink □ put someone or something to sleep □ sleep like a log □ sleep on something □ sleep something off □ sleep with someone

SLEEVE
□ have one's heart on one's sleeve □ have something up one's sleeve □ laugh up one's sleeve □ roll one's sleeves up □ wear one's heart on one's sleeve

SLICK
□ as slick as a whistle

SLIDE
□ let something slide

SLIP
□ get the slip □ give someone the slip □ let something slip by □ let something slip out □ let the chance slip by □ slip away □ slip of the tongue □ slip off □ slip one's mind □ slip out □ slip through someone's fingers □ slip up

SLIPPERY
□ as slippery as an eel

SLOUGH
□ slough something off

SLOW
□ Slow and steady wins the race. □ slow on the draw □ slow on the uptake □ slow someone or something down □ slow someone or something up □ take it slow

SLY
□ do something on the sly

SMACK
□ smack dab in the middle □ smack someone down

SMALL
□ big frog in a small pond □ engage in small talk

SMART
□ as smart as a fox

SMELL
□ smell a rat

SMILE
□ crack a smile

SMOKE
□ go up in smoke □ have a smoke □ Put that in your pipe and smoke it! □ smoke someone or something out □ Where there's smoke there's fire.

SMOOTH
□ smooth something out □ smooth something over

SNAG
□ hit a snag

SNAIL
□ at a snail's pace

SNAKE
□ snake-in-the-grass

SNAP
□ snap out of something □ snap something up □ Snap to it!

SNAPPY
□ Make it snappy!

SNEAK
□ sneak up on someone or something

SNEEZE
□ nothing to sneeze at

SNIFF
□ sniff someone or something out

SNIT
□ in a snit

SNOW
□ as white as the driven snow □ do a snow job on someone □ snowed in □ snowed under

SNOWBALL
□ have a snowball's chance in hell

SNUFF
□ snuff something out □ up to snuff

SNUG
□ as snug as a bug in a rug

SO
□ do so □ go so far as to say something □ have so □ in so many words □ never had it so good □ on someone's say-so □ So be it. □ So far, so good. □ So it goes. □ so long □ so much for someone or something □ so much the better □ so still you could hear a pin drop □ so to speak □ so-and-so □ so-so

SOAK
□ soak in □ soak something up □ soaked to the skin

SOBER
□ as sober as a judge

SOCIETY
□ pay one's debt to society

SOCK
- □ sock something away

SOFT
- □ as soft as a baby's bottom □ have a soft spot in one's heart for someone or something

SOIL
- □ soil one's hands

SOME
- □ and then some □ catch some Zs □ dig some dirt up on someone □ drum some business up □ give someone some skin □ in some neck of the woods □ knock some heads together □ raise some eyebrows □ to some extent □ to the tune of some amount of money □ use some elbow grease

SOMETIME
- □ drop around sometime

SON
- □ son of a bitch □ son of a gun

SONG
- □ buy something for a song □ go into one's song and dance about something

SOON
- □ A fool and his money are soon parted. □ as soon as possible □ had as soon do something □ had sooner do something □ just as soon do something □ no sooner said than done □ sooner or later □ would as soon do something

SORE
- □ sight for sore eyes □ stick out like a sore thumb □ touch a sore point □ touch a sore spot

SORROWS
- □ drown one's sorrows

SORT
- □ in bad sorts □ out of sorts □ something of the sort □ sort of something □ sort something out

SOUGHT
- □ much sought after

SOUL
- □ every living soul □ keep body and soul together □ not a living soul □ with all one's heart and soul

SOUND
- □ safe and sound □ sound someone out

SOUP
- □ as easy as duck soup □ as thick as pea soup □ everything from soup to nuts □ in the soup □ soup something up

SOUR
- □ strike a sour note

SOUTH
- □ down South

SOW
- □ sow one's wild oats

SOW'S
- □ Make a silk purse out of a sow's ear.

SPACE
- □ spaced out □ take up space

SPADE
- □ call a spade a spade

SPAIN
- □ build castles in Spain

SPAN
- □ spick-and-span

SPARE
- □ have something to spare □ in one's spare time

SPAZ
- □ have a spaz

SPEAK
- □ Actions speak louder than words. □ nothing to speak of □ on speaking terms with someone □ so to speak □ speak highly of someone or something □ speak of the devil □ speak off the cuff □ speak one's mind □ speak one's piece □ speak out of turn □ speak out on something □ speak up for someone or something □ speak up □ spoken for

SPEED
- □ at full speed □ speed someone or something up

SPELL
- □ spell something out □ spell trouble

SPICE
- □ Variety is the spice of life.

SPICK
- □ spick-and-span

SPILL
- □ cry over spilled milk. □ spill the beans □ take a spill

SPIN
- □ make someone's head spin □ spin one's wheels □ spin something off □ spin something out

SPIT
- □ be the spit and image of someone □ spit and image □ spit something up

SPITE
- □ cut off one's nose to spite one's face □ in spite of someone or something

SPLIT
- □ in a split second □ split hairs □

split people up □ split something fifty-fifty □ split the difference □ split up
SPOIL
□ To the victors belong the spoils. □ Too many cooks spoil the broth. □ Too many cooks spoil the stew.
SPONGE
□ throw in the sponge
SPOOK
□ spook someone or something
SPOON
□ born with a silver spoon in one's mouth
SPOT
□ have a soft spot in one's heart for someone or something □ hit the high spots □ hit the spot □ in a spot □ in a tight spot □ Johnny-on-the-spot □ on the spot □ put someone on the spot □ touch a sore spot □ X marks the spot
SPOTLIGHT
□ in the spotlight □ steal the spotlight
SPOUT
□ spout off about someone or something
SPREAD
□ spread it on thick □ spread like wildfire □ spread oneself too thin
SPRING
□ no spring chicken □ spring for something □ spring something on someone
SPRUCE
□ spruce someone or something up
SPUR
□ on the spur of the moment
SQUARE
□ do something fair and square □ square accounts with someone □ square off for something □ square peg in a round hole □ square someone or something away
SQUEAK
□ squeak by someone or something
SQUEEZE
□ put the squeeze on someone
SQUIRREL
□ squirrel something away
STAB
□ have a stab at something □ stab someone in the back □ take a stab at something
STACK
□ blow one's stack □ have the cards

stacked against one □ stack something up □ stack the cards against someone or something □ stack the deck against someone or something
STAG
□ go stag
STAGE
□ at this stage of the game □ in a stage whisper
STAKE
□ at stake □ burn someone at the stake □ pull up stakes □ stake a claim to something
STALL
□ stall someone or something off
STAMP
□ one's old stamping ground □ stamp someone or something out
STAND
(See also *STOOD.*)□ able to do something standing on one's head □ can't stand someone or something □ can't stand the sight of someone or something □ have one's heart stand still □ know where someone stands on someone or something □ make someone's hair stand on end □ not have a leg to stand on □ one-night stand □ stand a chance □ stand back of someone or something □ stand behind someone or something □ stand by someone □ stand by □ stand for something □ stand in awe of someone or something □ stand in for someone □ stand in someone's way □ stand on ceremony □ stand on one's own two feet □ stand one's ground □ stand out □ stand over someone □ stand pat □ stand someone in good stead □ stand someone to a treat □ stand someone up □ stand still for someone or something □ stand to reason □ stand up against someone or something □ stand up and be counted □ stand up for someone or something □ stand up to someone or something □ stand up with someone □ stand up □ take a stand against someone or something □ take the stand
STANDSTILL
□ come to a standstill
STARCH
□ take the starch out of someone
STARE
□ stare someone in the face

STARS

☐ get stars in one's eyes ☐ have stars in one's eyes ☐ thank one's lucky stars

START

☐ by fits and starts ☐ from start to finish ☐ get a head start on someone or something ☐ get a start ☐ get off to a bad start ☐ get one's start ☐ get someone or something started ☐ give someone a head start on someone or something ☐ give someone a start ☐ have a head start on someone or something ☐ have someone or something started ☐ off to a running start ☐ start from scratch ☐ start out as something ☐ start out ☐ start someone in as something ☐ start someone out as something ☐ start something up ☐ start something ☐ start the ball rolling ☐ start with a clean slate

STARTERS

☐ for starters

STATE

☐ lie in state ☐ pretty state of affairs

STATION

☐ as busy as Grand Central Station

STAY

☐ have no staying power ☐ stay after someone ☐ stay ahead of someone or something ☐ stay away from someone or something ☐ stay in touch with someone ☐ stay out ☐ stay up late

STEAD

☐ stand someone in good stead

STEADY

☐ go steady with someone ☐ Slow and steady wins the race.

STEAL

☐ steal a base ☐ steal a march on someone ☐ steal someone's thunder ☐ steal the show ☐ steal the spotlight

STEAM

☐ blow off steam ☐ let off steam ☐ steamed up ☐ under one's own steam

STEER

☐ steer clear of someone or something

STEM

☐ from stem to stern

STEP

☐ in step with someone or something ☐ out of step with someone or something ☐ step by step ☐ step down from something ☐ step into the breach ☐ step on it ☐ step on someone's toes ☐

step on the gas ☐ step out of line ☐ step something up ☐ step up ☐ take steps to prevent something

STERN

☐ from stem to stern

STEVEN

☐ be even-steven

STEW

☐ in a stew about someone or something ☐ stew in one's own juice ☐ Too many cooks spoil the stew.

STICK

☐ get the short end of the stick ☐ have one's words stick in one's throat ☐ have something stick in one's craw ☐ more than one can shake a stick at ☐ not hold a stick to someone or something ☐ Stick 'em up! ☐ stick around ☐ stick by someone or something ☐ stick one's foot in one's mouth ☐ stick one's neck out ☐ stick one's nose into something ☐ stick out like a sore thumb ☐ stick someone or something up ☐ stick someone with someone or something ☐ stick something out ☐ stick to one's guns ☐ stick together ☐ stick up for someone or something ☐ stick with someone or something ☐ stick-in-the-mud ☐ stuck on someone or something ☐ stuck with someone or something

STICKY

☐ have sticky fingers

STIFF

☐ bore someone stiff ☐ keep a stiff upper lip ☐ scare someone stiff

STILL

☐ have one's heart stand still ☐ hold someone or something still ☐ hold still for something ☐ hold still ☐ keep someone or something still ☐ keep still about someone or something ☐ keep still for something ☐ keep still ☐ so still you could hear a pin drop ☐ stand still for someone or something ☐ Still waters run deep.

STINK

☐ create a stink about something ☐ raise a stink about something

STIR

☐ cause a stir ☐ go stir crazy ☐ stir someone or something up ☐ stir up a hornet's nest

STITCHES

☐ keep someone in stitches

STOCK
☐ have something in stock ☐ in stock ☐ lock, stock, and barrel ☐ out of stock ☐ stock up on something ☐ take no stock in something ☐ take stock of something

STOMACH
☐ can't stomach someone or something ☐ get butterflies in one's stomach ☐ give one butterflies in one's stomach ☐ have butterflies in one's stomach ☐ have eyes bigger than one's stomach ☐ one's eyes are bigger than one's stomach ☐ turn someone's stomach

STONE
☐ A rolling stone gathers no moss. ☐ a stone's throw away ☐ cast the first stone ☐ have a heart of stone ☐ kill two birds with one stone ☐ leave no stone unturned ☐ run into a stone wall

STOOD
☐ should have stood in bed

STOOP
☐ stoop to doing something

STOP
☐ put a stop to something ☐ stop at nothing ☐ stop by someplace ☐ stop in someplace ☐ stop off someplace ☐ stop over someplace

STORE
☐ have something in store for someone ☐ mind the store ☐ set great store by someone or something

STORM
☐ kick up a storm ☐ take someone or something by storm

STORY
☐ cock-and-bull story ☐ make a long story short

STOW
☐ stow away

STRAIGHT
☐ get something straight ☐ go straight ☐ keep a straight face ☐ put something straight ☐ set someone or something straight ☐ straight from the horse's mouth ☐ straight from the shoulder ☐ vote a straight ticket

STRAIGHTEN
☐ straighten someone or something out ☐ straighten someone or something up ☐ straighten up

STRAPPED
☐ strapped for something

STRAW
☐ grasp at straws ☐ That's the last straw.

STREAK
☐ talk a blue streak

STREET
☐ down the street ☐ on easy street

STRENGTH
☐ on the strength of something

STRETCH
☐ stretch a point

STRICTLY
☐ strictly on the up and up

STRIDE
☐ hit one's stride ☐ reach one's stride ☐ take something in stride

STRIKE
☐ get two strikes against one ☐ go on strike ☐ have two strikes against one ☐ strike a bargain ☐ strike a happy medium ☐ strike a match ☐ strike a sour note ☐ strike it rich ☐ strike out at someone or something ☐ strike out ☐ strike someone funny ☐ strike someone out ☐ strike someone's fancy ☐ strike up a conversation ☐ strike up a friendship ☐ strike while the iron is hot

STRING
(See also STRUNG.)☐ control the purse strings ☐ have someone on the string ☐ pull strings ☐ string along with someone ☐ string something out ☐ tied to one's mother's apron strings ☐ with no strings attached

STROKE
☐ have a stroke ☐ stroke of luck

STRONG
☐ as strong as an ox ☐ use strong language

STRUGGLE
☐ struggle to the death

STRUNG
☐ strung out

STUBBORN
☐ as stubborn as a mule

STUFF
☐ know one's stuff ☐ stuff and nonsense ☐ stuff the ballot box

STUFFING
☐ beat the stuffing out of someone

STUMBLE
☐ stumble across someone or something ☐ stumble into someone or something ☐ stumble on someone or something

STUNT
☐ pull a stunt on someone
STYLE
☐ cramp someone's style ☐ go out of style ☐ in style ☐ out of style
SUBJECT
☐ subject to something
SUBSCRIBE
☐ subscribe to something
SUCH
☐ such as it is ☐ Such is life! ☐ such-and-such
SUCK
☐ suck someone in
SUDDEN
☐ all of a sudden
SUIT
☐ follow suit ☐ in one's birthday suit ☐ suit someone to a T ☐ suit up ☐ suit yourself
SUITCASE
☐ live out of a suitcase
SUM
☐ sum something up
SUN
☐ Make hay while the sun is shining.
SUNDAY
☐ in a month of Sundays ☐ in one's Sunday best ☐ Sunday-go-to-meeting clothes
SUNDRY
☐ all and sundry
SUPPLY
☐ in short supply
SURE
☐ for sure
SURFACE
☐ scratch the surface
SURPRISE
☐ take someone or something by surprise
SURVIVAL
☐ survival of the fittest
SUSPICION
☐ above suspicion ☐ under a cloud of suspicion
SWALLOW
☐ look like the cat that swallowed the canary ☐ swallow one's pride ☐ swallow something hook, line, and sinker
SWATH
☐ cut a wide swath
SWEAR
☐ swear by someone or something ☐

swear someone in ☐ swear something off
SWEAT
☐ break out in a cold sweat ☐ by the sweat of one's brow ☐ No sweat. ☐ sweat blood ☐ sweat something out
SWEEP
☐ make a clean sweep ☐ sweep one off one's feet ☐ sweep something up
SWEET
☐ have a sweet tooth ☐ short and sweet ☐ sweet on someone ☐ sweet talk someone ☐ take the bitter with the sweet
SWELLED
☐ get a swelled head ☐ give someone a swelled head ☐ have a swelled head
SWIM
☐ in the swim of things ☐ make someone's head swim ☐ out of the swim of things ☐ sink or swim ☐ swim against the current ☐ swim against the tide
SWINE
☐ cast pearls before swine
SWING
☐ get into full swing ☐ get into the swing of things ☐ in full swing ☐ not enough room to swing a cat ☐ swing into action ☐ swing something
SWITCH
☐ asleep at the switch
SWOOP
☐ at one fell swoop
SWORDS
☐ cross swords with someone
SYMPATHY
☐ extend one's sympathy to someone
SYSTEM
☐ all systems are go ☐ get something out of one's system
TAB
☐ pick up the tab
TABLE
☐ clear the table ☐ lay one's cards on the table ☐ put one's cards on the table ☐ set the table ☐ turn the tables on someone ☐ under the table
TABS
☐ keep tabs on someone or something
TACKS
☐ get down to brass tacks
TAIL
☐ can't make heads or tails of someone or something ☐ Get off someone's tail! ☐ have one's tail between one's

take the bitter with the sweet □ take the bull by the horns □ take the cake □ take the day off □ take the edge off something □ take the law into one's own hands □ take the liberty of doing something □ take the lid off something □ take the rap for someone or something □ take the stand □ take the starch out of someone □ take the trouble to do something □ take the wind out of someone's sails □ take the words out of one's mouth □ take time off □ take to one's heels □ take to someone or something □ take too much on □ take turns at doing something □ take up a collection □ take up arms against someone or something □ take up one's abode somewhere □ take up room □ take up someone's time □ take up space □ take up time □ take up with someone □ taken aback □ taken for dead □ That takes care of that. □ You can't take it with you.

TALES
□ tell tales out of school

TALK
□ all talk and no action □ be talked out □ engage in small talk □ have a heart-to-heart talk □ money talks □ sweet talk someone □ talk a blue streak □ talk back to someone □ talk big □ talk down to someone □ talk in circles □ talk oneself out □ talk shop □ talk someone down □ talk someone into doing something □ talk someone or something up □ talk someone out of doing something □ talk someone out of something □ talk someone's ear off □ talk someone's head off □ talk something out □ talk something over □ talk through one's hat □ talk turkey □ talk until one is blue in the face

TAMPER
□ tamper with something

TAN
□ tan someone's hide

TAPER
□ taper off doing something

TAR
□ beat the tar out of someone □ tar and feather someone □ whale the tar out of someone

TARGET
□ on target

TASK
□ take someone to task

TASTE
□ acquire a taste for something □ in bad taste □ in poor taste □ leave a bad taste in someone's mouth □ There's no accounting for taste.

TAT
□ give someone tit for tat

TAUT
□ run a taut ship

TEA
□ not someone's cup of tea

TEACH
□ teach someone a lesson □ You can't teach an old dog new tricks.

TEACHER
□ be the teacher's pet

TEAM
□ team up with someone

TEAPOT
□ tempest in a teapot

TEAR
□ tear into someone or something □ tear off □ tear one's hair □ tear someone or something down □ tear someone or something up □ tear something off □ wear and tear on something

TEARS
□ break out into tears □ burst into tears □ shed crocodile tears

TEE
□ tee someone off

TEETH
(See also *TOOTH.*)□ armed to the teeth □ as scarce as hen's teeth □ by the skin of one's teeth □ cut teeth □ fly in the teeth of someone or something □ get one's teeth into something □ grit one's teeth □ lie through one's teeth □ no skin off someone's teeth □ pull someone's or something's teeth □ scarcer than hen's teeth □ set someone's teeth on edge □ sink one's teeth into something □ take the bit in one's teeth

TELL
□ a little bird told me □ all told □ Tell it to the marines. □ tell on someone □ tell one to one's face □ tell people apart □ tell someone a thing or two □ tell someone off □ tell someone on someone □ tell someone where to get off □ tell tales out of school □ tell things apart □ tell time □ tell which is which □ Time will tell.

451

TEMPER
□ hold one's temper □ keep one's temper □ lose one's temper

TEMPERATURE
□ run a temperature

TEMPEST
□ tempest in a teapot

TENTERHOOKS
□ keep someone on tenterhooks

TERMS
□ come to terms with someone or something □ in no uncertain terms □ in terms of something □ on good terms with someone □ on speaking terms with someone

TERRITORY
□ cover the territory

TEST
□ put someone to the test

TETHER
□ at the end of one's tether

THAN
□ Actions speak louder than words. □ better late than never □ bite off more than one can chew □ easier said than done □ Half a loaf is better than none. □ have eyes bigger than one's stomach □ in less than no time □ less than pleased □ more often than not □ more than one can shake a stick at □ more to something than meets the eye □ no sooner said than done □ One's bark is worse than one's bite. □ one's eyes are bigger than one's stomach □ scarcer than hen's teeth □ There's more than one way to skin a cat. □ wear more than one hat

THANK
□ thank one's lucky stars □ thanks to someone or something

THEM'S
□ Them's fighting words.

THEN
□ and then some □ every now and then □ now and then □ then and there

THERE
□ hang in there □ here and there □ in there pitching □ neither here nor there □ not all there □ then and there □ There are plenty of other fish in the sea □ there is no doing something □ There will be the devil to pay. □ There's more than one way to skin a cat. □ There's no accounting for taste. □ Where there's

a will there's a way. □ Where there's smoke there's fire.

THICK
□ as thick as pea soup □ as thick as thieves □ get something into someone's thick head □ get something through someone's thick skull □ lay it on thick □ pour it on thick □ spread it on thick □ through thick and thin

THIEVES
□ as thick as thieves

THIN
□ on thin ice □ out of thin air □ pull something out of thin air □ skate on thin ice □ spread oneself too thin □ thin out □ thin something out □ through thick and thin □ vanish into thin air

THING
□ A little knowledge is a dangerous thing. □ do one's own thing □ do one's thing □ first thing in the morning □ First things first. □ get into the swing of things □ have a good thing going □ have a thing about someone or something □ have a thing going with someone □ in the swim of things □ just one of those things □ know a thing or two about someone or something □ not know the first thing about someone or something □ Of all things! □ out of the swim of things □ tell someone a thing or two □ tell things apart □ the in thing to do □ Things are looking up. □ too much of a good thing □ wash a few things out

THINK
□ come to think of it □ have another think coming □ put on one's thinking cap □ think a great deal of someone or something □ think a lot of someone or something □ think back on someone or something □ think highly of someone or something □ think little of someone or something □ think much of someone or something □ think nothing of someone or something □ think on one's feet □ think out loud □ think someone or something fit for something □ think something out □ think something over □ think something up □ think twice before doing something □ to someone's way of thinking

THIRD
□ get the third degree □ give someone the third degree

THORN
- be a thorn in someone's side

THOUGHT
- food for thought □ get second thoughts about someone or something □ have second thoughts about someone or something □ lose one's train of thought □ lost in thought □ on second thought □ Perish the thought.

THOUSAND
- one in a thousand

THREE
- like a three-ring circus

THRILL
- thrill someone to death □ thrill someone to pieces □ thrilled to death □ thrilled to pieces

THROAT
- cut someone's throat □ get a lump in one's throat □ have a lump in one's throat □ have one's words stick in one's throat □ jump down someone's throat □ ram someone or something down someone's throat □ shove someone or something down someone's throat

THRONE
- power behind the throne

THROUGH
- been through the mill □ break through something □ carry through on something □ come through □ fall through □ follow through on something □ get something through someone's thick skull □ get through something □ get through to someone □ get through with something □ go right through someone □ go through channels □ go through something □ go through the changes □ go through the motions □ go through the roof □ go through with something □ go through □ jump through a hoop □ leaf through something □ lie through one's teeth □ live through something □ make one's way through something □ pass through someone's mind □ pay through the nose for something □ pick one's way through something □ pull someone or something through something □ pull through □ put one through one's paces □ put someone through the wringer □ put something through its paces □ read something through □ run through something □ sail through some-

thing □ see something through □ see through someone or something □ shot through with something □ sit through something □ slip through someone's fingers □ talk through one's hat □ through and through □ through hell and high water □ through thick and thin □ through with someone or something □ thumb through something □ work one's way through college □ work through channels

THROW
- a stone's throw away □ throw a fit □ throw a monkey wrench in the works □ throw a party for someone □ throw caution to the wind □ throw cold water on something □ throw down the gauntlet □ throw good money after bad □ throw in the sponge □ throw in the towel □ throw one's weight around □ throw oneself at someone's feet □ throw oneself at someone □ throw oneself on the mercy of the court □ throw someone a curve □ throw someone for a loop □ throw someone for a loss □ throw someone off the track □ throw someone or something off □ throw someone out of something □ throw someone over □ throw someone to the wolves □ throw someone's name around □ throw someone □ throw something away □ throw something into the bargain □ throw something together □ throw something up to someone □ throw something up □ throw the book at someone □ throw up one's hands in despair □ throw up one's hands in horror □ throw up

THUMB
- all thumbs □ get someone under one's thumb □ have a green thumb □ have someone under one's thumb □ stick out like a sore thumb □ thumb a ride □ thumb one's nose at someone or something □ thumb through something □ thumbs down on someone or something □ twiddle one's thumbs

THUNDER
- steal someone's thunder

TICK
- as full as a tick □ as tight as a tick □ make someone or something tick □ what makes someone tick

TICKET
- round-trip ticket □ That's the ticket. □ vote a straight ticket

TICKLE

☐ tickle someone pink ☐ tickle someone to death ☐ tickle someone's fancy

TIDE

☐ swim against the tide ☐ tide someone over ☐ turn the tide

TIE

☐ fit to be tied ☐ have one's hands tied ☐ tie into something ☐ tie someone down ☐ tie someone in knots ☐ tie someone or something up ☐ tie someone's hands ☐ tie the knot ☐ tie traffic up ☐ tied down ☐ tied to one's mother's apron strings ☐ tied up ☐ with one hand tied behind one's back

TIGHT

☐ as tight as a tick ☐ as tight as Dick's hatband ☐ hold tight ☐ in a tight spot ☐ run a tight ship ☐ sit tight

TIGHTEN

☐ tighten one's belt

TIGHTROPE

☐ walk a tightrope

TILL

☐ have one's hand in the till ☐ till the cows come home

TILT

☐ at full tilt ☐ tilt at windmills

TIME

☐ ahead of time ☐ all in good time ☐ all the time ☐ at a set time ☐ at all times ☐ at the appointed time ☐ at the present time ☐ at the same time ☐ at this point in time ☐ at times ☐ bide one's time ☐ every time one turns around ☐ fight against time ☐ for the time being ☐ from time to time ☐ get a hard time ☐ get time for someone or something ☐ get time off ☐ get time to catch one's breath ☐ give someone a hard time ☐ hardly have time to breathe ☐ have a rough time of it ☐ have a whale of a time ☐ have no time for someone or something ☐ have the time of one's life ☐ have time for someone or something ☐ have time off ☐ have time to catch one's breath ☐ in due time ☐ in good time ☐ in less than no time ☐ in no time ☐ in one's spare time ☐ in the course of time ☐ in the nick of time ☐ in time ☐ It's about time! ☐ It's high time. ☐ keep good time ☐ keep time ☐ keep up with the times ☐ kill time ☐ live on borrowed time ☐ Long time no see. ☐ make good time ☐ make time with someone ☐ make up for lost time ☐ many is the time ☐ not able to call one's time one's own ☐ not give anyone the time of day ☐ on one's own time ☐ on time ☐ once upon a time ☐ one at a time ☐ out of time ☐ pass the time of day with someone ☐ pass the time ☐ race against time ☐ right on time ☐ run out of time ☐ take one's time ☐ take time off ☐ take up someone's time ☐ take up time ☐ tell time ☐ time after time ☐ time and again ☐ time and time again ☐ Time hangs heavy on someone's hands. ☐ Time is money. ☐ Time is up. ☐ time out ☐ Time will tell. ☐ two-time someone ☐ when the time is ripe ☐ while away the time

TIP

☐ on the tip of one's tongue ☐ tip someone off ☐ tip something over ☐ tip the scales at something

TIPTOE

☐ on tiptoe

TIRE

☐ sick and tired of someone or something ☐ tire someone out

TIT

☐ give someone tit for tat

TOE

☐ on one's toes ☐ step on someone's toes ☐ toe the line ☐ toe the mark ☐ tread on someone's toes ☐ turn up one's toes

TOGETHER

☐ Birds of a feather flock together. ☐ get it all together ☐ get it together ☐ get one's act together ☐ get together ☐ go together ☐ hang together ☐ keep body and soul together ☐ knock some heads together ☐ piece something together ☐ pull oneself together ☐ pull something together ☐ put something together ☐ put two and two together ☐ scrape something together ☐ slap something together ☐ stick together ☐ throw something together

TOKEN

☐ as a token of something ☐ by the same token

TON

☐ hit someone like a ton of bricks

TONE

☐ tone something down

TONGS
□ fight someone or something hammer and tongs □ go at it hammer and tongs

TONGUE
□ bite one's tongue □ Cat got your tongue? □ cause tongues to wag □ find one's tongue □ get a tongue-lashing □ give someone a tongue-lashing □ hold one's tongue □ keep a civil tongue in one's head □ on the tip of one's tongue □ slip of the tongue □ tongue-in-cheek

TOO
□ be too □ do too □ eat one's cake and have it too □ go too far □ have one's cake and eat it too □ have too many irons in the fire □ have too □ know something only too well □ spread oneself too thin □ take too much on □ too big for one's britches □ too close for comfort □ too good to be true □ Too many cooks spoil the broth. □ Too many cooks spoil the stew. □ too much of a good thing

TOOT
□ toot one's own horn

TOOTH
(See also *TEETH.*)□ An eye for an eye, a tooth for a tooth. □ fight someone or something tooth and nail □ go at it tooth and nail □ go over something with a fine-tooth comb □ have a sweet tooth

TOP
□ at the top of one's lungs □ at the top of one's voice □ blow one's top □ from top to bottom □ off the top of one's head □ on top of something □ on top of the world □ on top □ over the top □ sitting on top of the world □ top someone or something □ top something off with something □ top something off

TORCH
□ carry a torch for someone □ carry the torch

TOSS
□ toss one's cookies □ toss one's hat into the ring □ toss someone or something out □ toss something off

TOTAL
□ total something up

TOTEM
□ high man on the totem pole □ low man on the totem pole

TOUCH
□ get in touch with someone □ keep in touch with someone □ lose one's touch with someone or something □ lose touch with someone or something □ out of touch with someone or something □ stay in touch with someone □ touch a sore point □ touch a sore spot □ touch and go □ touch base with someone □ touch on something □ touch someone or something off □ touch something up □ touched by someone or something □ touched in the head

TOUGH
□ get tough with someone □ hang tough □ tough act to follow □ tough break □ tough it out □ Tough luck! □ tough nut to crack □ tough row to hoe

TOW
□ have someone or something in tow

TOWARD
□ go a long way toward doing something

TOWEL
□ throw in the towel

TOWER
□ live in an ivory tower

TOWN
□ all over town □ go to town □ night on the town □ out of town □ out on the town □ paint the town red

TOY
□ toy with someone or something

TRACK
□ cover someone's tracks up □ dead in someone's or something's tracks □ drop in one's tracks □ follow in someone's tracks □ get the inside track □ have the inside track □ jump the track □ keep track of someone or something □ lose track of someone or something □ make tracks somewhere □ off the beaten track □ off the track □ on the track of someone or something □ on the wrong track □ other side of the tracks □ the wrong side of the tracks □ throw someone off the track □ track someone or something down

TRADE
□ know all the tricks of the trade □ trade on something □ trade something in on something

TRAFFIC
□ tie traffic up

TRAIL
☐ blaze a trail ☐ on the trail of someone or something
TRAIN
☐ lose one's train of thought ☐ ride the gravy train
TRAP
☐ fall into a trap
TREAD
☐ tread on someone's toes
TREAT
☐ stand someone to a treat
TREATMENT
☐ get the red carpet treatment ☐ give someone the red carpet treatment
TREE
☐ bark up the wrong tree ☐ not able to see the forest for the trees ☐ up a tree
TREMBLING
☐ in fear and trembling
TRESPASSING
☐ no trespassing
TRIAL
☐ on trial ☐ send up a trial balloon ☐ trial and error
TRICK
☐ bag of tricks ☐ do the trick ☐ know all the tricks of the trade ☐ play tricks on someone ☐ pull a trick on someone ☐ use every trick in the book ☐ You can't teach an old dog new tricks.
TRIGGER
☐ quick on the trigger
TRIP
☐ round-trip ticket ☐ trip someone up
TROLLEY
☐ off one's trolley
TROUBLE
☐ ask for trouble ☐ borrow trouble ☐ drown one's troubles ☐ go to the trouble of doing something ☐ go to the trouble to do something ☐ look for trouble ☐ pour oil on troubled water ☐ spell trouble ☐ take the trouble to do something ☐ Trouble is brewing. ☐ trouble one's head about someone or something ☐ trouble oneself about someone or something ☐ trouble oneself to do something
TRUE
☐ come true ☐ dream come true ☐ hold true ☐ too good to be true ☐ true to form ☐ true to one's word

TRULY
☐ yours truly
TRUMP
☐ play one's trump card ☐ trumped-up
TRY
☐ take a try at something ☐ try one's hand at something ☐ try one's luck at something ☐ try one's wings ☐ try out for something ☐ try someone or something out ☐ try someone's patience ☐ try something on ☐ try something out on someone
TUCK
☐ nip and tuck
TUCKER
☐ all tuckered out ☐ best bib and tucker
TUNE
☐ call the tune ☐ can't carry a tune ☐ change someone's tune ☐ dance to another tune ☐ in tune with someone or something ☐ out of tune with someone or something ☐ sing a different tune ☐ to the tune of some amount of money ☐ tune someone or something out ☐ tune something in ☐ tune something up
TUNNEL
☐ see the light at the end of the tunnel
TURKEY
☐ go cold turkey ☐ talk turkey
TURN
☐ at every turn ☐ every time one turns around ☐ have turned the corner ☐ in turn ☐ not know where to turn ☐ not know which way to turn ☐ One good turn deserves another. ☐ out of turn ☐ speak out of turn ☐ take a new turn ☐ take a turn for the better ☐ take a turn for the worse ☐ take turns at doing something ☐ turn a blind eye to someone or something ☐ turn a deaf ear to something ☐ turn against someone or something ☐ turn around ☐ turn in ☐ turn into something ☐ turn of the century ☐ turn on a dime ☐ turn on someone ☐ turn on the waterworks ☐ turn one's back on someone or something ☐ turn one's nose up at someone or something ☐ turn out all right ☐ turn out to be someone or something ☐ turn out ☐ turn over a new leaf ☐ turn over in one's grave ☐ turn over ☐ turn someone or something down ☐ turn some-

one or something in □ turn someone or something into something □ turn someone or something off □ turn someone or something on □ turn someone or something out □ turn someone or something over to someone □ turn someone or something over □ turn someone or something up □ turn someone's head □ turn someone's stomach □ turn something around □ turn something to one's advantage □ turn the other cheek □ turn the tables on someone □ turn the tide □ turn to someone or something for something □ turn to □ turn turtle □ turn up one's toes □ turn up □ wait one's turn

TURTLE
□ turn turtle
TWICE
□ think twice before doing something
TWIDDLE
□ twiddle one's thumbs
TWINKLING
□ in the twinkling of an eye
TWIST
□ twist someone around one's little finger □ twist someone's arm
TWO
□ A bird in the hand is worth two in the bush. □ divide something in two □ game at which two can play □ get two strikes against one □ have two strikes against one □ in two shakes of a lamb's tail □ kill two birds with one stone □ know a thing or two about someone or something □ no two ways about it □ not care two hoots about someone or something □ put in one's two cents worth □ put two and two together □ stand on one's own two feet □ take someone down a notch or two □ take someone down a peg or two □ tell someone a thing or two □ That makes two of us. □ two-time someone
UNCERTAIN
□ in no uncertain terms
UNCLE
□ say uncle
UNDER
□ build a fire under someone □ cut the ground out from under someone □ get out from under someone or something □ get someone or something under control □ get someone under

one's thumb □ get something under one's belt □ get under someone's skin □ go under the knife □ go under □ have someone or something under control □ have someone under one's thumb □ hide one's light under a bushel □ hot under the collar □ keep something under one's hat □ keep something under wraps □ knuckle under to someone or something □ let grass grow under one's feet □ out from under something □ pull the rug out from under someone □ sail under false colors □ say something under one's breath □ snowed under □ take someone under one's wing □ under a cloud of suspicion □ under construction □ under fire □ under one's own steam □ under the circumstances □ under the counter □ under the table □ under the weather □ under the wire □ water under the bridge
UNDERSTAND
□ give someone to understand something □ given to understand □ reach an understanding with someone
UNDERWAY
□ get something underway □ get underway
UNGLUED
□ come unglued
UNKNOWN
□ be an unknown quantity
UNLIKELY
□ in the unlikely event of something
UNSEEN
□ buy something sight unseen
UNTIL
□ talk until one is blue in the face □ until all hours
UNTIMELY
□ come to an untimely end
UNTO
□ law unto oneself
UNTURNED
□ leave no stone unturned
UPON
□ call upon someone □ come upon someone or something □ fall upon someone or something □ feel put upon □ hit upon something □ incumbent upon someone to do something □ once upon a time □ prevail upon someone □ prey upon someone or something □ set upon someone or something □ take something upon oneself

UPPER
□ get the upper hand on someone □ have the upper hand on someone □ keep a stiff upper lip

UPROAR
□ create an uproar □ make an uproar

UPS
□ ups and downs

UPSET
□ upset someone's plans □ upset the apple cart

UPSHOT
□ the upshot of something

UPSIDE
□ upside down

UPTAKE
□ quick on the uptake □ slow on the uptake

USE
□ get used to someone or something □ have no use for someone or something □ It's no use doing something. □ make use of someone or something □ put something to good use □ use every trick in the book □ use one's head □ use some elbow grease □ use someone or something as an excuse □ use something up □ use strong language □ used to someone or something

UTTER
□ not utter a word

VACATION
□ on vacation

VAIN
□ do something in vain

VALUE
□ take something at face value

VANISH
□ vanish into thin air

VARIETY
□ Variety is the spice of life.

VENGEANCE
□ do something with a vengeance

VENT
□ give vent to something

VENTURED
□ Nothing ventured, nothing gained.

VERGE
□ on the verge of doing something □ verge on something

VICIOUS
□ in a vicious circle

VICTORS
□ To the victors belong the spoils.

VIEW
□ in view of something □ on view □ take a dim view of something □ with a view to doing something

VINE
□ die on the vine □ wither on the vine

VIRTUE
□ by virtue of something

VISIT
□ pay someone a visit

VOICE
□ at the top of one's voice □ give voice to something □ have a voice in something □ lower one's voice □ raise one's voice to someone

VOID
□ null and void

VOTE
□ vote a straight ticket □ vote someone in □ vote someone out □ vote something down

WADE
□ wade into something

WAG
□ cause tongues to wag □ tail wagging the dog □ wag one's chin

WAGON
□ fix someone's wagon □ on the wagon

WAIT
□ lie in wait for someone or something □ not able to wait □ on a waiting list □ wait on someone hand and foot □ wait one's turn □ wait up for someone or something □ wait-and-see attitude

WAKE
□ in the wake of something □ wake someone or something up

WALK
□ all walks of life □ get one's walking papers □ give one one's walking papers □ take a walk □ walk a tightrope □ walk all over someone □ walk away with something □ walk off with something □ walk on air □ walk on eggs □ walk out on someone or something □ walk the floor

WALL
□ bang one's head against a brick wall □ beat one's head against the wall □ climb the wall □ drive someone to the wall □ drive someone up the wall □ force someone to the wall □ go to the wall □ have one's back to the wall □ off the wall □ push someone to the wall

□ see the handwriting on the wall □ Walls have ears.

WALLOP
□ pack a wallop

WANT
□ want out of something

WAR
□ act of war □ all-out war

WARM
□ warm someone or something up □ warm the bench □ warm the cockles of someone's heart □ warm up to someone

WARPATH
□ on the warpath

WARRANT
□ sign one's own death warrant

WASH
□ come out in the wash □ wash a few things out □ wash one's hands of someone or something □ wash someone or something off □ wash someone or something up □ wash something down □ wash something out

WASTE
□ go to waste □ Haste makes waste. □ lay something to waste □ waste away □ waste one's breath □ waste someone

WATCH
□ A watched pot never boils. □ bear watching □ keep watch on someone or something □ keep watch over someone or something □ on watch for someone or something □ watch out for someone or something

WATER
□ as a duck takes to water □ come hell or high water □ dash cold water on something □ get one's head above water □ in deep water □ in hot water □ keep one's head above water □ like a fish out of water □ like water off a duck's back □ make someone's mouth water □ not hold water □ of the first water □ pour cold water on something □ pour oil on troubled water □ Still waters run deep. □ through hell and high water □ throw cold water on something □ water something down □ water under the bridge □ won't hold water

WATERFRONT
□ cover the waterfront

WATERLOO
□ meet one's Waterloo

WATERWORKS
□ turn on the waterworks

WAVES
□ make waves

WAY
□ all the way □ by the way □ by way of something □ come someone's way □ do something the hard way □ downhill all the way □ every which way □ find one's or something's way somewhere □ find one's way around □ find something out the hard way □ from way back □ get in someone's way □ get one's way with someone or something □ get out of someone's way □ get someone or something out of the way □ give way to someone or something □ go a long way toward doing something □ go all the way to somewhere □ go all the way with someone □ go out of one's way to do something □ have a way with someone or something □ have come a long way □ have it both ways □ have one's way with someone or something □ have the right-of-way □ in a bad way □ in a family way □ in one's own way □ in the family way □ in the way of someone or something □ in the worst way □ know one's way about □ know one's way around □ lead the way □ learn something the hard way □ look the other way □ make one's way through something □ make way for someone or something □ make way □ no two ways about it □ No way. □ not know which way to turn □ on someone's way □ on the way somewhere □ on the way to doing something □ one way or another □ one's way of life □ out of the way □ parting of the ways □ pave the way for someone or something □ pay someone's way □ pick one's way through something □ put someone or something out of the way □ put something in the way of someone □ rub someone the wrong way □ rub someone's fur the wrong way □ say something in a roundabout way □ see one's way clear to do something □ stand in someone's way □ take something the wrong way □ That's the way the ball bounces. □ That's the way the cookie crumbles. □ the other way round □ There's more

than one way to skin a cat. □ to someone's way of thinking □ Where there's a will there's a way. □ work one's way into something □ work one's way through college □ work one's way up □ worm one's way out of something □ yield the right-of-way

WAYSIDE

□ drop by the wayside □ fall by the wayside

WEAK

□ as weak as a kitten

WEAKNESS

□ have a weakness for someone or something

WEALTHY

□ Early to bed, early to rise, makes a man healthy, wealthy, and wise.

WEAR

(See also *WORN*.)□ If the shoe fits, wear it. □ none the worse for wear □ wear and tear on something □ wear more than one hat □ wear on someone □ wear one's heart on one's sleeve □ wear out one's welcome □ wear out □ wear someone or something down □ wear someone or something out

WEASEL

□ weasel out of something

WEATHER

□ fair-weather friend □ keep one's weather eye open □ lovely weather for ducks □ under the weather

WEAVE

□ weave in and out of something

WEDLOCK

□ born out of wedlock

WEEK

□ by the week □ week in, week out

WEEPERS

□ Finders keepers, losers weepers.

WEIGH

□ weigh on someone's mind □ weigh someone down □ weigh someone's words

WEIGHT

□ carry one's own weight □ carry the weight of the world on one's shoulders □ carry weight with someone □ pull one's weight □ put on weight □ throw one's weight around □ worth its weight in gold

WELCOME

□ wear out one's welcome □ welcome

someone with open arms □ welcome to do something

WELL

□ All's well that ends well. □ get well □ hail fellow well met □ know something only too well □ leave well enough alone □ let well enough alone □ well and good □ well-fixed □ well-heeled □ well-off □ well-to-do

WERE

□ as it were

WEST

□ out West

WET

□ all wet □ as mad as a wet hen □ get one's feet wet □ get wet □ wet behind the ears □ wet someone's whistle

WHACK

□ out of whack □ take a whack at someone or something

WHALE

□ have a whale of a time □ whale the tar out of someone

WHAT

□ come what may □ get what for □ get what's coming to one □ give someone what for □ have what it takes □ just what the doctor ordered □ know what's what □ know what's what □ no matter what □ practice what you preach □ What are you driving at? □ What difference does it make? □ What gives? □ What goes? □ What is sauce for the goose is sauce for the gander. □ what makes someone tick □ What of it? □ What's cooking? □ What's done is done. □ What's eating you? □ What's going on? □ What's gotten into someone? □ What's the good of something? □ What's the idea? □ What's up? □ What's with someone?

WHATEVER

□ for whatever it's worth

WHEEL

□ put one's shoulder to the wheel □ spin one's wheels

WHEN

□ cross a bridge when one comes to it □ when all is said and done □ When in Rome do as the Romans do. □ when it comes right down to it □ when it comes to something □ when least expected □ when one is good and ready □ When the cat's away the mice will play. □ when the time is ripe

WHERE
□ give credit where credit is due □ hit one where one lives □ know where someone stands on someone or something □ not know where to turn □ Put your money where your mouth is! □ tell someone where to get off □ where one is coming from □ where one lives □ Where there's a will there's a way. □ Where there's smoke there's fire.

WHEREWITHAL
□ have the wherewithal to do something

WHETHER
□ not know whether one is coming or going

WHICH
□ every which way □ game at which two can play □ know which is which □ know which side one's bread is buttered on □ not know which way to turn □ tell which is which

WHILE
□ every once in a while □ Make hay while the sun is shining. □ once in a while □ strike while the iron is hot □ while away the time

WHIP
□ whip something up

WHISKER
□ by a whisker

WHISPER
□ in a stage whisper

WHISTLE
□ as slick as a whistle □ blow the whistle on someone □ wet someone's whistle

WHITE
□ as white as the driven snow □ in black and white

WHO
□ He laughs best who laughs last. □ He who laughs last, laughs longest.

WHOLE
□ go whole hog □ make something up out of whole cloth □ on the whole

WHOM
□ to whom it may concern

WIDE
□ all wool and a yard wide □ come from far and wide □ crack something wide open □ cut a wide swath □ give someone or something a wide berth □ leave oneself wide open for something □ wide awake □ wide of the mark

WIG
□ flip one's wig

WILD
□ go hog wild □ run wild □ sow one's wild oats □ wild about someone or something □ Wild horses couldn't drag someone. □ wild-goose chase

WILDFIRE
□ spread like wildfire

WILL
□ against someone's will □ at will □ Give one an inch, and one will take a mile. □ of one's own free will □ That will do. □ There will be the devil to pay. □ Time will tell. □ When the cat's away the mice will play. □ Where there's a will there's a way. □ will not hear of something □ won't hold water

WILLIES
□ give someone the willies

WIN
□ Slow and steady wins the race. □ win by a nose □ win out over someone or something

WIND
□ get one's second wind □ get wind of something □ in the wind □ take the wind out of someone's sails □ throw caution to the wind □ wind down □ wind something up □ wind up by doing something □ wind up somewhere

WINDMILLS
□ tilt at windmills

WING
□ clip someone's wings □ on the wing □ take someone under one's wing □ try one's wings

WINK
□ as quick as a wink □ catch forty winks □ not sleep a wink □ take forty winks □ wink at something

WIPE
□ wipe someone or something out □ wipe someone's slate clean □ wipe something off □ wipe up the floor with someone

WIRE
□ down to the wire □ under the wire

WISE
□ as wise as an owl □ Early to bed, early to rise, makes a man healthy, wealthy, and wise. □ get wise to someone or something □ penny wise and pound foolish □ put someone wise to

461

someone or something □ wise up to someone or something

WISH
□ wish something off on someone

WITHER
□ wither on the vine

WITHIN
□ come within an ace of doing something □ come within an inch of doing something □ live within one's means □ within an inch of one's life □ within bounds □ within calling distance □ within hailing distance □ within limits □ within reason □ within someone's reach

WITHOUT
□ absent without leave □ do without someone or something □ get along without someone or something □ go without something □ goes without saying □ up the creek without a paddle □ without batting an eye □ without fail □ without further ado □ without question □ without rhyme or reason

WITS
□ at one's wits' end □ frighten one out of one's wits □ frighten the wits out of someone □ get one's wits about one □ have one's wits about one □ keep one's wits about one □ live by one's wits □ scare one out of one's wits □ scare the wits out of someone

WOLF
□ cry wolf □ keep the wolf from the door □ throw someone to the wolves □ wolf in sheep's clothing

WONDER
□ no wonder

WOOD
□ knock on wood

WOODS
□ babe-in-the-woods □ in some neck of the woods □ out of the woods

WOOL
□ all wool and a yard wide □ dyed-in-the-wool □ pull the wool over someone's eyes

WORD
□ Actions speak louder than words. □ at a loss for words □ beyond words □ by word of mouth □ eat one's words □ from the word go □ get a word in edgeways □ get a word in edgewise □ get the last word □ get the word □ go back

on one's word □ hang on someone's every word □ have a word with someone □ have one's words stick in one's throat □ have the last word □ in a word □ in other words □ in so many words □ keep one's word □ leave word with someone □ Mark my words. □ mince one's words □ Mum's the word. □ not breathe a word about someone or something □ not utter a word □ put in a good word for someone □ put something into words □ put words into someone's mouth □ say the word □ send word to someone □ take one at one's word □ take the words out of one's mouth □ Them's fighting words. □ true to one's word □ weigh someone's words □ word by word □ word for word □ words to that effect

WORK
□ all in a day's work □ All work and no play makes Jack a dull boy. □ all worked up over something □ at work □ get down to work □ get worked up over something □ have one's work cut out for one □ knock off work □ make short work of someone or something □ out of work □ take off from work □ work like a horse □ work on someone or something □ work one's fingers to the bone □ work one's way into something □ work one's way through college □ work one's way up □ work out for the best □ work out □ work someone or something in □ work someone or something up □ work someone over □ work something into something □ work something out □ work through channels

WORKS
□ get the works □ give someone the works □ gum up the works □ in the works □ shoot the works □ throw a monkey wrench in the works

WORLD
□ carry the weight of the world on one's shoulders □ come down in the world □ come up in the world □ dead to the world □ for all the world □ in a world of one's own □ in the world □ move up in the world □ not for anything in the world □ not for the world □ not have a care in the world □ not long for this world □ on top of the world □ out

of this world □ set the world on fire □ sitting on top of the world

WORM

□ open a can of worms □ The early bird gets the worm. □ worm one's way out of something □ worm something out of someone

WORN

□ worn-out

WORSE

□ for better or for worse □ go from bad to worse □ none the worse for wear □ One's bark is worse than one's bite. □ take a turn for the worse

WORST

□ at worst □ get the worst of something □ if worst comes to worst □ in the worst way

WORTH

□ A bird in the hand is worth two in the bush. □ An ounce of prevention is worth a pound of cure. □ for all it's worth □ for whatever it's worth □ get one's money's worth □ not worth a dime □ not worth a hill of beans □ not worth a red cent □ put in one's two cents worth □ worth its weight in gold □ worth one's salt

WOULD

□ as luck would have it □ look as if butter wouldn't melt in one's mouth □ would as soon do something □ wouldn't dream of doing something

WRAP

□ get something wrapped up □ have something wrapped up □ keep something under wraps □ wrap something up □ wrapped up in someone or something

WREAK

□ wreak havoc with something

WRENCH

□ throw a monkey wrench in the works

WRINGER

□ put someone through the wringer

WRIST

□ get a slap on the wrist □ give someone a slap on the wrist □ slap someone's wrist

WRITE

□ nothing to write home about □ That's all she wrote. □ write in for something □ write off for something □ write someone or something off □ write

someone or something up □ write something down □ write something out

WRONG

□ bark up the wrong tree □ get off on the wrong foot □ get out of the wrong side of the bed □ get up on the wrong side of the bed □ go wrong □ in the wrong □ on the wrong track □ rub someone the wrong way □ rub someone's fur the wrong way □ take someone or something wrong □ take something the wrong way □ the wrong side of the tracks

YARD

□ all wool and a yard wide

YEAR

□ advanced in years □ all year round □ along in years □ by the year □ get along in years □ on in years □ ring in the new year □ up in years □ year in, year out

YESTERDAY

□ not born yesterday

YIELD

□ yield the right-of-way

ZERO

□ zero in on something

ZONK

□ zonk out

ZOOM

□ zoom in on someone or something

Zs

□ catch some Zs

About the Author and Editor

Richard A. Spears, Ph.D. Associate Professor of Linguistics, North-western University. Specialist in Lexicography; English Language Structure; Phonetics; Language Standardization and Codefication; English as a Second or Foreign Language; American Culture.

Linda Schinke-Llano, Ph.D. Lecturer in Linguistics, Northwestern University. Specialist in Second Language Acquisition; Bilingual Education; English as a Second or Foreign Language.